THE CAMBRIDGE COMPANION TO
CHRISTIAN MYSTICISM

The Cambridge Companion to Christian Mysticism is a multiauthored interdisciplinary guide to the study of Western Christian mysticism, with an emphasis on the third through the seventeenth centuries. The book is thematically organized in terms of the central contexts, practices, and concepts associated with the mystical life in early, medieval, and early modern Christianity. Written by leading authorities and younger scholars from a range of disciplines, the volume provides a clear introduction to the Christian mystical life and articulates a bold new approach to the study of mysticism. The book looks beyond the term mysticism, which was an early modern invention, to explore the ways the ancient terms mystic and mystical were used in the Christian tradition: What kinds of practices, modes of life, and experiences were described as mystical? What understanding of Christianity and of the life of Christian perfection is articulated through mystical interpretations of scripture, mystical contemplation, mystical vision, mystical theology, or mystical union? What practices and experiences provided the framework within which one could describe mystical phenomena? And what topics are at the forefront of the contemporary study of Christian mystical practice and experience?

Amy Hollywood is Elizabeth H. Monrad Professor of Christian Studies at Harvard Divinity School. She is the author of *The Soul as Virgin Wife: Mechthild of Magdeburg, Marguerite Porete, and Meister Eckhart* (1995); *Sensible Ecstasy: Mysticism, Sexual Difference, and the Demands of History* (2002); and *Acute Melancholia and Other Essays* (forthcoming). She has written widely on topics medieval and modern and is currently engaged in an historical, philosophical, literary, and theological exploration of enthusiasm in the modern West.

Patricia Z. Beckman teaches in the Department of Religion and the Great Conversation program at St. Olaf College. Her research and writing explore medieval women's mystical teaching and practice, especially those of Mechthild of Magdeburg. She has served on the Council of the American Society of Church History and as senior Fellow for the Ford Foundation Difficult Dialogues project. She is an advocate for the public understanding, discussion, and debate of all things religious and historical.

CAMBRIDGE COMPANIONS TO RELIGION

This is a series of companions to major topics and key figures in theology and religious studies. Each volume contains specially commissioned chapters by international scholars, which provide an accessible and stimulating introduction to the subject for new readers and nonspecialists.

Other Titles in the Series

AMERICAN JUDAISM, *edited by* Dana Evan Kaplan

KARL BARTH, *edited by* John Webster

THE BIBLE, 2nd edition, *edited by* Bruce Chilton

BIBLICAL INTERPRETATION, *edited by* John Barton

DIETRICH BONHOEFFER, *edited by* John de Gruchy

JOHN CALVIN, *edited by* Donald K. McKim

CHRISTIAN DOCTRINE, *edited by* Colin Gunton

CHRISTIAN ETHICS, *edited by* Robin Gill

CHRISTIAN PHILOSOPHICAL THEOLOGY, *edited by* Charles Taliaferro and Chad V. Meister

CLASSICAL ISLAMIC THEOLOGY, *edited by* Tim Winter

JONATHAN EDWARDS, *edited by* Stephen J. Stein

FEMINIST THEOLOGY, *edited by* Susan Frank Parsons

THE JESUITS, *edited by* Thomas Worcester

JESUS, *edited by* Markus Bockmuehl

C. S. LEWIS, *edited by* Robert MacSwain and Michael Ward

LIBERATION THEOLOGY, *edited by* Chris Rowland

MARTIN LUTHER, *edited by* Donald K. McKim

MEDIEVAL JEWISH PHILOSOPHY, *edited by* Daniel H. Frank and Oliver Leaman

MODERN JEWISH PHILOSOPHY, *edited by* Michael L. Morgan and Peter Eli Gordon

MOHAMMED, *edited by* Jonathan E. Brockup

POSTMODERN THEOLOGY, *edited by* Kevin J. Vanhoozer

PURITANISM, *edited by* John Coffey and Paul C. H. Lim

THE QUR'AN, *edited by* Jane Dammen McAuliffe

KARL RAHNER, *edited by* Declan Marmion and Mary E. Hines

REFORMATION THEOLOGY, *edited by* David Bagchi and David Steinmetz

FREIDRICK SCHLEIERMACHER, *edited by* Jacqueline Mariña

SCIENCE AND RELIGION, *edited by* Peter Harrison

ST. PAUL, *edited by* James D. G. Dunn

THE TALMUD AND RABBINIC LITERATURE, *edited by* Charlotte E. Fonrobert and Martin S. Jaffee

HANS URS VON BALTHASAR, *edited by* Edward T. Oakes and David Moss

JOHN WESLEY, *edited by* Randy L. Maddox and Jason E. Vickers

THE CAMBRIDGE COMPANION TO
CHRISTIAN MYSTICISM

Edited by

Amy Hollywood
Harvard Divinity School

Patricia Z. Beckman
St. Olaf College

CAMBRIDGE
UNIVERSITY PRESS

32 Avenue of the Americas, New York NY 10013-2473, USA

Cambridge University Press is part of the University of Cambridge.

It furthers the University's mission by disseminating knowledge in the pursuit of education, learning and research at the highest international levels of excellence.

www.cambridge.org
Information on this title: www.cambridge.org/9780521682275

© Cambridge University Press 2012

This publication is in copyright. Subject to statutory exception and to the provisions of relevant collective licensing agreements, no reproduction of any part may take place without the written permission of Cambridge University Press.

First published 2012

A catalogue record for this publication is available from the British Library

Library of Congress Cataloguing in Publication data
The Cambridge companion to Christian mysticism / [edited by] Amy Hollywood, Harvard Divinity School, Patricia Z. Beckman, St. Olaf College
    p. cm. – (Cambridge companions to religion)
Includes bibliographical references and index.
ISBN 978-0-521-86365-0 (hardback)
1. Mysticism. I. Hollywood, Amy M., 1963–   II. Beckman, Patricia Z., 1967–
BV5082.3.C35   2012
248.2'2–dc23   2011046378

ISBN 978-0-521-86365-0 Hardback
ISBN 978-0-521-68227-5 Paperback

Cambridge University Press has no responsibility for the persistence or accuracy of URLs for external or third-party internet websites referred to in this publication, and does not guarantee that any content on such websites is, or will remain, accurate or appropriate.

Contents

Contributors page ix

Introduction 1
AMY HOLLYWOOD

Part I *Contexts*

1 Early Monasticism 37
DOUGLAS BURTON-CHRISTIE

2 Song, Experience, and the Book in Benedictine Monasticism 59
AMY HOLLYWOOD

3 New Forms of Religious Life in Medieval Western Europe 80
WALTER SIMONS

4 Early Modern Reformations 114
EDWARD HOWELLS

Part II *Key Terms*

5 Apophatic and Cataphatic Theology 137
ANDREW LOUTH

6 *Lectio Divina* 147
E. ANN MATTER

7 *Meditatio*/Meditation 157
THOMAS H. BESTUL

8 *Oratio*/Prayer 167
RACHEL FULTON BROWN

9 *Visio*/Vision 178
VEERLE FRAETERS

10 *Raptus*/Rapture 189
DYAN ELLIOTT

11 *Unio Mystica*/Mystical Union 200
BERNARD MCGINN

12 *Actio et Contemplatio*/Action and Contemplation 211
CHARLOTTE RADLER

Part III Contemporary Questions

13 Latin and the Vernaculars 225
BARBARA NEWMAN

14 Transmission 240
SARA S. POOR

15 Writing 252
CHARLES M. STANG

16 The Body and Its Senses 264
PATRICIA DAILEY

17 Mysticism and Visuality 277
JEFFREY F. HAMBURGER

18 Emotion 294
FIONA SOMERSET

19 Authority 305
MARY FROHLICH, RSCJ

20 Gender 315
ALISON WEBER

21 Sexuality 328
CONSTANCE M. FUREY

22 Time and Memory 341
PATRICIA DAILEY

Select Bibliography of Christian Mystical Texts up to around 1750 351

Select Bibliography of Modern Works Related to the Study of Western Christian Mysticism 357

Author and Artist Index 371

General Index 378

Contributors

Patricia Z. Beckman teaches in the Department of Religion and the Great Conversation program at St. Olaf College. Her research and writing explore medieval women's mystical teaching and practice, especially those of Mechthild of Magdeburg. She has served on the Council of the American Society of Church History and as senior Fellow for the Ford Foundation Difficult Dialogues project. She is an advocate for the public understanding, discussion, and debate of all things religious and historical.

Thomas H. Bestul is Professor of English at the University of Illinois at Chicago. He is the author of *Texts of the Passion: Latin Devotional Literature and Medieval Society* (1996) and the editor of *A Durham Book of Devotions* (1987) and *Walter Hilton's Scale of Perfection* (2000). With Franco Morenzoni and Greti Dinkova-Bruun he edited the *Opera omnia* of Alexander of Ashby (Corpus Christianorum, Continuatio Medievalis 188; Brepols 2004). He has written many articles on the prayers and meditations of Anselm of Canterbury and on other topics in medieval devotional literature.

Rachel Fulton Brown is Associate Professor of History at the University of Chicago. She is the author of *From Judgment to Passion: Devotion to Christ and the Virgin Mary, 800-1200* (2002) and coeditor with Bruce Holsinger of *History in the Comic Mode: Medieval Communities and the Matter of Person* (2007). She has published numerous articles on monastic and devotional prayer. Her current project is a study of the history and experience of saying the Hours of the Virgin.

Douglas Burton-Christie is Professor of Theological Studies at Loyola Marymount University where he teaches in the area of Christian spirituality. He earned his PhD in Christian Spirituality from the Graduate Theological Union in 1988 and his MA in Theology from Oxford University in 1980. His primary research interests are in the contemplative traditions of ancient Christian monasticism, spirituality and the natural world, and the discipline of Christian spirituality. He is the author of *The Word in the Desert: Scripture and the Quest for Holiness in Early Christian Monasticism* (1993) *and The Blue Sapphire of the Mind: Notes for a Contemplative Ecology* (2012), and is the founding editor of the journal *Spiritus: A Journal of Christian Spirituality*.

Patricia Dailey teaches in the Department of English and Comparative Literature at Columbia University. She has published essays in the *Journal of Medieval and Early Modern Studies*, *New Medieval Literatures*, *Women's Studies Quarterly*,

Le Secret: Motif et Moteur de la Litterature, *Les Imaginaires du Mal*, and *PMLA*. Her book, *Promised Bodies: Time, Language, and Corporeality in Women's Mystical Texts* (2012), focuses on temporality, embodiment, and language in medieval mystical texts and Anglo-Saxon poetry. She is the coeditor of the Brill *Companion to Hadewijch*. In addition to her work in medieval literature, she has translated works by Giorgio Agamben (*The Time That Remains*, 2005), Jean-François Lyotard, Antonio Negri, and Eric Alliez.

Dyan Elliott is the Peter B. Ritzma Chair in the Humanities, Department of History at Northwestern University. She is the author of *Spiritual Marriage: Sexual Abstinence in Medieval Wedlock* (1995); *Fallen Bodies: Pollution, Sexuality, and Demonology in the Middle Ages* (1999); *Proving Woman: Female Spirituality and Inquisitional Cultures in the Later Middle Ages* (2004); and *The Bride of Christ Goes to Hell: Metaphor and Embodiment in the Lives of Pious Women, 200–1500* (2012).

Veerle Fraeters studied Dutch language and literature at the Catholic University of Louvain. In 2002, she was appointed senior lecturer as an associate of the Ruusbroec Research Institute at the University of Antwerp. Her research is focused mainly on the area of medieval mysticism, and she has published primarily on visionary literature and female mysticism. She is currently collaborating with Frank Willaert on a new edition with a modern Dutch translation of the complete works of Hadewijch and with Patricia Dailey on *A Companion to Hadewijch*.

Mary Frohlich, RSCJ, is Associate Professor of Spirituality at Catholic Theological Union in Chicago. Her publications include essays on spirituality as a discipline, Carmelite spiritual writers, and topics in ecospirituality. Each year at the Summer Seminar in Carmelite Spirituality, she offers lectures and workshops with a particular focus on the women of Carmel. Other current research interests include mystical dimensions of "conversion to the Earth," the contributions of women in seventeenth-century French spirituality, and methodological issues in spirituality.

Constance M. Furey is Associate Professor of Religious Studies at Indiana University. She is the author of *Erasmus, Contarini, and the Religious Republic of Letters* (2005). She has also published articles on utopia, history, and the interest in the body and subjectivity in the study of religion. Her current book project explores how male and female writers of English Renaissance devotional poetry used the genre to reimagine friendship, marriage, patronage, authorship, and erotic love.

Jeffrey F. Hamburger is the Kuno Francke Professor of German Art and Culture at Harvard University. A Fellow of the Medieval Academy and an elected member of the American Academy of Arts and Sciences and the American Philosophical Society, he has written extensively on late medieval mysticism as well as medieval art, especially in Germany.

Amy Hollywood is the Elizabeth H. Monrad Professor of Christian Studies at Harvard Divinity School. She is the author of *The Soul as Virgin Wife: Mechthild of Magdeburg, Marguerite Porete, and Meister Eckhart* (1995); *Sensible Ecstasy:*

Mysticism, Sexual Difference, and the Demands of History (2002); and, forthcoming from Columbia University Press, *Acute Melancholia and Other Essays*.

Edward Howells is Lecturer in Christian Spirituality at Heythrop College, University of London. He is the author of *John of the Cross and Teresa of Avila: Mystical Knowing and Selfhood* (2002) and coeditor with Peter Tyler of *Sources of Transformation: Revitalising Christian Spirituality* (2010).

Andrew Louth is Professor Emeritus in the Department of Theology and Religion at Durham University and Visiting Professor at the Vriie Universiteit, Amsterdam. He is the author of *Greek East and Latin West, AD 681–1971* (2007); *Origins of the Christian Mystical Tradition: From Plato to Denys* (1996); *Discerning the Mystery: An Essay on the Nature of Theology* (1990); and books on Dionysius the Areopagite, Maximus the Confessor, and John Damascene and on the tradition of desert spirituality in the Christian tradition, Eastern and Western.

E. Ann Matter is the William R. Kenan Professor in the Department of Religious Studies at the University of Pennsylvania. Her teaching and scholarship focus on medieval and early modern spirituality in Western Christianity, with special attention to biblical exegesis and the importance of women authors.

Bernard McGinn is the Naomi Shenstone Donnelley Professor Emeritus at the Divinity School of the University of Chicago, where he taught from 1969 until his retirement in 2003. He has written extensively on the history of Christian apocalyptic traditions, as well as on spirituality and mysticism. He is currently completing the fifth volume of his projected seven-volume history of Christian mysticism under the general title *The Presence of God*. He also serves as the editor-in-chief of the Paulist Press series *The Classics of Western Spirituality* (123 volumes to date).

Barbara Newman is Professor of English, Religion, and Classics at Northwestern University. She is the author of *Frauenlob's Song of Songs* (2007); *God and the Goddesses: Vision, Poetry, and Belief in the Middle Ages* (2003); *From Virile Woman to WomanChrist* (1995); and many books and articles on Hildegard of Bingen and other religious women. She is currently working on a study of crossover between sacred and secular literature in the Middle Ages.

Sara S. Poor is Associate Professor of German Literature at Princeton University. She is author of *Mechthild of Magdeburg and Her Book: Gender and the Making of Textual Authority* (2004) and coeditor of *Women and Medieval Epic: Gender, Genre, and the Limits of Epic Masculinity* (2007). Her current research concerns the intersection of late medieval German narratives of clever women and the roles of women in the production of fifteenth-century devotional books.

Charlotte Radler is Associate Professor of Theological Studies at Loyola Marymount University. Her research interests include the mysticism of Meister Eckhart, women in medieval mysticism, and the construction of heresy and orthodoxy in early and medieval Christianity. Her work has appeared, among other places, in *The Journal of Religion, Vigilae Christianae, Spiritus*, and the *Journal of Buddhist-Christian Studies*. She is currently working on a book on the role of love in Meister Eckhart's thought.

Walter Simons is Professor of History at Dartmouth College. He is the author, most recently, of *Cities of Ladies: Beguine Communities in the Medieval Low Countries, 1200–1565* (2001) and editor, with Miri Rubin, of *The Cambridge History of Christianity*, vol. IV: *Christianity in Western Europe, c. 1100–c. 1500* (2009).

Fiona Somerset is Associate Professor of English at Duke University and coeditor of the *Yearbook of Langland Studies*. She is the author of *Clerical Discourse and Lay Audience in Late Medieval England* (1998) and editor of *Four Wycliffite Dialogues* (2009). Her *Classics of Western Spirituality* volume *Wycliffite Spirituality* (with J. Patrick Hornbeck II and Stephen E. Lahey) is slated for publication in 2012.She is finishing work on a new book on the writings of the Lollard movement, *Feeling Like Saints*.

Charles M. Stang is Assistant Professor of Early Christian Thought at Harvard Divinity School. His research focuses on the history and theology of Christianity in late antiquity, especially Eastern varieties of Christianity. He has edited, with Sarah Coakley, *Rethinking Dionysius the Areopagite* (2009). His book *Apophasis and Pseudonymity in Dionysius the Areopagite* is forthcoming in 2012 from Oxford University Press.

Alison Weber is Professor in the Department of Spanish, Italian, and Portuguese and Affiliate Professor in the Corcoran Department of History at the University of Virginia. She is the author of *Teresa of Ávila and the Rhetoric of Femininity* (1990) and edited *Book for the Hour of Recreation* by María de San José (2002) and *Approaches to Teaching Teresa of Ávila and the Spanish Mystics* (2009). Her articles have appeared in *Renaissance Quarterly, Hispanic Review, Sixteenth Century Studies, Publications of the Modern Language Association of America*, and other scholarly journals. She is currently working on a monograph on mysticism and perceptions of sanctity in early modern Spain.

Introduction
AMY HOLLYWOOD

In the ninth book of the *Confessions*, the Christian bishop Augustine of Hippo (354–430) writes of an experience he shared with his mother, Monica. The two were in Italy, preparing to travel back to their native North Africa. One day, deep in conversation, they wondered "what the eternal life of the saints would be like," concluding "that no bodily pleasure, however great it might be and whatever earthly light might shed luster upon it, was worthy of comparison, or even of mention, beside the happiness of the life of the saints." As they spoke, Augustine tells us, "the flame of love burned stronger" in them and raised them "higher toward the eternal God." Their thoughts ranged over all material things up to the heavens, and then beyond the material heavens to their own souls.

Yet for Augustine and Monica, the "eternal life of the saints" lay beyond even the realm of immaterial souls, in a place of "everlasting peace" governed by Wisdom. And so, Augustine explains, as he and his mother

> spoke of the eternal Wisdom, longing for it and straining for it with all the strength of our hearts, for one fleeting instant we reached out and touched it. Then with a sigh, leaving our spiritual harvest bound to it, we returned to the sound of our own speech, in which each word has a beginning and an ending – far, far different from your Word, our Lord, who abides in himself forever, yet never grows old and gives new life to all things.[1]

Augustine and Monica ascend together through the material and immaterial realms and then further upward, from the realm of the soul to that of the divine Word.

---

[1] Augustine, *Confessions*, trans. R. S. Pine-Coffin (Harmondsworth, UK: Penguin, 1961), bk. IX, sec. 10, pp. 197–8.

Augustine's account demonstrates his abiding debt to Neoplatonism. The pagan philosopher Plotinus (d. 270) describes the soul's movement into, through, and beyond itself to the universal Soul, from thence to Mind, and ultimately back into the One from which all things emanate and to which they aspire to return.[2] At the time of the vision at Ostia, however, Augustine was a committed Christian, and while he maintained crucial aspects of the Neoplatonic philosophical view, he also insisted on the necessity of divine mediation in order for the uplifting and return of the soul to its source to occur. Elsewhere he emphasizes the centrality of the incarnate Christ. Here he writes of Christ as the Word and as Wisdom. For Plotinus, the creation of all things occurs through the emanation of the One into the Mind, the Mind into Soul, the Soul into individual souls, and all into the realm of material creation. Augustine, as a Christian, insists that creation occurs directly through Christ as the Word who "gives new life to all things," and it is to this Word that all things will return.

Known as the vision at Ostia after the town in Italy in which the event occurred, this passage encapsulates themes that will play a vital role in the development of Western Christianity.[3] Four features, standing in dialectical relation to what might, at first sight, appear to be their opposites, lie at the heart of the Christian mystical life.[4] First, Augustine describes himself and his mother engaging in a process of uplifting and transcendence. For Augustine this process is grounded in the intellect, although love, signified here by the heart, is also crucial. Augustine emphasizes the transcendence of God and the transcending or uplifting

---

[2] For more on Neoplatonic theories of procession and return, see Andrew Louth's essay in this volume.

[3] Scholars continue to debate whether Augustine should be considered a mystic, with much hinging on what that designation is taken to entail. See Bernard McGinn, *The Presence of God: A History of Western Christian Mysticism*, vol. 1, *The Foundations of Mysticism: Origins to the Fifth Century* (New York: Crossroad, 1992), pp. 229–31 and the literature cited there.

[4] There have been many attempts to provide a phenomenological description of the primary feature of mysticism, and related attempts to create typologies of different kinds of mysticism. The most famous of the descriptive accounts is perhaps that of William James, which shares features with what I describe here. For James, mysticism is *always* marked by its ineffability and noetic quality; it is also often transient and passive. See William James, *The Varieties of Religious Experience* (Harmondsworth, UK: Penguin 1982 [1902]), pp. 380–2. I not only highlight slightly different features but also stress their constant interplay with what might, at first sight, appear to be their opposites. Hence I attempt to hold together the enormous range of phenomena that has been designated, either in premodern Christianity or in modernity, as mystical, without creating evaluative typologies or simply rejecting out of hand certain kinds of experience as inessential or representative of false mysticism.

motion of souls to God; others will double God's transcendence with claims to God's immanence to the soul in visionary or unitive experience. Centuries later, the Dominican preacher and theologian Meister Eckhart (d. 1328) will go even further, taking the Neoplatonic structure of emanation and return as the basis for the claim that God is simultaneously transcendent and immanent to all things.

Second, Augustine and Monica touch transcendent Wisdom only fleetingly. Throughout the course of Christian history, most of those who claim to have some experience of God's presence or of union with God admit, and often bemoan, the transience of such events insofar as they occur in human time. Others, however, claim to have more lasting rapturous engagements with God or, even more controversially, will claim to attain a permanent state of annihilation of the self and of unity with the divine ground of all things – a unity in which they share in God's eternal now. This view, which appears to have been held by the beguine Marguerite Porete (d. 1310), may have played a role in her condemnation. Yet it is one that will continue to resurface within the Christian tradition.

Third, Augustine explicitly contrasts his and his mother's momentary grasp of the divine Word to human speech. Augustine and Monica know that they are no longer touching Wisdom when they return "to the sound of [their] own speech, in which each word has a beginning and an ending." Human speech, unlike the divine Word, is temporal. In time, things have a beginning and an ending, whereas the divine Word is eternal and "abides in himself forever, yet never grows old." The limitation of human language for God is a recurrent theme within the Christian tradition and one that is often tied to the question of temporality. Yet there is also the need to find a language with which to praise God. In Augustine's discussion of his experience with his mother at Ostia, he points to the limitations of human speech to encompass divine Wisdom in part through a proliferation of metaphors from the realms of sight, taste, hearing, and thought. The interplay between the use of sensory images and intellectual concepts to name God and claims to God's unnameability lies at the heart of the Christian mystical tradition.

Finally, the experience recounted in the *Confessions* is deeply communal. Augustine comes to the Word in and through his conversation with his mother. They "reach out and touch" divine Wisdom together, and together they fall back into human speech, the "region of unlikeness" in which creatures live until they come to eternal life in God. Moreover, they name that which they seek in communal terms, speaking together of the "eternal life of the saints." For Augustine and Monica, to touch the Word is to touch and share in the life of the saints – the life of all those saved by Christ – and so to be part of a community grounded in God. Moreover, here and in other texts, Augustine emphasizes the importance of community and communal practice in the soul's movement toward God. Among Augustine's forebears and contemporaries, however, were those who claimed that the life of Christian perfection was best sought in solitude. How to bring this desire for solitude together with the communal nature of Christian life will be a recurring question, one that will play a central role in moments of rupture and transformation within the tradition.

In one scene, then, we find many of the most abiding and contentious aspects of the Christian mystical tradition, particularly as it is lived and practiced in the West from the third through the sixteenth centuries, the geographical and temporal focus of this volume.[5] In each instance, Augustine's description entails a position with regard to the nature of the human being's experience of God that borrows from the past and from his contemporaries and will be taken up by subsequent writers, either directly from Augustine or from other early Christian and pagan philosophical sources. In the texts and images discussed throughout this volume, we find a near constant interplay between God's transcendence and God's immanence in the experience of mystical vision, contemplation, or union; the transience of created time and the eternity of God; the necessity of naming God in order to praise God and the unnameability of God and, with that, of any experience of God; and the communal and the solitary nature of the pursuit of the Christian life.

Modern scholarship on Christian mysticism – and on mysticism understood as a more general religious phenomenon – often attempts to control its subject by emphasizing some features over others. Even more marked is the tendency to reduce complex phenomena, such as the interplay between transcendence and immanence or that between the communal and the individual, to one side of the pair, in the process often making evaluative judgments about what is central and what is peripheral to the mystical life or, even more damningly, what constitutes "true" as opposed to "false" mysticism.[6] As Veerle Fraeters, Dyan Elliott,

---

[5] Although a number of the essays collected here deal with early Christian materials from the East, the fate of the mystical and mysticism in medieval and modern Eastern Christianity unfortunately lies outside of the scope of the volume. For reflections on the distortions to which this leads, see Louth's essay in this volume.

[6] So, e.g., James omits "visual and auditory hallucinations," among other phenomena, because he deems them insufficiently "illuminative" to count as an essential aspect of the mystical life. James is far from alone in his desire to discount such experiences, although he has his own reasons for doing so. See James, *Varieties*, p. 408, n. 2.

Bernard McGinn, and Alison Weber show in their essays in this volume, this is a move that begins, at least in the West, during the Middle Ages. The goal of this book is to work against such simplifying maneuvers and so to insist on the various and multiple experiences of God recounted within a wide range of Christian texts.

There is a certain paradoxical quality to this enterprise, for the term mysticism that governs it and that names the canon of texts to which the volume attends is absent from almost all of the material it is taken to describe. Derived from the Greek, *muo*, which means to close, particularly the eyes, the adjectives mystic and mystical and the adverb mystically were used to modify an array of practices within the ancient Greek mystery religions, Greek Neoplatonic philosophy, and, most lastingly, Christianity. They then moved seamlessly from Greek into Latin and from thence into the Western European vernaculars. In their earliest Greek and Latin uses, mystic and mystical simply meant hidden.

According to Louis Bouyer, who offers the most detailed account of early usages, early Christian writers borrow the term from the Greek mystery religions in order to name the hidden reality underlying scripture and liturgy – namely, Jesus Christ, the reference of the most seemingly mundane and the most obscure biblical texts and the constant presence underlying the ritual life of Christian communities. Bouyer argues that only with Origen (d. 254) does an understanding of the mystical as a particular mode of theologizing or spiritual practice emerge. Origen designates as mystical the knowledge produced through allegorical interpretations of the Bible, because in such interpretation one seeks to uncover meanings hidden in or even by the literal meaning of the text.[7] This usage also marks a shift toward the experiential. The process by which one comes to know hidden things is designated as mystical rather than the things uncovered themselves. In uncovering the hidden meaning of scripture, by moving from what Origen calls the body (the literal meaning) of the text to its soul and spirit (both aspects of the allegorical), one is lifted up through the body to the soul and to that universal spirit in which we all share.[8]

Over the course of early and Western medieval Christian history, the experiential aspect of biblical interpretation takes on a life of its own. Increasingly we find the term mystical used to name not only Christ

[7] For more on the allegorical method of biblical interpretation, see E. Ann Matter's essay in this volume.
[8] See Louis Bouyer, "Mysticism: An Essay on the History of the Word," in *Understanding Mysticism*, ed. Richard Woods (Garden City, NJ: Image Books, 1980), pp. 42–55.

and Christ's teaching, which are the hidden truth of scripture, and the Eucharist (in which Christ is hidden under the visible bread and wine), but also stages of contemplation (in Greek, *theoria* and in Latin, *contemplatio*) leading to the vision of God, the vision of God itself, union with God (Greek, *henosis* and Latin, *unitas*), and theology (*theologia*, a Greek term taken over directly into Latin).[9] Early, medieval, and early modern Christian writers referred to all of these things as mystical, and it is to this array of practices – of mystical interpretation of scripture, mystical vision, mystical contemplation, mystical union, and mystical theology – that the substantive term mysticism, which begins to appear in the Western European vernaculars during the seventeenth and eighteenth centuries, refers.

The story of the modern articulation of the category of mysticism is only beginning to be written.[10] But what recurs in much of the modern literature is a tendency to emphasize transcendence, ineffability, and individuality and to understand mysticism as embracing inwardness and

---

[9] See McGinn, *Foundations of Mysticism*, esp. pp. 102, 105, 124, 128, 144, 171, 177, 210, and 252.

[10] There is, moreover, likely more than one story. For France, see Michel de Certeau, "'Mystique' au XVIIe siècle: Le problème de langage 'mystique,'" in *L'Homme devant Dieu: Mélanges offerts à Père Henri de Lubac* (Paris: Aubier, 1964), vol. 2, pp. 267–91; Michel de Certeau, "Mystic Speech," in *Heterologies: Discourse on the Other*, trans. Brian Massumi (Minneapolis: University of Minnesota Press, 1986), pp. 80–100; Michel de Certeau, "Mysticism," *Diacritics* 22 (1992): 11–25; and Michel de Certeau, *The Mystic Fable*, vol. 1, *The Sixteenth and Seventeenth Centuries*, trans. Michael B. Smith (Chicago: University of Chicago Press, 1992), pp. 72–112. On Germany, see Niklaus Largier, "Mysticism, Modernity, and the Invention of Aesthetic Experience," *Representations* 105 (2009): 37–60. Regarding the Anglophone world, see Leigh Eric Schmidt, "The Making of Modern 'Mysticism,'" *Journal of the American Academy of Religion* 71, no. 2 (2002): 273–302. Schmidt is right that a number of scholars – including Certeau – move too quickly from Certeau's claims about the emergence of the term mysticism (*mystique*) in seventeenth-century French Roman Catholic circles to its deployment by twentieth-century students of mysticism such as James and Evelyn Underhill. There is a "gaping eighteenth- and nineteenth-century hole" in this genealogy, and Schmidt's essay plugs in crucial pieces of the Anglo-American story. The interplay among (minimally) French-, Spanish-, Italian-, German-, Dutch-, and English-language discussions, and among theology, philosophy, and literature requires further research and analysis before we can begin to get a clear picture of whence and to what ends mysticism came to play such a vital role in modern religious studies, including theology, and in modern religious life. At the same time, it is necessary to insist that the word group does not limit the phenomenon. Practices and experiences often referred to in Christian texts as mystical also regularly occur without that specific appellation. After the Reformation, the term is used as often as one of abuse as of approbation, and yet the phenomena and the theological issues surrounding them by no means disappear. We need to avoid the mistake, then, of confusing word with concept and experience.

rejecting external forms.[11] For reasons that contemporary scholarship has yet fully to uncover, with the use of the substantive mysticism, and the notion of mystical theology as a specific mode of doing theology that stands independent of historical, biblical, or dogmatic theology, the Christian mystical tradition is often disengaged from the practices of biblical exegesis, liturgy, prayer, and contemplation with which it was always intimately bound in pre- and early modern Western Christianity.[12] The essays collected here insist that we return to a careful consideration of the specific forms of life within which and of the religious practices in the context of which the dialectical interplay between transcendence and immanence, time and eternity, naming and unnaming, and community and individuality that marks the Christian mystical life emerge and develop.[13]

Early, medieval, and early modern Christian mysticism can best be understood as a series of ongoing experiential, communal, and textual commentaries on and debates about the possibilities and limitations of encounters between God and humanity as they occur within history, the time and the place of the human as it is disrupted by the eternal God. The complex interplay between immanence and transcendence, time and eternity, nameability and unnameability, and community and individuality can best be articulated when due attention is given to the vital role of practice in Christian life. For in early, medieval, and early modern Christianity, the mystical senses, mystical visions, mystical contemplation, and mystical union took place, in the words of Niklaus Largier, "in the context of regulated forms of reading, preaching, prayer, and above all in the reading of scriptures and in the liturgical forms

---

[11] In many cases, in the very process of describing mysticism as marked by inwardness, transcendence, and ineffability, the very outward and communal practices supposedly antithetical to it are also described – Bible reading, hymn singing, communal exhortations, and engagement with the natural world. There are excellent examples of this in James, *Varieties*.

[12] Following Michel de Certeau's work, it has become common to refer to this tradition as retroactively constituted. Certainly a specific canon of texts is associated with the new coinage, mysticism, in the sixteenth and seventeenth centuries, yet recent work on textual transmission and translation suggests that a mystical canon was already in place by at least the later Middle Ages. See Newman and Poor in this volume.

[13] Although Schmidt suggests that a distinction can be made between the history of the term within the "study of religion" and "its genealogy as part of a history of Christian theology and exegesis," our suspicion is that the more we know about how the term mysticism is deployed across an array of languages, disciplines, and Christian and non-Christian communities in the seventeenth and eighteenth centuries, the more that distinction will erode. See Schmidt, "The Making of Modern 'Mysticism,'" p. 275, n. 1.

that enact, recall, and perform aspects of the scriptures and provide a general ... framework" for their interpretation.[14]

The phenomena grouped under the term mysticism, then, should first be approached in their specific historical settings, as that provides us with the best possibility of understanding these practices on something like the terms in which they were understood by those who wrote and lived them.[15] The monastic traditions in which these terms first occur were, from the beginning, attempts to generate the conditions and provide the practices by means of which monks and nuns, alone and in community, might best attain the life of Christian perfection, a perfection repeatedly named and described in terms of God's transforming presence.

For this reason, "Part I: Contexts" opens the book with four essays meant to give readers an understanding of the historically located forms of religious life in which mysticism emerged. What it means to be a Christian is always subject to debate, and in the periods covered by this volume, the ideals of Christian life were hotly contested. To be described as mystical was almost always to be associated with the highest aspects of the Christian life – hence the ideal form of life was very often the mystical one. But what this entailed changed over time, as the mystical life generated within the monasteries of the ancient and medieval Christian world gradually came to spread outside of the monastery walls, first to new religious orders and eventually to the laity.

Many of the practices and terms central to Western Christian mysticism emerge in the context of monasticism and the various reforms of the religious life that occur during the Middle Ages. "Part II: Key Terms" draws out some of the most vital of these, focusing on vocabulary central to early and medieval Christian articulations of the religious life. The writers to whom we attend throughout the volume wrote with great care. It is essential to listen carefully to their specific dialects, track the

---

[14] Largier, "Mysticism, Modernity," p. 40.
[15] In addition, we believe that this kind of historical work is the necessary condition for comparative study, whether across historical moments or religious traditions. The use of the term mystical to modify a range of phenomena associated with the religious life occurs most influentially and most lastingly in Christianity. Attempts to provide a general account of mysticism with transhistorical and interreligious power depend, therefore, on careful attention to the specificity of the Christian phenomena that are first described as mystical. Our intuition is that the most fruitful sites of comparison across the history of Christianity and between Christianity and other religions will be neither doctrinal nor phenomenological, but rather practical. The kinds of practices in which people pursue the religious life are likely to provide the most apt grounds for comparative work.

interrelationship between key concepts and practices, and show how terms function differently in different historical contexts.

"Part III: Contemporary Questions" turns to modern terms of analysis – or in some cases terms of analysis that, while available in one form or another in earlier historical moments, are so laden with contemporary presuppositions as to render a theoretically self-reflexive approach necessary. (We are thinking here of authority, the body and its senses, and vision – the latter of which is notably covered in both Parts II and III, albeit in quite different ways.) All of our historicist desires should not blind us to the fact that we ask our questions of old texts, questions that at times have only very faint analogues in the past. These engagements are vital to the ongoing making of – and often salutary breaks with – tradition.

The volume can be read and used in multiple ways. Some might choose to focus on particular temporal periods as they cut across the volume; others might want to work through the chronological chapters and then focus on issues of particular concern to them. Throughout, authors point to central primary sources, and we hope that the volume will be used in conjunction with the writings of the mystics. The volume was structured as a whole, but one with detachable parts, and there is no one way to link them. It is also marked by crucial absences. There is little attention to the Christian East after the sixth century or to Western developments after the eighteenth century. The size and scope of this volume did not allow of expansion to these essential aspects of the story of Christian mysticism. Both topics deserve their own volumes, the first a companion to this that focuses on Eastern Christian mysticism, the second a follow-up or continuation of the work done here that would tell the story of the mystical life in modernity. What follows, then, is meant only as a partial and imperfect guide to the riches provided by the essays themselves, with some indication of where future work might lead.

Chapter 1, "Early Monasticism," opens the book with Douglas Burton-Christie's account of some of the earliest and most formative texts from the monastic tradition. Burton-Christie emphasizes the ways in which the heights of spiritual experience are described within these writings as rooted "in a common life" and incorporated "into the texture and rhythms of daily living" (p. 4). The teachings of the desert fathers and mothers, as they come down to us through collections of sayings and lives, describe the regular and structured recitation of scripture, disciplined ascetic practice, and the practices of prayer, meditation, and contemplation by means of which monks and nuns struggle to be transformed in Christ. As Burton-Christie explains, "the early Christian monks were convinced that the practice of holding the Word at the center of one's consciousness led gradually toward a living encounter with the One speaking in and through the text" (p. 55) of scripture. Through this engagement with God's living Word, moreover, one might come to pure prayer – the contemplation of God alone. Hence we see already in early Christianity the interplay between speech and silence, the naming and unnaming of God that will run throughout the Christian tradition.

Amy Hollywood picks up the story of Christian monasticism in Chapter 2, "Song, Experience, and the Book in Benedictine Monasticism." Hollywood focuses on Western monasticism, which was largely governed by the sixth-century *Rule of Benedict*. The *Rule*, she argues, set the conditions within which the mystical life was pursued during much of the Western Middle Ages. Hollywood points to the centrality of communal prayer and reading to the monastic life and notes that early and medieval monastic texts wrote of experience (*experientia*) as the site of affective, intellectual, and spiritual transformation through the life of prayer. At the heart of the monastic life, both Burton-Christie and Hollywood show, lies the recitation of the Psalms. For monastic authors like John Cassian (d. ca. 435), whose *Institutes* and *Conferences* were required reading for monks and nuns living according to the *Rule of Benedict*, the recitation of the Psalms made it possible for "every love, every desire, every effort, every undertaking, every thought of ours, everything that we live, that we speak, that we breathe, ... [to] be God." Only then, according to Cassian, will the unity that exists between the Father and the Son "be carried over into our understanding and our mind so that, just as he loves us with a sincere and pure and indissoluble love, we too may be joined to him with a perpetual and inseparable love and so united with him that whatever we breathe, whatever we understand, whatever we speak, may be God."[16]

Hollywood goes on to show that the practices of prayer integral to Benedictine monasticism continued to play a role in the lives of those who seek spiritual grace, even among the laity and semireligious. This theme is further articulated in Chapter 3, "New Forms of Religious Life in Medieval Western Europe." Walter Simon's essay presents the range of new forms of religious life that emerged over the course of the late eleventh, twelfth, and thirteenth centuries. Fueled in part by

---

[16] John Cassian, *Conferences*, trans. Boniface Ramsey (New York: Newman Press, 1997) conf. 10, ch. 7, pp. 375–6; and John Cassian, *Conférences*, ed. Dom E. Pichery (Paris: Les Éditions du Cerf, 1955–9), vol. 2, conf. 10, ch. 7, p. 81.

an increasingly literate laity with greater leisure to attend to the religious life, the new religious movements often provided either greater attention on the part of the order to the religious needs of the laity or made modes of life devoted primarily to religion accessible to a broader range of people within society. As Simons shows, the new movements took four primary forms: (1) reforms of traditional Benedictine monasticism, with calls for a return to the simplicity and single-minded pursuit of religious perfection; (2) the adoption of another set of ancient texts known as the "Rule of Augustine," which, in at least some of its forms, allowed greater interaction between members of the order and the laity; (3) the formation of the orders of mendicant ("begging") friars, who pursued a life of active engagement with the secular world, preaching and caring for the souls of the laity; and (4) the engagement of many women and men in various informal modes of religious life. All of these forms of religious life were vital in transmitting and, in many cases, transforming earlier monastic ideals so as to make them available to a broader audience.

Simons demonstrates that these new religious movements were the site of intense mystical activity, in which increasingly radical claims were made about the nature and extent of the human capacity to be unified with God. Yet the sheer variety of mystical practices, texts, and experience belies any unifying vision of the mystical life during this period. As Simons shows, and the essays gathered in Part II elaborate, intense debates were waged concerning the nature of mystical vision, rapture, and union, the relative roles of action and contemplation in the ideal Christian life, the interplay between love and knowledge in the soul's movement to God, and many other issues. Yet it is worth noting that among the hallmarks of at least some of the mystical writings produced during the high and late Middle Ages in the West was a tendency toward the democratization of the religious life, a trend that will play a significant role in early modern transformations of Christianity.

In Chapter 4, "Early Modern Reformations," Edward Howells demonstrates the continuing – if often contested – power of this movement toward the democratization of the mystical life. Howells deftly outlines three central characteristics of the reform project that took over Western European Christianity during the late Middle Ages and early modern periods: (1) the democratization and laicization of the mystical life; (2) an optimism about the human capacity to achieve union with God, enabled in part by humanism; and (3) an increasing emphasis on "the authenticity of the inner life in the face of the deception and corruption of exterior forms of religion" (p. 119). As Howells notes, not all of these features were shared across the wide range of religious movements that marked the period. But in looking to these key sites of debate, Howells is able to demonstrate the continuities and ruptures between late medieval and early modern forms of mystical life, as well as the continuities and ruptures between and across the increasingly fragmented landscape of early modern Western Christianity. He shows that, contrary to some claims, the forms of life associated with Christian mysticism did not disappear in modernity, nor were they entirely foreign to Protestantism. Many of the practices and themes articulated within the magisterial and the radical reformations can be found, albeit in doctrinally different contexts, within late medieval and early modern Catholicism.

The essays collected in Part II elaborate on many of the concepts presented in Part I. Thus in Chapter 5, "Cataphatic and Apophatic Theology," Andrew Louth takes up an issue raised first by Burton-Christie. As Louth shows, ancient Israelite religion, Christianity, and ancient Greek Platonic traditions all share a concern with the interplay between affirmation and negation in relation to God. In the Hebrew scriptures and in the New Testament, there is a keen sense that God reveals Godself through revelation and that God remains mysterious, "leading to the negating of any affirmations about God" (p. 137). The specific language of cataphasis and apophasis, the saying and unsaying of the names of God, first comes into Christianity from a group of texts written in the sixth century under the pseudonym Dionysius the Areopagite, Paul's first convert among the Greeks. (As Charles Stang shows in his essay, "Writing," something vital is at stake in this pseudonym.) Louth emphasizes that for Dionysius, as for the traditions that follow him, both cataphasis and apophasis are required – there is no unnaming without a prior naming. In addition, sensory images and intellectual concepts are equally necessary and equally inadequate to the divine. As Louth puts it, "the denial and affirmation of images and concepts of God are equally radical: all are affirmed, all are denied" (pp. 141–2).

Dionysius operates within the Neoplatonic logic of emanation and return we saw at play in Augustine's *Confessions*. Cataphasis or the naming of God corresponds to God's emanation or procession, through which all things are created. Apophasis, the denial of those same names, provides a way of return into God as the source of creation. As Dionysius explains in his short treatise, *The Mystical Theology*, "the more we take flight upward, the more our words are confined to the ideas we are capable of forming; so that now as we plunge into that darkness which is beyond intellect, we shall find ourselves not simply running short of words but actually speechless and unknowing."[17] For Dionysius, the most divine knowledge of God comes through unknowing and "is achieved in a union far beyond mind, when mind turns away from all things, even from itself, and when it is made one with the dazzling rays, being then and there enlightened by the inscrutable depth of Wisdom."[18]

> Here renouncing all that the mind may conceive, wrapped entirely in the intangible and the invisible, he belongs completely to Him who is beyond everything. Here, being neither oneself nor someone else, one is supremely united in a complete inactivity of all knowledge.[19]

The paradoxical interplay between light and dark, knowing and unknowing, speech and silence that runs throughout Dionysius's work is integral to the mystical tradition, even in those times and places in which the Dionysian corpus was not known directly.

For Dionysius the primary sources for the names of God, both as affirmed and denied, are scripture and the liturgy, itself scripturally based. Over the course of the Western Middle Ages, monastic authors and authors from the new religious movements of the high and later Middle Ages devised countless schemata for understanding the religious life. The Augustinian canon, Hugh of Saint Victor (1096–1141), describes the mystical life as beginning with reading (*lectio*) and moving from there to meditation (*meditatio*), prayer (*oratio*), composition *(operatio)*, and contemplation (*contemplatio*). The Carthusian monk, Guigo II (d. 1193), similarly describes what he calls a "ladder of monks" by which one ascends through reading, meditation, prayer, and contemplation.[20] Other schema abound and none are definitive, yet all emphasize a set of features that the rest of Part II sets out to describe.

Everything begins with reading, and as E. Ann Matter shows in Chapter 6, "*Lectio Divina*," reading is the reading of scripture. Crucial

---

[17] Pseudo-Dionysius, *The Mystical Theology*, in *The Complete Works*, trans. Colm Lubhéid (New York: Paulist Press, 1987), ch. 3, p. 139.
[18] Pseudo-Dionysius, *The Divine Names*, in *The Complete Works*, ch. 7, n. 3, p. 109.
[19] Pseudo-Dionysius, *The Mystical Theology*, in *The Complete Works*, p. 137.
[20] Hugh of Saint Victor, *De meditando seu meditandi artificio*, PL 176, col. 993; Guigo II, *Ladder of Monks and Twelve Meditations: A Letter on the Contemplative Life*, trans. Edmund Colledge and James Walsh (Kalamazoo, MI: Cistercian Publications, 1981), pp. 67–8, 72–3; and Rachel Fulton Brown's essay in this volume.

to the early and medieval reception of scripture, Matter writes, is "the assumption that the words of scripture are just the outward shell of deep meanings hidden in the text, revealed through layers of allegorical reading" (p. 148). Cassian again was deeply influential on later traditions. He provided a fourfold account of the layers of meaning within the Bible. As Matter outlines, for Cassian there is

> the literal sense of the text (what was actually happening in the biblical narrative), the allegorical understanding of Christ and the Church, the tropological or moral sense of God and the Christian soul, and the anagogical sense, in which the text speaks of the ingathering of all things at the end of times. (p. 149)

Note that the word allegory was used to describe both the particular kind of interpretation that focused on the relationship between Christ and the church and all of the nonliteral interpretations of scripture. Again, Cassian's was just one, albeit a highly influential, schema. The primary point is that one began to be uplifted into the divine through the careful reading of, recitation of, and meditation on the Bible, whether through the liturgy, public recitation, or private reading.

Thus as Thomas H. Bestul shows in Chapter 7, "Meditatio/Meditation," *lectio divina*, the reading of scripture demanded by the *Rule of Benedict* and essential to all forms of monastic and religious life, led ineluctably to meditation (*meditatio*). Meditation, moreover, was never an end in itself, but always understood as a practice that would train one for prayer and contemplation. As Bestul notes, within the monastic tradition, "meditation was understood as both physiological and mental activity, with the goal of absorbing the complete meaning of the text, implanting it in the memory for future use" (p. 158). Over time, the term *meditatio* came also be used to refer to written works. Here the lines between *lectio*, *meditatio*, and *oratio* become blurred, for the writing of meditations was an act of scriptural exegesis (the meditation was often composed of an associative layering of biblical texts) and of prayer. At the heart of this tradition of the written meditation was the desire to arouse emotion. In its earliest instantiations, Bestul argues, the *meditatio* tradition emphasized self-knowledge and introspection as key to the uplifting of the soul into God. Grounded in scripture, in the words of Hugh of Saint Victor, these meditations "range along open ground" where they fix a "free gaze upon the contemplation of truth, drawing together now these, now those causes of things, or now penetrating into profundities."[21]

---

[21] Hugh of Saint Victor, *Didascalicon*, trans. Jerome Taylor (New York: Columbia University Press, 1961), ch. 3, n. 10, pp. 92–3. Cited by Bestul in this volume.

This form of reflective meditation was quickly overshadowed, however, by the enormous popularity of meditations focused on the life and death of Christ.[22] Coming to prominence during the thirteenth century, these meditations and the texts written to assist in them called on readers "to meditate on the events of Christ's life, *sicut praesens*, as though one were actually present at the scene. In this way emotion would be aroused, the presence of God deeply felt, and love for Christ increased" (p. 162). Bestul shows that the two strands of the *meditatio* tradition, the first focused on introspection and self-knowledge, the second on the life and death of Christ, came together in the work of the Franciscan theologian, Bonaventure (d. 1274). Bonaventure describes a threefold uplifting of the soul into God through meditation, prayer, and contemplation. The lives of Christ and of Saint Francis, who for Bonaventure engaged in the perfect imitation of Christ (*imitatio Christi*), organize Bonaventure's most famous meditative works. Francis is a model for Christ, and Christ, as the source of all creation and as incarnate, is the means by which the soul ascends to God. At the heart of Bonaventure's practice, Bestul explains, lies "a process of ascent to God beginning with contemplation of the traces of God in the visible world, then the traces of God within us, to consideration of God's unity and being, leading finally to repose of the soul in the love of God" (p. 164).

Prayer lies at the heart of the mystical life. It is made possible by the reading of and meditation on scripture. Yet it is also demanded of all Christians. This tension, as Rachel Fulton Brown argues in Chapter 8, "*Oratio*/Prayer," is at the heart of the exercise of prayer. It is tied to

---

[22] The essays collected here suggest a way to understand the relationship between the recitation of the Psalms so crucial to monastic and other forms of religious life and the development of the tradition of meditation on the life and death of Christ. As Matter notes, the Psalms were routinely interpreted as depicting the death and resurrection of Christ. Just as early Christian monks taught that all of the Psalter might be contained in a single verse (see Burton-Christie, Hollywood, and Brown), so also in the high and late Middle Ages and in the early modern period, one might come to understand the fullness of Christ's saving power through meditation on a single aspect of his Passion. If the Psalms were about Christ's death and resurrection, then meditation on extrabiblical texts in which scriptural passages were interwoven to generate a handbook for visualizing the life and Passion of Christ can easily be seen as a continuation, expansion, and transformation of existing practices. Methodist Passion hymns, then, might be understood as standing in a complex relationship of continuity with these practices. See, e.g., Phyllis Mack, *Heart Religion in the British Enlightenment: Gender and Emotion in Early Methodism* (Cambridge: Cambridge University Press, 2008), pp. 52–4. Mack argues that the goal of these hymns was not union with Christ but conversion. D. Bruce Hindmarsh, however, notes that Methodist hymnals dealt not only with the conversion experience but also charted "an ideal of spiritual progress." D. Bruce Hindmarsh, "'End of Faith as Its Beginning': Models of Spiritual Progress in Early Evangelical Devotional Hymns," *Spiritus* 10 (2010): 2.

a related paradox, that surrounding the nature of language for God, for if God can never be adequately named, then what words can or ought Christians use to worship God? Hence Cassian describes Abba Isaac, an early Christian desert father, as counseling him to pray using only a single psalm verse, "*Deus in adiutorium meum intende; Domine ad adiuvandum me festina*" ("O God make speed to save me; O Lord make haste to help me") (Ps 70:1; Vulgate 69:2), even as the monastic tradition of reciting all one hundred and fifty of the Psalms each week was being established. The Psalms were vital for those dedicated fully to the religious life and also, increasingly, for the laity. Yet while all Christians must pray, some might become virtuosi of prayer – this is the goal of the monastic and other forms of life devoted to Christian perfection within early, medieval, and early modern Christianity. Just as with meditation one begins with scripture and then moves through it to the production of new, scripturally grounded texts, so also with prayer. The Our Father, the Hail Mary, the Psalter, and other biblical texts were at the heart of the exercise of prayer, yet experts in prayer often produced new prayers through which others might come to experience God.

As both Burton-Christie and Brown show, Cassian's Abba Isaac explains that the monk can achieve, through prayerful meditation on a single line of the Psalms, an attentiveness in which the mind is set on fire and is "called forth in an unspeakable ecstasy of heart and with an insatiable gladness of spirit, and the mind, having transcended all feelings and visible matter, pours it out to God with unutterable groans and sighs."[23] This is *excessus mentis*, or fiery prayer, what Burton-Christie aptly describes as "an intense and often short-lived experience of ecstasy or rapture in prayer."[24] Here one comes, Burton-Christie explains, to "that sublime place that Abba Isaac claims one can know when the experiential grasp of the Word becomes fused with the experience of pure prayer – 'contemplation of God alone'" (p. 55). And here, most crucially, we move in and through *lectio*, *meditatio*, and *oratio* to contemplation, vision (*visio*), rapture (*raptus*), and union (*unio mystica*), those phenomena most often identified as mystical by modern scholars.

As Veerle Fraeters shows in Chapter 9, "*Visio*/Vision," *visio* is a complex term within early and medieval Western Christianity. Rooted in the tremendously influential typology provided by Augustine in his

---

[23] Cassian, *Conferences*, conf. 10, ch. 11, p. 385; Cassian, *Conférences*, conf. 10, ch. 11, p. 93.
[24] For this theme in Cassian, see also Columba Stewart, *Cassian the Monk* (Oxford: Oxford University Press, 1998), pp. 114–30.

Literal Commentary on Genesis, vision was routinely understood as threefold. Augustine distinguished between vision through the eyes of the body (*visio corporalis*), vision through the eye of the soul (*visio spiritualis*), and the highest form of sight, which he called intellectual vision (*visio intellectualis*). For Augustine, in this division concepts are higher and more adequate to the divine than are images, a view that stands in some tension with the position articulated by Dionysius, in which images and concepts are equally inadequate to God. This ambivalence runs throughout much of the Western Christian tradition, with some emphasizing the superiority of intellectual vision over all other kinds of vision and others insisting that one must transcend both the imagination and the intellect to contemplate God in ecstasy (*extasis* or *excessus mentis*). Yet all agreed that vision in all of its forms was a vital part of the soul's movement into God, for God as creator of all things could be known, albeit inadequately, through God's creations.

As Fraeters shows, women were seen as particularly apt to have visions and visionary experience was often at the heart of women's religious writing during the Middle Ages. Although liturgically and scripturally grounded, these visionary experiences legitimated women's writing; women could not be priests, and without that office, they were generally deemed unauthorized to engage in the interpretation of scripture so vital to the production of mystical texts. Classical and medieval conceptions of the sexed body, moreover, led many to believe that women were more liable to receive visions (whether divine or demonic) and so were more inclined to visions and rapture (*raptus*), to being rapt outside of the body or to experience their bodies and souls as "overpowered by the divine presence" (p. 189).

In Chapter 10, "*Raptus*/Rapture," Dyan Elliott usefully lays out the relationship, and subtle differences, between the medieval understanding of ecstasy and that of rapture; the latter connotes a certain violence on the part of the divine agent and a certain passivity on the part of the one who experiences God. Although Elliott notes that many texts do not clearly distinguish between ecstasy and rapture, she suggests that the more passive conception of the latter was strongly associated with women. These rapturous states, moreover, were often described as marking the body externally. Bodies levitated, emitted fragrant odors or ointments, were overcome with torrents of tears, or were so impassible that onlookers might stick a pin in the leg or pour molten lead over the feet of an enrapt person without drawing her out of her trance. These latter accounts come, however, from the hagiographical literature, literature that required some visible marking of sanctity on its subject. Yet as Elliott shows, such paramystical phenomena were increasingly associated with the mystical life in the Middle Ages (and they continue to be the subject of discussion in modernity).

As we have noted, among the contested issues in the modern study of Christian mysticism is precisely what counts as mystical. Are visionary experiences mystical? What about the kinds of extraordinary bodily experiences often associated with rapture in pre- and early modern literature? Are ecstasies and raptures essential to the mystical life or phenomena that one may experience, but that should be transcended in a higher experience of the divine? All of these questions have their roots in disagreements, sometimes overt and sometimes covert, over what constitutes the perfection of the Christian life. As Fraeters and Elliott both remark, for the men and women who described them, visions and raptures were generally not understood to be the apex of the religious life, although they might be a significant part of it. Yet as Bernard McGinn demonstrates in Chapter 11, "*Unio mystica*/Mystical Union," there were also important disagreements among those who understood union with God to be the height of the Christian life.

Although the phrase mystical union was rare before the seventeenth century, McGinn shows that many wrote of becoming one with God, with two primary conceptions of what such union entailed. As McGinn explains, some conceived of union "as a uniting of the Infinite Spirit with the finite spirit in a bond of love that emphasizes the distinction between creator and creature" (p. 204). It might feel to the soul as if it were one with God, but an ontological distinction between the soul and God continued to be in place. Thus Bernard of Clairvaux (d. 1153) draws on 1 Corinthians 6:17 ("*Qui autem adhaeret Domino unus spiritus est*" – "One who adheres to the Lord is one spirit with him") and asks, "when will [the soul] experience this kind of love, so that the mind, drunk with divine love and forgetting itself, making itself like a broken vessel (1 Cor 6:17), marches right into God, and adhering to him, becomes one spirit with him."[25] For Bernard, union occurs when the will of the soul fully submits itself to God's will. We come to be one with God when, through God's grace, we have so overcome our sinfulness as to have a will that fully adheres to God's will.

The language of *unitas spiritus*, McGinn explains, continues to be used throughout the medieval and modern periods. Yet there is a countertrend, one that first emerges clearly in northern Europe in the late

---

[25] Bernard of Clairvaux, *On Loving God*, in *Selected Works*, trans. G. R. Evans (New York: Paulist Press, 1987), X. 27, p. 195. Translation modified.

thirteenth and early fourteenth centuries (although there is evidence for similar views appearing contemporaneously south of the Alps). The beguines Hadewijch (active ca. 1250), Mechthild of Magdeburg (d. 1282), and Marguerite Porete (d. 1310), McGinn argues, "pioneered the use of the language of indistinction."

> Forms of daring, and even excessive, erotic language appeared; some mystics began to speak about forms of indistinction with God achieved by annihilating the created will and human individuality. Such understandings of union were often expressed in terms of the soul's regaining its true home, the precreational status it enjoys as an eternal idea in the mind of God. (p. 205)

Thus at a moment of intense erotic exchange between the soul and Christ in Mechthild's *The Flowing Light of the Godhead*, God says, "Lady Soul, you are so uttered formed to my nature that not the slightest thing can come between you and me."[26] Hadewijch has a vision in which an angel shows her an ideal, "full-grown" Hadewijch who is enclosed within God and has never fallen into sin.[27] Marguerite Porete argues that the free and annihilated soul – one who has not only overcome her own sinfulness and her own will, but who has also destroyed reason, will, and desire – exists there "where she was before she was."[28] Meister Eckhart takes up this language, placing it within a Neoplatonic framework of emanation, remaining, and return. Eckhart thus argues, as McGinn explains, for a union without distinction and "claims that, on some level, God and human are merged into what Meister Eckhart called *ein einic ein* ('a single/simple One')" (p. 204). The starkness of this language points to the centrality of apophasis for Eckhart. One must name and unname the soul just as one names and unnames God, for the soul shares in the unnameability of God in that ground where God's ground and the soul's ground are one ground.

In describing the simple and annihilated soul, Marguerite claims that such a soul "neither longs for nor despises poverty or tribulation, Mass or sermon, fasting or prayer."[29] (Eckhart uses similar language in

---

[26] Mechthild of Mageburg, *The Flowing Light of the Godhead*, trans. Frank Tobin (New York: Paulist Press, 1998), bk. 1, ch. 44, p. 62.

[27] Hadewijch, *The Complete Works*, trans. Mother Columba Hart (New York: Paulist Press, 1980), Vision 4, p. 274.

[28] Marguerite Porete, *The Mirror of Simple Souls*, trans. Edmund Colledge, J. C. Marler, and Judith Grant (Notre Dame, IN: University of Notre Dame Press, 1999), ch. 111, p. 134.

[29] Ibid., ch. 9, p. 20.

his vernacular sermons.) Although Marguerite immediately goes on to say that such a soul is so well ordered in God that it cannot ask for anything that is forbidden, the sacramental life of the church and the spiritual exercises central to the religious life play a role only in the soul's process of annihilation. Once the soul is free from will, reason, and desire, Marguerite insists, it will no longer require these practices. Perhaps more importantly, Marguerite describes those souls who achieve extraordinary experiences of God's love as occupying only the fourth state of the seven states to which the soul ought to aspire. This fourth state sounds very much like the realm of experience described in many of the essays in this volume, among them those by Fraeters and Elliott. Hence Marguerite claims that

> the fourth state is when the Soul is drawn up by the exaltation of love, into delight in the thoughts that come in meditation, and freed from all outward labors and from obedience to another, through the exaltation of contemplation, whereby the Soul becomes so vulnerable, so noble and delicate that she cannot endure anything to touch her, except only the touch of Love's pure delight, which makes her full of joy and lighthearted, and overweening in her abundance of love, in which she is the mistress of luster – that is, of the brightness – of her soul, which fills her wonderfully full of love of great fidelity, through that harmony of union which has given her possession of its delights.[30]

Having moved through meditation to contemplation and ecstatic union with God, the soul would seem to have achieved all it desires – and in a sense it has. Yet Marguerite calls for the annihilation of desire itself, which entails a movement past meditation, contemplation, rapture, and loving union into the abyssal negation of the soul.

Marguerite distrusts the special gifts of the spirit given in the fourth stage, for in them "Love's great brightness has so dazzled [the soul's] sight" that the soul comes wrongly to believe that she has plumbed the heights and depths of the spiritual life. In a similar way, Meister Eckhart at times seems to disdain extraordinary experiences of God's presence in contemplation, raptures, visions, or ecstasies. Yet, as Hollywood argues in discussing *experientia*, it is important to remember that Marguerite's and Eckhart's distrust is made in the context of widespread assertions of the existence and importance of these kinds of extraordinary experiences. Moreover, both Marguerite and Eckhart were condemned, and

[30] Ibid., ch. 118, pp. 142–3.

in the wake of those condemnations extraordinary experiences were pursued with even greater fervor. Most importantly, perhaps, all of the evidence we have suggests that Marguerite and Eckhart understood the practices of reading, meditation, prayer, and contemplation as essential to achieving the very union without distinction to which they call their readers. Debates about the relative importance of the experience of God's loving presence to the soul, of visions, raptures, or ecstatic union with God and the pursuit of detachment, annihilation, or unknowing begin, then, in the Middle Ages.

The issue of what practices were necessary to the religious life and what experiences constituted its highest achievement went hand in hand with debates about the relationship between action and contemplation. As Charlotte Radler argues in Chapter 12, "*Actio et Contemplatio*/Action and Contemplation," a key concern for those dedicated to the life of prayer and Christian perfection is how to bring together love of God, the putative aim of the contemplative life, with the love for one's neighbor also demanded by God within Christian revelation. The problem, presented allegorically through a reading of Luke 10:38–42, recurs throughout the monastic tradition and, as Radler shows, continues to play a vital role in the articulation of the ideal form of Christian life. Radler highlights the multiple ways in which the tension has been addressed, but gives particular attention to those who argue for what contemporary theologian Leonardo Boff has called "*contemplativus in liberatione*," or "contemplation while working towards liberation." Although the language of liberation may seem foreign to premodern and early modern texts, Radler shows that it beautifully echoes Eckhart's claim that in the union without distinction between God and the soul, the just work, which is the birth of the Son in the soul, is performed.

Radler's essay offers a nice pivot point, then, between Part II, focused on key terms derived from early Christian and medieval sources, and Part III, which explores a variety of conceptual and historical issues currently at the center of the study of Christian mysticism. As many of the essays in Part II demonstrate, the concerns crucial to pre- and early modern audiences continue to play a role throughout modernity and into the present. Yet the terms around which Part II is organized are ancient. In Part III, this is less clearly the case or, when ancient antecedents are available, authors focus on the particular form taken by contemporary debates. The essays are thus oriented toward contemporary historiographical and theoretical discussions, despite a continued attention to the historical specificity of the material with which each author engages.

There is a tendency in the scholarship on medieval devotional and mystical life to assume that the rise in the use of the vernacular denotes a certain democratization of the religious life. As Barbara Newman explains in Chapter 13, "Latin and the Vernaculars," Latin was the official language of the Western Christian Church, read and spoken throughout Western Europe by the clergy and other educated men – and some, most often religious, women. As reading and writing in the local vernacular languages became more prominent, a key question for religious leaders was what it was appropriate for lay Christians who read only the vernacular to learn from texts. Newman argues convincingly that while the use of the vernacular did make texts accessible to a broader audience, because of the difficulty of mystical texts and of the kind of life that they enjoined, which demanded ample leisure, self-discipline, and institutional support, the broad appeal of the vernacular did "not hold in the case of vernacular mystical books, which were read largely by religious women and their spiritual directors" (p. 229). Mystical texts written in the vernaculars, paradoxically, were more likely to have a broad readership if they were translated into Latin for which there was an international public of readers. Exploring the complexity of the interplay between vernacular and Latin textual production, Newman argues against any easy conclusions about their relative power and reach.

As Newman shows, Latin was an important vehicle for the dissemination of mystical texts originally written in the vernacular. A vernacular text like Henry Suso's (1295–1366) *The Little Book of Eternal Wisdom* might be translated into Latin (in this case by Suso himself). The resultant text, *Horologium Sapientiae* (*Wisdom's Clock*) differs from its original in important ways. By 1500, it had been translated into French, Dutch, Italian, English, Bohemian, Hungarian, Polish, Swedish, and Danish – although as Newman shows, when one turns to the surviving manuscripts, there are more in Latin than in all of the vernaculars combined. The continued importance of Latin and its centrality to the dissemination of mystical texts leads to the important question of how mystical texts were read and how they were transmitted across Europe.

In Chapter 14, "Transmission," Sara S. Poor takes up this issue, in the process pointing to the multiple meanings of transmission. First, God transmits God's word to the mystic. As Poor explains,

> the communication of God's truth in his own words as spoken to or through the mystic ... is thus embedded in mystical experience and text. Indeed, the act of recording revelations is the second act of

transmission and this act is mimicked in a third: the duplication and dissemination of mystical texts in manuscripts, an act that extends the conversation to others through reading and writing. In other words, the compulsion to talk about God's truth was also felt by clerics who wrote about mystical experience and by devout readers who made copies of writing by mystics and clerics and distributed them to others. (p. 241)

Transmission is a religious process, then, and it is one that occurs at multiple levels of experience and textual production.

Newman and Poor both engage in manuscript studies, an area of increasing scholarly interest to students of mysticism. If the act of transmission is vital to the mystical life, a point taken up in more theological terms by Charles M. Stang in Chapter 15, "Writing," then writing practices and the copying and transmission of texts become crucial to the study of mysticism. As Newman and Poor demonstrate, manuscripts functioned as transcripts of performances (e.g., songs, prayers, meditations, sermons, and other more complicated enactments of mystical ascent or annihilation); they were also intended to be performed, whether communally or individually. (Poor notes that the more widespread practice of private reading was among the important shifts brought about by the transition from manuscript to print culture, yet it is important to remember that private reading itself can be intensely performative.[31])

One of the most exciting aspects of Poor's work is the way in which she tracks the very different modes of reading mystical texts made visible by careful attention to the manuscript tradition. Modern readers tend to focus on the book with a single author, read in its entirety and in the order in which it appears in print. This is not the way, however, that people always read, nor was it the way in which many texts associated with the mystical life were intended to be read. Poor gives the example of Hildegard of Bingen's (1098–1179) *Scivias* (*Know the Ways of God*), which contains visions she claimed to have received from God. She dictated the visions in Latin to a scribe. *Scivias*, together with other of Hildegard's works, was collected together in a manuscript known as the *Riesenkodex* (*Giant Book*). The *Scivias* was copied in its entirety during the twelfth and thirteenth centuries, but by the fourteenth and fifteenth centuries, it was transmitted in increasingly smaller pieces.

---

[31] See, e.g., Jessica Brantley, *Reading in the Wilderness: Private Devotion and Public Performance in Late Medieval England* (Chicago: University of Chicago Press, 2007).

These shorter selections most often appeared in compilations of mystical texts, an important genre of writing in the later Middle Ages.

These compilations are most usefully read not as distortions of some putatively pure and intact original, but as theological and mystical productions. As Poor argues, "their increasingly fragmentary and individual quality was ... influenced by devotional practice" (p. 248). Just as Cassian's Abba Isaac recommended to Cassian and his friend Germanus that they focus their attention on a single verse of the Psalms, so many medieval mystical texts record and model "the practice of meditating on a short text about an image, vision, biblical passage, or piece of religious instruction" (p. 248). Detailed tables of contents led readers to texts that spoke to their specific situations. So whether we are dealing with a book written in many easily separable units, such as Mechthild of Magdeburg's *Flowing Light of the Godhead*, or a mystical compilation like *The Book of Divine Love* (1483) designed by Dorothea of Hof out of selections from other texts, both are compositions in their own right – compositions meant to be read in a specific, nonlinear, focused, and attentive manner (even though a broad movement through different stages of the mystical life may be evident in the manuscript's larger organization.)

The interplay between reading, meditation, prayer, contemplation, union, and writing is drawn out more fully by Charles M. Stang in Chapter 15, "Writing." Stang demonstrates conclusively what Poor suggests, which is that for at least some early and medieval Christians, writing is not simply a secondary phenomenon within the mystical life, but is also constitutive of it. Most striking, perhaps, is the case of the Dionysian Corpus, which, as we have mentioned, was produced under a pseudonym. Although produced during the sixth century, these texts purport to have been written by the Greek man, Dionysius the Areopagite, said to have been converted by Paul in the Acts of the Apostles. Many scholars have assumed that the use of the pseudonym was merely a way to gain increased prestige and authority. Stang argues, on the contrary, that the pseudonym is essential to the mystical path of naming and unnaming, cataphasis and apophasis, so vital to the corpus. As Stang puts it, "writing pseudonymously," in such a way that the author is "neither entirley himself nor someone else ... becomes for this author an erotic and ecstatic practice in the service of breaching the integrity of the singular self, unsaying that singular self, and thereby soliciting a deifying union with the unknown God." "If this is right," Stang concludes, "then writing as a spiritual practice in the service of mysticism takes its place at the inauguration of the negative or apophatic tradition" (p. 260).

The centrality of writing and transmission to the mystical life can be read in light of the dialectical tensions between transcendence and immanence, time and eternity, cataphasis and apophasis, and community and individuality found in Augustine's vision at Ostia. Although often mistakenly understood by modern scholars as secondary to the mystical life, writing and copying are, as Newman, Poor, and Stang show, intrinsic to it. Through mystical writing, God becomes immanent, eternity breaks into time, names are said and unsaid in a dialectical interplay through which the individual comes to God in and through community – either living communities of human beings or the communities created through the practices of reading and writing themselves.[32]

These texts, however, often present fundamental hermeneutical problems for the modern reader; the cataphatic naming of God, as Louth, Matter, Fraeters, and others show, involves the use of a wide array of images and concepts, and it is not always clear in what way they are meant to refer. Fraeters, in particular, demonstrates the wide range of sensory images, drawing not only from the realm of sight, but also from the realms of touch, taste, sound, and smell, on which mystical texts draw. Often biblically based, these images are said and unsaid in a dizzying array of synesthesic combinations. One goal of Patricia Dailey's complex argument in Chapter 16, "The Body and Its Senses," is to understand the precise theological character of such language within Western Christianity. Drawing on the Pauline distinction between the inner and the outer human being, Dailey demonstrates the way in which bodies – inner and outer, material and spiritual – become text. So for the beguine Hadewijch, God's presence "is strangely sensory" and "inhabits the senses while not being determinately sensible." God – under the guise of *Minne* (Love) – "passes, like a secret, through the senses, without form or figure, but permitting its taste" (p. 270). As Dailey explains, these sensory images allow Hadewijch to articulate the emotional and affective truth of that which she experiences, even as that experience cannot be fully embodied or made tangible. The inner senses, according to Niklaus Largier, whom Dailey cites, "constitute and construct a specific reality of the mind. Thus ... the invention and the rhetoric of the inner and spiritual senses allowed for the creation of an inner space of 'experience,' 'exploration,' and 'amplification' of the emotional as well as the sensory life of the soul."[33]

---

[32] For the indispensable idea of textual communities, see Brian Stock, *The Implications of Literacy: Written Language and Models of Interpretation in the Eleventh and Twelfth Centuries* (Princeton, NJ: Princeton University Press, 1983).

[33] Niklaus Larger, "Inner Senses, Outer Senses: The Practice of Emotions in Medieval Mysticism," in *Codierungen von Emotionen im Mittelalter/Emotions and Sensibilities in the Middle Ages*, ed. C. Stephen Jaeger and Ingrid Kasten (Berlin: De Gruyter, 2003), pp. 4–5.

Yet the language of the corporeal and of the spiritual senses, as Jeffrey F. Hamburger shows in Chapter 17, "Mysticism and Visuality," poses something of a challenge to those conceptions of religious perfection that insist on the ultimate unknowability of God. As Hamburger puts the question, "Given ... that the visible, let alone the invisible, is often said to defy verbal description, it must be asked why – and how – mystics 'see,' and why vision, however defined, is so indispensable to their way of framing the world and their experience of it" (p.277). Hamburger argues that images and other sensory claims not only make ideas accessible, but also endow them with enormous authority and authenticity. Such experiences are, moreover, theologically justified by the Incarnation – God become human, an embodied human – at the heart of the Christian tradition. Exploring the various theories of vision operative within the early and medieval Western Christian context, moreover, Hamburger demonstrates how vision became central to the Christian mystical tradition, even as these examples of what we would call cataphatic visionary theology often carry within them the process of their own unsaying. The two moments cannot be torn apart, for both are necessary to the movement into and of God.

In their articulation of the role of the inner senses in the development of the spiritual life, Christian writers prove themselves to be acute psychologists, for at the heart of their endeavors lies the attempt to cognitively and affectively reorient themselves and their readers toward God. Emotion and cognition go hand in hand, an insight central to the medieval texts discussed by Fiona Somerset in Chapter 18, "Emotion." As Somerset shows, medieval mystical writers were "emotion-artists ... specialists in the observation and description of emotion, and their writings provide especially rich sites for investigating the theory, practice, expression, and communication of emotional states" (p. 298). Mystical authors not only described but also incited emotion. Hence in the mid-fourteenth century, Richard Fitzralph labeled as "excitative speech" the rhetorical strategies by means of which mystical authors stir up feelings in themselves and their audiences. Furthermore, Somerset argues, in their attention to the finest detail of emotional states and to the varied means by which emotion can be generated, early and medieval Christian texts provide a useful counterpart to contemporary research, which attempts to distinguish between pan-cultural "basic emotions," socially constructed emotions, and higher cognitive states in which biological and cultural factors both play a role. Somerset suggests, following arguments in the contemporary philosophy of emotion, that what differentiates these more complex states might be the embedding of affect within narrative; so she argues, "perhaps it is narrative, rather than naming, that gives any textual rendition of emotion its intersubjective ground, while allegory, with its capacity to make the familiar strange, may give it flight."[34]

Throughout the essays collected here we see a recurrent emphasis on the spiritual senses – first of scripture, then by extension of the human person – and a close link between the senses and the emotions. The allegorical or spiritual interpretation of scripture – its spiritual sense – is associated with the body's five senses, although now moved from an outward, corporeal form to an inward, spiritual one. (At times, however, it is not entirely clear where to locate these sensory and intensely emotional experiences, a point leading to productive tensions in and between the essays collected here. See, in particular, Patricia Dailey's "The Body and Its Senses" and Constance Furey's "Sexuality.") The spiritual senses, we might say, are stirred up by the spiritual meaning of scripture – and throughout the early, medieval, and early modern Christian traditions, the spiritual senses are associated with what we have come to call the emotions. Sensory language, whether understood as corporal, spiritual, both, or something in between, is the language of the emotions and the emotions are at the heart of the religious life.[35] To make such a claim is by no means to downplay the centrality of cognition, for love is a way of knowing – and knowledge without love is empty.[36]

As Mary Frohlich argues in Chapter 19, "Authority," in naming the domain in which the transformation of the senses and the affective life occurs "the book of experience," the twelfth-century Cistercian, Bernard of Clairvaux opened an authoritative space to which every soul could lay claim (see also Hollywood's essay in this volume). Bernard appears to be the first to use the phrase when he argues in the third of his *Sermons on the Song of Songs* that one must look to the book of experience and compare it with the book of scripture in the hopes that one might bring

---

[34] I find myself wondering about this apparent antithesis, however, as the allegorical interpretation of the Bible is often a form of engendering narrative, telling stories about the believer and God and the often highly affective interplay between them.

[35] For a highly suggestive account of the interplay between figural language and emotion in eighteenth-century reappropriations of enthusiasm, see Shaun Irlam, *Elations: The Poetics of Enthusiasm in Eighteenth-Century Britain* (Stanford, CA: Stanford University Press, 1999), pp. 70–82. Irlam suggests that there is a sort of religious despair operative in this move, a despair that might usefully be compared to the "dark night of the soul" described in modernity by religious writers as diverse as John of the Cross and Thérèse of Lisieux. On this theme, see especially Mary Frohlich's essay in this volume.

[36] For two very different views of how love and knowledge come together in Western Christian mysticism, see the essays in this volume by Louth and McGinn.

one's own experience and that of the biblical text together. Yet Bernard's claim simply reflects on and validates the ongoing practice of reading, meditation, prayer, contemplation, and vision operative within the culture in which he wrote. Thus as Frohlich argues, among Bernard's contemporaries were powerful women and men who gained religious authority through the intensity of their experience. Bernard is among them, for although he makes no claim to visionary experience and little to rapture or union, the intensity of his language and the richness of its effects are unrivaled. Together with his friend, William of Saint Thierry, and others within and outside of the Cistercian order, Bernard's work lay at the heart of a highly affective understanding of the Christian life in which the spiritual senses were persistently drawn into play. Other women and men deployed the language Bernard provided in order to teach and write, often on the basis of more pointedly extraordinary experiences of God.

Bernard's central account of the mystical life occurs in his eighty-six sermons on the Song of Songs; his contemporary, Hildegard of Bingen, is only the most famous of those for whom their own visions became the text they wrote and on which they commented. Thus we see in the twelfth century two models of authority operating side by side, one that rests on office and appeals to scriptural authority and the teaching power of the church and the other to special gifts. Bernard, as abbot and priest, not only could but was required to preach the word of scripture. But Bernard used and enhanced his pedagogical office to make affective experience authoritative. In his call for each of his hearers to bring the book of scripture together with the book of experience, to sing with the bride of the Song of Songs, "Let him kiss me with the kisses of his mouth" (Sg 1:1), he helped to foster the conditions in which extraordinary experiences – visions, raptures, ecstasies, and exultations – became the basis for new books.

As Frohlich shows, during the twelfth century we see emerge a pattern that will play out repeatedly throughout the following centuries: some Christians, especially women, claimed religious authority on the basis of their extraordinary experiences of God's presence or of union with God. Some had books written about them. Others wrote books, sometimes for local communities, sometimes for broader audiences. Yet their safety and the success of their work tended to depend on the endorsement of male clerical authorities. (Hildegard wrote to Bernard seeking his approval – and through him, that of his former student, Pope Eugenius III.) By the fourteenth century, serious tensions emerged around women's claims to religious authority, with women increasingly forced to conform to the male-instituted practices by which one discerned what was a true and what was a false revelation.

Elliott and McGinn also discuss this process, the specifically gendered dimensions of which are articulated most fully by Alison Weber. As Weber notes in Chapter 20, "Gender," "as an abstraction, Christian mysticism is a religious experience for which sexual difference and gender roles are irrelevant." Yet although spiritual equality is a part of Christian doctrine (Galatians 3:28), "gender has had a profound impact on the perception of individual mystics and has played a fundamental role in determining how those individuals are remembered. Furthermore, gender roles have shaped the performance of mysticism – the acts, words, and gestures with which mystics have presented themselves to others" (p. 315). If, moreover, mysticism is its performance, as many of the essays collected here suggest, then the Christian mystical life is inevitably gendered. This is not to say that there is some transhistorical essence of femaleness or femininity and of maleness or masculinity that runs across the tradition. As Constance Furey shows, these dichotomies are inadequate to the multiple forms of embodiment visible within the Western Christian mystical tradition. Instead, Weber argues that gender has a history. If this is the case, than so does mysticism, even at those moments in which it pushes against the very boundaries of the historical. As Weber shows, "historically, mysticism has been remarkably protean in its capacity to challenge and confirm traditional gender roles, to open and foreclose opportunities for women, and to uplift and denigrate them" (p. 327). It has done so, moreover, in ways that push against any easy correlation of affective or corporeal mysticism with women or a putatively speculative mysticism with men. As the essays collected here suggest, it is not clear that such a distinction can account for the richness and variety of the Christian mystical tradition.

Throughout pre- and early modern Christianity, women were associated with the body, its porousness, openness, and vulnerability. Female bodies were believed to be more labile and changeable, more subject to affective shifts, and more open to penetration, whether by God, demons, or by other human beings. This slide, from claims to women's spiritual penetrability to that of her physical penetrability (and vice versa) is at the heart of Chapter 21, "Sexuality," in which Constance Furey makes a complex argument about the importance of sexuality to the study of Western Christian mysticism. As Furey shows, the porosity of the body might, at particular historical moments, be primarily associated with femaleness or femininity, yet the idea that the human being – body and soul – has porous boundaries is vital to all Christian mystical experience.

Furey notes that scholars are generally more comfortable talking about eroticism than about sexuality in relationship to the mystical tradition. *Eros* has "a proud pedigree," with no less a figure than Dionysius declaring God as *eros* and *eros* as the central power of "unifying, binding, and joining" all things in God. To the question, why then talk of sexuality, Furey responds,

> because if eroticism connotes yearning and fulfillment, arousal and frustration, deferral and satisfaction, the category of sexuality more specifically keeps our eyes trained on the physicality of these sensations and desires. In studying sexuality in Christian mysticism, we take our cue from the fact that many mystic writers wrote about somatic pleasure and pain, that they described bodies – their own bodies and the body of God – pierced, wounded, aroused, panting, bleeding, sucking, languishing, exulting, enlarging, and diminishing. (p. 330)

To get at the sexuality of pre- and early modern mystical texts, however, requires that we expand our conception of what sexuality entails. "The sexual language in mystical texts," Furey argues, "equates transcendence with embodied intersubjectivity" (p. 332). As a result, any easy dichotomies between transcendence and immanence or between community and individual are radically undermined by the intense focus on the porous boundaries between bodies and between body and soul.

At the heart of the sexuality of many mystical texts lies the centrality of relations and relationality to the mystical life. As Furey argues, describing the writings of Margery Kempe (d. aft. 1438) and Ann Lee (d. 1784), the founder of the Shakers, "the relationship with Christ is described as relational, as interactive and changeable, as constituted through aspirations and specific behaviors and the particularities of contact, of touch and reaction, between two beings" (p. 339). "Mystical sexuality is," she concludes, "about the intense pleasure and pain that bodies inflict and receive, and about the ecstasy, standing outside oneself, the rhythmic arousal and breathless pleasure that come from and in this experience" (p. 340).

Just as the sexuality of the mystical life fully enacts the intense interplay between immanence and transcendence in the experience of God, so Patricia Dailey demonstrates the temporal complexity of these experiences, the tension between their transient and enduring qualities. She records what occurs when the linearity of human time is confronted and transformed by the eternity of God. In Chapter 22, "Time and Memory," Dailey invokes the ideas of "unlived experience" and of "prememory," a kind of memory "oriented to something that claims to be before history and before space" (p. 342). Mystical experience is, for

Dailey, in some fundamental sense unlived, for it marks the eruption of the eternal into time. In describing visionary experience, she argues, "the vision is outside of time, in that the mystic's inner body or soul experiences an awareness or proximity to the divine, which may be beyond the grasp of language" (pp. 347–8). Hence the interplay of time and eternity replicate the interplay between the inscription of God in language and God's radical unnameability, between the embodied language that is the mystic's ecstatic and wounded corporality and the illegibility of that affectively riven corpus. As Dailey argues, the "temporal syncopation of event, meaning, and time has a similar structure to what Freud calls belatedness and Jean Laplanche calls afterwardness" (p. 348). Experience transforms the subject and with it that subject's history; all of one's life is recalibrated by the *now* such that all that preceded it is as if remembered for the first time. Dailey makes an even stronger, more explicitly theological claim, arguing that the "inversion of recall also shows that the memory does not find its origin in the mystic, but in God. It is not her memory, but the memory of God, in the strange sense of the subjective and the objective genitive." The mystic thus remembers God and her memory belong not to her, but to God Godself. "Memory," Dailey concludes, "is not merely a turning to the past or to time immemorial but also is a guide to the timelessness of the future" (p. 350).

A final word about the future – the future inscribed, and yet largely unspoken, within the essays collected here – the future of mysticism in modernity. In "Mysticism, Modernity, and the Invention of Aesthetic Experience," Niklaus Largier argues that, during the Protestant reformation, language associated with the mystical life was separated from the practices that gave it shape in early and medieval Christianity. Mystical tropes were projected "into a practice of writing and conversation ... evacuated of their objective claims, contained by the limits set up by Luther [between the secular and the religious], and adding to it the form of an experiential supplement that we might be tempted to qualify as aesthetic or subjective."[37] Largier is certainly right that the aesthetic realm took on many of the affective and figurative traits associated with the mystical life in early and medieval Christianity, yet I think he is mistaken in presuming that objective religious claims cease to be made in mystical terms.[38]

---

[37] Largier, "Mysticism, Modernity," p. 50.
[38] Shaun Irlam makes a similar case for eighteenth-century England, although he focuses his attention more sharply on the language of enthusiasm and its movement from a religious (and markedly perjorative) use to an approving aesthetic one. See Irlam, *Elations*.

As Largier notes, Martin Luther (1483–1646) articulates the distinction between the secular and the religious in the context of his debates with the radical wing of the reformation, in particular the Anabaptists and other religious and social revolutionaries. Labeling them *Schwärmer* or enthusiasts (the most common English translation of the term), Luther objects strenuously to their claims to offer "inspired," "mystical," or "prophetic" readings of the Bible. According to Largier,

> Luther produces a notion of the secular not as a realm that is subordinated to the religious, absolutely disassociated from it, or even opposed to it, nor primarily as a realm that is an expression of the faith of the believer ... but as an institutional context that is meant to contain and limit the use that can be made of the scriptures and of scriptural exegesis.... Thus, Luther also contains the formation of legitimate communities of readers, limiting the act of reading and the "freedom of a Christian" to the "inner man" or a contained religious community.[39]

On Largier's reading Luther privatizes religion in order to contain the religious and political claims of enthusiasts who read scripture allegorically, typologically, and prophetically – in other words, mystically. (The very term mysticism, as Leigh Eric Schmidt notes, first emerges in the English language in the context of mid-eighteenth-century critiques of enthusiasm.)[40]

Yet the practices in and by means of which mystical experience is inculcated continue to exist alongside of their rejection or transformation by the magisterial reformation, not only among Roman Catholics but also among Protestants. Although the terms mysticism and enthusiasm were largely perjorative and so avoided into the eighteenth century – and often beyond – the practices associated with them were not. Reading scripture, meditating on scripture and on one's own experience in relationship to scripture, visions and auditions, rapturous experiences of God's presence, and experiences of union with God continue to mark the Christian tradition up to the present day.[41] But that is another story,

---

[39] Ibid., pp. 42–3.

[40] Schmidt, "Making of Modern 'Mysticism,'" pp. 277–81. At least within the context of English-language speaking communities, mysticism and enthusiasm become almost inseparable terms.

[41] Within Protestant circles, practices of scripture reading, introspection, meditation, prayer, and writing were often directed toward conversion, itself often – although by no means always – understood as an intensely felt experience. Yet many also understood such practices as important to the life of sanctification or spiritual progress. Protestants for the most part steered clear of the words mystic and mystical, but this is not always

one the complexity of which might be more adequately accounted for against the background presented here.

the case. In addition, at times evangelicals and others speak explicitly about seeking union with God. For the various understandings of conversion operative in British Protestantism during one particularly fecund period, see D. Bruce Hindmarsh, *The Evangelical Conversion Narrative: Spiritual Autobiography in Early Modern England* (Oxford: Oxford University Press, 2005); for Protestant use of the term mystical, see Schmidt, "Making of Modern 'Mysticism,'" pp. 276–7; and for one use of the language of union and contemplation in early evangelicalism, Hindmarsh, "'End of Faith,'" p. 16. On the centrality of experience in Puritanism, among the early Quakers, Pietism, Methodism, various aspects of the Holiness tradition, and Pentecostalism, see Baird Tipson, "How Can the Religious Experience of the Past Be Recovered? The Examples of Puritanism and Pietism," *Journal of the American Academy of Religion* 43, no. 4 (1975): 695–707; Baird Tipson, "The Routinized Piety of Thomas Shepard's Dairy," *Early American Literature* 13, no. 1 (1978): 64–80; Phyllis Mack, *Visionary Women: Ecstatic Prophecy in Seventeenth-Century England* (Berkeley: University of California Press, 1992); Rosemary Moore, *The Light in Their Consciences: The Early Quakers in Britain 1646–1666* (University Park: Pennsylvania State University Press, 2000); Ann Taves, *Fits, Trances, and Visions: Experiencing Religion and Explaining Religion from Wesley to James* (Princeton, NJ: Princeton University Press, 1999); and Ted A. Smith, *The New Measures: A Theological History of Democratic Practice* (Cambridge: Cambridge University Press, 2007).

Part I

Contexts

1 Early Monasticism

DOUGLAS BURTON-CHRISTIE

INTRODUCTION

A story from the *Apophthegmata Patrum* provides an intriguing glimpse into the mystical impulse at the heart of early Christian monastic life.[1] "Abba Lot went to see Abba Joseph and said to him, 'Abba, as far as I can I say my little office, I fast a little, I pray and meditate, I live in peace and as far as I can, I purify my thoughts. What else can I do?' Then the old man stood up and stretched his hands towards heaven. His fingers became like ten lamps of fire and he said to him, 'If you will, you can become all flame.'"[2] The image of fire, employed to evoke a deep spiritual experience, is not uncommon in early monastic literature. But its meaning is not easy to determine. In texts such as the *Apophthegmata Patrum*, stories of monks touched or consumed by fire are often narrated simply, without comment or analysis. The precise nature of the experience remains hidden. However, in other early monastic texts, such as the writings of John Cassian (d. ca. 435), the experience known as *excessus mentis*, or fiery prayer, is given a more precise meaning; there it is associated with an intense and often short-lived experience of ecstasy or rapture in prayer.[3] Still other early monastic writers, most notably Evagrius of Pontus (d. 390), are more reserved about the role of fiery or ecstatic prayer in monastic life. When Evagrius speaks of "true prayer" or "pure prayer," he seems not to have in mind something that

---

[1] The dating of this document is complex and cannot be easily indicated by a single date. Some of the sayings are quite old (third to fourth century), although the collection as a whole likely dates to the fifth century.

[2] *Apophthegmata Patrum*, Abba Joseph of Panephysis 7, in *Patralogia Graeca* (*PG*) 65, col. 229CD. The Greek Text of the Alphabetical Collection is published in *PG* 65, cols. 71–440. For the collection in English translation, see *The Sayings of the Desert Fathers: The Alphabetical Collection*, trans. Benedicta Ward (Kalamazoo, MI: Cistercian Publications, 1984), p. 103. Citations to the *Apophthegmata Patrum* will be noted as *AP*, with the English translation from Ward, unless otherwise noted.

[3] See the excellent discussion in Columba Stewart, *Cassian the Monk* (Oxford: Oxford University Press, 1998), pp. 114–30.

is ecstatic or fiery in character. For Evagrius, true prayer has no form at all. Rather, because God is beyond all form, prayer must move beyond all mental representations and become completely "imageless."[4]

The story of Abba Lot's encounter with Abba Joseph, and the subsequent elaboration of the question of the true meaning of prayer by Cassian, Evagrius, and other early monastic writers, reveals the intense preoccupation among the monks with the question of how to encounter God honestly and deeply, how to discover that place within the soul where God could be known and loved – and how this could be best expressed in a life. Yet, even here within the earliest strands of the Christian monastic tradition, one sees considerable variation in expression and understanding of what this encounter might consist of, and how it should be understood and interpreted. Nor is it clear whether or to what extent such an experience was considered by the monks to be mystical.[5] To inquire into the meaning of mystical experience in the Christian monastic tradition, one is compelled to reckon with a range of expressions and understandings of spiritual experience so varied and complex as to make any simple account nearly impossible. Still, the monastic tradition has bequeathed to the larger tradition of Christian mystical discourse certain enduring motifs, ideas, and practices that must be accounted for in any attempt to understand the growth and development of Christian mysticism.

In what follows, I will focus my attention on Christian monastic origins, on those figures, texts, and communities that emerged in Egypt, Syria, the Judean desert, and Asia Minor between the third and fifth centuries CE.[6] I will give particular attention to *The Life of Antony*,

---

[4] See Evagrius of Pontus, *Evagrius of Pontus: The Greek Ascetic Corpus*, trans., intro., and comm. Robert E. Sinkewicz (Oxford: Oxford University Press, 2003), especially the section in "Chapters on Prayer," pp. 198–206. See also Antoine Guillaumont, *Un philosophe au désert: Évagre le Pontique* (Paris: Vrin, 2004); and Augustine Casiday, *Evagrius Ponticus* (New York: Routledge, 2006).

[5] It is not easy to determine the extent to which the early Christian monks understood their experience to be mystical. For the purposes of this discussion, I will proceed with the assumption that certain ideas and images that we might call protomystical almost certainly appear within early Christian monastic literature. Yet one should be cautious about assuming that later, more developed understandings of mystical experience can be found in this earlier tradition. On the development of the Christian mystical tradition, see Bernard McGinn, *The Presence of God: A History of Western Christian Mysticism*, vol. 1, *The Foundations of Mysticism: Origins to the Fifth Century* (New York: Crossroad, 1991); and Andrew Louth, *The Origins of the Christian Mystical Tradition: From Plato to Denys* (Oxford: Oxford University Press, 2007).

[6] The literature on this far-flung and varied movement is vast and complex. For an excellent introduction, with extensive bibliographies, see William Harmless, *Desert*

one of the most influential and enduring texts to have emerged from the early monastic period.⁷ This text has bequeathed to us many of the fundamental ideas and images that came to influence the shape of later monastic thought and practice. By examining this text, along with other contemporary monastic witnesses, we can gain entrée, albeit indirectly and partially, into many of the crucial themes that will define mystical experience in the later Christian monastic tradition.

MYSTICAL EXPERIENCE AND MONASTIC LIFE

Before proceeding, it is important to offer a working definition of mysticism and note some of the potential challenges of thinking about this notion within the context of the early Christian monastic world. Specifically, I want to consider what it means to acknowledge the extraordinary (and in some sense rare) character of mystical experience, while also taking into account the way such experience became woven into the fabric of ordinary monastic living.

The encounter between Abba Lot and Abba Joseph stands as a beacon – at once imaginatively alluring and daunting – illuminating the kind of profound, transformative experience open to the one who embarks upon the monastic way. But any real understanding of what it will mean to enter this fire, the reader understands implicitly, is only open to the one who walks the path. Elsewhere in the early monastic tradition, we see greater reticence toward speaking about such deep experience. In many instances, this reticence seems to be born of humility. The monk who has experienced something so profound has no desire to attribute this to himself, or to his own virtue, but rather always seeks to acknowledge the gratuitous character of the experience,

---

Christians: An Introduction to the Literature of Early Monasticism (Oxford: Oxford University Press, 2004).

[7] For a critical edition, see Athanasius, *Athanase d'Alexandrie: Vie d'Antoine*, ed. G. J. M. Bartelink (Paris: Éditions du Cerf, 1994) (hereafter cited as Athanasius, *VA*). For the English translation, see Athanasius, *The Life of Antony and the Letter to Marcellinus*, trans. Robert C. Gregg (New York: Paulist Press, 1980). Questions regarding the authorship, purpose, and meaning of this classic text have been fiercely debated in recent years. One of the results of this debate is that it is no longer possible to ignore the complex political aims of the text. Although these political aims are not central to my purposes here, any full appreciation of the *Life of Antony* must take them into consideration. See David Brakke, *Athanasius and Asceticism* (Baltimore, MD: Johns Hopkins University Press, 1998); Annick Martin, *Athanase d'Alexandrie et L'Église de l'Égypte au IVe siècle* (Rome: Palais Farnèse, 1996); and Samuel Rubenson, *The Letters of Antony: Origenist Theology, Monastic Tradition and the Making of a Saint* (Minneapolis, MN: Fortress, 1995).

its divine origin. There is also, I believe, something else that accounts for this reticence: a conviction on the part of the monks that particular experiences of God should not be separated from everyday living, especially from the push and pull of communal living that was for most monks at the heart of their understanding of what it meant to live the monastic life.[8]

This is not to say that the Christian monastic tradition refrained from speculating on the meaning of such experience, or even from developing an entire spirituality drawn from reflection on the heights or depths of spiritual experience. We see this already in early monastic writers such as Evagrius of Pontus and John Cassian. The later monastic tradition, represented by figures such as Bernard of Clairvaux (d. 1153), Isaac of Stella (d. 1169), Guerric of Igny (d. 1157), and Hildegard of Bingen (d. 1179), would also probe these dimensions of monastic experience deeply and with great delicacy. Still, one of the characteristic and enduring features of Christian monastic spirituality – including what we speak of as its mystical dimension – is its rootedness in a common life, its incorporation into the texture and rhythms of daily living. The most profound and transformative experiences of God were found not only in silence and solitude or in moments of ecstatic union, but also in common prayer, reading, manual labor, hospitality, and the endless opportunities to engage one's brothers or sisters in the flow of daily living.

We catch a glimpse of this in the story related concerning Abba Lot and Abba Joseph. Abba Lot describes his way of life thus: "I say my little office, I fast a little, I pray and meditate, I live in peace and as far as I can, I purify my thoughts." Here is a simple description of a way of life that includes a regular, structured practice of reciting scripture (sometimes understood as a personal and solitary practice, but often understood as part of a communal practice); disciplined ascetic practice aimed at helping the monk to bring to consciousness the myriad ways in which the body might either aid or hinder the search for God; regular prayer and meditation; and a conscious, disciplined effort to "purify the thoughts," understood by the monks to involve a long, sustained work – often in the company of an experienced elder – of attending to the deeper recesses of

---

[8] The irreducibly communal dimension of early Christian monasticism is thoughtfully examined in Graham Gould, *The Desert Fathers on Monastic Community* (Oxford: Oxford University Press, 1993). Lucien Regnault, *Day-to-Day Lives of the Desert Fathers in Fourth-Century Egypt* (Petersham, MA: St. Bedes, 2002), considers the concrete social and material context within which early Christian monasticism took hold.

consciousness where strong and hidden forces capable of undermining or aiding a monk's commitment to God might be reckoned with and hopefully purified. Even the seemingly innocuous reference to "living in peace" has an important bearing on our understanding of the wider context for the monk's experience of God. Here is an implicit reference to the daily round of living, which included manual labor, traveling to the local village to sell one's work, the acquisition of food and water, eating, drinking, sleeping, engaging visitors, settling disputes, and simply living in the company of others. All these dimensions of ordinary living, and many more besides, are found in the literature of ancient Christian monasticism. Yet only occasionally are they understood as having influenced the deeper experiences of God described by the monks. In drawing attention to this, I wish to underscore that whatever mystical experience meant in Christian monastic life, it always arose from and returned to this rich bed of ordinary living.[9]

In this regard, it is helpful to place the discussion of Christian monasticism that follows within the context of the broad understanding of mysticism offered by Bernard McGinn. For McGinn, mysticism can be understood in at least three different ways: "as a part or element of religion; ... as a process or way of life; and ... as an attempt to express a direct consciousness of the presence of God."[10] I wish to bear this in mind in the discussion that follows, in order to ground the examination of mystical experience in monastic life in relation to the entirety of that life. For if we reduce the meaning of mysticism to specific elements of monastic experience, and allow them to become detached from the fabric of the world out of which they arose and which they always informed, we risk losing the very heart of mystical experience in Christian monastic life.

Still, there is a tension here regarding the precise meaning of mystical experience. McGinn makes the case that in speaking of mysticism

---

[9] Our awareness of the social meaning and function of early Christian monastic practice owes much to Peter Brown's groundbreaking work, especially his article, "The Rise and Function of the Holy Man in Late Antiquity," *The Journal of Roman Studies* 61 (1971): 80–101. For an assessment of the legacy of Brown's work, see the special issue of *Journal of Early Christian Studies* 6, no. 3 (Fall 1998). For Brown's own critical examination of this essay and the subsequent scholarly research that emerged in its wake, see Peter Brown, "The Rise and Function of the Holy Man in Late Antiquity, 1971–1997," *Journal of Early Christian Studies* 6, no. 3 (Fall 1998): 353–76. On the broader challenge of understanding mystical experience as rooted in a concrete social world, see Philip Sheldrake, "Christian Spirituality as a Way of Living Publicly: A Dialectic of the Mystical and Prophetic," *Spiritus* 3, no. 1 (2003): 19–37.

[10] McGinn, *Foundations of Mysticism*, pp. xv–xvi.

as involving "an immediate consciousness of the presence of God," he underlines something that almost all Christian mystics claim, namely, that "their mode of access to God is radically different from that found in ordinary consciousness, even from the awareness of God gained through the usual religious activities of prayer, sacraments, and other rituals." What distinguishes this mode of consciousness from other, more ordinary forms of awareness, McGinn suggests, is that it is understood "as taking place on a level of the personality deeper and more fundamental than that objectifiable through the usual conscious activities of sensing, knowing and loving." It is understood as an experience of divine presence that is given "in a *direct and immediate way.*"[11]

How then are we to understand all the "mediated" forms of awareness (and practice) that lead to and emerge from such experience in Christian monastic life? Are these best understood simply as preparations for or departures from true mystical awareness? Or are they related in a more intimate and complex way to mystical consciousness? McGinn acknowledges that the lines between these different kinds of awareness and experience are not always sharply drawn, that because mysticism is always a "process or a way of life ... everything that leads up to and prepares for this encounter, as well as all that flows from or is supposed to flow from it for the life of the individual in the belief community, is also mystical, even if in a secondary sense."[12] Thus, although mystical experience should not be simply collapsed into or conflated with ordinary human consciousness, neither should it be separated from it artificially.

Such an approach to mystical experience can help us in our attempt to understand the particular contribution that monastic life and literature have made to Christian mysticism. For in this view, we are invited to take seriously not only the utterly mysterious and hidden dimensions of the monk's experience of God, but also the practices and disciplines that created the context for that experience and the expression of that experience in a life. The early Christian monastic experiment arose in the first instance as an endeavor to live in a particular way, oriented around and giving expression to a deep awareness of the presence of God. To understand the mystical character of monastic experience means taking into account monastic life as a whole, the social, embodied, and communal reality within which the felt presence of God emerged and took root. In what follows, I will examine this life in terms

---

[11] Ibid., p. xix. Emphasis mine.
[12] Ibid., p. xvi.

of three motifs that I believe are crucial to the entire monastic experience: *anachoresis*, or seeking the place of God; *prosoche*, or discernment and the struggle with the self; and *proseuche*, or dwelling in the place of God.

ANACHORESIS: SEEKING THE PLACE OF GOD

The Christian monk can be understood as one seeking the place of God. In Christian monastic literature, this quest was envisioned as an actual search for a place – a cell or a monastery – and as an imaginative process, a way of understanding the entire journey of monastic life, that is, the quest for God. This quest also contained and expressed a significant tension: the monk was one who lived in a monastery or a cell, for whom stability and commitment to a place were crucial values. But the monk's search for God also included and allowed for a certain restlessness, a recognition that setting off for a new place (whether understood as actual or metaphorical) was often necessary.

A monastery is first and foremost a place – not only a physical place but also a place of the imagination. Whether a simple monastic cell occupied by a hermit; a small, informal, gathering of monks (sometimes known as a *lavra*); or a larger, more structured community of monks living a common life under the authority of an abbess or abbot (which the early tradition sometimes referred to as a *coenobium*), the monastic place had a profound impact on the life and experience of the monk. In the earliest monastic tradition, the cell became an emblem of the monk's quest for God. One of the more memorable expressions of this ideal comes from Abba Moses, who in response to a brother's request for a word, told him: "Go, sit in your cell, and your cell will teach you everything."[13] The cell, in this view, was the place where the monk was to seek and find God in the long, often arduous *askesis* of silence and solitude. Dwelling, staying put, and entering into the space of the cell were means to go deeper in the monastic quest for God. Consequently, one finds frequent warnings against departing from the cell or monastery in early monastic literature.[14]

At the same time, early Christian monks were often wanderers who understood the spiritual life in terms of movement and yearning and

---

[13] *AP*, Moses 6; Ward, *Sayings*, p. 139.
[14] See, e.g., Antony's warning: "Just as fish die if they stay too long out of water, so the monks who loiter outside their cells or pass their time with men of the world lose the intensity of inner peace." *AP*, Antony 10; Ward, *Sayings*, p. 3.

recognized that no single place could encompass or contain their hunger for God. A serious critique of unbridled movement among monastics would eventually arise and be codified in Benedict of Nursia's (ca. 480–547) *Rule of St. Benedict* – the counsel against becoming a *gyrovague*, or one who moved aimlessly from monastery to monastery.[15] However, in the earliest tradition, there was a genuine appreciation of the need for movement, with monks setting out to seek counsel from an elder, to find a better or more appropriate place to live the monastic life, or in response to shifting social, ecclesial, and economic circumstances.[16] This deep impulse to move in order to discover God came to expression in various ideas and images in the Christian monastic tradition, such as John of Climacus's (d. ca. 606) famous *Ladder of Divine Ascent*, which envisioned the monk's life as a step-by-step ascent to God achieved by a long and difficult struggle against demonic forces, or Gregory of Nyssa's (d. 394) magnificent notion of *epectesis*, describing the soul's continuous and ever deepening yearning forward toward God.[17]

The *Life of Antony*, Athanasius of Alexandria's (d. 373) influential biography of the so-called founder of Christian monasticism, offers a good illustration of how this tension between place and movement played out in the early Christian monastic imagination.[18] The narrative depicts Antony as a young man living in a village in Egypt's Nile valley. His parents having recently died, he is now caring for his sister and reflecting on what he will do from this point forward. One day he wanders into church and hears a text being read aloud: "If you would be perfect ... come and follow me" (Mt 19:21). The text has a dramatic and life-altering effect on the young Antony. Athanasius relates that Antony felt as

---

[15] *The Rule of St. Benedict*, ed. Timothy Fry (Collegeville, MN: Liturgical Press, 1981), ch. 1: 10, p. 171.

[16] Graham Gould, "Moving on and Staying Put in the *Apophthegmata Patrum*," *Studia Patristica* 25 (1989): 231–7. On the larger issues relating to travel and movement among Christian monks and ascetics in the Late Antique world, see Daniel Folger Caner, *Wandering, Begging Monks: Spiritual Authority and the Promotion of Monasticism in Late Antiquity* (Berkeley: University of California Press, 2002); and Maribel Dietz, *Wandering Monks, Virgins, and Pilgrims: Ascetic Travel in the Mediterranean World, A.D. 300–800* (University Park: Pennsylvania State University Press, 2005).

[17] John Climacus, *Ladder of Divine Ascent*, trans. Colm Luibhéid and Norman Russell (New York: Paulist Press, 1982); and Gregory of Nyssa, *The Life of Moses*, trans. Everett Ferguson and Abraham J. Malherbe (New York: Paulist Press, 1978).

[18] See Douglas Burton-Christie, "The Place of the Heart: Geography and Spirituality in *The Life of Antony*," in *Purity of Heart in Early Ascetic and Monastic Literature*, ed. Harriet A. Luckman and Linda Kulzer (Collegeville, MN: The Liturgical Press, 1999), pp. 45–66.

though the scripture "had been read for him alone," and upon hearing it decided in that very moment to renounce his possessions and take up life as an ascetic. A second encounter with a text – "do not be anxious about tomorrow" (Mt 6:34) – provoked Antony to go even further. He placed his sister in charge of some "trusted virgins" and, having dispensed with all of his possessions, moved out to the edge of the village where he could devote himself completely to a life of prayer and fasting.

This initial stage of the story reveals some of the key elements of the monastic quest, including the fundamental importance of religious experience and the way the language of place and space signify the meaning of that experience. The narrative does not say explicitly what happened to Antony or what he experienced when he heard those biblical texts being read aloud in church (apart from the indication that he felt as though the texts had profound personal significance for him). But we can infer much from the action that ensues – a dramatic and life-altering choice to live for God alone. Although his initial choice is provisional and as yet untested, it is significant that Antony, on the strength of this initial experience, sets out along a path that will take him deep into the desert and into a long, tenacious, and solitary struggle over his soul. The early monastic texts are often reticent regarding the monks' experience of God, including the initial experiences of God that so often determined the shape of a monk's life. In addition, much monastic literature, especially hagiographical texts such as the *Life of Antony*, seeks to depict the monk's experience in a particular way, to suggest, for example, that the course of the monk's life was providentially preordained by God. All of this must be acknowledged as we seek to understand what kinds of experience lay at the heart of a monk's decision to take up the monastic life. Still, the *Life of Antony* provides us with intriguing clues about the character of this experience, some of which is corroborated elsewhere in the monastic literature.

In the present case, we see a young man seized by a message from God embedded in a scriptural text, touched so deeply by its message that he is unable to resist its claim upon his life. If we inquire as to the substance of that claim, we see that it centers on detachment and freedom, two key themes that will shape all subsequent monastic life. To let go of everything and live for God was at the heart of the monastic dream. Athanasius's narrative reminds us that such freedom was not merely a prospective hope, but was already woven into the monk's initial experience. In this sense, the monastic quest was understood less as an effort to achieve or realize something as yet unknown than as a gesture of uncovering more fully something already known and experienced.

Rhetorically and theologically, the *Life of Antony* depicts this most often through its reference to Antony's profound sense of the presence of Christ at the heart of his life. In Antony's struggles against the demons that afflict him in the desert, we hear again and again that it is not through Antony's effort alone, but rather through "the power of Christ *in* Antony," that he is able to vanquish the demons. Clearly, Antony's own agency as a person struggling to find his way through a difficult trial is honored and preserved when we consider his experience from this perspective. However, Athanasius leaves no doubt that the ultimate source of Antony's power is the divine Logos working through him. This is one of many instances in the *Life of Antony* where one senses the influence of Athanasius's anti-Arian agenda in his depiction of monastic spirituality.[19] Here it simply means that Antony must be seen as not merely relying on his own efforts to achieve ascetic detachment and freedom, but also must be understood as having been enlivened and empowered to succeed in this task by the dynamic, saving power of Christ in him. When, during the most intense and difficult moment of Antony's struggles with the demons, we are told that he looked up to see a light flooding into his cell, we are left in no doubt that this is the light of the divine Logos, the same Logos who will be described at Nicea as "God from God, Light from Light, True God from True God." The monk carries this light within him. It is his protection and power. It is at the core of his identity.

It is also the primary place in which the monk is called upon to dwell. In the depiction of the monastic journey, one understands that every step is oriented toward a fuller and deeper realization of the monk's identity in Christ. In Athanasius's narrative, this is described in terms of the monk's dynamic movement through space and time to a place of freedom. So the monk moves, initially renouncing village, home (*oikos*), and the entire domestic sphere, for the sake of an as-yet-undetermined life on the margins of the village, at the edge of the desert (*eremos*). After a time, he sets off again, traveling deeper into the wilderness, into a space of precariousness and solitude. He walks a path (*hodos*) that is filled with challenges and temptations with which he must reckon, eventually settling down in an old fortress and then moving to an abandoned tomb. The tomb becomes a crucible in which the monk makes himself vulnerable to the work of purification and renewal.

Antony would eventually find himself drawn to move even from this solitary place, the crowds having compelled him to set out into the

---

[19] See Robert C. Gregg and Dennis E. Groh, "Claims on the Life of St. Anthony," in *Early Arianism: A View of Salvation* (Philadelphia: Fortress Press, 1981), pp. 131–59.

furthest reaches of the eastern desert to seek a place of solitude wild and empty enough to enable him to live into his experience as deeply as possible. The narrative provides us with a sense of joyous recognition when Antony finally arrived at the place known as the "inner mountain." There Antony beheld "a very high hill. Below the hill there was water – perfectly clear, sweet and quite cold, and beyond there were plains, and a few untended date palms. Then Antony, as if stirred by God, fell in love with the place."[20] He lived "alone in the inner mountain devoting himself to prayers and the discipline" and continued to wrestle against demons. But Athanasius relates that "being alone in such a desert he was neither distracted by the demons who confronted him, nor was he frightened of their ferocity when so many four-legged beasts and reptiles were there. But truly he was one who, as Scripture says, having trusted in the Lord, was like Mount Sion, keeping his mind unshaken and unruffled."[21]

This image of a monk living in the deepest solitude of the desert, in perfect harmony with himself, God, and the place, became an emblem of the entire monastic quest.[22] Few monks who followed Antony would emulate the radically solitary character of his journey; yet the sense of what it meant to face oneself in solitude and to be transformed by this encounter captured in his story remained paradigmatic for Christian monastic life. As a place – both actual and imagined – the "inner mountain" came to be seen as a symbol of the monk's deepest penetration into the place of silence and solitude where God is to be sought and found.

PROSOCHE: DISCERNMENT AND THE STRUGGLE WITH THE SELF

What was the precise character of this journey into the place of silence and solitude? With what did the monk struggle in the effort to remain faithful to the original sense of having been called to follow this way?

---

[20] Athanasius, *VA*, pp. 49–50; Gregg, *Life of Anthony*, p. 68.
[21] Athanasius, *VA*, p. 51; Gregg, *Life of Anthony*, pp. 69–70.
[22] It should be noted that the *Life of Antony* presents a highly stylized portrait of early monastic life. As James Goehring and others have noted, at least one effect of this self-consciously literary and theological portrait was to create a sense of this solitary path as being *the* model of Christian monasticism. Careful historical analysis of early Christian monasticism has revealed a wide range of models and practices that suggests a need for a more subtle and critical reading of monastic origins. See James Goehring, "The Encroaching Desert: Literary Production and Ascetic Space in Early Egyptian Christianity," *Journal of Early Christian Studies* 1 (1993): 281–96. Still, the *Life of Antony*'s influence upon the ideas of monastic life remains formidable.

The literature of early Christian monasticism suggests that the monk's quest for the place of God involved an almost unbearably demanding and arduous process of relinquishment, a stripping away of the many layers of illusion and attachment that prevented the monk from arriving at an honest knowledge of self and God. Certain practices – especially attention to self (*prosoche*) and discernment of spirits (*diakrisis*) – became central to this quest and defined how the monk actually moved through the treacherous inner landscape toward a place of self-knowledge and freedom in God. The literature of early Christian monasticism articulated these practices in different ways, sometimes situating them as part of a narrative and at other times expressing them as a kind of spiritual taxonomy. In both cases, the aim was to illuminate and offer practical help regarding how the monk ought to face the myriad hidden forces within the soul – most often understood by the ancient monks as arising from the power of demons or thoughts – that prevented an honest and open engagement with the self and with God.

Early on in the *Life of Antony*, the monk's ascetic project is described in terms of *prosoche*.[23] Antony, says Athanasius, "began paying attention to himself."[24] The struggle with the self, however, is hardly simple in Athanasius's narrative; it is depicted as a long, sustained, and violent struggle to stand against the demons and to open himself to his own soul. In Antony's case, the descent into the desert in some ways mirrors the descent into himself. As he moves further into the desert, his struggles increase in depth and complexity. Athanasius tells us that after Antony had taken up habitation in some tombs outside his village, his progress provoked the enemy to such an extent that "approaching one night with a multitude of demons he whipped him with such force that he lay on the earth, speechless from the tortures. [Antony] contended that the pains were so severe as to lead one to say that the blows could not have been delivered by humans since they caused such agony."[25] What were these pains? Athanasius does not tell us. But the way they are described – "so severe as to lead one to say that the blows could not have been delivered by humans" – suggests something of how bewildering and frightening this experience was for the monk. Here is an agony so great that it cannot be accounted for by any simple reference to ordinary human experience. This is but one of many instances

---

[23] On the practice of *prosoche* within ancient philosophical practice and as crucial to early Christian monasticism, see Pierre Hadot, *Philosophy as a Way of Life*, trans. Michael Chase (Oxford: Blackwell, 1995), pp. 126–44.

[24] Athanasius, *VA*, p. 3; Gregg, *Life of Anthony*, p. 32.

[25] Athanasius, *VA*, p. 8; Gregg, *Life of Anthony*, p. 37.

in early Christian monastic literature where one senses just what the confrontation with the demonic in solitude really involved: the most demanding and far-reaching struggle with the self.

The question of how, precisely, to understand this struggle in the life of the monk has long occupied historians of the early monastic world. Certainly it is difficult to escape the sense that the demons can be understood on at least one level as representing elements of the monk's own psyche, expressed in vivid symbolic form. Peter Brown has argued that, for the early monks, the demonic was "sensed as an extension of the self. A relationship with the demons," he suggests, "involved something more intimate than attack from the outside: to be 'tried by the demons' meant passing through a stage in the growth of awareness of the lower frontiers of the personality. The demonic stood not merely for all that was hostile *to* [the monk]; the demons summed up all that was anomalous and incomplete *in* [him]."[26] This acute psychological understanding of the encounter with the demons is confirmed by the monks' own testimony. One day Abba Abraham asked Abba Poemen: "How do the demons fight against me?" Poemen responded: "The demons fight *against* you? ... Our own *wills* become the demons, and it is these which attack us in order that we may fulfill them."[27]

One senses here the terror that sometimes overcame the monks as they felt themselves being overwhelmed, even consumed by the power of the demonic. The willingness to allow oneself to become so vulnerable, to descend into the place of the greatest doubt and uncertainty, was a crucial part of the monastic practice of attention to self (*prosoche*) through which the monk eventually came to be transformed in Christ. The importance the monks attributed to this practice is expressed most clearly in the intricate and systematic taxonomy of the self found in the writings of Evagrius and Cassian, especially in their articulation and analysis of the "eight principal thoughts." Learning to become adept at recognizing and responding to these shifting and often-treacherous thoughts (*logismoi*), which revealed so clearly the competing impulses within the monk's inner life, became critical to the monk's journey toward an integrated and free self, alive in God.

[26] Peter Brown, *The Making of Late Antiquity* (Cambridge, MA: Harvard University Press, 1978), pp. 89–90. David Brakke cautions against understanding the presence of the demonic in early Christian monastic life in terms that are too exclusively psychological. David Brakke, *Demons and the Making of the Monk: Spiritual Combat in Early Christianity* (Cambridge, MA: Harvard University Press, 2006), pp. 7–14.

[27] *AP*, Poemen 67 [*PG* 65, col. 337C], emphasis added; Ward, *Sayings*, p. 176. See also Brown, *The Making of Late Antiquity*, p. 90.

In the opening section of the *Praktikos*, Evagrius describes the eight principal thoughts this way: "All generic types of thoughts fall into eight categories in which every sort of thought is included. First that of gluttony, then fornication, third avarice, fourth sadness, fifth anger, sixth acedia, seventh vainglory, eighth pride. Whether or not all these thoughts trouble the soul is not within our power; but it is for us to decide if they are to linger within us or not and whether or not they stir up the passions."[28] Here, Evagrius articulates the underlying framework through which he will examine, with tremendous subtlety and variation, the ever-shifting thoughts (*logismoi*) that move through the monk's soul and affect his capacity to know and love God. It was critical that the monk learn to understand the precise source of these thoughts and how they worked to undermine his resolve and sense of purpose, even his identity in God. This is because, as Brown has argued, "consent to evil thoughts, many of which were occasioned, in the first instance, by the dull creakings of the body – by its need for food and its organic, sexual drives – implied a decision to collaborate with other invisible spirits, the demons ... [their] pervasive presence, close to the human person, was registered in the 'heart' in the form of inappropriate images, fantasies, and obsessions."[29] These *logismoi* could be so potent and so debilitating that unless the monk cultivated the ability to identify, scrutinize, and struggle against them and even eventually to resolve them, prayer and knowledge of God would become impossible.

To cite but one example, if one understands the ascetic impulse toward detachment – captured emblematically in Antony's response to the radical call to discipleship of Matthew 19:21 – as expressing a desire for a single-minded existence focused on God, one can understand why the struggle to free oneself from attachments might be the cause of so much sadness in the life of the monk. "The monk with many possessions," says Evagrius, "carries around the memories of possessions as a heavy burden and a useless weight; he is stung with sadness and is mightily pained in his thoughts. He has abandoned his possessions and is lashed with sadness."[30] In another place, Evagrius describes the process through which sadness comes to afflict the monk this way: "When certain thoughts gain the advantage, they bring the soul to remember home and parents and one's former life. And when they observe that the soul does not resist but rather follows right along and disperses itself

---

[28] Evagrius, *Praktikos* 6, in *Evagrius of Pontus*, ed. Sinkewicz, pp. 97–8.

[29] Peter Brown, *The Body and Society: Men, Women and Sexual Renunciation in Early Christianity* (New York: Columbia University Press, 1988), p. 167.

[30] Evagrius, *Eight Thoughts* 3: 7, in *Evagrius of Pontus*, ed. Sinkewicz, p. 79.

among thoughts of pleasures, then with a hold on it they plunge it into sadness with the realization that former things are no more and cannot be again because of the present way of life. And the miserable soul, the more it allowed itself to be dispersed among the former thoughts, the more it has now become hemmed in and humiliated by these latter ones."[31]

The ultimate and devastating effect of this dispersion of thoughts, suggests Evagrius, is an inability to pray: "Sunlight does not penetrate a great depth of water; the light of contemplation does not illuminate a heart overcome by sadness."[32] One could also say the same of a heart overcome by anger, pride, gluttony, or any of the other *logismoi* that threaten to colonize the soul. For the monk to experience that profound and abiding sense of God's presence that was the great hope of monastic life, it was necessary to have arrived at a place of genuine freedom. Only a sustained commitment to pay attention to oneself and to search out the deep sources of the soul's chronic attachments could lead the monk to such a place. Among Antony's last words to his brothers were these: "Live as though dying daily, paying attention to yourselves."[33]

PROSEUCHE: DWELLING IN THE PLACE OF GOD

The mysterious process of reshaping one's consciousness, of becoming free of the obsessive preoccupations symbolized by the *logismoi*, was at the heart of the monastic understanding of prayer. In its most profound expressions, monastic prayer was simple. To pray was to recognize and open oneself to the presence of God. The specific techniques or approaches leading one to this place of deep prayer varied. But one thing remained constant: the early Christian monks grounded themselves in careful and sustained meditation on the Word of God.[34] Scripture constituted the foundation for the daily round of communal prayer

---

[31] Evagrius, *Praktikos* 10, in *Evagrius of Pontus*, ed. Sinkewicz, p. 98.
[32] Evagrius, *Eight Thoughts* 22, in *Evagrius of Pontus*, ed. Sinkewicz, p. 83.
[33] Athanasius, *VA*, p. 91; Gregg, *Life of Antony*, p. 97 (translation modified).
[34] On early Christian monastic reading of scripture, see Douglas Burton-Christie, *The Word in the Desert: Scripture and the Quest for Holiness in Early Christian Monasticism* (Oxford: Oxford University Press, 1993); Douglas Burton-Christie, "Listening, Reading, Praying: Orality, Literacy and Early Monastic Spirituality," *Anglican Theological Review* 83, no. 2 (Spring 2001): 5–25; Luke Dysinger, *Psalmody and Prayer in the Writings of Evagrius Ponticus* (Oxford: Oxford University Press, 2005); Steven D. Driver, *John Cassian and the Reading of Egyptian Monastic Culture* (New York: Routledge, 2002), esp. pp. 111–17 on prayer in relation to reading; and Elizabeth Clark, *Reading Renunciation: Asceticism and Scripture in Early Christianity* (Princeton, NJ: Princeton University Press, 1999).

practiced by the monks, as well as the source of protection and solace in the monk's internal struggle against the demons. Allowing oneself to be transformed by the Word was also understood as crucial to the experience of imageless or pure prayer in which God's presence pervaded the life of the monk utterly and completely. One should be careful, however, not to distinguish too sharply between and among these different modes of prayer. Although it is true that the "higher" reaches of prayer described by Cassian and Evagrius can seem far removed from the simpler and more concrete approaches to prayer one so often encounters in the early monastic literature, they were part of a continuous, if variegated, monastic spiritual culture. If the focus here is on the purer or rarer expressions of prayer, this is simply because they remind us of the ultimate aim of all monastic prayer, to bring the monk to what Evagrius calls the "place of God."

Part of what made the practice of rumination on the Word so important was its capacity to focus the monk's attention on the simple awareness of God. One saying from the *Apophthegmata Patrum* tells of a brother who, while reciting scripture with one of the elders, "forgot and lost track of a word of the psalm." The elder noticed this, and when the *synaxis* finished, he told the brother of his own practice. "When I recite the *synaxis*, I think of myself as being on top of a burning fire: my thoughts cannot stray right or left." He then asked the brother: "where were your thoughts, when we were saying the *synaxis*, that the word of the psalm escaped you? Don't you know that you are standing in the presence of God and speaking to God?"[35] One can see here how crucial attention, especially attention to the Word, was in cultivating a sense of the presence of God. Carelessness or inattention not only caused one to forget the words of scripture, but also opened the door to a stream of *logismoi* and caused one to become oblivious to the presence of God mediated through those words. It was this concern that led one elder to affirm: "if God reproaches us for carelessness in our prayers and distractions in our psalmody, we cannot be saved."[36]

The monks recognized that without an awareness of God's presence at the heart of one's life, there could be no meaningful resistance to the many *logismoi* that constantly threatened to dissipate one's consciousness, nor could there be a recognition of one's true identity. One

---

[35] *AP*, Anonymous 146 F., in "Histoires des solitaires égyptiens," *Revue d'orient Chrétien* 13 (1908): 50. For the English translation, see *Wisdom of the Desert Fathers: Systematic Sayings from the Anonymous Series of the Apophthegmata Patrum*, trans. Benedicta Ward (Oxford: SLG Press, 1986), p. 4.

[36] *AP*, Theodore of Enaton 3, *PG* 65, col. 197A; Ward, *Sayings*, p. 79.

arrived at such awareness and at the deep peace the monks called *hesychia* not merely by self-scrutiny and reflection, or by fierce resistance to thoughts and temptations. These are, after all, only the acts of the conscious and active mind. The monks knew the process of purification went much deeper. If to consent to *logismoi* meant consecrating oneself to demonic partners, then attainment of tranquility of mind and purity of heart meant consecrating oneself to the One whose presence is manifested in scripture.

Perhaps this helps to account for the monks' willingness to reduce the scope of their attention so radically, often to a single verse of scripture. In Cassian's *Conferences*, Abba Isaac advocates the continual repetition of a single verse from Psalm 70: "O God, make haste to save me, O Lord, make haste to help me." He notes that "the verse is an impregnable battlement, a shield and a coat of mail which no spear can pierce ... it will be a saving formula in your heart."[37] Why such trust in a single verse? A clue is provided in Isaac's allusion to the inner disposition that one should cultivate in ruminating upon the text. He contends that "a person who perseveres in *simplicity and innocence* ... is protected."[38] The person who meditates in such a spirit of concentrated attention is already on the way to realizing what he seeks – the deep inner clarity in which God can be apprehended. One sees a remarkable movement here, from the recitation of a text with the lips – a physical, embodied act often undertaken in the company of others – to a largely internal and hidden process known only to the monk. To keep the text always before one, "ceaselessly revolving it" within oneself, meant for Abba Isaac, "that continual meditation becomes finally impregnated in our soul."[39]

This ever-deepening grasp of the Word within the soul is precisely what the monks sought in their rumination upon scripture. At a certain point the Word became an "interior possession" and the monk no longer experienced any distance between the text, the One revealed in the text, and the person ruminating on the text. In another of Cassian's

---

[37] John Cassian, *Conférences* (Paris: Éditions du Cerf, 1955–9), conf. 19, ch. 10, p. 86. The texts are translated in *Western Asceticism*, ed. Owen Chadwick (Louisville, KY: Westminster John Knox, 1979); John Cassian, *The Conferences*, trans. John Boniface Ramsey (New York: Paulist Press, 1997); and John Cassian, *The Conferences*, trans. Colm Luibhéid (New York: Paulist Press, 1985). For this passage, see Chadwick, *Western Asceticism*, pp. 240–2.

[38] Cassian, *Conférences*, vol. 2, conf. 10, ch. 10, p. 91, emphasis added; Chadwick, *Western Asceticism*, p. 243.

[39] Cassian, *Conférences*, vol. 2, conf. 10, ch. 10, p. 90; Chadwick, *Western Asceticism*, p. 243.

Conferences, Abba Nestoros describes the mysterious process of transformation this way: "If these things [from scripture] have been carefully taken in and stored up in the recesses of the soul and stamped with the seal of silence, afterwards they will be brought forth from the jar of your heart with great fragrance and like some perennial fountain will flow from the veins of experience and irrigate channels of virtue and will pour forth copious streams as if from some deep well in your heart."[40] It is difficult to miss here the sense of inner transformation that was, for the early monks, at the heart of their practice of rumination on scripture. But how did it work exactly? How and in what way did such transformation occur?

The conference of Abba Isaac cited previously provides further insight into how this process of rumination worked and why the monks put such a great stake in it. Above all, it was because of their sense that the power and presence of God could be encountered and experienced here. Abba Isaac claims that this verse from Psalm 70 ("O God make haste to save me: O Lord, make haste to help me")

> carries within it all the feelings of which human nature is capable. It can be adapted to every condition and can usefully [be] deployed against every temptation. It carries within it a cry of help to God in the face of every danger. It expresses the humility of a pious confession. It conveys the watchfulness born of unending worry and fear. It conveys a sense of our frailty, the assurance of being heard, the confidence in help that is always and everywhere present ... this is the voice of ardor and charity. This is the terrified cry of someone who sees the snares of the enemy, the cry of someone besieged day and night and exclaiming that he cannot escape unless his protector comes to the rescue ... this verse keeps us from despairing of our salvation since it reveals to us the One to whom we call.[41]

It is striking to note how capacious scripture was seen to be, a single verse carrying within it and calling forth from the one who recites it "all the feelings of which human nature is capable." A complex array of emotions is compressed into and carried by this briefest of utterances: a cry for help, humility, watchfulness born of unending worry and fear, a sense of frailty, assurance, confidence, desire, love, or terror. The spiritual potency of this work is clear. It reveals, Abba Isaac claims, "the *One* to whom we call."

[40] Cassian, *Conférences*, vol. 2, conf. 14, ch. 13, p. 201; Cassian, *Conferences*, p. 518.
[41] Cassian, *Conférences*, vol. 2, conf. 10, ch. 10, p. 86; Chadwick, *Western Asceticism*, p. 242.

The early Christian monks were convinced that the practice of holding the Word at the center of one's consciousness led gradually but surely toward a living encounter with the One speaking in and through the text. Abba Isaac suggests that to engage in meditation on the Word in this way would lead the monk beyond the wealth of thoughts that constantly threatened to undermine his sense of God's presence and toward a place of simplicity or poverty of intention. The mind will go on grasping this single verse of scripture "until it can cast away the wealth and multiplicity of other thoughts, and restrict itself to the poverty of a single verse."[42] When it does so, the monk may well find himself in that sublime place that Abba Isaac claims one can know when the experiential grasp of the Word becomes fused with the experience of pure prayer – "contemplation of God alone."

This description of pure prayer is, like so many accounts of spiritual experience in early monastic literature, an approximation of something utterly mysterious and ultimately beyond expression. Yet, as is always the case in the Christian mystical tradition, language and images must be brought to bear upon the task of articulating what cannot, finally, be said or imagined. One of the most remarkable and compelling instances of this in early Christian monasticism is found in Evagrius's notion of pure prayer.[43] At the heart of Evagrius's understanding of pure prayer are two images: dwelling in "the place of God" and encountering a "sapphire-blue light," both of which draw upon his reflection on the account of the theophany in Exodus (24:10–11). Evagrius transposes the geographical image of Moses's encounter with God on Sinai to the inner life of the monk, so that the "place of God" becomes almost indistinguishable from the "place of prayer."[44] Reaching this place, however, requires a radical renunciation of all images, even the image of the

---

[42] Cassian, *Conférences*, vol. 2, conf. 10, ch. 11, p. 86; Chadwick, *Western Asceticism*, p. 243.

[43] See Columba Stewart, "Imageless Prayer and the Theological Vision of Evagrius Ponticus," *Journal of Early Christian Studies* 9, no. 2 (2001): 173–204. See also Antoine Guillaumont, "La vision de l'intellect par lui-même dans la mystique évagrienne," in *Études sur la spiritualité d l'Orient Chrétien* (Bégrolles-en-mauges, France: Abbaye de Bellefontaine, 1996), pp. 143–50; William Harmless and Raymond R. Fitzgerald, "The Sapphire Light of the Mind: The *Skemmata* of Evagrius Ponticus," *Theological Studies* 62 (2001): 493–529; Martin Laird, "The 'Open Country Whose Name Is Prayer': Apophasis, Deconstruction, and Contemplative Practice," *Modern Theology* 21, no. 1 (2005): 141–55; and Mette Sophia Bøcher Rasmussen, "Like a Rock or Like God? The Concept of *apatheia* in the Monastic Theology of Evagrius of Pontus," *Studia Theologica* 59, no. 2 (2005): 147–62.

[44] See Evagrius, *On Prayer* 56 and 57, in *Evagrius of Pontus*, ed. Sinkewicz, p. 198. Here "place of God" is juxtaposed to "place of prayer."

"place of God." This is because, as Columba Stewart notes, "the place of God is, by definition, 'unimaged,' meaning that the mind itself, when it becomes the place of God, is free of self-created imagery."[45] This is the meaning of Evagrius's claim that "the mind ... when it is in prayer ... is in a light without form, which is called the place of God."[46]

Here and elsewhere in Evagrius's writings one encounters what feels like an impossible paradox: the experience of pure prayer is utterly imageless, and yet it involves a vision of light and the sense of being drawn to dwell in "the place of God." This is a paradox that Evagrius insists must be accommodated if the monk is going to remain open to an experience of prayer that is true and deep. "When the mind has put off the old self and shall put on the one born of grace (cf. Col 3:9–10), then it will see its own state in the time of prayer resembling sapphire or the color of heaven; this state scripture calls the place of God that was seen by the elders on Mount Sinai" (Ex 24:9–11).[47] This vision of the monk completely subsumed into the life of God, living *in* God, is surely one of the most sublime and compelling expressions of spiritual experience in all of early monastic literature. Although its specific character is rooted in Evagrius's particular perspective on the monastic journey, it is consistent with the testimony about the ultimate end of monastic life that has come down to us from so many within the early Christian monastic tradition.

CONCLUSION

"Through fire everything changes. When we want everything to be changed we call on fire."[48] The image of the monk "all aflame" with which this essay began reminds us of how deeply committed the early Christian monks were to this kind of total transformation in God. Fire is certainly not the only image the monks used to convey their sense of this possibility, nor can one assign a single meaning to this image within early monastic experience. Still, it remains a compelling reminder of what the monks believed was possible for them. Seeking and finding

---

[45] Stewart, "Imageless Prayer," p. 197.
[46] Evagrius, *Reflections* 20, in *Evagrius of Pontus*, ed. Sinkewicz, p. 213.
[47] Evagrius, *On Thoughts* 39, in *Evagrius of Pontus*, ed. Sinkewicz, p. 180. See also *Reflections* 2: "If someone would want to behold the state of the mind, let him deprive himself of all mental representations, and then he shall behold himself resembling sapphire or the color of heaven (Ex. 24: 9–11). It is impossible to accomplish this without impassibility, for he will need God to collaborate with him and breathe into him connatural light" (*Evagrius of Pontus*, ed. Sinkewicz, p. 211).
[48] Gaston Bachelard, *The Psychoanalysis of Fire*, trans. Alan C. M. Ross (Boston: Beacon, 1987), p. 57.

the "place of God" meant allowing oneself to be consumed by God's mysterious and encompassing presence and opening oneself to the ever-deepening expression of this presence in one's life.

For generations to come, as the monastic experiment continued to unfold across the Christian East and West, the influence of ancient monasticism continued to reverberate strongly.[49] In the sixth century, Benedict of Nursia prescribed the reading of both the *Institutes* and *Conferences* in his *Rule*, ensuring that Cassian's spiritual vision as well as the stories and teachings of the early monks that he passed on would become woven deeply into Benedictine monastic life.[50]

Evagrius's influence is harder to trace, not least because of his controversial association with Origen's teachings, which resulted in the condemnation of some of his work. Nevertheless, his influence did make itself felt in the West – through Cassian, and through Latin translations of some of Evagrius's teachings. In the East, some of his writings in Greek survived under his own name, while others were attributed to Orthodox authors and enjoyed wide popularity in that form. In addition, his writing was translated into Syriac, Coptic, and Armenian, and key elements of his teaching play a role in the writings of Pseudo-Dionysius the Aeropagite (early sixth century) and Maximus the Confessor (d. 662). The *Apophthegmata Patrum* had a remarkably wide diffusion, making its way into the West through a Latin translation, but also eventually emerging in Coptic, Syriac, Armenian, Arabic, Ethiopian, and numerous other languages, a testimony to its enduring impact on Eastern Christian spirituality. Finally, Antony had a huge influence in both Eastern and Western Christianity, appearing as an iconic figure of great importance in the art and literature of the East and, through his presence in the *Golden Legend* of James of Voragine (d. 1298), becoming a significant object of devotion in the Christian West.

Antony's long sojourn in the solitude of the inner mountain, though only one of myriad images bequeathed to us by the early monastic tradition, remains uniquely emblematic of the depth and mystery of monastic life. Yet it is difficult in the end to say precisely or clearly what Antony and the other early Christian monks achieved. In part, this is because the greater part of their accomplishment remained, of necessity, hidden and obscure. When Athanasius describes Antony as "one who, as Scripture says, having trusted in the Lord, was like Mount

---

[49] See *The Encroaching Desert: Egyptian Hagiography and the Medieval West*, ed. Jitse Dijkstra and Mathilde van Dijk (Leiden, The Netherlands: Brill, 2006).

[50] See Amy Hollywood's and E. Ann Matter's contributions to this volume.

Sion, keeping his mind unshaken and unruffled," he hints at something that can never be fully known or understood, but that was crucial to Antony's witness – the depth of the inner freedom that the monk had achieved.[51]

The early monastic tradition was insistent that the "place of God" could be sought and even discovered by the monk who was prepared to embark on the long arduous journey of self-discovery. But ultimately the place remained hidden, not entirely knowable. The monks seemed to recognize and accept this. In their vision of the monastic life, they mapped out a way of living that promised the possibility of gaining a genuine and deep consciousness of God at the center of one's life. Still, they refrained from mapping everything, always preserving a space in the imagination where the mystery of God could be cherished. Antony's own journey into the solitude of the inner mountain became emblematic of this mystery. Abba Sisoes, who lived in the inner mountain for seventy-two years following Antony's death, never claimed to have penetrated the mystery of the place or of the one who had gone there before him. When a brother approached him on the mountain and asked him, "Have you already reached Abba Antony's stature, Father?" Abba Sisoes responded: "If I had one of Abba Antony's thoughts, I should become all flame."[52]

---

[51] Athanasius, *VA*, p. 51; Gregg, *Life of Antony*, p. 70.
[52] *AP*, Sisoes 9; Ward, *Sayings*, p. 214.

2 Song, Experience, and the Book in Benedictine Monasticism

AMY HOLLYWOOD

The various forms of monastic life that emerged in the third and fourth centuries of the Common Era all claimed to provide the space in which the life of Christian perfection might be most effectively pursued. The monks and nuns who became the self-described spiritual elite of Christianity lived under rules that told them when, why, where, and how to act. The most successful of these rules in Western Christianity, the sixth-century *Rule of Benedict*, is often praised for its flexibility and moderation, yet within it every aspect of the daily lives of the monks is carefully ordered. If we understand ritual as the repeated and formalized practice of particular actions within carefully determined times and places, the moment in which what we believe ought to be the case and what is the case in the messy realm of everyday action come together, then the Benedictine's life is one in which the monk or nun strives to make every action a ritual action.[1]

Between 400 and 700 CE at least thirty *regula*, or "rules of life," were written in Latin.[2] All of these Latin rules were grounded in earlier attempts to legislate the form of monasticism in which men or women – and sometimes men and women together – lived in an enclosed community under the leadership of an abbot or abbess. Known as cenobitic monasticism, this way of pursuing the ideal Christian life is described and prescribed in texts associated with Pachomius in Egypt (d. ca. 346), Basil the Great in Cappadocia (d. 379), and the North African bishop, Augustine of Hippo (d. 430). But it was the *Rule of Benedict*, together

---

[1] For this account of ritual, see Jonathan Z. Smith, "The Bare Facts of Ritual," in *Imagining Religion: From Babylon to Jonestown* (Chicago: University of Chicago Press, 1988), pp. 53–65.

[2] This paragraph is indebted to Bernard McGinn, *The Presence of God: A History of Western Christian Mysticism*, vol. 2, *The Growth of Mysticism: Gregory the Great through the Twelfth Century* (New York: Crossroad, 1994), pp. 27–31. For a fuller discussion of what McGinn calls "the mystical element in early monasticism," see pp. 34–79 (on Gregory the Great) and 119–46.

with variants written for the use of women, that became the centerpiece of monastic life in Western Europe during the Middle Ages.[3]

Making use of earlier documents, Benedict of Nursia (ca. 480–547) devised the rule for his own community at Monte Cassino.[4] The rule's enormous influence rests on a variety of factors. First, the *Rule of Benedict* prescribes the proper way to conduct one's daily life, yet with sufficient flexibility to allow it to serve in very different physical and spiritual contexts. Second, Benedict became a widely revered figure through the account of his life given by Pope Gregory the Great (ca. 540–604) in his *Dialogues* (593–94) – an account that describes Benedict's path to holiness through his embrace of monastic solitude and contemplation.[5] Finally, the *Rule* benefited from the patronage of the Carolingian monarchy of the early ninth century. As part of Carolingian attempts to unify the realm, Benedict of Aniane (d. 821) was called on to reform monastic houses. Benedict made use of the *Rule of Benedict*, which was

---

[3] Communities of women often used other rules, particularly that which came to be known as the Augustinian rule. Women who lived according to this rule were known as canonesses and often did not take permanent vows of poverty, chastity, and obedience as did Benedictine nuns. Women also often lived as recluses in the early, high, and late Middle Ages. Yet the influence of the *Rule of Benedict* is strong in all of these forms of life. Feminized versions of the *Rule* appear in manuscripts with other rules and many of its precepts are included in rules written for solitaries. The *Rule*'s outline for the weekly singing of the Psalms was also very influential on other forms of religious life for men and on cathedral liturgies, to which the laity would have had access. See Alison I. Beach, *Women as Scribes: Book Production and Monastic Reform in Twelfth-Century Bavaria* (Cambridge: Cambridge University Press, 2004), pp. 8–31 and 36. See also Penelope D. Johnson, *Equal in Monastic Profession: Religious Women in Medieval France* (Chicago: University of Chicago Press, 1991); and Bruce. L. Vernarde, *Women's Monasticism and Medieval Society: Nunneries in France and England, 890–1215* (Ithaca, NY: Cornell University Press, 1997). On the ubiquity of the Divine Office centered on the Psalms, see Margot E. Fassler, "Hildegard and the Dawn Song of Lauds: An Introduction to Benedictine Psalmody," in *Psalms in Community: Jewish and Christian Textual, Liturgical, and Artistic Traditions*, ed. Harold W. Attridge and Margot E. Fassler (Atlanta, GA: Society of Biblical Literature, 2003), p. 218.

[4] For detailed discussions of the sources of the rule, see *RB 1980: The Rule of Benedict*, ed. Timothy Fry (Collegeville, MN: The Liturgical Press, 1981). Further references will appear parenthetically within the text as *RB*. See also Bruce L. Vernarde, ed. and trans., *The Rule of Benedict*, Dumbarton Oaks Medieval Library (Cambridge, MA: Harvard University Press, 2011).

[5] As McGinn explains, Gregory depicts Benedict's life in three stages: "the retreat to a place of solitude (*ad locum dilectae solitudinis rediit*) at the outset, the living within himself (*habitavit secum*) of the early part of his career (*Dial.* 2.3), and the rapture above himself (*rapitur super se*) ... toward the end of his life." McGinn, *Growth of Mysticism*, p. 73. In Gregory's account of Benedict's life, monastic solitude, contemplation, visionary experience, and the highest sanctity available to one in this life go hand in hand. On Gregory's depiction of Benedict as a visionary, see also Veerle Fraeter's contribution to this volume.

then approved at the Synod of Aachen (817) as the standard rule for all monastic houses within the Carolingian empire.⁶

The *Rule of Benedict* and its account of the ideal Christian life were vital to the development of Western Christian mysticism. (In what follows, I will describe the *Rule* in its original form, which was designed for monks. Although some women complained that the rule did not meet their particular needs, the aspects of the *Rule* in which I am most interested, those parts dealing with prayer and devotional practice, were followed in very much the same way by men and by women.)⁷ The practices articulated there – practices Benedict passed down from the traditions of Eastern and Western monasticism to which he was heir – are those out of which mystical life most often emerges within the Western Christian tradition. As we see elsewhere in this volume, moreover, it is when these practices are adapted to new forms of religious life in semi- and nonmonastic settings that claims to extraordinary experiences of God's presence – and the apophasis or unsaying of these experiences – spread beyond the walls of the monastery.

This might seem to be a great deal to claim for a document that is largely concerned with ordering the daily life of a community, providing legislation for everything from the manner of selecting the abbot (*RB* 64) and the length of the novitiate (*RB* 58), to the proper time for meals (*RB* 41) and the amount of wine that should be drunk by the monks (*RB* 40). For many readers, the *Rule of Benedict* is most striking in its ascetic details. Benedict presumes that those who follow his rule will commit to lifelong continence, will eschew private ownership (*RB* 33), and, above all, will obey their abbot in all things. Silence is continually enjoined and laughter condemned. Sleep is curtailed; food, drink, and clothing are adequate but minimal; and contact with the world outside the monastery is highly regulated.

---

⁶ Strictly speaking there was no Benedictine order during this period, for each house existed as an autonomous unit under the authority of a local bishop or secular lord. The various Benedictine reform movements of the tenth and eleventh centuries attempted to loosen the ties between monasteries and local religious and political leaders in the service of religious independence and a return to the ideals of the *RB*, variously construed. For a general introduction, see C. H. Lawrence, *Medieval Monasticism: Forms of Religious Life in the Middle Ages* (London: Longman, 2000).

⁷ Complaints about the gendered nature of the *Rule of Benedict* were made most famously, perhaps, by Heloise (d. 1164) to Abelard (1079–1142). See Heloise's Letter Six and Abelard's First Reply and Abelard's Letter Eight in *The Letters of Abelard and Heloise*, trans. Betty Radice and M. T. Clanchy (Harmondsworth, UK: Penguin, 2003), pp. 93–111 and 130–210.

All of these details are held together, however, by the broad vision first articulated in the prologue. The prologue – and the *Rule* as a whole – is spoken in the voice of a father to his son.

> Listen carefully, my son, to the master's instructions, and attend to them with the ear of your heart. This is advice from a father who loves you; welcome it, and faithfully put it into practice. The labor of obedience will bring you back to him from whom you have drifted through the sloth of disobedience. This message of mine is for you, then, if you are ready to give up your own will, once and for all, and armed with the strong and noble weapons of obedience to do battle for the true King, Christ the Lord. (*RB* Prol. 1–3)

Obedience to the abbot, Christ's representative in the community, is at the core of the religious life.[8]

Obedience is made possible by stability. If a monk could simply choose to leave his monastery whenever he felt so inclined, he might easily move from one abbot to another and never achieve obedience. The *Rule* notes that there are four kinds of monk – the cenobites who live in community; the anchorites or hermits who live alone; the sarabaites, "the most detestable kind of monks," who live in small groups without a rule and without obedience to an abbot; and the gyrovagues, "who spend their entire lives drifting from region to region" and who, "slaves to their own wills and gross appetites," are "in every way ... worse than sarabaites" (*RB* 1). The problem with the sarabaites and gyrovagues is their lack of stability, hence their lack of obedience and resultant lack of humility. The *Rule* does allow that the life of the hermit or anchorite can be a valuable one, yet it demands that the monk first "have come through the test of living in a monastery for a long time" and thus been rendered self-reliant through obedience (*RB* 1).

According to the *Rule of Benedict*, the true monk begins as a cenobite, living in community under the rule of an abbot, that father who addresses them in the *Rule*. The monastery, the *Rule* tells us, is

> a school for the Lord's service. In drawing up its regulations, we hope to set down nothing harsh, nothing burdensome. The good of all concerned, however, may prompt us to a little strictness in order to amend faults and to safeguard love. Do not be daunted immediately

---

[8] This is a point that seemed to engender difficulties for those who wished to translate the *RB* for women. Can a woman be identified with Christ? See John E. Crean Jr., "*Voces Benedictinae*: A Comparative Study of Three Manuscripts of the Rule of St. Benedict for Women," *Vox Benedictina* 10, no. 1 (1993): 157–78.

by fear and run away from the road that leads to salvation. It is bound to be narrow at the outset. But as we progress in this way of life and in faith, we shall run on the path of God's commandments, our hearts overflowing with the inexpressible delight of love. Never swerving from his instructions, then, but faithfully observing his teaching in the monastery until death, we shall through patience share in the sufferings of Christ that we may deserve also to share in his kingdom. (*RB* Prol. 45–50)

Here, as in the opening lines of the *Rule*, we see one of the governing metaphors for the monastery, which is a "school for the Lord's service" ("*dominici schola servitii*"). The Latin *schola*, or schoolroom, was initially used for military schools. Later in the *Rule*, the monastery is described as a "training ground for eternal life." The monk learns there to engage in a warfare that is both physical and spiritual.[9]

Later Benedict will write of "the tools of the spiritual craft" ("*instrumenta artis spiritualis*") that are used in the "workshop" that is "the enclosure of the monastery and stability in community" (*RB* 4:75, 78). These tools, like the methods of warfare, are deployed toward the simultaneous ascent and descent that is humility:

> Accordingly, brothers, if we want to reach the highest summit of humility, if we desire to attain speedily that exaltation in heaven to which we climb by the humility of this present life, then by our ascending actions we must set up the ladder on which Jacob in a dream saw *angels descending and ascending* (Gn 28:12). Without doubt, this descent and ascent can signify only that we descend by exaltation and ascend by humility. Now the ladder erected is our life on earth, and if we humble our hearts the Lord will raise it to heaven. We may call our body and soul the sides of this ladder, into which our divine vocation has fitted the various steps of humility and discipline as we ascend. (*RB* 7:5–9)

---

[9] On the continuing role of violent imagery within the monastic context, particularly among the Cistercians, see Conrad Rudolph, *Violence and Daily Life: Reading, Art, and Polemics in the Cîteaux Moralia in Job* (Princeton, NJ: Princeton University Press, 1997); and M. Burcht Pranger, *The Artificiality of Christianity: Essays on the Poetics of Monasticism* (Stanford, CA: Stanford University Press, 2003). Bernard of Clairvaux in particular addressed himself to the knightly order. He called on knights to give up physical for spiritual arms and also wrote in praise of the Knights Templar, who dedicated themselves to God through their participation in the Crusades. See Bernard of Clairvaux, *In Praise of the New Knighthood: A Treatise on the Knights Templar and the Holy Places of Jerusalem*, trans. M. Conrad Greenia (Piscataway, NJ: Gorgias Press, 2010).

In the monastic life, one paradoxically ascends toward God by one's descent into humility before God, the abbot, and the religious community. The goal is "that *perfect love* of God which *casts out fear* (1 John 4:18)." For although the monk begins following the *Rule* and obeying the abbot out of fear, through the repeated practice of its injunctions he will come "to observe without effort, as though naturally, from habit, no longer out of fear of hell, but out of love for Christ, good habit and delight in virtue" (*RB* 7:67–9).

Love is inculcated through the workings of the Holy Spirit and the enactment of the *Rule*. Grace brings one to the *Rule*, the prescriptions of the *Rule* are the means of grace, and only through grace will the monk attain any part of the perfections the *Rule* enjoins.[10] The Benedictine life is made up of three components: communal prayer, private reading and devotion, and manual labor. I want first to focus on communal prayer. Although it may seem at first sight to be antithetical to the mystical life, for the monastic, communal prayer is the necessary precondition for any experience of the divine. Benedict, following John Cassian (ca. 360–435) and a host of other early monastic writers, argues that the monk seeks to attain a state of unceasing prayer.[11] Benedict cites Psalm 118 (119): "Seven times a day have I praised you" (Ps 118 [119]:164) and "At midnight I arose to give you praise" (Ps 118 [119]:62).[12] He calls on

---

[10] I cannot help thinking here of the words of "Amazing Grace," written by the Calvinist clergyman, John Newton (1725–1807):"Grace has led me safe thus far, and grace will lead me home." See D. Bruce Hindmarsh, "'End of Faith as Its Beginnings': Models of Spiritual Progress in Early Evangelical Devotional Hymns," *Spiritus* 10 (2010): 1–21, at p. 17. Hindmarsh's essay offers important insight into the continuing role of hymnody in Protestant, particularly evangelical, Christianity. On the Psalms specifically, see the essays by Serene Jones, Carlos Eire, Jaime Lara, Gilbert I. Bond, and Alexander Lingas in *Psalms in Community: Jewish and Christian Textual, Liturgical, and Artistic Traditions*, ed. Harold W. Attridge and Margot E. Fassler (Atlanta, GA: Society of Biblical Literature, 2003).

[11] For the centrality of the Psalms to early monasticism, see Brian Daley, "Finding the Right Key: The Aims and Strategies of Early Christian Interpretation of the Psalms," in *Psalms in Community: Jewish and Christian Textual, Liturgical, and Artistic Traditions*, ed. Harold W. Attridge and Margot E. Fassler (Atlanta, GA: Society of Biblical Literature, 2003), pp. 189–205, esp. pp. 190–2.

[12] According to Margot E. Fassler, Benedictines in the medieval West would have known the Psalms of the daily office in the second of Jerome's three Latin translations of the book. "This was a heavily Christianized version of the texts," Fassler explains, "primarily dependent on the Septuagint," a Greek translation of the Hebrew Bible, rather than on the Hebrew original. The numbering of this version of the Psalms, which is that found in the Benedictine Divine Office and in the Vulgate, differs from that in the Hebrew Bible and in modern translations done directly from the Hebrew. Hence the first number given refers to the Vulgate, the second to the Hebrew Bible and modern translations of the Psalms. In addition, Fassler notes that psalm verses in the liturgy of the Mass "were frequently taken from even earlier Latin translations." There was,

his monks to come together eight times a day for the communal recitation, chanting, or singing of the Psalms and other prayers and readings.[13] This is the work of God (*opus dei*) enjoined by the *Rule*. Each of the Psalms was recited once a week, with many repeated once or more a day. Benedict provides a detailed schedule for his monks, one in which the biblical injunction to always have a prayer on one's lips is enacted through the division of the day into the eight canonical hours: Vigils, Lauds, Prime, Terce, Sext, None, Vespers, and Compline.[14]

To many modern ears, the repetition of the Psalms, ancient Israelite prayers handed down by the Christian tradition in the context of particular, often Christological, translations and interpretations, will likely sound rote and deadening. Some modern Western conceptions of the mystical, spiritual, or religious life insist that it be an immediate and spontaneous engagement with the divine. From this perspective, one might well ask of the *Rule*: What of the immediacy of the monk's relationship to God? What of his personal feelings in the face of the divine? What spontaneity can exist in the monk's engagement with God within the context of such a regimented and uniform prayer life? If the monk is reciting another's words rather than his own, how can the feelings engendered by these words be his own and so be sincere?[15]

Yet for Benedict, as for Cassian on whose work he appears liberally to have drawn, the intensity and authenticity of one's feeling for God is enabled through communal, ritualized prayer, as well as through private reading and devotion (itself carefully regulated).[16] (Note that Cassian is describing the practice of prayer as it is undertaken by monks in solitude as well as in community. Benedict, by calling on his monks to read Cassian as a guide to the religious life, is folding his understanding of

---

then, no single book of the Psalms in the Latin West. Fassler, "Hildegard and the Dawn Song of Lauds," p. 218.

[13] For the tradition of singing the Psalms in Judaism and early Christianity, see Peter Jefferey, "Philo's Impact on Christian Psalmody," in *Psalms in Community: Jewish and Christian Textual, Liturgical, and Artistic Traditions*, ed. Harold W. Attridge and Margot E. Fassler (Atlanta, GA: Society of Biblical Literature, 2003), pp. 147–87.

[14] See the extremely helpful chart of the liturgical hours, worked out on the basis of the *RB*, in *RB 1980*, pp. 390–7.

[15] This question becomes particularly piquant when we note that the *RB* explicitly enjoins the monks to be brief in petitionary prayer. "Prayer should therefore be short and pure, unless perhaps it is prolonged under the inspiration of divine grace. In community, however, prayer should always be brief; and when the superior gives the signal, all should rise together" (*RB* 20:4–5).

[16] My account throughout is profoundly influenced by Jean LeClercq, *The Love of Learning and the Desire for God: A Study of Monastic Culture*, trans. Catherine Misrahi (New York: Fordham University Press, 1961).

prayer – and particularly the prayerful recitation of the Psalter – into the cenobitic life.) Proper performance of "God's work" in prayer requires that the monk not simply recite the Psalms. Instead, the monk was called on to feel what the psalmist felt, to learn to fear, desire, and love God in and through the words of the Psalms.[17] According to Cassian, we know God, love God, and experience God, when our experience and that of the psalmist come together:

> For divine Scripture is clearer and its inmost organs, so to speak, are revealed to us when our experience (*experientia*) not only perceives but even anticipates its thought, and the meaning of the words are disclosed to us not by exegesis but by proof. When we have the same disposition (*affectum*) in our heart with which each psalm was sung or written down, then we shall become like its author, grasping the significance beforehand rather than afterward. That is, we first take in the power of what is said, rather than the knowledge of it, recalling what has taken place or what does take place in us in daily assaults whenever we reflect on them.[18]

When the monk can anticipate what words will follow in a Psalm – not because he has memorized them, but because his heart is so at one with the psalmist that these words spontaneously come to his lips – then he knows and experiences God.[19]

---

[17] In his study of early Christian commentaries on the Psalms, Daley notes that they often seem explicitly geared toward "clergy or monks rather than congregations of 'ordinary' believers" and are less concerned with articulating the literal meaning of the texts or its moral and prophetic content than in facilitating "the *internalization* of these biblical prayers-in-verse, to enable the reader so to feel and grasp them, as works of divinely inspired poetry, that the reader's own thoughts and emotions, desires and passions, might be purified and transformed." Daley, "Finding the Right Key," p. 192.

[18] John Cassian, *Conferences*, trans. Boniface Ramsey (New York: Newman Press, 1997), conf. 10, ch. 11, p. 384. For the Latin, see John Cassian, *Conférences*, vol. 2, ed. Dom E. Pichery (Paris: Les Éditions du Cerf, 1955–9), conf. 10, ch. 11, p. 92.

[19] Experience is a notoriously difficult term. In this essay, I will simply trace some of the ways in which it is deployed in Christian monastic literature. Needless to say, I disagree rather strenuously with those who suggest, through their omissions, that nothing worthwhile is said about experience in the Middle Ages. See most recently, Martin Jay, *Songs of Experience: Modern American and European Variations on a Universal Theme* (Berkeley: University of California Press, 2005). Bernard McGinn eschews the term given its complexities and the misunderstandings to which it often gives rise – most notably that mysticism has to do with something called feeling that is other than or lies outside of reason. Yet consciousness, the term he prefers, seems to me to be just as, if not more, problematic. It is certainly as highly complex an idea as experience, and one that often connotes a kind of mastery and presence of the self to itself antithetical to many of the texts McGinn uses it to describe. See

The word translated here as "disposition" is derived from the Latin *affectus*, from the verb *afficio* – to do something to someone, to exert an influence on another body or another person, to bring another into a particular state of mind. *Affectus* carries a range of meanings, from a state of mind or disposition produced in one by the influence of another to that actual affection or mood itself. In many instances, *affectus* simply means love. At the center of ancient and medieval usages is the notion that love is brought into being in one person by the actions of another. For Cassian, as for later generations of monastic authors, our love for God is always engendered by God's love for us. God acts (*afficio*); humans are the recipients of God's actions (so *affectus* the noun is derived from the passive participle of *afficio*). The acquisition of proper dispositions through habit is itself the operation of the freely given grace that is God's love. There is no distinction here between mediation (through the words of scripture) and immediacy (that of God's presence), between habit and spontaneity, the impersonal and the personal, or feeling and knowledge.

The affects, moods, or dispositions engendered by God are not only those of love and desire. Fear, dread, shame, and sorrow, gratitude, joy, triumph, and ecstasy are all expressed in the Psalms and in the other songs found within scripture.[20] (In fact, as Abba Isaac explains to Cassian and Germanus in the *Conferences*, one single verse of the Psalms can contain all of these feelings: Psalm 70:1 [69:2], "O God, incline unto my aid; O Lord, make haste to help me."[21]) According to Cassian and other early Christian interpreters, the Psalms lay out the full realm of human

---

Bernard McGinn, ed., *The Essential Writings of Christian Mysticism* (New York: The Modern Library, 2006), pp. xv–xvi. For his understanding of consciousness, which is much more philosophically and theologically nuanced than I am able to do justice to here, see Bernard McGinn, "Mystical Consciousness: A Modest Proposal," *Spiritus* 8 (2008): 44–63.

[20] In a very important early commentary by Athanasius (d. 373), *Letter to Marcellinus on the Interpretation of the Psalms*, he argues that the book of Psalms "contains within itself the movements of each soul, their changes and adjustments, written out and thoroughly portrayed, so that if someone should wish to grasp himself from it, as from an image, and to understand on that basis how to shape himself, it is written there." As Daley argues, according to Athanasius, the Psalms are not simply mimetic but also therapeutic, for in singing them one can not only "learn ... about the motions and conditions of souls" but also "find in them the remedy and corrective measure for each of these motions." Athanasius, *Letter to Marcellinus on the Interpretation of the Psalms*, in *PG* 27, col. 20 and col. 25; as cited in Daley, "Finding the Right Key," pp. 200–1.

[21] Cassian, *Conferences*, conf. 10, ch. 10, p. 379; Cassian, *Conférences*, vol. 2, conf. 10, ch. 10, p. 89. For more on this passage, see the essays by Douglas Burton-Christie and Rachel Fulton Brown in this volume.

feeling and by coming to know God in and through these affects, the monk comes to know both himself and the divine.

> For we find all of these dispositions expressed in the psalms, so that we may see whatever occurs as in a very clear mirror and recognize it more effectively. Having been instructed in this way, with our dispositions for our teachers, we shall grasp this as something seen rather than heard, and from the inner disposition of the heart we shall bring forth not what has been committed to memory but what is inborn in the very nature of things. Thus we shall penetrate its meaning not through the written text but with experience (*experientia*) leading the way.[22]

What begins as a physical, affective, and cognitive experience leads to an inner transformation Cassian calls fiery prayer; the monk passes beyond the body and lets forth in his spirit "unutterable groans and sighs"; he feels "an unspeakable ecstasy of heart" and "an insatiable gladness of spirit."[23] Here prayer moves beyond images and affect even as it is their apotheosis. For Cassian, the entire body and soul of the monk is affected; he is transformed by the words of the Psalms so that he lives them and through this experience he comes to know, with heart and body and mind, that God is great and good.

For Cassian, Christians attain the height of prayer

> when every love, every desire, every effort, every undertaking, every thought of ours, everything that we live, that we speak, that we breathe, will be God, and when that unity which the Father now has with the Son and which the Son has with the Father will be carried over into our understanding and our mind, so that, just as he loves us with a sincere and pure and indissoluble love, we too may be joined to him with a perpetual and inseparable love and so united with him that whatever we breathe, whatever we understand, whatever we speak, may be God.[24]

---

[22] Cassian, *Conferences*, conf. 10, ch. 11, p. 385; Cassian, *Conférences*, vol. 2, conf. 10, ch. 11, p. 93.

[23] Cassian, *Conferences*, conf. 10, ch. 11, p. 385; Cassian, *Conférences*, vol. 2, conf. 10, ch. 11, p. 93.

[24] Cassian, *Conferences*, conf. 10, ch. 7, pp. 375–6; and Cassian, *Conférences*, vol. 2, conf. 10, ch. 7, p. 81. In Conference 10, Cassian depicts Abba Isaac telling him and his friend Germanus how to keep their minds from wandering from God. He suggests that the monk continually recite a single Psalm verse. Yet later in the Conference, Abba Isaac returns rather abruptly from the individual monk reciting an individual Psalm to the communal recitation of all of the Psalms and "the holy practices of the cenobium." He argues that these communal practices are also necessary to stabilizing

Although the fullness of fruition in God will never occur in this life, the monk trains himself daily, through obedience, chastity, poverty, and, most importantly, prayer, to attain it.[25]

Cassian's understanding of the role of the Psalms in the monastic life lays the foundation for monastic thought and practice throughout the Middle Ages. At the heart of Benedictine communal life, Cassian's understanding of prayer is also vital to the patterns of reading and private devotion prescribed by the *Rule of Benedict*. Reading, whether aloud in a communal setting or privately, is ubiquitous in the life of the monk, and the *Rule* is clear not only about its importance but also about what ought to be read. "For anyone hastening on to the perfection of monastic life," the *Rule* explains,

> there are the teachings of the holy Fathers, the observance of which will lead him to the very heights of perfection. What page, what passage of the inspired books of the Old and New Testaments is not the truest guide for human life? What book of the holy catholic Fathers does not resoundingly summon us along the true way to reach the Creator? Then, besides the *Conferences* of the Fathers, their *Institutes* and their *Lives*, there is also the rule of our holy father Basil. For observant and obedient monks, all these are nothing less than tools for the cultivation of virtues; but as for us, they make us blush for shame at being so slothful, so unobservant, so negligent. Are you hastening toward your heavenly home? Then with Christ's help, keep this little rule that we have written for

---

a wandering mind. A single line of the Psalms and the entire Psalter, the individual monk and the cenobium – ultimately Cassian suggests both must work together.

[25] I would take issue with the simplistic formulation of the relationship between belief and practice suggested by Louis Althusser. Althusser claims that Blaise Pascal said, "more or less: 'Kneel down, move your lips in prayer, and you will believe.'" Althusser's position is more complicated than these lines would suggest, but a quite simplistic reading of them has had an enormous influence in contemporary critical theory. The lines are often repeated in what becomes an almost behavioralist account of the efficacy of religious and other forms of practice. Lost is the insistence, in Cassian and other monastic writers, that one must look to one's own experience, think, reflect, meditate, and feel the words of scripture, working constantly to conform the former to the latter. See Louis Althusser, "Ideology and the Ideological State Apparatuses: Notes towards an Investigation," in *Lenin and Philosophy and Other Essays*, trans. Ben Brewster (New York: Monthly Review Press, 2001), p. 114. For a more recent analysis of monastic practice and the formation of the self, one deeply influenced by Jean LeClercq and attentive to the physicality of monastic practice, see Talal Asad, "On Discipline and Humility in Medieval Christian Monasticism," in *Genealogies of Religion: Discipline and Reasons of Power in Christianity and Islam* (Baltimore, MD: Johns Hopkins University Press, 1993), pp. 125–67.

beginners. After that, you can set out for the loftier summits of the teaching and virtues we mentioned above, and under God's protection you will reach them. Amen. (*RB* 73:2–9)[26]

In these, the closing lines of his rule, Benedict enjoins his monks to read and to study the *Rule* – but also the Bible and the writings of the "holy catholic Fathers," most prominent among them Cassian, author of the *Conferences* and the *Institutes*.[27]

The *Rule of Benedict* also calls on the monks to perform manual labor (*RB* 48).[28] For Benedict this no doubt largely entailed the work needed to feed and shelter the community. There are also provisions for nursing the monastery's sick (*RB* 36) and elderly (*RB* 37), for receiving guests (*RB* 53 and 56), and for the care of the boys who are assumed to be a part of the community (*RB* 37).[29] The presence of children in the

---

[26] Similar expectations were found in early rules for women, reinforcing and reinforced by the *RB*. Saint Jerome's (d. 420) letter to Laeta concerning the education of her daughter Paula was cited at length in Carolingian legislation for canonesses: "Let her treasures not be silks or gems, but manuscripts of the holy scriptures.... Let her first study the Psalter. Then let her gather wisdom for life in the proverbs of Solomon. Let her learn in Ecclesiastes to despise the vanities of the world. Let her follow in Job the example of virtue and patience. Then let her pass on to the gospels, never to be put aside once taken in hand. Let her also drink in the Acts of the Apostles and the Epistles with a totally willing heart, and then the rest of the New and Old Testament in their proper order." *Institutio sanctimonialium Aquisgranensis*, ed. A. Wermingholff, *Monumenta Germaniae Historica*, Concilia 2, pp. 453–4. Cited and translated in Beach, *Women as Scribes*, p. 20.

[27] On the reading of the rule to novices and to the community as a whole, see *RB* 58 and 66. On reading during meals, see *RB* 38. On private reading, see *RB* 42, 48, and 49. Cassian is recommended again in *RB* 42.

[28] The *Rule* enjoins manual labor, together with prayerful reading, as defenses against idleness, "the enemy of the soul" (*RB* 48). The bulk of the chapter, however, describes the proper way to engage in prayerful reading, suggesting that although manual labor is necessary to the upkeep of the community and a valuable defense against idleness, it may not have any great value in itself. This points to a tension running throughout the Christian monastic tradition and beyond between the need for action and the desire to live a life of contemplation. Arguably, by calling the monastic life of prayer the "work of God," the *Rule* refuses to distinguish between them. Yet concern about who will take care of the pastoral needs of the laity – or who will take care of the bodily needs of the monks – remains. On this issue, see McGinn, *Growth of Mysticism*, pp. 74–9 and 218–23; Giles Constable, *Three Studies in Medieval Religious Thought* (Cambridge: Cambridge University Press, 1995); and Douglas Burton-Christie's, Walter Simon's, and Charlotte Radler's essays in this volume.

[29] This points to a practice already in place at Monte Cassino and central to Benedictine communities – the gifting of children to the monastery by their families. The *RB* is at its harshest when describing the disciplining of boys. Not yet having attained the age of reason, the *RB* presumes that boys cannot be persuaded to the good and so must be physically disciplined (*RB* 30 and 63). What is the last resort when dealing with adult

monastery points to other kinds of manual labor, for not only must the boys be disciplined, they must also be taught to read if they are to enact the *Rule*. Benedict is not explicit, but monasteries throughout the Middle Ages were at the center of the production, transmission, and storing of knowledge. Monks and nuns worked as teachers, authors, and scribes. Book production throughout the period was extremely labor intensive and although, like all artisans (*RB* 57), those who engaged in the production of books must avoid pride, their labor was highly valued.[30] Monastic culture was, in its Western instantiations, a culture of the book as well as a culture of prayerful song.

At the heart of the monastic life, I have argued, lies the transformation of the monk's or nun's experience through his or her engagement with the Psalms and other texts performed – chanted or sung – during the Divine Office. This transformation goes hand in hand with that engendered through the reading of scripture and other religious texts (*lectio divina*, *RB* 48:1).[31] During Benedict's time, and with increasing complexity in the years to follow, the Divine Office involved not simply the Psalms but also other biblical texts and nonscriptural hymns and readings. The interweaving of biblical and nonbiblical sources, the particular order in which texts are organized, and the shifting temporality of song render the liturgy, in the words of the musicologist Susan Boynton, "a mode of performative exegesis."[32] Multiple interpretations of scripture are, Boynton argues, "literally performed through the juxtaposition, entwining and expansion of scriptural texts."[33]

---

monks is the first line of attack when dealing with children, although the monastic life for adults was also intensely physical. The humility the *RB* demands is expressed physically, particularly when a monk is disciplined. Hence the image of a monk prostrate before the abbot's feet and "the feet of all that they may pray for him" (*RB* 44) is as crucial to Benedictine monasticism as that of a monk, arms extended in prayer, singing to God. Benedict emphasizes the monk's humility by insisting on his physical posture – "his head must be lowered and his eyes cast down" (*RB* 7: 63).

[30] For one fascinating example of the esteem in which scribes were held by their communities, see the story of the female scribe, Diemut of Wessobrunn, in Beach, *Women as Scribes*, pp. 32–64.

[31] Given early monastic emphasis on interiorizing the word of God in the Divine Office and the often public nature of *lectio divina*, I think it is wrong to distinguish sharply between public liturgy and private devotion or between external performance and interior transformation. The ideal is not always achieved, but we need to recognize that it *is* the ideal around which Benedictine life is organized.

[32] Susan Boynton, "Performative Exegesis in the Fleury *Interfectio Puerorum*," *Viator* 29 (1998): 39–64.

[33] Susan Boynton, "Religious Soundscapes: Liturgy and Music," in *The Cambridge History of Christianity: Christianity in Western Europe c. 1100–c. 1500*, ed. Miri Rubin and Walter Simons (Cambridge: Cambridge University Press, 2009), p. 240.

Margot E. Fassler gives a fascinating glimpse of this process in her studies of Hildegard of Bingen's (1098–1179) musical compositions. As a Benedictine nun, Fassler notes, Hildegard would have heard Psalms and verses from individual Psalms in a number of different contexts and settings. Again, each psalm was sung in its complete form at least once a week in the Divine Office. These renditions were framed by antiphons or responses, sometimes verses from the psalm in question, sometimes "newly written texts created to link a given psalm to a particular hour of the day, to a feast, or to a season," and sometimes an Alleluia, a term from the Psalms, the singing of which might be short or extended, simple or complex.[34] The antiphon, Fassler argues, "comments upon the psalm text, transforming its meaning in the process."[35] A particular theological view – of the role of Mary in creation and salvation, for example – is performed through the juxtaposition of Psalms with antiphons.

This becomes clear when we look to the antiphons Hildegard wrote for a feast of the Virgin Mary as they stand in relationship to the *Rule of Benedict*'s prescription for the Psalms to be said at Lauds on Sundays and important feast days. As Fassler notes, the opening song for Lauds, Psalm 66, was performed without antiphony. The first antiphon written by Hildegard for the Marian Feast stands in productive counterpart to Psalm 92, the second psalm to be recited or sung during the hour. Hildegard has her nuns sing, "Today a closed gate is opened to us, that which the serpent choked in a woman. So the flower from the Virgin Mary gleams in the dawn."[36] Reference to the dawn immediately situates the antiphon in the hour of Lauds, which is the first of the day, meant to be performed as the sun rises. The centrality of Mary, moreover, provides a very specific reading of the generally Christologically interpretated Psalm 92 that follows: "The Lord hath reigned, he is clothed in beauty: the Lord is clothed with strength and hath girded himself" (Ps 92:1). The psalm still would have been heard as referring to Christ, but Mary and her role in the incarnation, Mary as the source of that fleshly clothing in which Christ comes, is highlighted. The "throne ... prepared from of old" (Ps 92:2) is the Virgin Mary as the throne of Wisdom, a common theme in Late Antique Christianity and in the twelfth century. When the nuns sing, "wonderful are the surges of the sea"

---

[34] Fassler, "Hildegard and the Dawn Song of Lauds," pp. 219–20.
[35] Ibid., p. 220.
[36] Ibid., p. 226. Fassler usefully provides the text for all of the Psalms sung at this hour and Hildegard's antiphons.

(Ps 92: 4) against the background of Hildegard's antiphon, Mary as "the star of the sea" is evoked. Finally, Fassler argues, "the final verse of Ps 92 includes the words 'holiness becomes thy house,' and this too would resonate with a Marian interpretation of the psalm text, Mary being the most common Christian type for the church, the house of the Lord."[37] Against the claim commonly made by modern scholars that medieval women were unable to engage in the interpretation of scripture because they were denied access to the priesthood and the schools, Fassler demonstrates how Hildegard's musical compositions and the antiphons she created for the Divine Office are an exegetically driven and musically performed theology.[38]

As the example of Hildegard shows, individual monastic houses developed increasingly complex versions of the Divine Office geared toward the particular needs and desires of the community and the larger world with which it interacted. Although Benedict prescribes only that the monk receive communion once a day and presumes that most of the monks will not be priests, monasteries for men became increasingly clericalized in subsequent centuries. The Mass joined the Divine Office as a vital aspect of the religious life of the monastery, which was increasingly understood by those within and those outside its walls as the site of intercession between the world and God. Although all clergy and religious were designated within medieval society as "those who pray," monks and nuns, as specialists dedicated increasingly solely to prayer and devotion, were generally seen as particularly potent intercessors. The secular clergy and the laity, particularly (although by no means only) the wealthy and powerful, gave material goods to monasteries in exchange for their prayers – and increasingly, in exchange for the performance of masses, with their own complex liturgies, on behalf of the souls of the dead.[39]

---

[37] Ibid., p. 235.
[38] See Margot E. Fassler, "Composer and Dramatist: 'Melodious Singing and the Freshness of Remorse,'" in *Voice of the Living Light: Hildegard of Bingen and Her World*, ed. Barbara Newman (Berkeley: University of California Press, 1998), pp. 149–75; and Margot E. Fassler, "Music for the Love Feast: Hildegard of Bingen and the Song of Songs," in *Women's Voices across Musical Worlds*, ed. J. Bernstein (Boston: Northeastern University Press, 2003), pp. 92–117.
[39] On these developments, see Barbara Rosenwein, *Rhinocerus Bound: Cluny in the Tenth Century* (Philadelphia: University of Pennsylvania Press, 1982). It is commonly argued that this transition was bad for nuns. For the argument and a vital challenge to it, see Fiona J. Griffiths, *The Garden of Delights: Reform and Renaissance for Women in the Twelfth Century* (Philadelphia: University of Pennsylvania Press, 2007), pp. 8–16.

The customaries produced by individual houses record their particular practices. Memorial books and necrologies begin to emerge in the eighth century, books that record the souls for whom the monks and nuns prayed – the dead from their own communities and the donors and patrons to whom the monastery had promised its prayers.[40] During the tenth and eleventh centuries, monasteries were at the center of various reform movements within the Church. Yet the central work of the Benedictines, or Black Monks as they were often called by contemporaries, was generally understood to be intercessory – and hence, critics argued, far from the spirit of the *Rule of Benedict*, which was geared toward the transformation of the individual soul in community.[41]

The story of these criticisms and the new orders to which they lead appears in the chapter that follows. I want to close, however, by pointing to continuities across the Benedictine tradition – continuities based on the centrality of song, experience, and the book to the monastic life. The complex relationship between song, experience, and book is brilliantly articulated by the Cistercian Bernard of Clairvaux (d. 1153) in his *Sermons on the Song of Songs*. In explaining the name of the biblical book, Bernard enumerates the scriptural songs, so vital to monastic experience – not only the Psalms but also the songs of Deborah (Jgs 5:1), Judith (Jdt 16:1), Hannah, Samuel's mother (1 Sm 2:1), the authors of Lamentations and of Job, and all of the other songs found throughout scripture. "If you consider your own experience (*experientiam*)," Bernard writes, "surely it is in the victory by which your faith overcomes the world (1 John 5:4) and 'in your leaving the lake of wretchedness and the filth of the marsh'(Psalm 39:3) that you sing to the Lord himself a new song because he has done marvelous works (Psalm 97:1)?"[42] As the modern annotation shows – annotation that would be unnecessary for a monastic audience – Bernard's text is a palimpsest of scriptural references. His mind and heart are so thoroughly imbued with the Bible through his monastic practice that he needs no other language with which to describe the movement of the soul toward God.

Following a tradition of interpretation of the Song of Songs that begins at least with Origen, Bernard argues that its title shows it to be

[40] See Patrick Geary, *Phantoms of Remembrance: Memory and Oblivion at the End of the First Millenium* (Princeton, NJ: Princeton University Press, 1996), pp. 120–30.
[41] See John Van Engen, "The 'Crisis of Cenobitism' Reconsidered: Benedictine Monasticism in the Years 1050–1150," *Speculum* 61, no. 2 (1986): 269–304. Van Engen both maintains this distinction and offers evidence that might, I think, count against it.
[42] Bernard of Clairvaux, *Sermons on the Song of Songs*, in *Selected Works*, trans. G. R. Evans (New York: Paulist Press, 1987), Sermon 1, V. 9, p. 213. For the Latin, see Bernard of Clairvaux, *Sancti Bernardi Opera*, ed. Jean LeClercq, C. H. Talbot, and H. M. Rochais, 8 vols. (Rome: Editiones Cistercienses, 1957–77), vol. 1, Sermon 1, V. 9, p. 72.

the preeminent of songs, the one through which one attains to the highest knowledge of God.⁴³ "This sort of song," Bernard explains, "only the touch of the Holy Spirit teaches (1 John 2:27), and it is learned by experience (*experientia*) alone."⁴⁴ In the third sermon of the series he calls on his listeners and readers to "read the book of experience" as they interpret the Song of Songs.

> Today we read the book of experience (*libro experientiae*). Let us turn to ourselves and let each of us search his own conscience about what is said. I want to investigate whether it has been given to any of you to say, "Let him kiss me with the kiss of his mouth." (Sg 1:1)⁴⁵

Bernard claims that it is through attention to "the book of experience" that the monk determines what he has of God and what he lacks.⁴⁶ Bernard calls on his fellow monks to see the gap between their experience of God's love and their love for God and then to meditate on, chew over, and digest the words of the Song so that they might come more fully to inhabit them. The soul should strive, Bernard insists, to be able to sing with the bride of the Song: "Let him kiss me with the kiss of his mouth."⁴⁷

---

43 On early and medieval Christian interpretation of the Song of Songs, see E. Ann Matter, *The Voice of the Beloved: The Song of Songs in Western Medieval Christianity* (Philadelphia: University of Pennsylvania Press, 1990); Denys Turner, *Eros and Allegory: Medieval Exegesis of the Song of Songs* (Kalamazoo, MI: Cistercian Publications, 1995); and Denis Reveney, *Language, Self and Love: Hermeneutics in Richard Rolle and the Commentaries on the Song of Songs* (Cardiff: University of Wales Press, 2001).

44 Bernard, *Selected Works*, Sermon 1, VI. 11, p. 214; Bernard, *Opera*, vol. 1, Sermon 2, VI. 11, p. 76.

45 Bernard, *Selected Works*, Sermon 3, I. 1, p. 221; Bernard, *Opera*, Sermon 3, I. 1, p. 100.

46 Bernard McGinn remarks that this is the first use of the expression "book of experience" of which he knows. Bernard McGinn, "The Language of Inner Experience in Christian Mysticism," *Spiritus* 1, no. 2 (2001): 162. A generation later, Alan of Lille (ca. 1128–1202) will refer to the book of experience (*liber experientiae*) as the human body, as opposed to the book of conscience (the mind) and the book of knowledge (scripture). This is quite distinct from Bernard's usage. See Gillian R. Evans, "The Book of Experience: Alan of Lille's Use of the Classical Rhetorical Topos in His Pastoral Writings," *Analecta cisterciensia* 32 (1976): 113–21. For more on Bernard, see Brian Stock, "Experience, Praxis, Work, and Planning in Bernard of Clairvaux: Observations on the *Sermones in Cantica*," in *The Cultural Context of Medieval Learning*, ed. John Emery Murdoch and Edith Dudley Sylla (Dordrecht, The Netherlands, and Boston: Reidel, 1976), pp. 219–68.

47 Note that experience does not refer solely or even primarily to the achievement of the kiss of the mouth, which we can understand as a unity of spirit between God and the soul. It refers instead to the entire range of human bodily, affective, and mental states. As Stock shows, moreover, "only a part of *experimentum* or *experientia* is given over to metaphysical, non-empirical, or spiritual notions" in Bernard's writing as a whole. Stock, "Observations," p. 225.

The very practice Cassian demands in a monk's engagement with the Psalms here serves as the basis for the more intense experience of the divine enabled by the Song of Songs. Bernard stresses that the Song is not for beginners, but for the advanced, that is, for those who have already come to experience the fear, contrition, gratitude, and love voiced in the Psalms. When Bernard asks his readers and listeners to "hear the demand of one who has experienced" the kiss of the kiss of Christ's mouth that is the Song of Songs, he again cites a Psalm: "Restore to me the joy of your salvation" (Ps 50:14). For himself, Bernard writes,

> a soul like mine, burdened with sins, cannot dare to say that, while it is still subject to fleshly passions (2 Tm 3:6), and while it does not feel the sweetness of the Spirit, and is almost wholly unfamiliar with and inexperienced in inner joys.[48]

Although "few," Bernard claims, can speak the words of the Song "wholeheartedly,"[49] his sermons are an attempt to engender – in himself and in his readers – just this wholeheartedness. Only in this way can the soul ever hope to experience the kiss and hence to speak with the bride in her experience of union with the bridegroom.

For Bernard, such a kiss is only ever fleeting in this life. Claims to more extended experiences of the divine presence and of the marking of that presence on the mind and body of the believer – in visions, verbal outcries, trances, convulsions, ecstasies, raptures, and other extraordinary experiences – will shortly follow (and will be particularly important in texts by and about women). They will spread, moreover, outside of the monastery and convent, into the world of the new religious orders, semireligious, and laity. Yet this experience will remain tied to scripture, liturgy, and prayer.[50] It will continue to be an experience of transformation in and through song and the book. There is much work to be done here, but my suspicion is that the visionary and ecstatic experiences described by figures like the Benedictines Hildegard of Bingen and

---

[48] Bernard, *Selected Works*, Sermon 3, I. 1, p. 221; Bernard, *Opera*, Sermon 3, I. 1, p. 100. Translation modified.

[49] Bernard, *Selected Works*, Sermon 3, I.1, p. 221; Bernard, *Opera*, Sermon 3, I. 1, p. 100.

[50] Visual images, whether in books, paintings, statuary, or other forms, also play a key role. See Jeffrey F. Hamburger, *The Rothschild Canticles: Art and Mysticism in Flanders and the Rhineland circa 1300* (New Haven, CT: Yale University Press, 1990); Jeffrey F. Hamburger, *The Visual and the Visionary: Art and Female Spirituality in Late Medieval Germany* (New York: Zone Books, 1998); Sara Lipton, "'The Sweet Lean of the Head': Writing about Looking at the Crucifix in the High Middle Ages," *Speculum* 80 (2005): 1172–1208; and Sara Lipton, "Images and Their Uses," in *The Cambridge History of Christianity: Christianity in Western Europe c. 1100–c. 1500*, ed. Miri Rubin and Walter Simons (Cambridge: Cambridge University Press, 2009).

Rupert of Deutz (ca. 1075–1129), the Cistercian nuns Gertrude the Great of Helfta (1256–1301/2) and Mechthild of Hackeborn (1241–99), and beguine writers like Hadewijch (mid-thirteenth century) and Mechthild of Magdeburg (ca. 1207–ca. 1282) are grounded temporally and substantively in the specific liturgies that filled their daily lives. (I also suspect that the same can be said for the visions and ecstasies found throughout Catholic and Protestant communities in modernity.[51])

Veerle Fraeters has demonstrated precisely this in her analysis of the beguine Hadewijch's *Book of Visions*. Fraeters insists that "medieval religious visions are not naïve renderings of spontaneous experiences." Rather, "like most thirteenth-century ecstatic visionaries, Hadewijch experienced her raptures within the sacred space of the church, and 'within' the words and rituals of the liturgy in which she participated with intense personal devotion."[52] Fraeters goes on to show that Hadewijch's Vision 9 is deeply indebted to the specific liturgical context in which it occurs. Hadewijch tells us that she had the vision during Matins on the feast of the Nativity of Mary, during which she was moved by the words from the Song of Songs (verses 1–10) that she heard in the third reading of the liturgy.

> Shortly afterwards, in the Second Nocturn, I saw in the spirit a queen come in clad *in a gold dress* (Ps 44:11); and her dress was all full of eyes; and all the eyes were completely transparent, like fiery flames, and nevertheless like crystal. And the crown she wore on her head had as many crowns one above the other as there were eyes in her dress; you shall hear the number when she herself declares it. Before the queen walked three maids.[53]

---

[51] In his study of the diary of American Puritan Thomas Shepard (1605–49), Baird Tipson shows how, for the Puritans, personal experience was a site of revelation, because only in it did God make known what his will was with regard to that particular individual. Yet it was crucial for Shepard and other Puritans, Tipson argues, that whatever spiritual testimony they might derive from their experience be tied to biblical texts. Shepard's fellow settler, Ann Hutchinson (1591–1643), who claimed to have "immediate revelation" from God, was roundly condemned – guilty, in the words of Governor John Winthrop of "the most desperate enthusiasm in the world." See Baird Tipson, "The Routinized Piety of Thomas Shephard's Diary," *Early American Literature* 13, no. 1 (1978): 64–80 at p. 67. For important distinctions between Puritan and Pietist practice and theology, and a model for the study of "experience," see Baird Tipson, "How Can the Religious Experience of the Past Be Recovered? The Examples of Puritanism and Pietism," *Journal of the American Academy of Religion* 43, no. 4 (1975): 695–707.

[52] Veerle Fraeters, "Handing on Wisdom and Knowledge in Hadewijch of Brabant's *Book of Visions*," in *Women and Experience in Later Medieval Writing: Reading the Book of Life*, ed. Anneke B. Mulder-Bakker and Liz Herbert McAvoy (New York: Palgrave Macmillan, 2009), p. 154.

[53] Hadewijch, *The Complete Works*, trans. Columba Hart (New York: Paulist Press, 1980), p. 285.

As Fraeters shows, the general content of this vision comes from Psalm 44, which was sung in the Second Nocturn of the Feast. The psalm, in its Vulgate rendering, describes a queen in gilded clothing followed by virgins. Fraeters suggests that the "dress all full of eyes" might be borrowed from Hildegard of Bingen, whose *Scivias* contains a famous image of a woman covered with eyes. Hadewijch lists "Hildegard, who saw all those visions," in her List of the Perfect, suggesting that she knew of Hildegard and so perhaps also of her visionary work.[54]

Fraeters goes on to provide a detailed analysis of Hadewijch's imagery in the vision, pointing to its sources in the book of Revelation.[55] The queen is Reason or Wisdom and she is associated with Christ, particularly in his apocalyptic role. (Eyes, fire, and crystal all appear together in Revelation 4:4–6, the description of the court of the Heavenly Jerusalem. Fiery eyes and multitudes of crowns appear in Revelation 19:11–12, where Christ is described coming in glory on a white horse.) The interplay of images, like the interplay of texts in Hildegard of Bingen's liturgical writing and Bernard of Clairvaux's sermons and commentaries, is exegetical, theological, and experiential.[56] For Hadewijch, I doubt that it would have made much sense to separate the three terms.

As Fraeters aptly argues, Hadewijch's *Book of Visions* "is an alternative form of experiential scriptural exegesis." Hadewijch describes, in Fraeters' words, an

> affective meditation during the reading of the opening lines of Psalm 44 [that] bring[s] her into rapture. In the course of that rapture the hidden sense of the scriptural texts is revealed to her in a visual way. The various elements comprising the visionary images and phrases point to texts and ideas that were triggered in Hadewijch's memory and that were in one way or another connected in her mind to that liturgical text. The written report of her ecstatic experience can then function, for Hadewijch's devotee(s), as an exegetical initiation into God's truth ... by meditating on the vision, the reader could, like Hadewijch during the primary visionary experience, become

---

[54] Fraeters, "*Book of Visions*," p. 157.

[55] Ibid., pp. 157–61.

[56] Hadewijch's visions, letters, and poems not only involve a dense interplay of images derived from the Bible, the liturgy, and the work of other mystics and visionaries, but also the unsaying or negation of those same images. Apophasis and cataphasis are joined in her work in and through experience. See the entries in this volume by Andrew Louth and Charles Stang, and also Amy Hollywood, "Mysticism and Transcendence," in *The Cambridge History of Christianity: Christianity in Western Europe c. 1100–c. 1500*, ed. Miri Rubin and Walter Simons (Cambridge: Cambridge University Press, 2009), pp. 304–5.

aware of the fact that *Sapientia Dei* [the Wisdom of God] resided inside their very own souls, and that it was their task to let it dwell there as queen, unhindered.⁵⁷

Hadewijch not only teaches her readers something about the nature of the soul – that the divine resides, and has always resided, within it – but also provides a script for the performance and the experience of that joyful knowledge. This knowledge, moreover, depends on an unsaying, an apophasis and a letting go of that very Reason or Wisdom to whom Hadewijch speaks in the Vision ("Then Reason became subject to me and I left her. But Love came and embraced me; and I came out of the spirit and remained lying until late in the day, inebriated with unspeakable wonders.").⁵⁸ Like Cassian's monks, who move between the prayerful meditation on and recitation of the Psalms to a fiery prayer in which all words and images are burnt away, Hadewijch points to multiple ways in which the divine can be encountered. She offers her visions and her songs to be read and sung in community, for through their naming and unnaming of God and of the soul, these texts promise to transform the lives of her readers into that joyful, tortured, loving divinity that is always already there – unknowing and unknown – within them.⁵⁹

---

⁵⁷ Fraeters, "*Book of Visions*," p. 161.
⁵⁸ Hadewijch, *Complete Works*, Vision 9, p. 286.
⁵⁹ This is the background against which we must read the apparent rejection of experience – or at least of extraordinary experiences grounded in either the inner or the outer senses – found in subsequent centuries in the writings of the beguine Marguerite Porete, the Dominican Meister Eckhart (d. 1328), the author of the *Cloud of Unknowing* (ca. 1380), Saint John of the Cross (1542–91), and Madame Guyon (1648–1717). Marguerite, e.g., is very clear that extraordinary experiences of God's presence, whether in visions, auditions, or ecstasies, mark a lower stage of the soul's movement into God. Yet her rejection of such experiences is grounded in her presumption that they exist and that they mark one possible moment of the soul's path to a union without distinction between God and the soul. She is very worried about people getting stuck in these – and I think implicitly also about people who feel tormented by the absence of such experiences in their lives. (The call to ritualize every aspect of one's existence – to make how things are and how they should be continuously coincide – is an unrelenting one, as Marguerite seemed to know well.) Yet whether her call for the annihilation of the soul or Eckhart's demand for radical detachment entails a rejection of experience – or even what that might mean – remains an open question, one that can only be adequately addressed when the centrality of experience within Christian thought and practice is properly understood. For one version of the argument against experience, see Denys Turner, *The Darkness of God: Negativity in Christian Mysticism* (Cambridge: Cambridge University Press, 1995). For another version of my argument with Turner, see Amy Hollywood, *Sensible Ecstasy: Mysticism, Sexual Difference, and the Demands of History* (Chicago: University of Chicago Press, 2002), p. 320, n. 1.

3 New Forms of Religious Life in Medieval Western Europe
WALTER SIMONS

Sometime in the early years of the eleventh century, a young Italian monk, called "Little John" because of his small stature, left his homeland to seek the true religious life in France. John traveled north at the invitation, we think, of his compatriot William of Volpiano, who in 987 entered the Benedictine monastery of Cluny in Burgundy, from there reformed Saint Bénigne of Dijon, and then founded Fruttuaria, the leading Cluniac house in northern Italy. Little John joined William at Saint Bénigne, which in the following years served as their basis for a wide-ranging renovation of monastic life in central and northern France. At the behest of Duke Richard II of Normandy, the two moved to Fécamp, where John became prior in 1017. He assumed the abbacy in 1028 and remained at the helm of Normandy's most prestigious monastery until his death fifty years later.

Abbot John of Fécamp, as he is known today, embodies in many ways the best of traditional Benedictine monasticism. A tireless administrator and disciplinarian, he solidified Fécamp's land holdings, took charge of Saint Bénigne along with his own abbey when the former experienced a leadership crisis, and reformed two other monasteries. An earnest scholar, John expanded Fécamp's school and library – in the 1070s, the library possessed eighty-seven manuscripts, virtually all acquired during his abbacy. He advised King William of Normandy, served a pope, and counseled an empress. He traveled to Jerusalem at a time when few Westerners ventured there. Amidst all that executive and inner-worldly action, he wrote extensively on the central, contemplative duties of the monk, offering a *Lament on Lost Leisure and Solitude* in which he longed for "the chaste and pure solitude, the sea of peace and rest where one enjoys intimacy with God."[1]

---

[1] John of Fécamp, *Lamentation*, in *Un maître de la vie spirituelle au XIe siècle: Jean de Fécamp*, ed. Jean LeClercq and Jean-Paul Bonnes, (Paris: Vrin, 1946), pp. 184–97 (quotation from p. 185). All translations are mine unless otherwise noted. References to Bernard McGinn, *The Presence of God: A History of Western Christian Mysticism*

John's "Little Book (*Libellus*) of Writings and Sayings of the Fathers for the Use Especially of Those Who Love the Contemplative Life" lays down an itinerary toward God that starts with meditations on the mystery of the Incarnation and Trinity, largely taken from Augustinian reflections, then gradually, through personal appeals to God, expresses the desire to witness the divine in heaven. But the soul also wishes to be granted a sample of that bliss in this life, as the soul "fixes its eyes of faith in you ... contemplates you ... and lets you, the highest and true good, the unending joy, spin under its heart."[2] Firmly grounded in the patristic tradition (the "Little Book" later circulated under Saint Augustine's name), John's works seem both timeless and fresh. No wonder that one of his many prayers, the elegant Oh Supreme High Priest (*Summe Sacerdos*), immediately found its way into contemporary missals and was later incorporated in the Tridentine missal as "the prayer of Saint Ambrose."[3] André Wilmart, the noted historian of medieval devotion, called John "the most remarkable spiritual writer of the Middle Ages before Saint Bernard."[4]

It is natural to compare John of Fécamp to Saint Anselm (ca. 1033–1109), that other great Italian monk, whose travels led him to Normandy half a century later.[5] The works of both men testify to the growing concentration on Christ's humanity and his passion that characterized much of eleventh-century thought. Like Anselm's "Meditations," John's prayers invoke an anguished response to Christ's torment as the sinner realizes he cannot possibly repay his debt. To articulate systematically that new Christological devotion and logically examine its theological implications – in other words, to start building the new scholasticism – that was a task that John left to the younger Anselm and to a new generation of scholars teaching at the burgeoning cathedral schools of northern France. John knew that, triggered by the renewed study of Aristotle's "old logic," "dialectics" exerted an unprecedented appeal on

---

(New York: Crossroad, 1990–), 4 vols., are abbreviated as *Presence* plus the volume number.
[2] John of Fécamp, *Libellus*, PL 40, col. 935.
[3] Jean-François Cottier, ed., *Anima mea: Prières privées et textes de dévotion du Moyen Âge latin* (Turnhout, Belgium: Brepols, 2001), pp. 101–11.
[4] André Wilmart, *Auteurs spirituels et textes dévots du Moyen Âge latin. Études d'histoire littéraire* (Paris: Librairie Bloud et Gay, 1932), p. 127. Véronique Gazeau, *Normannia monastica*, vol. 2 (Caen: Publications du CRAHM, 2007), pp. 105–10, has the most recent data on John's life and work. For Fécamp's library, see the sources cited below, note 6.
[5] As does Rachel Fulton, *From Judgment to Passion: Devotion to Christ and the Virgin Mary, 800–1200* (New York: Columbia University Press, 2002), pp. 162–3 and 190–1.

intellectuals, even in monastic schools.⁶ But for John, as for his monastic predecessors, *theologia* meant true knowledge of God achieved through meditation on scripture and the Fathers rather than by rational understanding, which was necessarily incomplete and unsatisfactory. The monk's goal remained the study and practice of *theoria* or *contemplatio*, which promised the first stirrings of eternal joy.⁷

The best way to pursue knowledge was only one of many hard questions facing monks during the eleventh and twelfth centuries. In a world that lacked well-educated laymen, monks were called upon to serve as teachers and preachers, political consultants and diplomats, arbiters of men and society – all roles that distracted contemplatives from their real vocation. The advances of the monastic reforms initiated by Cluny and Gorze during the tenth century resulted in requests that their leaders travel and reform other houses in the eleventh. By 1050, when the papacy began its push for a more combative, more centralized, "liberated" Church, monks often found themselves sent to far-flung places as papal legates or called to Rome, where they constituted the core of the renewed papal administration (*curia*) and even rose to the highest office. Virtually all the notable popes of the reformist era, from Stephen IX (1057–8) to Eugene III (1145–53), were Benedictine monks.

The "crisis of monasticism" that arose at this time has therefore less to do with the widespread decadence of monastic life (there is no need to take the heated rhetoric of certain reformers at face value) than with the remarkable achievements of their best practitioners, people like abbot Hugh of Saumur (1024–1109), "in his lifetime probably the most revered man in western Christendom,"⁸ and his angelic monks at Cluny, whom Peter Damian (ca. 1007–1072) described as having established "a paradise watered by the four streams of the Gospels and gushing with four rivers of spiritual virtues."⁹ Given the multiple

---

⁶ Data collected in Coloman Viola, "Aristote au Mont Saint-Michel," in *Millénaire monastique du Mont Saint-Michel*, vol. 2, ed. Raymonde Foreville (Paris: Lethielleux, 1967), pp. 289–312 (at pp. 291–5) and Geneviève Nortier, *Les bibliothèques médiévales des abbayes bénédictines de Normandie* (Paris: Lethielleux, 1971), pp. 196, 204, show that texts of the "old logic" were available in the nearby abbeys of Bec and Mont-Saint-Michel.

⁷ Compare John's *Confessio theologica* and his *Letter to Empress Agnes* in *Un maître*, ed. LeClercq and Bonnes, pp. 127–31 and pp. 211–17 (at p. 214), with the observations in Bernard McGinn, "Regina quondam ...," *Speculum* 83 (2008): 817–39. See also Fulton, *Judgment*, pp. 155–6.

⁸ According to one of the most perceptive specialists of the era, Gerd Tellenbach, *The Church in Western Europe from the Tenth to the Early Twelfth Century* (Cambridge: Cambridge University Press, 1993), p. 342.

⁹ Kurt Reindel, ed., *Die Briefe des Petrus Damiani*, vol. 3 (Munich: Monumenta Germaniae Historica, 1989), pp. 289–295, nr. 113, at pp. 289–90.

entanglements that had grown over the centuries between ascetics and the society they supposedly shunned, monks who strove, in line with Cluniac ideals, for the greater dignity of their vocation and the splendor of their liturgy invariably fell victim to their success. So many demands, so many perils for a monk's soul. This was the bind that prompted John of Fécamp's *Lament*: "It shames and horrifies me that I must appear in public assemblies, going into the city, talking to those in power, looking at women, mingling with the chattering masses and enduring so many other things that pertain to the world."[10]

Meanwhile, the world outside the monastery's walls was changing rapidly, growing more complex, and spurring new and unsettling questions. The agrarian revolution that occurred around the year 1000 and the subsequent urbanization of Europe challenged long-standing traditions of all kinds. As new fortunes and different social alignments took shape, the foundations of wealth and power received immense scrutiny, expressed in a greater emphasis on humility and poverty by those who wished to abandon the world. As new segments of the population gained access to literacy, they joined the debate over the perfect religious life and provided quite different answers than had earlier generations of Christians.

By the end of the eleventh century the old, Benedictine model of monastic life no longer satisfied all of these demands. Naturally, breaking away from it did not come easily for individuals and groups trained to respect authority and preserve stability at all costs. John's handling of tensions in his own community demonstrates this. Asked for an answer to the problems caused by the excessive intrusion of the world into the monk's physical and mental space, John fell back on the familiar theme of the spiritual desert, imagined not as a material space but as a state of being, the inner solitude that provided the stepping-stone to contemplation. When some of his monks rejected those teachings and fled Fécamp to live in greater physical seclusion, he reminded them of Saint Benedict's stark warning that the eremitical life was fraught with dangers and should be attempted only by experienced ascetics. Besides, John added, the *Rule of Benedict* states that nothing in the monastery shall be done without the express order of the abbot: obedience to his authority is the only safe road to "charity, the bond of perfection" (Col 3:14). His final message to rebels in the ranks was no less harsh: "The man who withdraws himself from obedience relinquishes Christ, who remained obedient to the Father until death (Phil 2:8). He who fights

---

[10] John of Fécamp, *Lamentation*, in *Un maître*, ed. LeClercq and Bonnes, p. 195.

against obedience acts against Christ; he who acts against Christ is the Antichrist."[11]

Yet, in the end, the old model splintered and was supplemented, one might say overrun, by multiple forms of religious life adopted after vigorous questioning and experiment. The renewal followed four different patterns that resulted in four types of religious life. Within the old monastic tradition, reformers usually aimed at restoring the Benedictine Rule to its pristine purity, trimming away those customs that had accumulated in the early Middle Ages or that were perceived as inimical to the original *Rule*. Among clerics (or "canons") living in community, a more rigorously ascetic lifestyle also spread, supported by a set of ancient texts known as "the Rule of Saint Augustine" (clerics who adopted this guideline became known as regular canons or "canons of Saint Augustine" in order to distinguish them from the traditional "secular" canons who followed the older, Carolingian "rule of Aachen"). Thirdly, in a more fundamental break with tradition, new movements shifted emphasis from the contemplative to an "active" life characterized by a continuous engagement with the secular world through preaching and by the rejection of all property as mendicant (i.e., "begging") friars. Finally, various groups embraced informal kinds of religious life. Here, the final results varied widely, from hermits and anchoresses to beguines (*beguinae*) and penitents, to the numerous experiments by clerics, laymen, and women, some of which were short-lived and thus left little trace in the historical record, while others, like the movement of Waldes and the Poor of Lyons, were declared heretical and persecuted.[12]

Before we discuss these four types of religious life in greater detail, a few preliminary remarks are in order. First, the differences between these orders or between the various types are real and significant but should not be exaggerated. Despite their often acerbic disputes, these movements had a great deal in common and borrowed constantly from

---

[11] John of Fécamp, *Letter to Rebellious Monks*, in *Un maître*, ed. LeClercq and Bonnes, pp. 218–20. For the centrality of obedience in Benedictine monasticism, see Ludo Milis, *Angelic Monks and Earthly Men: Monasticism and Its Meaning to Medieval Society* (Woodbridge, UK: The Boydell Press, 1992), pp. 70–2.

[12] For more on these changes, see Giles Constable, *The Reformation of the Twelfth Century* (Cambridge: Cambridge University Press, 1996); and Herbert Grundmann, *Religious Movements in the Middle Ages*, trans. Steven Rowan (Notre Dame, IN: University of Notre Dame Press, 1995) (original German publication in 1935). A general reference guide to male religious orders in the Middle Ages is André Vauchez and Cécile Caby, eds., *L'histoire des moines, chanoines et religieux au Moyen Âge: Guide de recherche et documents* (Turnhout, Belgium: Brepols, 2003).

each other. Customs of monks found their way into the regulations of the regular canons of Prémontré over the course of the twelfth century and later into those of the mendicant Dominicans. Heretical and orthodox movements shared goals or developed manifold ties of mutual influence, as in the case of the Waldensians, who took "vows" and thought of themselves as "brothers and sisters" belonging to an order much like those of the mendicant friars.[13]

Differences between "old" and "new" monasticism do not imply a contrast between conservative and progressive attitudes – insofar as these terms may be used at all in a medieval context. As was common in the Middle Ages, the newer movements thought of their innovations as a return to an older, more perfect existence. All modeled themselves on Christ, the apostles, and the first Christian communities described in the Acts of the Apostles (especially Acts 2:42–7 and 4:32–7). In reformist terminology, to seek the communal life (*vita communis*) or apostolic life (*vita apostolica*) was shorthand for pursuing monastic reform, just as the restoration of the "primitive Church" (*ecclesiae primitivae forma*) became the expressed ideal of the papal reform movement.[14] Some, like the hermit Stephen of Muret (d. 1124), who founded the order of Grandmont, went as far as to deny the need for any rules other than the gospels. He refused to be called a "monk" or a "canon" or by any title at all, in an effort to capture the lost innocence of the past.[15] The changes in religious life were thus initially not meant to adapt it to a changing society, for the secular world was deemed in irrevocable decline and beyond repair. Yet the concerns of the new movements did reflect broader societal trends: a critical stance against convention, interest in greater individual reflection and introspection, a desire for a more meaningful liturgy, and a greater sense of personal accomplishment through austerity. Gradually, first among the regular canons and hermits, then more systematically in the mendicant orders and informal movements, attention was paid to issues of pastoral theology, to the spiritual (and sometimes also material) needs of society at large.

Attitudes toward scholarship and learning diverged widely. Quite a few influential leaders of the new twelfth-century monasticism shared

---

[13] Peter Biller, "Christians and Heretics," in *The Cambridge History of Christianity*, vol. 4, *Christianity in Western Europe, c. 1100–c. 1500*, ed. Miri Rubin and Walter Simons (Cambridge: Cambridge University Press, 2009), pp. 170–86.

[14] Giovanni Miccoli, *Chiesa Gregoriana: Ricerche sulla riforma del secolo XI* (Florence: La Nuova Italia, 1966), pp. 225–99; Constable, *Reformation*, pp. 159–60.

[15] Jean Becquet, ed., *Scriptores ordinis Grandimontenses* (Turnhout, Belgium: Brepols, 1978), pp. 5, 121.

with traditionalists like John of Fécamp a distrust of intellectual labor performed in the novel, scholastic fashion, in part because they rejected the urban culture with which cathedral schools were associated, but also out of a desire to restrain that learning and balance it with manual labor. Peter Damian, Bruno the Carthusian (ca. 1030–1101), Bernard of Clairvaux (1090–1153), and Norbert of Xanten (ca. 1080–1134) all received excellent educations at top schools before withdrawing from the world. They and their most ardent followers criticized the use of "dialectics," not because they objected to rational argument (which would be absurd in the context of the medieval learned tradition) but rather to caution against the frivolous pleasures of logical "subtleties" and manifest doctrinal errors.[16] The regular canons of Saint Victor and the mendicant orders, which were founded and grew in close contact with university life, rarely expressed such reservations. But neither did they abandon the purely contemplative. In these newer movements there was place for both mysticism and scholasticism, sometimes even in the work of a single individual.

This said, we can discern a few important institutional changes over time. In traditional Western monasticism before the tenth century, every monastic house enjoyed considerable autonomy. Religious "orders" in the modern sense did not exist. One of the greatest innovations offered by Cluny was its gradual development from a personal union between Cluny's abbot and its daughter-houses into a juridical union of monasteries, thus forming an "order" closer to the present sense of the word, an evolution more or less completed by the twelfth century (opinions differ on the precise chronology). All of the new religious movements discussed in this chapter (with the natural exception of those of the informal, fourth type) forged close ties between individual houses or even became single juridical entities, although the extent to which this occurred varied greatly and contemporary canon law often assumed greater legal unity than practice mandated. The mendicant orders were the most highly centralized and can best be imagined as international organizations with local dependencies. Unlike monks, individual friars made their profession to the superior official of the entire order and not to a local house; they (and their books!) were thus movable at will and often were transferred between houses and

---

[16] For an early example, see the case of the regular canon Manegold of Lautenbach's treatise "Against Wolfelmus." Robert Ziomkowski, trans., *Manegold of Lautenbach, Liber Contra Wolfelmum* (Louvain, Belgium: Peeters, 2002). See also Ludo Milis, "The Regular Canons and Some Socio-Religious Aspects about the Year 1100," in *Religion, Culture and Mentalities in the Medieval Low Countries: Selected Essays*, ed. Jeroen Deploige et al. (Turnhout, Belgium: Brepols, 2005), pp. 169–80.

even between provinces. In consequence, the mendicants enjoyed much greater uniformity of custom, education, and spirituality than did the members of older orders, although some of these, like Cîteaux, always had a high regard for liturgical uniformity.

An important shift also occurred in the social background of religious movements around the year 1100, as new types of lay brothers (*conversi*), gained entry into the Cistercian and other orders, and again around 1200, with the breakthrough of the mendicants, beguines, and other "informal" groups. Traditionally, monks came from the landed aristocracy that dominated early medieval society. "Donated" to the monastery by their families at a young age as "oblates," they received an education in the cloister, were ordained when reaching adulthood, and became choir monks, assisted by a substantial number of lay servants from the lower classes, who were not considered part of the monastic community proper. In contrast, the newer orders preferred to recruit their clerical members as adults and employed a discrete category of lay brothers, usually taken from the lower knightly and the peasant classes. These lay brothers were illiterate and barred from becoming monks. While they led a religious life according to a rule and thus belonged to the monastic community in the broader sense, they tended to dwell in separate quarters and performed only manual tasks. The presence in the monastery of lay monks, however, quickly affected the intellectual life of the clerics. Out of concern for the spiritual well-being of these laymen, monks and canons of the new orders began to translate suitable Latin texts into vernacular languages. Members of the mendicant orders and other movements born in the thirteenth-century cities recruited from a much broader spectrum of the population, including the urban middle classes and the urban proletariat. Efforts to initiate lay members of the community into the religious life thus gave rise to robust traditions of pedagogy and translation. Old and new texts – including works of mysticism – became available for those who did not know Latin.

REFORM OF THE BENEDICTINE MODEL

When in 1098, Robert of Molesme and his band of refugees from traditional Benedictinism established their "new monastery" in the woods of Cîteaux, they claimed that they simply "desired to observe the Rule of Saint Benedict more strictly and more faithfully than they did in the past."[17] Cîteaux tried to limit contact with the feudal world: it accepted

[17] Jean Marilier, *Chartes et documents concernant l'abbaye de Cîteaux, 1098–1182* (Rome: Editiones Cistercienses, 1961), pp. 49–51, n. 23; for context, see Chrysogonus

donations of unsettled land but not tithes, serfs, tenants (hence the need to use lay brothers), or the care of parishes and pilgrims. The elaborate office of the Cluniac monks was pared down to shorter sequences alternating with meditative reading of scripture and other holy books (*lectio divina*) and manual labor. During the next decades, the "white monks" of Cîteaux (discarding the black robes of traditional Benedictines for habits of undyed cloth to mark their simplicity and purity) developed a more comprehensive ethos of austerity and authenticity by banning ornamentations from their churches and manuscripts and by restoring the old "Ambrosian" hymnary. At the heart of the new movement lay the writings of a remarkably talented generation of authors, chief among them Bernard, the first abbot of Cîteaux's daughter house, Clairvaux, best known for his sermon cycles (on the Song of Songs and in praise of the Virgin Mary) and his didactic works on monastic piety, theology, and ecclesiology.[18]

Bernard and his contemporaries defined the Cistercian self-image by spelling out new norms of ascetic life and the reward that they would yield: the restoration of a prelapsarian disposition for God's love. *Caritas* is a central theme in Cistercian spirituality – love of God, but also love of neighbor, particularly as experienced within monastic group discipline. Early Cistercian writers examined that love along two axes of inquiry consistent with broader developments in twelfth-century culture. A first, psychological-anthropological approach looked at the dynamics of interpersonal relationships (notably between monks) and inner reflection. A second, more poetic and metaphysical approach was nourished by imaginative identification with the human Christ and the Virgin Mary. The physical and spiritual solitude (*eremum*) so important to the early Cistercians functioned as the setting. There, the monk's supreme virtue – humility – laid the foundation for the ascent toward God, which they viewed as an inherently mystical process.

Very early in his monastic career, Bernard made the connection between the pursuit of the authentic *Rule of Saint Benedict* and union with the divine explicit by presenting his *On the Stages of Humility and Pride* as a commentary on the *Rule's* chapter 7, which enjoins renunciation of one's will and features the well-known image of Jacob's ladder as humanity's vehicle toward God. Bernard develops that theme,

---

Waddell, *Narrative and Legislative Texts from Early Cîteaux: An Edition, Translation, and Commentary* (Brecht, Belgium: Cîteaux, 1999).

[18] The standard edition of Saint Bernard's work is *Sancti Bernardi Opera*, ed. Jean LeClercq, C. H. Talbot, and Henri Rochais (Rome: Editiones Cistercienses, 1957–77), 8 vols.

linking it with Paul's rapture to portray ascetic and disciplinary conversion as a precondition for shedding one's carnal being and accepting God's charity. He then envisages the important role of the Trinity in the transformation of the soul:

> The Son of God, the word and wisdom of the Father, took mercy on our intellectual faculty, called reason, "weighed down by the body" (Wis 9:15), a prisoner of sin, blinded by ignorance, given over to external things, and He raised it by His power ... and caused it to sit in judgment on itself.... From this first alliance of the Word and reason humility was born. Then the Holy Spirit honored with a visit the second faculty, the will, contaminated by the poisonous flesh.... The Spirit filled it with mercy and ... made it a friend of those who were enemies. From this second alliance love grew.... The Father finally bound this perfected soul to Him as a bride in such a way that reason shall not think of itself, nor will of its neighbor, but the blessed soul delighted only in saying: "The King has taken me into his chamber" (Cant 1:3).... There, for a brief while, "as it were for half an hour" (Apoc 8:1), the soul finds rest and sleeps in the embrace that was so much longed for. But "her heart watched" (Cant. 5:2), filled with the secrets of truth that will nourish her memory when she comes to herself. There she sees the invisible and hears the ineffable "which it is not granted to man to utter" (2 Cor 12:4).[19]

To explain and celebrate that necessarily spiritual process, Bernard later mobilized a wealth of imagery drawn from scripture and human experience, as in his *Sermons on the Song of Songs* and the iconic *On Loving God*.

Much of that imagery is unambiguously erotic. The sermon cycle on the *Song of Songs* immediately seizes on the first verse ("Let him kiss me with the kiss of his mouth") in order to bring home how intense and extraordinary the perfect love of God is. The Incarnation is the ultimate kiss, the "union of the divine and man" that makes possible the union of the divine and the soul. This union, the "kiss of his mouth," comes as a reward, "not for the souls of children and novices or of those who have just recently left the secular world" but for "those who have made progress, have enriched their mind through hard work and who

---

[19] Bernard of Clairvaux, *Liber de gradibus humilitatis et superbiae*, n. 21, in *Sancti Bernardi Opera*, vol. 3, pp. 31–2. *Presence*, II, p. 191 notes that the Trinitarian aspects of Bernard's mystical thought are less pronounced in his later writings.

with God's help have reached the age of marriage [an age of deserving, not of years]."²⁰ In his mature work, Bernard repeatedly states that the experience of that reward must be brief, "a moment." In the concluding pages of *On Loving God*, Bernard asks:

> When will this "flesh and blood" (Matt 16:17), this "earthen vessel" (2 Cor 4:7), this "earthly habitation" (Wis 9:15) achieve this? When will this sort of attraction (*affectus*) be felt, so that drunken by divine love the mind forgets itself and becomes in its own view "as a vessel that is destroyed" (Ps 30:13), hastening towards God and clinging to him, becoming "one with him in spirit" (1 Cor 6:17)? ... I would say: that man is blessed and holy to whom this experience is granted, such a rare thing in mortal life, even if it happens only once, quickly, barely for the space of a moment.²¹

Bernard's "bridal mysticism" strikes us today as extraordinarily sensual but was deeply rooted in the experience of monastic life, with its calculated tension between material abstinence and imaginative longing, between ascetic routines and the barrages of sensory images unleashed over and over again during choir chant and *lectio divina*.

Bernard is such a towering figure that his fellow Cistercians of the era could easily be neglected, although they often exercised considerable influence on Christian and monastic spirituality. Some of them knew Bernard personally, like William (1085–1148), the Benedictine abbot of Saint Thierry at Rheims, who transferred to the Cistercians of Signy in 1135 and became Bernard's biographer, or Bernard's favorite student, Guerric, a canon who became Cistercian abbot of Igny (ca. 1078–1157). Others, like the Englishman Isaac, later abbot of Stella (or l'Étoile, on the Île de Ré, d.1169), converted to Cistercian monastic life as students at the cathedral schools of northern France after Bernard's famous Paris sermon in 1139/40. Another Englishman, Aelred of Rievaulx, was encouraged by Bernard to write his *Mirror of Charity* for Cistercian novices (1110–67).²²

The Cistercian order enjoyed massive success in the mid- to late twelfth century when it expanded from Burgundy across western and

---

[20] Bernard of Clairvaux, *Sermones super Cantica Canticorum*, n. 1 and 2, in *Sancti Bernardi Opera*, vol. 1, pp. 3–14 (quotations from pp. 8 and 7, respectively).

[21] Bernard of Clairvaux, *Liber de diligendo Deo*, X, 27, in *Sancti Bernardi Opera*, vol. 3, p. 142.

[22] See *Presence*, II, pp. 225–323; Paul Verdeyen, *La théologie mystique de Guillaume de Saint-Thierry* (Paris: FAC-éditions, 1990); and Dániel Deme, ed. *The Selected Works of Isaac of Stella: A Cistercian Voice from the Twelfth Century* (Aldershot, UK: Ashgate, 2007).

central Europe. Subsequently, its most creative minds were found not in France (or England, where the order had build about 80 houses by 1152) but in southern Italy, home of the Calabrian hermit, abbot, and visionary Joachim of Fiore (1132–1202),[23] the Low Countries, and Germany, where the monastery of Villers (founded by Saint Bernard in 1146) and the convent of Helfta (1229), to name only the most important, became influential centers of spirituality in the thirteenth century.[24]

Several other monastic reformers of the age chose to retain the *Rule of Benedict* and generated small congregations that spread only regionally, among them those of Camaldoli (c. 1010), Vallombrosa (1036), and Fontevrault (1099). Others built on the *Rule* to formulate their own monastic customs with lasting success, as did the Carthusians. Founded at La Grande Chartreuse by Bruno of Cologne during the 1080s, but truly developed only by his successor, Guigo, in the first years of the twelfth century, the Carthusian order combined the eremitical with the coenobitical lifestyles, requiring monks to spend the day alone, praying, working, eating, and sleeping in their individual cells, while gathering in church for Vespers and the night office, and meeting as a community on Sundays and major feast days.[25] Throughout the centuries, it never wavered from its original structures and customs. It survived without any apparent upheavals in large part because new members were chosen only after a careful and long selection process. Consequently, Carthusian communities were always small (12 monks was a common number), drawing their members from the upper layers of society, thus bringing in sufficient wealth to ensure the monastery's economic viability. The papal administration and canon law regarded the Carthusians as the strictest of all religious orders, a distinction that contributed to its excellent reputation.[26] From the beginning, Carthusians were devoted to religious scholarship as part of their daily routine, concentrating on the study of contemplation. As is their practice today, Carthusians did not commonly circulate

---

[23] On this prolific author, see now Julia Eva Wannenmacher, *Hermeneutik der Heilsgeschichte: De septem sigillis und die sieben Siegel im Werk Joachims von Fiore* (Leiden, The Netherlands: Brill, 2005). For Joachim's complicated relationships with the Cistercian order, see Valeria de Fraja, *Oltre Cîteaux: Gioacchino da Fiore e l'Ordine florense* (Rome: Viella, 2006).

[24] *Presence*, IV, pp. 267–82; Martinus Cawley, trans., *Send Me God: The Lives of Ida the Compassionate of Nivelles, Nun of La Ramée, Arnulf, Lay Brother of Villers, and Abundus, Monk of Villers, by Goswin of Bossut* (Turnhout, Belgium: Brepols, 2003).

[25] See most recently, *San Bruno di Colonia: un eremita tra Oriente e Occidente. Secondo convegno internazionale, Serra San Bruno, 2–5 ottobre 2002* (Soveria Manelli, Italy: Rubettino, 2004).

[26] Jacques Hourlier, *L'Âge classique (1140–1378): Les religieux* (Toulouse, France: Cujas, 1974), pp. 246–7.

their work or, if they did, wrote anonymously, although exceptions do exist, most notably the prolific scholar and *"doctor ecstaticus,"* Denis the Carthusian (Dionysius van Rijkel, 1403–71).[27] The order's greatest contribution to the history of Christian mysticism, particularly during the fourteenth and fifteenth centuries, may have been in the copying and translation of spiritual texts for internal use and for the outside "market." Some of the oldest mystical sources in Dutch, German, and English owe their distribution at least in part to Carthusians.[28]

REGULAR CANONS

Dissatisfaction with traditional monastic life naturally led some to suggest alternatives to the *Rule of Benedict*. Such a revolutionary change could only be made by presenting it as a return to an even more ancient norm – the writings of Saint Augustine, in particular three texts attributed to him that alone or together formed the so-called Augustinian "Rule": the "Rule" (*Praeceptum*), the "Regulations for a Monastery" (*Ordo Monasterii*), and the instructions for religious life found in his *Letter* 211.[29] The attraction of these texts lay as much in their clear apostolic echoes ("First, because this is the purpose of your community: Live in this house in harmony, be one of mind and heart in God"[30]) as in their flexibility, for they suited all kinds of religious lifestyles, from utter seclusion to active engagement with the cure of souls. Known as "regular canons," those who observed the Augustinian rule debated these options with just as much vigor as did monks. The main fault line ran between congregations, among them that of Prémontré, who favored the strict asceticism of the "new way of life" (*ordo novus*), an asceticism akin to that found in the Cistercian order, and those who adopted a moderate form of the Augustinian tradition known as the "old

---

[27] A critical edition of his works is under way in the *Corpus Christianorum, Continuatio Mediaeualis*. See Kent Emery Jr., ed., *Dionysius Cartusiensis, Opera Selecta* (Turnhout, Belgium: Brepols, 1991), vol. 1.

[28] Erik Kwakkel, *Die Dietsche boeke die ons toebehoeren: De kartuizers van Herne en de productie van Middelnederlandse handschriften in de regio Brussel (1350–1400)* (Louvain, Belgium: Peeters, 2002); Jessica Brantley, *Reading in the Wilderness: Private Devotion and Public Performance in Late Medieval England* (Chicago: University of Chicago Press, 2007).

[29] For the complicated history of these texts, see Luc Verheijen, *La Règle de saint Augustin* (Paris: Études augustiniennes, 1967), 2 vols.; Luc Jocqué, "Regole canonicali," in *Dizionario degli Istituti di Perfezione* (Rome: Edizioni Paoline, 1983), vol. 7, cols. 1496–1517.

[30] *Praeceptum*, 2, ed. Verheijen, *La règle*, vol. 1, p. 417; and compare Acts 4:32.

way of life" (*ordo antiquus*). Some congregations took an intermediate position, as did those of Arrouaise and Saint Victor. Also subject to debate was the degree to which the congregation should concentrate on pastoral care, always a key question in the life of clerics. Sometimes regular canons combined several options: the order of Prémontré, for instance, started in eremitical austerity but allowed for pastoral work thanks to its founder, Norbert of Xanten (c. 1080–1134), a celebrated preacher who ended his life engrossed by missionary ambitions as archbishop of Magdeburg. Over time, many Premonstratensian monasteries took charge of rural parishes and small towns in Germany and the Low Countries.[31]

Regular canons on the ascetic and contemplative end of the spectrum naturally shared with monks a profound interest in the most perfect reform of religious life, seen as a precondition for true knowledge of God. An author like Hugh of Fouilloy (d. 1172/74), the leader of a small congregation with eremitical origins in Picardy, wrote *On the Cloister of the Soul* and several other works of contemplative spirituality and was much appreciated by Cistercians.[32] Canons like the Premonstratensians Anselm of Havelberg (ca. 1095–1158) or Philip of Harvengt (d. 1183), on the other hand, tended to view reform in ecclesiastical terms, as part of a larger institutional and social enterprise that implied a commitment to action in the world.[33] Nevertheless, whatever their stance on the active life (*vita activa*), regular canons, more than monks, thought of their task as one that included teaching within their communities.[34] After all, even the reclusive Hugh of Fouilloy, who refused the abbacy of Saint Denis of Rheims because it was too close to the center of power (the archbishop's see and the schools of

---

[31] The only modern, comprehensive history of any of these orders is Ludo Milis, *L'ordre des chanoines réguliers d'Arrouaise. Son histoire et son organisation, de la fondation de l'abbaye-mère (vers 1090) à la fin des chapitres annuels (1471)* (Bruges, Belgium: De Tempel, 1969), 2 vols. See also Ludo Milis, "Hermits and Regular Canons in the Twelfth Century," in *Religion, Culture, and Mentalities*, pp. 181–246.

[32] Ivan Gobry, *Le De Claustro Animae d'Hugues de Fouilloy* (Amiens, France: Eklitra, 1995) (publication of a 1965 Sorbonne thèse complémentaire); Walter Simons, "Deux témoins du mouvement canonial au XIIe siècle: les prieurés de Saint-Laurent-au-Bois et Saint-Nicolas de Regny et leurs démêlés avec l'abbaye de Corbie," *Sacris Erudiri* 24 (1980): 203–44.

[33] Jay T. Lees, *Anselm of Havelberg: Deeds into Words in the Twelfth Century* (Leiden, The Netherlands: Brill, 1998); Philip of Harvengt, *De institutione clericorum*, PL, vol. 203, cols. 665–1206. Anselm and Philip emphasized the priestly function of canons.

[34] As argued by Caroline Walker Bynum, *Docere Verbo et Exemplo: An Aspect of Twelfth-Century Spirituality* (Missoula, MT: Scholars Press, 1979).

Rheims), wrote a little treatise for the spiritual education of lay brothers in his monastery.[35]

The didactic interests of the mature canonical movement of the twelfth century are best exemplified in the order of Saint Victor, initiated by William of Champeaux in 1108, when he resigned from his positions as archdeacon of Paris and master of Notre Dame and retreated to the shrine of Saint Victor outside the city walls. After William became bishop of Chalons (1113), the young community of regular canons grew under its first abbot, Gilduin, in close symbiosis with the burgeoning Parisian schools on the left bank. By the end of the twelfth century, Saint Victor headed a rather loose-knit network of houses in France, the Low Countries, the British Isles, and Scandinavia. It owed its reputation in no small part to the brilliance of several teachers at the motherhouse, who had been drawn there from diverse regions of Europe (as were the students in Paris). The Germans Hugh "of Saint Victor" (d. 1141) and Adam (d. 1143) were followed in the next generation by Achard (d. 1170/1) and Andrew (d. 1175), both Englishmen; Richard, from Scotland (d. 1173); and Geoffrey (d. 1194).[36]

We now think of William of Champeaux mainly as a rhetorician and logician – the man who famously "lost" the debate over universals, if we can believe the testimony of the "winner," Peter Abelard.[37] But William was also an accomplished theologian, having studied with Anselm of Laon, a pioneer of newer forms of theology at the turn of the twelfth century. William's *Sentences* answered questions of doctrine according to a new technique, based on classroom comparisons of biblical passages, biblical glosses, and patristic sources. Rather than accumulating texts reflectively and associatively in the manner of much monastic theology, students now arranged such pronouncements systematically to form logical units. Scholars at the abbey of Saint Victor were ideally placed to develop and complete this effort thanks to the abbey's library, its close ties to the royal administration, its multiple contacts with the schools (the Victorines became regular confessors of Parisian students), and its engagement with the Jewish intelligentsia.[38]

---

[35] Willene B. Clark, *The Medieval Book of Birds: Hugh de Fouilloy's De avibus* (Binghamton, NY: MARTS, 1992); Friedrich Ohly, *Sensus spiritualis: Studies in Medieval Significs and the Philology of Culture* (Chicago: University of Chicago Press, 2005), pp. 68–135; Simons, "Deux témoins," pp. 236–9.

[36] See Jean Longère, ed., *L'abbaye parisienne de Saint-Victor au Moyen Age* (Paris: Brepols, 1991) and subsequent volumes in the series *Bibliotheca Victorina*.

[37] Abelard, *Historia Calamitatum*, 2nd ed., ed. Jacques Monfrin (Paris: Vrin, 1965), p. 65.

[38] On these developments, see Beryl Smalley, *The Study of the Bible in the Middle Ages*, 3rd ed. (Notre Dame, IN: University of Notre Dame Press, 1982), pp. xii, 83–195;

In his *On the Sacraments*, Hugh of Saint Victor presented a comprehensive overview of Christian doctrine organized chronologically from creation to the end of time. His (and Abelard's) student, Peter the Lombard (d. 1160), chose a logical and topical arrangement in his *Sentences*, which became the basic textbook of scholastic theology around 1200.[39] To be sure, the Victorines were a long way from promoting anything like the disputational pyrotechnics that would characterize classic scholasticism. They followed quite closely in the tradition of monastic theology with its emphasis on exegesis. In the prologue of his *On the Sacraments*, Hugh describes his enterprise as moving beyond literal or historical interpretation toward the more advanced learning found in allegory (*ad secundam eruditionem quae in allegoria est*), which was to be followed by tropological understanding – a very traditional view.[40] Nonetheless, he and other Victorines pushed monastic theology to its limits.

Richard of Saint Victor, in his *Commentary on the Vision of Ezekiel*, scoffed at "those who, supposedly out of respect, try not to do anything that was not previously done by the Fathers," and Andrew argued that, had Jerome taken a similar view, he would not have devoted his entire life to scripture. "Sure," he said, "careful search will find the truth, but in a manner that suggests even more search will find more truth. Nobody can find it all."[41] Rainer Berndt has drawn attention to Andrew's exegetical method of generating real "questions" (*quaestiones*) in the new style and composing short dissertations suitable for systematic "compendia" (*summae*), even though he stuck to literal or historical exegesis.[42] Although Hugh's mode of argument was traditional, he did

---

Joachim Ehlers, "Das Augustinerchorherrenstift St. Viktor in der Pariser Schul- und Studienlandschaft des 12. Jahrhunderts," in *Aufbruch, Wandel, Erneuerung: Beiträge zur 'Renaissance' des 12. Jahrhunderts*, ed. Georg Wieland (Stuttgart, Germany: Frommann-Holzboog, 1995), pp. 100–22; Constant J. Mews, "*Logica* in the Service of Philosophy: William of Champeaux and his Influence," in *Schrift, Schreiber, Schenker: Studien zur Abtei Sankt Viktor in Paris und den Victorinern*, ed. Rainer Berndt (Berlin: Akademie Verlag, 2005), pp. 77–117.

[39] Hugh of Saint Victor, *De Sacramentis*, PL 176, cols. 174–615. I have not yet seen the new edition by Rainer Berndt, *De sacramentis Christianae fidei* (Münster, Germany: Aschendorff, 2008). Paul Rorem, *Hugh of Saint Victor* (Oxford: Oxford University Press, 2009) offers a brief overview of Hugh's work.

[40] Hugh of Saint Victor, *De Sacramentis*, PL 176, col. 183.

[41] Richard of Saint Victor, *Prologus in visionem Ezechielis*, PL 196, col. 527; Andrew of Saint Victor, *Prologus in Isaiam*, in Smalley, *Study*, p. 378. For a translation of Richard, see Smalley, *Study*, p. 108. See also Richard's *Exposition on the Tabernacle of the Covenant*, PL 196, col. 211.

[42] Rainer Berndt, *André de Saint-Victor, exégète et théologien* (Paris: Brepols, 1991), p. 250.

probably more than anyone else in his age (with the obvious exception of Abelard) to construct theology as an organized discipline of the whole of revelation (including the created world), not just "knowledge of God reached through study and meditation," as John of Fécamp had maintained less than a century earlier.[43] Accordingly, the Victorine masters covered a wide range of fields and subjects, from exegesis to moral theology, from the *artes* to liturgical poetry.

It is only in this context that we can truly understand Victorine mysticism. As Hugh explains in *On the Sacraments*, the final purpose of the human hermeneutical enterprise is the restoration of humanity to its original, prelapsarian perfection:

> At the top stands the divine, to which Scripture leads us through allegory or tropology, the former providing the right faith, the latter the right action (*operatio*). In these consist knowledge of truth and love of virtue, and this is the true restoration of humanity.[44]

This restoration will in turn mean arrival at "the homeland, and the joy of [celestial] happiness."[45] Like most of his patristic and early medieval predecessors, Hugh clearly envisages the last stages of this restoration as a measured process, intellectual as well as spiritual. That is, the return will be carried out through meditation and contemplation. He suggests how this can be done in such works as *Noah's Ark* and in lectures collected as *The Little Book on the Making of the Ark*, using key biblical symbols as guides for the internalization of externally gathered knowledge, or, more briefly put, for the appropriate conditioning of the soul.[46] These complex (and often hermetic) handbooks should be read in tandem with the soliloquy on *The Arrha of the Soul*, which adopts bridal imagery to describe the soul's grace-given affective powers

---

[43] Dominique Poirel, "Pierre Abélard, Hugues de Saint-Victor et la naissance de la 'théologie,'" *Perspectives médiévales* 31 (2007): 45–86; McGinn, "Regina," pp. 834–5. Charles H. Buttimer, ed., *Hugonis de Sancto Victore Didascalicon de studio legendi* (Washington, DC: Catholic University of America Pres, 1939), p. 119 (the passage outlines Hugh's later *On the Sacraments*). For John of Fécamp, see note 7.

[44] Hugh of Saint Victor, *De Sacramentis*, PL 176, col. 185.

[45] Ibid., col. 184.

[46] Edited in PL 176, cols. 617–80 and 681–704, and critically in Richard of Saint Victor, *De Archa Noe. Libellus de formatione arche*, ed. Patrice Sicard (Turnhout, Belgium: Brepols, 2001). For very divergent interpretations of the latter work, see Patrice Sicard, *Diagrammes médiévaux et exégèse visuelle: Le Libellus de formatione arche de Hugues de Saint-Victor* (Paris: Brepols, 1993); and Conrad Rudolph, *"First, I Find the Center Point": Reading the Text of Hugh of Saint Victor's The Mystic Ark* (Philadelphia: American Philosophical Society, 2004).

and dwells more extensively on the final, ecstatic stage of humanity's restoration.[47]

Richard of Saint Victor devoted more sustained attention to the intricacies of contemplation in a series of subtle works that, like Hugh's, build on allegorical and tropological exegesis. He starts his *The Mystical Ark* (or *Benjamin Major*) by recalling Hugh's distinctions between *cogitatio* (careless wandering of the mind), *meditatio* (the focused mental search for truth), and *contemplatio*, which he defines as "the free insight of the mind, suspended with wonder in the manifestations (*spectacula*) of wisdom, or for certain, in the words of the most distinguished theologian of our age [Hugh], 'the penetrating and free fixation of the mind extended over all things for insight.'"[48] Richard then discusses six kinds (*genera*) of contemplation, underpinning a progression from the sensible world through the internal world of rational knowledge to the divine mysteries, which are contemplated at the highest level above (*supra*) reason. That is, the divine mysteries are understood only by a gift from God, beyond (*praeter*) and even possibly against (*contra*) reason. Finally, Richard explains the three modes of contemplation, differentiating them according to the part played by human capacity and that played by divine grace: humans are capable of expanding (*dilatio*) the mind; they can lift their mind (*sublevatio*) with God's help, as in prophecy, or they can leave (*alienatio*) their mind in ecstasy, which is solely God's work "breaking through" human experience.

Richard illuminates each of these aspects of contemplation – and many more omitted here – through a biblical figure, symbol, or verse that personifies or illustrates the material but is also intended as a vehicle for further reflection and deeper understanding. Moreover, he manages to undergird this multifaceted and multidimensional – if highly esoteric – presentation with references to the human psyche that seem drawn from personal experience or, at the least, speak vividly to the individual student of contemplation. He follows the same procedure in *On the Twelve Patriarchs* (or *Benjamin Minor*), which is centered on

[47] Edited by Hugh B. Feiss, Patrice Sicard et al., *L'oeuvre de Hugues de Saint-Victor*, vol. 1 (Turnhout, Belgium: Brepols, 1997), pp. 209–300.
[48] Richard of Saint Victor, *De gratia contemplationis ... dictum Benjamin Major*, PL 196, cols. 63–192, at col. 67. Richard's reference must be to Hugh. See the latter's *Homilies on Ecclesiastes*, PL 175, col. 117 and the *De modo dicendi et meditandi libellus*, sometimes attributed to Hugh (PL 176, col. 879). Richard's major works have been translated, with a very useful introduction, in Richard of Saint Victor, *The Twelve Patriarchs; the Mystical Ark; Book Three of the Trinity*, ed. Grover Zinn (New York: Paulist Press, 1979).

the story of Jacob's sons and other members of his household, including Leah and Rachel, traditionally understood as allegories of the active and the contemplative lives. Richard follows this traditional reading, but emphasizes the interaction between individual and group, contemplation and preaching or instruction. He then combines these stories with that of the Transfiguration of Christ, suggesting that visions of light may mark the transition from internal peace to ecstasy.[49]

Two additional points bear mention. First, since the 1908 publication of Pierre Rousselot's influential *The Problem of Love in the Middle Ages*, there has been a tendency to contrast Hugh of Saint Victor's "physical" concept of love, in which love of God is an extension of love of self, to Richard's "ecstatic" concept, which stresses the opposition between love of self and love of God.[50] This is evidently an exaggeration. As Dominique Poirel has argued, Hugh urges us to recognize the limitations of the love of self while identifying the aspects of that same love that, at a crucial moment in the human's progression, allow for transcending and sublimating it.[51] It is true, however, that Richard, far more so than Hugh, addressed the intensity of the contemplative ascent, devoting a (short) treatise to *The Four Degrees of Violent Charity*.[52]

Second, the influence of the texts attributed to Dionysius the Areopagite on the Victorine school is still under investigation.[53] As is well-known, John Scot Eriugena's ninth-century Latin translations of the Dionysian corpus solicited little interest before the twelfth century. Hugh of Saint Victor's long *Commentary on the Celestial Hierarchy*, written for teaching purposes, was the first since Eriugena's commentary on that book.[54] Paul Rorem argues that apart from Hugh's statement that love of God is superior to knowledge of God – a statement he makes in a comparison between the seraphim and cherubim that is highly dependent on Eriugena – the imprint of the Pseudo-Dionysius on

[49] Edited by Jean Châtillon et al., *Richard de Saint-Victor. Les douze patriarches ou Beniamin minor* (Paris: Éditions du Cerf, 1997).

[50] Pierre Rousselot, *Pour l'histoire du problème de l'amour au Moyen Age* (Münster, Germany: Aschendorff, 1908); Pierre Rousselot, *The Problem of Love in the Middle Ages: An Historical Contribution*, trans. Alan Vincelette and Pol Vandevelde (Milwaukee, WI: Marquette University Press, 2002).

[51] Hugh of Saint Victor, "Introduction" [to *De Arrha Anime*] in Feiss, Sicard et al., *L'oeuvre de Hugues de Saint-Victor*, pp. 211–24 at pp. 218–23.

[52] Richard of Saint Victor, *De quatuor gradibus violentae charitatis*, PL 196, cols. 1207–25; Richard of Saint Victor, "On the Four Degrees of Violent Love," trans. Andrew B. Kraebel, in *On Love: A Selection of Works by Hugh, Adam, Achard, Richard, and Godfrey of St. Victor*, ed. Hugh Feiss (Turnhout, Belgium: Brepols, 2011).

[53] For this important tradition, see the essays in this volume by E. Ann Matter, Bernard McGinn, Andrew Louth, and Charles M. Stang.

[54] Hugh of Saint Victor, *Commentarius in Hierarchiam Coelestem*, PL 175, cols. 113–256.

Hugh's thought is rather small.⁵⁵ Yet given Hugh's penchant for using visible symbols or images to reveal invisible truths, and a certain preoccupation with angelic imagery (even more intensively explored by Richard), the Dionysian influence may run deeper. At any rate, the works of the Pseudo-Dionysius continued to inspire the next generation of Victorines (Richard and Achard), and during the thirteenth century, a canon of Saint Victor and founder of Saint Andrew at Vercelli, Thomas Gallus (d. 1246), completed a new, comprehensive exposition of the Dionysian corpus, as well as a short introduction, widely regarded as authoritative in the late Middle Ages.⁵⁶

THE MENDICANTS

The two main focal points of reform during the late eleventh and twelfth centuries – poverty and instruction – were brought to their logical conclusion by the mendicants (or friars), who broke with traditional monasticism in the early days of the thirteenth century. Whereas monks and regular canons were individually poor but often owned considerable property as communities, the mendicants adopted the principle of collective poverty, essentially living off the generosity of the faithful. Their natural habitat was the city, where they could hope to support themselves from alms and realize their spiritual goal by converting the populace to a more deeply experienced Christian faith. Like the Victorines, whose urban location anticipated mendicant life, the friars engaged closely with higher education. When the followers of Saint Dominic Guzman (ca. 1171–1221) cast about for the best places to establish monasteries after the founding of their order of Friars Preachers in the Languedoc in 1215, they first headed to Paris and Bologna, the two main university centers in Europe. The Dominicans believed that studies at the highest level were necessary for first-rate preaching and confession and were also essential in order to distinguish heresy from

---

⁵⁵ Rorem, *Hugh*, pp. 167–76. Zinn, *Richard*, pp. 4, 26–7, 33, suggests a larger role for the Pseudo-Areopagite in Richard's thought by way of Hugh. See also *Presence*, II, pp. 375–6 and Dominique Poirel's forthcoming new edition of Hugh's *Commentary* as well as his *Hugues de Saint-Victor et le réveil dionysien du XIIe siècle* (Turnhout, Belgium: Brepols, 2010).

⁵⁶ Robert Javelet, "Thomas Gallus et Richard de Saint-Victor mystiques," *Recherches de théologie ancienne et médiévale* 29 (1962): 206–33; Robert Javelet, "Thomas Gallus et Richard de Saint-Victor mystiques," *Recherches de théologie ancienne et médiévale* 30 (1963): 88–121; James McEvoy, ed., *Mystical Theology: The Glosses by Thomas Gallus and the Commentary of Robert Grosseteste on "De Mystica Theologia"* (Louvain, Belgium: Peeters, 2003).

orthodoxy – perhaps the most important part of the early Dominican ministry and obviously crucial for their work as inquisitors from the 1230s onward.

The early Franciscans put greater emphasis on personal devotion and regarded learning as a potential source of pride. Saint Francis of Assisi (1181/2–1226), a layman without much Latin education, even worried that study might "extinguish the spirit of prayer and piety," as he noted in a letter to Saint Anthony of Padua granting him permission to teach theology to the brethren. Francis feared that learned knowledge might be a cause for self-deception.[57] Yet despite these concerns, he recognized the need for trained clergymen among his followers, and in the generation after his death his order of Friars Minor resolutely turned to the schools, greatly spurred by the conversion of secular masters like Alexander of Hales (1236).

A similar transformation occurred in the Order of the Virgin Mary of Mount Carmel (Carmelites), originally a group of hermits in Palestine that reorganized along mendicant lines and moved to Western Europe during the 1240s, and in the Friars Hermits of Saint Augustine (Augustinian friars), created in 1256 as a federation of various eremitical movements. By the 1270s, all of these orders operated as mendicants. They were engaged in the apostolate – preaching and exhorting laypeople, hearing confessions, and otherwise caring for the souls of the faithful – and were centrally led and closely allied with papal authority.[58] These were large organizations; at the end of the thirteenth century, some thirty-five thousand Franciscans lived in Europe and the Near East.[59]

The novelty of mendicancy and the encroachment of the mendicant orders on territory under the official charge of the secular clergy generated controversy and even resistance. In response, each mendicant order fashioned a distinctive spiritual profile that legitimized its mission and defined its message. The Franciscans built a powerful metanarrative

---

[57] Francis of Assisi, *Epistola ad sanctum Antonium*, in *Fontes Franciscani*, ed. Enrico Menestò and Stefano Brufani (Assisi, Italy: Edizioni Porziuncola, 1995), p. 55 (Francis was alluding to his *Regula Bullata*, c. 5, in ibid., p. 175); *Admonitiones*, c. VII, in ibid., p. 29.

[58] Good introductions to the vast literature are C. H. Lawrence, *The Friars: The Impact of the Early Mendicant Movement on Western Society* (London: Longman, 1994); and Frances Andrews, *The Other Friars: The Carmelite, Augustinian, Sack and Pied Friars in the Middle Ages* (Woodbridge, UK: The Boydell Press, 2006).

[59] Based on the number of houses (1,421) suggested in Girolamo Golubovich, *Biblioteca bio-bibliographica della Terra Santa e dell'oriente francescano*, vol. 2 (Quaracchi, Italy: Collegium S. Bonaventurae, 1913), pp. 250–1.

around their charismatic founder; the Dominicans identified themselves as teachers of the Word; Augustinian friars drew on the legacy of Saint Augustine and the Desert Fathers; and the Carmelites harked even further back to the Old Testament Elijah or united around the popular cults of the Virgin Mary.[60] As highly centralized organizations sensitive to social perceptions, the mendicants mobilized enormous resources and disseminated their images widely by means of their historiographical writings, collections of exempla (stories ready-made for preaching), pastoral handbooks, and distinctive liturgies.[61]

Mendicant spirituality, while innovative, also tapped into wider currents of piety, as Saint Francis shows. When Francis divested himself of all possessions and urged penance, he meant to follow the example of Christ and renounce the world, not to contend with the effects of commercial capitalism. (Contrary to a common misconception still held today, his followers were only marginally active in charitable work.) Francis's "radicalism" is the coalescence of a series of practices and beliefs that first appear in the eleventh and twelfth centuries and that emphasize the imitation of the human Christ, including his life and suffering. Seeing Francis within this context helps explain the specific form of his ecstatic experience in his last years, when he received the stigmata in a vision of a crucified seraphim.[62] The vision transformed his body into the image of the dying Christ – the sort of literal, physical, and emotive mirroring that, together with popular devotions to the Christchild (which largely postdate Francis's life), became a signature characteristic of Franciscan Christology. Stigmatization was a new paramystical phenomenon, to become exclusively female later in the century. It represents one of the many points of contact between Franciscan thinking about the humanity of Christ and the somatic aspects of late medieval spirituality often associated with women.[63]

---

[60] Andrew Jotischky, *The Carmelites and Antiquity: Mendicants and Their Pasts in the Middle Ages* (Oxford: Oxford University Press, 2002).

[61] See, e.g., Bert Roest, *Franciscan Literature of Religious Instruction before the Council of Trent* (Leiden, The Netherlands: Brill, 2004).

[62] Thomas of Celano, *Vita prima sancti Francisci*, II, 3, in *Fontes*, ed. Menestò and Brufani, pp. 369–70.

[63] Giles Constable, "The Ideal of the Imitation of Christ," in his *Three Studies in Medieval Religious and Social Thought* (Cambridge: Cambridge University Press, 1995), pp. 143–248, at pp. 190–1 and 207–17. As with any aspect of Francis's life, the differences between his own views and the later portrayals are not always easy to discern in the sources. On the impact of the imitation of Christ on Dominicans, also quite significant, see Kent Emery Jr. and Joseph Wawrykow, eds., *Christ among the Medieval Dominicans: Representations of Christ in the Texts and Images of the Order of Preachers* (Notre Dame, IN: University of Notre Dame Press, 1998).

When Saint Bonaventure (d. 1274) described the stigmata in his "Major Reading" (*Legenda Maior*; the "official" life of Francis), he spoke of them as the "seal of Christ, the Supreme Pontiff," authenticating the saint's words and deeds as "divine truth" (*sacramentum*), and as the "likeness of the Crucified written out on parts of his body by the finger of the living God" (Jn 11:27).[64] Like all academically trained friars, Bonaventure's imagery moves effortlessly from the world of urban notaries validating documents, to the Bible, to patristic teaching on the sacraments and the classical metaphor of a mental image stored in memory like the wax imprint left by a signet ring. Just as the *Legenda Maior* portrays Francis as made after the exemplar that is Christ, Bonaventure's wide-ranging theological works, guided by an Augustinian Aristotelianism, present creation and the incorporeal world as an imprint of God's thought. In *The Mind's Road to God*, Bonaventure uses Saint Francis's vision of the six-winged seraphim to construct a simple plan for the six-stage ascent to God, starting with sensation of the material world, followed by internal speculation on the Trinity reflected in the soul, and ending with contemplation of God in mystical union, a "falling asleep" with God. Bonaventure's mystical theology integrates elements from the Augustinian, Bernardine, and Victorine traditions, but also draws on Dionysian thought as it was available to Bonaventure through thirteenth-century translations and commentaries.[65]

The Dominican friar Saint Thomas Aquinas (d. 1274), Bonaventure's exact contemporary, is not usually associated with mysticism but displayed a vivid interest in its findings. Thomas continued the intellectual reading of the Pseudo-Dionysius (sometimes combined with new Neoplatonic materials based on Proclus and others) conducted at the University of Paris and the Dominican house of study (*studium*) in Cologne since the days of his master, Albert the Great (d. 1280), in the 1240s. Citing the Areopagite widely throughout his work, Aquinas even produced his own commentary on *The Divine Names*.[66]

---

[64] *Legenda maior*, 13, in *Fontes*, ed. Menestò and Brufani, pp. 893 and 897.

[65] Bonaventure, *Itinerarium mentis in Deum*, ed. Philotheus Boehner, with a rev. ed. by Zachary Hayes (St. Bonaventure, NY: Franciscan Institute Publications, 2002). The Latin is published here with an English translation. See also J. G. Bougerol, *Introduction à saint Bonaventure* (Paris: Vrin, 1988); and *Presence*, II, pp. 87–112.

[66] L. Michael Harrington, ed., *A Thirteenth-Century Textbook of Mystical Theology at the University of Paris: The "Mystical Theology" of Dionysius the Areopagite in Eriugena's Latin Translation with the Scholia Translated by Anastasius the Librarian and Excerpts from Eriugena's "Periphyseon"* (Louvain, Belgium: Peeters, 2004); Fran O'Rourke, *Pseudo-Dionysius and the Metaphysics of Aquinas* (Leiden,

The most innovative mystic among the Dominicans, Meister Eckhart (ca. 1260–1328), born in Thuringia, may have studied with Albert the Great in Cologne in the late 1270s; he certainly was teaching at Paris from 1293 to 1294/95, 1302 to 1303, and 1311 to 1313, with the last, unusual reappointment serving as an indication of his high standing as a theologian. Intermittently, and from 1313 until 1328, he worked as a Dominican official and preacher in Saxony, Bohemia, and the Rhineland. He ended his days at the papal court of Avignon defending himself against accusations of heresy, which had been launched against him beginning in 1325. Pope John XXII condemned as heretical several statements attributed to Eckhart on March 27, 1329, about a year after Eckhart's death. His thought has remained controversial ever since, even though his immediate Dominican followers, Henry Suso (d. 1366) and John Tauler (d. 1361), moderated and qualified some of his teachings. As befitted a member of his order, Eckhart always wrote primarily as a teacher and preacher, using the technical Latin of mature scholasticism and a vernacular (but also rather technical) Middle High German dialect intended for larger audiences.[67]

Rejecting the extravagant calls for bodily asceticism made by many in the high Middle Ages, Eckhart always gave priority to internal self-denial as the prime vehicle for the transformation of the soul. Detachment (*abegescheidenheit*) is necessary for a "breaking through" (*durchbrechen*) into the divine ground. At the base of his thought stands a Neoplatonic view of creation in which all things exist only in God, emanate from him in their created form, and flow back to him. Through an ethical, material, and psychological letting go (*gelâzenheit*) of all things, including the notion of self, the human becomes aware of the "ground" (*grunt*) in the soul that, as uncreated, "is" God. That process summons the intellect (*vernünft*) but in turn requires a cessation of intellectual activity in order to reach the essential, hidden ground. The human is made "*at* the image of God" (*ad imaginem Dei*), as in traditional Christian thought, and, inasmuch as the soul is uncreated, it "*is* the image of God" (*imago Dei*). Exemplar and image relate to each

---

The Netherlands: Brill, 1992). For Albert the Great's mysticism, see *Presence*, IV, pp. 12–27.

[67] Bernard McGinn, *The Mystical Thought of Meister Eckhart: The Man from Whom God Hid Nothing* (New York: Crossroad, 2001); and *Presence*, IV, pp. 81–296 are now the best introductions to Eckhart's life, work, and legacy through Suso and Tauler. Eckhart's work is in Meister Eckhart, *Die deutschen und lateinischen Werken*, ed., Josef Quint, Josef Koch et al. (Stuttgart and Berlin, Germany: Kohlhammer, 1936–), 9 vols. to date.

other as an object reflected in a mirror – they are similar, but the image draws its existence from the archetype. In the end, the two are joined, as he put it in the conclusion of his German Sermon 69, on John 16:16:

> The image [manifested by the Word] and the image [a property of the intellect aware of God] are so completely one and joined together that one cannot comprehend any distinction between the two.... I say further: God in his omnipotence cannot understand any distinction between them, for they are born together and die together.[68]

Although Eckhart presented his views within the framework of Christian salvation history, the potential dissonance with Christian doctrine was great. His concept of union without distinction presented multiple problems, but it is striking that opposition against him became manifest only during the 1320s and initially targeted his popular preaching, the "sermons to simple and uneducated people, which could lead the audience in error," as the Dominican general chapter of 1325 put it.[69] We can understand that reaction only in light of the growing unease in the Church about spiritual currents among Eckhart's audience: the nuns, beguines, and other laywomen and laymen he was known to address, and to whom we must now turn.

INFORMAL RELIGIOUS MOVEMENTS

Reform of religious life was not only the work of monks, canons, and mendicants. Over the course of the twelfth century, laypeople began to explore ways to lead a more conscious Christian life without taking formal religious vows. The movements they generated appeared in every corner of Latin Christianity but earlier, and in greater numbers, in the more urbanized regions that form an arch reaching from the Low Countries in the north across the Rhineland and the Lake Constance area down to northern and central Italy. These were places of intensive commercial but also cultural exchange, crucially benefiting from a high degree of lay literacy. The men and women known as Humiliati/e, for instance, who were active in northern Italy, earned papal recognition in 1201 as a tripartite religious order composed of clerics, cloistered members, and laypeople living at home.[70] Groups of lay penitents,

---

[68] Eckhart, *Predigt 69*, in *Die ... Werke: Die deutschen Werken*, vol. 3, ed. Quint and Koch, pp. 159–80. For the English translation, see Meister Eckhart, *Teacher and Preacher*, ed. Bernard McGinn (New York: Paulist Press, 1986), p. 314.
[69] Bernard M. Reichert, ed., *Acta capitulorum generalium*, vol. 2 (Monumenta Ordinis Praedicatorum Historica, vol. IV) (Rome: Propaganda Fidei, 1899), pp. 160–1.
[70] Frances Andrews, *The Early Humiliati* (Cambridge: Cambridge University Press, 1999).

known since the 1170s, organized themselves during the thirteenth century under the auspices of the Franciscans as a "Third Order" (after the Friars Minor and the "second" order of Saint Clare for nuns) and became "tertiaries."[71] Solitary isolation by recluses also broke away from monastic tradition and became an urban phenomenon, famously in England, but also on the continent.[72]

The large proportion of women involved in such movements was noted by contemporary observers. Many women first flocked to the reformed orders (Herman of Tournai wrote around 1150 that "more than ten thousand women" joined the Premonstratensians[73]), which could hardly accommodate them all. The opportunities for cloistered women to direct and shape their own destiny were always more limited than those of men. Because women could not be ordained, they needed the assistance of clerics for important sacraments and for a few other rituals. Not as well funded as monasteries for men (although there were important exceptions) and encumbered by greater restrictions on their interactions with the world, nunneries often struggled to find an acceptable scope of action. One symptom of the early reformers' taste for experiment (and the great influence of the apostolic ideal) was their use of syneisactism, an arrangement by which men and women lived religiously in close proximity to each other. Most orders (Prémontré and Cîteaux among them), however, gradually insisted on a wider separation between houses of monks and nuns. Some even went so far as to refuse to accept the care of nuns altogether. This is an area in which normative theory and concrete practice diverged considerably, however, and until the mid-thirteenth century, new foundations for women continued to be inspired by the reformed monks and regular canons, while the mendicants started their own branches for nuns (the Order of Saint Clare and that of the Dominican nuns).[74] All of these houses, including those

---

[71] Giovanna Casagrande, *Religiosità penitenziale e città al tempo dei communi* (Rome: Istituto Storico dei Cappuccini, 1996). For Dominican tertiaries, see Maiju Lehmijoki-Gardner, Daniel E. Bornstein, and E. Ann Matter, eds. and trans., *Dominican Penitent Women* (New York: Paulist Press, 2005).

[72] Ann K. Warren, *Anchoresses and Their Patrons in Medieval England* (Berkeley and Los Angeles: University of California Press, 1985); Anneke B. Mulder-Bakker, *Lives of the Anchoresses: The Rise of the Urban Recluse in Medieval Europe* (Philadelphia: University of Pennsylvania Press, 2005).

[73] Herman of Tournai, *De Miraculis S. Mariae Laudunensis liber III*, vol.12, ed. R. Wilmans, *Monumenta Germaniae Historica, Scriptores* (Hanover, Germany: Hahn, 1856), pp. 653–60 at p. 659.

[74] The large literature on this subject cannot be described in full here. See most recently Constable, *Reformation*, pp. 68–75; Bruce L. Venarde, *Women's Monasticism and Medieval Society: Nunneries in France and England, 890–1215* (Ithaca, NY: Cornell University Press, 1997); Walter Simons, *Cities of Ladies: Beguine Communities in*

controlled by mendicants, were in principle cloistered and reserved for women of the propertied elite, either noble or of the urban patriciate, because their only means of existence came from endowments.

Around 1200, women in the southern Low Countries (roughly covering the area of modern Belgium) and the Rhineland began to practice a devout life "in the world," alone (as recluses, enclosed anchoresses, or in their family) and in small groups, devoted to the care of the sick, teaching, and the promotion of penance. Their lives were not unlike that of Saint Francis. These beguines (*beguinae*) never formed a single order but gradually congregated locally to form independent communities or beguinages, which acquired and rented out homes to individual women, elected their own superiors, and by the end of the thirteenth century, adopted local rules or statutes to regulate the internal life of the community. At that time, the movement had spread across continental northern Europe, from Marseilles in southern France to the Baltic coast.[75] Beguines came from all walks of life but mainly from the middle and lower classes. Although they always lived simply, they did not observe rules of individual or collective poverty. In most communities, physically able beguines were expected to earn their own living in the urban textile industry, as nurses, or in other professions. In the most populous cities of the Low Countries, beguinages could house several hundred women; the largest on record, the "beguine court" (*begijnhof*) of Saint Catherine's in Mechelen, had about 1,500 beguines during the sixteenth century. Overall, more than three hundred beguine communities have been attested to in the southern Netherlandish provinces alone.

Such communities offered an opportunity to explore religious life for whole segments of the female population previously denied access to it. Economic and social motives made many women join who had little or no interest in a religious commitment and may not even have been particularly pious. Because beguines took no solemn vows, they were free to leave the community if they so desired. Some "returned to the world," possibly for marriage. Others who found the free combination of the active and contemplative life in beguinages unsatisfactory

the *Medieval Low Countries 1200–1565* (Philadelphia: University of Pennsylvania Press, 2001), pp. 19–20, 109–10; and Fiona J. Griffiths, *The Garden of Delights: Reform and Renaissance for Women in the Twelfth Century* (Philadelphia: University of Pennsylvania Press, 2007).

[75] Simons, *Cities*, pp. 24–90; Jean-Claude Schmitt, *Mort d'une hérésie: L'Église et les clercs face aux béguines et béghards du Rhin supérieur du XIVe au XVe siècle* (Paris: Mouton, 1978); Frank-Michael Reichstein, *Das Beginenwesen in Deutschland: Studien und Katalog* (Berlin: Koster, 2001).

(and were of the right social class) left to enter convents. Seven of the fourteen religious women (*mulieres religiosae*) celebrated in the famous hagiographies of beguines written in the Low Countries during the thirteenth century ended their lives as nuns. The *vitae*, written by monks and friars for an audience of contemplatives, were likely not read in beguinages.[76] Still, beguine life obviously met a real need. In some cities of Belgium, it survived even until the late twentieth century.

The study of mysticism was part of beguine life from the start. The earliest communities formed around charismatic women who acted as inspirational teachers. The terms *magistra* and *martha*, commonly used for beguine leaders, recall the dual root of beguine life, the latter alluding to the humble worker who teaches by example, the former to the learned instructor of the monastic or eremitical tradition. Hadewijch served as a beguine teacher in the region of Brabant, although we do not have any documentary evidence to identify her exact group or even to assign precise dates to her (the mid-thirteenth century seems likely).[77] In her Middle-Dutch *Letters*, *Poems in Couplets* (*Mengeldichten*), and *Visions*, she initiates younger or less advanced students in the art of love (*minne*). Her *Poems in Stanzas* (*Strofische Gedichten*), less obviously didactic, are songs of *minne* in the courtly tradition. *Minne* is the only possible road to God, triggered by an innate desire but thwarted by the awareness of human "smallness." Ecstatic union is nevertheless possible, presented in strikingly sensory language using rich Christological, Eucharistic, Trinitarian, and angelic imagery, as in *Vision Seven*. After receiving the Eucharist, Hadewijch writes,

> [The Man] came himself to me, embraced me completely and pressed me to him, and all of my limbs felt his in all their joy, as much as my heart and my humanity wished, so that I was externally satisfied

---

[76] See my "Holy Women of the Low Countries: A Survey," in *Medieval Holy Women in the Christian Tradition c. 1100–c. 1500*, ed. Alastair Minnis and Rosalynn Voaden (Turnhout, Belgium: Brepols, 2010), pp. 625–62.

[77] The century-old discussion on Hadewijch's historical identity is ongoing. Rob Faesen, "Was Hadewijch a Beguine or a Cistercian Nun: An Annotated Hypothesis," *Cîteaux: Commentarii Cistercienses* 55 (2004): 47–63, revisits the old view that she was a Cistercian, but I believe the internal evidence found in her work points against it. Nor do I subscribe to the argument in Hans Wilbrink, *Amplexio Dei: De Omarming Gods. Vergelijkend onderzoek van de mysticologische en sociologische profielen van Hildegard van Bingen en Hadewijch van Brabant* (Maastricht, The Netherlands: Shaker Publishing, 2006), pp. 271–88, that she lived in the city of Liège. For a brief overview of her work, see *Presence* III, pp. 199–222, which also lists the critical editions. Selections of her work in rather loose translations (but with fine commentary) can be found in Hadewijch, *The Complete Works*, trans. Mother Columba Hart (New York: Paulist Press, 1980).

and completely filled. I was even able to sustain it for a while....
And then it seemed to me as if we were one without distinction.
That was all on the outside, in seeing and tasting and feeling ...
and I was so much given over into my Beloved that I melted away
in him, and nothing was left of me. Afterwards I was transported
[internally].[78]

Hadewijch may have been the first of the medieval mystics to invoke – repeatedly – her uncreated self as the ground for a perfect union and for her authority to teach about it, perhaps most memorably in *Vision Twelve*, where she approaches the divine "countenance ... that cannot be seen unless ... one is cast into the deep abyss" and is found worthy, "swallowed into the abyss, where I received the certainty that I was received in these forms in my Beloved, and my Beloved was in me."[79] At the end of her *Visions*, she even appears to place herself in a gallery of other "perfect," including a select group of saints like Augustine and Bernard, but also several contemporary beguines and hermits.[80]

Still in the Low Countries, but in the French-speaking province of Hainaut, the beguine Marguerite Porete (d. 1310) also employed the courtly love idiom but understood the mystical process very differently than did Hadewijch. Her famous *Mirror of Simple Souls* is a dynamic allegory of the soul's struggle to be simple and free, not only from the concerns of the world – an ascetic commonplace – but also from all will and desire. Even stronger, the *Mirror* describes a quest for the annihilation of the soul, a return into sheer nothingness (the precreated state), which opens her up to "the all." Such a one has no use for charity, the sacraments, the works of "holy Church," or even the work of contemplation, all of which Marguerite associates with the active life. (Nevertheless, she does suggest that the annihilated soul cannot wish anything that goes against divine will.[81])

That two beguine authors separated by a distance of fifty miles and hardly half a century could hold such different views should caution us

---

[78] Hadewijch, *De visioenen van Hadewijch*, vol. 1, ed. Jozef Van Mierlo (Louvain, Belgium: De Vlaamsche Boekenhalle, 1924), pp. 78–9.
[79] Ibid., pp. 126, 134.
[80] Ibid., pp. 179–92, possibly the most enigmatic (and disputed) of all her writings.
[81] Marguerite Porete, *Le mirouer des simples ames/Margaretae Porete, Speculum simplicium animarum*, ed. Romana Guarnieri and Paul Verdeyen (Turnhout, Belgium: Brepols, 1986); Marguerite Porete, *The Mirror of Simple Souls*, trans. Edmund Colledge, J. C. Marler, and Judith Grant (Notre Dame, IN: University of Notre Dame Press, 1999). See Amy Hollywood, *The Soul as Virgin Wife: Mechthild of Magdeburg, Marguerite Porete, and Meister Eckhart* (Notre Dame, IN: University of Notre Dame Press, 1995); and *Presence*, III, pp. 244–65.

against understanding beguine mysticism as homogeneous – a caution only reinforced by consideration of Beatrice of Nazareth's (Brabant, d. 1268) *Seven Manners of Loving*, Mechthild of Magdeburg's (Saxony, d. ca. 1282) *The Flowing Light of the Godhead*, the so-called Hadewijch II's (Brabant, possibly 1270s) continuation of Hadewijch's *Poems in Couplets*, the *"Rule" for the True Lovers* (Picardy, ca. 1300), or the anonymous sermons, songs, and poems written in these circles and preserved in Dutch, French, and German.[82] Even less can we speak of a uniform women's mysticism or feminine mysticism, as is made evident if we cast our net wider and also examine the beguines' Italian counterparts, women like Angela of Foligno (d. 1309) or Catherine of Siena (d. 1380), the Cistercian and Dominican sisters in German lands, or the Béguins of southern France (tertiaries inspired by the Franciscan John Paul Olivi).[83]

Let me, by way of conclusion, suggest a few common threads in the thicket of texts that emerge from these diverse new movements and trace the reactions they provoked in the final centuries of the Middle Ages. First, the increased use of the vernacular as vehicle of expression not only expanded the number of potential participants but also transformed and enriched mystical discourse.[84] We have already encountered Eckhart's *grunt*, Hadewijch spoke of her *orewoet* (torment, insanity), and Mechthild talked of *vliesen* (flowing). Although medieval Latin had obvious strengths (its pedigree and putative universality), the vernacular could be more flexible and often inspired new poetic forms of expression, as for instance in the work of the Italian Franciscan

---

[82] Jos Huls, ed., "Seuen maniren van minnen" van Beatrijs van Nazareth. *Het mystieke proces en mystagogische implicaties* (Louvain, Belgium: Peeters, 2002), 2 vols.; Mechthild von Magdeburg, *Das Fliessende Licht der Gottheit*, ed. Gisela Vollmann-Prose (Frankfurt: Deutscher Klassiker Verlag, 2003); Mechthild of Magdeburg, *The Flowing Light of the Godhead*, trans. Frank Tobin (New York: Paulist Press, 1998); Saskia Murk-Jansen, *The Measure of Mystic Thought: A Study of Hadewijch's Mengeldichten* (Göppingen, Germany: Kümmerle, 1991); Karl Christ, ed., "La Règle des Fins Amans: Eine Beginenregel aus dem Ende des XIII. Jahrhunderts," in *Philologische Studien aus dem romanisch-germanischen Kulturkreise: Karl Voretzsch ... dargebracht*, ed. B. Schädel and Werner Mulertt (Halle, Germany: Max Niemeyer, 1927), pp. 173–213 (note that Tanya Stabler Miller, "What's in a Name? Clerical Representations of Parisian Beguines (1200–1328)," *Journal of Medieval History* 33 (2007): 60–86, at p. 75, connects the *Règle* to Parisian clerics); Wybren Scheepsma, *The Limburg Sermons; Preaching in the Low Countries at the Turn of the Fourteenth Century*, trans. David F. Johnson (Leiden, The Netherlands: Brill, 2008).

[83] See the sections on Italy and the German Territories in Minnis and Voaden, eds., *Medieval Holy Women*; and Louisa A. Burnham, *So Great a Light, So Great a Smoke: The Beguin Heretics of Languedoc* (Ithaca, NY: Cornell University Press, 2006).

[84] See Barbara Newman's contribution to this volume.

Jacopone da Todi (d. 1306).[85] In recent years, scholars have also begun to examine the performative aspects of such texts: song, dance, dialogue, and even silence stood at the disposal of the mystic as teacher within these circles.[86]

Second, because the more informal movements lacked solid institutional structures, our information about the individuals involved and their work can be fragmentary. Even the largest beguinages, which expanded into veritable walled neighborhoods complete with church, hospital, and service buildings for beguine use, lacked collective libraries. Manuscripts were considered private property, circulating quite freely among individual women and men and were thus also less likely to be preserved *in situ*. Much work remains anonymous and hard to date or place in context; much is still unpublished.[87] Consequently, it can be difficult to determine how ideas and systems of thought were transmitted. There is an understandable tendency to prioritize the written tradition, but it cannot explain everything. In some cases, informal, oral tradition must also be in play. In addition, we should not assume that the current of influence always flows from the Latin and clerical to the vernacular and lay. Meister Eckhart's preaching to nuns and beguines must be imagined as a two-way street: his sermons likely met with responses from his beguine and lay audiences or were intended to address beguine thought in the first place. There is little doubt that Eckhart was familiar with Porete's thinking (and possibly with Hadewijch's), and Hadewijch's influence on such later clerical mystics like John Ruusbroec (d. 1381) is indisputable.[88]

The preceding observations lead inexorably to the even more obvious issue of religious authority.[89] The ambitions of nonconventional

---

[85] See most recently Enrico Menestò, ed., *La vita e l'opera di Iacopone da Todi* (Spoleto, Italy: Fondazione Centro italiano di studi sull' alto Medioevo, 2007).

[86] Mary A. Suydam and Joanna E. Ziegler, eds., *Performance and Transformation: New Approaches to Late Medieval Spirituality* (New York: St. Martin's Press, 1999); Anikó Daróczi, *Groet gheruchte van dien wondere: spreken, zwijgen en zingen bij Hadewijch* (Louvain, Belgium: Peeters, 2007).

[87] See my "Staining the Speech of Things Divine: The Uses of Literacy in Medieval Beguine Communities," in *The Voice of Silence: Women's Literacy in a Men's Church*, ed. Thérèse de Hemptinne and María Eugenia Góngora (Turnhout, Belgium: Brepols, 2004), pp. 85–110.

[88] Some of these questions are explored in Bernard McGinn, ed., *Meister Eckhart and the Beguine Mystics: Hadewijch of Brabant, Mechthild of Magdeburg, and Marguerite Porete* (New York: Continuum, 1994); *Presence*, IV, p. 99; Paul Verdeyen, "Mystiek in de Nederlanden vóór Ruusbroec," in *Jan van Ruusbroec 1293–1381* (Brussels, Belgium: Koninklijke Bibliotheek Albert I, 1981), pp. 1–14; and Geert Warnar, *Ruusbroec: Literatuur en mystiek in de veertiende eeuw* (Amsterdam: Athenaeum–Polak and Van Gennep, 2003).

[89] See Mary Frohlich, Veerle Fraeters, Dyan Elliott, and Alison Weber in this volume.

movements greatly raised the stakes for a Church increasingly emphasizing the powers of its teaching authority or *magisterium*. Because mysticism is fundamentally a "speaking" of the essence of God, its realization by lay individuals or nuns, who were not authorized to preach or teach on such matters, posed the question on what authority such teachings might be based. That question hovers behind both the multiplication of paramystical phenomena (revelations, prophecies, clairvoyance, or stigmata) and the intensified efforts to authenticate them.[90]

It is not easy to weigh the exact role gender played in these debates, but it would be hard to overestimate it. Since the beginning of the reform, a fascinating dynamic developed, linking religious men and women of various kinds and across the boundaries of orders or congregations in complex relationships that were tense, even tinged with suspicion, and mutually enriching. Men increasingly acknowledged that women, "free" from the institutional demands of the clerical office, could make original contributions to Christian spirituality.[91] Such contacts were not new (John of Fécamp had also attended to the religious formation of nuns[92]), but they proliferated from the twelfth century onward at various levels of the clergy and in different religious orders. Inspired by the new pastoral theology, these sympathizers supported the first beguines against detractors (*beguina* was originally a term of derision, denoting a "fake devotee") and throughout the thirteenth century helped circulate their ideas, even if as hagiographers; they also distorted women's lives – by emphasizing external, bodily aspects over the interior ones, for instance.[93] Fictional dialogues between learned master and simple beguine became something of a literary trope in the thirteenth century, contrasting scholastic reason and experiential knowledge, with

---

[90] See the literature cited in *Presence*, IV, pp. 513–14 as well as Alain Boureau, *Satan the Heretic: The Birth of Demonology in the Medieval West* (Chicago: University of Chicago Press, 2006).

[91] Here, too, studies abound. See, e.g., Caroline Walker Bynum, *Holy Feast and Holy Fast: The Religious Significance of Food to Medieval Women* (Berkeley and Los Angeles: University of California Press, 1987); Jeffrey F. Hamburger, *The Visual and the Visionary: Art and Female Spirituality in Medieval Germany* (New York: Zone Books, 1998); Catherine M. Mooney, ed., *Gendered Voices: Medieval Saints and Their Interpreters* (Philadelphia: University of Pennsylvania Press, 1999); John Coakley, *Women, Men, and Spiritual Power: Female Saints and Their Collaborators* (New York: Columbia University Press, 2006); and Dyan Elliott, *Proving Woman: Female Spirituality and Inquisitional Culture in the Later Middle Ages* (Princeton, NJ: Princeton University Press, 2004).

[92] Fulton, *From Judgment to Passion*, pp. 166–8.

[93] Amy Hollywood, "Inside Out: Beatrice of Nazareth and Her Hagiographer," in Mooney, ed., *Gendered Voices*, pp. 78–98.

the beguine often coming out on top.⁹⁴ Just how far this could go is demonstrated by the German *Sister Catherine Treatise* (from the first half of the fourteenth century), preserved in at least seventeen manuscripts, in which a beguine, Catherine, helps her confessor reach a prolonged state of mystical union.⁹⁵

In real-life cases of conflict, a woman's deference to authority (a disposition conspicuously absent from the fictional dialogues) could possibly save her, but around 1300 the implications had extended so far beyond the purely theological that Marguerite Porete's apparent disregard for the sacraments and her seemingly antinomian statements were deemed intolerable. Her local bishop, Guy of Cambrai, condemned the *Mirror* between 1296 and 1306, had her book burned in Valenciennes, and warned her never to disseminate it again. Arrested for circulating another version of her book, Marguerite was defiant and, after a long inquisitorial trial, was executed in Paris as a lapsed heretic in 1310.⁹⁶ Shortly afterward, the Council of Vienne (1311–12) decreed against beguines suspected of similar doctrines, leading to widespread investigations and often the suppression of their communities until the 1320s. New accusations against beguines and beghards (male followers of the beguine lifestyle, sometimes itinerant) were made for another century in various parts of northern Europe.⁹⁷

New religious movements originating in subsequent decades took these lessons to heart. Some of the followers of Geert Grote (d. 1384), known as the "New Devout," adopted a mode of religious life close to that of beguines but often expressed reservations about more speculative mystical beliefs as well as claims to rapture. Although the work of John Ruusbroec, Gerlach Peters (d. 1411), and Henry Mande (d. 1431) greatly expanded mystical culture among the laity (as well as among the clergy), they always took pains to observe the limits of orthodoxy

---

⁹⁴ Simons, *Cities of Ladies*, pp. 118–32, with a discussion of the etymology of the word *beguina* and an overview of internal disagreements within the clerical body. It should be noted that already in 1236 Robert le Bougre, an inquisitor in the diocese of Cambrai, executed a beguine for (in the words of Hadewijch) her "just *minne*" (Hadewijch, *Visioenen*, vol. 1, p. 189).

⁹⁵ Franz-Josef Schweitzer, *Der Freiheitsbegriff der deutschen Mystik* (Frankfurt: Peter Lang, 1981), pp. 321–70; "The Sister Catherine Treatise," in *Meister Eckhart: Teacher and Preacher*, pp. 349–87. The text presents multiple problems of interpretation that cannot be discussed here.

⁹⁶ See now Sean Field, *The Beguine, the Angel, and the Inquisitor: The Trials of Marguerite Porete (d. 1310) and Guiard of Cressonessart* (Notre Dame, IN: University of Notre Dame Press, 2012).

⁹⁷ Simons, *Cities*, pp. 132–7.

and promote sacramental devotion.[98] These concerns were generally shared by the Observant reforms in monastic and mendicant orders that occurred during the late fourteenth and fifteenth centuries.[99]

Not since the beginning of Western monasticism had there flourished such widespread and productive interest in religious perfection as during the twelfth through fifteenth centuries. At times chaotic and contradictory, the renewal of religious life unquestionably enriched Western Christianity as it built on older conventions while questioning their limitations. As the mystical thought of these movements shows, the new religious landscape was decidedly more diverse – in itself an alarming thought for a world striving for a singular perfection.

---

[98] John van Engen, *Sisters and Brothers of the Common Life: The Devotio Moderna and the World of the Later Middle Ages* (Philadelphia: University of Pennsylvania Press, 2008).

[99] Bert Roest, "Observant Reform in Religious Orders," in *Christianity*, ed. Rubin and Simons, pp. 446–57.

4 Early Modern Reformations
EDWARD HOWELLS

INTRODUCTION

In the study of the Reformation, attention has turned in recent decades to the reform character of the late medieval period as the positive basis of Reformation thought and institutional change, against older views that emphasized only decline as the background to reform.[1] This has the advantage not only of improved accuracy but also of including a wider range of changes under the umbrella of Reformation. It brings Roman Catholicism within the purview of the Reformation, not merely as a reactionary force against Protestant changes (a Counter-Reformation) but also as engaged in its own reforms (a Catholic Reformation).[2] It permits profound connections to be drawn between Roman Catholicism and Protestantism in producing the Reformation. At the same time, the Reformation can no longer be seen as a single change or group of changes emanating from one historical event, such as Luther's theological breakthrough, but is instead a plural confluence of changes covering the late medieval and early modern periods with a common reform character. Rather than beginning with Luther, therefore, I shall approach the Reformation as a collection of changes – reformations – beginning in the late medieval period. I shall focus on three facets of reform – democratization and laicization, humanism, and interiority. I shall then turn to a number of concrete contexts and figures as representative of the development of mysticism between 1500 and 1700: Martin Luther, Teresa of Avila and John of the Cross, Hans Denck, the Moravians and the Quakers, and Pierre de Bérulle.

[1] Steven E. Ozment, *The Age of Reform 1250–1550: An Intellectual and Religious History of Late Medieval and Reformation Europe* (New Haven, CT: Yale University Press, 1980), pp. 9–20.
[2] H. O. Evennett, *The Spirit of the Counter-Reformation* (Cambridge: Cambridge University Press, 1968), ch. 1.

DEMOCRATIZATION AND LAICIZATION

Bernard McGinn has drawn attention to a democratization of Christian life that begins in the thirteenth century, affecting mysticism especially.³ It starts with a change in the understanding of the relation between the world and the cloister. The late medieval understanding of the apostolic life (*vita apostolica*) shifted from an ideal of flight from the world into secluded and remote monasteries to the possibility of living religious life in the city and engaging in apostolic work among the laity, practices put forward first by the Augustinian canons and then by the new mendicant orders, the Dominicans and Franciscans.⁴ Religious life was democratized in the sense that, in this new form, it was lived among the people rather than set apart from them. This gave it an influence that crossed the boundary between religious and lay in new ways. The beguines of the thirteenth century, for example, occupied a position between lay and enclosed religious life. A new kind of religious order for women, though never fully approved, beguines made no lifelong vows and supported themselves through secular work. Some were cloistered, while some wandered and preached.⁵ There was also the development of third orders, laity who attached themselves to a religious order, taking on some of its spiritual discipline, while remaining in secular life. This increased contact and fluidity between religious and lay life had the effect of putting the goals of spiritual perfection and unmediated relationship with God before a wider public, producing an enormous growth in mystical literature and practices, which continued through the fourteenth and fifteenth centuries. The expansion of the towns and the market economy contributed to the change, as well as the increasing use of the vernacular and growing literacy among the public and, during the late fifteenth century, the rise of the printing press.⁶

---

3   Bernard McGinn, "Mysticism," in *The Oxford Encyclopedia of the Reformation*, ed. Hans J. Hillerbrand (Oxford: Oxford University Press, 1996), pp. 119–24; Bernard McGinn, *The Presence of God: A History of Western Christian Mysticism*, vol. 3, *The Flowering of Mysticism: Men and Women in the New Mysticism (1200–1350)* (New York: Crossroad, 1998), ch. 1.
4   M.-D. Chenu, *Nature, Man and Society in the Twelfth Century: Essays on New Theological Perspectives in the Latin West* (Toronto: University of Toronto Press, 1997), chs. 6 and 7. Also see Walter Simons in this volume.
5   R. W. Southern, *Western Society and the Church in the Middle Ages* (Middlesex, UK: Penguin, 1970), ch. 7.
6   Lester K. Little, *Religious Poverty and the Profit Economy in Medieval Europe* (Ithaca, NY: Cornell University Press, 1978); Ozment, *Age of Reform*, ch. 5.

Catherine of Genoa (1447–1510) is one of numerous late medieval women who gained a popular following on the basis of her ecstatic experiences and mystical teaching. She was a married laywoman who combined her secular life with contemplation and the care of the sick. A religious confraternity gathered around her from 1497, comprising thirty-six lay brothers, four priests, and a prior, who engaged in regular prayer, assemblies and services, the Eucharist, confession and penance, and who also committed themselves to work among the poor and sick. This confraternity is regarded as the seedbed of the Catholic Reformation, giving birth to the Oratory of Divine Love, founded in Rome sometime around 1517, and the Theatine Order, founded in 1524.[7]

The democratization of religious life was also found among the Protestant Reformers. Martin Luther's (1483–1546) call for the secularization of monks – secular in the medieval sense referring to those who do not live according to a monastic rule – and his departure from the monastery and marriage can be regarded as further outworking of the democratization of religious life. Luther was not simply reacting against monasticism, but also wanted all to have the spiritual benefits of religious life. When he read and approved popular fourteenth-century German mystical works such as John Tauler's sermons and the *Theologia Deutsch* (*German Theology*), he took them as guides to Christian life as a whole, rather than as specialist texts for a spiritual elite.[8] Religious life and teaching, especially mystical works, had moved from being the preserve only of those who entered monasteries. Though they worked out their solutions in different ways, both Protestant and Catholic reformers wanted to make personal transformation available to all and to break down the barriers between contemplation and action.

HUMANISM

A particular driving force was given to reform with the rise of humanism. Humanism arose out of new interest in the classical Greek and Roman authors. The focus was on learning the languages and critical skills necessary for the study of ancient texts, as well as on rhetoric.

---

[7] John C. Olin, *The Catholic Reformation: Savonarola to Ignatius Loyola: Reform in the Church, 1495–1540* (New York: Harper and Row, 1969), pp. 16–17.

[8] Heiko A. Oberman, "*Simul Gemitus et Raptus*: Luther and Mysticism," in *The Dawn of the Reformation* (Grand Rapids, MI: Eerdmans, 1992), p. 140.

Arguably humanism was less concerned with ideas than with an educational program of study of the Latin and Greek classics and with the kind of humanity that was formed by this program. It took hold in many universities in the late medieval period and was the basis on which important new foundations were made, such as the University of Alcalá founded by Cardinal Cisneros in Spain in 1508, where the study of the Bible in the original languages produced the Complutensian Polyglot Bible, exemplifying the new linguistic and critical-textual approach, characterized by philological exactness and attention to the original languages.[9] The effect of humanism on mysticism came indirectly, through the reform movements that it helped to inspire.

Desiderius Erasmus (ca. 1469–1536), the most famous humanist scholar of the Reformation period, promoted a popular ethical reform of the church, advocating a return to the primitive simplicity he found in the New Testament and the early church, against religious ceremonial, the doctrinal control of the Inquisition, and scholastic abstraction and argument. At the heart of his vision was an understanding of the dignity of the human person as capable of high moral standards through the practice of simple inward piety, a point that applied to every Christian, religious or lay. This ethic was typical of Catholic reforming circles in Italy and Spain during the late fifteenth and early sixteenth century. It fed into the reforms of the religious orders during the sixteenth century. The reform of the Franciscans in Spain, for instance, led by Cardinal Cisneros (1435–1517), brought a renewal of the ideal of primitive simplicity and of the interior life that then inspired Teresa of Avila's (1515–82) reform of the Carmelites.

Teresa of Avila sought to return the Carmelite Order to observance of its primitive rule, removing more recent accretions of wealth and custom. She drew on new popular writing on prayer in the vernacular, much of it produced by Franciscans. Francis of Osuna's (ca. 1492–ca. 1540) *Third Spiritual Alphabet*, which influenced Teresa, is a good example, teaching a method of prayer for individuals beginning with interior withdrawal or "recollection" and leading to states of "devotion," "quiet," and "union with God."[10] Such mystical works favored interior and mystical prayer as a spiritual path for all.

[9] For an analysis of the distinctive features of humanism in this period, see Charles Trinkaus, *In Our Image and Likeness: Humanity and Divinity in Italian Humanist Thought*, vol. 1 (Notre Dame, IN: University of Notre Dame Press, 1995), pp. xii–xxvii; and ibid., vol. 2, pp. 761–74.

[10] Francisco de Osuna, *The Third Spiritual Alphabet*, trans. Mary E. Giles (New York: Paulist Press, 1981). Teresa of Avila, *Life*, ch. 4, para. 7, *The Collected Works of St.*

Heiko Oberman suggests that both nominalism and mysticism took their high anthropology from humanism, while also possessing a "contradictory" neo-Augustinian stress on the incapacity of human nature without grace.[11] Though humanism drew on pagan sources, its emphasis on the dignity of human nature, found for instance in the humanist scholar Pico della Mirandola's (1463–93) treatise *On the Dignity of Man*, had its parallel in theological and mystical works. This needs some qualification: it was not high anthropology so much as the availability of the new sense of humanity that had a parallel effect on mysticism. In mystical works, we see the parallel in growing optimism about the availability of union with God, which encouraged women and the laity, for instance, increasingly to seek such states.[12]

The proliferation of mystical writings during the fifteenth and sixteenth centuries was aided by humanist education, as the move to translate and make available mystical texts drew on skills encouraged and developed by humanists. Many mystical writings of the period show a rhetorical and literary skill that was learned in a humanist culture, for instance John of the Cross's or Luis of León's (1528–91) poetry, or Benet of Canfield's (1562–1611) style in his *Rule of Perfection*.[13] Humanists also, in general, stood against the attempts of the Inquisition to control ideas, seeking to preserve academic freedom in the universities, especially in Spain, sometimes becoming the allies of mystics under investigation.[14] A further respect in which humanism influenced mysticism was in the revival of Neoplatonism, seen for instance in the innovative mysticism of Nicholas of Cusa (ca. 1400–64).[15] In summary, humanism's influence

---

Teresa of Avila, vol. 1, trans. and intro. Kieran Kavanaugh and Otilio Rodriguez (Washington DC: Institute of Carmelite Studies, 1987), p. 67.

[11] Heiko A. Oberman, "Some Notes on the Theology of Nominalism: With Attention to Its Relation to the Renaissance," *Harvard Theological Review* 53 (1960): 47–76.

[12] This is evident from attempts by the church authorities during late-sixteenth-century Spain to restrict women and lay readers of spiritual texts. E.g., Jodi Bilinkoff notes that the Inquisitor Valdés told Luís de Granada that the reason his *Treatise on Prayer* (1554) and *Guide of Sinners* (1556–7) had been placed on the index of forbidden books was not for doctrinal reasons, but simply because he had encouraged the "wives of carpenters" in the ways of contemplation. See Jodi Bilinkoff, "St. Teresa of Avila and the Avila of St. Teresa," *Carmelite Studies* 3 (1982):53–86.

[13] Kent Emery Jr., *Renaissance Dialectic and Renaissance Piety: Benet of Canfield's Rule of Perfection* (Binghamton, NY: Center for Medieval and Early Renaissance Studies at the State University of New York, 1987), p. 26.

[14] On Luis of León's support of Teresa of Avila, see Gillian Ahlgren, *Teresa of Avila and the Politics of Sanctity* (Ithaca, NY: Cornell University Press, 1996), pp. 117–18, 138–40.

[15] Louis Dupré, *Passage to Modernity: An Essay in the Hermeneutics of Nature and Culture* (New Haven, CT: Yale University Press, 1993), pp. 188–9.

on mystical theology and practice was in the increasing availability of an enlarged (though graced) sense of human capacity in relation to God, which together with new literary and rhetorical skills furthered the process of democratization.

INTERIORITY

There was no identifiable movement favoring interiority, but as a spiritual theme, interiority was a significant feature of the age of reform and important in the development of mysticism. Rowan Williams has pointed out that whether we consider Erasmus or Luther, Teresa of Avila or John of the Cross (1542–91), we see a common focus on the authenticity of the inner life in the face of the deception and corruption of exterior forms of religion.[16] Though Teresa of Avila and John of the Cross supported the Roman Catholic Church in their work of reform, they (unwittingly) shared with Luther a suspicion of the deceptive nature of human religiosity when it is divorced from an authentic interior union with Christ. There was a prevailing sense of tension in reform circles about the relationship between the interior life and exterior, public life. It is around this tension that the difficulties faced by mysticism in meeting the challenges of reform were played out. This is not to say that mysticism can be simply identified with interiority and opposed to exterior concerns. Rather, in the remainder of this chapter, I shall focus on the creative dynamic between the inner sources of mysticism, on the one hand, and its exterior life as an aspect of reform, on the other, noting the tensions and the new ways in which the inner and outer were put together, producing new forms of reformation mysticism.

Interiority had always been a definitive aspect of mysticism, in that the key shift in mystical transformation was from the ordinary mediation of prayer, spiritual practices, and the sacraments to a more direct, face–face relationship with God, often called union with God. Bernard McGinn pinpoints this central feature of mysticism as "immediate consciousness of the presence of God," marking the shift from the mode of access to God found in ordinary consciousness.[17] Union with God is interior because it is contrasted with access to God through

---

[16] Rowan Williams, "Religious Experience in the Era of Reform," in *Companion Encyclopedia of Theology*, ed. Peter Byrne and Leslie Houlden (London: Routledge, 1995).

[17] Bernard McGinn, *The Presence of God: A History of Western Christian Mysticism*, vol. 1, *The Foundations of Mysticism: Origins to the Fifth Century* (New York: Crossroad, 1991), p. xix.

exterior, mediated means; it is consciousness of the intimate relationship that God has with the soul, as creator, without any mediating elements between the soul and God. The relationship between the interior and the exterior is therefore complex even before the new influences of democratization, laicization, and humanism are introduced. At the same time, exterior forms of religion can never be altogether jettisoned: they are vital for the cultivation of an "immediate consciousness" of God. This transformation of consciousness requires exterior practices, giving a paradoxical character to mysticism that is seen, for instance, in the way that it is both an affirmation of the world in its exterior forms and a withdrawal from the world in its interior immediacy with God. With the move of mysticism increasingly out of the cloister and into the world in the late medieval and Reformation period, this tension between the interior and the exterior also shifted, producing cracks, breaks, and new varieties of resolution.

A good way to map out this tension between the interior springs of mysticism and its exterior integration in the church and society is to note three major condemnations of mysticism that punctuated the period from 1300 to 1700. First, the condemnation of the heresy of the so-called Free Spirits at the Council of Vienne in 1311 and 1312; second, the activity of the Inquisition in Spain during the sixteenth century against the *alumbrados* ("illuminated ones"); and third, the condemnation of Quietism in France in 1699.[18] A central feature of all three condemnations was a perceived antagonism between the mystics' claims for unmediated union with God and the mediated structures of the church and the sacraments. Meister Eckhart, for instance, whose posthumous condemnation in 1329 was connected with the condemnation of the Free Spirits, was criticized for stating that there was an uncreated aspect of the soul indistinct from God.[19] This deepening of mystical union to a point of ontological indistinction between the soul and God reflected an increasing interiority in late medieval mysticism. Many of the articles of condemnation focus on the effect that this had on outer practices. Eckhart is accused of denying the value of prayer, good works, and exterior activity.

The main concern expressed in the condemnation of Quietism nearly four hundred years later was, similarly, over the putative tension

---

[18] McGinn, "Mysticism," p. 119.
[19] Meister Eckhart, *Meister Eckhart: The Essential Sermons, Commentaries, Treatises, and Defense*, trans. Bernard McGinn and Edmund Colledge (New York: Paulist Press, 1981), pp. 77–81.

between an interior union with God and exterior action.[20] This was connected to the earlier, mid-sixteenth-century condemnations of the *alumbrados* in Spain, in which the authorities sought to restrict the practice of mental prayer, forbidding it to suspect groups, including women religious. This was, in effect, an attempt to shut down these groups' access to the interior realm. Rowan Williams, Gillian Ahlgren, and others have noted that Teresa of Avila is unusual in this repressive context for her success in bringing her rich interior life together with exterior reforming activity.[21] She found a way to overcome the tensions between mystical interiority and exterior life, which had been pushed to the breaking point by the Inquisition; she succeeded, where others failed, to use mysticism in her pursuit of exterior religious reform. Against this example, the condemnations reveal the increasing strain between the interior sources of mysticism and the exterior forms of its cultivation and expression.

Yet it is possible to take this argument too far. It was not the case that mysticism was faced with an irreconcilable opposition between all forms of exterior social or ecclesial life and the interior life with God. Steven Ozment tends to this view in *Mysticism and Dissent*, his study of the Radical Reformation. Mysticism is a "challenge, always in theory if not in daily practice, to the regular, normative way of religious salvation," Ozment argues, because it is concerned with "more intimate communications from God than those which the eyes and ears behold in the sermons, sacraments, ceremonies and writings of the church."[22] The problem with this approach is that it ignores the equally important exterior element of mysticism, as dependent on communities of practice for its cultivation and expression. The tension between the interior and the exterior, though increasing during the fifteenth, sixteenth, and seventeenth centuries, and a *central* cause of dissent in the Radical Reformation, was a creative one, producing new outward forms of mysticism, rather than marking a retreat to a wholly separate interior. Ozment is right to regard the tension between the interior and the exterior as a useful tool for understanding mysticism in early modernity, but there was no irreconcilable opposition between them. Mysticism

---

[20] Louis Cognet, *Post-Reformation Spirituality*, trans. P. J. Hepburne-Scott (London: Burns and Oates, 1959), pp. 134–6.
[21] Rowan Williams, *Teresa of Avila* (London: Geoffrey Chapman, 1991), ch. 1; Ahlgren, *Politics of Sanctity*, esp. ch. 1; Jodi Bilinkoff, *The Avila of Saint Teresa: Religious Reform in a Sixteenth-Century City* (Ithaca, NY: Cornell University Press, 1989), esp. ch. 5.
[22] Ozment, *Mysticism and Dissent*, pp. 1–3.

continued to generate exterior forms, which played a positive and creative role in reform, not just a negative and critical one. I now turn to some examples of these new trajectories.

TERESA OF AVILA AND JOHN OF THE CROSS (SIXTEENTH-CENTURY SPAIN)

Teresa of Avila met John of the Cross in 1567, while he was a young Carmelite studying at the University of Salamanca. She invited him to join her in the reform of the order, which she had begun with the foundation of Saint Joseph's monastery in Avila in 1562. Teresa and John were united in their desire to train Carmelites in mystical prayer through a renewal of primitive community discipline and individual spiritual direction. They were driven by a high optimism about the possibility for the transformation of the human person into the likeness of God.

Tensions are evident in their conceptions of the spiritual life. John frames his *Ascent of Mount Carmel* and *Dark Night* using a dialectic of darkness and light, reflecting his paradoxical combination of a high anthropology of humanity transformed in mystical union with an Augustinian pessimism about the capabilities of unaided human nature. The sensory and spiritual deprivation of the "dark night of the soul" is paradoxically combined with the "light" of unmediated contact with God.[23] Similarly, though without the metaphor of darkness, Teresa emphasizes the shift from natural states of prayer to supernatural states using the language of ecstasy. The pain and disruption of ecstasy, like the deprivation of dark night, are regarded as the grace of mystical contact with the transcendent God.[24] The result for both mystics is to put their anthropology under great strain, as the interior of the soul enters into mystical contact with God, while the exterior is left behind, paralyzed in ecstasy or plunged in the oblivion of the dark night.[25] The effect, at this crucial stage of mystical transformation, is to set the mystic apart from involvement in the outside world, leaving the interior, as John writes, "hanging in mid-air."[26]

---

[23] See John of the Cross, *Dark Night*, bk. 2, ch. 5, para. 2, in *The Collected Works of Saint John of the Cross*, trans. Kieran Kavanaugh and Otilio Rodriguez (Washington, DC: Institute of Carmelite Studies, 1979), p. 335.
[24] See Teresa of Avila, *Life*, ch. 10, para. 1, p. 105.
[25] Edward Howells, *John of the Cross and Teresa of Avila: Mystical Knowing and Selfhood* (New York: Crossroad, 2002), pp. 1–8.
[26] John of the Cross, *Dark Night*, bk. 2, ch. 6, para. 5, p. 339.

It would be hard to find a stronger statement of the discontinuity between interior life with God and exterior engagement in the world. The need to challenge the exterior realm as spiritually deceptive and lacking in authenticity stands at the heart of the Carmelites' project. But instead of rejecting special forms of religious life, they sought a radical reform of the order, making it an engine house for mystical transformation.

The painstaking resolution of the tension between interior union and exterior reformation is charted in Teresa's writings, as she moves from a purely ecstatic view of union with God as an escape from the world, in her first major work, the *Life* (1562–5), to a reconciled view of union as combining action and contemplation in the *Interior Castle* (1577). The change comes about through intense work on her initially divided anthropology, whereby she reaches an understanding of Christ as already present, though unrecognized, in the center of the soul before mystical transformation begins, rather than as exterior to the soul and reached only in ecstatic union. This means that when the soul, in union, joins Christ in the center, there is not just an unmediated awareness of the presence of God, but an overflow of the Christ-life within her to her body and to the world in exterior good works.[27] This was the breakthrough that Teresa required to make sense of her work as a reformer. She could then see the work of reform as flowing seamlessly from, even if still in tension with, her life in union with God. A parallel but less pronounced progress is seen in John's writings as he moves from the key moment of withdrawal in the suffering of the dark night to the reintegration of the soul with exterior activity in the later stages of the mystical journey.[28]

This combination of the interior and the exterior is clear in Teresa's model of community. On the one hand, her reformed communities are constituted in reaction to a society and church ridden with divisive concepts of honor, racial persecution of Jews and Muslims, and the oppression of women as intellectually and morally inferior to men. Her reaction is an interior one, setting her understanding of union with God as a relationship of mutuality and friendship over against the inequalities of her outer circumstances. On the other hand, she finds a way to

---

[27] Teresa of Avila, *Interior Castle*, in *The Collected Works of St. Teresa of Avila*, vol. 2, bk. 7.
[28] John of the Cross, *The Spiritual Canticle*, stanza 31, para. 4, p. 532 and stanza 36, para. 4, pp. 546–7; John of the Cross, *Living Flame of Love*, stanza 1, para. 36, p. 595. The parallel move can be seen in Teresa of Avila, *Interior Castle*, bk. 7, ch. 3, para. 8–9, pp. 440–1 and bk. 7, ch. 4, para. 10–11, pp. 447–8.

channel her interior life into a new model of community, specifying that her communities must be communities of equals, free from considerations of wealth or social status, having everything in common, and observing strict enclosure in order to cultivate the life of prayer free from divisive external social interference.[29] Thus she moves from a reactive and interior conception of the religious life to a kind of social reform, intended as a corrective to Spanish society and the church, making concrete the mystical insight that God is with the soul in an equal union of love. Her interior journey becomes part of the wider Catholic Reformation, in continuity with Spanish religious reforms earlier in the century, yet only by means of mystical insights that remain critical of and in tension with that society.

Thus Teresa and John combine extreme interiority with exterior reforming activity. The dialectic of inner and outer is accentuated to its breaking point in Teresa's ecstasies and John's dark night. But this tension is reconfigured as a new kind of equal relationality, moving beyond the apparently destructive opposition between interior and exterior, to a creative reform of the Order. Drawing on traditional currents in late medieval mysticism to develop a deep interiority, they then move out of this interior in a reforming activity at once critical of and in continuity with the Catholic Reformation.

LUTHER (1483–1546)

Luther was engaged in a similar democratizing agenda, though with the laity at its center. His view was unusual in two respects. First, he wanted to abolish all hierarchy between religious, priests, and laity, arguing that the distinctions were of function only, not degrees of spiritual perfection.[30] Second, he emphasized faith as the full attainment of justification, as opposed to seeing justification as a journey, through works and further grace, to a higher goal of perfection or union with God.[31] The latter had serious consequences for conceptions of Christian perfection. If the completion of Christian life (this side of heaven) is in the attainment of a single step of faith, the further step of mystical transformation into God is ruled out.

---

[29] Bilinkoff, *The Avila of Saint Teresa*, pp. 123–51.
[30] Martin Luther, *The Freedom of a Christian*, in *Martin Luther: Selections from His Writings*, ed. John Dillenberger (New York: Doubleday, 1961), pp. 63–5.
[31] Steven E. Ozment, "*Homo viator*: Luther and Late Medieval Theology," in *Reformation in Medieval Perspective*, ed. Steven E. Ozment (Chicago: Quadrangle Books, 1971), pp. 142–54.

At the root of Luther's theology was his focus on the "alien" nature of the grace given in faith. God is hidden from us and wills to be unknown by us, even in faith. All we see of God is his "clothing and display" in his Word, which is found clearly only in scripture.[32] The object of faith is the concrete form of the human Christ, revealed through scripture, who then "covers" our sinful nature with his perfect flesh.[33] Righteousness comes from nothing we contribute but only from God, imputed as "passive" or "alien" righteousness, from outside our nature.[34] Ontologically, there is no sharing or likeness of natures between God and human, and no participation of human nature in the divine nature, except in the person of Christ, who becomes our "covering," remaining external to us rather than transforming us interiorly. From this follows Luther's famous *simul justus et peccator* (at once just and a sinner): we are truly given God's righteousness and are fully justified, but we remain sinful (this side of heaven), only "covered" in justice by Christ.[35]

For the Council of Trent, seeking to summarize the Catholic response to Luther later in the sixteenth century, this was a rejection of the reality of justification as something that changes the human person within.[36] But there was a strong current of mystical interiority in Luther's thought. His emphasis on the external Christ is offset by the language of "union with Christ":

> Faith ... unites the soul with Christ as a bride is united with her bridegroom. By this mystery, as the Apostle teaches, Christ and the soul become one flesh [Eph 5:31–2]. And if they are one flesh and there is between them a true marriage ... it follows that everything they have they hold in common, the good as well as the evil. Accordingly the believing soul can boast of a glory in whatever Christ has as though it were its own, and whatever the soul has Christ claims as his own.[37]

Christ and the soul share all that they possess. The justice that Christ has in full becomes the soul's possession in the relational sense of bridal

---

[32] Martin Luther, *The Bondage of the Will*, in *Selections*, ed. Dillenberger, pp. 190–1.
[33] Martin Luther, *The Commentary on Galatians*, in *Selections*, ed. Dillenberger, p. 112.
[34] Ibid., pp. 106–7.
[35] Ibid., p. 111.
[36] Council of Trent, "Decree on Justification," ch. X, in *The Christian Faith: In the Doctrinal Documents of the Catholic Church*, ed. J. Neuner and J. Dupuis (London: Collins Liturgical, 1983), para. 1937.
[37] Luther, *The Freedom of a Christian*, in *Selections*, ed. Dillenberger, p. 60.

union, contrary to Catholic misunderstanding at Trent. The difference from previous understandings of mystical union, however, is that the soul possesses everything that Christ possesses relationally, without becoming Christ in a union of likeness. For Luther, to seek anything beyond a relationship with God mediated by faith is to deny the democratic singularity of faith and the God-given limits of human nature in the order of redemption. "High mysticism," as Oberman calls it – the infusion of contemplation in unmediated contact with God, including claims to extraordinary personal experience – is ruled out, as beyond the appointed means of access to God through faith alone.[38] Instead of bringing the full interiority of mystical union, as an ontological transformation, into the center of Christian life – the route taken by Teresa and John – Luther uses the same democratic imperative to argue for the exclusion of such ontological transformation. His understanding of justification by faith – of the *"simul"* – renders it impossible for our nature to be raised into unmediated likeness with God's being. Human beings must remain outside God, united to God only through the external Christ. The same is true of John Calvin (1509–64), who speaks of "union with Christ" and uses the term "mystical union," while excluding the ontological transformation of human nature.[39] This was typical of the magisterial Reformers.

But the mystical interior remains in evidence in Luther's thought. Further mystical resonances reached him through the *Theologia Deutsch* (*The German Theology*), the key text for German mysticism in the late medieval period, and through Tauler.[40] The *Theologia Deutsch* taught a kind of resignation and self-abandonment (*Gelassenheit*) that leads to an interior union with the Father, understood as suffering the cross of Christ.[41] Through "becoming nought," self-will is vanquished and the will is left in freedom and rest, finding its true source in the Father, who is revealed in the soul, in a union of the soul with the Father.[42] Luther took from this an emphasis on the interior suffering of the cross and on the need to transcend human boundaries in "darkness," a view that he recognized as derived from Dionysius, even as he rejected Dionysius's

---

[38] Oberman, "*Simul Gemitus et Raptus*," pp. 142–3.
[39] Dennis E. Tamburello, *Union with Christ: John Calvin and the Mysticism of St. Bernard* (Louisville, KY: Westminster John Knox Press, 1994), ch. 5.
[40] Alois Haas, cited by Bernard McGinn, *The Presence of God: A History of Western Christian Mysticism*, vol. 4, *The Harvest of Mysticism in Medieval Germany (1300–1500)* (New York: Crossroad, 2005), p. 392.
[41] *Theologia Deutsch*, chs. 7–8, in *Late Medieval Mysticism*, ed. Ray C. Petry (London: SCM, 1957).
[42] Ibid., ch. 51, 53.

"speculations."[43] He denied only the ontological participative element of Dionysian union, rejecting Tauler's Eckhartian anthropology of the divine ground in the soul (*Seelengrund*).[44] Instead of seeing the negativity and suffering of the interior of the soul in ontological terms, as an interior penetration into the divine nature, he saw this negativity as motivating the soul to flee to God, who remains exterior, hidden on the cross.[45] Ontological union is meticulously avoided.

Luther begins a trajectory that, while containing mystical elements, cuts off the key ontological aspect of the late medieval and early modern mystical tradition. Yet faith is the attainment of a democratized form of interiority that transforms all Christians. The area of faith was broadened, making a new kind of union with Christ and the existential intensity of mystical interiority widely available and extending it to those in the secular realm.

THE RADICAL REFORMERS

Different solutions to the tension between reform and the heritage of late medieval mysticism were being experimented with during the sixteenth century. There is such diversity among the so-called radical reformers that they are hard to categorize. At the heart of the Radical Reformation, however, may be identified the democratizing agenda with which we are now familiar, although here understood as interior access to the Holy Spirit and the "inner Word," rather than, as with the magisterial reformers, as access to the external means of scripture and the historical Christ. The radical reformers split away from both the magisterial reformers and the Catholics for a variety of reasons linked to their rejection of exterior forms in favor of interior access to the truth. The first Anabaptists, for instance, separated from Zwingli in Zurich over the payment of taxes, objecting to the town council's failure to forbid the practice of the Catholic mass.[46] They withdrew into communities of the elect, marked by adult baptism and uncompromised by dealings with the secular government. They rejected any spiritual

---

[43] Oberman, "*Simul Gemitus et Raptus*," pp. 131–3.

[44] Ibid., p. 138; and see also Bernard McGinn, "*Vere tu es Deus absconditus*: The Hidden God in Luther and Some Mystics," in *Silence and the Word: Negative Theology and Incarnation*, ed. Oliver Davies and Denys Turner (Cambridge: Cambridge University Press, 2002), p. 111.

[45] McGinn, "*Vere tu es Deus absconditus*," pp. 94–114.

[46] James M. Stayer, Werner O. Packull, and Klaus Depperman, "From Monogenesis to Polygenesis: The Historical Discussion of Anabaptist Origins," *Mennonite Quarterly Review* 49 (1975): 93–4.

hierarchy between pastor and laity, stressing the immanence of God in every person. They did not want their freedom from the old Catholic hierarchies to be replaced by new mediating bodies and rejected the close relationship with the state adopted by the magisterial reformers.[47] Groups of radicals spread over South Germany, Austria, Switzerland, and the Netherlands during the 1520s and 1530s, with various theological and social emphases, some in conflict with each other. These reformers did share, however, certain attitudes toward medieval and early modern mystical traditions.

A central example of the mysticism of the Radical Reformation is to be found in a key early figure in southern Germany, Hans Denck (ca. 1500–27). Denck was repeatedly expelled by Lutheran city councils for his public insistence on the interior authority of the spiritual person and the invisibility of truth, over and above outward forms, especially that of scripture.[48] The greatest mystical influence on Denck, as on Luther, was the *Theologia Deutsch*. From it, he took the view that inner freedom is gained by the "letting go" (*Gelassenheit*) of attachment to external circumstances, following Christ's example of subjugating self-will to the Father's will and yielding willingly to adversity when it comes. "God's breaking, as it seems to us, is the best making," Denck writes, and thus we appropriate "the bitter cross."[49] But unlike Luther, Denck takes up the *Theologia Deutcsh*'s Neoplatonic scheme of flowing back into the Father. When it seems God has forsaken us and we are in hell, the dawn breaks and we see God as he is, born in us as in Jesus.[50] This theme of the birth of the Word in the soul (*Gottesgeburt*) was prominent in late medieval German mysticism, closely connected to the *Seelengrund*, the breaking through of awareness of the divine ground in the soul. Denck speaks of "God's seed," the "little spark" of uncreated divine love in the soul, and of God being within the soul "without intermediary," an awareness of which is attained through being brought to nought, in the bitter taste of Christ's life.[51]

---

[47] George Huntston Williams, *Radical Reformation*, 3rd ed. (Kirksville, MO: Sixteenth Century Journal Publishers, 1992), p. 1.

[48] Ozment, *Mysticism and Dissent*, pp. 116–36.

[49] Hans Denck, *Whether God Is the Cause of Evil*, in *Spiritual and Anabaptist Writers*, ed. G. H. Williams and A. M. Mergal (Philadelphia: Westminster Press, 1957), p. 95.

[50] *Theologia Deutsch*, chs. 51, 53. See Hans Denck's *Divine Order*, in *Selected Writings of Hans Denck 1500–1527*, ed. E. J. Furcha (Lewiston, NY: Edwin Mellen Press, 1989).

[51] Variously in Denck's *The Law of God*, *Divine Order*, and *Concerning Genuine Love*, in Denck, *Selected Writings*, ed. E. J. Furcha.

For radicals such as Denck, the full interiority of late medieval mysticism, as immediate participation in Christ's human-divine union, remains central to their conception of the religious life. Scripture and the preaching of Christ take precedence over the authority of tradition, but they are in turn subjugated to the authority of the interior realm. For Denck, the priority given to the interior realm was problematic, cutting off the exterior altogether. He refused, for instance, to say whether he was fully an Anabaptist, on the grounds that the Holy Spirit alone has the whole truth; only in the last year of his life did he concede that there may be a link between inner and outer baptism, which might furnish an argument against infant baptism.[52] He was distraught at the disagreements among Anabaptists at the "Martyr's Synod" in Augsburg in August 1527, and abandoned Anabaptism, saying that it could not be the will of God because it led to strife. Yet he had no suggestion as to how agreement might be found, other than repeated claims for the authority of the inner spiritual person. It appears that the interior and the exterior could not be reconciled in his thought in ways that might lead to an effective program of reform. The divisiveness and fragmentation of much of the Radical Reformation seems to owe something to this appropriation of mystical interiority in its full, ontological depth, without developing sufficient means of adjudicating rival claims that might mediate between interior inspiration and exterior life.

Other radicals were more successful, however, in finding new external forms that adjudicated effectively between differing claims to interior authority. In general, radicals sought a return to the primitive community life of the New Testament, many groups seeking a restoration of the community of goods described in Acts 2 and 4. Among south and central German Anabaptists, the mystical piety of *Gelassenheit* was channeled into renunciation of ties to material possessions in a communist spirituality. The group that came to be called the Moravians lived in economic units of about five hundred people and engaged in advanced craft production. They came to be an enduring example of this movement.[53] Their democratic, lay spirituality was centered on the interior, immediate relationship of the soul with Christ, attained by journeying through trials to a life-changing personal experience of Christ. Count von Zinzendorf (1700–60), who revitalized the Moravians in the early eighteenth century, spoke of the "moment" in which Christ was

---

[52] Denck, *Divine Order*, in Denck, *Selected Writings*, ed. E. J. Furcha.
[53] James M. Stayer, "Anabaptists," in *The Oxford Encyclopedia of the Reformation*, vol. I, p. 33.

"before the vision of one's heart, before the eyes of one's spirit, before one's inner man," in the manner of John in Revelation 1:10: "I was in the Spirit on the Lord's day."[54] Scripture and reason were regarded as valuable but radically inferior to this interior immediacy of the soul with Christ.

George Fox (1624–91), whose preaching led to the formation of the Society of Friends, or Quakers, in mid-seventeenth-century England, based his teaching on a similar "experimental knowledge" of Christ, which he contrasted with anything that can be obtained from other people, or "in the natural state, or ... from history or books."[55] The strong tension between the fire of Christ within and exterior forms was mediated for the Quakers not by forming a community segregated from the world – they remained engaged in secular society and employment – but by their distinctive communal practice. Here, an apophatic rejection of words was combined with a high theological anthropology of immediate interior participation in the divine-human union – the "light" or "seed" within – and discerned through the communal meeting, which was designed to channel this hidden source of inspiration into exterior life.

The meeting became an effective tool of spiritual discernment, allowing the interior light to be mediated in distinctive forms of life. Differing individual inspirations or "leadings" were subject to communal discernment in the "business meeting," which began and ended with silence and was understood as an act of worship. Unity was sought without voting, by coming to agreement on decisions in common once individuals had spoken. All were permitted to contribute, including women. Though conflicts arose and central organization was increasingly imposed from above during the seventeenth century, the local meeting remained the focus of authority, producing distinctive Quaker practices and social action.[56] An interior mysticism was thus cultivated and given exterior expression. For both the Quakers and the Moravians, the priority of interior mystical inspiration was retained, but also reconstituted in new forms of community.

[54] Nicolas Ludwig, Count von Zinzendorf, "From Nine Public Lectures 1746," in *Pietists: Selected Writings*, ed. Peter C. Erb (New York: Paulist Press, 1983), p. 319.

[55] George Fox, *George Fox: An Autobiography*, ed. Rufus M. Jones (Philadelphia: Friends' Book Store, 1903), pp. 82–3.

[56] See Michael J. Sheeran, *Beyond Majority Rule: Voteless Decisions in the Religious Society of Friends* (Philadelphia: Philadelphia Yearly Meeting of the Religious Society of Friends, 1983), pt. I; and Rosemary Moore, *The Light in Their Consciences: The Early Quakers in Britain 1646–1666* (University Park: Pennsylvania State University Press, 2000).

Early Modern Reformations 131

Thus the radicals were true heirs to late medieval mysticism in their stress on the immediate union of the soul with Christ as an interior, spiritual possession, contrasted with the exterior mediation of scripture, tradition, church authority, and practices. In some cases, this tension failed to move beyond sheer opposition, but gradually, exterior forms were developed in which to safeguard and cultivate the new inspiration. Denck's emphasis on the interior gave no concrete outlet to mysticism, but others developed new exterior forms that sustained its paradoxical character, such as the Moravians' segregated lay community and the Quakers' silent meeting.

PIERRE CARDINAL DE BÉRULLE (1575–1629)

We have seen that the age of reform produced a tension between interior union and a democratizing agenda that required new exterior forms in order to attain viable new settings for mystical faith and practice. Within Roman Catholicism, there were attempts, such as those of Teresa of Avila and John of the Cross, to reestablish the link between mystical life and the existing ecclesiastical apparatus, though these were hampered by anxiety over questions of doctrine.[57] At the end of the sixteenth century, the mantle of Catholic reforming innovation passed from Spain to France. An example of the way in which the exterior structures of reform were combined with the interior springs of mysticism is found in the work of Pierre de Bérulle. An aristocrat related to Barbe Acarie (later Marie of the Incarnation, 1566–1618) and part of her famous Parisian *salon* of spiritual reformers, Pierre de Bérulle was the founder of the French Oratory (1611) for the training of priests, France's response to the educational reforms of the Council of Trent.[58] Bérulle, an admirer of Teresa's writings, was also instrumental in bringing Spanish nuns from Teresa's monasteries to Paris in order to begin the reform of the French Carmelites on the Teresian model (1604). Bérulle was a public figure and a cardinal, engaged in controversies with French Protestants and in French politics. Yet he was also a prolific mystical writer. His thought is characterized by a dilemma. On the one hand, Bérulle draws on late medieval and early modern conceptions of mysticism, which he encountered in popular mystical compendia. On the other hand, there is an emphasis on meditation on Christ's life and passion, which he

---

[57] Michel de Certeau, *The Mystic Fable, vol. 1, The Sixteenth and Seventeenth Centuries*, trans. Michael B. Smith (Chicago: Chicago University Press, 1992), p. 86.
[58] Cognet, *Post-Reformation Spirituality*, pp. 69–76.

adopted from the now highly popular *Spiritual Exercises* of Ignatius Loyola (1491–1556).

Bérulle sought to put the human Christ first, as a corrective to the problematic separation of the interior from the exterior that he perceived in much mysticism of the period. In his greatest mystical work, the *Discourse on the State and Grandeurs of Jesus* (1623), he begins with incarnation as the point of divine-human unity both given in revelation and the focus of our devotion.[59] We enter into the incarnation by meditating, in Ignatian fashion, on the "states" of Jesus's life and matching them to our own, particularly his states of adoration and servitude.[60] The "states" draw us into the human-divine union at Christ's center, but only through a concrete relationship between our humanity and Christ's humanity, and never as an interior reality alone.

Bérulle's emphasis on the "states" centers on the kenosis (emptying) of Christ in radical dispossession, which is the model for our own *anéantissement*, or self-abnegation. The influence of late medieval mysticism, with its emphasis on the inner suffering of the cross, is clear here. But from, our side of the relationship with Christ, *anéantissement* remains a concrete, human attitude rather than a simple unmediated possession of divinity. It is only in "pure relationship" with Christ – a human relationship of complete self-abnegation – that we join Christ in his ontological union with the Father. The full depth of interior mystical union is granted, but interiority is tied inseparably to relational sharing at the human level. In this, Bérulle has an interesting connection with Luther, setting the concrete contingencies of the relationship of the human pilgrim with the humanity of Christ "between" the soul and God. But he then argues that, if the relationship is constituted by complete mutual dispossession, it can be both fully human and a sharing of the interior life of Christ in his divine relationship with the Father.

Bérulle's ability to hold together the interior and the exterior in his mystical anthropology allows him to extend his mysticism into a program of reform. This can be seen in three ways. First, Bérulle brings mystical interiority to the heart of his reform of the clergy in founding the French Oratory, which in turn led to other new congregations of clergy in France. As well as introducing the educational objectives of Trent, these congregations spread a mystical spirituality characterized

---

[59] Pierre de Bérulle, *Discourse on the State and Grandeurs of Jesus* 1:2, in *Bérulle and the French School: Selected Writings*, trans. Lowell M. Glendon (New York: Paulist Press, 1989), p. 109.

[60] Bérulle, *Grandeurs* 2:5, p. 117; 2:6, p. 121; 2:13, p. 126; and 6:1, pp. 138–9.

by interior *anéantissement* and exterior devotion to the human Christ. Importantly, this was mysticism not just for contemplatives, but for those primarily engaged in the active life, resulting in a democratization of mysticism beyond that found in Teresa of Avila and John of the Cross. Second, Bérulle used his idea of the "states" to make room for a variety of human vocations, all seen as joining in the mystical life, by referring the different vocations to the various aspects of Christ's life. Every person has a distinct "state" of life to which they are called, linked immediately to the incarnation, and this is part of the organization of creation into different orders, on the model of Dionysius's hierarchies.[61]

Third, Bérulle's firm linkage between human relationality and mystical transformation carries a democratizing potential with radical implications. In arguing that mystical transformation is attained by practicing Christ-like relationality at the human level, characterized by *anéantissement*, he implies that mysticism could be extended beyond the realm of individual relationship with Christ into the wider world of relationships between ordinary human beings. The same kind of relationality on the model of Christ could be lived in relation to any other human, in any place. According to Bérulle's logic, this kind of human relationality would necessarily be accompanied by the same mystical transformation. Bérulle did not go this far: instead, in line with much of the spirituality of his day, he focused on the individual relationship with Jesus and not on its extension to life in the world. But the germ of a full democratization of mysticism was present. The mystical is not tied to a form of life but only to a quality of human relationality; it is this that makes it available to the clergy and not just to those living a formal contemplative life. By the same token, it could be extended to the laity. This was a possibility that, in Roman Catholicism, would only come to fruition with the Second Vatican Council and in the work of theologians central to that council, among them Karl Rahner.[62]

CONCLUSION

Under the combined influences of democratization, laicization, humanist optimism concerning the spiritual possibilities of the human person, and an increasing emphasis on the interior realm as the locus

---

[61] Fernando Guillén Preckler, *"État" chez le cardinal de Bérulle: Théologie et Spiritualité des "États" Bérulliens* (Rome: Università Gregoriana, 1974), pp. 54–5, 165–7.
[62] Philip Endean, *Karl Rahner and Ignatian Spirituality* (Oxford: Oxford University Press, 2001), esp. ch. 3.

of mystical transformation, mysticism changed in the Reformation period, adopting new forms. These may be characterized according to the examples that we have seen. In Roman Catholicism, mysticism tended to be democratized through an intensification of interiority that challenged previous exterior forms, paradoxically allowing a greater union of contemplation with action and furthering the late medieval desire to unite the two forms of life. The reforms of Teresa of Avila and John of the Cross were both conscious reactions to conventional models of social and religious organization and attempts to achieve new integration of contemplation with action. Pierre de Bérulle extended this mystical reform further, moving mysticism into the active sphere, and offering the possibility of a fully democratized mysticism of Christ-like relationality lived out in the world of ordinary human relationships. In the magisterial Reformation, Luther extended mysticism by restricting it, removing the ontological depth of interior union with Christ, but expanding faith into a mystical attainment of Christ's experience on the cross, especially his suffering and darkness, attainable by all. In the Radical Reformation, in spite of great diversity, there was a common harnessing of the inner life of Christ, in the full mystical sense of penetration into the divine-human unity, at first against unwanted institutional authority and exterior forms of practice, but then in new forms of community. Radicals such as the Moravians and the Quakers developed new forms of community that channeled this mystical interiority into distinctive practices. Thus medieval mystical traditions were carried into the Reformation period in a variety of ways. The increasing tension between an interior, unmediated sphere of union with God and the exterior forms of language, practice, and custom by which mysticism was cultivated and expressed produced breaks with earlier periods, but also gave rise to new possibilities, in keeping with the new diversity of church life.

Part II
Key Terms

5 Apophatic and Cataphatic Theology
ANDREW LOUTH

The terminology of "apophatic" and "cataphatic" theologies, that is, the use of negation (*apophasis*) and affirmation (*kataphasis*) in our ways of talking about God, was introduced into Christian theology by the probably early-sixth-century author who wrote under the pseudonym of the Apostle Paul's convert, Dionysius the Areopagite (generally referred to as Pseudo-Dionysius). It was, however, only terminology that Dionysius introduced; the use of negation and affirmation in relation to God had a long history, longer even than Christianity, reaching back into the traditions of the Hebrew scriptures and classical Greek philosophy to which Christian theology had early laid claim. Human beings have always affirmed something of God, either as a result of speculation about the divine or as an affirmation of revelation about God – the Hebrew scriptures contain records claiming to be God's self-revelation, and followers of other religious traditions have both claimed similar revelations and celebrated the divine in hymnic aretalogies, that is, lists of divine virtues. But this affirmation of the divine has always been hedged about by a sense of the mysteriousness of the divine, leading to the negating of any affirmations about God, thereby bearing testimony to the inadequacy of any human conception of God. So a Hebrew prophet exclaims in God's name, "To whom then will you compare me, that I should be like him? says the Holy One" (Is 40:25) and even the revelation of God's name to Moses – "I am that I am" (Ex 3:14) – is an affirmation about God inviting or even requiring an apophatic interpretation. Similarly, within the Greek philosophical tradition, we find Plato asserting in the *Timaeus* that "to discover the Father and Maker of the universe would be some task, and it would be impossible to declare what one had found to everyone" and in *The Republic* that the Idea of the Good, for Plato the highest reality, is "beyond being."[1]

---

[1] Plato, *Timaeus* 28C and *The Republic* 509B, in Plato, *The Complete Works*, ed. John M. Cooper (Indianapolis, IN: Hackett, 1997), pp. 1235–6, 1129–30.

This sense that God is beyond anything we can affirm of him, so that cataphatic theology needs to be qualified by apophatic theology – or, more radically, grounded on apophatic theology – is found (without the specific terminology) in several of the Greek Fathers. Beginning with Clement of Alexandria (ca.150–ca. 215), it is especially strong in the Cappadocian Fathers – Basil of Caesarea (ca. 330–79), his friend Gregory of Nazianzos (330–90), and his younger brother Gregory of Nyssa (ca. 335–ca. 394) – and in their younger contemporary, John Chrysostom (ca. 347–407). Basil introduces the distinction between God's essence and his activities or energies (*energeiai*), declaring that "from his activities we know our God, but his very essence we do not profess to approach. For his activities descend to us, but his essence remains unapproachable." In addition, Basil notes that "knowledge of the divine essence is a sense of his incomprehensibility."[2] Especially in his *Life of Moses*, Gregory of Nyssa sees the ascent of the soul to closer union with God as an advance into an ever-deepening darkness in which the soul is more and more aware of God's utter transcendence and unknowability.

A similar sense of the overwhelming mystery of God is found in John Chrysostom, especially in a series of sermons he preached called *On the Incomprehensibility of God*. For Chrysostom, our knowledge of God is shrouded by a sense of his incomprehensibility: "For I know that God is everywhere and that he is everywhere in his whole being. But I do not know how he is everywhere."[3] This incomprehensibility, however, is not merely a sense of the limitations of reason; it is rather a matter of fear and awe. Commenting on the verses of Psalm 138 – "Knowledge of you has amazed me ... I will confess to you, that you have amazed me fearfully" (Ps 138.6, 14) – he speaks of the "fearful wonder," the sense of vertigo (*ilingos*), at the realization that he has an "incomprehensible Master." Chrysostom exclaims, "His judgments are inscrutable, his ways are unsearchable, his peace surpasses all understanding, his gift is indescribable, what God has prepared for those who love him has not entered into the heart of man, his greatness has no bound, his understanding is infinite."[4] Negative adjectives are formed in Greek by the use of the alpha-privative (e.g., incomprehensible = *akataleptos*);

---

[2] Basil of Caesarea, Letter 234 in *The Letters*, vol. 3, trans. Roy J. Deferrari (Cambridge, MA: Harvard University Press, 1930), pp. 371–7.
[3] John Chrysostom, *On the Incomprehensible Nature of God*, trans. Paul W. Harkins (Washington, DC: The Catholic University of America Press, 1982), I.19, pp. 57–8.
[4] Ibid., I.30, p. 64.

John develops here, and elsewhere, an apophatic theology that might be called a theology of the alpha-privative.

In introducing the terminology of apophatic and cataphatic theology Dionysius was simply introducing a terminology for an already well-established approach to theology. He did not invent this terminology, however, but borrowed (like much else) from the great fifth-century Neoplatonist, Proclus (410 or 412–85), *diadochos* (i.e., Plato's successor) at the Academy at Athens. The importance of negation in our knowledge of God, or the One, was recognized by Plotinus, following Plato. The Neoplatonists, led by Plotinus, found a good deal more apophatic theology in the Platonic dialogues than scholars do nowadays (or indeed, did their predecessors, the so-called Middle Platonists), notably in the latter section of the *Parmenides* concerned with the consequences of positing or denying the One. But it fell to Proclus to introduce the terminology of apophatic and cataphatic theology.

In the second book of his *Platonic Theology*, Proclus says that, according to Plato, the One is elder than intellect or being, and that Plato shows, on the one hand, that the One can be revealed "through analogy (*di' analogias*) and through likeness to what is posterior [to the One]," and, on the other, that "through negations (*dia ton apophaseon*) its transcendence over everything can be shown." Proclus suggests that the first way, that of analogy, is discussed by Plato in the analogy of the sun in the *Republic* (506D–509C), in which the first principle is considered as the Good; the second way, the apophatic, is treated in the second part of the *Parmenides*, in which the first principle is considered as the One. Proclus continues:

> It seems to me that the latter of these modes manifests the procession (*proodos*) from the One of everything else, above all the divine orders, for the reason why it is transcendent over everything that comes into being from it is because the cause is more elevated than any of its effects, and for this reason it is none of all these, because everything proceeds from it. For it is the principle (*arche*) of everything, both beings and non-beings. But the first of these modes gives an image of the return (*epistrophe*) to it of everything that has proceeded from it. Because of the likeness that every rank of being has with the One, there is a monad which is analogous to the Good, which plays for the whole of the series that is united to it the role that the Good plays in relation to the orders of gods, and this likeness is without doubt the reason for the return of everything to the One. Beings do not simply proceed thence, but they return to that

One, and while the procession of everything reveals to us the ascent to the first by way of negations, the return reveals that by way of analogies.[5]

Proclus goes on to warn against interpreting the negations (*apophaseis*) as privations (*stereseis*), or the analogies as identities: both misinterpretations, he says, will frustrate the "journey which raises us towards the first principle." The analogies, he says, are hints or suggestions that point us toward the One, while the negations do not simply contradict affirmations (here Proclus uses the word *kataphasis*), rather, because they are closer to the first principle, they, as it were, underlie and generate affirmations. There are two points to note about Proclus's exposition. First, apophatic and cataphatic (or, for Proclus, analogical) theology belong together (they complement each other) and, furthermore, apophatic theology undergirds cataphatic theology (they do not simply balance each other). Second, the pair constituted by apophatic and cataphatic theology matches the pair procession and return, procession corresponding to apophatic theology and return corresponding to cataphatic theology.

This is very much what we find in Dionysius's use of apophatic and cataphatic theology. They are a pair, and they match the pair, procession-return, though Dionysius switches the match – for Dionysius, apophatic theology corresponding to return and cataphatic theology to procession. Dionysius also emphasizes, as Proclus does, that negations applied to God do not mean that God lacks some quality or another, but that he transcends it. He expresses this conviction by supplementing adjectives prefixed by the alpha-privative with adjectives prefixed by *hyper-* ("beyond").

Dionysius's most explicit discussion of apophatic and cataphatic theology is found in chapter 3 of his short treatise, *Mystical Theology*, which is entitled in some manuscripts, "What Are the Cataphatic Theologies, and What the Apophatic." The cataphatic theologies (in the sense of ways of talking about God) descend from affirmations about the being of God, who is both one and three, through the Incarnation, to the concepts we use of God and the images that scripture applies to him. The further we descend with cataphatic theology, following the way of procession, the more verbose our explanations become, whereas when we trace the way of return, the way of apophatic theology, "the more we take flight upward, the more our words are confined to the ideas we are

---

[5] Proclus, *Platonic Theology* II.5, in *Théologie Platonicienne*, vol. 2, ed. H. D. Saffrey and L. G. Westerink (Paris: Les Belles Lettres, 1974), pp. 37–9. My translation.

capable of forming; so that now as we plunge into that darkness which is beyond intellect, we shall find ourselves not simply running short of words but actually speechless and unknowing."⁶

Dionysius also discusses the nature of apophatic and cataphatic theology elsewhere, for instance in the *Divine Names*, in which he says,

> God is therefore known in all things and as distinct from all things. He is known through knowledge and through unknowing. Of him there is conception, reason, understanding, touch, perception, opinion, imagination, name, and many other things. On the other hand he cannot be understood, words cannot contain him, and no name can lay hold of him. He is not one of the things that are and he cannot be known in any of them. He is all things in all things and he is no thing among things. He is known to all things from all things and he is known to no one from anything.... This is the sort of language we must use about God, for he is praised from all things according to their proportion to him as their Cause. But again, the most divine knowledge of God, that which comes through unknowing, is achieved in a union far beyond mind, when mind turns away from all things, even from itself, and when it is made one with the dazzling rays, being then and there enlightened by the inscrutable depth of Wisdom.⁷

This expresses very clearly two aspects of Dionysius's theology: the complementarity of apophatic and cataphatic theology and the more fundamental truth expressed by the way of negation. The key term here is that of "cause" (*aitia*) applied to God. It is in virtue of God being the cause of all that everything has a relationship to God. Because there is an analogy, in virtue of the relationship everything has to its cause, every affirmation can be made in same way of God. But the term *cause* is also the key to Dionysius's apophatic theology. For God as cause really is the "cause of all," and for that reason does not belong to "the all": "he is not one of the things that are." In virtue of this, any attribute applied to God must be denied of him: he does not belong to the realm from which our concepts and images are derived.

There are some other consequences of Dionysius's understanding of apophatic and cataphatic theology that should be mentioned. The denial and affirmation of images and concepts of God are equally radical: all

---

⁶ Pseudo-Dionysius, *The Mystical Theology*, in *The Complete Works*, trans. Colm Luibhéid (New York: Paulist Press, 1987), ch. 3, p. 139.
⁷ Pseudo-Dionysius, *The Divine Names*, in Pseudo-Dionysius, *The Complete Works*, ch, pp. 108–9, n. 3.

are affirmed, all are denied. It follows that conceptual images are not privileged, and so, as Christos Yannaras has said, "the apophatic attitude leads Christian theology to use the language of poetry and images for the interpretation of dogmas much more than the language of conventional logic and schematic concepts."[8] It is in praising him that we celebrate what we can affirm of God, not merely by logical predication. For Dionysius theology is doxology.

This understanding of apophatic and cataphatic theology became part of the heritage of Byzantine theology. The most striking evidence for this is to be found in the liturgical poetry of the Byzantine Church, which developed in the centuries following Dionysius. Dionysius's cumbersome language of "beyond being" (*hyperousios*), "beyond deity" (*hypertheos*), and "beyond goodness" (*hyperagathos*) was gleefully picked up by the poets, and became common in Byzantine hymnography; it serves to celebrate a mystery beyond conceptual expression.

Dionysius's pairing of apophatic and cataphatic theology is developed in a quite original way by Maximus the Confessor, the greatest of Byzantine theologians, who lived a century or more after Dionysius. In his meditation on the Transfiguration of Christ, Maximus sees in the blinding light that flows from the face of Christ a negation of human comprehension that thus grasps the Divine Person there revealed, while the radiance of his garments symbolizes the cataphatic revelation of God's glory. Light is naturally experienced as illuminating, but it can also be experienced as overwhelming – as a blinding darkness, Dionysius's "darkness beyond radiance" (*hyperphotos gnophos*), rendered into English by the seventeenth-century poet Henry Vaughan as "dazzling darkness." The experience of God as light, of which the Transfiguration is a preeminent type, is thus an experience that can be understood as combining the cataphatic and apophatic, both revealing and withdrawing beyond comprehension – or revealing precisely as unknowable mystery, as Dionysius himself interprets the Incarnation.

The experience of light becomes increasingly central to Byzantine mysticism: an experience uniting apophasis and cataphasis. At the turn of the millennium, there is the powerful and controversial figure of Symeon the New Theologian (949–1022). Three centuries later, claims by monks of the monastic communities of Mount Athos ("hesychasts") to experience God himself in uncreated light, as at the Transfiguration, led to full-blown controversy. Gregory Palamas (ca. 1296–1359) defended

---

[8] Christos Yannaras, *Elements of Faith: An Introduction to Orthodox Theology* (Edinburgh: T. and T. Clark, 1991), p. 17.

the experience of the hesychasts and his conviction of the unknowability of the divine essence by developing the distinction made centuries earlier by Basil the Great between God's essence, which is unknowable, and his activities or energies in which he makes himself known.

The West only came to learn of the notions of Dionysius when his works were translated into Latin, first in the ninth century by Abbot Hilduin of the abbey of Saint Denys (who now combined the identities of the martyr of Paris, the early bishop of Athens and Paul's convert, and the author of the Dionysian corpus) – a translation later in that century revised by John Eriugena, and again revised in the twelfth century by John the Saracen. Eriugena's own highly elaborate theology incorporated much of the Dionysian vision, including the twin concepts of apophatic and cataphatic theology, but his influence was limited. The real influence of Dionysius and his notion of apophatic and cataphatic theology only occurred during the twelfth century, profoundly influencing the Victorines and their successors.

The West, however, had its own tradition of the incomprehensibility of God, powerfully articulated by Augustine (d. 430), innocent of the Dionysian terminology. During the twelfth century, the recently recovered Dionysian vision came to be seen with eyes formed on Augustinian premises. Dionysius fed the developing scholastic tradition and the reaction to that found in the so-called mystical tradition of the late Middle Ages. For the scholastics, the distinction between apophatic and cataphatic theology became a logical dialectic by which theological language was refined; for the mystics, the distinction between cataphatic and apophatic became a gulf between a superficial theology of affirmation, which was thought to reduce God to rational categories and a loving abandonment to God in a felt experience of darkness, disorientation, bewilderment, and ecstasy. In this mystical tradition, cataphatic and apophatic are torn apart: the cataphatic reduced to the operations of the reasoning mind, the apophatic to be explored only by love, which in its longing after God penetrates the darkness. So the author of the fourteenth-century *Cloud of Unknowing* asserts that "of God himself can no man think.... Whence he may well be loved, but not thought. By love may be he gotten and holden; but by thought never."[9]

The different ways of interpreting Dionysius that emerge in the West may be symbolized by the way in which Dionysius's *Divine Names* became the focus for a scholastic exercise in predication of God's properties, while the *Mystical Theology* became a handbook for

---

[9] *Cloud of Unknowing*, ed. James Walsh (New York: Paulist Press, 1981), p. 6.

the mystic. The author of *The Cloud* knew (or made) a translation into Middle English of the edition of the *Mystical Theology* (which he called *Hid Divinitie*) that included a commentary interpreting the treatise as a guide to the darkness of unknowing, in which the soul is inwardly united with God in ecstatic love. In the West, the mystical tradition continued (and continues) to harbour suspicions about an all-too-cataphatic scholastic theology, to which it opposes its own practice of a loving pursuit of God. The contrast should not be overdrawn; the greatest scholastics, such as Bonaventure (d. 1274), Thomas Aquinas (d. 1274), and Meister Eckhart (d. 1328), preserve at the heart of their theology a sense of the apophatic, though the mistrust of scholasticism in the emerging late medieval mystical tradition is fairly consistent.

During the twentieth century, appeal to apophatic theology became characteristic of much Eastern Orthodox theology, both among the Russians, expelled from their homeland by the Communist Revolution and encountering in the West a rather-too-confident and overdefined Roman Catholic theology, and among other Orthodox, seeking to escape the just-as-overdefined Orthodox theology that had emerged as Orthodoxy sought to understand itself during the seventeenth century in distinction from Western Catholicism and Protestantism. These modern Orthodox understandings of apophatic theology were articulated in significantly different ways. The Romanian theologian, Father Dumitru Stăniloae, regarded the apophatic as the obscurely felt presence of God, experienced in a multitude of ways – in worship, in prayer, in the sense that our everyday experience of life has an undefinable element manifest in a sense of providential guidance or being checked – that we try, inadequately, to articulate in the cataphatic language of revelation and theology. It is by no means confined to the mystical, or perhaps better, the mystical needs to be redefined to embrace not only experiences of awe and ecstasy but also our obscure sense of being guided, checked, and snatched out of ourselves by experiences of beauty, love, and attention.

The Greek theologian Christos Yannaras makes a distinction between what he calls an "apophaticism of essence" and an "apophaticism of the person." The former apophaticism is well-known in the Western philosophical/theological tradition and took the form of a dialectic between cataphatic and apophatic theology, in which the apophatic checks the cataphatic and leads to knowledge of God by way of analogy. The latter apophaticism is the tradition of the Greek East, and speaks instead of the inexhaustibility of our understanding of the personal, of the person encountered in an experience of ecstatic self-transcendence in love (*eros*). Yannaras finds this apophaticism in the Greek Christian tradition reaching from the Cappadocian Fathers, through Dionysius and Maximus, to Gregory Palamas, who, with his distinction between essence and energies, safeguarded the apophaticism of the person.

Furthermore, this apophaticism of the person provides a response to the challenge to the whole Western philosophical tradition posed by Friedrich Nietzsche (1844–1900) and Martin Heidegger (1889–1976) (as well as Jean-Paul Sartre [1905–80]), a challenge that Yannaras interprets as exposing the emptiness of the Western concept of God, reduced to a being among beings, albeit very exalted. For Yannaras, Nietzsche, Heidegger, and Sartre face, with some courage, the only alternative they can find to this empty concept of God – the nihilism of a literally godless world. This is, Yannaras argues, the inexorable entailment of the apophaticism of essence; the alternative is to be found in the apophaticism of the person, which reveals a universe of persons, irreducible to one another, and finding meaning in their mutual ecstatic encounter in love, a love whose reality is grounded in the creative, self-emptying love of God.

Perhaps the exponent of Orthodox apophatic theology best known in the West is the Russian émigré theologian, Vladimir Lossky, who died in Paris in 1958, before Yannaras discovered his theological vocation or Stăniloae became known outside Romania. For Lossky, Orthodox theology is characterized by its sense of the apophatic, in contrast to an all-too-cataphatic Western theology. He expounds the apophatic, closely following Dionysius, emphasizing the primacy of the apophatic as undergirding anything we might say about God cataphatically. Like Stăniloae and Yannaras, the apophatic discloses a sense of the mystery of the person, which is grounded in the mystery of the three-personed Trinity. But here his sense of the place of the apophatic takes on a quite distinctive dimension. As he puts it in his epoch-making book, *The Mystical Theology of the Eastern Church*:

> Apophaticism, so far from being a limitation [to knowledge], enables us to transcend all concepts, every sphere of philosophical speculation. It is a tendency towards an ever-greater plenitude, in which knowledge is transformed into ignorance, the theology of concepts into contemplation, dogmas into experience of ineffable mysteries. It is, moreover, an existential theology involving man's entire being, which sets him upon the way of union, which obliges him to be changed, to transform his nature that he may attain to the

true gnosis which is contemplation of the Holy Trinity. Now, this "change of heart", this *metanoia*, means repentance. The apophatic way of Eastern theology is the repentance of the human person before the face of the living God.[10]

In conclusion, the distinction between apophatic and cataphatic theology, based on a logical distinction drawn by Aristotle, transferred to theology by the Neoplatonists, adopted in Christian theology by Dionysius the Areopagite, proved astonishingly fruitful, not least because it gave words to something fundamental to the human – and not just Christian – encounter with God, to what Rudolf Otto called the *mysterium tremendum atque fascinosum*. It expressed a revelation that overwhelms, an engagement that leaves a sense of withdrawal, for there is always more to experience; it calls on the imagination to interpret a richness of experience that cannot be reduced to rational categories, a richness that borders on – or rather clearly transgresses – the paradoxical, as in the widespread imagery and experience of a "dazzling darkness." It has quarried in the West a sense of the inward, already opened up by the questing spirit of Augustine. It has paved the way for a sense of the personal, based on an experience of ecstatic encounter in love. Its baffling affirmation of a God who "is not" resists the too-human tendency, never fully checked in the West, to be satisfied with a God who too comfortably "is," and then is too easily dispensed with. Its capacity to hold one before the inexhaustible depths of the reality of God, who is more real than anything we can know or imagine, is not likely to have been exhausted.

---

[10] Vladimir Lossky, *The Mystical Theology of the Eastern Church*, trans. Fellowship of Saint Albans and Saint Sergius (London: James Clarke and Co., 1957), p. 238.

6 Lectio Divina

E. ANN MATTER

There is a profound connection between medieval Christian mysticism and the traditions of biblical exegesis that grew up over the course of the Middle Ages; *lectio divina*, the prayerful study of scripture, lies in the middle. This system of meditation on passages in the Bible, sometimes extended to texts based on biblical passages and redolent of biblical language, is rooted in ancient ascetic discipline and is still practiced by Christians today, but it had its most important and formative period in the monastic world of the Middle Ages, when prayerful study and recitation of parts of the Bible was part of the everyday experience of monks and nuns.

It is important to understand what sort of Bible inspired the *lectio divina*. First of all, in the monastery, the Bible was mostly known through liturgy and devotional practices. As the great scholar of medieval monasticism Jean LeClercq pointed out, medieval monastics needed to know how to read so that they could participate in the *lectio divina*, and this *lectio* was primarily engaged through reading out loud. Later, in the world of the medieval schools and incipient universities, *lectio divina* came to be understood as part of *sacra pagina*, the study of the Bible for its own sake and for the sake of knowledge of the text, as well as texts that were directly inspired by the Bible, such as devotional treatises and homilies. But in the monastic world, *lectio divina* is centered on spiritual experience, especially the arousal of compunction, the desire for heaven.

It is also important to realize that the medieval Bible was physically different from a modern Bible. The Christian Bible came together over the first three centuries of the tradition, a composite of the inherited Jewish scriptures, originally in the Greek version known as the Septuagint, with the addition of the specifically Christian New Testament books. The medieval Bible was not often found in one complete volume, what is called a pandect. When we think of a Bible, we probably think of a book, one book; but for medieval Christians, the

Bible was more like a "*biblioteca,*" a library. Only in a few high points of medieval culture was there an effort to copy the Bible in one collection; for the most part, biblical books circulated in manuscripts of one book or several examples of one type of book. There were many copies of the Psalms in book form, and perhaps even more one-volume copies with the four canonical Gospels – Matthew, Mark, Luke, and John. This is because Psalms and Gospels were used in liturgies. Other codices (and the Christian Bible was transmitted in codices – bound books – rather than in the older scroll format) might contain Genesis, the books of Solomon (Proverbs, Ecclesiastes, and the Song of Songs), or the letters of Paul. Because the Bible was received in parts, different parts took on different roles in Christian devotional traditions.

The Psalter was an especially important book because the Benedictine tradition organized each day around the Divine Office, eight (mostly short) prayer services that punctuated the monastic routine carefully described in *The Rule of Saint Benedict*. This tradition developed from the devotions of the Desert Fathers and Mothers of the fourth century and was largely made up of prayerful recitation of Psalms. In the Benedictine tradition, all 150 Psalms were sung every week, so the words, images, and cadences of the Psalms were engrained in the spiritual imagination of monastics. In the later Middle Ages, laypeople followed this model with abbreviated cycles of prayer (usually three a day, also mostly recitation of Psalms) set forth in Books of Hours, and so also shared in this Psalm-oriented spirituality.

The Psalms are ready-made vehicles for meditation because they are heartfelt outpourings of human emotions, praise, exultation, sorrow, and despair, directed to God. But the medieval Christian reception and understanding of the Psalms shows another aspect of the tradition of *lectio divina*, the assumption that the words of scripture are just the outward shell of deep meanings hidden in the text, revealed through layers of allegorical reading. The third-century exegete Origen of Alexandria (185–254) made a huge impression on the tradition of biblical understanding in Eastern and Western Christianity with his homily and commentary on one of the most enigmatic books of the Bible, the Song of Songs. Origen's expositions (extant in translated fragments and in the work of other early Christian theologians) assume that the Song of Songs is really about the love between God and the church or God and the human soul.

Another multifaceted system of interpretation was set forth by Augustine of Hippo (354–430) in his handbook to the interpretation of spiritual signs, *On Christian Doctrine*. Such theories of interpretation were deeply tied to ancient devotional practices, as is seen in the fact that the most influential system of levels of meaning was expounded by an abbot very close to the desert traditions, John Cassian (d. ca. 435). Cassian posited as many as four potential readings for any verse of scripture: the literal sense of the text (what was actually happening in the biblical narrative), the allegorical understanding of Christ and the Church, the tropological or moral sense of God and the Christian soul, and the anagogical sense, in which the text speaks of the ingathering of all things at the end of times. Cassian's senses of scripture became standard, but the prevailing idea, that scripture was multivocal, is the main point. According to Augustine and Cassiodorus (d. ca. 585), whose commentaries on the Psalter set the standard for a thousand years, the Psalms are truly about the death and resurrection of Christ, so the Christian meditating on those ancient texts is taken up into a mimetic experience of dying and rising with Christ.

The heart of the experience of the *lectio divina* is the participatory sharing in the deep meaning of scripture that is only made possible by understanding the resonances to allegorical meanings beyond the letter of the text. This is partly revealed through the tradition of allegorical exegesis shaped by Origen, Augustine, Cassian, and others, and partly by the use of the Bible in liturgy. Just as a medieval monastic would know the Psalter by heart, she or he would also know what texts resonated with other texts liturgically. So the beautiful and plaintive poems on the destruction of Jerusalem known as the Lamentations of Jeremiah were sung at the time of utter liturgical devastation after the stripping of the altar on Maundy Thursday, after which the altar remains dark until the Resurrection of Jesus is liturgically celebrated at the Easter Vigil at midnight on Holy Saturday. These services are known as the Tenebrae, and are celebrated as the three lessons of the First Nocturn of Matins on Maundy Thursday, Good Friday, and Holy Saturday. By their very liturgical settings, they carry an interpretation of the texts sung, but the purpose of the interpretation is to serve the devotional discipline.

This is, obviously, a very different approach to scripture than is found in modern Bible scholarship, and yet the medieval commentators often took all of this spiritual tradition into account when they wrote an exposition of a biblical text. Here is where biblical interpretation, *lectio divina*, and mystical theology come together, in a tradition of biblical exegesis that really needs to be understood as a type of Christian mysticism. Some of the most sophisticated biblical interpretations of medieval Christianity are found in texts that are ranked among the jewels of Christian mysticism – or to put it the other way around, some of the classics of mystical theology are actually interpretations of biblical passages, set out in the style of the *lectio divina*.

For example, the account of the creation of the world at the beginning of Genesis is a text that inspired many commentaries in the devotional mode tending toward mystical expositions. Augustine tried to grapple with this text no fewer than five times over the course of his long life, but one extended treatment, the last part of the *Confessions*, presents his interpretation as a prayer, a meditation on God, eternity, and being. This prayer develops throughout the last three books of the work, but blossoms into a line-by-line exposition of Genesis 1 in Book 13. Here is Augustine on Genesis 1:1–2:

> Here in an enigmatic image (1 Corinthians 13:12) I discern the Trinity, which you are, my God. For in the beginning of our wisdom, which is your wisdom, Father, begotten of your self, equal to you and coeternal, that is, in your Son, you "made heaven and earth" (Gen 1:1). We have said a lot about "the heaven of heaven" (Ps 113:24), about "the earth invisible and unorganized," and about the "dark abyss." It is dark because of the disordered flux of spiritual formlessness; but it became converted to him from whom it derived the humble quality of life it had, and from that illumination became a life of beauty. So it was the heaven of that heaven which was subsequently made to take its place between water and water (Gen 1:7). And now where the name of God occurs, I have come to see the Father who made these things; where the "Beginning" is mentioned, I see the Son by whom he made these things. Believing that my God is Trinity, in accordance with my belief I searched in God's holy oracles and found your Spirit to be borne above the waters. There is the Trinity, my God – Father and Son and Holy Spirit, Creator of the entire creation.[1]

Here, very much in the spirit of *lectio divina*, Augustine's meditation on the first day of creation leads him to the contemplation of the Triune God. This text greatly influenced later medieval commentaries on the beginning of Genesis, like Bonaventure's (1221–74) *Collations on the Hexameron*, which also uses meditation on creation as a way to teach proper theology and a deeper connection with God.

The biblical text that provided the greatest opportunity for mystical contemplation was the Song of Songs. The enigmatic quality of

---

[1] Augustine of Hippo, *Confessions*, trans. Henry Chadwick (Oxford: Oxford University Press, 1991), XIII. v. 6, p. 276.

these eight love poems, which contain no clear sacred history or moral teaching and do not mention God, opened up allegorical possibilities for Jewish exegetes, who tended to read the Song of Songs as the love between God and Israel. Origen, who had studied with Jewish scholars in Caesarea of Palestine, developed a Christianized version of this type of interpretation on two levels, reading these passionate poems as allegories of the love between Christ and the Church, or the love between God and the Christian soul. All medieval Christian commentaries on the Song of Songs start by assuming Origen's approach to the text, and some branch out in far more complicated directions. Some of these commentaries, while ingenious in their expositions, are clearly exhibitions of scholarly prowess and are not part of the devotional tradition associated with *lectio divina*. But some medieval and early modern commentaries on the Song of Songs truly deserve to be counted among the most important Christian mystical texts.

The most famous of these is the collection of eighty-six sermons on the Song of Songs by the twelfth-century Cistercian abbot, Bernard of Clairvaux (1090–1153), a series of meditations on the text to the beginning of chapter 3. These are short, fervent lessons on the spiritual life based in the text, but digressing into many aspects of the soul's journey to God. The digressions explain why, in so many sermons, Bernard did not get through even half of the Song of Songs; Bernard wrote them over the last eighteen years of his life, leaving them unfinished at his death in 1153. They were probably written for the novices at the monastery of Clairvaux and use the enigmas of the Song of Songs as vehicles for meditation on many paradoxes of the monastic life. In Sermon 43, on Song of Songs 1:12, "My beloved is to me a little bundle of myrrh that lies between my breasts," Bernard links myrrh to the bitterness of the cross and explains that the Passion of Christ must be lovingly embraced from the front, not carried on the back, where it becomes a burden. Even more creative is Sermon 3, a meditation on the opening line of the Song of Songs: "Let him kiss me with the kiss of his mouth," in which the Latin words "osculare," "to kiss," "osculo," "kiss," and "os," "mouth" make up the three kisses by which the Christian comes close to God. The kiss of the feet is human abjection and repentance, the kiss of the hand is conversion and discipleship, and the kiss of the kiss of the mouth is divine union with God. These sermons have been important guides to the spiritual path for centuries, playing as great a part in the shaping of later medieval mysticism as Bernard's more openly didactic work *On Loving God*, in which the spiritual path by which human beings learn to love God and to aspire to become one with him is described.

The classical description of the mode of performing the *lectio divina* dates from the same period as Bernard's sermons, right around the middle of the twelfth century; it is attributed to Guigo (Guy) the Carthusian (mid-twelfth century) and is variously called *The Ladder of Paradise* or *The Ladder of Monks*. Guy's insight is based on Jacob's vision in Genesis 28:12 of angels ascending and descending a ladder to God, bringing human prayers to heaven and God's answers to earth. Guy understood that this ladder was meant for those in cloisters, seeking the contemplative life. He saw four rungs on this ladder: reading, meditation, prayer, and contemplation. Reading is looking diligently into Holy Scripture with all one's will and intelligence. Meditation is based on having the proper skill to search deep into the mind to find what had been concealed. Prayer is the devout wish of the heart for good rather than for evil. Contemplation is lifting up the heart to God to taste a bit of heavenly consolation. In a wonderful metaphor of eating, Guy says, "Reading (*lectio*), as it were, puts the food whole into the mouth, meditating chews it and breaks it up, prayer extracts its flavor, contemplation is the sweetness itself which gladdens and refreshes."[2] In other words, in *lectio divina* one ruminates on the scripture like a cow chews her cud. Medieval monastics made collections of verses from works like the *Moralia in Job* of Gregory the Great (d. 604) combined with their own reflections, showing the stages of *lectio* and a more privately engaged *meditatio*. The *Ladder of Monks* had a wide diffusion, was translated into vernacular languages, and is still a basic guide for those who wish to practice *lectio divina*.

This combination of passionate longing for God and a step-by-step process for arriving at divine union is also found in the *Spiritual Exercises* of the German nun Gertrude the Great of Helfta (1256–1302). Gertrude's community at Helfta in Saxony was strongly influenced by the Cistercian spirit and followed the Cistercian version of the Benedictine Rule; therefore it is not surprising that she has been influenced by Bernard. Gertrude's *Exercises*, a collection of meditations, rituals, prayers, instructions on how to pray, chants, hymns, and litanies, are ruminations on spiritual themes based in scripture. There are seven exercises, set up as the seven steps of a monastic spiritual life.

The first four exercises are linked to the liturgical rites of baptism and the vesting, consecration, and profession of a nun. The last four link the seven-day offices (not including Matins) to seven stages of a

---

[2] Guigo (Guy) the Carthusian, *The Ladder of Monks and Twelve Meditations: A Letter on the Contemplative Life*, trans. Edmund Colledge and James Walsh (Kalamazoo, MI: Cistercian Publications, 1981), pp. 82–3.

monastic life. Exercise 5, "The exercise of divine love," is a step-by-step guide to union with God. The exercise begins with a sober command for a spiritual discipline of withdrawal and meditation:

> As often as you want to be at leisure for love, withdraw your heart from all inordinate affection, hindrances, and phantasms, choosing the day and the opportune time for this purpose – at least three hours on that day, that is in the morning, at noon, and in the evening – making amends for never having cherished your Lord God with all your heart, your soul and with all your virtue. And now with all affection, all devotion and intention, may you join yourself to God in prayer, as if you saw the spouse Jesus himself present, who assuredly is present in your soul.[3]

A bit further on, in a wash of language from the Song of Songs and three different Latin words for love, Gertrude cries out for the heavenly embrace:

> Ah! Admit me to the secret of your charity [caritatis], Lo! My heart already burns for the kiss of your love [amoris]. Open for me the private bed-chamber of your beautiful cherishing-love [dilectionis]. Lo! My soul thirsts for the embrace of intimate union with you.[4]

After the *Ladder of Monks*, there are many examples of *lectio divina* in this mode, texts that quake with passionate longing for God's embrace and yet also provide a guidebook for how to get there. Perhaps the most influential author who shows both of these characteristics is the sixteenth-century Spanish mystic, John of the Cross (1542–91). Two of his works, *The Ascent of Mount Carmel* and *The Dark Night of the Soul* are based on a mystical poem of his own composition. This poem is a stunning example of the use of biblical language in Christian mysticism: a song of the soul's happiness in having passed through the dark night of faith, in nakedness and purgation, to union with its beloved.

> 1. One dark night,
> fired with love's urgent longings
> – ah, the sheer grace! –
> I went out unseen,
> my house being now all stilled.

---

[3] Gertrude the Great of Helfta, *Spiritual Exercises*, trans. Gertrude Jaron Lewis and Jack Lewis (Kalamazoo, MI: Cistercian Publishers, 1989), p. 73.
[4] Ibid., p. 77.

2. In darkness and secure,
by the secret ladder, disguised,
– ah, the sheer grace! –
in darkness and concealment,
my house being now all stilled.

3. On that glad night,
in secret, for no one saw me,
nor did I look at anything, with no other light or guide
than the one that burned in my heart.

4. This guided me
more surely than the light of noon
to where he was awaiting me
– him I knew so well –
there in a place where no one appeared.

5. O guiding night!
O night more lovely than the dawn!
O night that has united
the Lover with his beloved,
transforming the beloved in her Lover.

6. Upon my flowering breast
which I kept wholly for him alone,
there he lay sleeping,
and I caressing him
there in a breeze from the fanning cedars.

7. When the breeze blew from the turret,
as I parted his hair,
it wounded my neck
with its gentle hand,
suspending all my senses.

8. I abandoned and forgot myself,
laying my face on my Beloved;
all things ceased; I went out from myself,
leaving my cares
forgotten among the lilies.[5]

The passionate language of this poem comes right from the Song of Songs, and the interpretation echoes the ancient spiritual level described

---

[5] John of the Cross, *Selected Writings*, trans. Kieran Kavanaugh (New York: Paulist Press, 1987), pp. 55–6.

by Origen, depicting the marriage of God and the soul. But the fierce longing and the graphic consummation emphasize, even insist on, the mystical union in a way that makes the threefold kiss of Bernard of Clairvaux seem tentative.

The fact that the poem appears twice is also quite interesting, because its role is different in each context. *The Ascent of Mount Carmel* is a long treatise, carefully structured around the idea of a spiritual ascent that can be undertaken only after purgation; each step is carefully planned. This is *The Ladder of Monks* in a far more sophisticated elaboration, with a clear goal of mystical union. These steps have become well-known in the study of Christian mysticism because they were adapted by Evelyn Underhill as a universal "mystic's path": awakening, purification, illumination (including voices, visions, recollection, and contemplation), ecstasy and rapture, the dark night of the soul, and, finally, the unitive life.[6] In this scheme, after awakening to the spiritual life, the soul turns toward God, reaps some rewards, but then inevitably finds itself in the dark night of the soul, a time of trial and desolation, before finding the true unitive life with God. John's shorter treatise, *The Dark Night of the Soul*, is a description of this desolate stage, a description that is spelled out in a verse-by-verse commentary on the poem. The context of *The Dark Night* lights up (so to speak) the paradoxes of the poem: the darkness that is light, the leaving that is coming home, the wound that is sweetness. These are all characteristics of another type of *lectio divina* – apophatic meditation on scripture.

The tradition of apophatic theology, that is, the theology that speaks away from rather than affirms, has its most formal foundation in the writings of an anonymous Syrian theologian who wrote around the year 500 and who is known as Dionysius the Areopagite. Two of his works, *The Divine Names* and *The Mystical Theology*, are biblically based meditations on how God can only be known by the things he is not, that is, in paradox. These were popular texts in the Latin West, where they were translated successively from the ninth century on and commented on by many famous scholars, including Hugh of Saint Victor (1096–1141) and Thomas Aquinas (ca.1225–74). The *Mystical Theology*, notable for its succinct explanation of these mysteries of unsaying, was translated into Middle English, perhaps by the same fourteenth-century author who scholars think may have been a Carthusian monk and who wrote the Middle English mystical classic, *The Cloud of Unknowing*. John of the Cross probably knew either the *Cloud of Unknowing* (which

---

[6] See Evelyn Underhill, *Mysticism* (New York: Dutton, 1965).

had been translated into Latin and was widely diffused) or *The Mystical Theology*, or both, as his paradoxical language, especially the repeated theme of the luminous darkness, was bequeathed to Western Christian mysticism through this Dionysian line. The importance of apophasis for *lectio divina* is in how it underlines the importance of spiritual experience rather than intellectual understanding. The Pseudo-Dionysian texts, deeply rooted in scripture, thus became the exemplars for a *lectio divina* of unknowing. This is a specialized, even rarefied, taste in meditative practice, to be sure, but one that had adherents in every century after the ninth and that led to John's insights into "the dark night" through which a mystic must pass, in which God is present in the absolute desolation of loss.

Lectio divina is a method by which reading and interior exploration of scripture can open the soul to the possibility of union with God. It grew out of the earliest era of communal asceticism, flowered in the monastic world of the Middle Ages, and is still practiced today. *Lectio divina* always is closely related to traditions of biblical interpretation because it is based on a deep moralizing understanding of scripture, what John Cassian called the "tropological sense." It was the impetus for centuries of biblical learning and a key to understanding some of the most important works of medieval theology.

7 *Meditatio*/Meditation
THOMAS H. BESTUL

In the Christian tradition, *meditatio* (meditation) has long been considered an essential element of the contemplative life. Meditation is almost always seen as training or preparation for the higher activity of prayer or contemplation, an intermediate stage rather than an end in itself. In considering meditation, it is useful to distinguish between meditation as a practice or spiritual exercise and meditation as a written form. The latter includes narratives that often are or claim to be the product of the writer's personal experience and serve the didactic function of providing models to imitate or inspiration for those seeking to practice meditation in pursuit of the contemplative life. It would be mistaken, however, to consider *meditatio* as a well-defined literary genre or formal category in the Middle Ages. The term is loosely applied to a range of works in both prose and verse and is often not used in connection with works for which it would seem appropriate, at least according to the modern understanding of the term. The element of private self-examination seems to be a common denominator, but there is considerable variation.

In the early Middle Ages, meditation as an activity is almost exclusively associated with monasticism, and later developments reflect these monastic origins. The monastic rules of the early Middle Ages mention *meditatio* as a spiritual exercise most frequently in connection with the reading of a text, as Jean LeClercq explains,[1] and it is clear that the term means something other than its modern sense of private thought or solitary reflection. In early monasticism, *meditari*, the Latin verb related to *meditatio*, usually means the private recitation of a text, with a view toward memorizing it. The text most likely to be meditated upon in this fashion was a biblical text, often the Psalms, which were

---

[1] Jean LeClercq, *The Love of Learning and the Desire for God: A Study of Monastic Culture*, 3rd ed., trans. Catherine Misrahi (New York: Fordham University Press, 1982), pp. 15–17. LeClercq's treatment of meditation in early monasticism, upon which the discussion here is based, remains indispensable.

central to the liturgical life of the monastery. It is important to note that meditation in this sense is never free-form speculation or associational thinking but is always tied specifically to a text. In monastic writing of the early Middle Ages, *meditatio* was associated with two other related activities, *lectio* (reading) and *oratio* (prayer), which followed one upon another. *Lectio* occurred first, and was the reading of the scriptures aloud or listening to them being read aloud, as prescribed in the Benedictine *Rule*; this was followed by *meditatio*, in which the text read was gone over with concentrated intensity, perhaps murmured aloud. Meditation was understood as both physiological and mental activity, with the goal of absorbing the complete meaning of the text, implanting it in the memory for future use.[2] Once this was done, the soul could then be disposed for the ultimate experience, *oratio*, that is, prayer, or communion with God.

Although the term *meditatio* should be understood in its monastic context as described, works were written in the early period that are meditational, in approximately our modern sense of the term, even though they are not formally styled as meditations. These were mainly works of personal introspection and self-examination, the outstanding example of which is Augustine's (d. 430) *Confessions*. Another work of Augustine's, the *Soliloquies*, was also influential, especially in the later development of meditation as a written form. The *Soliloquies* is a dialogue between a first-person narrator and his soul. Augustine was imitated in the seventh century by Isidore of Seville (d. 636), whose *Synonyma* follows the model of Augustine's *Soliloquies*, and is sometimes given that title in the early manuscripts.[3] Isidore's treatise is a reflective philosophical monologue with passages of moral examination. These two works of Isidore and Augustine were well-known throughout the early Middle Ages, although they inspired few direct imitators.

Anselm of Canterbury (d. 1109) was apparently the first to apply the term *meditatio* to a written work, in his *Orationes sive meditationes* (*Prayers and Meditations*), a collection of devotional writings written for the most part while he was prior of the Norman monastery of Bec during the 1060s and 1070s. The earlier monastic tradition as well as the work of Augustine lies behind Anselm's development of the *meditatio* as a form of devotional writing. In Anselm's usage, *oratio* and *meditatio* are not as clearly distinguished as in the earlier monastic treatises, but

---

[2] See Mary Carruthers, *The Book of Memory: A Study of Memory in Medieval Culture* (Cambridge: Cambridge University Press, 1990), pp. 162–76.
[3] For a text of the *Synonyma*, see *PL* 83, col. 827–68.

in general the meditations have a more personal or autobiographical emphasis than the prayers, as can be seen from the opening line of the first meditation – "I am afraid of my life; for when I examine myself carefully, it seems to me that my whole life is either sinful or sterile" – and the title of the second – "A Lament for Virginity Unhappily Lost."[4] Anselm conceives of meditation as a private, interior, and deeply emotional act of self-examination, rather than the preparatory discipline of the early monastic tradition. Anselm's work marks a departure from what had gone before, although in the depth of his introspection he reconnects with Augustine, and precedents for his emotional fervor may be found earlier in the desert fathers, Cassian, and certain Anglo-Irish prayers of the eighth century. Much of what is novel in Anselm had been anticipated, to a lesser extent, in the devotional writing of his fellow Norman and near contemporary, John of Fécamp (d. 1078).[5] Yet in the intense affectivity of his meditative writing can be seen the evidence of the transformation in piety that occurs at the end of the eleventh century and continues in the twelfth, a piety marked by new emphases on personality and the dynamics of inner psychology.

Anselm states in the prologue to his collection that the purpose of the prayers and meditations is to be read in order to stir up the mind of the reader to fear and love of God and to provoke self-examination. They are to be read quietly, not skimmed or hurried through, but taken a little at a time, with deep and thoughtful meditation. Moreover, it is not necessary to read all of them or even to start at the beginning, but to read only so much as may be found effective in stirring up the spirit of the reader to prayer.[6]

It is Anselm's description of the purpose of devotional writing and its relation to private reading that offers an insight into his own conception of the term *meditatio*, which in turn forms a basis for the ways in which that term may have been understood in the later Middle Ages. Central to Anselm's conception is the relation between private reading and the arousal of emotion. Anselm's prologue, in a sense, defines devotional literature, specifically the *meditatio*, in terms of its capacity to arouse in the reader fervent religious emotions, especially regret for sin and love of God. From this definition, certain stylistic imperatives seem

---

[4] For Meditation 1, see Anselm, *The Prayers and Meditations of St. Anselm*, trans. Benedicta Ward (Harmondsworth, UK: Penguin Books, 1973), p. 221. For Meditation 2, see ibid., pp. 225–9.
[5] See G. R. Evans, "*Mens Devota:* The Literary Community of the Devotional Works of John of Fécamp and St. Anselm," *Medium Aevum* 43 (1974): 105–15.
[6] Anselm, *Prayers and Meditations*, trans. Ward, p. 89.

to follow, among them the use of a vivid, realistic style as being most likely to produce the desired result.

During the twelfth century, treatises appear that analyze the act of meditation in greater depth and detail than can be found in the monastic rules of the early Middle Ages. These treatises reflect the emphasis of the age on subjectivity, and they articulate more thoroughly and systematically the relation of meditation to reading, prayer, and contemplation. These writings often have a practical as well as a theoretical emphasis, being handbooks on how to meditate as well as analytical explorations. At the same time, works variously titled meditations are circulated in monastic circles. Examples are the enormously popular *Meditations* falsely attributed to Augustine but written during the late eleventh century, possibly by John of Fécamp; the *Meditations* of the Carthusians, Guigo I of Chartreuse (d. 1136) and Guigo II of Chartreuse (d. 1193); and the *Meditations* of William of Saint Thierry (d. 1148).[7] Other meditational writing from the period includes major contributions from the Cistercians Bernard of Clairvaux (d. 1153), whose *Sermons on the Song of Songs* are really an extended discourse on all aspects of the mystical and contemplative life, and Aelred of Rievaulx (d. 1167), especially the treatise *On Jesus at the Age of Twelve* and part 3 (the "Threefold Meditation") of his *Rule of Life for a Recluse*.[8]

An influential early analysis of meditation is found in the widely popular *Scala claustralium* (*The Ladder of Monks*) of Guigo II of Chartreuse.[9] Making extended use of metaphors of climbing and ascent traditionally used to describe the stages of the contemplative life, Guigo defines four spiritual activities, leading from one to another in an ascending order. These are *lectio*, *meditatio*, *oratio*, and *contemplatio*, which together form the "ladder" by which monks can become closer to God.

---

[7] The pseudo-Augustinian meditations are in *PL* 40, cols. 901–42. See also *Les méditations selon S. Augustin*, trans. Jean-Clair Giraud (Paris: Migne, 1991). For Guigo I, see Guigo I, *The Meditations of Guigo I, Prior of the Charterhouse*, trans. A. Gordon Mursell (Kalamazoo, MI: Cistercian Publications, 1995). For Guigo II, see Guigo II, *The Ladder of Monks and Twelve Meditations: A Letter on the Contemplative Life*, trans. Edmund Colledge and James Walsh (Kalamazoo, MI: Cistercian Publications, 1981). For William of Saint Thierry, see William of Saint Thierry, *On Contemplating God; Prayer; Meditations*, trans. Sister Penelope (Kalamazoo, MI: Cistercian Publications, 1977).

[8] Bernard, *On the Song of Songs*, trans. Killian Walsh and Irene Edmonds (Kalamazoo, MI: Cistercian Publications, 1971–80), 4 vols. Both works of Aelred are in Aelred of Rievaulx, *Treatises: The Pastoral Prayer*, trans. Theodore Berkeley, Mary Paul Macpherson, and R. Penelope Lawson (Kalamazoo, MI: Cistercian Publications, 1971).

[9] See Guigo II, *Ladder*, trans. Colledge and Walsh.

Meditatio is defined as "the busy application of the mind to seek with the help of one's own reason for knowledge of hidden truth."[10]

Guigo's treatise reflects and popularizes the rationalization of the elements of the contemplative life, including meditation, formulated under the influence of the writings on mystical theology of the Pseudo-Dionysius at the Abbey of Augustinian Canons of Saint Victor in Paris. The major figures are Hugo of Saint Victor (d. 1141) and Richard of Saint Victor (d. 1173), the first of whom defined meditation as follows:

> Meditation is sustained thought along planned lines: it prudently investigates the cause and the source, the manner and the utility of each thing. Meditation takes its start from reading but is bound by none of reading's rules or precepts. For it delights to range along open ground, where it fixes its free gaze upon the contemplation of truth, drawing together now these, now those causes of things, or now penetrating into profundities, leaving nothing doubtful, nothing obscure.... There are three kinds of meditation: one consists in a consideration of morals, the second in a scrutiny of the commandments, and the third in an investigation of divine works.[11]

More simply, Aelred of Rievaulx defined three types of meditation: on the memory of Christ in the past, the experience of things in the present, and the expectation of what lies ahead in the future. Meditation will arouse the emotions, the emotions will arouse desire, and desire will stir up tears.[12] Somewhat later, Alexander Nequam (d. 1217), writing under Victorine influence, states that the first subject of meditation is humanity, then other created beings, and finally, the Creator. In meditating on humanity, the meditator considers the dignity of human nature as well as its fragility; in meditation on the external world, he recognizes the vanity of things as well as their utility; and in meditation on higher things, he contemplates the humanity of the Savior as well as his divinity.[13]

These analytical approaches to meditation are somewhat overshadowed during the thirteenth century by the rise in popularity of focused meditation on the humanity of Christ, particularly on the events of his Passion, although it is important to observe that the conception of

---

[10] Ibid., p. 68.
[11] Hugh of Saint Victor, *Didascalicon*, trans. Jerome Taylor (New York: Columbia University Press, 1961), 3.10, pp. 92–3.
[12] Aelred, *Rule of Life for a Recluse* 33, in *Treatises*, trans. Macpherson, p. 102.
[13] Alexander Nequam, *Commentary on Proverbs* (unpublished), Oxford, Jesus College MS. 94, fol. 57r.

meditation as a disciplined activity leading to memory of the text as preparation for contemplation persists until the end of the Middle Ages.[14] Meditation on Christ's humanity is especially associated with the spirituality of the new Franciscan order, but its roots can be found much earlier, in, for example, Aelred of Rievaulx and Anselm of Canterbury.[15] This meditation was strongly affective, and although the earlier meditative themes of self-knowledge and introspection remain a part of it, emphasis is on the creation of concrete visual images with the aid of the faculty of the imagination. The goal was to meditate on the events of Christ's life, *sicut praesens*, as though one were actually present at the scene. In this way, emotion would be aroused, the presence of God deeply felt, and love for Christ increased.

The most influential Franciscan writer of meditations of this type was Bonaventure (d. 1274), whose two treatises on the Passion, the *Lignum vitae* (*The Tree of Life*), a meditation on the life, death, and resurrection of Christ, and the *Vitis mystica* (*The Mystical Vine*), or *Tractatus de passione domini* (*Treatise on the Passion of Our Lord*), were widely read.[16] But the most popular of the meditative works belonging to the Franciscan tradition is the *Meditationes vitae Christi* (*Meditations on the Life of Christ*), a work written in Italy at the end of the thirteenth century that was much influenced by Bonaventure and usually attributed to him in the Middle Ages.[17] This is a lengthy series of affective meditations on the whole life of Christ, but the heart of the work is the chapters on the Passion, which were often extracted and circulated separately. The prologue contains an important discussion and rationale for the method of meditation based on visual imagery. The meditator must place him- or herself "in the presence of whatever is related as having been said or done by the Lord Jesus, as if you were hearing it with your own ears and seeing it with your own eyes, giving it your total mental response."[18]

---

[14] See Carruthers, *Memory*, pp. 167–70.
[15] See Anselm, *Prayer to Christ* (Oratio 2), in Anselm, *Prayers and Meditations*, trans. Ward, pp. 93–9; Aelred, *Rule of Life for a Recluse*, pt. 3 ("Threefold Meditation on Life of Christ"), in *Treatises*, trans. Macpherson, pp. 79–102.
[16] Both are translated in José de Vinck, *The Works of Bonaventure I: Mystical Opuscula* (Paterson, NJ: St. Anthony Guild Press, 1960).
[17] The work may be by John of Caulibus. See *Meditations on the Life of Christ*, trans. Francis X. Taney, Anne Miller, and C. Mary Stallings-Taney (Asheville, NC: Pegasus Press, 2000); and Sarah McNamer, "The Origins of the *Meditationes vitae Christi*," *Speculum* 84 (2009): 905–55.
[18] Stallings-Taney, *Meditations*, p. 4.

The *Meditations on the Life of Christ* was enormously popular in the later Middle Ages. Translated into the vernacular, it appealed to both lay and clerical audiences. In terms of meditative literature, it was perhaps the first, and certainly the most widely disseminated, crossover success. It should be noted that the *Meditations* was addressed to a woman, like many other devotional works in the period after about 1200. This fact is a reflection of the expanded audience for devotional texts of all kinds occasioned by the increase in literacy, particularly among laypersons of the aristocratic and bourgeois classes, and the growth of opportunities for private leisure and devotion.

Bonaventure and the *Meditations on the Life of Christ* provided models for many later works. In the same rich tradition are such late-thirteenth or early-fourteenth-century works as the popular *Stimulus amoris* (*The Goad of Love*) – also attributed to Bonaventure but probably by James of Milan – and the *Arbor vitae crucifixae Christi* (*The Tree of Life of the Crucified Christ*) of the Franciscan Ubertino da Casale (d. ca. 1329–41).[19] The summit was reached in the *Vita Christi* (*Life of Christ*) of Ludolph of Saxony (d. 1377), a vast compilation drawn from multiple sources with a preface explaining the benefits of meditation on the humanity of Christ.[20]

The method of meditation making use of physical images as a stage leading to contemplation of higher intangible matters, from the visible to the invisible, is known as the *via positiva*, or positive way. Although this type of meditation was dominant in the later Middle Ages, another strain existed alongside it, known as the *via negativa*, or negative way.[21] Here, because God is unknowable and transcendent, any involvement with the physical or concrete is seen as a hindrance instead of a help in meditation, and the higher stages of contemplation are most likely to be reached when one rids oneself, to the extent possible, of all images and sensory impressions that compromise the ineffability of the divine.

Even though affective meditation on the humanity of Christ may have been the dominant expression of late medieval piety, systematic approaches to meditation emphasizing self-knowledge and introspection, a heritage of the rationalization of meditation begun by the Victorines, are found in the later periods. The two strands come together

---

[19] James of Milan, *Stimulus amoris Jacobi mediolanensis*, 2nd ed. (Quaracchi, Italy: Collegium S. Bonaventurae, 1949); Ubertino, *Arbor vitae crucifixae Christi* (1485; repr., Turin: Bottega d'Erasmo, 1961).
[20] Ludolphus, *Vita Christi*, ed. L. M. Rigollot (Paris: Palme, 1870), 4 vols.
[21] See Andrew Louth's essay in this volume.

and reach their culmination in the great treatises of Bonaventure. In his *Itinerarium mentis ad deum* (*Journey of the Mind to God*), for example, he refers to the *Mystical Theology* of the Pseudo-Dionysius (early sixth century) and describes a process of ascent to God beginning with contemplation of the traces of God in the visible world, then the traces of God within us, to consideration of God's unity and being, leading finally to repose of the soul in the love of God.[22] In the first chapter of his *De triplici vita* (*On the Threefold Life*), Bonaventure describes purgation, illumination, and perfective union as successive stages of contemplative life. These are to be realized through the spiritual activities of meditation, prayer, and contemplation. Meditation is the means by which the soul is cleansed, enlightened, and perfected; it involves remembrance of sin, consideration of the human condition, and consideration of what is good.[23] Following Dionysian-Victorine teaching, the spiritual journey is envisioned as a progression from the concrete and material to the invisible, toward unity with God in love. To achieve the journey, meditation is followed by prayer, then contemplation. Prayer is the means by which our misery is deplored, God's mercy is implored, and worship rendered. Contemplation is the means by which true wisdom is attained. In the *Soliloquium de quatuor mentalibus exercitiis* (*Soliloquy on Four Mental Exercises*), Bonaventure in a dialogue with his soul states that the objective of the devout mind ought to move from interior things to exterior, then from lower things to higher. The higher things are the ineffable delights and eternity of the divine.[24]

Some of these ideas are more popularly expressed in the *Meditations* attributed in the Middle Ages to Bernard but written probably sometime during the thirteenth century.[25] The *Meditations* circulated extensively under the prestige of Bernard's name, and was, like the *Meditations on the Life of Christ*, one of the most popular religious works of the later Middle Ages. Like that work, it was widely read by lay and clerical audiences. The theme of the *Meditations* is self-knowledge as the beginning of wisdom. This is a commonplace from classical antiquity that is found frequently in the works of twelfth-century authors who wrote on meditation and contemplation.[26] The *Meditations* begin with the phrase,

---

[22] See Bonaventure, *Mystical Opuscula*, in *Works*, trans. de Vinck, p. 9.
[23] Bonaventure, *Mystical Opuscula*, in *Works*, trans. de Vinck, pp. 64–72.
[24] Bonaventure, *Soliloquium*, prologus, in *Decem opuscula ad Theologiam Mysticam Spectantia*, 4th ed. (Quaracchi, Italy: Collegium S. Bonaventurae, 1949), pp. 44–5.
[25] The Latin text is printed in *PL* 184, cols. 485–508.
[26] See Pierre Courcelle, *Connais-toi toi-même: De Socrate à saint Bernard* (Paris: Études Augustinennes, 1974–75), 3 vols.

"Many know much, but do not know themselves." As in Bonaventure (and the Victorines), the recommended course of meditation is to proceed from exterior things to interior, and to ascend from lower things to higher; through knowledge of self, one can attain knowledge of God.

Meditation, and the contemplative life in general, is in the Middle Ages above all a clerical, primarily monastic pursuit. Yet as early as the eleventh century, as seen in the treatises and correspondence of Anselm of Canterbury and John of Fécamp, there is a sensitivity to the contemplative aspirations of laypeople, especially of noble women.[27] During the fourteenth century, and increasingly during the fifteenth, a strong desire emerged among the laity, particularly among the aristocracy and the newly emergent and increasingly literate bourgeois class, to participate in some form of the contemplative life and to share its benefits. Guides to meditation and meditative works aimed in whole or part at lay or mixed audiences became increasingly available, often in the form of translations from Latin into the vernacular languages of Western Europe.[28] The abundant devotional writing deriving from the lay and clerical movement known as the *devotio moderna*, which originated in the Low Countries during the late fourteenth century and flourished during the fifteenth, illustrates the broadened social context for meditation and contemplation quite well.[29]

In terms of mysticism, the one constant that can be attached to the various manifestations of meditation and considerations of it as a spiritual activity is that it is regarded as an intermediate stage, preceded by a more elementary, if essential, practice, such as the attentive reading of scripture, and followed by a stage that in some form or another leads to closer communion with God. It is important to note that those who advocated the utility of mental images in meditation would not see such visual meditation as an end in itself, but would regard images as a concession to human weakness, with the goal always

---

[27] See Thomas Bestul, "Antecedents: The Anselmian and Cistercian Contributions," in *Mysticism and Spirituality in Medieval England*, ed. William F. Pollard and Robert Boenig (Woodbridge, UK: Boydell and Brewer, 1997), pp. 9–10; and Sarah McNamer, *Affective Meditation and the Invention of Medieval Compassion* (Philadelphia: University of Pennsylvania Press, 2009).

[28] See the chapters by Valerie Edden, "The Devotional Life of the Laity in the Late Middle Ages," and Thomas Bestul, "Walter Hilton," in *Approaching Medieval English Anchoritic and Mystical Texts*, ed. Dee Dyas, Valerie Edden, and Roger Ellis (Cambridge: D. S. Brewer, 2005), pp. 35–49, 87–100.

[29] See John Van Engen, *Sisters and Brothers of the Common Life: The Devotio Moderna and the World of the Later Middle Ages* (Philadelphia: University of Pennsylvania Press, 2008).

to proceed from the visible to the invisible. None of the writers we have discussed would claim that experience of the divine would necessarily follow upon meditative activity, no matter how assiduously pursued: the attainment of the higher levels of contemplation cannot be earned but is a gift of God's grace.

8 *Oratio*/Prayer

RACHEL FULTON BROWN

Prayer, in the Christian tradition, is an exercise almost by definition riddled with contradiction. The tension goes back to the Gospels; it is, likewise, at the root of many contemporary debates over the purpose of the liturgy and the role of individual experience in developing a relationship with God. For medieval Christians, as for the Fathers on whom they relied, prayer was something that everyone, even the unlettered knowing only the words of the Our Father (*Pater Noster*) or the Hail Mary (*Ave Maria*), was expected to be able to achieve. At the same time, it was also considered an art or discipline requiring long experience and great skill that even specialists (e.g., monks and nuns) could not realize without grace.[1] Irreconcilable as these two extremes of practice and experience might seem today, for early and medieval Christians, at least, this much was clear: to be a Christian meant to be one who prayed. Yet, then as now, many struggled to explain not only how one should pray but also, and even more urgently, why.

Throughout the Middle Ages, prayer, at its most basic level, was defined as an act of speech and, therefore, of reason; as Cassiodorus (d. ca. 585) put it, "prayer (*oratio*) is spoken reason (*oris ratio*)."[2] Yet, in its purest form, prayer would seem to go beyond reason, as the Augustinian canon Hugh of Saint Victor (d. 1141) explained: "pure prayer (*pura oratio*) is when out of an abundance of devotion the mind is so inflamed that, about to make a request to God, it is so transformed before the magnitude of his love it even forgets its petition."[3] Formally speaking, the

---

[1] For the expectation that the "unlettered," those not schooled in Latin, should know the Our Father and the Hail Mary, see *Medieval Popular Religion, 1000–1500: A Reader*, ed. John Shinners (Peterborough, ON: Broadview, 1997), pp. 5, 13, 17, 29–31, 56, 61. For prayer as an art or discipline, see John Cassian, *Conferences*, trans. Colm Luibhéid (New York: Paulist Press, 1985), conf. 10, ch. 8, pp. 130–1.

[2] Cassiodorus, *Expositio in Psalmum*, 38.14 [sic], PL 70, col. 285.

[3] Hugh of Saint Victor, *De modo orandi* c. 2, PL 176, col. 980; Hugh of Saint Victor, *L'oeuvre de Hugues de Saint-Victor 1: De institutione novitiorum, De virtute orandi, De laude caritatis, De arrha animae*, ed. P. Sicard, H. B. Feiss, D. Poiriel, and H. Rochais (Turnhout, Belgium: Brepols, 1997), p. 136.

most perfect prayer was (and, arguably, is) without contest that which the Lord Jesus Christ taught to the apostles (Mt 6:9–13; Lk 11:2–4); according to Augustine of Hippo (d. 430), "if you go over all the words of holy prayers, you will find nothing which cannot be comprised and summed up in the petitions of the Lord's Prayer."[4] Nevertheless, not only the Old Testament Psalms, but also the various hymns, chants, and other similar pieces "made by the Holy Spirit" for "the worship of the church," that is, the Mass, the Hours of the Divine Office, and other formal rites of the liturgy, were reckoned as integral to the practice of prayer.[5] In addition, there were numerous so-called private prayers composed by authors like the Benedictine abbots John of Fécamp (d. 1078) and Anselm of Bec (d. 1109) taken up by clergy and laity alike in the course of their devotions.[6] Yet, again, there were those, like the Yorkshire hermit Richard Rolle (d. 1349) or the anonymous fourteenth-century author of the *Cloud of Unknowing*, who insisted that prayer, insofar as it was spoken corporeally at all, might best be effected with but a single word, for example, "Jesus," "Sin," or "God."[7] Disciplined or spontaneous, rational or affective, prolix or concise, communal or solitary, vocal as well as mental or only in the mind: these were but some of the tensions attending the efforts of medieval Christians, as John of Damascus (d. 749) would put it, "to raise up [their minds] to God."[8]

Some of these tensions had their source in scripture. To begin with, there was the Lord's injunction not to be "like the hypocrites," who loved to pray in public where others might see them; true prayer, Christ seemed to say, is that which is practiced in secret, alone (Mt 6:5–6). Yet the apostles had come together in prayer (Acts 1:14: "*unanimiter in oratione*"); likewise, James advised his brethren, "Pray for one another,

---

[4] Augustine, Epistola 130 (A.D. 412), to Proba, in *A Select Library of the Nicene and Post-Nicene Fathers of the Christian Church*, vol. 1, *The Confessions and Letters of St. Augustin, with a Sketch of His Life and Work* (New York: Christian Literature Publishing Co., 1886), ch. 12.22, p. 466.

[5] For the prayers of the Church as inspired by Holy Spirit, see Walter Hilton, *The Scale of Perfection*, trans. John P. H. Clark and Rosemary Dorward (New York: Paulist Press, 1991), bk. 2, ch. 42, p. 289.

[6] On the tradition of private prayer as exemplified by Anselm and John, see Jean-François Cottier, *Anima mea: Prières privées et texts de devotion du Moyen Age latin. Autour des* Prières ou Méditations *attribuées à saint Anselme de Cantorbéry (XIe-XIIe siècle)* (Turnhout, Belgium: Brepols, 2001).

[7] On "Sin" and "God" as prayers, see *The Cloud of Unknowing*, trans. A. C. Spearing (Harmondsworth, UK: Penguin, 2001), chs. 37–40, pp. 60–4.

[8] John of Damascus, *De fide orthodoxa* 3.24, cited by Thomas Aquinas, *Summa theologiae*, 5 vols. (Ottawa, ON: Studii Generalis O. Pr., 1941–5), 2a 2ae q. 83 a. 1, 3:1841b: "Oratio est ascensus mentis in Deum."

that you may be saved" (Jas 5:16). But this was only the beginning, as the apostle Paul averred, "For we do not know how to pray as we ought" (Rom 8:26). Prayers, it would seem, should be brief, as Christ commanded: "in praying, do not speak much, as the *ethnici* do" (Mt 6:7). Yet he also told a parable to the effect that the faithful should "pray always and not faint" (Lk 18:1), in example of which Jesus spent whole nights in prayer (Lk 6:12). Likewise, Paul wrote: "Pray without ceasing" (1 Thes 5:17) and "do all things to the glory of God" (1 Cor 10:31). Nor was it certain whether prayers should be spoken aloud, because, if spoken, they could hardly be secret (Mt 6:6). Overriding all such practical concerns, however, was the question whether Christians should pray at all, when, as Christ assured his disciples, "your Father knows what you need before you ask him" (Mt 6:8; cf. Mt 6:32). Yet again, Christ had said: "Ask, and it will be given to you; seek, and you will find; knock, and it will be opened to you" (Mt 7:7).

So Christians prayed, not, as Origen of Alexandria (d. ca. 254) explained, because they expected thereby to change God's mind about that which his providence had foreknown and his will foreordained, but rather so as to prepare themselves "to partake of the Word of God ... who is never absent from prayer, and who prays to the Father with the person whose Mediator He is."[9] As Augustine put it: "Our Lord and God does not wish that our will should tell him what it is impossible for him not to know; but he wishes our desire to be exercised in prayers, whereby we may be able to receive what he is preparing to give."[10] "For we pray," the Dominican Thomas Aquinas (d. 1274) concurred, citing Gregory the Great (d. 604), "not that we may change the Divine disposition, but that we may impetrate that which God has disposed to be fulfilled by our prayers, in other words, 'that by asking, men may deserve to receive what Almighty God from eternity has disposed to give.'"[11] Of all things, that which God is most disposed to give to those who have – as the Augustinian canon Walter Hilton (d. 1396) put it, "purified [themselves] by the fire of desire in devout prayer" and so made themselves "able and ready like a clean vessel to receive" – is his grace. "Although," Walter continued, "it is true that prayer is not the cause

---

[9] Origen, *On Prayer* 10.2, in Origen, *An Exhortation to Martyrdom, Prayer, and Selected Works*, trans. Rowan A. Greer (New York: Paulist Press, 1979), pp. 100–1.

[10] Augustine, *Epistle 130*, in Hilton, *Scale*, ch. 8.17, p. 167, n. 87; and see also Augustine, *Confessions and Letters*, p. 464.

[11] Aquinas, *Summa theologica* 2a 2ae q. 83 a. 2, citing Gregory, *Dialogi* 1.8, trans. Fathers of the English Dominican Province, 3 vols. (New York: Benziger Brothers, 1947–1948), vol. 2, p. 1539.

for which our Lord gives grace, nevertheless it is a way by which grace, freely given, comes to a soul."[12]

Accordingly, that Christians should pray was, theologically speaking at least, relatively clear. How best to ensure that their prayers had their intended effect was another matter. It was one thing, after all, to say with Paul that the "Spirit helps us in our weakness ... [and] intercedes for us with sighs too deep for words" (Rom 8:26), or with Origen that "our mind would not even be able to pray unless the Spirit prayed for it as if obeying it."[13] The apostle was also understood to have indicated that prayers might take various forms: supplications (*obsecrationes*), prayers (*orationes*), intercessions (*postulationes*), and thanksgivings (*gratiarum actiones*) (1 Tm 2:1). One way to read such distinctions was with respect to stages of spiritual development. As John Cassian (d. ca. 435) opined, supplication or confession "seems especially appropriate for beginners ... goaded by the memory of past sin," while prayer or promises are "appropriate for those making progress in the acquisition of virtue and in the exaltedness of their souls." Intercessions or pleas are "suitable for those who live as they have promised to do, who see the frailty of others and who speak out for them because of the charity that moves them," and thanksgiving "suits those who have pulled the painful thorn of penitence out of their hearts and who in the quiet of their purified spirit contemplate the kindness and mercy that the Lord has shown them in the past, that He gives them now and that He makes ready for them in the future."[14]

Another way to read such distinctions was as formal rhetorical modes.[15] As the schoolman Peter the Chanter (d. 1197) put it, in an effort to goad his fellow clerics into taking seriously their responsibility as prayer experts and, thus, prayer models, "the *orator* is an artisan (*artifex*) for whom knowledge (*scientia*) is necessary."[16] His Victorine counterpart Hugh was even more particular. As the Augustinian master explained in his oft-copied *De modo orandi* (*Concerning the Manner of Praying*), "There are three kinds of prayer (*species orationis*)": *supplicatio*, or "humble and devout prayer (*precatio*) without determination of

---

[12] Hilton, *Scale*, bk. 1, ch. 24, p. 97.
[13] Origen, *On Prayer* 2.4, in Origen, *Exhortation*, p. 85.
[14] Cassian, *Conferences*, conf. 9, ch. 15, pp. 109–10.
[15] On prayer as a rhetorical art, see Barbara Jaye, *Artes orandi* (Turnhout, Belgium: Brepols, 1992).
[16] Peter, "De oratione et speciebus illius," in *The Christian at Prayer: An Illustrated Prayer Manual Attributed to Peter the Chanter (d. 1197)*, ed. Richard C. Trexler (Binghamton, NY: Medieval and Renaissance Texts and Studies, 1987), ll. 300–2, p. 26.

petition (*petitio*)"; *postulatio*, or "undetermined narration (*narratio*) for a determined petition"; and *insinuatio*, or "indicating what is wanted without petition but solely through narration." Each of these modes of prayer may be further subdivided by style (high, middle, or low), matter (*materia*), and affect (*affectus*).[17] Formally speaking, according to Hugh's schema, pure prayer (*pura oratio*) is the most sublime of the three *genera* of *supplicatio*. *Captatio*, or winning the goodwill of the audience is the lowest, and *exactio*, or the reiteration of one's cause is the middle. The difference is determined by affect, "because *captatio* has perfected fear, *exactio* trust, and *pura oratio* love," which affect, in turn, is determined by verbal form. Although *captatio* uses both nouns (*nomina*) and verbs (*verba*) and *exactio* depends more upon verbs, *pura oratio* is formed through nouns alone, "for as much as it is imperfect in its outward signification, so much the more is it filled inwardly with an abundance of love."[18]

Yet, as Hugh would be the first to acknowledge, such carefully crafted prayer by itself, however perfect or pure, was hardly enough to count as "real" prayer. Not, it should be said, because it was bound up with "letters and syllables, dictions and spoken prayers" (in Peter the Chanter's words), that is to say in more modern terms, "artificial" and, therefore, by implication "inauthentic" or "indirect" efforts to express "the inner experience of religion, the experience of awe, trust, surrender, yearning and enthusiasm" at the heart of "genuine" prayer.[19] Rather, and understandably, because prayer was something that it was very hard to do well. In addition to models (e.g., the Lord's Prayer), it required preparation and practice; nor, or so most spiritual advisors recognized, was it practicably possible to pray "without ceasing," that is, without growing tired and needing a break. According to Hugh, prayer as a practice came third, after reading (*lectio*) and meditation (*meditatio*) but before composition (*operatio*) and contemplation (*contemplatio*), in the five-stage process of spiritual ascent.[20] Although there were variations on this schema – for Guigo II the Carthusian (d. 1193), prayer was the third of four rungs on the "ladder of monks" (*lectio*, *meditatio*, *oratio*, and *contemplatio*), and for the Franciscan

[17] Hugh, *De modo orandi*, c. 2, PL 176, col. 979.
[18] Ibid., cols. 979–80.
[19] Peter, *De oratione*, ll. 300–1, in *The Christian at Prayer*, p. 179. On "genuine" prayer as "the inner experience of religion," see Friedrich Heiler, *Prayer: A Study in the History and Psychology of Religion* (Oxford: Oxford University Press, 1932), pp. xv–xxiv *passim*.
[20] Hugh of Saint Victor, *De meditando seu meditandi artificio*, PL 176, col. 993.

Bonaventure (d. 1274), prayer was the second of three stages on the "triple way" (*meditatio, oratio,* and *contemplatio*) – all were clear, as the *Cloud of Unknowing* put it, "that no thinking [i.e., Meditation] can be achieved by beginners and those making progress unless reading or listening [i.e., Lection] comes first, and no prayer [i.e., Orison] can be achieved without thinking."[21]

Not only beginners but also the more experienced made use of prayer as a tool in this way. One might begin, as Abba Isaac counseled Cassian and Germanus, with a simple formula. For monks, like Cassian, this might be as little as a single verse from a psalm. Isaac suggested what was to become the opening prayer of the Divine Office: "*Deus in adiutorium meum intende; Domine ad adiuvandum me festina*" (Ps 69:2, "O God make speed to save me: O Lord make haste to help me").[22] Laypeople, too, might start with the Psalms, either in full or, as the Princess Adelaide's request to Anselm for a *florilegium* of Psalms made clear, in abbreviated form.[23] Arguably, in a pattern somewhat more likely by the later Middle Ages at least they might begin with "the psalter of our Lady," which was made up of the fifteen Our Fathers and 150 Hail Marys of the rosary.[24] Then there were the prayers without number circulating, from at least the Carolingian period, either appended to psalters (so-called *libelli precum*) or in self-standing (i.e., nonliturgical) devotional collections such as the ninth-century Book of Cerne (Cambridge, University Library, MS L1.1.10) or the fifteenth-century book of Robert Thornton (Lincoln Cathedral Library, MS 91 [A.5.2]), to say nothing of the Psalms and prayers included in the Books of Hours.[25]

---

[21] Guigo II, *Ladder of Monks and Twelve Meditations*, trans. Edmund Colledge and James Walsh (Kalamazoo, MI: Cistercian Publications, 1981), pp. 67–8, 72–3; Bonaventure, *De triplici via*, in Bonaventure, *Opera omnia*, ed. Collegii a S. Bonaventura, 10 vols. (Quaracchi, Italy: Ex Typographia Collegii S. Bonaventurae, 1882–1902), vol. 8, pp. 3–18; *Cloud*, ch. 35, p. 59.

[22] Cassian, *Conferences*, conf. 10, ch.10, p. 132.

[23] Cottier, *Anima mea*, pp. xliii–lvi.

[24] On these devotions, see Anne Winston-Allen, *Stories of the Rose: The Making of the Rosary in the Middle Ages* (University Park: Pennsylvania State University Press, 1997).

[25] On the Book of Cerne, see Michelle P. Brown, *The Book of Cerne: Prayer, Patronage and Power in Ninth-Century England* (Toronto: University of Toronto Press, 1996). For Robert Thornton's devotional miscellany (ca. 1430–50), see C. Horstmann, *Yorkshire Writers: Richard Rolle and his Followers*, 2 vols. (Woodbridge, UK: D. S. Brewer, 1999), vol. 1, pp. 184–411. On the *Libelli precum*, see Cottier, *Anima mea*, pp. 276–9.

The nun Gertrude of Helfta (d. 1301/2) found one such prayer "in a book" during the winter of the first or second year when she had begun to receive "favors," that is, visions of and conversations with her Beloved, Christ the Lord. "I was so pleased," she averred, "with this little prayer that I repeated it often with great fervor; and you, who never refuse to grant the requests of the humble, were to grant me the effects of the prayer," to wit, "Lord Jesus Christ, Son of the living God.... Inscribe with your precious blood, most merciful Lord, your wounds on my heart ... that you may become the only sweetness of my heart." Not long after, Gertrude recalled: "I felt, in my extreme unworthiness, that I had received supernaturally the favors for which I had been asking in the words of the prayer.... I knew in my spirit that I had received the stigmata of your [i.e., Christ's] adorable and venerable wounds interiorly in my heart, just as though they had been made on the natural places of the body."[26]

As with all such disciplined practices, results varied, depending on the practitioners' experience and relative level of skill. "For example," the Cistercian Stephen of Sawley (d. 1252) observed of his experience in saying the Psalms and other prayers of the monastic office, "there are those who are well-trained in the spiritual life. They extract from the psalms meanings which may be mystical, moral or anagogical. From them they fashion pleasant meditations which produce an aversion for the things of the world and a longing for the things of heaven. To them time spent reciting the psalmody – no matter how long and drawn out – always seems to pass quickly, and the burden seems light." Others of the monks, less skilled, might spend only so long "as the word is on their lips" thinking about even the literal meaning of the texts, occupying themselves "during the pauses" (i.e., in the alternations of the psalm verses from one side of the choir to the other) with "greetings to the Blessed Mary or ejaculations like, 'God, be merciful to me, a sinner', (Lk 18:13) in order to stop the mind's wanderings." Then there were those "simpler souls" who had "not been given the gift of understanding the psalms, but [found] themselves, in so far as the understanding of the psalms and prophecies go, in 'dark, misty rain-clouds' (Ps 17:12)." These would spend their time in choir making pictures in their minds of events from the life of Christ or, for example, during Lauds, saying the five Psalms in honor of Christ's wounds. All, Stephen concluded,

---

[26] Gertrude of Helfta, *The Herald of Divine Love*, trans. Margaret Winkworth (New York: Paulist Press, 1993), bk. 2, chap. 4, pp. 99–100.

"make very good use of the time" as evidenced by their progress in virtue, despite the fact that only some were able to access in proper meditative fashion the deeper meanings of the Psalms.[27]

The key, or so Hilton warned, was not to attempt a mode of prayer beyond one's immediate spiritual strength. For those newly converted, or just turned to the religious life, the spoken prayer "made especially by God," such as the Our Father, or "by the ordinance of holy church," such as the recitation of Psalms and other prayers in the Divine Office, was best, "for a person needs a firm staff to hold him up if he cannot run easily by spiritual prayer because his feet of knowing and loving are infirm through sin." Only later, and with "the grace of devotion by the gift of God," might one expect to be able to pray, still speaking, "but without any particular set of words," following only the "affections of the heart."[28] Such prayer, in Hilton's tripartite schema, belongs to "the higher degree of the second part of contemplation," when "those who by the grace of Jesus Christ and long labor in body and spirit feel rest of heart and cleanness in conscience, so that nothing pleases them so much as to sit still in bodily rest, to pray to God always, and to meditate on our Lord."[29] "Anyone," Walter continued, "with the skill to pray often like this ... will acquire more virtues in a little while than someone else as good will get in a long time without this, for all the bodily penance that he could do." The third kind of prayer, "in the heart alone and without speaking," was more strenuous still, "for there are many souls who are unable ever to find rest of heart in prayer, but struggle with their thoughts all their lifetime, hindered and troubled by them."[30] Yet for those who could overcome the temptations and vanities of the mind and think only on God, their souls would become altars, burning with the fire of love, every word that they secretly prayed "like a spark springing out of a firebrand, warming all the powers of the soul, turning them into love, and filling them with light." Such prayer, in Walter's experience, rises like incense to heaven (see Ps 140:2); it is "a rich offering, all filled with the fatness of devotion" and "makes a soul at home and in fellowship with Jesus and with all the angels of heaven."[31]

Without question, the way was difficult, but, as Walter and all those like him who had found themselves able to endure the labor knew, the

---

[27] Stephen of Sawley, *On the Recitation of the Divine Office*, in Stephen of Sawley, *Treatises*, trans. Jeremiah F. O'Sullivan (Kalamazoo, MI: Cistercian Publications, 1984), pp. 125–7.
[28] Hilton, *Scale*, bk. 1, chs. 27–30, pp. 98–101. See also *Cloud*, ch. 39, pp. 62–3.
[29] Hilton, *Scale*, bk. 1, ch. 7, p. 81.
[30] Hilton, *Scale*, bk. 1, chs. 32–3, pp. 102–4.
[31] Hilton, *Scale*, bk. 2, ch. 42, pp. 290–1.

rewards were correspondingly great. "Prayer," as one late medieval English treatise, possibly the work of Richard Rolle, put it, "generously adorns our souls with flowers of sweetness, with the beauty and the sweetness of the fruit falling into humble hearts – that is, [the fruit which is the power] to gaze freely on the lovely face of God in all humble virtues, with the beams of his radiance illumining every pure conscience and all humble hearts."[32] Prayer opened the heart and illumined the mind, washed the soul clean of its sins and inclined it to the love and praise of God.[33] As Augustine put it, "the very effort involved in prayer calms and purifies our heart ... so that the vision of the pure heart may be able to bear the pure light, divinely shining, without any setting or change."[34] Accordingly, or so Rolle cautioned, "here some are reproved that rather take heed to meditation than to prayer, not knowing that God's speech is fired, and with it the filth of sin is cleansed, and the minds of those praying are enflamed with love. They say that they will first meditate and so stable their hearts, but they are stabled the later in that they are not comforted by prayer."[35] Prayer, as both Augustine and Rolle insisted, was indispensable as a preparation for turning the mind and the heart to God.

At its most powerful, prayer was a challenge, but it was also a comfort, offering not only cleansing from but also protection against all those "distractions" and "waverings of heart" (in Rolle's words) that made it so difficult to pray. More particularly, "prayer strikes at the fiend ... and makes him to fall and flee ... for shame of himself it drives him away as a coward wholly overcome."[36] Prayer was the shield of faith, the breastplate of justice, the helmet of salvation, and the sword of the Spirit with which the faithful armed themselves so as to be ready to "pray at all times in the Spirit, with prayer and supplication" (cf. Eph 6:14–18), lest they be led into temptation along the paths of the enemy.[37] It was, as Cassian put it, "an indomitable wall for all those struggling against

---

[32] (Rolle), "On Prayer," in *Yorkshire Writers*, ed. Horstmann, vol. 1, p. 297. The translation is by Barbara Newman, personal communication.

[33] (Rolle), "On Prayer," ed. Horstmann, in *Yorkshire Writers*, vol. 1, pp. 299–300; and cf. Bonaventure, *De triplici via*, cap. 2, ed. Collegii a S. Bonaventura, vol. 8, pp. 8–11.

[34] Augustine, "De sermone in Monte," trans. William Findlay, in *A Select Library of Nicene and Post-Nicene Fathers of the Christian Church*, ed. Philip Schaff, vol. 6, *St. Augustin: Sermon on the Mount; Harmony of the Gospels; Homilies on the Gospels* (New York: Christian Literature Publishing, 1886), bk. 2, chap. 3.14, p. 38.

[35] Rolle, *The Mending of Life or The Rule of Living*, trans. Richard Misyn into Middle English, trans. Miss Comper into modern English, 2nd ed. (Christian Classics Ethereal Library, accessed via NetLibrary, August 31, 2006), ch. 7, p. 7.

[36] (Rolle), "On Prayer," ed. Horstmann, in *Yorkshire Writers*, vol. 1, p. 299.

[37] Hrabanus Maurus, *Homilia XIX: In litaniis*, in PL 110, col. 39.

the onslaught of demons, an impenetrable breastplate and the sturdiest of shields."[38] As Rolle observed, "with busy prayers truly we overcome fiends.... They are enfeebled and as it were without strength, while we, strong and not overcome, bide in prayer."[39]

"Pray always," Christ had taught his disciples, "but be brief." According to Cassian, "there lies true sacrifice ... the saving oblation, the pure offering, the sacrifice of justification, the sacrifice of praise."[40] Prayer, as "the holy man says," is "a lovely sacrifice to god (*deo sacraficium*), solace to the angels (*angelis solacium*), and torment to the fiend (*diabolo tormentum*)."[41] Whatever else it might be, prayer, above all, was an act of worship, an offering rising like incense to God. As Thomas Aquinas put it: "By praying man surrenders his mind to God, since he subjects it to Him with reverence and, so to speak, presents it to Him.... Wherefore just as the human mind excels exterior things, whether bodily members, or those external things that are employed for God's service, so too, prayer surpasses other acts of religion [in showing honor to God]."[42] It was as the psalmist had written: "Let my prayer rise up like incense before your face and my hands like the evening offering" (Ps 140:2).

Prayer, in short, for early and medieval Christians, was a great mystery, an asking beginning in reason, but also an offering ending in love, an act of worship or sacrifice (God directed) as much as a confession or appeal for help (directed to self), an act of speaking often consisting, as Augustine noted, "more in tears than in words."[43] It was an intentional exercise, a "labor," as Hilton put it, that might take a lifetime to accomplish ("pray without ceasing"), but it was also a surrender, perfect only in the moment, to paraphrase Cassian, "when the orator was no longer conscious of himself and of the fact that he was actually praying."[44] Then as now, there were those who were skeptical, for whom spoken prayer at least seemed at best a "mere repetition of sacred formulae," at worst a "vain exercise of words."[45] For all those, however, like Augustine,

---

[38] Cassian, *Conferences*, conf. 10, ch. 10, p. 133.
[39] Rolle, *Mending of Life*, ch. 7, p. 7.
[40] Cassian, *Conferences*, conf. 9, ch.36, p. 124.
[41] "The Abbey of the Holy Ghost," ed. Horstmann, in *Yorkshire Writers*, vol. 1, pp. 327–8.
[42] Aquinas, *Summa theologica*, 2a 2ae q. 83 a. 3, trans. Fathers of the English Dominican Province, vol. 2, p. 1540.
[43] Augustine, Epistola 130, to Proba, in *The Confessions and Letters*, ch. 10.20, p. 465, with slight changes.
[44] Cassian, *Conferences*, conf. 9, ch. 31, p. 120.
[45] On the (supposed) vanities of verbal prayer, see William James, *The Varieties of Religious Experience: A Study in Human Nature* (Harmondsworth, UK: Penguin, 1982, originally published 1902), p. 464, citing Auguste Sabatier, *Esquisse d'une Philosophie de la Religion d'après la psychologie et l'histoire*, 2nd ed. (Paris: Fischbacher, 1897), pp. 24–6.

Cassian, Hugh, Gertrude, Hilton, and Rolle, with long practice in the rigors and delights of communal liturgy and solitary devotions, of verbal as well as mental prayer, the apparent contradiction between the method (speech) and the goal (kindling of the heart) was simply a matter of experience, impossible to describe for those who had not yet tasted it, unmistakable for those who had.

9 *Visio*/Vision
VEERLE FRAETERS

EARLY MEDIEVAL REFLECTIONS ON VISION

How exactly did the visionary prophets of the Hebrew Bible perceive God's Word? What did Saint Paul mean when he described "a person being transported to the third heaven, in or out of the body, I do not know?" In chapter 12 of his treatise *On the Literal Meaning of Genesis*, Saint Augustine (d. 430), reflecting about such questions, develops a typology of vision that became very influential throughout the Middle Ages, not least because Saint Isidore of Seville (d. 636) reproduced it in the chapter on prophets in his extremely popular *Etymologia*.[1] Augustine's classification of vision deals not so much with seeing as knowing. He is interested in the epistemological question of how a human being can know and correctly understand the meaning of God's Word. In line with Neo-Platonic philosophers, he uses the metaphor of vision in order to consider, in an intelligible way, the invisible process of cognition.

Augustine distinguishes three kinds of vision. The lowest form is seeing by means of the eye, the external organ of vision (*visio corporalis*). This material seeing is inadequate to perceive God's eternal truth; the viewer's position in time and in space necessarily limits his perspective. When one turns away from outer seeing to inner seeing – a turning away Augustine calls rapture (*raptus*) – a higher, spiritual form of vision is accessed (*visio spiritualis*).[2] With the inner eye, an organ of perception of the human soul, one can see images presented to the imagination (*imaginatio*), which is the faculty of the human soul that stores information perceived by the individual sense organs and binds it into a coherent mental representation. Cognition at this level remains inadequate to grasp eternal ideas because it is mediated by images (*enigmata* or *phantasmata*). The highest form of (in)sight is intellectual vision

---

[1] Augustine, *The Literal Meaning of Genesis*, in Augustine, *On Genesis*, trans. Edmund Hill and Matthew O'Connell (New York: New City Press, 2002), ch. 12, pp. 464–75.
[2] See Dyan Elliott's and Patricia Dailey's contributions to this volume.

(*visio intellectualis*) by the eye of the mind, the organ of perception of the intellect (*intellectus* or *mens*), which is the highest faculty of the rational soul (*anima rationalis*). The intellect is transpersonal in nature and through its close affinity with God – it was thought to be an image of God (*imago Dei*) – it is capable of receiving the grace of divine illumination and directly perceiving divine truth.

Primarily interested in the veracity and trustworthiness of the different forms of vision, Augustine marks spiritual seeing as an ambiguous middle category, located between corporeal seeing, which is fallible, and intellectual seeing, which is infallible. Biblical instances, such as the visions of Ezekiel and Revelation, show that visions can be divine revelations. Yet insights acquired through the eye of the imagination might just as well be phantasms or have been instigated by evil demons. Augustine's emphasis on the primacy of unmediated intellectual vision over symbolic spiritual vision remains influential. It was reproduced in numerous texts, including *On the Spirit and the Soul* (*De spiritu et anima*), a compilation circulated under the name of Augustine that was written by the Cistercian Alcher of Clairvaux (ca. 1160). Alcher adds that spiritual vision is certainly infallible when the seer is rapt from outer to inner vision by an angel, as was the case with John when he received the Book of Revelation. In such instances a temporary fusion of angelic and human consciousness takes place.[3]

Alcher's view concurs with that of another authority from the early Middle Ages whose ideas about *visio* influenced later medieval contemplatives and mystics. In his widely disseminated writings, Saint Gregory the Great (d. 604) stresses the great importance of spiritual vision. The Bible and the lives of the desert fathers and saints of the early Church testify to the fact that vision is the essential tool with which God communicates to his chosen ones. Gregory states in *Moralia in Job* that the eyes of the heart (*cordis oculis*) or, as he sometimes calls them, the eyes of the mind (*mentis oculis*), are the seat of understanding, the organ with which the human mind can conceive or apprehend God's message.[4] A contemplative person can be touched by the power (*virtus*) of an angel and transported into the spiritual dimension, where he temporarily participates in the universality and eternity of the divine gaze. In book 2 of the *Dialogues*, Gregory presents Saint Benedict of Nursia (ca. 480–547) as the prototype of the contemplative mystic and his so-called cosmic

---

[3] Alcher of Clairvaux (ps. Augustinus), *De spiritu et anima* 24, in *PL* 40, col. 797.
[4] Gregory the Great, *Morals on the Book of Job*, trans. John Henry Parker Oxford, (London: J.G.F. and J. Rivington, 1844), 3 vols.

vision as an exemplum of spiritual vision.[5] As Gregory tells it, while praying, Benedict was transported into God (*raptus in Deo*). He saw a light breaking through the clouds, bright beyond comparison, and he contemplated the whole universe from God's point of view – God being the glorified Christ into whom saints and martyrs are taken up after their death. Benedict thus enjoyed the beatific vision (*visio beatifica*), which all virtuous souls will contemplate forever at the end of time (Rv 22:4). The writings of Gregory profoundly inspired the mystics of the twelfth century, who share his high esteem of visionary experiences in the context of a life of prayer.

MONASTIC MYSTICISM AND VISION

The monastic movements of the twelfth century put private meditation on God's Word (*lectio divina* and *meditatio*) at the center of spiritual life. This meditational praxis facilitated the grace of contemplation (*contemplatio*) in which one sees the face of God. To contemplate is to understand God's Word in the same spirit in which it was written, as William of Saint Thierry (d. 1148) argues in his famous *Golden Epistle* (1136) to the monks of the Carthusian monastery Mont-Dieu.[6] Investment in such a contemplative praxis makes sense only if one believes that "seeing God face to face" is possible, despite the word spoken by God to Moses: "no man shall see me and live" (Ex 33:20). In Meditation 7 on Psalm 26 (27):8 William writes, "Neither Paul nor your beloved disciple could see Your face, and yet, when I hear David speak like this of a face to face, hearing another hope in You, I cannot give up hope."[7] William hopes that seeing God face to face may be possible in an ecstasy in which one transcends the limits of humanity, and thus of one's mind.

The power that makes such an ecstasy possible is love. Following Gregory and others, William understands the bride of the Song of Songs as the ideal model for the contemplative monk. Wounded by the arrow of love (Sg 2:5), she burns with incessant desire to see her beloved. The contemplative soul burning with excessive desire to see God may be transported into God and is bound to him in the unity of spirit: "Love

---

[5] Gregory the Great, *Dialogues*, trans. Odo John Zimmerman (New York: Fathers of the Church, 1959), bk. 2.

[6] William of Saint Thierry, *The Golden Epistle: A Letter to the Brethren at Mont Dieu*, trans. Theodore Berkeley (Kalamazoo, MI: Cistercian Publications, 1971).

[7] William of Saint Thierry, *On Contemplating God; Prayer; Meditations*, trans. Penelope Lawson (Kalamazoo, MI: Cistercian Publications, 1971), p. 137.

is a strong inclination of the will toward God.... But 'unity of spirit' with God for the man who has his heart raised on high is the term of the will's progress toward God. No longer does it merely desire what God desires, not only does it love him, but it is perfect in its love, so that it can will only what God wills."[8] The highest cognitive faculty lies in love, which has the rapturous power to carry human beings beyond themselves and merge with the divine other.

The Victorines taught their novices similar things about mystic contemplation. In his commentary on Revelation, Richard of Saint Victor (d. 1173) develops a typology of vision that differs significantly from the Augustinian one.[9] It is not triadic but dyadic in nature, distinguishing corporeal vision from spiritual vision. The highest form of spiritual vision is, according to Richard, anagogic in nature: the soul temporarily contemplates the glorified Christ and understands everything from his point of view. During such an anagogic spiritual vision, the soul takes part in the beatific vision (*visio beatifica*) of the saints and martyrs. Yet like the Cistercian mystics, the Victorines also situated true cognition of God no longer in contemplation at the level of the intellect, but rather in the capacity to transcend one's mind (*excessus mentis*). In chapter 12 of *Benjamin major*, Richard uses the biblical passage of the Queen of Sheba meeting Solomon as a simile for the process of meditation.[10] First the queen is looking for Solomon and she listens (*prius quaerit et audit*); this is meditation. She then sees him and understands (*postea videt et intelligit*); this is contemplation. Next her seeing him stupefies her (*stupet*) and makes her transcend her spirit (*a spiritu deficit*); this is ecstasy (*extasis, excessus mentis*).

Extreme admiration for Solomon's wisdom carries the queen beyond herself. Richard identified three inner dispositions that facilitate ecstasy: desire (*desiderium*), exemplified by the bride in the Song of Songs; admiration (*admiratio*), exemplified by the Queen of Sheba; and jubilation (*jubilatio, exsultatio*), exemplified by David, the presumed poet of the Book of Psalms. These affective dispositions generate the dynamic power necessary for a human being to momentarily transcend the limits of her own mind and experience union with the divine. The wisdom that resides in this union can no longer be discussed in terms of visuality and cognition, because the subject-object relation these imply

---

[8] William of Saint Thierry, *The Golden Epistle*, ch. 257, p. 94.
[9] Richard of Saint Victor, *In apoc.* 1, in *PL* 196, cols. 684–7. My translation.
[10] Richard of Saint Victor, *Benjamin major* 5, 12, in *PL* 196, cols. 180–2; Richard of Saint Victor, *The Twelve Patriarchs; The Mystical Ark; Book Three of the Trinity*, trans. Grover Zinn (New York: Paulist Press, 1979), pp. 326–7.

has been transcended. Terms from the primary register of the sensorium were better qualified. The seeing of God fades to make way for synaesthetic and gustatory metaphors, often taken from the Song of Songs: kissing and touching, tasting, drinking and becoming inebriated, and melting together in union. In his *Sermons on the Song of Songs*, which deeply influenced later generations of mystics, William's close friend Bernard "the mellifleus" of Clairvaux (d. 1153), exploited this affective register to the fullest.

Recognizing the value of affect as an agent of mystical union, the monks cultivated meditation techniques meant to inflame the heart. Because of this, images took pride of place. Whereas discursive words have to be mentally processed and understood before they can move the heart, images were thought to be able to touch and move the heart immediately, thus providing an added value in devotional practices. Images, real ones as well as visualizations and spiritual visions, elicit intensity or the fire of compunction (*ardor compunctionis*) that has the power to engage the viewer in an anagogical movement from the visible to the invisible (*per visibilia ad invisibilia*), all the way into the divine in its Trinitarian nature. The use of images was therefore given an important place in meditational practices that aimed to facilitate a breakthrough of the grace of contemplation and of mystical union in which all images fall away. The main biblical models of this new mode of meditation were women: the bride of the Song of Songs, inebriated by the ardent desire to see and meet her lover, and the Queen of Sheba, stupefied by wonder on seeing the greatness of King Solomon. It therefore comes as no surprise that the texts and practices of the twelfth-century monastic mystics inspired the religious women of the thirteenth century.

FEMININE ECSTATIC MYSTICISM AND VISION IN THE TWELFTH AND THIRTEENTH CENTURIES

These views on ecstatic vision and mystical union, developed in an elitist milieu of cloistered monks, were appropriated, along with the accompanying meditational practices, by religious and semireligious circles of devout women. This process of appropriation implied modifications, the most striking one being the fact that visions seem to have played a much more substantial role for women than for men. The predominant role of visions is witnessed in texts by and about women mystics. The lives of the thirteenth-century holy women (*mulieres sanctae*) of the Low Countries and the Rhineland abound with visions. Clearly, the hagiographers considered the rapturous experiences of these women to be an important element in the construction of their sanctity. Holy women's private revelations were not only an important motif in hagiographies: they were also collected into separate books written in either Latin or in the vernacular. The *Book of Visions* (*Liber visionum*) of the Benedictine nun Elisabeth of Schönau (d. 1164) was the first and widely distributed example of this new genre. These books of visions might be written by the visionary, as is the case of the Middle Dutch *Book of Visions* by the beguine Hadewijch of Brabant (mid-thirteenth century), or in collaboration with cosisters, as is the case of the *Revelations* of Gertrude of Helfta (d. 1301/2). Yet most often, the literary fixation and dissemination of women's revelations resulted from a collaboration between the female visionary and a male spiritual mentor who authorized her experiences in the eyes of the wider reading public. Elisabeth's *Book of Visions*, for example, was edited and promoted by her brother-theologian Egbert of Schönau.

Having visions was thus considered a hallmark of sanctity, especially for women. Visionary experience was, to a certain degree, considered to be gender specific.[11] Because of their inferior bodily constitution – the female body was thought to be moist and cold rather than dry and hot – the image of God (*imago Dei*) was believed to manifest less brightly in the minds of women than in the minds of men. Yet spiritually both sexes were considered equal: the passion of Christ liberated both sexes from original sin, and men and women were called to contemplate God. Women's temperamental constitution, however, was thought to make them more receptive to the visitation of angels, which could transport their souls into the spiritual world where Christ, Mary, the saints, and the martyrs might reveal God's will and word directly to them. Given these views, it is perhaps natural that significantly more visionary testimonies of religious women – nuns, beguines, and anchoresses – have survived than those of men.

Their privileged and direct relation with God allowed charismatic women to be, in the eyes of the community, a locus where the spiritual and the worldly, the dead and the living, might meet. They were seen to take to heart, in an exemplary way, the advice of Saint Paul to be zealous for spiritual gifts, especially the gift of prophecy, so that they might edify the church by revealing to it God's hidden word (1 Cor 14:1–14; see also Rv 19:10). As prophets, they had religious authority *ex gratia* (by grace), which was considered by many to be equal to if not more

---

[11] See also the contributions to this volume by Dyan Elliott, Alison Weber, and Mary Frohlich.

valuable than the religious authority *ex officio* (by right of office) held by clerics. Private people as well as secular and religious authorities consulted visionary women in order to access information of all kinds: the whereabouts of the souls of the deceased, insight into God's view on ecclesial political issues, and the true spiritual meaning of disputed biblical passages. Holding such an authoritative position as prophet within the community could lead to conflicts and compromises, as is shown by another widely read text by Elisabeth of Schönau, her *Book of Revelations on the Company of the Martyrs of Cologne*. Elisabeth was asked by the local authorities to confirm, by way of her visions, the identity and provenance of numerous bodies found in an old cemetery outside Cologne, thought to be those of Saint Ursula and her company. Elisabeth had to overcome her own skepticism and reluctance before accepting the task. Yet her visionary communication with the long-dead saints and martyrs confirmed what the authorities hoped, and Elisabeth thus became, on the basis of her acknowledged visionary power, the arbiter and facilitator of the cult of Saint Ursula in Cologne.[12]

Yet for many mystic women the gift of clairvoyance had no real value in itself. "Beautiful revelations and miracles have happened to you during your days.... Exterior miracles and gifts that had begun to be worked in you, you refused to accept from me.... You forsook them because of Love, and you want nothing else than myself," Christ tells Hadewijch during one of her raptures.[13] In line with the meditational praxis of the Cistercian and Victorine love mystics, women mystics like Hadewijch, Beatrice of Nazareth (d. 1268), Mechthild of Magdeburg (d. ca. 1282), and the Helfta nuns sought to contemplate God face to face so that their own souls might gradually be transformed into a perfect likeness of the divine exemplar. Whereas for cloistered monks like Bernard of Clairvaux, the private *lectio divina* was one primary context for this praxis, many women focused on the corporate ceremony of the liturgy celebrated in the public space of the church. The ritual of the liturgy provided them with a perfect setting for private devotions, in which visualization and ecstatic vision played a key role. The textual space of the Divine Office was filled with exactly those biblical texts that had inspired their monastic predecessors: the Psalms, the Song of Songs, and the sapiential books. This gave women plenty of opportunity for *lectio divina* and for meditating on God's Word, longing to experience

---

[12] Elisabeth of Schönau, *The Complete Works*, trans. Anne L. Clark (New York: Paulist Press, 2000), p. 213.

[13] Hadewijch, *The Complete Works*, trans. Columba Hart (New York: Paulist Press, 1980), p. 270.

the grace of contemplation and see their Love face to face. The space of the liturgy was filled with sacred objects and images that provided visual anchors to enhance their affective longing for the Beloved. Christ was represented on images such as the crucifix and was believed to be present in the host. The Eucharist especially triggered ecstatic visions; from women's visionary writing it can be inferred that they had visions mainly during matins or mass on the major liturgical feasts. During the thirteenth century, communion was offered only on these days. Clearly, it was the affective longing for union with Christ through the consummation of the body of Christ in the Eucharist (*Corpus Christi*) that triggered the grace of *visio Dei* and of mystical union.

Thirteenth-century visionary literature of and about women reflects this specific liturgical setting. Most books of visions are ordered according to the liturgical calendar. The individual visionary reports start with an indication of the liturgical day and hour and, in some cases, even the scriptural text chanted or recited at the moment the visionary was transported into the spirit and was given a vision. During her ecstatic contemplation, the visionary perceives with the internal senses of the soul, which was thought, since the patristic age, to be analogous to the senses of the body and, at the same time, opposed to them in that the soul's sensorium can only become active when the bodily senses are muted. The sight and hearing of the inner senses are especially active: the soul sees images (*visio*) and hears sounds (*auditio*), and the blessed in heaven speak to her (*allocutio*). Given the liturgical setting of ecstasy, visionary imagery is often linked to the liturgical moment at which the vision took place. The vision reveals the hidden sense of the liturgical text on which the visionary was meditating. In the case of women with a well-stocked and well-stimulated memory, what is seen during the vision is fed not only by the specific liturgical text of the day, but also by other texts and images that are triggered during the visionary's affective ruminations on the text. Consequently, the visions of well-read beguines and nuns like Hadewijch and the Helfta nuns display a high degree of intertextual dialogue between scripture and a wide array of other religious and classical texts. These women therefore can rightly be understood as engaged in an "experiential hermeneutics" or an "imaginative theology."[14]

[14] For "experiential hermeneutics" see Otto Langer, "Zum Begriff der Erfahrung in der mittelalterlichen Frauenmystik," in *Religiöse Erfahrung: Historische Modelle in christlicher Tradition*, ed. Walter Haug and Dietmar Mieth (Munich: Fink, 1992), pp. 229–46. For "imaginative theology" see Barbara Newman, *God and the Goddesses: Vision, Poetry, and Belief in the Middle Ages* (Philadelphia: University of Pennsylvania Press, 2003), pp. 294–304.

The revelations women receive during contemplation are not limited to an understanding of God's Word. The divine message primarily concerns their personal vocation as the bride of God and their salvific role for others. In her *Book of Visions*, Hadewijch explains to the anonymous spiritual friend for whom she writes that her rapturous contemplations function as mirrors in which she can discover to what degree her soul has become a perfect image of her Beloved. Yet the visions are also agents that progressively facilitate her transformation toward spiritual perfection: "Each time then and always I received new gifts, which made known to me how far I had then advanced, and to what stages of development I had been raised."[15] Through visionary communication, Hadewijch becomes conscious of her spiritual authority and her spiritual mission. In a society in which women were not allowed to preach publicly, a God-given instruction to publicize their experiences and insights was necessary – together with clerical mentorship – to overcome social barriers. Mechthild of Magdeburg received her *Schreibbefehl* (commandment to write) directly from God during ecstasy.[16] Hadewijch is told several times during her visions, by God, Mary, and other heavenly dwellers, that she is to guide others to spiritual perfection.[17] One way in which she answered that vocation was to write.

In the last vision recorded in her *Book* it is revealed to Hadewijch that she has reached the place for which she was chosen, namely the choir of the seraphim, in closest proximity to God. She is shown that her soul's bridal dress fully possesses all virtues and that her throne is so transparent that God's will can work through it unhampered: her similitude to the Beloved is complete. Other mystic visionaries are also transported during their ecstasy to the most privileged place in medieval spiritual topography: the choirs of the highest angelic triad, where the contemplative angels – thrones, cherubim, and seraphim – enjoy the endless vision of God's countenance. The anonymous Cistercian cleric who wrote the *Life* of Beatrice of Nazareth explains that Beatrice was often transported into the heavenly sphere of the seraphim and that her ecstatic raptures did not differ from the experience of Paul when he was caught up to the third heaven. The hagiographer specifies that in her blissful raptures she contemplates the face of the glorified Christ and temporarily shares in the beatific vision.[18] Hadewijch was also brought

---

[15] Hadewijch, *Complete Works*, p. 304.
[16] Mechthild of Magdeburg, *The Flowing Light of the Godhead*, trans. Frank Tobin (New York: Paulist Press, 1998), p. 96.
[17] Hadewijch, *Complete Works*, pp. 284, 301.
[18] *The Life of Beatrice of Nazareth*, trans. Roger De Ganck (Kalamazoo, MI: Cistercian Publication, 1991), pp. 205, 208.

during her raptures before "that Countenance of God with which he will satisfy all the saints and all men for the full length of his eternity."[19] From that anagogic perspective she sees "everything as it is in God and as far as it is in God and as far as it is God."[20]

Yet again, most women mystics do not consider vision the most powerful and most empowering spiritual experience. The revelation of divine justice and love disclosed to them in the vision of God's countenance intensifies their admiration, jubilation, and desire to the point that they transcend their mind (*excessus mentis*) and merge with their Beloved. During this ultimate ecstasy, the inner senses of hearing and seeing active during the vision can no longer operate independently. The soul liquifies, and its sensory channels fuse into one synaesthetic sensation of joyful bliss. This experience of mystical union is ineffable. When women mystical writers refer to it, they use nuptial imagery, metaphors of liquification, and the language of touch and taste. For Hadewijch, "the most secret name of *Minne* (Love) is Touch,"[21] and she calls the fruit of mystical fruition "the full taste of cognition."[22] Like vision, union harbours knowledge. Yet, although the visionary revelation is understood by the mind, the truth hidden in mystical union is apprehended through participation: the mystic is in God and shares in God's Trinitarian enjoyment of himself. In such union "out of the spirit," one is closer to God and knows God more deeply than any vision "in the spirit" allows. As Hadewijch tells her friend at the end of her *Book of Visions*: "Once I lay for three days and the same number of nights in entrancement of spirit at the Countenance of our Beloved; and this has often lasted for that length of time; and also for the same length of time entirely out of spirit, lost there to myself and to all persons, in fruition of him: to know how in fruition he embraces himself. To be out of the spirit and to be in him – this surpasses all that one can have from him and all that he himself can accomplish; and then one is not less than he himself is."[23]

EPILOGUE

At the end of the thirteenth century, feminine ecstatic visionary mysticism spread from its nucleus in the Southern Low Countries and the Rhineland to other regions in Europe. In Lyon, the Carthusian prioress

[19] Hadewijch, *Complete Works*, p. 297.
[20] Ibid., p. 286.
[21] Ibid., p. 91.
[22] Ibid., p. 282.
[23] Ibid., p. 305.

Margaret of Oingt (d. 1310) wrote her visionary experiences in Latin and in the vernacular. In Italy, Angela of Foligno (d. 1309) dictated her ecstatic visions to a Franciscan friar. In Bavaria, the Dominican nun Margaret Ebner (d. 1351) was encouraged by her clerical mentor to record her revelations. The accent slowly shifted from love mysticism, in which the Eucharist was the emblematic trigger of union with the Beloved, to passion mysticism, in which the cross was the first and foremost focus of the visionary's affectionate gaze (a practice illustrated beautifully in the visions of the anchorite Julian of Norwich [d. after 1416]).

The meditational practices that underlie visionary mysticism were popularized. For less educated women, prescribed visualizations such as the pseudo-Bonaventuran *Meditations on the Life of Christ* replaced the personal rumination of a liturgical text. The formulaic visions thus produced, for example, in the *Book* of the housewife Margery Kempe (d. after 1438), lacked the exegetical complexity and mystical profundity that characterized earlier visionary literature. The ongoing democratization of spiritual life, together with controversies over the prophecies of Bridget of Sweden (d. 1373), led the Catholic Church to establish a protocol for distinguishing between true and false visions (*discretio spirituum*).[24] The Church thus went back to Augustine, who in his treatise *On the Literal Meaning of Genesis* was cautious about spiritual vision, because the spiritual world is inhabited not only by God and his angels but also by demons. With the implementation during the fifteenth century of the discernment of spirits, claims to visionary and prophetic gifts were suspect unless proven to be, through canonical investigation, authentic divine revelations. This policy favored a new type of visionary, one very different from the twelfth-century contemplatives and the women mystics of the thirteenth and fourteenth century, who were well versed in reading religious texts and well trained in meditational techniques. The ideal visionary of the postmedieval era is instead an uneducated girl, like the miller's daughter, Bernadette Soubirous (d. 1879), who saw Mary appear at the grotto of Massabielle outside Lourdes, weeping over the sins of modernity.

---

[24] See also Dyan Elliott's contribution to this volume.

10 *Raptus*/Rapture

DYAN ELLIOTT

In contemporary discourse, rapture has become shorthand for the apex of sexual pleasure, which is a far cry from its original sense. The Latin word *raptus* literally means "seized" or "captured." In a medieval context, this term was used to denote both the trance-like state of abstraction induced by proximity to the Godhead and the crime of rape. The evolution of medieval mystical discourse eventually provides a bridge between these two extremes, anticipating the erotic hybrid of modern parlance.

The mental abstraction associated with mystical rapture is not unique to the Christian tradition. In Neoplatonic circles, terms like *exstasis* (literally standing outside oneself) or *excessus mentis* (departure of the mind) implied being raised above one's normal understanding in the contemplation of the divine. In contrast to these more neutral terms, rapture conveys the idea of being physically overpowered by the divine presence – a meaning that becomes increasingly prominent over time as a result of medieval theology's progressive emphasis on the body. From a theological standpoint, a contemplative's alienation from the senses was interpreted as a function of the body's frailty, as it was considered fatal for postlapsarian humankind to see God directly (Ex 33:23).[1] Because embodiment is intrinsic to human nature, many theologians perceived the physical abstraction associated with rapture to be unnatural,[2] while some, such as Thomas Aquinas (d. 1274), emphasized

---

[1] Peter Lombard, *Collectanea in Epistolae D. Pauli, In Ep. 2 ad Cor.*, v. 2, in *PL* 192, col. 82; Alexander of Hales, *Quaestiones disputatae "Antequam esset frater"* (Florence: Ad Claras Aquas, 1960), q.68, memb. 3, c. 9, vol. 3, p. 1348. For a more detailed discussion of this terminology, see Barbara Newman, "What Did It Mean to Say 'I Saw'? The Clash between Theory and Practice in Medieval Visionary Culture," *Speculum* 80 (2005): 6–41; and Dyan Elliott, "The Physiology of Rapture and Female Spirituality," in *Medieval Theology and the Natural Body*, ed. Peter Biller and Alastair Minnis (Woodbridge, UK: York Medieval Press in association with Boydell and Brewer, 1997), pp. 142–4.

[2] Peter Lombard, *Collectanea in Epistolae D. Pauli, In Ep. 2 ad Cor.*, v. 1, in *PL* 192, col. 80; and compare, Thomas Aquinas, *Summa theologicae*, trans. Roland Potter (London: Blackfriars, 1970), 2a 2ae q. 175, art. 1, rep. obj. 1, vol. 45, p. 97.

its implicit violence. Although Aquinas would argue that it was precisely the quality of violence that distinguished rapture from conditions like ecstasy, not all religious writers would maintain this distinction.[3]

There were a number of supposed incidents of ecstasy or rapture in the Hebrew Bible and the New Testament. According to theologian Alexander of Hales (d. 1245), Adam experienced a rapture during the creation of Eve, regaining normal consciousness with the understanding that he was intended to rule over woman (Gn 2:22). Moses was understood to undergo rapture when he was moved to speak in a quasiprophetic mode (12 Nm 6–8). The same can be said for the visionary John, who was described as "in the spirit," when ordered by God to record the revelation he saw (Rv 1:10–11).[4] Likewise, Peter apprehended a vision during the course of a trance or "departure of the mind" (*mentis excessus*, Acts 10:10).[5] Despite the undeniable parallels between such occurrences, however, they nevertheless lent themselves to a ranked order of merit. Augustine (d. 430) set forth three types of vision arraigned in ascending hierarchy: the corporeal sight of the eyes, the spiritual sight of the imagination, and the intellectual sight of the mind, which functioned entirely without images.[6] The first two types of vision were vitiated by the body; the third was not. Thus the experiences of Peter and John were contingent upon mental images, perceived as a limitation. Pride of place was reserved for Paul's description of a man (presumably himself) who was "caught up (*raptum*) to the third heaven," where he heard "secret words which it is not granted to man to utter" (2 Cor 12:2, 4).[7] According to many scholastic theologians, a true rapture was dependent on intellectual vision alone.[8] This rigorous standard

---

[3] Aquinas, *Summa theologicae* 2a 2ae q. 175, art. 2, rep. obj. 1, vol. 45, p. 101.
[4] Alexander of Hales, *Quaestiones disputatae "Antequam esset frater,"* q. 68, memb. 11–12, vol. 3, pp. 1360–3.
[5] See Aquinas, *Summa theologicae* 2a 2ae q. 173, art. 3, resp., vol. 45, pp. 62–3; and Vincent of Beauvais, *Speculum naturale* c. 100, vol. 1 of 4 (Douai: B. Belleri, 1624), col. 1907.
[6] Augustine, *On the Literal Meaning of Genesis*, in Augustine, *On Genesis*, trans. Edmund Hill and Matthew O'Connell (New York: New City Press, 2002), bk. 12, pp. 464–75. See Newman, "What Did It Mean to Say 'I Saw'?" pp. 14–41; and Veerle Fraeters's essay in this volume.
[7] All biblical quotations are from the Douai-Reims translation of the Latin Vulgate.
[8] See Vincent of Beauvais, *Speculum naturale* c. 100, cols. 1906–7. The famous "rapture" at the end of the world in which the living and dead will be raised for judgment – the "rapture" that looms so large in contemporary evangelical sources – was an altogether separate phenomenon (1 Cor 15:51). On this see Peter Lombard, *Sententiae in IV libris distinctae* 4.43.6.4, 3rd ed. *Spicilegium Bonaventurianum*, IV–V (Rome: College of St. Bonaventure ad Claras Aquas, 1981), vol. 2, p. 515.

produced certain tensions in medieval religious circles regarding what constituted an authentic spiritual experience.

The spirituality of the early Middle Ages did not favor philosophical contemplation, let alone the altered states of being that fostered revelations. There is the occasional exception: the nun Baudonivia, for example, recounts how the Frankish Radegund (d. 587) was visited by visions of Christ.[9] But it is in the high and later Middle Ages that rapture will come to the fore as compelling evidence for a heightened spiritual state.[10] Latin Christendom's increased affluence, in conjunction with church reform, gave rise to a spirituality that was characterized by increased asceticism and heightened emphasis on interiority. This trend is epitomized by the Cistercian movement, one of the new monastic orders recognized for both its greater austerity and its renewed commitment to the contemplative life. The writings of the Cistercian abbot, Bernard of Clairvaux (d. 1153) were especially important in fostering a spirituality that was conducive to mystical rapture. His treatise *On Loving God* outlines seven stages of ascent leading to union with God. Moreover, his series of sermons on the Song of Songs expatiate at length on the fruit of this union in terms of the mystical marriage between Christ and the human soul represented by the bride.[11] The bride's intimate contact with the celestial bridegroom results in an ecstasy in which "the soul does not deny that it is inebriated but with love, not wine."[12] There was a long tradition of Christian exegesis identifying the human soul with the bride of the Song of Songs; since the fourth century, however, the virginal nun, who was publicly veiled as Christ's bride, had become the most visible repository of this image.[13]

[9] Baudonivia, *The Life of the Holy Radegund* 2.3, 2.20, in *Sainted Women of the Dark Ages*, ed. and trans. Jo Ann McNamara and John Halberg (Durham, NC: Duke University Press, 1992), pp. 88, 101.

[10] For an overview, see Bernard McGinn, *The Presence of God: A History of Western Christian Mysticism*, vol. 3, *The Flowering of Mysticism: Men and Women in the New Mysticism (1200–1350)* (New York: Crossroad, 1998).

[11] Bernard of Clairvaux, *On the Love of God*, in Bernard of Clairvaux, *Treatises II*, trans. Robert Walton (Kalamazoo, MI: Cistercian Publications, 1974), pp. 93–132; and Bernard of Clairvaux, *On the Song of Songs*, I–IV, trans. Kilian Walsh and Irene Edmonds (Kalamazoo, MI: Cistercian Publications, 1971–80). Also see E. Ann Matter, *The Voice of My Beloved: The Song of Songs in Western Medieval Christianity* (Philadelphia: University of Pennsylvania Press, 1990), pp. 123–33.

[12] Bernard of Clairvaux, *Song of Songs*, Sermon 49, n. 1, vol. 3, p. 22; and also see Jean LeClercq's introduction, *Song of Songs*, vol. 1, p. xxiii.

[13] See Caroline Walker Bynum, *Jesus as Mother: Studies in the Spirituality of the High Middle Ages* (Berkeley: University of California Press, 1982), pp. 110–69; and René Metz, *La Consecration des vierges dans l'eglise romaine: etude d'histoire de la liturgie* (Paris: Presses universitaires de France, 1954).

Another important font for the understanding of mystical ecstasy were the works attributed to a certain Dionysius, whom the Eastern church associated with the judge of the Athenian Areopagus converted by Paul (Acts 17:34), and whom the West further identified with a third-century Gallic martyr. These works were probably written by a Syrian monk during the early sixth century, so the anonymous author is now commonly referred to as Pseudo-Dionysius. His complex mystical theology centers around the concept of reunion with an essentially unknowable God through a three-stage ascent of illumination, purification, and perfection or union. Ecstasy is associated with love, which takes us out of ourselves and draws us toward the object of love, which is God.[14] Although the work of Dionysius was introduced to the Western church during the ninth century through the translations of the Carolingian theologian John Scotus Eriugena (ca. 815–77),[15] the impact of his thinking was felt in the later Middle Ages when, directly or indirectly, it influenced writers as diverse as Hugh of Saint Victor (d. 1141), Bonaventure (d. 1274), Albert the Great (d. 1280), Marguerite Porete (d. 1310), Meister Eckhart (d. ca. 1328), Henry Suso (d. 1366), and the anonymous author of the fourteenth-century *Cloud of Unknowing*.

For both Bernard and Dionysius, the condition of ecstasy was entirely shorn of bodily effects. This excluded mental images as well, which were ultimately dependent on the imagination, and hence the senses.[16] Even so, the overall influence of these writers fostered two different traditions of mysticism. These traditions were by no means mutually exclusive, and some mystics incorporated elements of both. Yet certain tensions arose over questions such as the presence of images in revelations and, more generally, the impact and importance of trance-like states on the body.

The love mysticism of Bernard was not destined to remain the sole preserve of a cloistered audience of men. The end of the twelfth century saw the emergence of the beguines – a group of pious laywomen from the Low Countries whose religiosity was deeply shaped by Cistercian spirituality.[17] In the prologue to the life of Mary of Oignies (d. 1213),

---

[14] Bernard McGinn, *The Presence of God: A History of Western Christian Mysticism*, vol. 1, *The Foundations of Mysticism: Origins to the Fifth Century* (New York: Crossroad, 1991), pp. 157–82. See the translations by Colm Luibhéid and Paul Rorem in Pseudo-Dionysius, *The Complete Works* (New York: Paulist Press, 1987).

[15] Bernard McGinn, *The Presence of God: A History of Western Christian Mysticism*, vol. 2, *The Growth of Mysticism: Gregory the Great through the Twelfth Century* (New York: Crossroad, 1994), pp. 82–3.

[16] Elliott, "Physiology of Rapture," pp. 144–9.

[17] Simone Roisin, "L'efflorescence cistercienne et le courant féminin de piété au XIIIe siècle," *Revue d'histoire ecclésiastique* 39 (1943): 342–78. On the beguine movement,

one of the first women to be associated with the beguine movement, her confessor James of Vitry (d. 1240) describes a series of women whose exceptional piety was rewarded by raptures and other divine consolations.[18] Moreover, James soon discovers during the course of his travels that the beguine lifestyle was not unique: there were pious enclaves spontaneously arising all over Europe associated with parallel mystical phenomena.[19]

The fact that the kind of mystical spirituality conducive to rapture first appeared among a community of women was not accidental: although Francis of Assisi (d. 1226) is arguably the most famous of medieval mystics, receiving the stigmata (the wounds of Christ) during the course of a rapture, women were much more inclined to experience mystical phenomena like rapture than were men. Women's mystical propensity made sense to the medieval mind. Rapture was construed as a function of human frailty, which was understood to be epitomized in women. Not only did Paul introduce the philosophical bias into the faith, prizing spirit over matter, but he further aligned man with the spirit and woman with the body (Eph 5:28–9). The medical tradition corroborated the tendency to regard the female body as inferior to the male: softer, wetter, porous, malleable, unsealed, and hence, impressionable. This physical inferiority rendered women especially susceptible to outside spiritual influences, good and bad.[20]

There was considerable variety in the experience of rapture and the revelations that ensued during the course of rapture. Yet there are some

---

see Ernest McDonnell, *The Beguine and Beghards in Medieval Culture* (New York: Octagon, 1969); and Walter Simons, *Cities of Ladies: Beguine Communities in the Medieval Low Countries, 1200–1565* (Philadelphia: University of Pennsylvania Press, 2001).

[18] James of Vitry, *The Life of Mary of Oignies*, trans. Margot King, in *Mary of Oignies: Mother of Salvation*, ed. Anneke Mulder-Bakker (Turnhout, Belgium: Brepols, 2006), prologue, chs. 6–8, pp. 45–9.

[19] James of Vitry, Epistle 1, in James of Vitry, *Lettres de Jacques de Vitry*, ed. R. B. C. Huygens (Leiden, The Netherlands: Brill, 1960), esp. pp. 72–5.

[20] See Caroline Walker Bynum, "The Female Body and Religious Practice in the Later Middle Ages," in *Fragmentation and Redemption: Essays on Gender and the Human Body in Medieval Religion* (New York: Zone Books, 1991), pp. 181–238; Elliott, "The Physiology of Rapture," pp. 157–73; Dyan Elliot, *Fallen Bodies: Pollution, Sexuality, and Demonology in the Middle Ages* (Philadelphia: University of Pennsylvania Press, 1999), pp. 35–60; Nancy Caciola, *Discerning Spirits: Divine and Demonic Possession in the Middle Ages* (Ithaca, NY: Cornell University Press, 2003), pp. 131–57; Nancy Caciola, "Breath, Heart, Guts: The Body and Spirits in the Middle Ages," in *Demons, Spirits, Witches: Communicating with the Spirits*, ed. Gábor Klaniczay and Éva Pócs (Budapest: Central European University Press, 2005), pp. 21–39, esp. 23–7; and Gábor Klaniczay, "The Process of Trance: Heavenly and Diabolical Apparitions in Johannes Nider's *Formicarius*," Collegium Budapest, Discussion Paper Series, 65 (June 2003): 1–81.

areas of common ground. Caroline Walker Bynum has demonstrated the importance of Eucharistic devotion to female spirituality, stressing women's acceptance of their traditional assimilation with the flesh and the ways this complemented their role as providers of food – as much by virtue of the biological function of lactation as by domestic responsibilities. This created a point of identification with the broken (hence feminized) flesh of Christ, which, like the lactating bodies of women, became a source of food during the course of the Mass.[21] For many female mystics, the reception of the host, and hence a closer union with Christ, triggered rapture.

Additionally, women's raptures were often structured around a flexible love story in which the *dramatis personae* were the mystic and God. Barbara Newman has demonstrated that such narratives first arose among the beguines, who combined the love mysticism of the Cistercians with the tradition of *fine amour* (courtly love) to form a new tradition, which she designates *la mystique courtoise*.[22] Many of these women were laywomen, some of whom had been married at one time. Nevertheless these women dared to construe themselves as lovers in pursuit of divine love or as its particular object, even encroaching on virgin territory by assuming the auspicious title of bride. The expansion of the bridal prerogative corroborates Bernard's influence by further appropriating the imagery associated with the Song of Songs at the expense of the virginal nun.[23] Yet this increased emphasis on biologically sexed women as the beloved of Christ also countermanded Bernard's destabilization of the gendered persona of the bride.

The strategic structuring of a mystical experience as a romantic narrative, with ecstasy as a kind of consummation, would eventually be adopted in some form by many, if not most, female mystics. Moreover, the Middle Ages would witness a progressive somatization of this imagery. During the course of a rapture, Catherine of Siena (d. 1380) participated in a visionary ceremony in which she wed Christ with a ring fashioned from his foreskin.[24] The Prussian mystic Dorothea of Montau

---

[21] Caroline Walker Bynum, *Holy Feast and Holy Fast: The Religious Significance of Food to Medieval Women* (Berkeley: University of California Press, 1987).

[22] Barbara Newman, *From Virile Woman to WomanChrist: Studies in Medieval Religion and Literature* (Philadelphia: University of Pennsylvania Press, 1995), ch. 5.

[23] For the correlation between mystical experiences and married women's guilt over their sexual past, see Dyan Elliott, *Spiritual Marriage: Sexual Abstinence in Medieval Wedlock* (Princeton, NJ: Princeton University Press, 1993), pp. 231–45.

[24] Catherine of Siena, Epistle 39, in *The Letters of St. Catherine of Siena*, trans. Suzanne Noffke (Binghamton, NY: Medieval and Renaissance Texts and Studies, 1988), vol. 1, p. 128.

(d. 1394) suffered from an illness that caused open sores to erupt on her body, which she associated with the "wounds of love" administered by her spiritual bridegroom.[25] Moreover, Dorothea, following in the footsteps of her role model, Bridget of Sweden (d. 1373), likewise experienced a mystical pregnancy.[26] At the far end of such increasingly concrete enactments we find the Renaissance nun Benedetta Carlini (d. 1661), whose publicly staged espousals with Christ created a scandal that prompted an ecclesiastical inquest.[27]

During the course of a mystical revelation, the body of the enrapt saint frequently constituted a spectacle in the hagiographical literature. Francis of Assisi was raised far enough from the ground for Brother Leo to walk beneath his feet; Lutgard of Aywières (d. 1246) was also said to levitate; Christina the Astonishing (d. 1224) curled up like a hedgehog and rolled around like a hoop, while a beautiful sound emanated between her neck and throat;[28] and divine love made Vanna of Orvieto (d. 1306) sweat so profusely that she shed her clothes.[29] Meanwhile, onlookers often felt compelled to test the body of the enrapt individual to assess the authenticity of an ecstasy. Usually this was limited to some gentle poking by the confessor. But the unfortunate Douceline

---

[25] On Dorothea's spirituality and wounds, see Richard Kieckhefer, *Unquiet Souls: Fourteenth-Century Saints and Their Religious Milieu* (Chicago: University of Chicago Press, 1984), pp. 22–33.

[26] *Acta et processus canonizacionis Beate Birgitte*, ed. Isak Collijn (Uppsala, Sweden: Almquist and Wiksells, 1924–31), p. 500; John of Marienwerder, *Vita Dorotheae Montoviensis Magistri Johannis Marienwerder*, ed. Hans Westpfahl, in *Forschungen und Quellen zur Kirchen- und Kulturgeschichte Ostdeutschlands*, vol. 1 (Cologne and Graz: Böhlau, 1964), 6.17e, p. 313; cf. 6.22.e, p. 321.

[27] The transcription of the inquest appears in the appendix of Judith Brown's *Immodest Acts: The Life of a Lesbian Nun in Renaissance Italy* (New York: Oxford University Press, 1986).

[28] Little Flowers of St. Francis, in *St. Francis of Assisi: Writings and Early Biographies; English Omnibus of the Sources for the Life of St. Francis*, ed. Marion Habig (Chicago: Franciscan Herald, 1973), pt. 2, consideration 2, pp. 1440–1; Thomas of Cantimpré, "The Life of Lutgard of Aywières," ch. 1.10, in Thomas of Cantimpré, *The Collected Saints' Lives: Abbot John of Cantimpré, Christina the Astonishing, Margaret of Ypres, and Lutgard of Aywières*, ed. Barbara Newman, trans. Margot King and Barbara Newman (Turnhout, Belgium: Brepols, 2008), pp. 224–5; "The Life of Christina of Saint Trond," chs. 16, 35, in Thomas of Cantimpré, *Collected Saints' Lives*, pp. 136, 145–6. See also Walter Simons, "Reading a Saint's Body: Rapture and Bodily Movement in the Vitae of Thirteenth-Century Beguines," in *Framing Medieval Bodies*, ed. Sara Kay and Miri Rubin (Manchester, UK: University of Manchester, 1994), pp. 10–23; and Elliott, *Proving Woman*, pp. 183–8.

[29] Giacomo Scalza, *Leggenda latina della B. Giovanna detta Vanna d'Orvieto del Terz' Ordine di S. Domenico*, ed. and trans. V. Marreddu (Orvieto, Italy: Sperandeo Pompei, 1853), ch. 5, pp. 13–18.

of Digne (d. 1274) had molten lead poured over her feet at the orders of Charles of Anjou.[30] She did not flinch until her rapture was over.

The tradition indebted to Dionysian mysticism did not lend itself to outward displays of embodied spirituality, including spectacular visions. This is even true of authors like Marguerite Porete, who adopt versions of the romantic framework alluded to previously.[31] Yet this ostensibly less flamboyant tradition had scandals of its own. Marguerite was accused of propounding that mystical union with the divine had the effect of divinizing the individual, making her impervious to sin. She was condemned by an ecclesiastical tribunal and executed.[32] Moreover, the beguine movement was accused of harboring a parallel set of beliefs, which ecclesiastical authorities referred to as the "Heresy of the Free Spirit," and was subsequently persecuted.[33]

Even so, the mystical tenets associated with Dionysius tended to attract a more educated clientele that frequently had close links with university circles. Thus the clerical credentials of a mystical writer like Meister Eckhart, who was influenced by Marguerite Porete and whose writings raised similar suspicions of heresy, may have helped to ensure that he did not share her fate.[34] He died while still appealing his

---

[30] Felipa of Porcelet, *The Life of Saint Douceline, A Beguine of Provence*, trans. Kathleen Garay and Madeleine Jay (Woodbridge, UK: D. S. Brewer, 2001), 9.16, pp. 51–2. On this text, see Sean Field, "Agnes of Harcourt, Felipa of Porcelet, and Marguerite of Oingt: Women Writing about Women at the End of the Thirteenth Century," *Church History* 76 (2007): 298–329.

[31] See Barbara Newman, "The Mirror and the Rose: Marguerite Porete's Encounter with the *Dieu D'Amours*," in *The Vernacular Spirit: Essays on Medieval Religious Literature*, ed. Renate Blumenfeld-Kosinski et al. (New York: Palgrave, 2002), pp. 105–23. But for the differences between Marguerite's spirituality and the somatic piety of many women, see Amy Hollywood, *The Soul as Virgin Wife: Mechthild of Magdeburg, Marguerite Porete, and Meister Eckhart* (Notre Dame, IN: University of Notre Dame Press, 1995), pp. 109–12; and Amy Hollywood, "Suffering Transformed: Marguerite Porete, Meister Eckhart, and the Problem of Women's Spirituality," in *Meister Eckhart and the Beguine Mystics*, ed. Bernard McGinn (New York: Continuum, 1997), pp. 87–113.

[32] For the passages that the ecclesiastical authorities found especially problematic, see Marguerite Porete, *The Mirror of Simple Souls*, trans. Ellen Babinsky (New York: Paulist Press, 1993), chs. 19, 21, 58; pp. 101, 103–4, 135. The documents for the trial of Marguerite and the cleric who attempted to defend her are edited by Paul Verdeyen, "Le Procès d'inquisition contre Marguerite Porete et Guiard de Cressonessart (1309–1310)," *Revue d'histoire ecclésiastique* 81 (1986): 47–94.

[33] See Robert Lerner, *The Heresy of the Free Spirit in the Later Middle Ages* (Berkeley: University of California Press, 1972); and Bernard McGinn, *The Presence of God: A History of Western Christian Mysticism*, vol. 4, *The Harvest of Mysticism in Medieval Germany, 1300–1500* (New York: Crossroad, 2005), pp. 48–79.

[34] On Marguerite's potential influence on Eckhart, see Maria Lichtman, "Marguerite Porete and Meister Eckhart," in *Meister Eckhart and the Beguine Mystics*, ed.

condemnation. Occasionally we find ecclesiastical authorities recasting somatic mystical experiences to conform to a more palatable conception of rapture. Bonaventure, for example, who became master general of the Franciscan order, regarded Francis as "an example of perfect contemplation."[35] Yet Bonaventure insisted that a contemplative shun all images in meditation, even though a speaking crucifix was pivotal in Francis's own conversion.[36] By the same token, Bonaventure remained hostile to visions, believing them "more to be feared than desired," despite the fact that Francis's stigmata were administered by a seraph during the course of an ecstasy.[37]

Because mystical rapture accords a direct experience of God independently of the church, there was never a time when these experiences were not treated with caution, if not with down right suspicion. During the thirteenth century there were already incidents in which Satan appeared as an angel of light, or even as Christ, during the course of a female mystic's revelations.[38] William of Auvergne (d. 1249), archbishop of Paris, also raised the possibility of an individual being raptured into evil.[39] Such concerns grew with time. Over the course of the fourteenth century, the university authorities' growing apprehension about the proliferation of mystical ecstasies and the difficulty of deciphering between divine and diabolical inspiration came to be expressed in treatises on spiritual discernment aimed at assessing the authenticity of a given mystical experience.[40] Like Bonaventure, John Gerson (d. 1429), chancellor of the University of Paris, believed that contemplation enlisting

McGinn, pp. 65–86. For a discussion of the exceptions made for mystical clerics, see Robert Lerner's "Ecstatic Dissent," *Speculum* 67 (1992): 33–57.

[35] Bonaventure, *Itinerarium mentis ad Deum* 7.3, as cited by McGinn, *The Flowering of Mysticism*, p. 34

[36] Thomas of Celano, *Second Life* 1.6.10, in *St. Francis of Assisi: Writings*, pp. 370–1.

[37] Bonaventure, *Sententiae* dist. 9, art.1, q. 6, as cited by McGinn, *The Flowering of Mysticism*, p. 111. On Francis's reception of the stigmata, see *Legends of the Three Companions* 17.69–70, in *St. Francis of Assisi: Writings*, pp. 953–4; *Little Flowers of St. Francis* pt. 2, consideration 3, in *St. Francis of Assisi: Writings*, p. 1449; and see also Thomas of Celano, *First Life* 2.19.112–15, in *St. Francis of Assisi: Writings*, pp. 325–30.

[38] See Stephen of Bourbon, *Anecdotes historiques, légendes et apologues tirés du recueil inédit d'Etienne de Bourbon*, ed. A. Lecoy de la Marche (Paris: Librairie Renouard, 1877), pp. 198–9. See Elliott, *Fallen Bodies*, pp. 52–6; and Dyan Elliot, "True Presence/False Christ: Antinomies of Embodiment in Late Medieval Spirituality," *Mediaeval Studies* 64 (2002): 241–65.

[39] Elliott, *Proving Woman*, pp. 253–4; and Elliot, "Physiology of Rapture," pp. 149–51.

[40] See Rosalynn Voaden, *God's Words, Women's Voices: The Discernment of Spirits in the Writing of Late-Medieval Women Visionaries* (Woodbridge, UK: Boydell Press, 1999); Caciola, *Discerning Spirits*, pp. 285–309; and Elliott, *Proving Woman*, pp. 257–84.

mental images was dangerous and hence was extremely apprehensive of female mystics and their clerical supporters. He further emphasized the parallels between rapture and delusional trance-like states brought on by illness.[41] Gerson ultimately would shape the genre of spiritual discernment into an instrument for suppressing female visionaries. His efforts in this direction culminated in the treatise *On the Proving of Spirits*, which challenged the recent canonization of Bridget of Sweden at the Council of Constance (1415).[42]

The medieval era presents a number of particular challenges to understanding the female mystic's spiritual experiences because she was, more often than not, illiterate, and the task of recording her revelations usually fell to one of her admirers. Moreover, this difficulty is complicated by the requirements of pious humility, which dictated reluctance over revealing revelations.[43] As is apparent in the rapport between James of Vitry and Mary of Oignies, the confessor, who was privy to the mystic's inner life, tended to be the most likely conduit for these experiences. John Coakley, who has studied a number of such relationships, stresses the collaborative nature of such partnerships.[44] But there is little doubt that, at times, the clerical voice overwhelmed the mystic's experience. Beatrice of Nazareth (d. 1268) is one of the rare mystics for whom we have two accounts of the same experience: her own and that of her clerical amanuensis. As Amy Hollywood has demonstrated, the cleric is much more inclined to emphasize the bodily nature of Beatrice's experiences than did the mystic herself.[45] Karen Scott observes similar discrepancies in points of emphases between Catherine of Siena and her confessor, Raymond of Capua. While Raymond tends to emphasize paranormal phenomena, such as Catherine's reception of the stigmata or her mystical death, Catherine stresses active works

---

[41] Elliott, *Proving Woman*, pp. 203–211, 277–8.
[42] John Gerson, "The Concept of 'Discretio spirituum,'" in John Gerson, *"De probatione spirituum" and "De distinctione verarum visionum a falsis,"* trans. Paschal Boland (Washington, DC: Catholic University Press, 1959). On Gerson, see Brian Patrick McGuire, *Jean Gerson and the Last Medieval Reformation* (University Park: Pennsylvania State University Press, 2005).
[43] Dyan Elliott, "*Dominae* or *Dominatae*?: Female Mystics and the Trauma of Textuality," in *Women, Marriage, and Family in Medieval Christendom: Essays in Memory of Michael M. Sheehan, C.S.B.*, ed. Constance Rousseau and Joel Rosenthal (Kalamazoo, MI: Medieval Institute Publications, 1998), pp. 50–3.
[44] John Coakley, *Women, Men, and Spiritual Power: Female Saints and Their Male Collaborators* (New York: Columbia University Press, 2006).
[45] Amy Hollywood, "Inside Out: Beatrice of Nazareth and Her Hagiographer," in *Gendered Voices: Medieval Saints and their Interpreters*, ed. Catherine Mooney (Philadelphia: University of Pennsylvania Press, 1999), pp. 78–98.

like charity and peacemaking.[46] In the cases of Angela of Foligno and Dorothea of Montau, moreover, the clerical hand does not simply bias the narrative produced, but also arguably imposes a distinct interpretation of the mystical experiences on the women.[47]

The recent work of scholars such as Christina Mazzoni and Amy Hollywood demonstrates that the experiences of medieval mystics have engaged and continue to engage intellectuals in disciplines as diverse as medicine, psychoanalysis, and philosophy.[48] Recently, medievalists have turned to the anthropological work on ecstatic religions, stressing the parallels between rapture and various forms of trance or spirit possession in other cultures.[49] Yet it is with good reason that Michel de Certeau describes mysticism as the "language of the unsayable":[50] one of the hallmarks of the authentic mystical experience is the impossibility of its communication. So even if anthropological or medical breakthroughs fully explain the phenomenon of rapture, it is still impossible for the average reader, medieval or modern, to fathom an experience the very essence of which is its inscrutability.

---

[46] Karen Scott, "Mystical Death, Bodily Death: Catherine of Siena and Raymond of Capua on the Mystic's Encounter with God," in *Gendered Voices*, pp. 136–67; see also F. Thomas Luongo, *The Saintly Politics of Catherine of Siena* (Ithaca, NY: Cornell University Press, 2006).

[47] See Catherine Mooney, "The Authorial Role of Brother A. in the Composition of Angela of Foligno's Revelations," in *Creative Women in Medieval and Early Modern Italy: A Religious and Artistic Renaissance*, ed. E. Ann Matter and John Coakley (Philadelphia: University of Pennsylvania Press, 1994), pp. 34–63; Elliott, "Authorizing a Life: The Collaboration of Dorothea of Montau and John Marienwerder," in *Gendered Voices*, ed. Mooney, 168–91; and Coakley, *Women, Men, and Spiritual Power*, pp. 193–310.

[48] Cristina Mazzoni, *Saint Hysteria: Neurosis, Mysticism, and Gender in European Culture* (Ithaca, NY: Cornell University Press, 1996); Amy Hollywood, *Sensible Ecstasy: Mysticism, Sexual Difference, and the Demands of History* (Chicago: University of Chicago Press, 2002).

[49] I. M. Lewis, *Ecstatic Religion: An Anthropological Study of Spirit Possession and Shamanism* (Harmondsworth, UK: Penguin, 1971). See Caciola, "Possession Phenomena, Possession Systems," in *Communicating with the Spirits*, ed. Klaniczay and Pócs, pp. 84–151; and Barbara Newman, "Possessed by the Spirit: Devout Women, Demoniacs, and the Apostolic Life in the Thirteenth Century," *Speculum* 73 (1998): 733–70.

[50] Michel de Certeau, "Mysticism," *Diacritics* 22 (1992): 17.

11 *Unio Mystica*/Mystical Union

BERNARD MCGINN

Although union language is not the only way of understanding how to attain some form of direct contact with God in this life, it has played a central role in the history of Christian mysticism. The notion that a human being can become one with a god or gods seems to depend on how one views divinity. When the gods are conceived of as stronger beings within the world system, the boundaries between the divine and the human realm are porous, allowing for various kinds of intermingling of superior and inferior beings. The emergence of belief in a single divine source of all things, a transcendent God or Supreme Principle, might seem to preclude the possibility of uniting with that principle. In the face of such transcendence, the proper response of humans should be worship, not desire for communion. Yet paradoxically, the growth of a strong sense of the difference between the one God and the limited world of creatures seems to have encouraged, rather than suppressed, desire to become one with God.

In the wake of the critique of the Olympian gods by Greek philosophers, uniting with the source of all things took on an increasingly important role in Greek philosophical religion. Many of the issues involved in union with the Supreme God were explored by Greek philosophers between ca. 300 BCE and 300 CE. The richest development is found in Plotinus (205–70 CE), whose *Enneads* set forth a sophisticated doctrine of attaining indistinct union, not only with ultimate existence, or Intellect, but even with the One hidden beyond the realm of all visible and invisible reality. Plotinus's view of such "oneing" (*henôsis*) is, at times, expressed in personal terms: "But there is our true love, with whom we also can be united, having a part in him and truly possessing him, not in the flesh from outside. But 'whoever has seen, knows what I am saying,' that the soul then has another life and draws near, and has already come near and has a part in him."[1]

---

[1] Plotinus, *Enneads*, 7 vols. (Cambridge, MA: Harvard University Press, 1987), vol. 7, p. 339.

Belief in a single omnipotent God also evolved among the ancient Jews, as reflected in the texts that came to form the Hebrew Bible. Here, the distinction between the God "who made heaven and earth" (Gn 1:1) and human beings who are part of this creation erected a barrier to language about uniting with the "Holy One, Blessed be He." God sometimes appeared to his favored friends, although the Hebrew Bible reflects different views on whether God is ever really visible to humans. If language of uniting with God is foreign to the authors of what Christians called the Old Testament, later Christian teaching on mystical union still made use of many texts from the book that stressed the desirability of direct experience of God, for example, "Taste and see that the Lord is sweet" (Ps 33:9).

The root of Christian conceptions of union with God is found in the writings that form the New Testament. This message about God's loving concern with humanity manifested through sending his only Son into the world allowed for a new form of relationship with God. Although God as Father remains transcendent ("No one has ever seen God" [Jn 1:18a]), he has now become accessible in the Incarnate Word ("but now his only-begotten Son, who abides in the bosom of the Father, has made him known" [Jn 1:18b]). In the texts of John and Paul, salvation is equated with becoming united to Jesus Christ, the God-man, established as Savior of the world through his death and resurrection. In the Johannine writings, union is expressed in vegetative metaphors ("I am the vine, you are the branches" [Jn 15:5]), and, more daringly, in terms of Jesus's union with his Father ("that they all may be one, as you Father are in me and I in you, that they may also be one in us " [Jn 17:21]). In Paul's epistles, the language of union is even more to the fore – "in Christ" is a central motif of Pauline thought. Believers become one with Christ in baptism, the Eucharistic meal, and every aspect of the life they share with the crucified Lord. As Paul says in Galatians 2:19–20: "I have been crucified with Christ, and I live now not with my own life, but with the life of Christ who lives in me." The believer's union with Jesus Christ is effected through the "Spirit of Christ," who is sent to dwell in the hearts of the faithful (Rom 5:5, 8:1–9; 2 Cor 3:17–18; Gal 4:6; Phil 1:19). In 1 Corinthians 6:17, Paul attacks Christians who commit fornication as sinning against the union of their bodies with Christ, noting that "anyone who is joined to the Lord is one spirit with him," a text often cited by later writers to support their understanding of mystical union.

Christian teaching concerning mystical union, therefore, was a natural outgrowth of the New Testament, one whose development was influenced by Greek philosophical speculation on becoming one with the First Principle. A Christological reading of some Old Testament texts, especially the interpretation of the marriage of the bride and bridegroom in the Song of Songs as an allegory of the union of Christ and the Church, as well as of Christ and the believer, also contributed to the evolution. This is evident in the writings of Origen (190–254), the first theorist of Christian mysticism. His *Commentary on the Song of Songs*, the source of much later mystical writing, stressed many of the central motifs of the tradition, such as contemplation, divinization, and union. Given the erotic model of the uniting of lovers in the Song of Songs, Origen concentrated on how the yearning drive of *erôs*, involving both loving and knowing, leads the soul to friendship with God and fellowship with Jesus, that is, a union that preserves the distinction between Creator and creature. Origen cited 1 Corinthians 6:17 in support of his view of the union of spirits as the goal of the Christian life.[2] His Pauline view of "union of spirits" (*unitas spiritus*) was shared by many later patristic mystics, such as Ambrose of Milan (d. 397).

Although the erotic model of mystical union pioneered by Origen remained central to Christian views of union with God, late antique writers developed other modes of understanding this central theme. At least two were to have considerable influence. The first is the language of indistinct union. Neoplatonic mystics like Plotinus had explored how the soul, or at least its higher self, could attain indistinction with the One. For many believers, such a union seemed to compromise the Christian doctrine of creation. (This is why Augustine's mystical teaching does not use unitive language.) Other mystics, however, especially among the early monastics, used language that invited believers to aspire to becoming absolutely one with God on some level of existence. The *Homilies* ascribed to the early Egyptian monk Macarius appear to come from Syrian ascetics of the late fourth century. Although the teaching they present is more practical than speculative, these sermons contain the earliest uses of the phrase mystical (i.e., hidden) union in Christian literature (e.g., *Homilies* 10.2, 15.2).[3] Evagrius Ponticus (d. 390), the first great monastic mystical theologian, was more speculative. Evagrius went beyond Origen in his teaching on the highest stage of the return to God, what he called essential contemplation (*theôria*) of the Trinity. He taught that the naked intellect (*nous*), purified of the passions that

---

[2] Origen, *The Song of Songs: Commentary and Homilies*, trans. Rowan A. Greer (New York: Paulist Press, 1957), pp. 41, 53.
[3] Pseudo-Macarius, *The Fifty Spiritual Homilies and the Great Letter*, ed. George A. Maloney (New York: Paulist Press, 1992), pp. 89, 108.

block the way to God, is able to become one with the very "science of the Trinity." Evagrius's descriptions of how created minds merge with the Trinity feature language that implies a goal of oneness without distinction. In his *Letter to Melania*, Section 6, he says: "When minds flow back to him like torrents into the sea, he changes them all completely into his own nature, color, and taste. They will no longer be many, but one in his unending and inseparable unity, because they are united and joined with him."[4] A similar form of indistinct union appears in the Dionysian Corpus, treatises ascribed to Paul's Athenian disciple (see Acts 17:34), but that were actually written in monastic circles around 500 CE.[5] In the *Mystical Theology*, Dionysius uses Moses's ascent of the mountain to encounter God in cloud and darkness (Ex 19 ff.) as a model for mystics. Moses undergoes purification in order to gain contemplation of the place where God dwells. Finally, he reaches the state of "mystical union" (*henôsis mystikê*), a condition that can only be indirectly expressed through negative language. "Here," he says, "renouncing all that the mind may conceive, wrapped entirely in the intangible and the invisible, he belongs completely to Him who is beyond everything. Here, being neither oneself nor someone else, one is supremely united in a completely unknowing inactivity of all knowledge."[6]

The late-fourth-century Cappadocian, Gregory of Nyssa (ca. 335–ca. 394), was an important source for the apophatic, or negative, aspect of Dionysian mysticism. Gregory presents another way of understanding union, what he called "mingling," "sharing," and "fellowship" with God. Like Origen, Gregory wrote a commentary on the Song of Songs in the form of fifteen homilies, and, like Dionysius, he pointed to Moses as the ideal mystic in his *Life of Moses*.[7] Both works, while adapting an erotic model of yearning for union and the language of darkness, express a form of mysticism characterized by what Gregory called *epektasis*, or eternal "straining forward" into God (see Phil 3:13). This is a form of attaining God that is unitive rest and, at the same time, unbounded desire for greater contact with the infinite God who always exceeds the limits of created spirits. The central message of the Song of Songs is the

---

[4] Quotation from Bernard McGinn, *The Presence of God: A History of Western Christian Mysticism*, vol. 1, *The Foundations of Mysticism: Origins to the Fifth Century* (New York: Crossroad, 1991), p. 154.
[5] Pseudo-Dionysius, *The Complete Works*, trans. Colm Luibhéid (New York: Paulist Press, 1987).
[6] Pseudo-Dionysius, *The Complete Works*, pp. 137, and 65, 109.
[7] Gregory of Nyssa, *The Life of Moses*, trans. Abraham J. Malherbe and Everett Ferguson (New York: Paulist Press, 1978).

marriage, or "mingling of the human soul with God," realized in erotic *epektasis*. In the first of his homilies on the Song of Songs, Gregory says that the bride is the exemplar for "all others in whom the desire for God is deeply embedded: they never cease to desire, but every enjoyment of God they turn into the kindling of a still more intense desire."[8]

These biblical and patristic roots formed a rich source for tradition. Although the phrase mystical union was quite rare until the seventeenth century, many mystics spoke about becoming one with God and devoted effort to analyzing the modes of union and discriminating between correct and incorrect understandings of such uniting. For heuristic purposes, we can say that conceptions of union fall into two broad camps: (1) union conceived of as a uniting of the Infinite Spirit with the finite spirit in a bond of love that emphasizes the distinction between creator and creature, and (2) union of indistinction that claims that, on some level, God and human are merged into what Meister Eckhart called *ein einic ein* ("a single/simple One"). There was a considerable variety of ways of conceiving these modes of union, and many mystics used language and images expressing both forms.

Expositions of union with God reached a high level of sophistication during the twelfth century, especially among the Cistercians. Bernard of Clairvaux (1090–1153) composed a series of *Sermons on the Song of Songs* that analyzed *unitas spiritus* with great subtlety as an affective and operational union of the soul with Christ, the Divine bridegroom.[9] In his *Treatise on Loving God*, the abbot presented four degrees of the ascent of love to union with God, described by three metaphors taken from the seventh-century monk, Maximus the Confessor. Becoming one with God is like a drop of water dissolved in a vat of wine, an iron heated in a fire until it becomes totally enflamed, or air transformed into sunshine. The metaphors might suggest some kind of fusion or identity with God, but Bernard is quick to caution that "the human substance remains, but in another form."[10] Bernard's friend, William of Saint Thierry (ca. 1085–1148), also used the Pauline *unitas spiritus* text to understand

---

[8] Gregory of Nyssa, *Commentary on the Song of Songs*, trans. Casimir McCambley (Brookline, MA: Hellenic College Press, 1987), p. 51.

[9] There is a translation of Bernard's mystical masterpiece in the four volumes, Bernard of Clairvaux, *Sermons on the Song of Songs*, trans. Killian Walsh and Irene Edmonds (Kalamazoo, MI: Cistercian Publications, 1971–80). For important passages on union, see, e.g., Sermons 2.2, 67.8, 71.6–10, and 83.3 (*On the Song of Songs*, vol. 1, p. 9; vol. 4, pp. 12, 52–6, 182–3).

[10] For a translation and commentary, see Bernard of Clairvaux, *On Loving God*, trans. Emero Stiegman (Kalamazoo, MI: Cistercian Publications, 1995). The passage cited is from 10.28 (p. 30); see also 15.39 (p. 41).

union with God, exploring how union produced "a love that itself was a form of understanding" (*amor ipse intellectus est*). William's view of union was more Trinitarian than Bernard's, because he identified the Holy Spirit as the kiss that binds the Divine Lover and human beloved in the Song of Songs. Like all Christian mystics, William held that full union will only be attained in heaven, but we can begin to share in the life of the three persons who are one God on earth through the action of the Holy Spirit who "is the unity of the Father and the Son; and is also the love and likeness of God and man."[11]

The new mysticism that appeared at the beginning of the thirteenth century featured innovative forms of religious life, especially the mendicants and the beguines, as well as new kinds of teaching. The goal of union was now conceived of as open to all believers and capable of being realized in all walks of life. Mystical texts in the vernacular proliferated, many written by women. Forms of daring, and even excessive, erotic language appeared; some mystics began to speak about forms of indistinction with God achieved by annihilating the created will and human individuality. Such understandings of union were often expressed in terms of the soul's regaining its true home, the precreational status it enjoys as an eternal idea in the mind of God. Beguine mystics, such as Hadewijch (active ca. 1250), Mechthild of Magdeburg (d. 1282), and Marguerite Porete (d. 1310), pioneered the use of the language of indistinction. Hadewijch and Mechthild mingled traditional language reflecting the idea of an erotic *unitas spiritus* and motifs and metaphors suggesting a state of indistinction. Hadewijch, for example, considered the soul and God as mutual abysses. A passage from her Letter 18 speaks of how the soul and God can only find fruition and sufficiency in the abyss of the other – "Soul is a way for the passage of God from the depths of his liberty, that is, into his inmost depths, and God is a way for the passage of the soul into its liberty, that is, into his ground that cannot be touched without contact with the soul's depth."[12] Mechthild's *Flowing Light of the Godhead* contains many accounts of erotic union, but she sometimes goes beyond this to suggest a deeper oneness. In a love drama in the *Flowing Light* (bk.1, ch. 44), God says, "Lady Soul, you are so utterly formed to my nature that not the slightest thing can come between you

---

[11] William of Saint Thierry, *The Enigma of Faith*, ed. John D. Anderson (Kalamazoo, MI: Cistercian Publications, 1973), p. 39. See also William of Saint Thierry, *Exposition on the Song of Songs*, trans. Columba Hart (Kalamazoo, MI: Cistercian Publications, 1989).

[12] Hadewijch, *The Complete Works*, trans. Columba Hart (New York: Paulist Press, 1980), Letter 18, p. 86.

and me."¹³ The most daring teaching about annihilation of the will as necessary for attaining a union of indistinction is found in Marguerite Porete's *Mirror of Simple Annihilated Souls*. Both she and her book were so controversial that they were condemned to the flames as heretical by the Inquisition in 1310.¹⁴

Growing use of the language of indistinction by no means meant the end of the more traditional understanding of union in terms of *unitas spiritus*. The Franciscan mystic Bonaventure (d. 1274) discussed the different ways in which the term union can be understood in Christian discourse. His own teaching, as found in the *Mind's Journey into God*, wove many strands of mysticism into a new Franciscan robe, influenced by the reading of the Dionysian Corpus pioneered by Thomas Gallus (d. 1246). For Gallus, the soul's goal of dark union with God is a passage beyond all forms of knowledge of God into a supreme affectivity (*apex affectionis/affectio principalis*) where uniting (*unitio*) takes place. Gallus's understanding of union is a variant of the traditional erotic model, but his conception of the path is new in its stress upon the cutting off of all intellectual operations at the highest level.¹⁵ This understanding of union is also found in the fourteenth-century English classic, the *Cloud of Unknowing*.¹⁶

Renewed study of the Dionysian Corpus produced another interpretation, the intellective Dionysianism pioneered by Albert the Great (d. 1280), who argued that, although God lies beyond affirmation and negation, as Dionysius taught, and although both loving and knowing are used in the path to union, a heightened form of intellect plays the dominant role. According to the Dominican, Dionysius teaches "how it is necessary to be united to God by intellect and to praise him by word."¹⁷ Albert's Dionysianism was taken up by Meister Eckhart (ca. 1260–1328), perhaps the foremost exponent of the union of indistinction in the Christian tradition.

---

¹³ Mechthild of Magdeburg, *The Flowing Light of the Godhead*, trans. Frank Tobin (New York: Paulist Press, 1998), bk. 1, ch. 44, p. 62.

¹⁴ See Marguerite Porete, *The Mirror of Simple Souls*, trans. Ellen Babinsky (New York: Paulist Press, 1993), e.g., ch. 118, pp. 189–94.

¹⁵ On Thomas Gallus's view of union, see Bernard McGinn, *The Presence of God: A History of Western Christian Mysticism*, vol. 3, *The Flowering of Mysticism: Men and Women in the New Mysticism (1200–1350)* (New York: Crossroad, 1998), pp. 78–87.

¹⁶ Anonymous, *The Cloud of Unknowing*, ed. James Walsh (New York: Paulist Press, 1981).

¹⁷ This passage is found in Bernard McGinn, *The Presence of God: A History of Western Christian Mysticism*, vol. 4, *The Harvest of Mysticism in Medieval Germany (1300–1500)* (New York: Crossroad, 2007), p. 13.

Eckhart's teaching on union is rooted in his master metaphor of the ground (*grunt*), the fused identity of God and the soul. "God's ground is the soul's ground, and the soul's ground is God's ground"; or, to frame the same doctrine in terms of ocular identity: "The eye with which I see God is the same eye with which God sees me" (see, e.g., German Sermons 5b, 12, and 15).[18] Although an equivalent Latin term for *grunt* was lacking, Eckhart expressed the same teaching in his scholastic works in his expositions of divine unity understood as the dialectical indistinction that distinguishes the divine nature from all other things. Two of the essential themes of Eckhart's preaching flow from the indistinct oneness of the ground. The first is his teaching about the birth of the Word in the soul. Because we are eternally one with God in the ground, that is, because "God's existence must be my existence and God's self-identity (*istikeit*) is my self-identity," then, just as the Father is always giving birth to the Son, so too "He gives me birth, me, his son and the same Son."[19] The second theme is the "breaking through" into the hidden ground, or absolute unity, which in one sense lies beyond even the Trinity of Father, Son, and Spirit. The "spark" of the soul, Eckhart says, is not content with the Trinity, or even with the divine essence, "but it wants to know the source of this essence, it wants to go into the simple ground, into the quiet desert into which distinction never gazed, not the Father, nor the Son, nor the Holy Spirit."[20] Thus, on the deepest level, there is no distinction between God and the soul: "Between man and God there is not only no distinction, there is no multiplicity either. There is nothing but one."[21] Nevertheless, Eckhart, like most identity mystics, insisted that absolute oneness continues to coexist with the distinction between creator and creature – distinction and indistinction are reciprocal concepts.

Twenty-eight extracts from Eckhart's teaching were condemned by Pope John XXII in 1329, including several on the birth of the Word and the lack of distinction in God. This condemnation, along with that of Porete and the 1312 conciliar attack on the errors of the so-called Free Spirit heretics, introduced a debate on the differences between true and

---

[18] Many of Eckhart's sermons, as well as selections from his Latin writings, can be found in Meister Eckhart, *The Essential Sermons, Commentaries, Treatises, and Defense*, trans. Edmund Colledge and Bernard McGinn (New York: Paulist Press, 1981); and Meister Eckhart, *Teacher and Preacher*, ed. Bernard McGinn (New York: Paulist Press, 1986). For Sermon 5b and 15, see *The Essential Sermons*, pp. 183, 192; for Sermon 12, see *Teacher and Preacher*, p. 270.

[19] Sermon 6, in Eckhart, *The Essential Sermons*, p. 187.

[20] Sermon 48, in ibid., p. 198.

[21] Sermon 40, in Eckhart, *Teacher and Preacher*, p. 301.

false mysticism that was to last for more than three centuries. Proper understanding of union with God played a central role in these disputes. Expressions of union of indistinction were a priori suspect, though some mystics continued to employ them in qualified ways. This is evident in the writings of Eckhart's followers, Henry Suso and John Tauler. Both of these Dominicans made extensive use of Eckhartian themes, but their understanding of indistinct union gave greater weight to the ongoing ontological difference between God and the soul, making indistinction into a mental category. For the advanced soul, as Suso put it, "a powerful annihilating bursting into the Nothing removes all difference in the ground, not of essences, but on the part of our perception."[22]

An original doctrine of union appeared in the writings of the Flemish canon, John Ruusbroec (d. 1381), a contemporary of Eckhart's followers. Ruusbroec knew some sermons by Eckhart and denounced them as dangerous, even heretical. Nevertheless, his own teaching on becoming one with God owed something to Eckhart's indistinction. Ruusbroec described three interdependent forms of union here and in heaven, a teaching that incorporated the *unitas spiritus* model and aspects of Eckhartian teaching on *unitas indistinctionis*. Throughout his treatises, but especially in his late *Little Book of Enlightenment*, Ruusbroec distinguishes (1) union with an intermediary (uniting with God through grace and the traditional rituals of the church), (2) union without an intermediary (the direct encounter with God in the depths of the soul), and finally, (3) "union without difference or distinction ... where the three persons give way to the essential unity and without distinction enjoy essential blessedness.... There all the elevated spirits in their superessence are one enjoyment and one beatitude with God without difference."[23] Ruusbroec's attempt to synthesize the various forms of mystical union was criticized, in his lifetime and later. Jean Gerson (d. 1429) attacked Ruusbroec during the first decade of the fifteenth century; Gerson even expressed doubts about the language used by Bernard of Clairvaux. Nevertheless, Ruusbroec's teaching about a superessential union was mediated to later mystics through his own works in translation and those of his followers.

Discussion and debate over mystical union continued into the early modern period of the sixteenth and seventeenth centuries. Some of the

---

[22] Henry Suso, *The Little Book of Truth*, in *The Exemplar, with Two German Sermons*, trans. and ed. Frank Tobin (New York: Paulist Press, 1989), ch. 5, p. 320.
[23] John Ruusbroec, *The Little Book of Enlightenment*, in *The Spiritual Espousals and Other Works*, trans. James A. Wiseman (New York: Paulist Press, 1985), p. 265.

radical Protestant reformers used the language of indistinct union, but most Protestant mystics, such as Johann Arndt (d. 1621) and the seventeenth-century Puritan mystics, tended to employ traditional expressions of love union. In the Catholic world, the need for careful discrimination of proper ways of expressing union is evident in the major schools: the Spanish mysticism of the sixteenth century and the French mysticism of the seventeenth. Teresa of Avila (d. 1582) was a profound analyst of the psychology of mystical states, but her understanding of union, although it shifted from her earlier to later works, fundamentally adhered to the traditional erotic model drawn from the Song of Songs.[24] Her friend John of the Cross (d. 1591), like Ruusbroec, worked out a synthesis of various ways of understanding union, though he was also careful to insist on the ongoing ontological difference between creator and creature. Like the mystics of indistinction, John taught that mystical transformation of the self requires an annihilation of the ordinary modes of knowing and loving in order to attain oneness with the Trinity in what he called "the center of the soul." Union begins in the stage of betrothal and reaches its culmination in "spiritual marriage." In both manifestations it can be said of God and the soul that "each is the other and that both are one."[25] Because "the soul's center is God," the more the soul penetrates the center, the more its activity becomes divine. John insists, however, that the soul taken in itself remains a created reality. Because the soul now loves in a divine way, however, it seems to be God. As a passage from the *Spiritual Canticle* explains, "This thread of love binds the two ... with such firmness and so unites and transforms them and makes them one in love, that, although they differ in substance, yet in glory and appearance the soul seems to be God and God the soul."[26]

The French mystics of the seventeenth century represent the last great chapter of traditional analysis of mystical union. Despite the influence of medieval and Spanish mysticism on these writers, the French School created by Cardinal Bérulle (d. 1629) was an original development. Bérulle's view of mystical union involved adherence to the "states," or salvific mysteries, of Jesus that produces an unmediated relational unity. In his *Discourse on the States and Grandeurs of Jesus* he explains his notion of unity in the single mystical person of the Word made flesh as

---

[24] Teresa of Avila, *The Interior Castle*, trans. Kieran Kavanaugh and Otillo Rodriguez (New York: Paulist Press, 1979). See esp., bk. 7.1–2, pp. 172–82.
[25] John of the Cross, *Spiritual Canticle* 12.7, in *The Collected Works of John of the Cross*, trans. Kieran Kavanaugh and Otillo Rodriguez (Washington, DC: ICS Publications, 1991), pp. 517–18.
[26] John of the Cross, *Spiritual Canticle* 31.1, in ibid., p. 595.

the product of love: "For love transports us out of ourselves into him and, what is more, it makes us like he is in himself, by divinizing and transforming us into God."[27]

The central figure of French mysticism was Francis de Sales (d. 1622), the author of the last great mystical summa, the *Treatise on the Love of God*, published in 1616. The work, remarkable more for its synthesis than for its originality, contains a summary of the traditional view of the *unitas spiritus*.[28] Erotic union with God was also explored by the main female mystics of the time, such as the Ursuline nun, Marie of the Incarnation (d. 1672), and the controversial Madame Guyon (d. 1717), although the latter also employed the language of mystical annihilation in her voluminous writings. Guyon was central to the Quietist Controversy (1675–1700), a late chapter in the conflict over false mysticism. Although mystical union was not the most prominent aspect of the Quietist debates, the key topics, such as the proper understanding of modes of contemplation, holy indifference, and pure love, implied the themes of annihilation and mystical indistinction that had been at issue for centuries. The 1699 papal letter condemning Guyon's supporter, Archbishop Fénelon (d. 1715), specified twenty-three errors in his writings, including the claim that "in the state of the contemplative or unitive life every motive of interested fear or hope is lost."[29] The long history of understandings of mystical union and debates over its proper expression have provided abundant material for the study of mysticism in recent scholarship.

---

[27] Pierre Bérulle, *Discourse on the States and Grandeurs of Jesus*, 9.1 in *Bérulle and the French School*, trans. Lowell M. Glendon (New York: Paulist Press, 1989), p. 148.

[28] Saint Francis of Sales, *Treatise on the Love of God*, trans. Henry Benedict Mackey (Westminster, MD: Newman Press, 1953), pp. 301–24.

[29] Fénelon's understanding of mysticism is found especially in his *Maxims of the Saints*, available in François Fénelon, *Selected Writings*, ed. Chad Helms (New York: Paulist Press, 2006), pp. 209–97.

12 *Actio et Contemplatio*/Action and Contemplation

CHARLOTTE RADLER

For most Christian mystics, the experience of the presence of God not only alters their interior journey but also radically transforms their exterior life. Leonardo Boff outlines a new vision for sanctity and mystical union with God that entails being contemplative while working toward liberation. This call to be *contemplativus in liberatione*, echoing Jerónimo Nadal's characterization of Ignatius of Loyola's spirituality as *simul in actione contemplativus* ("contemplative while in action"), involves a critique of reductive configurations of the relationship between *ora et labora* ("pray and work") that devolve into polarizations or spiritual monophysitisms (traditionally the term monophysitism refers to the "heretical" belief that Christ has only one [Greek *monos*] nature [Greek *physis*], as his humanity is absorbed and transfigured by his divinity; in this particular context, it signifies a one-sided emphasis on either action or contemplation).[1] For Boff, the summons to be contemplatives in liberation expresses a synthesis of prayer in action that holds the two poles together dialectically, "treating them as two spaces that are open to one another and imply each other."[2] Boff's discussion highlights tensions that Christian mystics have wrestled with as they have articulated the relationship between *actio* and *contemplatio*. Yet the assertion that a dichotomy between action and contemplation is characteristic of the Christian mystical traditions (mirroring a putative dichotomy between body and soul, world and church) is controverted by an examination of several seminal Christian thinkers.

In this essay, I examine the divergent yet continuous attempts at constructing the relationship between action and contemplation found in the writings of Augustine (354–430), Meister Eckhart (1260–1328),

---

[1] Leonardo Boff, "The Need for Political Saints: From a Spirituality of Liberation to the Practice of Liberation," *Cross Currents* 30, no. 4 (Winter 1980/1): 371–2; Jerónimo Nadal, *Epistolae P. Hieronumi Nadal*. IV. "P. Hieronumi Natalis in Examen Annotationes" (Madrid, Spain: Typis Gabrielis Lopez del Horno, 1905), 66, p. 651.

[2] Leonardo Boff, "The Need for Political Saints," p. 373.

Ignatius of Loyola (1491–1556), Thomas Merton (1915–68), Dorothee Soelle (1929–2003), and Leonardo Boff (b. 1938). Augustine's understanding of the relationship between action and contemplation shares an assumption that was widespread in patristic thought. It favors contemplation as the highest goal, but acknowledges that the realities of this life necessitate oscillation between the two. In the late medieval and early modern periods, Eckhart and Ignatius reconstitute the relationship between action and contemplation, for they envision their dynamic union. In the twentieth century, Merton develops a nondualist conception of the relationship between world and monastery, action and contemplation. In the twenty-first century, Soelle forges an inclusive vision of mysticism and, resonating with Boff's insight, links mysticism with the praxis of liberation and resistance.

Christian concern for the relationship between action and contemplation did not arise in a vacuum. Greek philosophical, theological, and political traditions constitute one intellectual horizon for interpreting Christian views. Christian thinkers assumed the Greek distinction between *praxis* – active participation in the public life of the *polis* – and *theōria* – the philosophical pursuit of truth. In the Western Christian tradition these modalities of life came to be known as the *vita activa* and the *vita contemplativa*. Etymologically, the Latin term *actio* comes from the verb *agere*, to do, while *contemplatio* stems from the verb *contemplari*, which originally meant to mark out a space for the augurs to read the augeries. Christian theological traditions disrupt the classical template by depoliticizing the concept of *praxis* to mean the active love of neighbor and by refiguring the meaning of *theōria* to mean a contemplative experience of the divine presence. They maintain that the perfect earthly life is a balance between the contemplative experience of God and the life of charity. Action and contemplation are no longer seen as alternative ways of living, but, to varying degrees, as integrated and mutually transforming aspects of the life of the Christian.

Beginning at least with Origen (d. ca. 254), the story of Jesus's visit to Mary and Martha (Lk 10:38–42; Jn 12:1–8) becomes a central locus for understanding the relationship between action and contemplation, Martha signifying the former and Mary the latter. In Luke's version of the narrative (Lk 10:38–42), Jesus is received in the house of Martha. While Martha is busy serving, Mary sits at Jesus's feet and listens to his words. Martha grows frustrated with her sister's lack of assistance and implores Jesus to ask Mary to help her. Jesus replies that "only one thing is necessary. Mary has chosen the best part, and it will not be taken away from her" (Lk 10:42). John's account of the story (Jn 12:1–8) differs from

Luke's rendering: as Martha serves, Mary pours an expensive ointment over Jesus's feet and wipes them with her hair. Although Judas reprimands her action, Jesus praises it. The varied interpretations of these texts reflect the changing concerns and values of different interpreters and their communities. The narrative does not offer a straightforward template for understanding the interrelationship between *actio* and *contemplatio* but gives rise to diverging readings.

AUGUSTINE: LOVING CONTEMPLATION, LOVING ACTION

Augustine of Hippo advocates a mixed life of action and contemplation with a hierarchical relationship between the two: although works are necessary and good, they are subordinate to the delights of contemplation by which the soul ascends toward a vision of God. Nevertheless, Augustine's hierarchical ordering is partially based upon his construal of action as transient activity and contemplation as eternal repose. The realities of this life nevertheless call for a balanced life in which contemplation is necessarily suspended by the demands of charity and one's actions become rightly ordered through contemplative love. Augustine outlines three forms of life – the contemplative, active, and mixed – exhorting the virtue of balance: "As to these three modes of life ... he may choose any of them without detriment to his eternal interests.... No man has a right to lead such a life of contemplation as to forget in his own ease the service due to his neighbour; nor has any man a right to be so immersed in active life as to neglect the contemplation of God."[3]

Augustine refracts the question of the relationship between action and contemplation through his doctrine of the whole Christ (*totus Christus*), with Christ as head and the Church as body. According to the teaching of *totus Christus*, Christ unites with humanity in the incarnation in order to transfigure humanity in his body. Augustine conceptualizes *totus Christus* in such a way that daily life becomes the format for the continuing conformation to Christ; consequently, human beings should not abandon everyday life. The incarnate Christ – in whom action and contemplation organically converge – immerses himself in the human condition in love and solidarity, and, by immersing itself in works of mercy, humanity acts through Christ's same love and solidarity.

---

[3] Augustine, *The City of God*, trans. Marcus Dodds (New York: The Modern Library, 1950), 19.19, pp. 697–8.

As there is unity between action and contemplation, there is unity in the twofold commandment to love God with all one's heart, soul, and mind, and the neighbor as oneself (Mt 22:34–40). Love, hence, has a "double face."[4] Augustine boldly identifies love of God and love of neighbor without conflating them. Both are the same unifying love, but with a comprehensive range that includes two very distinct objects: "But, if you love your brother, perhaps you love your brother and don't love Christ? How can that be ...? When you love Christ's members, then, you love Christ.... Love, then, cannot be separated.... But unless the heat of charity blazes up, there can be no fusion of many into one. Because we love God, that is how we know that we love the sons of God."[5] Because God is united to humanity through the incarnation, Christ is present in one's fellow human beings, and one loves God in loving others.

Augustine discusses the agile "ambidexterity" necessary in everyday life through the Martha and Mary *topos*, for Martha and Mary lived together in one house and united in their reception of Jesus in their home: "So there remained in that house, which welcomed the Lord, two kinds of life in two women; both innocent, both praiseworthy; one laborious, the other leisurely.... So there were in that house these two kinds of life, and the very fountain of life himself."[6] However, even though both vocations are essential in order to host and serve Christ, Martha and Mary serve in distinct ways. Martha attends to the fleshly needs – food and drink – of the incarnate Christ. But while Martha feeds Jesus, Mary feeds on the eternal word of Christ.[7]

Following earlier interpretations, Augustine also sees the active Martha and contemplative Mary as mirroring the sisters Leah and Rachel in the Hebrew scriptures. Although Augustine appropriates these *topoi* in traditional ways, he also reinscribes their meaning: Leah and Martha denote the present church, while Rachel and Mary represent the church to come. Whereas the former signify the service and administration that currently sustain the Christian community, the latter connote the future tranquility to be enjoyed by the Christian community in eternity. Augustine presents them as two interlocking phases in the historical trajectory of the church. He explains his reapplication of Martha and Mary, "So you see ... that in these two women who were both dear to the

---

[4] Tarcisius van Bavel, "Double Face of Love," *Augustinian Studies* 17 (1986): 169–81.
[5] Augustine, *Homilies on the First Epistle of John*, trans. Boniface Ramsey (Hyde Park, NY: New City Press, 2008), 10.3, III/14, pp. 148–9.
[6] Augustine, *Sermons*, trans. Edmund Hill (Brooklyn, NY: New City Press, 1992), 104.4, III/4, p. 83.
[7] Ibid., 103.2–3, III/4, pp. 76–7.

Lord, both lovely people, both disciples of his; ... in these two women two kinds of life are represented: present life and future life, toilsome and restful, miserable and beatific, temporal and eternal life."[8] Martha's valuable charity toward her neighbor is an inescapable duty in this present age troubled by desperate need, but it is an age that will eventually cease. Mary has chosen the better part because it is everlasting and suffused with perfect love. "You [Martha] have chosen a good part, but she [Mary] a better one," Augustine writes. "What you have chosen comes to an end. You are serving the hungry, serving the thirsty, making beds for people to sleep on, offering your house to those who wish to stay there. All these things come to an end.... 'Mary has chosen the better part, which will not be taken away from her.' She has chosen to contemplate, chosen to live on the Word."[9] While Mary is at rest and at eternal peace in the homeland, Martha labors with the ephemeral business of the exile on her pilgrimage to find peace. In the final stillness of the contemplative vision in the afterlife – when our restless hearts find rest in God – Leah becomes Rachel and Martha becomes Mary. However, the metaphorical pattern is more complex because Augustine does not posit a bifurcation between time and eternity, for the future breaks into the present life and the lives of the two sisters are entwined. Mary is a multivalent signifier, who in her person illustrates how contemplative experiences in the present life (albeit fragmentary, as if through an aperture) stretch toward permanence and fullness in eternity.

MEISTER ECKHART: A LIVING UNION OF ACTION AND CONTEMPLATION

Meister Eckhart's reconfiguration of the dialectical union of action and contemplation constitutes an original integration and sanctification of the world of action. In his complex mystical theology, Eckhart – a Dominican teacher, preacher, and spiritual director – construes the relationship between action and contemplation through the praxis of detachment (*abegescheidenheit*). According to Eckhart, there is a dialectical continuity between God and world that ruptures any static duality between Creator and creation. Through detachment, a practice intimately linked to Eckhart's larger apophatic method, the human being cuts away extraneous attachments to awaken to its simple and divine identity. The process of detachment dethrones the autonomous self and uncovers

---

[8] Ibid.,104.4, III/4, p. 83.
[9] Ibid.,169.17, III/5, p. 234. See also, e.g., Augustine, *The Trinity* 1.20.

the shared ground of being, a transcendent and transparent nothingness from whence one comes and to which one will return. This recognition has implications for the way in which Eckhart reimagines the relationship between action and contemplation, because it is by overcoming a myopic solipsism that one can truly be and act in the world. By deconstructing the autonomous "I," the human being adopts God's will and freedom. "If our will becomes God's will, that is good." Yet Eckhart jolts his audience by radicalizing his claim: "if, however, God's will becomes our will, that is far better."[10] Eckhart suggests that this person and God are so united that they are more one than God and the Trinity. Through detachment, the human being so conforms to God that its being, will, and action form a comprehensive unity and transform the world. True detachment means that a person has God wherever she is, be it in the bustling streets or the tranquility of a cell. Eckhart thus assimilates the interior and exterior dimensions of existence in what has been called his this-worldly mysticism.[11]

In his mystical theology, Eckhart posits a living union and harmonious continuity between the active life and the contemplative life, as actions abound from the inner divine source. "One ought not to avoid or escape or deny the interior," he tells his Dominican novices, "but one should learn to work in it and with it and from it precisely so that one lets inwardness break out into activity and activity lead into inwardness, and one becomes accustomed to act freely.... [I]f both could exist in one that would be the best, so that one could work together with God."[12] Eckhart's subversive reading of the Mary and Martha story in German Sermon 86 captures cogently this dynamic union between action and contemplation. (Though Eckhart's reading in many ways breaks with the preceding tradition, Giles Constable holds that his privileging of Martha over Mary was not unprecedented, albeit unusual.[13]) Perfectly detached and acting out of a "well-exercised ground" (*ein wol geüebeter grunt*), Martha epitomizes true spiritual maturity as she serves Christ and actually practices life.[14] Martha was what she did and did what she

[10] Meister Eckhart, "Sermon 25," in Meister Eckhart, *Die deutschen Werke*, vol. 2, ed. Josef Quint (Stuttgart and Berlin, Germany: W. Kolhhamer Verlag, 1936–), pp. 8–9. My translation.

[11] Reiner Schürmann, *Meister Eckhart: Mystic and Philosopher* (Bloomington, IN: Indiana University Press, 1978), p. 47.

[12] Meister Eckhart, "Traktat 2: Liber 'Benedictus': Die rede der underscheidunge," in Eckhart, *Die deutschen Werke*, vol. 5, p. 291. My translation.

[13] Giles Constable, *Three Studies in Medieval Religious and Social Thought* (Cambridge: Cambridge University Press, 1995), p. 116.

[14] Meister Eckhart, "Sermon 86, 'Intravit Iesus in quoddam castellum,'" in Eckhart, *Die deutsche Werke*, vol. 3, p. 481.

was and so attained the noblest form of knowing. Because she remains grounded in her being (which is also God's being), her everyday activity and service do not uproot her but bring her blessedness and joy. Mary, conversely, sits blissfully at Christ's feet without exercising any activity; her addiction to this delightful feeling interrupts the flow from interiority to exteriority.

Eckhart's critical appraisal of Mary's character deconstructs a dualistic paradigm and forges a synthesis of action and contemplation. His rereading also disproves accusations of quietism, as he ends the sermon by criticizing those wishing to be free of work. Only by living and practicing virtue can the human being fully follow Christ. Unlike Augustine, who contends that Martha ultimately becomes Mary, Eckhart configures a model whereby Mary ultimately becomes Mary, that is, as she recovers her own ground she truly becomes what she always was. Thus, although Mary must become Martha before she becomes Mary, it is too facile to argue that Eckhart merely inverts the Augustinian paradigm. Rather, as Martha becomes Martha through detachment and activity "without a why" (*sunder warumbe*), Mary finally becomes Mary through the same practices. Eckhart's refusal to metamorphose Mary into Martha or Martha into Mary conveys his understanding of the vocation of detached life: be and do what you are, as you are, in essence, carrying all truth within you.[15]

Though the posthumous condemnation of tenets of Eckhart's thought in 1329 complicated his reception, Eckhart's mystical theology indicates a ripe theological, philosophical, and social climate that transformed thinking about *actio* and *contemplatio*. The richness of the Christian mystical traditions allows for several coexisting paradigms, but from Eckhart on we see attempts at integrating action into the spiritual life rather than constructing it as an addendum to contemplation. Ignatius of Loyola, although a very different kind of thinker than Eckhart, offered one particularly influential model for this integration of action and contemplation.

IGNATIUS OF LOYOLA: CONTEMPLATION IN ACTION

Ignatius of Loyola founded the Society of Jesus in 1534 with the mandate to promote the greater glory of God and the good of souls.[16] In fulfilling

---

[15] See Meister Eckhart, "Sermon 5b, 'In hoc apparuit,'" in Eckhart, *Die deutsche Werke*, vol. 1, p. 95.

[16] Ignatius of Loyola, *The Constitutions of the Society of Jesus*, trans. George E. Ganss (New York: Paulist Press, 1991), no. 360, pp. 294–5.

this apostolic mission, Jesuits would undertake obedient service and active engagement with the world that were "not only the equivalent of the union and recollection of uninterrupted contemplation, but even more acceptable to Him, proceeding as they do from a more active and vigorous charity."[17] This vigorous charity was guided by an *indiferençia* that withdraws from the world and an active mind and discerning heart that seek and find God in all things.[18] Prayer conforms the human will to God's will through love and pure intention and renders service the substance and goal of contemplative experience.

Ignatius configures a continuous flow between contemplation and action, just as Mary and Martha are united and mutually aid each other. The purpose of *The Spiritual Exercises* is to engender an intimate spiritual awareness of God that orders one's life for service. The participant imagines the Nativity and accompanies Mary and Joseph, "contemplating them, and serving them in their needs, just as if I [the participant] were there."[19] Contemplation removes all temporal and spatial distance and confers on the participant an active presence as a witness – experiencing the Nativity through the senses – to the mystery. But in a multidimensional motion, Ignatius stretches the activity within contemplation from the biblical scene to the participant's own time and place, allowing the narrative events to become textured events that break into the participant's life. This intersection is transformative – "a kind of osmosis" – and compels the participant to become an apostle who follows Christ and asks "Lord, to whom shall we go?"[20] Hence, Ignatius, similar to Eckhart, rehabilitates history and the world as he maps a mystical discourse and practice in which God's greater glory is sought in contemplative action through loving service of the neighbor.

THOMAS MERTON: OPENNESS, ACTION, AND CONTEMPLATION

In the writings of Thomas Merton, again, the putative binary between the active and contemplative lives and, more particularly, between the

---

[17] Ignatius of Loyola, *Letters of St. Ignatius of Loyola*, trans. William J. Young (Chicago: Loyola University Press, 1959), Letter 2383, IV, 127, p. 255.

[18] Ignatius of Loyola, *The Spiritual Exercises*, trans. George E. Ganss (New York: Paulist Press, 1991), no. 23, p. 130; Ignatius, *The Constitutions of the Society of Jesus*, no. 288, p. 292.

[19] Ignatius of Loyola, *The Spiritual Exercises*, no. 114, p. 150.

[20] William J. Young, *Finding God in All Things* (Chicago: Henry Regnery Company, 1958), p. 94.

world and monastery dissolves. He reimagines the meaning and relation of such concepts in a daring fashion that appropriates and reframes Eckhart's mysticism. Like Eckhart, Merton also democratizes and universalizes the mystical journey, configuring it as accessible to everyone everywhere.

Merton's experience on the corner of Fourth and Walnut, the shopping district in Louisville, Kentucky, is an epiphany: "I was suddenly overwhelmed with the realization that I loved all those people, that they were mine and I theirs, that we could not be alien to one another even though we were total strangers. It was like waking from a dream of separateness, of spurious self-isolation in a special world, the world of renunciation and supposed holiness."[21] This experience constitutes a profound realization not only of the unity of all things but also of the interconnectedness of all human beings, a realization that dismantles the idea of a dichotomy between world and monastery. Merton refutes the notion that monks are somehow located outside of contingent everyday existence, separated for God and with special access to God. "Though 'out of the world' we are in the same world as everybody else, the world of the bomb, the world of race hatred, the world of technology, the world of mass media, big business, revolution, and all the rest."[22]

Merton further reflects on the interpenetration of self and world: "I am the world just as you are! Where am I going to look for the world first of all if not in myself?"[23] This insight ruptures a materialist and externalized understanding of the world: "As long as I assume that the world is something I discover by turning on the radio or looking out of the window I am deceived from the start. As long as I imagine that the world is something to be 'escaped' in a monastery ... I am dedicating my life to an illusion."[24] The world is not a vast, material space from which the "I" is separated and which the "I" can observe as an object external to itself. Instead, world and self suffuse in a perichoretic (mutually coinhering and permeating) movement free of stasis and bifurcation. Merton promotes a dialectical balance between the active and contemplative lives, "In the contemplative life, action exists for the sake of contemplation and vice versa."[25] He therefore urges contemplatives to be open to the

---

[21] Thomas Merton, *Conjectures of a Guilty Bystander* (Garden City, NJ: Doubleday, 1989 [1966]), p. 156.
[22] Ibid., p. 157.
[23] Thomas Merton, "Is the World the Problem?" in *Contemplation in a World of Action* (Garden City, NJ: Doubleday and Company, 1971 [1965]), p. 145.
[24] Ibid.
[25] Thomas Merton, "Openness and Cloister," in ibid., p. 141.

world, which requires "being aware of and responsive to the real situation of people in the world, the critical problems in the world."[26]

DOROTHEE SOELLE: CONTEMPLATION IN RESISTANCE

Influenced by Eckhart, contemporary feminist discourse, and eco- and liberation theologies, the mysticism of Dorothee Soelle neither privileges mystical epistemology nor bifurcates mystical experience and social justice. Like Eckhart and Merton, Soelle begins with the bold assertion that everyone is a mystic, "in the sense of a demand on life that cannot be relinquished," thereby radically democratizing mysticism and valorizing everyday life.[27] She reads mystical theology through the lens of social reality and the demands of justice, and she reinterprets the goal of the mystical journey as resistance to the trivialization of life and sexist, ecocidal, imperialistic, and xenophobic values. In her judgment, mystical theology explodes dichotomies between mystical and political, transcendent and immanent, and inner and outer. She therefore concurs with Eckhart's reading of the Mary and Martha story, in which he brings together contemplation and action, theory and praxis, by "conceiving of Mary in Martha."[28]

In mystical union, the soul attains a new vision of the world that obviates segregation between action and contemplation. Such a mysticism of wide-open eyes frees human beings from the three powers that imprison them – the ego, possession, and violence – and has emancipatory practical and secular import. Mysticism, for Soelle, brings together action and contemplation by engendering resistance – the third mystical stage, marking the progression through earlier stages (the *via positiva* of amazement and the *via negativa* of letting go) – that transforms the external world, prophetically challenging patriarchal thinking, and democratically communicating suffering, communion, and joy. The mystical call to *gang uz dir selbst uz* ("go out of yourself") therefore manifests itself not as a private or esoteric experience but as praxis or a *via transformativa* that effectuates change in the world.[29] Mystical experience is necessarily transformative because it always brings about a different relationship to the world and reflects human dependence and interdependence in relation to the rest of creation.

[26] Ibid., p. 138.
[27] Dorothee Soelle, *The Silent Cry: Mysticism and Resistance* (Minneapolis, MN: Fortress Press, 2001), p. 15.
[28] Ibid., p. 200.
[29] Ibid., p. 93.

LEONARDO BOFF: CONTEMPLATION IN LIBERATION

We may now return to Leonardo Boff's rereading of action and contemplation within the Christian mystical traditions. He adopts an integrative model, but, similarly to Soelle, reworks it in the direction of liberation theology. By critiquing and reappropriating previous mystical and monastic traditions and by destabilizing the hegemony of a privileged Eurocentrism, he offers a provocative and transgressive model that speaks meaningfully to current socioeconomic realities in much of central and Latin America. He radicalizes Ignatius's conception of contemplatives in action by summoning us to be contemplatives in liberation (*contemplativus in liberatione*). This implies a recasting of sanctity that includes both a struggle against one's passions and against the mechanisms of exploitation. The notion of *contemplativus in liberatione* maintains a dynamic unity between action and prayer that facilitates the lived experience of the presence of God. Boff abrogates the compartmentalization of contemplation and liberation in favor of an integration whereby contemplation is incorporated in the concrete process of liberation. Such a fruitful synthesis of "prayer *in* action, *within* action and *with* action" will, Boff asserts, propel God's Kingdom of truth, love, and justice.[30]

Thus to be *contemplativus in liberatione* means to be in a sustained dialectical oscillation between liberation and contemplation: one's commitment to the process and praxis of liberation is born out of prayer, yet this same commitment and practice points back to prayer. Boff elucidates the dialectical motion, "The pole of liberating practice sends us back to the pole of prayer as the source which sustains our strength in the struggle and guarantees Christian identity in the process of liberation.... This is what it means to be '*contemplativus in liberatione*.' Contemplation is not carried out only within the sacred space of prayer, nor in the sacred precinct of the church; purified, sustained and nurtured by living faith, it also finds its place in political and social practice."[31]

CONCLUSION

This brief survey suggests continuities and discontinuities among Christian mystics in their attempts to render productive the tension between action and contemplation. Depending upon different theological

---

[30] Leonardo Boff, "The Need for Political Saints," p. 372.
[31] Ibid., p. 374.

sensibilities and changing historical contexts, one sees, alternately, the privileging of contemplation, the retrieval of the value of action, or the emergence of social justice as central to the mystical life. However the particular emphases may shift, there is a consistent attempt among Christian mystics to struggle with the challenge of cultivating a quality of awareness that is both grounded in God's mystical presence and open to authentic engagement with the world; the relationship between contemplation and action is ultimately dialectical and synthetic, a way of living in the world and in God that is simple and whole.

Part III
Contemporary Questions

13 Latin and the Vernaculars
BARBARA NEWMAN

The year 1215 marks a watershed in church history, for in that year the Fourth Lateran Council decreed that all believers must confess their sins and receive the Eucharist at least once a year. Flanked by the founding of the Franciscan order in 1210 and the Dominicans in 1217, the decree "Omnis utriusque sexus" ("Everyone of either sex") was more symbol than cause of the great pastoral initiative that had already been underway for half a century. No longer could "the Church" be conceptualized as a collective of priests, monks, and nuns, for henceforth the laity constituted the *raison d'être* of the clergy. It was to teach laypeople their faith, pray for them, nourish them with word and sacrament, absolve their sins, and in a word, save them, that "religious professionals" existed at all. Thus, in the wake of Fourth Lateran, it became possible and necessary to ask, with new urgency, just what was appropriate for a lay Christian to know.

This pastoral initiative coincided with the first stages of a far-reaching change in the relationship between Latin and Europe's burgeoning vernaculars. Latin had been and would long remain the language of a learned elite – an international community including regular and secular priests, monks and nuns, friars, university students and teachers, clerics in secular employment such as court bureaucrats, and a sprinkling of humanist intellectuals. The language had a distinguished history stretching from Virgil to the latest scientific tract or papal bull, and its universality enabled texts written in Ireland to be read in Poland, and authors from Sweden to find an audience in Sicily or Spain. Although it had ceased well before 1000 to be anyone's mother tongue, Latin functioned much as English now does to make a global community, or at least the idea of one, possible. But it had its limits. Like other classical languages (e.g., Hebrew, Arabic, Sanskrit), it was hard enough to learn

---

I thank Rachel Fulton Brown, Richard Kieckhefer, Robert Lerner, Sara Poor, John Scofield, John Van Engen, and Nicholas Watson for their many helpful suggestions.

that merely acquiring it conferred privilege, and its status as the medium of a sacred text assured the priority of writing over speech even among those who actually spoke it.[1]

Until at least 1200, to be *litteratus* meant to be literate in Latin – a skill with many gradations of competency, extending from passive understanding through liturgical performance, grammatical knowledge, and oral fluency to various levels of compositional ability.[2] (Writing, or the technology of producing manuscripts, was a separate skill; even highly literate authors dictated to professional scribes.) Conversely, not to know Latin was to be *illitteratus*, a term whose synonyms included *rusticus* (a peasant) and *idiota* (a layman). But as the vernaculars developed written traditions, this slowly began to change. These literatures ripened at differing rates – first Occitan and Old French, then High and Low German (and its relative, Dutch), Italian, and English (reborn as "Middle English" after the decline of an illustrious pre-Conquest literature). In contrast to Latin, the vernaculars were "mother tongues" that privileged speech. The earliest secular literature in these languages was meant for performance: love songs, epics, bawdy tales, and romances. Early vernacular manuscripts are first of all scripts, or transcripts, from the minstrel's repertoire. But the production of such manuscripts kept pace with the rise of vernacular literacy, for learning to read is much easier in one's native tongue. By the time of Fourth Lateran, the potential vernacular audience had grown to the point where our pastoral question entailed a rider: what was it appropriate for a lay Christian to learn *from writings*? By 1500, that audience had grown exponentially. Swelling the ranks of non-Latinate readers were religious women (nuns, beguines, recluses, and tertiaries) and a wide swath of aristocrats, merchants, and artisans. Among the nobility, reading may have been a more common pastime for leisured women than their warrior husbands.[3] Among the

---

[1] Walter Ong, *Orality and Literacy: The Technologizing of the Word* (London: Methuen, 1982); Brian Stock, *The Implications of Literacy: Written Language and Models of Interpretation in the Eleventh and Twelfth Centuries* (Princeton, NJ: Princeton University Press, 1983).

[2] Eamon Duffy, *The Stripping of the Altars: Traditional Religion in England, c. 1400–c. 1580* (New Haven, CT: Yale University Press, 1992), pp. 210–32. See also Katherine Zieman, *Singing the New Song: Literacy and Liturgy in Late Medieval England* (Philadelphia: University of Pennsylvania Press, 2008); and Linda Olson and Kathryn Kerby-Fulton, eds., *Voices in Dialogue: Reading Women in the Middle Ages* (Notre Dame, IN: University of Notre Dame Press, 2005), especially the essays of Katherine Zieman, Margot Fassler, Elizabeth Schirmer, and Steven Justice, pp. 307–94.

[3] Susan Bell, "Medieval Women Book Owners: Arbiters of Lay Piety and Ambassadors of Culture," *Signs* 7 (1982): 742–68; Joel Rosenthal, "Aristocratic Cultural Patronage and Book Bequests, 1350–1500," *Bulletin of the John Rylands Library* 64

merchant class, readers included more men, who needed written records for business.

The question of lay religious knowledge was delicate because, as medieval clerics well knew, a little learning is a dangerous thing. Everyone agreed on certain basic prayers (the Our Father, the Hail Mary, the Apostles' Creed) and items of catechetical knowledge (3 theological and 4 cardinal virtues, 7 deadly sins, 8 beatitudes, 10 commandments). But there agreement ended, for a gulf yawned between those who opted for a minimalist version of the question ("how much *must* a lay Christian know to be saved?") and those who preferred a maximalist version ("how much *should* a lay Christian know to attain spiritual perfection?").[4] The minimalist version was safe but dull: a sound knowledge of "mere Christianity" would, with luck, keep the layperson out of hell without luring him into heresy. The maximalist version was optimistic but dangerous: since Christ had chosen unlettered fishermen for his apostles and an ex-prostitute for his closest friend, why should the laity not have access to all the Church's theological treasures? A popular exemplum held that a simple woman could love God more than the greatest cleric and thereby acquire greater perfection; so why should she be denied the fruits of the cleric's learning?[5] On the other hand, what if such a woman were to decide that, having already attained perfection through love, she no longer needed the cleric at all – neither his learning nor his priesthood nor his sacraments, nor indeed his church? The question is not hypothetical: a "beguine clergesse" named Marguerite Porete was burned at the stake in Paris on June 1, 1310 because, it was claimed, she taught precisely that.[6]

(1982): 522–48; Carol Meale, ed., *Women and Literature in Britain, 1150–1500* (Cambridge: Cambridge University Press, 1993); David Bell, *What Nuns Read: Books and Libraries in Medieval English Nunneries* (Kalamazoo, MI: Cistercian Publications, 1995); June McCash, ed., *The Cultural Patronage of Medieval Women* (Athens: University of Georgia Press, 1996); D. H. Green, *Women Readers in the Middle Ages* (Cambridge: Cambridge University Press, 2007).

[4] See Nicholas Watson, "Censorship and Cultural Change in Late-Medieval England: Vernacular Theology, the Oxford Translation Debate, and Arundel's Constitutions of 1409," *Speculum* 70 (1995): 822–64, esp. pp. 840–6 on the Oxford translation debate.

[5] F. P. Pickering, "Notes on Late Medieval German Tales in Praise of *docta ignorantia*," *Bulletin of the John Rylands Library* 24 (1940): 121–37; see also the exemplum "Meister Eckhart's Daughter," in *Meister Eckhart: A Modern Translation*, trans. Raymond Blakney (New York: Harper and Row, 1941), pp. 252–3.

[6] Robert Lerner, *The Heresy of the Free Spirit in the Later Middle Ages* (Berkeley: University of California Press, 1972), pp. 68–78; Suzanne Kocher, *Allegories of Love in Marguerite Porete's Mirror of Simple Souls* (Turnhout, Belgium: Brepols, 2008), pp. 26–46; Sean L. Field, *The Beguine, the Angel, and the Inquisitor: The Trials of Marguerite Porete and Guiard of Cressonessart* (Notre Dame, IN: University of Notre Dame Press, 2012).

Marguerite's fate casts a paradoxical light on our question, for she herself wrote a French mystical dialogue called *The Mirror of Simple Souls*. All but one late vernacular copy perished with her.[7] Yet the text was translated anonymously into Latin, and with that version as intermediary, two Italian translations materialized, one ascribing the book to Queen Margaret of Hungary. Marguerite's French text was also rendered into Middle English, and by that route, into a second Latin version by Richard Methley.[8] By a quirk of fate, the Middle English version is in some ways closer to Marguerite's original than the sole surviving Middle French text.[9] In these translations, the *Mirror* outlived its author, continuing to find new audiences until, in 1946, Marguerite and her book were finally reunited.[10] In a crowning irony, the monks of Downside Abbey sponsored a modernized edition of the medieval English text in 1927, adorned with the *nihil obstat* and *imprimatur* of the very Church that had sent its author to the flames.[11]

Marguerite believed that even murderers could be saved; but the soul that merely dies to sin and attains a state of grace is saved "uncourteously," in contrast to noble "annihilated" souls who "live only in the will and desire of Love."[12] Despite her aristocratic self-consciousness, however, Marguerite was a democrat with regard to language. She saw no correlation between nobility of soul and knowledge of Latin, and thus no reason to refrain from teaching the most abstruse theology in the vernacular. Her inquisitors thought otherwise. But the interesting question for our purposes is not only whether such vernacular texts as the *Mirror* should be allowed to exist, but also how many readers actually wanted

[7] Although three or four French manuscripts survived into the sixteenth century, only one is still extant. Ruusbroec's critique of Marguerite hints at the existence of a possible Dutch translation that, if it ever existed, is now lost.

[8] Marguerite Porete, *Le mirouer des simples ames*, ed. Romana Guarnieri, and *Speculum simplicium animarum*, ed. Paul Verdeyen, both in CCCM 69 (Turnhout, Belgium: Brepols, 1986); *The Mirrour of Simple Soules: A Middle English Translation*, ed. Marilyn Doiron, *Archivio italiano per la storia della pietà* 5 (1968): 241–355; Laura Saetveit Miles, "Richard Methley and the Translation of Vernacular Religious Writings into Latin," in *After Arundel: Religious Writings in Fifteenth Century England*, ed. Vincent Gillespie and Kantik Ghosh (Turnhout, Belgium: Brepols, 2012), pp. 449–66.

[9] Robert E. Lerner, "New Light on *The Mirror of Simple Souls*," *Speculum* 85 (2010): 91–116.

[10] Romana Guarnieri, "Lo *Specchio delle anime semplici* e Margherita Poirette," *L'Osservatore Romano*, June 16, 1946, p. 3; Romana Guarnieri, "Il Movimento del Libero Spirito, Testi e Documenti," *Archivio italiano per la storia della pietà* 4 (1965): 353–708.

[11] Clare Kirchberger, ed., *The Mirror of Simple Souls, by an Unknown French Mystic of the Thirteenth Century*, translated into English by M. N. (London: Burns, Oates, and Washbourne, 1927). *Nihil obstat* ("nothing stands in the way") signifies the approval of an ecclesiastical censor; *imprimatur* ("let it be printed") is the official Catholic declaration that a book is free of doctrinal error.

[12] Marguerite, *Mirouer*, ch. 62, pp. 180–2.

them. Mystical writings fall at the maximalist end of the spectrum, for the practices described and recommended in them require a high degree of leisure, interiority, self-discipline, and institutional support (even recluses needed license from their bishop and proof of sufficient financial resources to provide for a lifetime of enclosure). Despite the vogue for mystical texts in the late Middle Ages, therefore, no cleric would have dreamed of requiring such high-level spiritual practices from the laity – and in any case, lay readers cared much more about the seven works of mercy and the craft of dying than they did about esoteric speculations on the Trinity. Although the vernacular audience for books like the *Mirror* did grow, it remained tiny in comparison with either the Latin readership of such works or the lay audience for pastoral and secular literature. Hence the paradox that, although vernacularity implies broad access, what holds true for other categories of writing does not hold in the case of vernacular mystical books, which were read largely by religious women and their spiritual directors. This coterie audience within any single language community, or even across several, never equaled the international public of Latin readers.

In the sinuous history of mystical texts, each has its own unpredictable destiny, but some broad patterns emerge. The twelfth century was the great age of Latin mystical writing, dominated by the German Benedictines (Rupert of Deutz, Hildegard of Bingen, Elisabeth of Schönau), the Cistercians (especially Bernard of Clairvaux, William of Saint Thierry, and Aelred of Rievaulx), the Victorines (especially Hugh and Richard), and, to a lesser degree, the Carthusians.[13] Some of these writers, above all Bernard (d. 1153) and Richard of Saint Victor (d. 1173), were enormously influential. Their ideas were paraphrased, popularized, diffused in sermons, and discussed among friends. Lambert li Bègues, a parish priest of Liège and precursor of the beguine movement, was charged with heresy in 1175 for translating the Acts of the Apostles and the *Life of St. Agnes* into French verse for his parishioners.[14] It was only in the thirteenth century, however, that such scriptural paraphrases as well as mystical treatises circulated widely in French.[15] In

---

[13] The best guide is Bernard McGinn, *The Presence of God: A History of Western Christian Mysticism*, vol. 2, *The Growth of Mysticism: Gregory the Great through the Twelfth Century* (New York: Crossroad, 1994).

[14] Walter Simons, "'Staining the Speech of Things Divine': The Uses of Literacy in Medieval Beguine Communities," in *The Voice of Silence: Women's Literacy in a Men's Church*, ed. Thérèse de Hemptinne and María Eugenia Góngora (Turnhout, Belgium: Brepols, 2004), pp. 85–110.

[15] Kocher, *Allegories of Love*, p. 77. For the Song of Songs tradition in vernacular mysticism, see Friedrich Ohly, ed., *Das St. Trudperter Hohelied: eine Lehre der liebenden*

the twelfth century, the overwhelming majority of suitable readers still knew Latin.

By around 1200, however, Bernard's important *Sermons on the Song of Songs* and William of Saint Thierry's *Golden Epistle* (usually ascribed to Bernard) were available in French versions.[16] Fearing heresy, the papal legate to Liège demanded in 1203 that "all books concerning the Holy Scriptures, written in French or Dutch, be handed over to the bishop, and he will return those he has seen and deemed worthy to be returned."[17] By 1210 the vernacular audience – and the fear – had increased to the point that a Parisian synod forbade the ownership of all French theological books, even the Our Father and the Creed, except for saints' lives.[18] But the bishops failed to stem the tide, for by 1274, the Franciscan polemicist Guibert of Tournai was complaining to the Council of Lyon about beguines who translated scripture and delighted in theological subtleties. He claimed to have examined "a French Bible whose exemplar is publicly available at the stationers' shops in Paris for the copying of heresies and errors, dubious and awkward interpretations." Guibert wanted all such books destroyed and their translators locked up, "lest the divine word be cheapened by vernacular speech."[19]

Meanwhile, the Latin mystical tradition continued to flourish in the thirteenth century with such writers as Bonaventure (d. 1274), who fused scholastic theology and contemplation at the highest level.[20] More

---

Gotteserkenntnis (Frankfurt am Main, Germany: Deutscher Klassiker Verlag, 1998); and Tony Hunt, ed., *Les Cantiques Salemon: The Song of Songs in MS Paris BNF fr. 14966* (Turnhout, Belgium: Brepols, 2006).

[16] Robert Taylor, "The Old French 'Cistercian' Translations," in *Medieval Translators and Their Craft*, ed. Jeanette Beer (Kalamazoo, MI: Medieval Institute Publications, 1989), pp. 67–80.

[17] "Omnes libri romane vel teotonice scripti de divinis scripturis in manum episcopi tradantur et ipse quos viderit reddendos reddat." Cited in Wybren Scheepsma, *The Limburg Sermons: Preaching in the Medieval Low Countries at the Turn of the Fourteenth Century*, trans. David F. Johnson (Leiden, The Netherlands: Brill, 2008), p. 363.

[18] "De libris theologicis scriptis in Romano precipimus, quod episcopis diocesanis tradantur et *Credo in Deum*, et *Pater noster* in Romano preter vitas sanctorum, et hoc infra purificationem, quia apud quem invenientur pro heretico habebitur." Heinrich Denifle et al., eds., *Chartularium Universitatis Parisiensis*, 4 vols. (Paris: Delalain, 1889–97), vol. 1, p. 70. A Dominican canon from the 1220s also prohibited friars from translating "sermones vel collationes vel alias sacras scripturas de latino ... in vulgari." G. Meersseman, "Les Frères Prêcheurs et le mouvement dévot en Flandres au XIIIe siècle," *Archivum Fratrum Praedicatorum* 18 (1948): 105.

[19] Guibert of Tournai, *Collectio de scandalis Ecclesiae*, ed. Autbertus Stroick, *Archivum Franciscanum Historicum* 24 (1931): 61–2.

[20] Bonaventure, like Augustine and Bernard, was an author whose prestigious name lent its luster to many pseudonymous works, including the widely read and much translated *Meditationes vitae Christi* (*Meditations on the Life of Christ*).

surprisingly, two nuns at the Saxon monastery of Helfta, Gertrude the Great (d. 1301/2) and Mechthild of Hackeborn (d. 1299), composed massive visionary books in Latin, assisted only by their fellow nuns. Thanks to their wealth and privilege, elite nunneries in the Empire managed to preserve their Latinate culture well into the fourteenth century, long after most nuns in Europe had abandoned it.[21] By and large, however, the thirteenth and fourteenth centuries represent the heyday of mystical writing in the vernacular, much of it by women. Among the most innovative authors were Hadewijch (thirteenth century) in Dutch, Mechthild of Magdeburg (d. 1282) in German, Marguerite Porete in French, and Julian of Norwich (d. after 1416) in English. Significantly, some women's texts were so prized that clerics translated them into Latin, as in Marguerite's case – thus facilitating a multiethnic readership, along with the prestige and the implied (if sometimes misleading) seal of orthodoxy conferred by the learned tongue.

Periodic outbreaks of repression, clerical caution, and the chances of manuscript transmission have preserved some mystical texts only in Latin, although they were first written or dictated in the vernacular. Around the time of Guibert of Tournai's broadside, the Flemish nun Beatrice of Nazareth's (d. 1268) autobiography was recast as a Latin *vita* by a priest who probably destroyed its original to avoid persecution.[22] The great Franciscan mystic Angela of Foligno (d. 1309) dictated in Italian to her scribe, "Brother A.," who transcribed her speech in his safer though admittedly inadequate Latin.[23] Almost a century later, Bridget of Sweden (d. 1373) experienced the same destiny. Although early in her career she had promoted the translation of religious texts into Swedish, the fragments of her own writing in the vernacular pale beside the vast tomes of Latin revelations carefully edited by her confessor, Alfonso of Jaén.[24] All

[21] Barbara Newman, "The Visionary Texts and Visual Worlds of Religious Women," in *Crown and Veil: Female Monasticism from the Fifth to the Fifteenth Centuries*, ed. Jeffrey F. Hamburger and Susan Marti (New York: Columbia University Press, 2008), pp. 151–71; Anna Harrison, "'Oh! What Treasure Is in This Book?' Writing, Reading, and Community at the Monastery of Helfta," *Viator* 39, no. 1 (2008): 75–106.

[22] Roger DeGanck, trans., *The Life of Beatrice of Nazareth, 1200–1268* (Kalamazoo, MI: Cistercian Publications, 1991), pp. xxviii–xxxii. Around the same time an orthodox layman, James of Maerlant, was repeatedly interrogated for his Dutch rhymed Bible and a poem on the Trinity.

[23] Catherine M. Mooney, "The Authorial Role of Brother A. in the Composition of Angela of Foligno's Revelations," in *Creative Women in Medieval and Early Modern Italy: A Religious and Artistic Renaissance*, ed. E. Ann Matter and John Coakley (Philadelphia: University of Pennsylvania Press, 1994), pp. 34–63.

[24] Some of these revelations were subsequently translated into Italian at the request of Bridget's fellow prophet, Catherine of Siena. Alfonso was also among the promoters of Catherine's sainthood.

three women are now officially *sancta* or *beata*, titles granted to none of the four whose vernacular texts survive.[25]

In the fourteenth century, we find learned men self-consciously producing both Latin and vernacular works for differing audiences. Meister Eckhart (d. 1328), a German Dominican who died while under investigation for heresy, is the most famous case in point. His academic writings in Latin were not particularly controversial, but his German mystical sermons – preached to laity of both sexes, though especially popular with women – were intensely so. Eckhart taught in Paris shortly after Marguerite Porete's execution, lodging in the same friary as her chief inquisitor, and recent studies suggest that her book influenced his vernacular writings – an influence that, for obvious reasons, he did not footnote.[26] The rapid spread of Eckhartian and "Free Spirit" ideas prompted Emperor Charles IV in 1369 to a repressive decree directing inquisitors to confiscate and burn suspect theological texts in German.[27]

Like Eckhart, his disciple Henry Suso (d. 1366) was deeply involved in the direction of nuns and beguines, writing in German for that audience. In an early work, *The Little Book of Truth*, Suso defended some of Eckhart's controverted positions, only to be accused at a chapter in 1330 of "soiling the whole country with [this] heretical garbage." That charge may have moved him to adopt a simpler devotional piety in *The Little Book of Eternal Wisdom*. To attract a broad clerical readership for that book and perhaps also to escape further prosecution, Suso then crafted a Latin version of it, entitled *Horologium Sapientiae* (*Wisdom's Clock*).[28] A comparison of Suso's German original with his Latin adaptation clearly reveals the difference in intended audience. In both texts, the figure of Eternal Wisdom is dual-gendered (masculine as Jesus, feminine

---

[25] The mere survival of vernacular mystical texts by women constituted proof against an official cult, except for the Italian saints Catherine of Siena and Catherine of Genoa.

[26] Edmund Colledge and J. C. Marler, "'Poverty of the Will': Ruusbroec, Eckhart and *The Mirror of Simple Souls*," in *Jan van Ruusbroec: The Sources, Content and Sequels of His Mysticism*, ed. Paul Mommaers and Norbert De Paepe (Leuven, Belgium: Leuven University Press, 1984), pp. 14–47. See also the essays of Maria Lichtmann, Amy Hollywood, and Michael Sells in *Meister Eckhart and the Beguine Mystics*, ed. Bernard McGinn (New York: Continuum, 1994), pp. 65–146. Eckhart most likely knew a Latin version of Marguerite's book, suggesting that it was translated during her lifetime.

[27] Lerner, *Heresy*, p. 134; Paul Frédéricq, ed., *Corpus documentorum inquisitionis haereticae pravitatis Neerlandicae*, vol. 1 (Ghent, Belgium: Vuylsteke, 1889), pp. 214–17, no. 212. The decree targets beguines, beghards, and other "lay or almost lay persons ... who wish to know more than they should" (*plus quam oportet volentes sapere*), stating further that "it is not canonically permitted for laity of either sex to use even vernacular books of any kind concerning sacred Scripture."

[28] Henry Suso, *The Exemplar, with Two German Sermons*, trans. Frank Tobin (New York: Paulist Press, 1989), pp. 32–5.

as Sapientia), but the German emphasizes the masculine figure while the Latin highlights the feminine. Suso assumed heterosexual readers who would respond with greater love to a representation of the Divine in the opposite gender.[29]

This case also illustrates the role of Latin as an intermediary between vernaculars. By 1500, the hugely popular *Horologium* had been translated into French, Dutch, Italian, and English, with numerous exemplars of each – not to mention Bohemian, Hungarian, Polish, Swedish, and Danish. Yet the two hundred manuscripts extant in all these vernaculars combined still fall short of the number surviving in Latin. In England, the manuscript tradition sometimes confused Suso with his like-minded contemporary, Richard Rolle (d. 1349), who was also devoted to the Holy Name of Jesus and wrote both Latin and vernacular works. In the later Middle Ages, the English developed a taste for continental mystical texts, almost always translated from the Latin (except in the case of Porete's *Mirror*). In addition to the *Mirror* and Suso's *Horologium*, we have Middle English versions of Mechthild of Hackeborn; excerpts from Ruusbroec; an "Elizabeth of Hungary" who may have been Suso's friend, Elisabeth of Töss; Catherine of Siena's *Dialogue*; and Bridget of Sweden's *Revelations* – all by way of Latin intermediaries.[30] The role of Latin as a clearinghouse for vernacular mystical texts contrasts tellingly with the patterns of translation we find in secular literature. French courtly romances, for example, were adapted routinely into German, Dutch, Italian, English, and other tongues – once even into Hebrew[31] – without passing through Latin. This intermediary role points to the identity of the religious translators, virtually always clerics who felt more comfortable in Latin and would have seen no reason to read any vernacular but their own. It was not just the authority and international reach of Latin

---

[29] Heinrich Seuse, *Büchlein der Ewigen Weisheit*, in Henry Suso, *Deutsche Schriften*, ed. Karl Bihlmeyer (Stuttgart, Germany, 1907; repr., Frankfurt: Minerva, 1961), pp. 196–325; Henry Suso, *Horologium Sapientiae*, ed. Pius Künzle (Freiburg, Switzerland: Universitätsverlag, 1977); Barbara Newman, *God and the Goddesses: Vision, Poetry, and Belief in the Middle Ages* (Philadelphia: University of Pennsylvania Press, 2003), pp. 206–22.

[30] Alexandra Barratt, ed., *Women's Writing in Middle English* (London: Longman, 1992), pp. 49–107; Rosalynn Voaden, ed., *Prophets Abroad: The Reception of Continental Holy Women in Late-Medieval England* (Woodbridge, UK: D. S. Brewer, 1996); Joyce Bazire and Eric Colledge, eds., *The Chastising of God's Children and The Treatise of Perfection of the Sons of God* (Oxford: Blackwell, 1957), pp. 83–7; Jocelyn Wogan-Browne et al., eds., *The Idea of the Vernacular: An Anthology of Middle English Literary Theory, 1280–1520* (University Park: Pennsylvania State University Press, 1999), pp. 235–8, 258–65, 288–91.

[31] Curt Leviant, ed. and trans., *King Artus: A Hebrew Arthurian Romance of 1279* (Syracuse, NY: Syracuse University Press, 2003).

that inspired their confidence, but also its presumably greater precision. As Eckhart's example shows, only a finely honed theological vocabulary permitted the subtle *distinctiones* that kept error at bay, enabling wary readers to distinguish between strong claims about the indwelling divine presence and potentially heretical claims of pantheism or autotheism.[32]

Translators often worked to the interests of particular readers. One fascinating case is provided by Mechthild of Magdeburg's text, *The Flowing Light of the Godhead*, composed in Low German. Shortly after the beguine's death, a Dominican translated most of her book into Latin as *Lux divinitatis* (*The Light of Divinity*), prefacing it with an elaborate defense of female prophecy, yet suppressing Mechthild's name because the true "author is the Father, Son, and Holy Spirit." Although the Latin version is essentially faithful, it tones down Mechthild's critiques of the clergy, tidies up the haphazard order of her book, and tempers her eroticism by translating courtly into biblical idioms. Around 1345, the spiritual director Henry of Nördlingen discovered Mechthild's original work and found it deeply moving. Calling it "the loveliest German I have ever read," Henry wished to send it to his friend Margaret Ebner (d. 1351), a mystical writer at the convent of Maria Medingen, and other "friends of God" in their circle.[33] These nuns were quite competent in Latin. Henry had earlier advised them to copy Suso's *Horologium Sapientiae*, and in another letter he recommended the *Summa* of Thomas Aquinas.[34] Unfortunately, though, he did not have the *Lux divinitatis* at hand, nor could the nuns read Mechthild's original because they spoke High German, not Low German. So Henry undertook the task of translating

---

[32] Compare Scheepsma, *Limburg Sermons*, pp. 397–8.

[33] Mechthild von Magdeburg, *Das fliessende Licht der Gottheit*, ed. Gisela Vollmann-Profe (Frankfurt am Main, Germany: Deutscher Klassiker Verlag, 2003); Mechthild of Magdeburg, *Lux divinitatis*, in *Revelationes Gertrudianae ac Mechtildianae*, vol. 2, ed. Monks of Solesmes (Poitiers, France: Oudin, 1877); Sara S. Poor, *Mechthild of Magdeburg and Her Book: Gender and the Making of Textual Authority* (Philadelphia: University of Pennsylvania Press, 2004), pp. 85–94; Patricia Z. Beckman, "The Power of Books and the Practice of Mysticism in the Fourteenth Century: Heinrich of Nördlingen and Margaret Ebner on Mechthild's *Flowing Light of the Godhead*," *Church History* 76 (2007): 61–83; John Coakley, *Women, Men, and Spiritual Power: Female Saints and Their Male Collaborators* (New York: Columbia University Press, 2006), pp. 156, 296–7.

[34] Heinrich von Nördlingen, "Briefe an Margaretha Ebner," in Philipp Strauch, ed., *Margaretha Ebner und Heinrich von Nördlingen: Ein Beitrag zur Geschichte der deutschen Mystik* (Tübingen, Germany, 1882; repr., Amsterdam: Schippers, 1966), pp. 228–9, 238. The *Summa* itself was also translated in the fourteenth century; a single manuscript from Weingarten survives. B. Q. Morgan and F. W. Strothmann, eds., *Middle High German Translation of the* Summa Theologica *by Thomas Aquinas* (Stanford, CA: Stanford University Press, 1950).

from one dialect to another, in a partial exception to the rule of Latin intermediaries – remarking that this required two years of burdensome labor. Like the Latin, his Middle High German version suppresses Mechthild's name, yet he tells Margaret to venerate her with prayers and prepare for reading her book by reciting seven Paternosters, seven Ave Marias, and seven *Veni sancte Spiritus* (Come, Holy Spirit) – all in Latin, of course. Moreover, by 1346 Henry had discovered the *Lux divinitatis* and was asking Margaret to send him the Latin text through another friend.[35] Mechthild's case thus suggests the complex imbrication of Latin and vernacular in the transmission of mystical texts, as well as the close-knit coteries in which they circulated. Both the *Lux divinitatis* and Henry of Nördlingen's translation survive, while Mechthild's original is lost.

Perhaps no factor short of canonization determined the influence of medieval mystics, over the long haul, more than their availability in Latin. Hadewijch of Brabant, a brilliant poet and mystical theologian probably a generation older than Mechthild, never made the cut. She too was translated into High German; a fragment survives at Einsiedeln, the same Swiss monastery that preserves Mechthild's book. But Hadewijch's impact remained minimal until her works came to the notice of a later Dutch mystic, John Ruusbroec (d. 1381), who silently adopted her Trinitarian doctrine and other core ideas.[36] Ruusbroec in turn found Latin translators through whom he – and indirectly, Hadewijch – entered the wider Catholic tradition, culminating in the Spanish Counter-Reformation mystic, John of the Cross (d. 1591).[37] Another Dutch example makes the point even more sharply. Ruusbroec's most famous translator, Geert Grote (d. 1384), may or may not have been a mystic. But as the founder of a movement called the *Devotio Moderna* (New Devotion) or, in its institutional form, the Sisters and Brothers of the Common Life,

---

[35] Henry of Nordlingen, "Briefe," pp. 246–9.
[36] Hadewijch, *The Complete Works*, trans. Columba Hart (New York: Paulist Press, 1980), pp. 14–15; Georgette Epiney-Burgard, "L'influence des béguines sur Ruusbroec," in *Jan Van Ruusbroec: The Sources, Content, and Sequels of His Mysticism*, ed. Paul Mommaers and Norbert De Paepe (Leuven, Belgium: Leuven University Press, 1984), pp. 68–85; Jessica Boon, "Trinitarian Love Mysticism: Ruusbroec, Hadewijch, and the Gendered Experience of the Divine," *Church History* 72 (2003): 484–503. Ruusbroec's circle is responsible for copying the few extant manuscripts of Hadewijch's works.
[37] John Ruusbroec, *The Spiritual Espousals and Other Works*, trans. James Wiseman (New York: Paulist Press, 1985), pp. 32–4; Bazire and Colledge, eds., *The Chastising of God's Children*, pp. 83–7. Jean Gerson's damaging attack on *The Spiritual Espousals* was indirectly an attack on Hadewijch's theology, though no one realized this at the time.

his influence was incalculable.[38] By promoting both scribal work and the writing of meditations as a spiritual exercise, Grote inspired a whole library of devotional literature in Latin and Middle Dutch, little known outside the Netherlands.

There is, however, one exception. Around 1420 an anonymous New Devout author began to circulate, in Latin, a work called *The Imitation of Christ* – a collection of spiritual teachings not unlike others in the movement, though written with incomparably greater eloquence and authority. Now ascribed to Thomas à Kempis, the book became an instant classic – "the most influential devotional book in Western Christian history," in John Van Engen's words. Though penned only a generation before printing, it survives in 750 manuscripts and some three thousand editions, fifty of them before 1500. The text passed into Dutch, German, French, and Italian so quickly that the author's nationality was long in doubt.[39] Lady Margaret Beaufort collaborated on the first English version in 1502; by 1700 *The Imitation* was available in Japanese, Arabic, Armenian, and neoclassical French verse. This veritable orgy of translation testifies to the reach and accessibility of the vernaculars. But it testifies no less to the authority of Latin, the hub from which all versions radiate outward like spokes on a wheel.

No Anglo-Latin writer after Aelred of Rievaulx in the twelfth century enjoyed anything like the international influence of Bonaventure, Suso, or Thomas à Kempis. Of the vernacular mystics, however, Walter Hilton (d. 1396), like Richard Rolle, composed Latin as well as English works. His *Scale of Perfection*, though written in English, has a Latin title (*Scala perfectionis*) in many manuscripts and was actually translated into Latin by a Carmelite, Thomas Fishlake.[40] The author of *The Cloud of Unknowing*, though he wrote only in English so far as we know, was nonetheless a skilled translator. His *Benjamin* is adapted from Richard

---

[38] John Van Engen, *Sisters and Brothers of the Common Life: The Devotio Moderna and the World of the Later Middle Ages* (Philadelphia: University of Pennsylvania Press, 2008).

[39] John Van Engen, ed. and trans., *Devotio Moderna: Basic Writings* (New York: Paulist Press, 1988), pp. 8–10; Uwe Neddermeyer, "*Radix studii et speculum vitae*: Verbreitung und Rezeption der 'Imitatio Christi' in Handschriften und Drucken bis zur Reformation," in *Studien zum 15. Jahrhundert: Festschrift für Erich Meuthen zum 65. Geburtstag*, ed. Johannes Helmrath, Herbert Müller, and Helmut Wolff (Munich: Oldenbourg, 1994), vol. 1, pp. 457–81.

[40] Michael Sargent, "Walter Hilton's *Scale of Perfection*: The London Manuscript Group Reconsidered," *Medium Aevum* 52 (1983): 189–216; Walter Hilton, *The Scale of Perfection*, trans. John Clark and Rosemary Dorward (New York: Paulist Press, 1991), pp. 18–19, 56–7.

of Saint Victor's *Benjamin Minor*, and *Deonise Hid Divinite* eloquently translates Dionysius the Areopagite's *Mystical Theology* – from a Latin intermediary, not the Greek. (The semantic distance separating "mystical theology" from "hid divinity" shows how greatly "equivalent" terms can differ in resonance.) *The Cloud* itself was Latinized twice, once by Richard Methley.[41] But neither Julian of Norwich nor Margery Kempe (d. after 1436), today the best-loved and most-studied English mystics, gained a Latin audience or, indeed, much of an audience at all. Their relative obscurity owed less to gender than to the fact that neither belonged to a religious order, and – even more to the point – both composed late enough to risk censorship in the increasingly intolerant climate of the fifteenth century. Julian wrote just before, and Kempe well after, another act of ecclesiastical repression: a decree by the archbishop of Canterbury in 1409 banned all new vernacular writing on biblical subjects. Though aimed at suppressing the proto-Protestant, decidedly nonmystical heresy of the Lollards, the "Constitutions of Arundel" had a chilling effect on religious writing of many kinds.[42]

The fifteenth century marked an age of retrenchment. Favored mystical texts continued to circulate as both Latin and vernacular manuscripts were copied in greater numbers than ever. But in this domain there was little new composition. Mystics, prophets, visionaries, and would-be saints of all sorts, especially women, came under intense scrutiny, and their purported revelations no longer found a welcoming clerical public. The careers of the two most prolific writers of the age, Jean Gerson (d. 1429) and Denis the Carthusian (d. 1471), offer revealing glimpses into its spirit. Gerson, chancellor of the University of Paris and a key figure in the conciliar movement, wrote voluminously in both Latin and French; one scholar describes him as the first public intellectual.[43] His attitude toward mysticism was deeply ambivalent. On the one hand, he deplored the aridity of scholastic thought without spirituality, wished

---

[41] John Clark, ed., *The Latin Versions of the "Cloud of Unknowing,"* Analecta Cartusiana 119/1-2 (Salzburg, Austria: Institut für Anglistik und Amerikanistik, 1989); Richard Methley, *Divino Caligo Ignorancia: A Latin Glossed Version of the Cloud of Unknowing*, ed. John Clark, Analecta Cartusiana 119/3 (Salzburg, Austria: Institut für Anglistik und Amerikanistik, 2009).

[42] Watson, "Censorship and Cultural Change." For a different view see Kathryn Kerby-Fulton, *Books under Suspicion: Censorship and Tolerance of Revelatory Writing in Late Medieval England* (Notre Dame, IN: University of Notre Dame Press, 2006), pp. 397–401.

[43] Daniel Hobbins, "The Schoolman as Public Intellectual: Jean Gerson and the Late Medieval Tract," *American Historical Review* 108 (2003): 1308–35; Daniel Hobbins, *Authorship and Publicity before Print: Jean Gerson and the Transformation of Late Medieval Learning* (Philadelphia: University of Pennsylvania Press, 2009).

to deepen the prayer lives of university students, and wrote treatises on contemplation for his sisters. His last work, finished days before his death, was a commentary on the Song of Songs.[44] On the other hand, Gerson profoundly distrusted such female mystics as Catherine of Siena and the newly canonized Bridget, whom he blamed for the papal schism. He lamented the popularity of unauthorized revelations, and his influential tracts on the discernment of spirits put visionary spirituality on the defensive, where it has remained ever since.

Like Gerson, Denis the Carthusian was both a schoolman and a contemplative, deeply attracted to twelfth-century writers and (unlike Gerson) prone to ecstasies. Born in the heartland of the thirteenth-century beguine mystics, the alarmingly prolific Denis wrote more than 150 works – exegetical, scholastic, pastoral, and mystical – summing up the entire Catholic tradition to date. But all were in Latin, and despite his fame as a churchman and scholar, this cloistered monk neither sought nor found a vernacular audience.[45] Both Gerson and Denis strove rather to re-Latinize mysticism and revitalize clerical spirituality. We might add Nicholas of Cusa (d. 1464), the philosopher and theologian who professed "learned ignorance" – but only in Latin. Meanwhile, both religious and lay readers increasingly favored a new kind of manuscript, the devotional miscellany, in which named authors in any language retreat behind the more generalized authority of the tradition.[46]

In retrospect, the flowering of medieval vernacular mysticism was a brilliant but fragile phenomenon. It fostered a hunger and thirst for "the sweetness of God"[47] beyond cloister walls and enabled an untold number of souls to be "saved courteously," in Marguerite Porete's terms. It also produced extraordinary texts in many tongues, justly admired as much for their beauty as their spiritual teachings. But it did not spell

---

[44] Brian Patrick McGuire, *Jean Gerson and the Last Medieval Reformation* (University Park: Pennsylvania State University Press, 2005), p. 319.

[45] Kent Emery Jr., ed., *Dionysii Cartusiensis Opera Selecta: Prolegomena*, CCCM 121–121a (Turnhout, Belgium: Brepols, 1991). The critical edition to follow this two-volume preliminary work has yet to appear.

[46] Duffy, *Stripping of the Altars*, pp. 68–77; Poor, *Mechthild of Magdeburg*, pp. 134–8; Nikolaus Staubach, "Der Codex als Ware: Wirtschaftliche Aspekte der Handschriftenproduktion im Bereich der *Devotio moderna*," in *Der Codex im Gebrauch*, ed. Christel Meier et al. (Munich: Wilhelm Fink, 1996): 143–62; Anne Winston-Allen, *Convent Chronicles: Women Writing about Women and Reform in the Late Middle Ages* (University Park: Pennsylvania State University Press, 2004), pp. 182–4; Barry Windeatt, "Constructing Audiences for Contemplative Texts: The Example of a Mystical Anthology," in *Imagining the Book*, ed. Stephen Kelly and John Thompson (Turnhout, Belgium: Brepols, 2005), pp. 159–71.

[47] Rachel Fulton, "'Taste and See that the Lord Is Sweet' (Ps. 33:9): The Flavor of God in the Monastic West," *Journal of Religion* 86 (2006): 169–204.

a decline in the authority of Latin. To be sure, vernacular texts could do many things that Latin texts could not. They could address an ever-growing lay and female public, enabling many more women's voices to be heard. They could mediate between ecclesiastical tradition and secular experience, inspiring fresh thought and remarkably powerful new modes of expression. But it was only after the Protestant and Catholic Reformations, not to mention the triumph of print, that the vernaculars truly gained the dominance they enjoy in contemporary scholarship.[48]

---

[48] As late as 1744, the German *Revelations* of Margaret Ebner (d. 1351) were translated into Latin to promote her beatification, which finally occurred in 1979. Meri Heinonen, "Brides and Knights of Christ: Gender and Body in Later Medieval German Mysticism" (PhD diss., University of Turku, Finland, 2007), p. 37.

14 Transmission

SARA S. POOR

In his recent history of Christian mysticism, Bernard McGinn appeals to the model of conversation to characterize a new mysticism emerging during the twelfth and thirteenth centuries.[1] The transmission or manuscript circulation of mystical texts grows out of this conversation. Mystics have visions in which they converse with God, and, obeying his command or that of his priestly agent, they transmit his words to others. For example, Hildegard of Bingen (1098–1179) opens her *Scivias* (short for *Scito Vias Domini* [Know the Ways of God]) with a declaration in which she reports a voice from heaven telling her to "speak therefore of these wonders, and being so taught, write them and speak."[2] Hildegard's contemporary, Elisabeth of Schönau (1129–64), was also graced with visions that a guiding angel explained to her and that her brother Ekbert recorded in a series of books. Ekbert reports that Elisabeth was "compelled by familial love and by order of the abbot to explain in intimate detail the whole thing to this cleric."[3] A century later, at the beginning of Mechthild of Magdeburg's (ca. 1210–82) *The Flowing Light of the Godhead*, God is quoted as saying: "This book I hereby send as a messenger to all religious people, both the bad and the good."[4] Later in the book, Mechthild refers to her confessor having commanded her to write.[5] Finally, Henry Suso (1295–1366) received a divine command to share his mystical path. In the preface to his "Life," he reports that a nun in his spiritual care (Elsbeth Stagel, d. ca. 1360) had begun composing it without

---

[1] Bernard McGinn, *The Presence of God: A Study of Western Christian Mysticism*, vol. 3, *The Flowering of Mysticism: Men and Women in the New Mysticism (1200–1350)* (New York: Crossroad, 1998), p. xiii.

[2] Hildegard of Bingen, *Scivias*, trans. Columba Hart and J. Bishop (New York: Paulist Press, 1990), p. 59.

[3] Elisabeth of Schönau, *The Complete Works*, trans. Anne L. Clark (New York: Paulist Press, 2000), p. 42.

[4] Mechthild of Magdeburg, *The Flowing Light of the Godhead*, trans. Frank Tobin (New York: Paulist Press, 1998), p. 39.

[5] Ibid., bk. IV, ch. 2, pp. 143–4.

his knowledge. When he discovered this "theft," he reproached her and burned the pages she had with her, but when about to burn a second batch of pages, "this was hindered by a celestial message from God which prevented it."[6] Transmission – the communication of God's truth in his own words as spoken to or through the mystic – is thus embedded in mystical experience and text. Indeed, the act of recording revelations is the second act of transmission and this act is mimicked in a third: the duplication and dissemination of mystical texts in manuscripts, an act that extends the conversation to others through reading and writing. In other words, the compulsion to talk about God's truth was also felt by clerics who wrote about mystical experience and by devout readers who made copies of writings by mystics and clerics and distributed them to others.

The story the manuscripts tell about these textual conversations can be summarized as follows: mystical works are transmitted initially in their entirety and often the messenger subordinates his or her own authorship to the divine message. The more distant from the author's lifetime, the more the texts are excerpted and included in compilations. Particularly with famous figures like Bernard of Clairvaux or Hildegard of Bingen, the name of the author becomes increasingly significant: it is often attached even to texts the person did not write. Yet as fragmentary compilations themselves become excerpted to form new compilations, authorial naming becomes less important. Further, because the circulation of these texts is usually connected to a project of reforming religious practice – often with the larger goal of preventing heretical error – the authority of the texts lies not in their divinely inspired authors but in the presumption of divine (orthodox) content. The apparent consequence of this reduced emphasis on named authority was that anyone (i.e., even the laity or women) could work with the divine words. In the context of fifteenth-century reform movements, traditional hierarchies like that between priests and the nuns in their charge became inverted. Nuns could collect and reassemble the divine words of others to make devotional books of their own and, in so doing, step into the role of learned teacher. What is more, fragmentary compilation could become a textual strategy used to camouflage the transmission of potentially dangerous texts.[7]

[6] Henry Suso, *The Exemplar, with Two German Sermons*, trans. Frank Tobin (New York: Paulist Press, 1989), p. 63.
[7] For an expanded discussion of several aspects of the argument presented here, see Sara S. Poor, "Women Teaching Men in the Medieval Devotional Imagination," in *Partners in Spirit: Men, Women, and Religious Life in Germany, 1100–1500*, ed. Fiona J. Griffiths and Julie Hotchin (New York: Brepols, forthcoming).

Before the invention of the printing press (1450), secular and religious texts were written down by hand onto parchment and then by the fifteenth century, onto paper. Gathered together in quires, the manuscript pages (*folios*) were then later bound into books (*codex*) with bindings made usually of leather-covered wood. Scholars generally trace a single text's transmission, taking note of how many manuscripts or codices contain copies of that text. Exploring where the manuscripts were produced, by whom and for whom, how many of them remain extant, and what kinds of books they are, scholars speculate about the popularity of a given text, its readers, its function, and the literary culture in which it participates. As Barbara Newman notes in her contribution to this volume, manuscripts originally functioned primarily as transcripts of performances (songs, ballads, rhymed tales, religious services, and sermons), but by the fifteenth century, they were increasingly produced to be read on an individual basis. Mystical texts in particular, because they are focused on the individual's relation to and interaction with God, were read for purposes of personal devotion and contemplation.[8] The advent of paper technology (around 1400) made book production easier and less costly. Simultaneously, attitudes toward books and writing shifted. Manuscripts were increasingly regarded as tools to be used rather than as treasures to be cherished; literacy rates were also increasing, particularly among the laity; and among the devout (monastic and lay), reading, writing, and book production were ways in which individuals could effectively pursue their meditations and do good works at the same time.

Central to our story, then, is the larger number of manuscripts produced in and surviving from the fifteenth century. If most of the now canonical medieval mystics wrote down their revelations and sermons between the twelfth and fourteenth centuries, their writings flourished during the fifteenth century, a tendency that parallels a wider trend in Europe in the late Middle Ages. For example, there are between 120,000 and 130,000 manuscripts from German-speaking areas that survive from the Middle Ages (both Latin and German); about 60 percent are from the fifteenth century and roughly 10 to 15 percent of these are written in German. Similar figures are in evidence (though fewer total manuscripts) for France, Italy, and England.[9]

---

[8] See the essay by Thomas Bestul in this volume.
[9] Uwe Neddermeyer, *Von der Handschrift zum gedruckten Buch: Schriftlichkeit und Leseinteresse im Mittelalter und in der frühen Neuzeit. Quantitative und qualitative Aspekte*, 2 vols. (Wiesbaden, Germany: Harrassowitz, 1998), for Germany, vol. 1, pp. 85–7; for the rest of Europe, vol. 1, pp. 91–2.

As these statistics indicate, most surviving medieval manuscripts are in Latin – indeed, most mainstream religious writing in the Middle Ages was written in Latin. The rise in the number of surviving manuscripts can be attributed to the increasingly inextricable connection between writing and religious reform.[10] Texts with monastic rules and guidelines for daily religious life were produced in order to promote proper and more uniform devotional practices. For reform efforts were almost always aimed at renewing "authentic" observance of the monastic rule in the face of evidence of its flagrant disregard among monks and nuns. This type of textual production was also aimed at preventing and correcting heresy. Despite these efforts to make theology and religious practices more uniform (and uniformly orthodox), however, the manuscripts transmitting devotional texts, particularly those written in vernaculars, become increasingly fragmentary and disjointed. Despite warnings not to excerpt devotional and visionary writings because of the danger of heretical error, the fifteenth-century manuscript is almost always a compilation of texts excised from other longer texts, sometimes unattributed or misattributed, compilations in which mystical texts appear consistently.[11]

The mystical texts transmitted in these later manuscripts are almost all in conversation with the writings of the twelfth-century popularizer of the Cistercian order, Bernard of Clairvaux (1090–1153). Bernard's main message was that every soul could find in itself a way to experience the presence or consciousness of God. However, although he directed his writings to his fellow monks living a life withdrawn from the world, his message was soon disseminated beyond this monastic context. By 1953, Jean LeClercq had documented close to 1,500 extant manuscripts of Bernard's Latin writings in European libraries. Of these, 450 were in the German-speaking regions, more than four hundred in France, and 170 in England. Six hundred of the 1,500 date to the twelfth century, and for most of these manuscripts, the provenance (where the manuscript was written, who owned it, and where it ended up) is known.[12] During

---

[10] Klaus Schreiner, "Verschriftlichung als Faktor monastischer Reform: Funktionen von Schriftlichkeit im Ordenswesen des hohen und späten Mittelalters," in *Pragmatische Schriftlichkeit im Mittelalter: Erscheinungsformen und Entwicklungsstufen (Akten des Internationalen Kolloquiums 17.–19. Mai 1989)*, ed. Hagen Keller, Klaus Grubmüller, and Nikolaus Staubach (Munich: Wilhelm Fink, 1992).

[11] The author of the *Cloud of Unknowing*, e.g., warns that "if a man save one part [of this text] and not another, he might easily be led into error" (my translation). Quoted in Barry Windeatt, "Constructing Audiences for Contemplative Texts: The Example of a Mystical Anthology" in *Imagining the Book*, ed. Stephen Kelly and John J. Thompson (Turnhout, Belgium: Brepols, 2005), pp. 159–71, at p. 160.

[12] Ulrich Köpf, "Die Rezeptions- und Wirkungsgeschichte Bernhards von Clairvaux. Forschungsstand und Forschungsaufgaben," in *Bernhard von Clairvaux: Rezeption*

the twelfth and thirteenth centuries, it is also possible to identify countless compilations of shorter texts attributed to Bernard. For example, a Belgian, William of Saint Martin (of Tournai; fl. 1250), put together an anthology of Bernard's writings under the title *Flores Bernardi* (*The Flowers of Bernard*) that survives in more than one hundred manuscripts and that has been continually printed since 1472.[13] Bernard's *flores* can also be found in compilations by other authors – for example, Vincent of Beauvais's (d. ca. 1264) *Speculum historiale* (*Mirror of History*) has one entire section filled with sayings drawn from the writings of Bernard.

As the statistics for Germany suggest, in general there were many more Latin manuscripts made and circulated than vernacular ones. There is only one Old French translation of Bernard's *Sermons on the Song of Songs* (*Cantica Canticorum*), for example.[14] Werner Höver has researched the transmission of a medieval German translation of Bernard's *Sermons on the Song of Songs*, of which there are nine extant manuscripts, five complete, and four containing only parts.[15] But Ulrich Köpf notes that entire sets of sermons like those on the Song of Songs are much less prevalent in the vernacular transmission than are isolated sermons. Most common are short excerpts or sayings extracted from sermons and tracts.[16] In addition, the transmission of short vernacular texts attributed to Bernard that were not actually written by him attests to the extent of his influence and authority beyond the world of monastic readers of Latin.

While Bernard wrote about the mystical relationship allegorized in the Song of Songs, his contemporary, Hildegard of Bingen, recounts direct communication from the divine in her *Scivias* (*Know the Ways of God*). Hildegard claims to have received the visions described in this book, as well as their exegesis, from a heavenly light. She dictated the Latin words of God to her scribe, who then later transferred his transcription from wax

---

und Wirkung im Mittelalter und in der Neuzeit, ed. Kaspar Elm (Wiesbaden, Germany: Harrassowitz, 1994), pp. 5–65, at pp. 9–10.

[13] Ibid., p. 15.

[14] Stewart Gregory, ed., *La Traduction en Prose Française du 12e Siècle des Sermones in Cantica de St. Bernard* (Atlanta, GA: Rodopi, 1994).

[15] Werner Höver, *Theologia Mystica in altbairischer Übertragung: Bernhard von Clairvaux, Bonaventura, Hugo von Balma, Jean Gerson, Bernhard von Waging und andere: Studien zum Übersetzungswerk eines Tegernseer Anonymus aus der Mitte des 15. Jahrhunderts* (Munich: C.H. Beck, 1971).

[16] Köpf, "Rezeptions- und Wirkungsgeschichte Bernhards," p. 18. See also, Werner Höver, "Bernhard von Clairvaux," in *Die deutsche Literatur des Mittelalters Verfasserlexikon*, vol. 1, ed. Kurt Ruh, Gudolf Keil, Werner Schröder, Burghart Wachinger, and Franz Josef Worstbrock (Berlin: de Gruyter, 1978), pp. 753–62.

tablets to parchment. Hildegard is also author of several other significant works, most of which are collected together in a manuscript known as the *Riesenkodex* (*Giant Book*). The production of this codex was most likely overseen by Hildegard, yet later scribes only rarely copied the entire collection. There was significant interest in Hildegard's individual works during her lifetime; the *Scivias*, for example, was copied and circulated reasonably widely, though not as widely as Bernard's writings. There are ten extant manuscripts that transmit the text whole and another thirteen mentioned by her contemporaries that are no longer extant. By the fourteenth and fifteenth centuries, however, the text is transmitted much less frequently and in smaller and smaller pieces.[17] Similar to the case of Bernard, there are a number of texts associated with Hildegard that she did not write; John Tauler (ca. 1300–61) and Henry of Nördlingen (ca. 14th century) refer to her in sermons and letters, and there are vernacular texts in German associated with her legend as a prophetess and saint.[18] With both Bernard and Hildegard, as the texts shrink in size, the name that bears and transmits authority gains in importance.

The divine authority associated with particular names becomes an organizing principle in some of the compilations that transmit mystical texts. For example, in London, British Museum Ms Additional 37790, a mid-fifteenth-century manuscript, collects the following English texts: (1) Richard Rolle's (ca. 1300–49) *De emendatione vitae* (*On the Mending of Life*); (2) Rolle's "*Liber de incendio amoris*" (*Book of the Fire of Love*); (3) a pseudo-Bernard tract; (4) Julian of Norwich's (1342–ca. 1416) "Shewings" (the short text); (5) a treatise on the perfection of God, by John Ruusbroec (1293–1381); (6) excerpts from two other Rolle texts; (7) one section from chapter four of the English abridged version of Henry Suso's *Horologium Sapientiae* (*The Clock of Wisdom*); (8) Marguerite Porete's (d. 1310) *Mirror of Simple Souls* (though not attributed to her here); (9) excerpts from a book of diverse devotional tracts attributed to Saint Augustine of Canterbury (d. 604); (10) an anonymous text on contemplation; (11) an anonymous extract from a text on compassion; and (12) a text on the visions of Saint Bridget of Sweden (d. 1373). The catalogue description reveals that six of the nine texts (1–5 and 9) are explicitly attributed to an author; for number 8, the translator mentions three named authorities who have seen the text and approved of it; and

---

[17] Michael Embach, *Die Schriften Hildegards von Bingen* (Berlin: Akademie Verlag, 2003), pp. 82–3.
[18] Ibid., pp. 422–57.

number 12 names Saint Bridget as a visionary authority.[19] Regardless of the compiler's intentions, this grouping has the effect of constructing a tradition that is defined according to divinely inspired authorship.

But authorship becomes less and less important in the increasingly fragmentary fifteenth-century compilation of vernacular devotional texts. The transmission of Mechthild's book also follows this pattern: there is only one complete manuscript (dating to the fourteenth century). Of the nineteen manuscripts transmitting fragments, ten are from the fifteenth century; fourteen of the nineteen fragmentary manuscripts transmit only a few chapters from Mechthild's book and eleven of these fourteen transmit only an excerpt from one chapter.[20] Further, the more fragmentary the transmission, the fewer attributions of authorship appear. Mechthild's book is initially translated during her lifetime from Middle Low German (a dialect of central Germany) into Latin in order to promote her writings to a more universal audience. In the prologue to this translation, Mechthild is named and explained: readers are encouraged to view God as the author of the book and not Mechthild, who is compared to biblical women prophets in order to justify her authorial role. The Middle Low German is later translated into Middle High German (a dialect of southern Germany); virtually all of the existing German manuscripts stem from this translation.[21] In one of the manuscripts containing large selections from her book, Mechthild is named as a saint. But in the eleven manuscripts that include just one selection, names of authors are no longer important. Eight of these eleven manuscripts contain a collection of Bernardian and Eckhartian sayings. Shifting our focus from Mechthild as author to this collection as a unit, we find that it suffers the same fate as Mechthild's book; it is first transmitted whole in the fourteenth century, and then in the fifteenth century, it is broken

---

[19] Marleen Cré, *Vernacular Mysticism in the Charterhouse: A Study of London, British Library, MS Additional 37790* (Turnhout, Belgium: Brepols, 2006), pp. 17–18.

[20] Five of this total of twenty have been discovered and documented in the past five years. For the most recent and thorough account of the Mechthild manuscript transmission, see Balázs J. Nemes, *Von der Schrift zum Buch – vom Ich zum Autor: Zur Text- und Autorkonstitution in Überlieferung und Rezeption des "Fliessenden Lichts der Gottheit" Mechthilds von Magdeburg.* (Tübingen, Germany: A. Francke Verlag, 2010). For the complete manuscript list, see pp. 487–8.

[21] There is one German manuscript that translates the Latin version back into Middle High German in 1517 (Rw). See ibid., p. 488. On some newly discovered fragments that predate the 1345 Middle High German translation, see Natalja Ganina and Catherine Squires, "Ein Textzeuge des 'Fliessenden Lichts der Gottheit' von Mechthild von Magdeburg aus dem 13. Jahrhundert Moskau, Bibl. der Lomonossow-Universität, Dokumentensammlung Gustav Schmidt, Fonds 40/1, Nr. 47," *Zeitschrift für deutsches Alterum und deutsche Literatur* 139 (2010): pp. 64–86.

up for new compilations that neither acknowledge the original compiler as author nor preserve its integrity as a collection.[22]

This pattern of transmission brings us back to the relationship between the production of writing and religious reform, for the manuscripts transmitting these fragmentary compilations are closely connected with the so-called observance reform. This movement arose primarily from within religious orders whose leaders saw the need to return to a strict observance of monastic rule. It began in Italy among Franciscans and Augustinians and developed simultaneously among Dominicans and Benedictines throughout Spain, France, and the German-speaking territories, as well as eastward into Poland, Bohemia, and Austria. The desire for reform was motivated by the spiritual bankruptcy and division left in the wake of war, plague, natural disaster, and the political strife relating to the papal schism during the second half of the fourteenth century, conditions that diverted both men and women from attending to spiritual matters.

Although efforts were made to renew men's and women's religious houses, it was primarily the reform of nuns that led directly to the increased production and popularity of vernacular devotional literature, particularly in the German-speaking regions.[23] Although most women's communities were self-governed, they nevertheless required priests to administer the sacraments, celebrate mass, preach, and hear confession. Yet even before the establishment of newer reformed convents, in the province of Teutonia (southern German-speaking regions) women's convents outnumbered men's houses by three to one, an imbalance that persisted into the fifteenth century. During the fourteenth century, in Alsace and Swabia, there were twenty Dominican friaries responsible for the care of sixty-three women's convents.[24] Reform-minded women filled the void left by this imbalance with medieval devotional books, pressing their spiritual advisors for transcripts of sermons, copies of devotional tracts, and other material suitable for religious meditation. The

---

[22] For an edition of this compilation, see Karin Schneider, *Pseudo-Engelhart von Ebrach das Buch der Vollkommenheit* (Berlin: Akademie Verlag, 2006).

[23] For an overview of literature making this claim as well as a qualification of it, see Balázs J. Nemes, "*Dis buch ist iohannes schedelin*: Die Handschriften eines Colmarer Bürgers aus der Mitte des 15. Jahrhunderts und ihre Verflechtungen mit dem Literaturangebot der Dominikanerobservanz," in *Kulturtopographie des deutschsprachigen Südwestens im späteren Mittelalter: Studien und Texte*, ed. Barbara Fleith and René Wetzel (Berlin: De Gruyter, 2009), pp. 157–214.

[24] Regina D. Schiewer, "Sermons for Nuns of the Dominican Observance Movement," in *Medieval Monastic Preaching*, ed. Carolyn Muessig (Leiden, The Netherlands: Brill, 1998), p. 75.

manuscript evidence speaks for itself: while only about 10 percent of the houses in a given order accepted strict observance, 90 percent of extant German religious manuscripts can be traced to reformed houses.[25]

This context further explains the increased production of fifteenth-century vernacular devotional books. Their increasingly fragmentary and individual quality was also influenced by devotional practice. A text like Mechthild's *Flowing Light* – a work made up of seven "books" each containing between twenty-five and fifty chapters of varying length – both records and models the practice of meditating on a short text about an image, vision, biblical passage, or piece of religious instruction. These books were not meant to be read from front to back. Rather, with a detailed table of contents, readers could select shorter readings for meditations appropriate to varying situations. The fragmentary style of a large book of revelations like Mechthild's was carried over into compilations of unattributed devotional texts in the fifteenth-century observant context.

The need for written spiritual guidance in the absence of priests, combined with the material factors mentioned earlier (the advent of paper and changing attitudes toward book use), the devotional practice of meditating on short texts, and the resulting reduced emphasis on naming authors created a situation in which traditional hierarchies like priest over nun or author over text could be inverted. This situation, in which the authority of the divine Word outweighs the authority of a human author (mystic or cleric), and in which anonymity was, after all, theological practice, opened the door for women's active participation in a religious literary culture in which female authority was doctrinally a contradiction in terms.

My final example epitomizes this situation: a compilation designed by Dorothea of Hof that she calls "The Book of Divine Love" (1483). Although it consists entirely of quotations from texts by Henry Suso, Otto of Passau (fl. 1380), Thomas Peuntner (d. 1429), Marquard of Lindau (d. 1392), and John Nider (1380–1438), it is a composition in its own right.[26] At the end of this composition, Dorothea appends two dialogues: a "Dispute between the loving soul and our Lord" and a text entitled "Here follows an instruction by one who asks after the quickest way." The latter of these two dialogues, known in the scholarship as the "Sister Catherine Treatise," is especially significant.[27] In the dialogue, a sermon

[25] Ibid., p. 78.
[26] Einsiedeln, Stiftsbibliothek, Ms. 752. Margit Brand, *Studien zu Johannes Niders deutschen Schriften* (Rome: Istituto Storico Domenicano, 1998), pp. 90–3.
[27] "The 'Sister Catherine' Treatise," in Meister Eckhart, *Teacher and Preacher*, trans. Bernard McGinn with Frank Tobin and Elvira Borgstadt (New York: Paulist Press, 1986), pp. 347–87.

on sin given by a learned father-confessor to his "spiritual daughter" (most likely a beguine, or lay religious woman) becomes, because of her insistent questions, a conversation about how to achieve most quickly the state of nonidentity and openness to God's presence advocated by mystics like Meister Eckhart.[28] Although the confessor cautions her against taking this way because she is a woman, the daughter defies him, goes into exile, returns transformed into "nothing," and becomes his teacher. A conversation between a confessor and a lay religious woman advocates a radical negative theology and concludes with an inversion of the standard power dynamic between priest and his female charge.

In a certain sense, Dorothea, who is herself a lay religious woman, models the inversion dramatized in this final dialogue. The main part of her book, a composition in which she incorporates the words of famous preachers into an original work, can be compared to the spiritual daughter's sermons to the priest at the end of the dialogue. Dorothea writes specifically in her prologue that the book is meant to comfort suffering souls; although her instruction is not directed at priests, it is clearly meant specifically to perform the function the priests are not there to perform – the pastoral care of troubled souls. What better way to take up this task than to compose her "sermons" with quotations from famous preachers? Yet Dorothea does not name any of these men in her book. Her table of contents simply lists the main topic of each lesson – the danger of sin, for example, or the benefits of praising God. The holy words of each lesson are the source of textual authority here, not the names of the preachers who authored them. In effacing the names of the earthly sources, Dorothea claims the authority of a father-confessor, yet simultaneously (strategically?) she reasserts God's authority as supreme.

The table of contents does not list the final dialogue, however, which may amount to an additional undermining of traditional hierarchies. The Sister Catherine Treatise and the negative theology it teaches were associated with the so-called Heresy of the Free Spirit condemned by the Church in the fourteenth century. One scholar suggests that Dorothea refrained from listing this text in the contents in order to hide its presence in the collection from suspicious eyes.[29]

[28] There is a short legend called "Meister Eckhart's Daughter" from which the inspiration for the Sister Catherine Treatise was probably drawn. See Kurt Ruh, "Eckhart-Legenden," in *Die deutsche Literatur des Mittelalters: Verfasserlexikon*, vol. 2, ed. Wolfgang Stammler and Kurt Ruh (Berlin: de Gruyter, 1980), pp. 350–4.

[29] Otto Simon, *Überlieferung und Handschriftenverhältnis des Traktates "Schwester Katrei": Ein Beitrag zur Geschichte der deutschen Mystik* (Halle, Germany: Ehrhardt Karras, 1906), p. 33. More recently, scholars have disputed this association. See, e.g., Undine Bruckner, "Dorothea Von Hof: *das buoch der götlichen liebe und summe der*

However, despite including and camouflaging the potentially dangerous dialogue, Dorothea chooses not to embrace the path to nonidentity it promotes. She not only identifies herself and expresses her spiritual ambitions but also records specific information about her life: the dates of her birth, marriage, and spiritual conversion, even supplying details like her husband's name and her surrender of all her worldly clothes. She is obviously not nothing or no one. What seems more important is the mutually instructive relationship between the confessor and the daughter, a relationship that is inextricably tied up with the production of books in the observant context and that must also have played a role in the production of Dorothea's compilation.

Dorothea's book shows that, by the fifteenth century, the appeal of the daughter becoming confessor outweighs, at least for some, that of the negative mystical theology of complete detachment. Circulation of several similar, more secular stories during the fifteenth century suggests that this pattern of the simple female soul becoming a teacher of trained theologians was a *topos* of popular devotional culture. There were at least three other texts about conversations between a woman and a learned superior circulating during the fifteenth century in similar types of compilation manuscripts: "The Young Woman of Two and Twenty," "The Pious Miller's Wife," and "The Young Beguine of Paris."[30] In the first of these, a woman comes to town and asks for the learned master of theology, who is unnerved because his advice is usually requested

---

tugent. A Study of a Konstanz Laywoman's Compilation of German Spiritual Texts from the 14th and 15th Centuries, with Two Editions" (PhD diss., Oxford University, 2008). Scholars have also questioned the association between the Sister Catherine Treatise and the Heresy of the Free Spirit. See, e.g., Bernard McGinn, *The Presence of God: A History of Western Christian Mysticism*, vol. 4, *The Harvest of Mysticism in Medieval Germany (1300–1500)* (New York: Crossroad, 2005), pp. 344–9.

[30] For "The Young Woman of Two and Twenty," see F. P. Pickering, "Notes on Late Medieval German Tales in Praise of *Docta Ignorantia*," *Bulletin of the John Rylands Library Manchester* 24, no. 1 (1940): 127–9. See also Kurt Ruh, "Das Frauchen von 22 (21) Jahren," in *Die deutsche Literatur des Mittelalters: Verfasserlexikon*, vol. 2, ed. Wolfgang Stammler and Kurt Ruh (Berlin: de Gruyter, 1980), pp. 858–60. For "The Pious Miller's Wife," see Kurt Ruh, "Die fromme (selige) Müllerin," in *Die deutsche Literatur des Mittelalters: Verfasserlexikon*, vol. 2, ed. Wolfgang Stammler and Kurt Ruh (Berlin: de Gruyter, 1980), pp. 974–7; and Heinrich Kaufringer, *Werke*, vol. 1, ed. Paul Sappler (Tübingen, Germany: Niemeyer, 1972), pp. 198–206. The dialogue in "The Young Beguine of Paris" is between the beguine and Christ. "Van den Begingin van Paris," in *Geistliche Gedichte des XIV. und XV. Jahrhunderts vom Niderrhein*, ed. Oskar Schade (Hanover, Germany: Carl Rümpler, 1854), pp. 333–60. See also Hartmut Beckers, "Beginchen Von Paris," in *Die deutsche Literatur des Mittelalters: Verfasserlexikon*, ed. Wolfgang Stammler and Kurt Ruh (Berlin: De Gruyter, 1978), pp. 667–71.

by local students. This woman is married, but she demonstrates such a devout frame of mind that the master asks her to confess the secret of her success. After she enlightens him, he confesses that in all his fifty years of teaching, he has never achieved the perfection that she has as a married woman. The other two texts tell a similar story. The extent of these texts' circulation is not yet completely established, but there are at least thirty known manuscripts containing "Young Woman of Two and Twenty," fifty of "The Pious Miller's Wife," and at least five manuscripts and numerous early modern print versions of "The Young Beguine of Paris." The wide popularity of this paradigm is emblematic of the situation of women religious within the observance movement and their active role in the production of devotional books. It seems likely that this paradigm helped women like Dorothea successfully negotiate the powerful compulsion to transmit the truth about union with God.

15 Writing

CHARLES M. STANG

In Evelyn Underhill's popular study, *Mysticism* (1911), she defines mysticism as "experience in its most intense form."[1] A mystic writes, Underhill argues, because she is "often a literary artist as well" and is able to clothe her intense experience in symbolic language so as "to stir our own deeper selves in their sleep."[2] On this understanding, mystical *scriptio* is the experiential report mystics give us to read, with the hope that our practice of reading will awaken the desire and perhaps even the capacity to enjoy such experiences as they do. *Scriptio* serves *lectio*, which in turn serves *experientia*. No doubt this is in part true. Mystics have left reports – often opaque and indirect – of their own visions of and encounters with the divine. Yet this account has at least two flaws. First, to define mysticism as the reception of a certain kind of intense experience is questionable, as if mysticism were simply the accumulation of discrete, extraordinary "experiences" to be delimited and then described, however poorly. Second, it is not fair to the historical record to suggest that mystical writing is only a kind of vehicle (form) for the transfer of a certain experiential cargo (content).

I wish instead to suggest that mystical writing can serve as a spiritual exercise in the service of soliciting an encounter with the mystery of God. Bernard McGinn insists that we "remember that mysticism is always a process or a way of life" and that "everything that leads up to and prepares for this encounter [between God and the human] ... is also mystical."[3] Underhill's account of writing would place it always in the wake of the mystical encounter, whereas McGinn suggests that writing constitutes part of the devotional life of the mystic and thereby prepares

---

[1] Evelyn Underhill, *Mysticism: A Study in the Nature and Development of Man's Spiritual Consciousness* (London: Methuen, 1911), p. 82.
[2] Ibid., p. 80.
[3] Bernard McGinn, *The Presence of God: A History of Western Christian Mysticism*, vol. 1, *The Foundations of Mysticism: Origins to the Fifth Century* (New York: Crossroad, 1991), p. xvi.

for and invites that event.⁴ His brief description of mysticism as a "way of life" recalls Pierre Hadot's styling of ancient philosophy as a way of life, a program of "spiritual exercises" whose aim is to remake the philosopher in conformity with ultimate reality.⁵ Hadot highlights writing as one of the principal spiritual exercises of ancient philosophy. Thus for Hadot, while philosophical writing does aim to communicate to others – reading is another principal spiritual exercise – writing serves also (perhaps first and foremost) to remake the writer herself. I suggest that we follow McGinn's allusion to Hadot and approach mystical writing as a spiritual exercise, an *askêsis* wherewith the writer remakes herself for an encounter with God. In answer to the question, "why do mystics write?" I would suggest that they write in order to become mystics.

In what follows, I briefly trace the Eastern and Western Christian trajectories of mystical *scriptio*. In the East, we begin with Philo, move through John Chrysostom and "Pseudo" Dionysius the Areopagite, and conclude by passing beyond the Greek world to an East Syrian mystic by the name of John of Dalyatha. This Eastern trajectory inclines toward the late antique period. In the West, however, while we begin with Augustine, we quickly find ourselves squarely in the medieval period, considering the Carthusian background to the thirteenth-century mystic Marguerite d'Oingt's practice of *scriptio divina*.

THE EASTERN TRAJECTORY

Philo (ca. 15–10 BCE–ca. 45–50 CE)

The first mystic to whom we turn is Philo of Alexandria, who may strike the reader as strange because he is not a Christian but a first-century Hellenistic Jew. Nevertheless Philo exerts, along with Plotinus, an immeasurable influence on the Christian mystical tradition. One of his most famous descriptions of a mystical encounter is found in *Who Is the Heir of Divine Things?* (*Quis rerum divinarum heres?*).⁶ This treatise is an allegorical reading of Genesis 15:2–18, in which Abram, who is not yet Abraham, laments his lack of an heir, and God promises him that his offspring will be as the stars in heaven. Philo, however, allegorizes

---

⁴ See also Derek Krueger, *Writing and Holiness: The Practice of Authorship in the Early Christian East* (Philadelphia: University of Pennsylvania, 2004).
⁵ Pierre Hadot, *Philosophy as a Way of Life: Spiritual Exercises from Socrates to Foucault*, trans. Michael Chase (Oxford: Blackwell, 1995).
⁶ Philo, *On the Confusion of Tongues, On the Migration of Abraham, Who Is the Heir of Divine Things?, On Mating with the Preliminary Studies*, trans. F. C. Colson and G. H. Whitaker (Cambridge, MA: Harvard University Press, 1932).

Abram's lament such that Abram comes to speak for anyone who wishes to inherit divine things: "Who then shall be the heir? Not that way of thinking which abides in the prison of the body of its own free will, but that which, released from its fetters into liberty, has come forth outside the prison walls, and if, we may so say, has left behind itself."[7] Playing on the notion that an heir is someone who comes forth from a parent, Philo insists that only he who comes forth out of himself can ever inherit the divine. Philo transforms divine inheritance into an ecstatic asceticism exemplified by Abram:

> Therefore, my soul, if thou feelest any yearning to inherit the good things of God, leave not only thy land, that is the body, thy kinsfolk, that is the senses, thy father's house, that is speech, but be a fugitive from thyself also and issue forth from thyself. Like persons possessed and corybants, be filled with inspired frenzy, even as the prophets are inspired.[8]

This passage begins with an allegorical reading of Genesis 12:1, in which God says to Abram, "Go from your land and your kindred and your father's house to the land that I will show you." Philo reads land, kindred, and home as body, sense, and reason, and thus God's command – "leave!" – as an imperative to lead an ecstatic *askêsis*.

Ecstasy makes an appearance later in the treatise, when Philo unpacks Genesis 15:12, "As the sun was going down, a great ecstasy fell on Abram; lo, and a dread and great darkness fell upon him." This prompts Philo to distinguish between four types of ecstasy: (1) "a mad fury" produced by natural causes; (2) an "extreme amazement" at sudden and unexpected events; (3) a "passivity of mind, if indeed the mind can ever be at rest"; and (4) "the best form of all ... the divine possession or frenzy to which the prophets as a class are subject."[9] Obviously, Philo is most interested in the fourth type and explains that the setting of the sun in Genesis 15:12 refers to the setting of Abram's rational faculty and the rising of the divine light. The rational faculty is figured as the sun at noon, when all is illuminated and we are entirely ourselves, in ourselves. When this sun sets, however, "a dread and great darkness" falls. This darkness is the overwhelming light of the divine, which we experience as darkness because we are accustomed to the weaker, derivative light of our own making, namely reason. With this darkness falls "ecstasy and

---

[7] Philo, *Who Is the Heir?*, LXVIII, p. 317.
[8] Ibid., XIV, p. 317.
[9] Ibid., LI, pp. 409–10.

divine possession and madness" and the "divine spirit" forces the eviction not only of reason but also of the mind (*nous*).

This enthusiasm for ecstasy as divine possession finds an interesting echo in another work of Philo on Abram, now Abraham, one that bears directly on our understanding of writing as a spiritual exercise serving a mystical enterprise. In *On the Migration of Abraham* (*De Migratione Abrahami*), Philo reflects on his own life of writing, confessing how he suffers frustrations just as all writers do. But he also confesses that

> on other occasions, I have approached [my writing] empty and suddenly become full, the ideas falling in a shower from above and being sown invisibly, so that under the influence of Divine possession I have been filled with corybantic frenzy and been unconscious of anything, place, persons present, myself, words spoken, lines written. For I obtained language, ideas, an enjoyment of light, keenest vision, pellucid distinctness of objects, such as might be received through the eyes as a result of clearest showing.[10]

If we read Philo's description of the divine possession he experiences while writing together with his description of Abrahamic ecstasy in *Who Is the Heir?*, then Philo would seem to be confessing that through the practice of writing he suffers a mystical encounter with God, the eviction of his own self by the divine. Just as in *Who Is the Heir?* he spoke of serial selves – divine following upon human, in *On the Migration* he describes successive subjectivities, kenotic and plenary. Philo says that he suffered this swing from empty to full "suddenly" – an adverb that for a Jewish Platonist suggests a variety of connections, biblical and Platonic, all of them associated with the manifestation of God.[11] But what is most interesting for our purposes is not that Philo would seem to have suffered a sort of mystical ecstasy he usually reserves for prophets, but that he experienced such a mystical encounter while writing.

John Chrysostom (347–407 CE)

Chrysostom's seventh-century biographer records a miraculous meeting between the apostle Paul and John, his Antiochene admirer.[12] As the

---

[10] Philo, *On the Migration*, VII, pp. 152–3.
[11] For a summary of the biblical and philosophical use of the term suddenly (*exaiphnês*), see Alexander Golitzin, "'Suddenly, Christ': The Place of Negative Theology in the Mystagogy of Dionysius Areopagites," *Mystics: Presence and Aporia*, ed. Michael Kessler and Christian Sheppard (Chicago: University of Chicago, 2003), pp. 22–3.
[12] *De vita sancti Joannis Chrysostomi* 27, in François Halkin, *Douze récits byzantins sur Saint Jean Chrysostome* (Brussels, Belgium: Société des bollandistes, 1977), pp. 142–8;

story goes, Chrysostom had a portrait of Paul on the wall of his room in Constantinople, and he would speak with the portrait as if it were alive, often putting exegetical questions to the apostle. One night his secretary Proclus peeked through the door while Chrysostom was hard at work on a homily about one of Paul's letters. He saw a man standing over Chrysostom's shoulder, whispering in his right ear as he wrote. Chrysostom seemed unaware of the visitor and only later did his secretary realize that the man whom he saw was the same man from the portrait, namely Paul: "the man I saw speaking with you looked just like this man. Indeed, I think it is he!"[13] This legend went on to produce a rich iconographical tradition in Byzantium, perhaps the most stunning of which is an illustrated medieval manuscript in which the bodies of Chrysostom, who is seated, and Paul, who is standing over him, form a single letter, kappa, which begins a new sentence.[14] This legend, together with Chrysostom's own remarks on his practice of writing, will prove important for our purposes. For according to the legend and Chrysostom, he was able, through writing, to summon Paul into the present, such that their authorial voices and even their bodies became so intertwined that it was difficult to differentiate them.

Throughout his homilies about Paul, Chrysostom seeks quite literally to summon the apostle into the present: privately through his devotional reading and writing, publicly through his preaching. In her study of these homilies, Margaret M. Mitchell aptly characterizes John's homiletics as an "inherently necromantic art."[15] Furthermore, she likens his efforts to summon Paul to a kind of "time travel": "not his own trek back in time but Paul's movement forward ... creates [Chrysostom's] encounter with the Paul he knows."[16] Chrysostom confesses that he is often diverted from his own ends by Paul, who "takes possession" of him as he speaks:

> But why am I troubled? Summoning great force I must flee, lest again Paul, taking possession of me, might lead me away from the text I have set forth to preach on. For you well know how repeatedly

cited in Margaret M. Mitchell, *The Heavenly Trumpet: John Chrysostom and the Art of Pauline Interpretation* (Tübingen, Germany: Mohr Siebeck, 2000), pp. 35–6.
[13] Halkin, *Douze récits*, p. 147; cited in Mitchell, *The Heavenly Trumpet*, p. 36. See also Paul A. Holloway, "Portrait and Presence: A Note on the *Visio Procli* (George of Alexandra, Vita Chrysostomi 27)," *Byzantinische Zeitschrift* 100, no. 1 (2007): 71–83.
[14] British Library Add. Ms. 36636, fol. 179r; Plate 6 in Mitchell, *The Heavenly Trumpet*, p. 507.
[15] Mitchell, *The Heavenly Trumpet*, p. xix.
[16] Ibid., p. 393.

at other times, meeting me as I was going about my sermon, he took possession of me and I became diverted right in the middle of my sermon, and he so seized me that I was persuaded by him to wreck the sermon.[17]

In a pair of homilies on Ephesians, Chrysostom confesses that "we cannot bear to resist" such a possession.[18] He invites his audience into his own possession: "What is happening to me? I wish to be silent, but I am not able."[19] He suggests that the chain that once bound Paul in prison the apostle now uses to bind him: "Paul's chain has become very long, and held us very tightly fast.... This chain pulls those who are bound with it to heaven, as though it were a crane. Just like a secured gold cord, Paul's chain pulls them up to heaven itself."[20] Despite the confusion and the consequent loss of control over his own voice, Chrysostom nevertheless views these episodes as anagogical, as Paul enabling his ascent to heaven. Reflecting on Chrysostom's descriptions of these episodes, Mitchell remarks, "In Chrysostom's interpretation of Paul the identities, personalities and voices of the two men, like their faces in the miniature portrait, become conformed to one another. Thus in Chrysostom's discourse on Paul we have a complex interweaving of the two persons, the two selves, of Paul and Chrysostom."[21]

This interweaving is the very aim of his time-traveling necromancy. Put another way, Chrysostom understands himself as pursuing a course of "the imitation of Paul" (*imitatio Pauli*). The mandate to imitate Paul comes from the apostle, who in several places exhorts his readers to "be imitators of me" (1 Cor 4:16, 11:1; Gal 4:12). Paul, however, insists that he only serves as a means to an end – in Mitchell's words a "mimetic intermediary," for his exhortation to "become imitators of me" is coupled with the reminder, "just as I am of Christ!" (Gal 4:16). For Chrysostom, Paul's own "imitation of Christ" (*imitatio Christi*) is grounded in his confession in Galatians 2:20 that "it is no longer I, but Christ who lives in me." The fact that Christ broke into the "I" of Paul guarantees the chain of *imitatio Christi*, guarantees that the person

---

[17] John Chrysostom, *ego dominus deus feci lumen* 3 [56.146]; Mitchell, *The Heavenly Trumpet*, p. 69.
[18] John Chrysostom, *homiliae in epistulam ad Ephesios (hom. 1–24)* 9.1 [62.69]; Mitchell, *The Heavenly Trumpet*, pp. 69, 184.
[19] John Chrysostom, *homiliae in epistulam ad Ephesios (hom. 1–24)* 8.8 [62.66]; Mitchell, *The Heavenly Trumpet*, p. 184, n. 267.
[20] John Chrysostom, *homiliae in epistulam ad Ephesios (hom. 1–24)* 8.8 [62.66]; Mitchell, *The Heavenly Trumpet*, p. 184, n. 266.
[21] Mitchell, *The Heavenly Trumpet*, p. 42.

we are imitating in Paul is Christ. As Mitchell puts it, it is Paul's own "Christ-infusion" that makes Paul worthy of such imitation. The literary practices to which John devotes himself conform him to Christ through Paul, conform him to the point that he is as interwoven with the apostle as the apostle confesses to have been with Christ.

The reader may wonder what if anything this has to do with writing and Christian mysticism. If Bernard McGinn is strictly correct that mysticism is "an attempt to express a direct consciousness of the presence of God," Chrysostom's endeavors would not seem to count as mystical. After all, his encounter with God (as Christ) is ineluctably indirect, that is, mediated – in his case mediated through the apostle Paul. On the contrary, I would suggest that the example of Chrysostom serves as a reminder that many Christian mystics encounter the mystery of God indirectly through the apostles, saints, and their contemporaries, holy men and women. Chrysostom is seeking to solicit through Paul the same mystical "Christ-infusion" to which the apostle famously confesses in Galatians 2:20. More germane to our purposes here, however, is the fact that Chrysostom pursues this mystical Christ-infusion through his practice of reading and, more to the point, writing. His pen summons a "Paul-infusion" and so with it a Christ-infusion.

"Pseudo" Dionysius the Areopagite (ca. late 5th–early 6th century)

In the early sixth century in Syria there began to circulate a collection of writings allegedly authored by Dionysius the Areopagite, the learned pagan judge whom Paul is said to have converted with his famous speech to the court of the Areopagus in Athens (Acts 17). I say that these texts were "allegedly authored" by Dionysius rather than "attributed" to him because the author literally assumes the identity of this famous disciple of Paul, writing to his fellow disciple Timothy, witnessing to the dormition of Mary, and counseling John the evangelist in exile on Patmos. In the late nineteenth century, two German scholars definitively demonstrated that the author of this collection was no first-century Athenian judge but a late-fifth- or early-sixth-century pseudepigrapher heavily indebted to Neoplatonism, especially the fifth-century philosopher Proclus.

Scholars have been split as to whether it is best to interpret the Dionysian corpus against the backdrops of Neoplatonism or late ancient Eastern Christian traditions.[22] Scholars are united, however, in agreeing

---

[22] For the critical edition of the Greek text, see Beate Regina Suchla, ed., *Corpus Dionysiacum I* (Berlin: de Gruyter, 1990); and Günter Heil and Adolf Martin Ritter, eds., *Corpus Dionysiacum II* (Berlin: de Gruyter, 1991). For the English translation,

that the corpus is one of the most influential texts in the history of Christian mysticism, and that its longstanding influence was bolstered by its presumed apostolic pedigree. The corpus exhorts its reader to pursue an astringent contemplative regimen in which one "says" (*kataphasis*) and "unsays" (*apophasis*) in perpetuity the divine names in hopes of soliciting a deifying encounter with an utterly transcendent, ineffable God, none other than the "unknown God" whom Paul proclaims in Athens. Shocking to some modern readers, this mystical enterprise is firmly embedded in an elaborately articulated ecclesiastical hierarchy (which is itself a reflection of the celestial hierarchy) with its own, complementary economy of deification in which the currency is the deifying light of Christ. Owing to the importance it places on the transcendence of God and the consequent necessity of perpetual unsaying or negation, the Dionysian corpus is widely regarded as the font of the negative way (*via negativa*) in Christian mysticism – also called negative or apophatic theology.

The pseudonym, Dionysius the Areopagite, and the corresponding influence of Paul together constitute the best interpretive lens for understanding the Dionysian corpus and its author.[23] It is crucial first, however, to realize that the mystical enterprise of the Dionysian corpus has an anthropological dimension. In short, unsaying the names of God requires the unsaying of the human self and its faculties; to suffer union with the unknown God requires that we become unknown to ourselves and thereby open to the God who is otherwise than we are. For Dionysius, love is the instrument for this apophasis of the self. *Erôs* is the love that stretches us to the point of splitting and thereby clears room for the descent of that unknown God, whom we receive in the deifying light of Christ. Paul is, not surprisingly, the exemplar here, for it is Paul "the great lover" who is ecstatic for God (2 Cor 5:13) and displaces himself so as to make a place for Christ (Gal 2:20).[24] The other exemplar is Moses, who at the summit of Sinai, enshrouded in the "darkness of

---

see Pseudo-Dionysius, *The Complete Works*, trans. Colm Luibhéid (New York: Paulist Press, 1987).

[23] See Charles M. Stang, *Apophasis and Pseudonymity in Dionysius the Areopagite* (Oxford: Oxford University Press, 2012); Charles M. Stang, "Dionysius, Paul and the Significance of the Pseudonym," in *Rethinking Dionysius the Areopagite*, ed., Sarah Coakley and Charles M. Stang (Oxford: Wiley-Blackwell, 2008), 11–25; Charles M. Stang, "'Being Neither Oneself nor Someone Else': The Apophatic Anthropology of Dionysius the Areopagite," in *Apophatic Bodies: Negative Theology, Incarnation and Relationality*, ed., Chris Boesel and Catherine Keller (New York: Fordham University Press, 2009), pp. 59–75, 381–90.

[24] Pseudo-Dionysius, *Divine Names*, 4.13, p. 82.

unknowing ... belongs completely to him who is beyond everything ... being neither [entirely himself] nor someone else."[25] In both cases, there is a negative mystical anthropology in which the human is not annihilated by the infusion of the divine, but doubled, simultaneously self and other, oneself and someone else.

The question is whether this mystical anthropology provides us any insight into writing as a spiritual exercise. I suspect that the author's decision to write under a pseudonym may align with and even contribute to the mystical enterprise laid out in his work. Not unlike Chrysostom, the author is engaged in a kind of time travel, but whereas Chrysostom summons Paul into his present, this author transports himself back into the bosom of the apostle by assuming the identity of his disciple, Dionysius the Areopagite. By becoming an imitator of Dionysius, who in turn was an imitator of the Christ-infused Paul, the author also writes himself into the presence of the divine. But the author's identification with the historical Dionysius the Areopagite is not seamless. He infamously cribs from Proclus and occasionally strays close to contemporary Christological controversies. The pseudonymous author is "neither himself nor someone else," neither the sixth-century Syrian whom we assume he was nor the first-century Athenian whose identity he assumes. His practice of pseudonymous writing renders him two in one. In this regard, his writing under a pseudonym aligns closely with his apophatic anthropology: writing pseudonymously, in which he is neither entirely himself nor someone else only because he is both himself and someone else, becomes for this author an erotic and ecstatic practice in the service of breaching the integrity of the singular self, unsaying that singular self, and thereby soliciting a deifying union with the unknown God. If this is right, then writing as a spiritual practice in the service of mysticism takes its place at the inauguration of the negative or apophatic tradition within Christian mystical theologies.

This survey of the Eastern trajectory would be incomplete without at least a glance further eastward, beyond the Greek world, to the Syriac-speaking Christian communities. It is there that we find John of Dalyatha, an eighth-century East Syrian (or "Nestorian") mystical theologian from the monasteries of Mesopotamia. In one of his letters to the "solitaries," he confesses that:

> The pen burns from the strength of your fire, O Jesus, and my right hand has stopped writing; my eyes are scorched by the rays of your

[25] Pseudo-Dionysius, *Mystical Theology* 1.3, p. 137.

beauty. The ground on which I have been proceeding has been altered before me. My intelligence has been astonished by the marvel which You provoke and henceforth I know myself as not existing.[26]

In the East Syrian tradition, fire often represents the baptismal restoration of the garment of light or the "robe of glory" lost in the Fall. Following Dionysius, however, the fire is also the deifying light of Christ that, while first experienced in baptism, can descend suddenly, as it did for Paul and as it does here for John of Dalyatha, in an extraordinary flash. John is consumed by this deifying fire that "scorches" his senses and his intelligence and quite literally renders him naught. What is of most interest is that he suffers the paradoxical knowledge of his nonexistence while he is writing. Although he says that his hand has stopped writing, we know that eventually he picks up his burning pen again to write this letter. Moreover, his knowledge of his nonexistence persists beyond this extraordinary event ("henceforth I know myself as not existing"). Here again we see the dense interweaving of mystical union, negative anthropology, and writing as a spiritual exercise.

THE WESTERN TRAJECTORY

Augustine of Hippo (354–430)

Augustine has more to say about language and its discontents, and the spiritual practices of reading and writing, than any of the other Latin Fathers. Early in his *Confessions*, Augustine dedicates his writing to God's service;[27] we learn later that those books he wrote at Cassiciacum "were indeed now written in your service."[28] But how did Augustine understand his writing as serving God? Near the end of the *Confessions* Augustine offers at least one answer to that question: "Why then do I set before you an ordered account of so many things? It is certainly not through me that you know them. But I am stirring up love for you in myself and in those [*sed affectum meum excito in te et eorum*] who read this, so that we may all say, 'Great is the Lord and highly worthy to be praised' [Ps 47:1]."[29] For Augustine writing his *Confessions* is a means of first exciting his own and then his readers' love (*affectus*) for God.

---

[26] John of Dalyatha, Letter 4:6 in *The Letters of John of Dalyatha*, trans. Mary T. Hansbury (Piscataway, NJ: Gorgias, 2006), p. 26.
[27] Augustine, *Confessions*, trans. Henry Chadwick (Oxford: Oxford University Press, 1991), bk. I.15.24, p. 18.
[28] Ibid., bk. IX.4.7, p. 159.
[29] Ibid., bk. XI.1.1, p. 221.

In his famous account of the vision at Ostia – often interpreted as his description of a mystical encounter – Augustine remarks that his and his mother's "minds were lifted up by an ardent affection [*ardentiore affectu*] towards eternal being itself."³⁰ If writing stirs up our affection for God, and affection is what lifts us up so far as to "touch" (*attingere*) eternal being, then Augustine also would seem to have developed already some understanding of mystical *scriptio* in the *Confessions*.

The Carthusians (11th–13th centuries)

Drawing on the reflections on the art of the scribe in such figures as Cassiodorus (ca. 485–ca. 585) and Isidore of Seville (ca. 560–636), the architects of the Carthusian order in the late eleventh and twelfth centuries provide a crucial example of the role of reading and writing as the center of the devotional live of their monks. Whereas the Benedictines insisted that God was met in the communal life of the monks, especially in the Divine Office, the Carthusians endorsed a spirituality of the cell and celebrated solitude and silence. Not surprisingly, reading and writing (specifically scribal transcription) become characteristically Carthusian spiritual exercises. As the Carthusian prior Guigo I (1083–1136) remarks, echoing Augustine on *affectus*, "For as many books as we write, so many heralds of truth we seem to us to make, hoping for a reward from the Lord for all those ...who will have been inflamed with desire [*ad desiderium*] of the heavenly country."³¹

This Carthusian esteem for writing – what Stephanie Paulsell calls "*scriptio divina*" – comes to fruition in the twelfth and thirteenth centuries among a handful of women mystics who apply this understanding of writing as a devotional practice not only to scribal transcription but also to their own authored texts.³² The most striking example of the three whom Paulsell investigates is perhaps the least well-known. Marguerite of Oingt (d. 1310), although less famous than the visionary Hildegard of Bingen (1098–1179) or the condemned beguine Marguerite Porete (d. 1310), advances one of the clearest articulations in the Latin West of *scriptio divina*. She inherits Guigo II's (d. 1193) "ladder of monks" in

---

³⁰ Ibid., bk. IX.10.24, p. 171.
³¹ Guigo I, *Consuetudines*, 28.3–4; cited in Stephanie Paulsell, "*Scriptio divina*: Writing and the Experience of God in the Works of Marguerite d'Oingt" (PhD diss., University of Chicago, 1993), p. 122.
³² My discussion of the Carthusians and Marguerite d'Oingt borrows largely from Paulsell's dissertation. See also Stephanie Paulsell, "Writing and Mystical Experience in Marguerite d'Oingt and Virginia Woolf," *Comparative Literature* 44, no. 3 (Summer 1992): 249–67; and Stephanie Paulsell, "*Scriptio divina*: Women, Writing and God" *The Spire* 26, no. 1 (Fall 2005): 10–17.

which the solitary ascends to God by way of four rungs: *lectio, meditatio, oratio,* and *contemplatio.* At the highest rung, *contemplatio,* Marguerite confesses to have one night "been lifted up in our Lord" and that "when she returned to herself, she had all these things written in her heart in such a manner that she was not able to think about other things, but her heart was so full that she was not able to eat, nor drink, nor sleep until she was in so great a state of weakness that the doctors judged her to be near death."[33] In this encounter, echoing Jeremiah 31, Marguerite becomes the site of a divine *scriptio,* her heart the surface on which God writes. She responds by transcribing the divine text in her heart and thereby taking on God's creative writing as a model for her own. Not only does her writing purge the congestion that was killing her, but also by the addition of a new rung, *scriptio,* Marguerite transforms Guigo's ladder of ascent into a circle or spiral by resolving to read and meditate on her own text.

Finally and paradoxically, by transcribing the divine text inscribed in her own heart, Marguerite purges God from her heart and is thereby saved from the suffocation of his presence and experiences his grace operating in her. As she explains, rather defensively, in her *Page of Meditations (Pagina meditationum)*: "you ought to consider that I have in myself neither the understanding nor the clerical office by which I would know how to draw out these things from my heart, nor to write without another copy [before me] unless the grace of God had been operating in me."[34] For Marguerite, *scriptio divina* draws her nearer to God, but in such a way as to live in that proximity rather than to be extinguished by it. *Scriptio divina* is for her a discipline with which she can negotiate the overpowering presence of the divine not merely by relieving the pressure of that presence but also by responding to it creatively. As Paulsell concludes, "for Marguerite, God's writing leads to her own writing, and her own writing leads always back to God. The spiritual life and the creative life are, for her, one."[35]

---

[33] Marguerite of Oingt, *Les Oeuvres de Marguerite d'Oingt,* ed. Antonin Duraffour (Paris: Societé d'edition "Les belles letters," 1965), p. 142.
[34] Ibid., p. 72.
[35] Paulsell, "*Scriptio divina,*" p. 146.

16 The Body and Its Senses
PATRICIA DAILEY

We cannot presume to know to what medieval mystical texts refer when they call attention to the body. In the Christian tradition, the body is not presented as a united whole but is divided into at least two parts, inner and outer, united only in an unknowable future. When medieval mystical texts write of the body, they require that we make sense of the body in its multifaceted nature. Within these texts, human beings are composed of both inner and outer bodies and inner and outer senses, a model that finds its paradigmatic expression in the writings of Origen (ca. 185–254) and Augustine (354–430). In the *Confessions* and *On the Trinity*, Augustine draws upon the anatomy of the outer body to provide an intellectual physiognomy for the soul and its forms of apprehension. For Augustine, just as the outer body has eyes, ears, and other sensory organs, the inner body, the sign of the interior human being, has inner ears and inner eyes, and memory, part of its most spiritually nutritive element, which functions like a stomach, distilling the inner from the outer, the eternal from the temporal, the "I" from the eternal "thou" who punctuates Augustine's prose and his person.[1] Impressions are distilled from the outside in. From the limited human perspective, a kind of sensing is converted into knowing or striving for the inner spiritual life.

Augustine does not invent the tradition; the notion of an inner human being is present in Hellenic thought and is linked to the soul and the afterlife. In Greek, it is often referred to as *nous* (mind) or *psyche* (the soul) and is tied to that part of creaturely existence that persists beyond physical death.[2] In 2 Corinthians 4:16, the apostle Paul articulates this

---

[1] "We might say that the memory is a sort of stomach for the mind, and that joy or sadness are like sweet or bitter food." Augustine, *Confessions*, trans. R. S. Pine-Coffin (New York: Penguin, 1961), bk. 10, 14, p. 220.

[2] David E. Aune suggests that the difference between Hellenistic eschatology and Judeo-Christian apocalyptic eschatology lies in the tendency for the former to emphasize the individual, while the latter places its emphasis on the community at large. The body

distinction between earthly and heavenly dwellings in terms of the difference between the "outer human being" (*ho exo anthropos*) and the "inner human being" (*ho eso anthropos*), the former characterized as a temporal earthly vessel that operates by means of things seen, and the latter as that aspect of the human being that renews itself according to the promised measure of eternal life. The relation between Hellenistic eschatology, Neoplatonic philosophy, and Pauline theology (the latter two being sources for Augustine's model) is complex and much debated, yet suffice it to say that the inner human being referred to by Paul in varied contexts is characterized by its persistence beyond death and is often described in contrast to the perishable vessel (*ostrakinon skeuous*, 2 Cor 4:7) or earthly house (*epigeios oikia*, 2 Cor 5:1) of physical existence.

Augustine recapitulates this Pauline distinction in far more specific – and now Latin – terms, linking capacities of the mind or the soul (*mens*), which are constitutive of the inner, to ideational and mnemonic capacities that allow human beings an even greater proximity and likeness to God and to the image of God in which they are created (*imago dei*). For Origen, as for Augustine, the inner and outer persons are described in terms of inner and outer bodies, of which "one was made in the image of God and the other was formed from the mud of the earth."[3] Knowledge and experience of the divine are illuminated through the senses of the inner body primarily through the reading of scripture. In his *Commentary on the Song of Songs*, Origen writes that "in the divine Scriptures by synonyms, that is, by similar designations and sometimes by the same words, both the members of the outer man and the parts and desires of the inner man are designated and that they are to be compared with one another not only with respect to the designations but also with

that one will assume in the afterlife is a corporate, collective body, often referred to in the plural. Aune argues against a purely Platonic reading of the inner human being, showing that the inner and outer are different but not opposing. See David E. Aune, "Anthropological Duality in the Eschatology of 2 Corinthians 4:16–5:10," in *Paul Beyond the Judaism/Hellenism Divide*, ed. Troels Engberg-Pedersen (Louisville, KY: Westminster John Knox Press, 2001), p. 218. For more on the inner person in Paul see, Hans Dieter Betz, "The Concept of the 'Inner Human Being' in Paul's Anthropology," *New Testament Studies* 46 (2000): 351–41.

[3] Origen, *Commentary on the Epistle to the Romans, Books 1–5*, trans. Thomas P. Scheck (Washington, DC: Catholic University of America Press, 2001). Bernard McGinn argues that "the spiritual senses as employed by Origen, Gregory of Nyssa and other patristic and medieval Christian mystics can be seen as forms of affective intentionality that display their analogical relation to outer sensation through a variety of linguistic transformations." Bernard McGinn, "The Language of Inner Experience in Christian Mysticism," *Spiritus* 1 (2001): 157–71 at p. 158.

respect to the realities themselves."[4] The inner is closer to divinity and becomes the ultimate repository for the indwelling of the divine, transforming the outer as it gains in spiritual substance. The inner person is the ultimate destination point for human beings and for their reading of the spiritual senses of scripture. "Everything is consummated in the inner man," as Henri de Lubac said of the history and mystery of Christ; "Everything is done to conduct us to 'the inner parts,' to make us observe the Law 'according to the inner man.' The soul is 'the temple of God, in which the divine mysteries are celebrated.'"[5]

The indwelling and proximity of the divine, however, are not granted to all in the same way and to the same degree. Theodore of Mopsuestia (ca. 350–428) carefully notes in his commentary on Psalm 51:11 that God's indwelling is selective and requires a kind of attunement of the mind and soul: "He comes near in disposition to those who are worthy of such nearness and he goes far away from sinners. It is not a matter of being separated or coming nearer in actual nature; in both cases what happens is a question of attitude of mind."[6] Christian mystical theology and practice exemplify the ultimate attempt to solicit the indwelling of the divine; it performs (willingly or unwillingly, passively or actively, affectively or intellectually) closeness or unity with the divine, and it does so by calibrating the outer according to the inner, the physical body to the spiritual or figural body, through a form of imitation (*imitatio*). In this instance, understanding the outer body (what we, as contemporary readers think of as the body) requires that we read and comprehend it in quite a counterintuitive way, that is, as a sign of the inner body.

Reading the body, reading it as something other than its most immediate referent, in a way designed to cultivate its spiritual form, is often a pivotal moment within mystical experience. In her conception of *mynd*, Julian of Norwich (ca. 1342–1416) asks to be given not only physical wounds but "the wound of true contrition, the wound of loving compassion, and the wound of longing with my will for God."[7] The wounds signify a spiritual meaning that confers true form and teaches us how

---

[4] Origen, "The Prologue to the Commentary on The Song of Songs," in *An Exhortation to Martyrdom, Prayer, and Selected Works*, trans. Rowan A. Greer (New York: Paulist Press, 1979), p. 220.

[5] Henri de Lubac, *Medieval Exegesis*, vol. 2, *The Four Senses of Scripture*, trans. E. M. Macierowski (Grand Rapids, MI, and Edinburgh, Scotland: William Eerdmans and T. and T. Clark, 2000), p. 139.

[6] Theodore of Mopsuestia, "On the Incarnation VII," in *Documents in Early Christian Thought* (Cambridge: Cambridge University Press, 1975), p. 59.

[7] Julian of Norwich, *Showings*, trans. and ed. Edmund Colledge and James Walsh (New York: Paulist Press, 1978), p. 179.

to read the physical. In her first vision, as Julian, with Mary "spiritually in her bodily likeness," is shown Christ's passion, she is also given the sense of what these showings mean, that is, how they should be read.[8] Her experience consists of a form of reading (what is shown to her by God) and exegesis. She converts one likeness into another, reading the image of the physical as the spiritual and scriptural. If we read her body only as an immediate physical materiality, we miss the double nature of Julian's reading, how she constitutes meaning for her body, and what the body becomes – spiritual text and scripted performance. The body's doubleness finds its source in the figure it seeks to imitate: Christ. The letter and the body are tightly interwoven through the act of reading, given the mediating importance of the Word in understanding the flesh.

For mystics like Julian, reading is not limited to bodily wounds. Julian reads objects (e.g., the hazelnut and rain drops), reading in them spiritual truth. Michel de Certeau has shown us how for the mystic everything becomes an occasion for reading, attests to some sign, and is some kind of divine signal, even the smallest detail. As Bernard of Clairvaux (ca. 1090–1153) illustrates, reading and affective (or loving) response constitute the most effective way of moving from the outer to the inner body, from bodily agitation or entrapment to inner meditative and spiritual contemplation and mystical experience. In the language of the twelfth-century Victorines, reading (*lectio*) allows for meditation (*meditatio*), prayer (*oratio*), operation (*operatio*), and, finally, contemplation (*contemplatio*). By reading then, I intend not only the reading of texts but also the reading of and meditation on devotional images, pious and exemplary behavior, impressions proffered by one's senses (internal and external), and the mystic's body and life by the hagiographer.[9] Reading presents the opportunity not only for the exegesis of scripture but also for the exegesis of experience and the cultivation – and construction – of the inner body and the inner senses.[10] It enables a bridge

---

[8] Ibid., p. 182.

[9] D. H. Green's understanding of the nature of reading includes reading images and meditating on Christ's body, "even if uneducated and unable to read it in the literal sense." D. H. Green, *Women Readers in the Middle Ages* (Cambridge: Cambridge University Press, 2007), p. 45.

[10] The inner senses are traditionally thought of as five: sight, hearing, smell, taste, and touch. They are not limited to those, however, and, depending on the text, can include the heart, the inner person, a sense of the soul, and more. See Karl Rahner, "Le Début d'une doctrine des cinq sens spirituals chez Origène," *Revue d'ascétique et de mystique* 13 (1932): p. 118. In his *Mystical Ark*, Richard of Saint Victor elaborates on Hugh's notion of three eyes: the eyes of the flesh, reason, and contemplation. See Richard of Saint Victor, *The Twelve Patriarchs; The Mystical Ark; Book Three of the Trinity*, trans. Grover Zinn (New York: Paulist Press, 1979), pp. 149–370; and Hugh of Saint

between the inner and outer bodies; it renders them coherent, in touch with one another by means of an awareness of divinity, and in this way, anticipates the unity of inner and outer bodies in and through divinity. Reading is also a means of writing; it produces a form of inscription into its material, thus allowing the body to become part of its intended script.

For Bernard of Clairvaux, William of Saint Thierry (ca. 1085–1148), Hugh of Saint Victor (1096–1141), Richard of Saint Victor (ca. 1123–73), Bonaventure (1221–74), and many others during the twelfth and thirteenth centuries, the inner senses are characterized by an idiom drawn from the sensorium of the Song of Songs. While Origen introduces the notion of the spiritual senses, which are then elaborated over the following centuries, what I would like to emphasize here is that the inner senses are often conceived of as divine gifts that allow the "honey" of scripture to be extracted from the letter and tasted by the inner human being so that it might be renewed in the image of the Trinity. Understanding is an embodied sensibility mediated by the letter. For William of Saint Thierry,

> this is the sense of taste which the Spirit of understanding has made for us in Christ; that is, the understanding of God's Scriptures and mysteries.... When we begin not only to understand, but in some way also to touch with our hands and to feel the inner sense of the scriptures, and the power of God's mysteries and sacraments, then Wisdom begins to offer her riches. This touching and feeling is produced by the inner senses when these are well practiced in the art of reading the soul's secrets and the hidden action of God's grace.[11]

Twelfth- and thirteenth-century commentaries on the Song of Songs and the echoes of these commentaries heard in women's mystical texts reverberate with a sensual language that often joins corporeality with spiritual understanding.

Victor, *On the Sacraments of the Christian Faith*, trans. Roy J. Deferrari (Cambridge, MA: Medieval Academy of America, 1976).

[11] William of Saint Thierry, *On the Nature and Dignity of Love*, trans. Geoffrey Webb and Adrian Walker (London: Mowbray, 1956), pp. 44–5. The Carthusian abbot, Guigio II (d. 1193), transposes the steps of reading (*lectio*), meditation (*meditatio*), and prayer (*oratio*) into digestive registers: "Reading, as it were, puts food whole into the mouth; meditation chews it and breaks it up; prayer extracts its flavor; contemplation is the sweetness itself which gladdens and refreshes." Guigo II, *The Ladder of Monks and Twelve Meditations*, trans. Edmund Colledge and James Walsh (Kalamazoo, MI: Cistercian Publications, 1979), p. 69.

The thirteenth-century Brabant mystic Hadewijch (mid-thirteenth century), for example, writes that "Love impels us to long desiringly for her / And to taste her without knowing her essence."[12] To see, taste, and hear inwardly become synonymous, generally speaking, with a form of spiritual understanding that does not assume absolute knowledge of the divine but does know something of the divine. For the Franciscan friar Rudolf of Biberach (ca. 1270–1326), taste is understood as an act of affective contemplation of the Eucharist (by means of the *affectus*), which can accomplish union in and of itself.[13] The goal of affective mysticism is not to excite the outer body into a Bacchic frenzy, but to allow one's affective and thus embodied experience to stimulate the construction of the inner body and then to allow the heart, innards, or inner senses to speak and act through the outer body. Gregory the Great (ca. 540–604) similarly notes that "the book which filled the innards (*viscera*) became as sweet honey in the mouth because those who have learned truly to love Almighty God in the innards (*visceribus veraciter*) of their heart know how to speak sweetly about Him."[14] The inner is developed so that it may become a reality that dominates, scripts, and bestows sense on the outer. For these wise men, William of Saint Thierry tells us, the outer body is transformed; "Just as holiness of life and the transfiguration of the inner man become visible in them ... so are their bodies also transfigured in our sight."[15]

For Hadewijch, the kind of reality that the inner senses and *Minne* (Love) produce is a gift that enriches her world by converting meaning into a new spiritual register and an undermining force that depletes her world of its previous sense of the real. The arrival of *Minne* occasions

---

[12] Hadewijch, *Liederen*, ed. and trans. Veerle Fraeters and Frank Willaert (Groningen, The Netherlands: Historische Uitgeverij, 2009), p. 240.

[13] See Rudolf von Biberach, *De septem itineribus aeternitatis*, ed. Margot Schmidt (Stuttgart-Bad Cannstatt, Germany: Frommann-Holzboog, 1985); and Gordon Rudy, *Mystical Language of Sensation in the Later Middle Ages* (New York: Routledge, 2002), p. 112.

[14] Gregory the Great, *The Homilies of St. Gregory the Great on the Book of the Prophet Ezekiel*, trans. Theodosia Gray (Etna, CA: Center for Traditionalist Orthodox Studies, 1990), p. 114, with slight modification.

[15] William of Saint Thierry, *On the Nature and Dignity of Love*, p. 56. See also William's reading of charity as the eye that sees God: "Charity ... is the eye by which God is seen. The soul, like the body, has five senses, but whereas the body is joined to the soul by means of its senses, with life as mediator, the soul has five senses wherewith it may be joined to God, with charity as mediator." Ibid., pp. 8–29. Reason and love are also described as the two eyes of the soul. For more on William see James Walsh, "Guillaume de St. Thierry et les sens spirituels," *Revue d'ascétique et de mystique* 35 (1959): 27–42.

the "doubling" of her senses, thus showing the gifts of divinity to which she had previously been immune. The new meaning that accompanies this doubling makes any knowledge of *Minne* even more elusive. In her thirtieth song, she writes,

> Minne first made me rich,
> She doubled my senses,
> and showed me all of her winnings.
> But why now does she disappear before me like a traitor?
> She doubled my senses,
> and now I wander in stranger's land.[16]

Minne makes Hadewijch a wanderer in a foreign, alien, or strange land; the world that lies outside of union with God, dominated by the outer, is no longer privy to the spiritual certainty she knew in the visions, but has to operate through faith alone and, like Job, through the absence of the divine.

Inasmuch as the new reality *Minne* bestows is strangely sensory, it inhabits the senses while not being determinately sensible. It passes, like a secret, through the senses, without form or figure but permitting its taste:

> It has no form, no figure.
> It is only tasted by us creatures
> It is the material of my bliss.
> [...]
> Never was so wretched a desert created
> As Minne can make in her landscape!
> For she impels us to desire her
> And to taste her without knowing her essence,
> She shows herself as she takes flight;
> We seek her, but she remains unseen.[17]

While Hadewijch's visions chronicle what promises to be present in the inner body and the world it belongs to, the world of the outer body is marked by absence, longing, and a memory of *Minne*, often described as an insatiable hunger or a touch that irreversibly alters the person it

---

[16] Hadewijch, *Liederen*, p. 240. Translation mine. Columba Hart's translation loses the exactitude of the Middle Dutch's "doubling" of the senses (not "joy" as she translates it). For a more accurate published translation see Marieke van Baest, *Poetry of Hadewijch* (Leuven, Belgium: Peeters, 1998), p. 213.

[17] Hadewijch, *Liederen*, Lied 22, p. 184. Translation mine.

affects, like the lovelorn bride in the Song of Songs.[18] Her inner body affirms *Minne's* truth in visions, yet the poems, anchored as they are in a time outside of union, affirm an emotional and affective truth that cannot be embodied or made fully tangible. In this sense, while language and embodiment are inextricable from one another, they cannot be reduced to one another.

In Niklaus Largier's reading of the inner and outer senses, the inner body is not merely an allegorical construct; rather, language produces or enables an embodied effect.[19] Allegory helps construct an inner space that creates affectively embodied access to the divine. For Largier, this happens through the use of emotion in prayer and meditation:

> although the inner or spiritual senses correspond to the five outer senses (in fact they are named in analogous ways), they are not to be seen as a set of allegorical poetic means of expressing and representing spiritual experience. Rather, the texts argue, they constitute and construct a specific reality of the mind. Thus ... the invention and the rhetoric of the inner and spiritual senses allowed for the creation of an inner space of "experience," "exploration," and "amplification" of the emotional as well as the sensory life of the soul.[20]

In what Largier calls a "phenomenology of emotion," medieval texts deploy a rhetoric of affective engagement that serves to engage the physical and emotional in a divine register.[21] Outer and inner are not

[18] Hadewijch brings to life the travails of the bride as William of Saint Thierry describes them in his *Exposition on the Song of Songs*: "And in the Bride's inner self, while she knows it not, the Bridegroom feeds upon what causes her torment, when she accepts no consolation apart from the embrace and the kiss and the sweetness of mutual union." The bride, according to William, shows the "inner perfume of unceasing desire" and "sometimes crucified with desire and sometimes enjoying and delighting in love, and always crucified with desire as long as she cannot enjoy the delights of love, [she] is powerless to obtain from you the stability in you of eternal joy." William of Saint Thierry, *Exposition on the Song of Songs*, trans. Columba Hart (Kalamazoo, MI: Cistercian Publications, 1989), pp. 140–1, 145. Similarly, centuries earlier Origen equates the bride's movement to the lord's inner chamber or treasure house to the soul's introduction into the hidden sense (*sensus*) of Christ.

[19] Niklaus Largier, "Inner Senses, Outer Senses; The Practice of Emotions in Medieval Mysticism," in *Codierungen von Emotionen im Mittelalter/Emotions and Sensibilities in the Middle Ages*, ed. C. Stephen Jaeger and Ingrid Kasten (Berlin: De Gruyter, 2003), p. 8.

[20] Ibid., pp. 4–5. Largier gives an overview of the history of the inner senses in Origen and Gregory of Nyssa and their development in medieval mysticism. He argues that the emphasis on the inner sense denaturalizes the outer senses, liberates them, and then allows for their reinvestment in a different tenor.

[21] Niklaus Largier, "Medieval Mysticism," in *The Oxford Handbook of Religion and Emotion*, ed. John Corrigan (Oxford: Oxford University Press, 2008), pp. 365–6.

given; the inner must be cultivated, even as the inner senses are understood to be passive recipients of the divine. Inner touch, sight, taste, and even hearing require a kind of fine-tuning, although they are ultimately instruments, not of the human being, but of the divine as it reverberates through him in the rumination of scripture. By letting the outer body be mediated or regulated by its inner form, one reaches embodied spiritual perfection.[22] When analyzing and reading the more "corporeally" minded aspects of medieval mystical texts, we have to be careful to understand the complexity of their relation to textuality, materiality, and agency and their implications for identity, especially because the inner body attributed to the mystic cannot be called his or her own.

No study of the body in medieval mystical texts would be complete without reference to Caroline Walker Bynum's seminal work on high and late medieval devotional and religious life. In *Holy Feast and Holy Fast: The Religious Significance of Food to Medieval Women* (1987) and *Fragmentation and Redemption: Essays on Gender and the Body in Medieval Religion* (1991), Bynum insists on the centrality of materiality to medieval Christians, describing the feminization of the flesh and its link to Christ and countless instantiations of lactation, mastication, laceration, and other bodily metaphors and experiences. According to Bynum, "many medieval assumptions linked woman and flesh and the body of God. Not only was Christ enfleshed with flesh from a woman; his own flesh did womanly things: it bled, it bled food and it gave birth."[23] As Bynum notes elsewhere, the vocabulary of the inner senses and its reality are also heard in these texts:

> Mechthild of Magdeburg spoke of mystical union as "eating God." And Ida of Louvain was able to eat Christ almost at will by reciting John 1.14. For, whenever she spoke the words *Verbum caro factum*

---

[22] Even for those seemingly less corporeal mystics like Marguerite Porete, the emphasis on reading the senses can be seen in the form of the book. Largier suggests that the focus on reading and dialogue may be a rewriting of the Song of Songs, in which the inner senses and "sensory experiences we are told about unfold in a process of reading, or more precisely, in the practice of the mediation of the text, in its contemplative reproduction, and finally in the rewriting of the text." Amy Hollywood argues that embodiment is transformed through reading, because "the process of writing the book transforms or transfigures the author in the same way that the Soul is transformed in the text, and the same transformation is meant to be brought about in the reader." Amy Hollywood, *The Soul as Virgin Wife: Mechthild of Magdeburg, Marguerite Porete, and Meister Eckhart* (Notre Dame, IN: Notre Dame University Press, 1995), p. 114. Thus the ultimate corporeality is represented by the corporeality of the book.

[23] See Caroline Walker Bynum, *Holy Feast and Holy Fast: The Religious Significance of Food to Medieval Women* (Berkeley: University of California Press, 1987).

est – which she inserted into the Hours whenever possible – she tasted the Word on her tongue and felt flesh in her mouth; and when she chewed it, it was like honey, "not [her biographer tells us] a phantasm but like any other kind of food." This example makes clear to the modern reader how insistently Christ's humanity was thought of as flesh, as food (*corpus, caro, carnis*), eaten in the eucharist.... Moreover, the incorporation of self into Christ, or of Christ into self was so much a matter of flesh swallowing flesh that women who were not able to eat still received and digested Christ's physicality.[24]

What I would like to suggest here is that the mystic may think of her flesh in relation to Christ's not only because of the nature of the flesh, but because of the dual nature of Christ as Word made flesh and the underlying promised unity of Word and flesh in the perfected inner body. Eating is partially synonymous with understanding, making her identification not only bodily but also cognitive. If we read her body only according to the outer body, we miss the desired referent and the desired transformation of the outer into its perfected inner form. The insistence on the flesh, embodiment, and materiality in women's mystical texts may not be as markedly (and essentially) different from what we find in the texts of their male counterparts if we read the body in the light of its intended honeyed referent – in its desired reflection of the inner body, which performs a more perfect union with Christ, and which the outer body seeks to become like and conform to in the afterlife.[25] When Ida of Louvain's (ca. 1065–1139) hagiographer depicts her performing the consumption of the Eucharist, she is also scripting her performance, reciting the verse in John, and clearly alluding to the "honey" of exegesis. As her biographer notes, Ida's full recitation of the Johannine "The word was made flesh" ("*Verbum caro factum est*") continues with "and lived among us" ("*et havitavit in nobis*"), showing that the host in which it dwells is also not singularly "hers" but a third-person plural that points to a collective identity.[26] Ida's body might have less to do with a fleshy "incorporation" or "mutual interpenetration" of God into the self, than with a desired or understood expropriation of the self into the mystical body (*corpus mysticum*) by means of her imitation.

---

[24] Caroline Walker Bynum, "Women Mystics and Eucharistic Devotion in the Thirteenth Century," *Women's Studies* 11 (1984): p. 188.
[25] Hollywood, *The Soul as Virgin Wife*, p. 25.
[26] Acta Sanctorum Full-Text Database, April 2, p. 164, http://acta.chadwyck.com (accessed January 22, 2012).

To use another example from a nonhagiographical text, when Marguerite of Oingt (ca. 1210) has a vision of a tree with leaves upon which are inscribed the names of the five senses, although it may, as Bynum argues, "be hard to imagine a more graphic illustration of the medieval conviction that those who love Christ should respond to all of his body with all of theirs," we should also remember that the senses are words represented in Latin; "the experiences which seem to be transmitted directly through the senses thus seem to be mediated by writing" as they do the understanding necessary for accessing the meaning of the written form.[27] As David Aers notes, the constitutive means whereby the body becomes materially significant in medieval mystical texts may have less to do with sex or gender than with the power that renders the body significant and signifying. Destabilizing the category of the body should, he argues, lead us to "explore the processes, performative acts, and powers in and through which they become fixed, normative, seemingly inevitable."[28] Although reading "according to the letter," that is in a literal or carnal fashion, may be ascribed in the Middle Ages to the way in which women read as a subversive technique, this kind of sentiment is often defined by the patriarchy it seems to subvert.

As male-authored texts of the period exhibit an increasing emphasis on the tactile nature of the inner body and the inner senses, women's emphases on embodied forms of devotion appeal to the categories applied to textual interpretation and the spiritual sense of reading, especially in the eyes of their hagiographers. If we read both natures in Christ's body, the desired materiality of the body of the mystic who reads herself in Christ's likeness becomes complicated by the text or Word it imitates. In a nuanced critique of Bynum's identification of women's mysticism with the flesh, Amy Hollywood argues that although women writers of the thirteenth century emphasize a suffering that is tied to embodiment, they "refuse the purely bodily designation of this suffering, and with it the emphasis on physicality and physical asceticism found in the hagiographical tradition; they attempt to associate primarily not with

---

[27] Caroline Walker Bynum, *Fragmentation and Redemption: Essays on Gender and the Human Body in Medieval Religion* (New York: Zone Books, 1991), p. 91; Renate Blumenfeld-Kosinski, "The Idea of Writing as Authority and Conflict," in Margaret of Oingt, *The Writings of Margaret of Oingt*, trans. and ed. Renate Blumenfeld-Kosinski (Cambridge: D. S. Brewer, 1997), p. 83.

[28] David Aers, "Humanity of Christ: Reflections on Orthodox Late Medieval Representations," in David Aers and Lynn Staley, *Powers of the Holy: Religion, Politics, and Gender in Late Medieval English Culture* (University Park: Pennsylvania State University Press, 1996), p. 35.

the body of Christ but with the humanity designated by that body."²⁹ Hollywood thus reads embodiment in a way that is not strictly tied to its materiality, but rather is tied to its signifying capacity. In looking at the different ways that bodily suffering is treated in the writing of women mystics and their male hagiographers, Hollywood highlights an ambiguity in the treatment of bodily suffering, showing how male biographers tend to emphasize the outer body and the "objective and the external," while the women emphasize the inner body and, in the case of Christina the Astonishing (1150–1224), "a realm of feeling or sensation separable from the body itself, yet not yet fully identified with the soul." Thus the emphasis on the purely bodily nature of redemptive suffering often "reflects contemporary male expectations and desires."³⁰

In his article, "Desire for the Past," Nicholas Watson echoes Hollywood, noting that given the framing of Bynum's *Holy Feast and Holy Fast*, "the book's argument makes more use of the *vitae* of holy women than of their writings," representing less the "feelings of the holy women ... but [more] ... those of the men who described them."³¹ This tendency to focus on the material represented rather than the means of its representation, he argues, overlooks textuality and may not adequately describe the ways in which acting out divinity and Christ's Passion diffuses the relation between the subject and his or her body. In his reading of the Life of Elizabeth of Spalbeek (1246–1304), written by Philip of Clairvaux, Watson notes that "Elizabeth can be a *miraculum* in this text only insofar as she is not an agent. While Philip knows he is watching a performance, it is God who is the real actor, inspiring a re-enactment of Christ's Passion which 'this virgyne ... figures and expounes ... in hir body'; what fascinates him, in this life that is 'alle mirakill', is the fusion of sign and signified, text and exposition, body and word."³² The body's signifying capacity is not attributed to the intention of the performer, but to an agency, like that of the inner body, that is ascribed to God. Finally, if we read this with the overtones of the inner body, of how the outer body is being scripted to conform to the inner body, then any sense of its materiality must involve the materiality of the letter.

---

²⁹ Hollywood, *The Soul as Virgin Wife*, p. 25.
³⁰ Ibid., pp. 48–9.
³¹ Nicholas Watson, "Desire for the Past," in *Maistresse of My Wit: Medieval Women, Modern Scholars*, ed. L. D'Arcens and J. F. Ruys (Turnhout, Belgium: Brepols, 2004), p. 165. D. H. Green argues that Elizabeth's body becomes a "book" to be read by the illiterate, to be read by the "inner eyes" or the "mind." See Green, *Women Readers in the Middle Ages*, pp. 46–7.
³² Watson, "Desire for the Past," p. 168.

I have pointed out a doubleness at the heart of embodiment in medieval mysticism in order to complicate the meaning of embodiment and of the senses for us as contemporary readers. Whether the body, in its multiplicity as inner and outer, designates humanity, imitates Christ, enacts a text, or reifies ecclesiastical structures, its materiality is intimately bound to the Word it seeks to exemplify and the act of reading and reflection that gives its sense.

17 Mysticism and Visuality
JEFFREY F. HAMBURGER

"Mysticism and visuality": the topic presents, as Gilbert and Sullivan might have put it, "a most ingenious paradox." By definition, the ineffable lies beyond representation of any sort, be it visual or verbal. In its root sense, the word mysticism derives from the Greek "*muo*," "to remain silent" or "to close the lips or eyes." What place can there be for any discourse on the visible in the context of a system of thought that, by definition, is predicated on obscurity and blindness? The paradox extends from sight to speech: were mystics to fall silent, there would not be any mystical literature. Yet when they speak, they very often are called to describe what they see. The description of mystical vision might be considered a special subgenre of ekphrasis, a rhetorical mode predicated on the assumption that, in defiance of the aphorism to the contrary, a thousand words are worth a single picture. Given, however, that the visible, let alone the invisible, is often said to defy verbal description, it must be asked what – and how – mystics "see," and why vision, however defined, is so indispensable to their way of framing the world and their experience of it.[1]

My observations assume that not only the form but also the content of mystical experience, whatever claims its practitioners might make to the contrary, are conditioned by historical context.[2] For an art historian, the most obvious way of insisting on the impact of context, however construed, is to point out the numerous instances in which works of art shaped and structured the experience of onlookers. To define the problem in such straightforward terms, however, is too simplistic; images are shaped in complex ways by the experience, expectations, class, and gender of their audiences. For the material discussed here, the audience

---

[1] In lieu of the large literature, I cite only Barbara Newman, "What Did It Mean to Say 'I Saw'? The Clash between Theory and Practice in Medieval Visionary Culture," *Speculum* 80 (2005): 1–43. For her comments and criticism, I am indebted to Hildegard Elisabeth Keller.

[2] See Steven T. Katz, ed., *Mysticism and Language* (Oxford: Oxford University Press, 1992).

is, above all, monastic, although by the later Middle Ages it expands to comprehend the laity. Given that writings in (and on) the monastic tradition have often interpreted manifestations of the visible as concessions to lay piety, linking visualization with vernacularization, it is important to stress that this essay's emphasis lies elsewhere: on the value attached to the visible within monastic exegesis, theology, and practice.[3]

The focus of this essay is Christian mysticism – specifically, Christian mysticism of the Western Middle Ages. Yet the history of Christian attitudes toward the ineffable and invisible cannot be understood without a glance back at Jewish traditions. Jewish scripture is not silent on the subject of the visible and visuality.[4] Nonetheless, especially as characterized by Christianity, which is the relevant context here, it ultimately insists, or is said to insist, on God's invisibility, his status as the hidden God, the *Deus absconditus* (Is 45:15: "*vere tu es Deus absconditus Deus Israhel salvator*" [Verily thou art a hidden God, the God of Israel the savior]).[5] This is the God whom Moses cannot see face to face, who shows him only his "back parts" (Ex 33:20–3: "Thou canst not see my face: for man shall not see me and live....And when my glory shall pass, I will set thee in a hole of the rock, and protect thee with my right hand, till I pass: And I will take away mine hand, and thou shalt see my back parts: but my face thou canst not see.") Moses's vision is presented and granted as a privilege (cf. Ex 33:13–14), but from a Christian perspective, the prophet is denied the ultimate vision of God face to face that is the birthright of every true believer, in keeping with Paul's proclamation in 1 Corinthians 13:12: "We see now through a glass in a dark manner; but then face-to-face."

A German History Bible, dated 1467, illustrates this specifically Christian retrospective on Moses's vision with an image that reverses the logic of the icon by taking very literally the words spoken by God ("*so wirst dü mein hintertailsehen*") (see Fig. 1).[6] Ironically, his "back

[3] For background, see Jeffrey F. Hamburger, "The Visual and the Visionary: The Changing Role of the Image in Late Medieval Monastic Devotions," *Viator* 20 (1989): 161–82, reprinted in Jeffrey F. Hamburger, *The Visual and the Visionary: Art and Female Spirituality in Late Medieval Germany* (New York: Zone Books, 1998).

[4] See, in general, Kalman P. Bland, *The Artless Jew: Medieval and Modern Affirmations and Denials of the Visual* (Princeton, NJ: Princeton University Press, 2000). Also see Herbert L. Kessler and David Nirenberg, eds., *Judaism and Christian Art: Aesthetic Anxieties from the Catacombs to Colonialism* (Philadelphia: University of Pennsylvania Press, 2011).

[5] See Jeffrey F. Hamburger, "Body vs. Book: The Trope of Visibility in Images of Christian-Jewish Polemic," in *Ästhetik des Unsichtbaren: Bildtheorie und Bildgebrauch in der Vormoderne*, ed. David Ganz and Thomas Lentes (Berlin: Reimer, 2004), pp. 112–45.

[6] See Ferdinand Hutz, *Die Vorauer Volksbibel: Faksimile-Wiedergabe aller 51 Seiten des Buches Exodus aus dem Codex 273 der Stiftsbibliothek Vorau* (Graz, Austria: ADEVA, 1986). I employ the modern foliation.

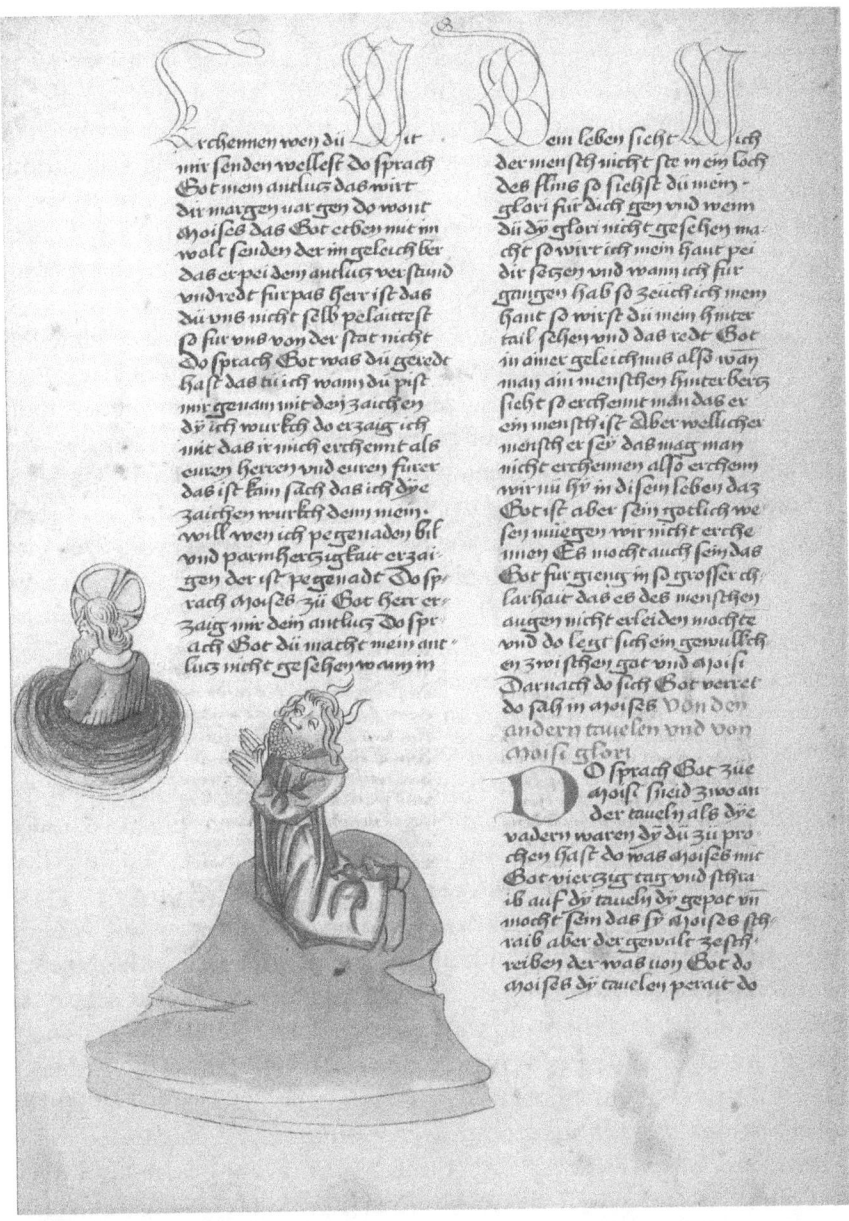

Figure 1. God showing Moses his back parts. Vorauer Volksbibel, 1467 (Stiftsbibliothek Vorau Codex 273, f. 96v). Photo: after Hutz.

parts" are precisely what the image omits, as the deity emerges from a cloud that looks more like a pool of water. Although God's face is in profile and his back in three-quarter view, his halo stands parallel to the picture plane and hence is not subject to reversal. This is the *Deus absconditus* of Jewish scripture, yet the cross-halo represents an immutable truth, a reminder that full vision is accessible only to Christians. In this instance, the image rewards the reader by showing that any believing Christian will, in the fullness of time, come to see more than Moses ever could.

Images served as means, not simply of making ideas accessible but also of endowing them with authority, authenticity, and immediacy. Very often such images frame themselves explicitly in terms of vision. A fourteenth-century French frontispiece to the *Bible historiale* identifies the monarch with the wise king Solomon by showing the patron, Charles V of France, having taken the place of Moses (who cowers at the upper right in what Exodus describes as a "hole in the rocks"), gazing wide-eyed into the tabernacle, which opens to reveal, not the solitary Jehovah, but now the Trinitarian Godhead (see Fig. 2).[7] In contrast, in Christian scripture, the tables are turned by the Incarnation: God does not merely manifest himself in human history by means of signs and symbols (e.g., as in Ex 13:21, a pillar of cloud or a pillar of fire), he enters into history in person, in the flesh. In keeping with the classic formulation of Christian doctrine, "from Christ the human being to Christ the Lord" (*"per Christum hominem ad Christum dominum"*), the Incarnation establishes a bridge between empirical and what, for lack of a better word, could be called transcendental experience. The opening of John's Gospel (Jn 1:14), a passage to which magical powers were attributed throughout the Middle Ages, summarizes this teaching in words that underscore the preeminent role of vision in leading the faithful to a revelation that surpasses understanding: "And the Word was made flesh, and dwelt among us (and we saw his glory, the glory as it were of the only begotten of the Father)." This definitive statement of faith is not, however, without an element of equivocation: *"et vidimus gloriam eius gloriam quasi unigeniti a Patre plenum gratiae et veritatis."* "As it were" – in other words, not quite the real thing. An element of mystery beyond the power of vision remains.

[7] For fuller discussion, see Jeffrey F. Hamburger, "The Medieval Work of Art: Wherein the 'Work'? Wherein the 'Art'?," in *The Mind's Eye: Art and Theological Argument in the Middle Ages*, ed. Jeffrey Hamburger and Anne-Marie Bouché (Princeton, NJ: Princeton University Press, 2005), pp. 374–412; and Jeffrey F. Hamburger, "Rewriting History: The Visual and the Vernacular in Late Medieval History Bibles," in *Retextualisierung in der mittelalterlichen Literatur*, ed. Ursula Peters and Joachim Bumke (Berlin: Erich Schmidt, 2005), pp. 259–307.

Mysticism and Visuality 281

Figure 2. Frontispiece to Old Testament, *Biblehistoriale* of Charles V, Paris, ca. 1370 (Bibliothèque de l'Arsenal, Ms. 5212, fol. 1r). Photo: Bibliothèque de France.

The *quasi* that opens John's Gospel contains within it the potential for all of Christian art, be it verbal or visual (or, for that matter, musical). John Tauler (ca. 1300–61) reminds his readers of this fact when, in a sermon on the illustrations to Hildegard of Bingen's *Liber Scivias*, he concludes by noting that "whatever nature does, that always has some stain [*flecken*] and is not yet completely pure."[8] By "stain," Tauler means less the stain of sin, although that connotation is implicit in his term, than the fact of representation itself. Any representation of divine glory necessarily falls short of the mark. Nonetheless, without imaginative representations worshippers would be unable to project themselves into the mysteries of the faith. Sometimes framed as a

[8] For a fuller discussion, see Jeffrey F. Hamburger, "The 'Various Writings of Humanity': Johannes Tauler on Hildegard of Bingen's *Liber Scivias*," in *Images and Objects: Visual Culture and the German Middle Ages*, ed. Kathryn Starkey and Horst Wenzel (London: Palgrave Macmillan, 2005), pp. 161–205. See Ferdinand Vetter, ed., *Die Predigten Taulers aus der Engelberger und der Freiburger Handschrift sowie aus Schmidts Abschriften der ehemaligen Strassburger Handschriften* (repr., Dublin-Zurich: Weidmann, 1968), p. 380, lines 13–16: "*Wissest: was die nature wúrket, das hat alwegen etwas flecken, und es enist nút vollen luter.*"

grudging pastoral concession to the illiterate (otherwise known as the "*idiotae*," for whom, according to canon law, images took the place of books), images and visualization nonetheless had an established place in Christian thought.[9] How could it have been otherwise? The doctrine of the Incarnation provided the best argument for those seeking to justify the use of images against those who characterized them as idols: if God had truly taken on human form, then surely he could be portrayed just like any other man.

As a religion of the book, Christianity, like Judaism, is rooted in scripture. In the visions of the Apocalypse, as in those of the Old Testament prophets on which it is modeled (and which had an impact on medieval iconography no less profound than that of the Gospels), vision provides a vehicle for transporting the soul to God or for God to manifest himself to humanity. Christianity sought to distinguish itself from Judaism in part on the basis of the abrogation of the second commandment, according to which humanity should make no graven images.[10] The existence of images, let alone their legitimacy, in turn required at least a limited affirmation of vision and visual experience, closely linked to Christianity's affirmation (in the face of dualist doctrines) of creation and history. Right from the start, one sees that vision, and mystical visuality along with it, had apologetic as well as theological dimensions. They hence belong as much to social history as to the history of art, literature, and spirituality.

In the context of an essay written for a modern handbook, it is revealing to turn to an earlier *vade mecum*, John Altensteig's *Vocabularius theologie*, published in Hagenau in 1517.[11] Scanning its entries, one looks in vain for any equivalent to mysticism, let alone anything that might be likened to visuality as it has been defined in modern discourse, a historicized account of the process and protocols of perception. Recognizing the root of contemplation in vision, Altensteig notes

---

[9] See, most recently, Herbert L. Kessler, "Gregory the Great and Image Theory in Northern Europe during the Twelfth and Thirteenth Centuries," in *A Companion to Medieval Art: Romanesque and Gothic in Northern Europe*, ed. Conrad Rudolph (Oxford: Blackwell, 2006), pp. 151–72.

[10] Herbert L. Kessler, "'Pictures Fertile with Truth': How Christians Managed to Make Images of God without Violating the Second Commandment," *Journal of the Walters Art Gallery* 49–50 (1991–2): 53–6; and, more generally, Herbert L. Kessler, *Spiritual Seeing: Picturing God's Invisibility in Medieval Art* (Philadelphia: University of Pennsylvania Press, 2000).

[11] Johann Altensteig, *Vocabularius theologie coplectes vocabulo(rum) descriptioes & significatus ad theologiam utilium & alia quibus prudes & diligens lector multa abstrusa & obscura theologo(rum) dicta dissolvere & ... intelligere poterit* (Hagenau, Germany: Heinrich Gran for Johann Rynman of Öhringen, 1517).

that, according to Richard of Saint Victor (d. 1173), *contemplatio* can be defined as "the suspension of the mind with admiration in a certain arresting mirror (or reflection) of wisdom (*est mentis quidam conspicua in sapientiae spectacula cum admiratione suspensio*)." He goes on, however, to define contemplation more broadly in terms of the other senses, not just sight but also taste (*degustare*), a metaphor that would have meant more to monastics who likened reading to mastication.[12] Vision (*visus*), according to Altensteig, tends toward blindness: "I am unwilling, he said, to see Christ: it is enough if I will see him in glory" ("*Nolo inquit hic videre christum: satis est ipse in gloria si videro*"). His definition of the next term, *visibile*, predictably focuses on its apophatic opposite – "The invisible: that which cannot be seen" ("*Invisibile: quod non potest videre*"). He adds that, according to Bonaventure (1221–74), there are three reasons why things cannot be seen: on account of defective organs, a lack of light, or the intellect's inability to perceive spiritual things (*spiritualia*). Given that Altensteig writes on the eve of the Reformation, it is not surprising to find an entry titled "De imaginibus." Warning against idolatry, he trots out the age-old *ratio triplex*, the threefold argument for the necessity of images. Images instruct, edify, and commemorate, because he affirms, citing Horace's *Ars poetica*, "our affect is more excited by sight than by hearing" ("*affectus noster plus excitari visu quam auditu*").[13] Visuality is defined in part by the place of vision within a hierarchy of the senses, in which vision by no means always occupied or attained the top tier.

Altensteig's understanding of vision and its limits is rooted in scripture – witness the Ark of the Covenant, which literally veils scripture in a Russian doll-like series of sequestered chambers that only heighten spiritual desire. As late as the sixteenth century, the Flemish illuminator Simon Bening comments on Christian interpretations of such desires, defined in terms of penetrating vision.[14] Drawing on medieval precedents, he pairs two images in a prayer book (see Fig. 3): on the left, a close-up of the Crucifixion, and, on the right, the rent veil of the tabernacle, which opens to reveal the ark containing the covenant that, along with the prohibition on images, is abrogated at the moment of Christ's death.

---

[12] See Friedrich Ohly, *Süsse Nagel der Passion: Ein Beitrag zur theologischen Semantik* (Baden-Baden, Germany: Koerner, 1989); and Rachel Fulton, "'Taste and see that the Lord is sweet' (Ps. 33:9): The Flavor of God in the Monastic West," *Journal of Religion* 86 (2006): 169–204.

[13] Creighton Gilbert, *The Saints' Three Reasons for Paintings in Churches* (Ithaca, NY: Clandestine Press, 2001).

[14] Discussed further in Hamburger, "Body vs. Book."

Close scrutiny reveals that Christ's side wound – according to legend, the source of the spurting blood that healed the blind Longinus – is hidden by the slight torsion in Christ's torso that presents his flank to the eyes of Mary and John.[15] For the viewer, the opening has been displaced onto the rent veil to the right, which, in keeping with Paul's words in Hebrews 10:19–20, represents the torn, sundered flesh of Christ: "having therefore, brethren, a confidence in the entering into the holies by the blood of Christ; A new and living way which he hath dedicated for us through the veil, that is to say, his flesh." Beneath the veil of the flesh lies the truth of the Logos. The image does not reveal this truth; rather, it constructs it. The record of such constructions in terms of vision could be said to represent the history of Christian visuality. Images do not merely reflect visual experience; rather, they shape the experience of perception. Further still, even in the absence of art theory, they provide an implicit commentary on the role, status, and legitimacy of images and visual experience as such. These issues, far from incidental to a history of Christianity, are as central as the doctrine of the Incarnation.

Bening's polemical miniature reveals that Christianity is founded on the desire, even the necessity, to make the Word visible. In Exodus (33:20), God says to Moses, "Thou canst not see my face: for there shall no man see me, and live." Paul takes up the same topic when he declares, "Eye hath not seen, nor ear heard, neither hath it entered into the heart of men, what things God hath prepared for them that love him" (1 Cor 2:9). In spite of such pronouncements, or precisely in order to contravene them, the John of the Epistles (1 Jn 3:2) declares, "It does not yet appear what we shall be, but we know that when he [Christ] appears we shall be like him, for we shall see him as he is." With fullness of vision comes not just knowledge but also identification and transformation. Faith, far from being blind, aspires to a fullness of vision that goes beyond anything that can be imagined from a merely human perspective. Mysticism, at least mysticism understood as the experiential cognition of God ("*cognitio Dei experimentalis*"), cannot, it turns out, be imagined without recourse to the visible, however it is defined.

Theologians and mystics resorted to theories of vision to account for the workings of the imagination, revealing in the process something

---

[15] Close examination of the leaf, which was inaccessible to me when I published it previously, suggests that the area in question may have been damaged and/or repainted in part, so that the absence of the side wound must be taken *cum grano salis*. Nonetheless, the fact remains: Mary and John view Christ's body from behind, rather than from his right side, let alone from the traditional positions to either side of the cross.

Figure 3. Simon Bening, Christ on the Cross, cutting from a Spanish prayer book, ca. 1509–10 (Private collection, on deposit at the Pierpont Morgan Library, New York). Photo: author.

of their attitudes toward art and visual experience.[16] In schematic terms, the principal theories of vision can be grouped under the headings of intromission and extromission. Both theories are invoked in mystical texts, not simply by way of analogy but also in order to ground religious realities in human experience and, vice versa, to characterize such experience as but the first step in an upward-leading ascent. In a sermon for Christmas, Tauler compares the process of mystical union to the process by which the eye perceives an image on the wall: "For if two are to become one, one must be passive, whereas the other must act. If, for instance, my eye is to receive an image on the wall, or anything whatever, it must first be free from other images; for if there remained an image of color, it could not receive another.... In short, whatever should receive must first be empty, passive, and free."[17] Meister Eckhart

[16] See Robert S. Nelson, ed., *Visuality Before and Beyond the Renaissance: Seeing as Others Saw* (Cambridge: Cambridge University Press, 2000); Suzannah Biernoff, *Sight and Embodiment in the Middle Ages* (Houndmills, New York: Palgrave-Macmillan, 2002); and *La visione e lo sguardo nel Medio Evo/View and Vision in the Middle Ages* (Florence, Italy: Sismel, 1997–8).

[17] Vetter, *Die Predigten Taulers*, p. 9, line 34 through p. 10, line 3 (sermon 1); and John Tauler, *Sermons*, trans. Maria Shrady (New York: Paulist Press, 1985), p. 38.

(d. 1328) states, "An eye is nobler in itself than an eye that is painted on a wall."[18] Eckhart's choice of image is hardly coincidental; the eye he has in mind is none other than the all-seeing eye of God.[19] The disembodied eye also stands for the intellect that, in striving for union with God, comes to see all. Elsewhere, Eckhart states, "The eye with which I see God is the same eye with which God sees me: my eye and God's eye are one eye, one seeing, one knowing and one love."[20] In keeping with the Neoplatonist underpinnings of his thought, Eckhart characterizes the eye's activity primarily (although not exclusively) in terms of extromission, that is, the notion that the eye grasps the object of perception by emitting an effluent, variously characterized as a "visual fire" or "ray," that coalesces with sunlight before extending toward the object of perception.[21] Eckhart's theory of vision is notably at odds with theories current in his day, which, whatever the differences among them, were predicated on the idea of intromission, that is, of rays emanating from the object somehow imprinting themselves on the mind through the medium of the eye.

Eckhart's mysticism demonstrates the extent to which the apophatic theology of the Pseudo-Dionysius, which insisted that God was beyond all predication, continued to make its presence felt, especially in the Rhineland. Even there, however, to paraphrase one of Eckhart's immediate successors, the Dominican Henry Suso (ca. 1295–1366), images could be used to drive out images. An illustration to Suso's *Exemplar*, culminating in the geometric representation of the triune Godhead represented as three concentric circles seen beyond the veil of the tabernacle, seeks to demonstrate this process (see Fig. 4). Suso's writings demonstrate the extent to which in the High and later Middle Ages, not to mention in the early modern period, mystical and visionary spirituality increasingly converge in mendicant and, more surprisingly, in Cistercian piety, leading to a broad-based affirmation of the legitimacy of images that in no way

---

[18] Meister Eckhart, Sermon 9, in Meister Eckhart, *Eckhart: Werke I-II*, ed. Nikolaus Largier and trans. Josef Quint, 2 vols. (Frankfurt: Deutscher Klassiker Verlag, 1993), vol. 1, p. 112, lines 2–3.

[19] For the eye of God, see Gudrun Schleusener-Eichholz, *Das Auge im Mittelalter*, 2 vols. (Munich: Fink, 1985), vol. 2, pp. 1076–1110.

[20] For the passage that drew his critics' ire and that he, in turn, defended, see Meister Eckhart, Sermon 12, in Eckhart, *Werke*, ed. Largier, vol. 1, p. 148, lines 31–4; and Meister Eckhart, *Sermons and Treatises*, trans. Maurice O'C. Walshe, 3 vols. (London: Watkins, 1981–7), vol. 2, p. 87.

[21] For Eckhart on vision, see Schleusner-Eichholtz, *Das Auge*, vol. 1, pp. 116–28; John E. Crean, "Mystical 'Schauen' in Meister Eckhart and Jan van Ruusbroec," *Monatshefte* 62 (1970): 37–44; and the commentary of Largier, s.v. "Auge."

Mysticism and Visuality 287

Figure 4. The Mystical Way, Heinrich Seuse, *Exemplar*, Strasbourg, ca. 1370 (Strasbourg, Bibliothèque Nationale et Universitaire, Ms. 2929, f. 82r). Photo: Bibliothèque Nationale et Universitaire.

can be written off as a concession to popular piety. Images increasingly become constitutive of certain kinds of mystical experience.

The theological roots of this development are broad and deep. As in so many other respects, however, the twelfth century can be seen as a turning point. Augustine's commentary on Genesis had established the threefold hierarchy of corporeal, spiritual, and intellective vision as the framework for all medieval discussions of the subject.[22] Yet Altenstaig's harking back to Hugh of Saint Victor (1096–1141) also points to the influence of Victorine theology. The reinterpretation of a single verse in Paul's Epistle to the Romans (1:20) permits one to trace the Victorine reevaluation of the visible and, along with it, nature, human history, and the literal (as opposed to the allegorical) sense of scripture.[23] A touchstone in medieval debates over the status and experience of the visible world, this passage from Paul provides the classic argument against image worship in terms that relate the experience of the visible to the knowledge of the invisible: "For the invisible things of him, from the creation of the world, are clearly seen, being understood by the things that are made; his eternal power also, and divinity: so that they [idolators] are inexcusable." In effect, Paul presents a version of the argument from design, arguing that any intelligent observer, independent of Christian revelation, should be able to discern that behind the world's visible appearances there has to stand an eternal, if invisible, creator. Christian commentators went so far as to argue that in referring, not to God's invisibility, but rather to the "invisible things [plural] of God" (invisibilia dei), Paul referred to the Trinity, another way of linking the visible (Christ the Son) to the invisible (God the Father).

Victorine exegetes, however, gave Paul's formulation an unexpected twist, laying the foundation for a new vision that attributed the capacity to point the intellect toward God to the faculty of sight. The technical term given to this way of reading the world was speculation (speculatio). In his treatise De operibus trium dierum (On the Works of Three Days), which also circulated under the title Tractatus super invisibilia (Treatise on Invisible Things), Hugh of Saint Victor provides a detailed account of the perceptual process by which a person should be led from visible things to invisible things (per visibilia ad invisibilia), arguing that history, that is, scripture, and the book of nature are written by the hand of God. To be sure, the visible world represents no more than the first stage in the mind's ascent to God, but, in a fundamental shift, it now represents an indispensable stepping-stone along the way. Paraphrasing Paul, Hugh argues that the person who sees nature but who fails to discern the hand of its creator beyond its visible forms is like the illiterate

---

[22] See Veerle Fraeters's essay in this volume.
[23] For fuller discussion, see Jeffrey F. Hamburger, "Speculations on Speculation: Vision and Perception in the Theory and Practice of Mystical Devotions," in Deutsche Mystik im abendländischen Zusammenhang: Neu erschlossene Texte, neue methodische Ansätze, neuetheoretische Konzepte, ed. Walter Haug and Wolfram Schneider-Lastin (Tübingen, Germany: Niemeyer, 2000), pp. 353–408.

who, upon viewing figures in an open book, is unable to understand their significance. This is the classic definition of speculative reasoning summarized by Alan of Lille (d. 1202/3) in his famous verses: "Every creature in the world is, for us, like a book and a picture and also a mirror" ("*Omnis mundi creatura / Quasi liber est pictura / Nobis est, et speculum*"). In this way of reading, vision provides a platform from which the right-thinking viewer can rise to the vision of God. Nature has become a veil and a mirror.

The Victorine turn had implications for mysticism as well as exegesis. By the late Middle Ages, taking Victorine exegesis as their point of departure, various commentators and mystics had turned Paul's premises entirely on their head. Gertrude of Helfta's *Legatus divinae pietatis* (*Herald of Divine Love*), written ca. 1300, begins with an apology for her visions based on Richard of Saint Victor (erroneously identified as Hugh), which in turn is based on Paul:[24]

> But, as invisible and spiritual things cannot be understood by the human intellect except in visible and corporeal images, it is necessary to clothe them in human and bodily forms. This is what Master Hugh demonstrates in the sixteenth chapter of his discourse on *The Inner Man*: "In order to refer to things familiar to this lower world and to come down to the level of human weakness, Holy Scripture describes things by means of visible forms, and thus impresses on our imagination spiritual ideas by means of beautiful images which excite our desires."

This apology for images lays the ground for what follows. In the vision related in book 2, chapter 8, Gertrude again speaks of "the invisible things of God ... manifest to the intelligence by the exterior things of creation."[25] By the end of book 2, the only section of the *Herald* that can be reliably attributed to Gertrude, she turns the Gregorian dictum on its head.[26] Rather than characterizing images as the bible of the illiterate, she argues that "just as students attain to logic by way of the alphabet, so, by means of these painted pictures [*istas velut depictas*

---

[24] Gertrude of Helfta, *Oeuvres spirituelles*, vol. 2, *Le Héraut (Livres I et II)*, ed. Pierre Doyère (Paris: Le Cerf, 1968), I. i. 3–4, pp. 124–27; Gertrude of Helfta, *The Herald of Divine Love*, trans. Margaret Winkworth (New York: Paulist Press, 1993), pp. 54–5. The passage quoted by Gertrude, which has remained unidentified by all her editors and translators, comes from chapter 15 of Richard of Saint Victor's *Benjamin minor*; see Richard of Saint Victor, *Les Douze Patriarches ou Beniamin minor*, ed. and trans. by Jean Châtillon, Monique Duchet-Suchaux, and Jean Longère (Paris: Le Cerf, 1997).

[25] Gertrude of Helfta, *Héraut*, II. viii. 4, p. 266; Gertrude, *Herald*, p. 107.

[26] Gertrude of Helfta, *Héraut*, II. xxiv. 1, p. 351; Gertrude of Helfta, *Herald*, p. 135.

imaginationes, by which she means her visions], as it were, they may be led to taste within themselves that hidden manna, which it is not possible to adulterate by any admixture of material images and of which one must have eaten to hunger for it forever."[27] Gertrude's "by means of" (*velut*) indirectly invokes John's "as it were" (*quasi*): the reader can, as it were, taste hidden manna (note, once again, the relationship of taste to sight). Her words also draw on a passage in Paul (Heb 5:12–14), in which the apostle declares that "you are become such as have need of milk; and not of strong meat. For every one that is a partaker of milk, is unskillful in the word of justice: for he is a little child. But strong meat is for the perfect." Whereas Paul describes his words as milk for those too weak for the meat of words "hard to be intelligibly uttered" (Heb 5:11), Gertrude, in contrast, describes her pictorial visions as the hidden manna of Revelation (2:17).

Different types of mystical spirituality cultivated different forms of visuality. Vision was strictly controlled in monastic environments; different groups adopted (or were compelled to adopt) different protocols of vision.[28] These rules were anything but abstract and were often subject to change, according to circumstances. Visuality was closely linked to corporeal discipline. Under strict enclosure, which was increasingly common following the tellingly titled bull, *Periculoso* (named after its opening words, "Wishing to provide for the dangerous and abominable situation of certain nuns"), issued in 1298 by Pope Boniface VII, nuns were to shun any contact with the outside world or with male clergy, a move that also curtailed access to the Eucharist, a focal point of female visionary piety.[29] In part because enclosed women were denied frequent visual contact with the consecrated host, convent chronicles brim over with accounts of women gazing at the priest holding the Christ Child in his hands at the moment of the elevation.[30] On occasion, the enclosed woman "sees" the host through the wall, as if

---

[27] Gertrude of Helfta, *Héraut*, II. xxiv. 1, p. 351; Gertrude of Helfta, *Herald*, p. 135.
[28] See Hamburger, *The Visual and the Visionary*.
[29] See, most recently, Carola Jäggi, *Frauenkloster im Spätmittelalter: Die Kirchen der Klarissen und Dominikanerinnen im 13. und 14. Jahrhundert* (Petersberg, Germany: Michael Imhof Verlag, 2006).
[30] See Karl Bihlmeyer, ed., "Mystisches Leben in dem Dominikanerinnenkloster Weiler bei Eßlingen im 13. und 14. Jahrhundert," *Württembergische Vierteljahrshefte für Landesgeschichte* N.F. 25 (1961): 61–93, esp. p. 81; and Ruth Meyer, *Das "St. Katharinentaler Schwesternbuch": Untersuchung, Edition, Kommentar* (Tubingen, Germany: Niemeyer, 1995), p. 117, lines 21–4. The desire to see the consecrated host was hardly peculiar to nuns; see Edouard Dumoutet, *Le désir de voir l'Hostie et les origines de la dévotion au Saint-Sacrement* (Paris: Beauchesne, 1926).

with X-ray vision.³¹ Other accounts stress that the nun in question saw the Corpus Christi "with bodily eyes" ("*mit leiplichen augen*"), not with spiritual sight.³² Some women relied on sounds made by outsiders, who knocked on the wall dividing the choir from the lay church, signaling when they should stand to see the elevated host.³³ Only the exceptional nun does not seize every opportunity to gaze at Christ. The fourteenth-century chronicle of Adelhausen reports that the lay sister Gûte Tuschelin refused to join her companions in the kitchen and the infirmary as they rushed to a window to witness the elevation of the host, even though, strictly speaking, they were excused from attendance at Mass.³⁴ At Saint Katharinental, Elsbeth of Stoffeln "had the habit of standing in her place in the stalls when the convent took communion so that she could see him well." Elsbeth's actions are reported without disapproval; she is rewarded with a vision.³⁵

The Eucharist has often been held up as a focal point of visual piety in the High and later Middle Ages, although its importance can be exaggerated.³⁶ In theory, if not always in practice, the consecrated host remained a point of passage, not an end in itself.³⁷ In the words of an anonymous Carthusian writing toward the end of the fifteenth century who summarizes a long tradition of theological commentary, in particular in this passage, Jean Gerson "that which you see with the eye of the body is not our lord, but that which you see with the eye of your heart, that is the lord our God."³⁸ Similar theological tags were often inscribed on images, reminding viewers that "the form is neither God nor man,

---

31 Franz Mittermaier, ed. "Lebensbeschreibung der sel. Christina von Retters," *Archiv für mittelrheinische Kirchengeschichte* 17–18 (1965–6): 209–51, 203–38, at p. 243.
32 Bihlmeyer, "Weiler," p. 72.
33 Ibid., p. 81.
34 Johannes König, ed., "Die Chronik der Anna von Munzingen, geschrieben von Johannes Hull, 1433, nach der ältesten Abschrift mit Einleitungen und Beilagen," *Freiburger Diözesan-Archiv* 13 (1880): 129–236, esp. p. 169.
35 Birlinger, "Mystisches Leben," p. 167.
36 See the cautionary comments of Thomas Lentes, "'As far as the eye can see...': Rituals of Gazing in the Late Middle Ages," in *The Mind's Eye*, ed. Hamburger and Bouché, pp. 360–73.
37 See Caroline Walker Bynum, "Seeing and Seeing Beyond: The Mass of St. Gregory in the Fifteenth Century," in *The Mind's Eye*, ed. Hamburger and Bouché, pp. 208–40.
38 Basel, Öffentliche Bibliothek der Universität Basel, Ms. A VIII 37, f. 3r. For a fuller discussion of this manuscript, see Jeffrey F. Hamburger, "The Writing on the Wall: Inscriptions and Descriptions of Carthusian Crucifixions in a Fifteenth-Century Passion Miscellany," in *Tributes in Honor of James H. Marrow: Studies in Late Medieval and Renaissance Painting and Manuscript Illumination*, ed. Jeffrey F. Hamburger and A. S. Korteweg (Turnhout, Belgium: Brepols, 2006), pp. 231–52.

Figure 5. The *connubium spirituale*, *Rothschild Canticles* (Yale University, Beinecke Rare Book Library, Ms. 404, f. 66r). Photo: Beinecke Rare Book and Manuscript Library.

which you here do behold. / But here the God and Man, of whom you by that form are told" ("*Nec deus est, nec homo, presens quem cernis imago / Sed deus est et homo, presens quem signat imago*").[39]

Eucharistic piety is only one arena in which vision looms large. Bridal mysticism is another. Bridal mysticism has its roots in the Marian liturgy's application of the Song of Songs, first, to the marriage of Christ and Church or the Virgin, then, by extension, to the union of Christ and the loving soul. As in the case of exegesis, so too in that of the visual arts: only beginning in the twelfth century do we see any systematic attempt to translate the metaphorical imagery of the Song of Songs into a coherent picture of the soul's union with God. These efforts culminate in the later Middle Ages in a mystical miscellany known as the *Rothschild Canticles*, in which an eroticized image of the spiritual

---

[39] See Ragne Bugge, "*Effigiem Christi, qui transi, semper honora*: Verses Condemning the Cult of Sacred Images in Art and Literature," *Acta ad Archeologiam et Artium Historiam Pertinentia* 6 (1975): 127–39, esp. pp. 133–4. Also see Herbert Kessler, *Neither God nor Man: Words, Images, and the Medieval Anxiety about Arts* (Freiburg im Breisgau: Rombach Verlag, 2007).

nuptials (*connubium spirituale*) provides perhaps the best antecedent for Giovanni Bernini's (1598–1680) *Ecstasy of St. Teresa* (see Fig. 5).[40]

Perhaps the ultimate paradox, when speaking of mysticism and visuality, is that a discourse that by definition shuns the senses came, throughout the course of the medieval millennium, not only to legitimize but also even to redeem them. Given the incarnational emphasis of late medieval piety, one must use the word *redeem* advisedly, if cautiously, given that mysticism's sensory and, at times, sensual side was never without controversy. The sensory was integrated into the spiritual. In the spirit of "as it were," illusionistic strategies, some driven by the desire for divine presence, only served to make images more persuasive. Changing attitudes toward works of art form a part of this picture. Not even the Reformation was able to undo the effects of this affirmation of the visual.

[40] See Jeffrey F. Hamburger, *The Rothschild Canticles: Art and Mysticism in Flanders and the Rhineland circa 1300* (New Haven, CT: Yale University Press, 1990), pp. 106–10.

18 Emotion

FIONA SOMERSET

What might be the most fruitful avenues for new research on emotions within mysticism? How might that research benefit from the enormously increased attention to emotion over the past forty years in a wide range of humanities, social science, and life science fields (including cognitive science, sociology, neuroscience, evolutionary biology, psychology, philosophy, anthropology, literature, history, religious studies)? Any attempt to address these questions must acknowledge at the outset that emotion, like mysticism, is a term of relatively recent invention, and that like mysticism, the term emotion is notoriously difficult to define and to situate culturally and historically.[1] If this volume as a whole demonstrates that mysticism is a capacious category rather than a tightly defined and universally applicable term, then this chapter aims to do the same work for emotions. In the process, though I will never entirely abandon the term emotions, I will also use terms such as affect, excitation, passion, and feeling where these allow a closer engagement with writers of the past.

Attuning ourselves to the terms mystical writers themselves used to talk about feeling will be especially important because of an insight that recent researchers often seem to think is fresh and new, but that many medieval thinkers certainly shared:[2] as any attempt to make analytic distinctions between aspects of human functioning such as memory, reason, will, bodily sensation, and emotion must acknowledge, even as it artificially separates these processes, these operations are radically interactive, deeply mutually enmeshed.[3] Even if medieval theorists assign

---

[1] Thomas Dixon, *From Passions to Emotions: The Creation of a Secular Psychological Category* (Cambridge: Cambridge University Press, 2003).
[2] Simo Knuuttila, *Emotions in Ancient and Medieval Philosophy* (Oxford: Oxford University Press, 2004).
[3] A. O. Rorty, "Enough Already with 'Theories of the Emotions,'" in *Thinking about Feeling*, ed. Robert C. Solomon (Oxford: Oxford University Press, 2004), pp. 269–78; William Reddy, *The Navigation of Feeling: A Framework for the History of Emotions* (Cambridge: Cambridge University Press, 2001), esp. pp. ix–137.

functions to separate faculties given specific locations in the soul or body (e.g., the will, the imagination, and the common sense), they never suggest that any of these faculties might operate in isolation: feeling involves sensory as well as emotional and cognitive aspects, for example; excitation is a physical as well as emotional, volitional, and intellectual response; and passion is a general term for sensations or effects the body or mind undergoes, in contrast to its own self-initiated actions.

Mystical writers are aware of these theories, but if anything they push their implications further as they strive, in their aspirations toward the divine, to describe possibilities beyond the typical expectations of their culture, or even outside human capacity as they perceive it. Consider, for example, Marguerite Porete's (d. 1310) effort to describe how the Soul, once annihilated and entirely dissolved into God, has abandoned the exercise of all its own capacities:

> Love explains clearly, who says that the Soul brought to Nothing is without herself when she has no feeling or work from nature, nor any from within, nor shame or honor, nor any fear of anything which may happen, nor any affection for the divine goodness; and when she no longer knows where her will is housed, but is rather constantly without will. Then it is that she is brought to nothing, without herself. This is no wonder: she is no longer for herself, for she lives by the divine substance.[4]

Sensation, activity, perception, emotion, will, and knowledge are all abandoned: the Soul is brought to nothing and is "without herself." Marguerite's description of the annihilated soul's self-abandonment, here and in more detail elsewhere, itemizes faculties while also describing the complexity of their interactive operation. Marguerite strives to explain an experience of radical self-emptying that can be evoked only with difficulty, perhaps successfully only for those who have experienced it, but that cannot (or so Marguerite's personification of Reason frequently complains) be comprehended by reason alone.

Granted, there do seem to have been periods in history when many imagined we would be better off if we were creatures of pure reason; emotion has often been undervalued. In particular it has received little credit (except as a possible impediment) in much of logic and the philosophy of language. Yet Marguerite's example illustrates that the new emphasis in current research, which insists that emotions are an

---

[4] Marguerite Porete, *The Mirror of Simple Souls*, trans. Edmund Colledge, J. C. Marler, and Judith Grant (Notre Dame, IN: University of Notre Dame Press, 1999), p. 136.

essential aspect of complex processing along the body/mind continuum and in every human interaction, is not as novel as many researchers tend to suggest. Mystical writers often similarly oppose the tendencies they see in contemporary learned discourse by stressing the importance of love over knowledge (though they insist on both) and placing special emphasis on emotions and sensations.

Richard Fitzralph's mid-fourteenth-century explanation of the rhetorical category that he labels "excitative speech" is a description of this aspect of mystical discourse. In insisting that mystical language goes beyond the merely ratiocinative, Fitzralph in addition reminds us of a key difference between mystical writers and theorists of emotion, medieval as well as contemporary. While theorists aim to name, describe, and analyze feelings, this is not the sole (even if it is often a partial) goal of mystical writers. They aim as well to stir feelings up, both in themselves and in their audiences:

> When some saint speaks excitatively, that is, so as to excite himself and others toward devotion, it does not seem to be required that his statement should be strictly true, but only that it should be useful (provided of course that he speaks without expressly impugning faith) because he does not intend to discuss or assert what he says, but to edify. Saint Bernard's statement in this place [referring to a description of Christ begging door to door] was of this sort, as it seems to many; just as in the meditation about the compassion of the blessed glorious virgin he says "who will give to my head water and to my eyes a well that I may weep day and night until lord Jesus Christ should appear to his servant," not intending to say that it is true that he needs so much water or that his eyes need a well, but so that he should provoke tears in himself and so that others attending to his devotion should similarly be provoked to tears.[5]

Affect-laden language produces tears; naming this somatic response is a conventional metonymy for any more detailed description of the bodily sensations and emotions excited by Bernard's description or the fervent devotion they provoke.[6] But the feelings created in the audience are at least as important, if not more important, than the feelings described

---

[5] My edition and translation. See Fiona Somerset, "Excitative Speech: Theories of Emotive Response from Richard Fitzralph to Margery Kempe," in *The Vernacular Spirit*, ed. Renate Blumenfeld-Kosinski, Duncan Robertson, and Nancy Bradley Warren (New York: Palgrave, 2002), pp. 59–79.

[6] Piroska Nagy, "Religious Weeping as Ritual in the Medieval West," *Social Analysis* 48, no. 2 (2004): 119–37.

by the writer. Through reading and meditation not only the self but also other readers go through the emotional processes that the writing incites. The process described is one that sidesteps strict truth and the standards of proof required in ordinary or scholastic language in favor of creating fellow-feeling.

Fitzralph's emphasis on the different truth-value of affective language is partly a product of his circumstances: the work in which he explains this theory is his defense against accusations by the friars in the papal curia. Yet many mystical writers who are not under this sort of acute pressure similarly stress that affective language obeys different rules than ratiocinative discourse and place special emphasis on the reading audience's emotional response. Feeling – consisting of what we might call emotion, as well as bodily sensation and interior disposition more broadly – plays a part in authenticating and authorizing the writer's account. It also plays a part in authenticating the reading audience.

For Fitzralph's contemporary Richard Rolle, for example, in the prologue to his *The Burning of Love* (*Incendium Amoris*), excitative language both addresses a broader audience than commonsense or scholastic discourse might reach and selects out the members of that audience best disposed toward loving God, regardless of their level of education:

> [God] is not known through disputation but through doing and loving. But I reckon that what is discussed here could not be understood by those intellectuals, who are supreme in all sorts of learning, but inferior when it comes to loving Christ. So I have forborn to write for them unless, putting behind and forgetting everything related to the world, they burn to be subjected to nothing but longing for the Creator alone. For the more knowledgeable they are, the more apt they would be, in principle, for loving, if they readily despised themselves and rejoiced to be despised by others. Consequently, because I here [excite] all people to love, and try to manifest both the superfervent and the supernatural effect of love, the title chosen for this book is *The Burning of Love*.[7]

Rolle's "burning of love" is emotion, sensation, and will together, as he explains earlier in his prologue by recounting his own experience. Here, he aims to excite the same feelings and actions in his readers. Doing and loving are more important qualifications for sharing Rolle's experience than knowledge – not that knowledge disqualifies readers, but it tends

---

[7] Somerset, "Excitative Speech"; see also Nicholas Watson, *Richard Rolle and the Invention of Authority* (Cambridge: Cambridge University Press, 1991).

to hamper their proper self-disposition toward love by making them too proud. Bernard McGinn has suggested that the relationship later medieval mystical texts have with their readers is typically conflicted in just this sort of way. Early mystical writings are more likely to present divine union as universally available to all Christians, but they do not have to deal with the implications of this claim because they are typically written for very selective monastic audiences. For writers after 1200, attaining the heights of contemplation is a special grace, not a universal privilege, and typically they labor both to include a wider range of readers than might have been the audience for earlier mystical writings, and to emphasize that only the best-qualified readers will succeed.[8]

Feeling is the main ground on which this conflict is played out. Partly in consequence, partly as cause, mystical writers are emotion-artists: they are specialists in the observation and description of emotion, and their writings provide especially rich sites for investigating the theory, practice, expression, and communication of emotional states. They not only reflect the received views on emotion of the culture in which they were produced but engage productively with these views and help to shape them, often in ways that influence not only their immediate context, but a range of other places and times in which their writings come to be read with close attention – including the here and now. If there is still anyone who believes that the emotions of past cultures were childlike or unsophisticated in comparison with our own, then mystical writings can help to convince them otherwise.[9] Indeed, mystical writing about emotions is at least as sophisticated (though not always in identical ways) as the most recent insights arrived at over the past forty years of intensive study of emotions by means of putatively more "enlightened" speculation and experimental science.

A recent article by the psychologist James R. Averill is a welcome attempt to consider what mystical writings might contribute to new research on emotions. Averill is one of the more prominent proponents of the theory that emotions are socially constructed – we will turn to consider the alternative against which he contends in a moment. Averill is interested in exploring the implications of the idea that emotions may not always be the same: the expression and even the experience of

---

[8] Bernard McGinn, *The Presence of God: A History of Western Christian Mysticism*, vol. 3, *The Flowering of Mysticism: Men and Women in the New Mysticism (1200–1350)* (New York: Crossroad, 1998), pp. 12–13.

[9] Barbara H. Rosenwein, "Worrying about Emotions in History," *American Historical Review* 107 (2002): 921–45. See also Barbara H. Rosenwein, *Emotional Communities in the Early Middle Ages* (Ithaca, NY: Cornell University Press, 2006).

emotions may vary from individual to individual, as well as from social group to social group. In a recent research study, he uses "mysticism" as one of the criteria for evaluating individual differences in emotion and its expression under the rubric of "emotional creativity":

> Religion can be, and often is, a source of profound and creative emotional experiences, from the depths of despair to the heights of ecstasy (James, 1902/1961). Among the creative emotional reactions often associated with religion is mystical experience. "When love has carried us above and beyond all things, above the light, into the Divine Dark, there we are wrought and transformed by the Eternal Word Who is the image of the Father; and as the air is penetrated by the sun, thus we receive in idleness of spirit the Incomprehensible Light, enfolding us and penetrating us." That is the way Jan van Ruysbroeck [sic], the 14th century Flemish mystic, described his experiences (quoted in Laski, 1961, p. 428).[10] Needless to say, full-blown mystical experiences are rare – but no more rare than full-blown anxiety attacks. And in more mild degree, mysticlike experiences are not unusual. In a national survey, Greeley (1974) found that 35% of Americans reported having had such experiences repeatedly. Nor are mystical experiences confined to the religiously inclined, but can be found among all people in all walks of life and of secular as well as religious orientation.[11]

For Averill, mystical experience is a creative emotional reaction associated (though not necessarily so) with religion: he quotes Ruusbroec by way of illustration of a kind of experience he suggests that many, even if not all, of us have felt. An example from the medieval Christian past explains an emotional experience in the broadly secular American present.

From the point of view of a student of mysticism, there are some obvious problems here. Religious experience and emotion cannot be so easily treated as equivalent: whatever the relation between love and divine union or presence, the two are not the same.[12] Ruusbroec's allegorical journey into the Divine Dark uses metaphor and simile to describe the transcendence of emotion and volition as if it were a series of transformed

---

[10] For a newer translation of the same passage from *The Sparkling Stone*, see John Ruusbroec, *The Spiritual Espousals and Other Works*, intro. James A Wiseman (New York: Paulist Press, 1985), pp. 171, lines 2–11.
[11] James R. Averill, "Individual Differences in Emotional Creativity: Structure and Correlates," *Journal of Personality* 67, no. 2 (1999): 331–71, pp. 350–1.
[12] See Amy Hollywood's introduction to this volume.

and transforming bodily sensations. His narrative description emphasizes the continuities along this range of vividly evoked physical and mental experiences. There is far more than just emotion operative here, and at the height of the experience, emotion seems to be left behind. Averill also seems conflicted in his insistence on how frequently "mysticlike experiences" occur, even as he uses the term mysticism to label extraordinary emotional creativity: this is perhaps a secularized, contemporary version of the conflict over audience and accessibility exhibited by Rolle and discussed by McGinn. What is more, it seems odd, if not contradictory, for Averill to stress individual emotional differences within a social group while insisting that secularized "mysticlike experience" in the present and "full-blown mystical experiences" in the past differ only in degree, but not in kind. Surely if individuals differ in their emotional experience and expression, then so do cultures. Still, Averill's hunch that mystical writings reveal "emotional creativity" seems worth pursuing. So does his sense that they might contribute usefully to the larger debate in which his research is engaged.

For students of mysticism, just as for many historians and cultural anthropologists who begin from the premise that the cultures they study are different from our own, it may seem very odd that anyone would want to make the claim, against Averill, that emotions are in at least some respects always and everywhere the same. Mystical writers confront us with emotional alterity. The difficulty of analysis is not to decide whether there are differences to explore, but rather how to explain them through forms of investigation that supplement or substitute for our own emotional expectations: which aspects of a mystical writer's emotional alterity are typical of her or his culture, which are conventions of the mystical works and styles of religious expression familiar to the author, and which the idiosyncratic products of a given writer's emotional artistry? Nevertheless, the debate over the basic nature of emotions has been a lively and contentious one spanning many fields of inquiry, and as we will see, it cannot be reduced to a simple conflict between difference and sameness.

Cultural anthropologists and some psychologists, philosophers, and historians, Averill among them, stress the socially constructed nature of emotion, such that different points in history, different cultures, different communities, different genders, and even different individuals or the same individual in different contexts might express and experience emotions differently and according to different social rules.[13] Some

---

[13] For introductory discussion see Reddy, *Navigation of Feeling*; and Rosenwein, "Worrying about Emotions."

research psychologists and evolutionary biologists, on the other hand, have sought to isolate "basic emotions," each associated with a specific facial expression and involving measurable autonomic nervous system arousal, including, at minimum, versions of surprise, fear, anger, disgust, sadness, and joy. Researchers have sought to demonstrate that these "affect program responses" are common across cultures and to some extent also shared with primates and other animals and that they are evolved, adaptive behaviors: emotions are at the very least pancultural, and, according to the claims of some, universal.[14]

These views have sometimes – especially by research psychologists – been seen as locked in ideological conflict with one another, such that one must choose sides and proceed on the basis of either one hypothesis (emotions are always the same) or the other (emotions vary). But this need not be the case. The philosopher Paul Griffiths has made the most elaborate effort to reconcile these two views.[15] Griffiths contends that the overarching category of emotion clumps together three very different phenomena: (1) affect program responses (the pancultural "basic emotions"); (2) socially sustained pretenses (the extreme case of socially constructed emotions); and (3) higher cognitive states, which are culturally variable and have social as well as biological elements. Thus it is true both that emotions are always the same and that they vary, but each claim is only true of some kinds of emotion. Any attempt to study emotions across these categories through introspection and by analyzing everyday language without reference to recent experimental science will merely recycle the stereotypes of "folk psychology."[16] Griffiths's three-part taxonomy is illuminating in that it helps us see how different are the methods and goals of those who focus on basic emotions and those who focus on socially constructed emotions. But it does not seem to me tenable to claim, as Griffiths does, that these researchers address entirely different objects of study. After all, Griffiths admits that some examples of an emotion such as anger might fit under each of his three categories, and that each category is dependent upon the previous ones. Instead, it seems to me that these two groups are engaged in different

[14] See Paul Ekman, "Basic Emotions" and "Facial Expressions," in *Handbook of Cognition and Emotion*, ed. Tim Dalgleish and Mick Power (Chichester, NY: John Wiley and Sons, 1999), pp. 45–60, 301–20.
[15] See also Jenefer Robinson, "Emotion: Biological Fact or Social Construction?" and Jesse Prinz, "Embodied Emotions," in Solomon, *Thinking about Feeling*, pp. 28–43, 44–58; and Antonio Damasio, *The Feeling of What Happens: Body and Emotion in the Making of Consciousness* (New York: Harcourt Brace, 1999), pp. 130–9.
[16] Paul E. Griffiths, *What Emotions Really Are: The Problem of Psychological Categories* (Chicago: University of Chicago Press, 1997).

yet potentially complementary pursuits – each facilitated by its working assumptions – on the same rather lumpy and variegated terrain.[17]

Mystical writings can usefully intervene in this debate. They pose an implicit challenge to Griffiths's proposal that any introspective account of emotions merely reproduces the stereotypes of folk psychology. Writers of mystical works may not have access to the most recent research findings on the amygdala, but still they are anything but unwitting recyclers of the platitudes of ordinary language. The excessiveness of mystical emotions and their expression cannot be fully explained away by cultural difference. Mystical writers open up a way to rethink the tendency in many fields of inquiry (including those more receptive to the view that emotions are culturally variable) to view any occasion in which feelings are described or expressed as representative and culturally normative. In turn, these normative tendencies of analysis highlight the ways in which it is productive for scholarship on mysticism to focus upon extraordinary emotional artistry.

Another difficulty of analysis that arises in this pursuit, however, as it does in many fields of inquiry that aim to study emotions, is that of finding evidence of the emotions we want to discuss. In the here and now of human social interaction, emotions are typically mediated at least in part through language, even if they also involve the interpretation of nonverbal cues such as facial expression, stance, and gesture.[18] Any description or theoretical discussion of emotion is, of course, linguistic. The emotions visible in texts are obviously only available in written language. But where and how can emotions be found in textual evidence? Moments when emotions are explicitly named have been the focus of nearly all work by historians who study emotion, even the most insightful and innovative; much of that work has, in addition, proceeded by isolating individual emotions for study and, in some cases, positioning them within a larger taxonomy.[19] Yet as we noted at the outset, an insight shared by mysticism and by recent research on emotion is that

---

[17] For another response to Griffiths, see Jesse Prinz, "Which Emotions Are Basic?" in *Emotion, Evolution, and Rationality*, ed. Dylan Evans and Pierre Cruse (Oxford: Oxford University Press, 2004), pp. 69–87.

[18] Bella M. DePaulo and Howard S. Friedman, "Nonverbal Communication," in *Handbook of Social Psychology*, 4th ed., ed. Daniel T. Gilbert, Susan T. Fiske, and Gardner Lindzey (Boston and New York: McGraw Hill, 1998), vol. 2.

[19] See, in addition to the historical studies already cited, Barbara H. Rosenwein, ed., *Anger's Past: The Social Uses of an Emotion in the Middle Ages* (Ithaca, NY: Cornell University Press, 1998); Daniel Lord Smail, *The Consumption of Justice: Emotions, Publicity, and Legal Culture in Marseille, 1264–1423* (Ithaca, NY: Cornell University Press, 2003); and David Konstan, *The Emotions of the Ancient Greeks: Studies in Aristotle and Classical Literature* (Toronto: University of Toronto Press, 2006).

isolative analysis can carry us only so far. Certainly, every one of the examples from mystical writing that we have examined illustrates this point. Porete's description of the annihilated soul's self-abandonment itemizes faculties while also describing the complexity of their interactive operation. Rolle's "burning of love" is emotion, sensation, and will together, as explained in terms of his own experience earlier in his prologue. Fitzralph's tears are a conventional metonymy for emotions, bodily sensation, and physical action all at once, together demonstrating the workings of the divine. Ruusbroec's allegorical journey into the Divine Dark uses metaphor and simile to describe the transcendence of emotion and volition in terms of transforming bodily perceptions in a way that emphasizes the continuities along this range of physical and mental experience. We would gain little insight by picking out an individual emotion (say, love) as our focus, or even by picking out the full range of emotion words, for example, in Porete, shame, honor, fear, and affection.

The apparent dilemma of how to analyze emotions other than by picking out the words that describe them is not really a dilemma at all once we remember that all talk is talk about feeling. Even if emotion has sometimes been systematically ignored, there is no human communication in which affect is absent. Our task is not to search through the written record for feelings that may not be there, but instead to choose the occasions where they are most visible. One way to select our materials (though there are surely others) would be to focus on moments where some sort of special appeal is made to feeling. These will include occasions where emotions are named; moments when especially evocative, lyrical, and figural language is used (as analyzed by Fitzralph); or where feeling is evoked in narrative or through allegory (as by Ruusbroec). Further, this method of analysis gains support not only from the traditional tools of literary criticism but also from recent work by analytic philosophers, including some who tend toward universalizing analyses of emotion. Ronald de Sousa has suggested that what differentiates human from animal emotions (as well as one emotion from another) may be precisely the acquisition of a narrative form: we tell ourselves and each other stories about our feelings as a way of explaining our world and our behavior.[20] Peter Goldie examines in detail how just this sort of telling ourselves and each other stories, pervasive in everyday social life,

---

[20] Ronald de Sousa, "Emotions: What I Know, What I'd Like to Think I Know, and What I'd Like to Think," in *Thinking about Feeling*, ed. Solomon, pp. 61–75, esp. pp. 63, 73–5.

is a way of relating and inviting emotional responses.[21] David Velleman claims that what gives a narrative its shape is, above all, its "emotional cadence," or the chain of emotional responses, each arising from the last, that it evokes. He speculates that the most enduring and thought-provoking narratives may often be those that leave our feelings, and those of the characters of the story, least specified and most unresolved.[22] Perhaps it is narrative, rather than naming, that gives any textual rendition of emotion its intersubjective ground, while allegory, with its capacity to make the familiar strange, may give it flight.

---

[21] Peter Goldie, "Narrative and Perspective: Values and Appropriate Emotions," in *Philosophy and the Emotions*, ed. A. Hatzimoysis (Cambridge: Cambridge University Press, 2003), pp. 201–20.

[22] J. David Velleman, "Narrative Explanations," *The Philosophical Review* 112, no. 1 (2003): 1–25.

19 Authority

MARY FROHLICH, RSCJ

The core meaning of authority is "the power of authorship." Thus authority in human societies has to do with being able to maintain, create, or modify relationships and the flow of benefits that they structure. In Christian theology, the ultimate source of this power resides in God, and it is mediated through Jesus, the Holy Spirit, the scriptures, and the church. Yet the meaning given to each of these terms, and the way they are played out in social structures and relationships, changes radically in different eras and cultures. For example, in traditional societies, authority resides in the elders, revered ancestors, and the canon of *Auctoritates* that are presumed to have a special intimacy with the divine. A Christian mystic, for example, would gain authority and the influence by demonstrating association with Christ, the clergy, the saints, and the Bible. In modernity, on the other hand, authority is more often identified with comprehensive expertise or with sheer force (whether physical, emotional, or rhetorical). In this case, the mystic's influence is likely to derive from a demonstration of unusual insight or of apparently supernormal powers.

One of the key distinctions in relation to how mysticism functions within social networks is that between popular or charismatic authority and elite or institutionalized authority. Popular authority operates at a grassroots level and involves offering people something they want – often healing, safety, personal affirmation, a meaningful story to live by, or a sense of belonging. Popular authority is often in tension with elite authority, which operates in a universalized framework and asserts systematic procedures for determining who may have authority. When people identified as having extraordinary knowledge of God gain a popular following, representatives of elite authority tend to react by striving either to gain control of the movement or to destabilize it. This pattern is played out over and over again in the history of Christian mysticism.

In view of this, a much debated question has been whether ultimately mysticism is inherently subversive toward elite authority or tends more toward conserving established religious structures. Gershom Scholem opened a discussion about this by asserting that "all mysticism has two contradictory and at the same time complementary aspects, a conservative and a revolutionary one."[1] Subsequently, Steven Ozment contended that any claim of personal experience of God will tend to conflict with established authority, while Steven Katz argued for the view that mystical experience is always generated within the parameters of a specific tradition and aims to conserve it. More recently, Bernard McGinn proposed a more complex relational perspective in which a combination of inherent and situational factors must be weighed in order to assess the impact of any given instance of a mystical claim to authority.

Since the 1980s, much of the scholarship on the relation between authority and mysticism has been done by feminist scholars with an interest in reclaiming historical examples of female authority and in deconstructing the structures of patriarchy. Caroline Walker Bynum's *Holy Feast and Holy Fast: The Religious Significance of Food to Medieval Women* was a groundbreaking work that stressed the positive creativity and self-affirmation of medieval women mystics. Bynum continues to take a somewhat sanguine view of how women have been able to create and claim forms of authority even within misogynist systems. For her and for many others who have followed her lead, a significant area of research has been the reconsideration of historical figures, especially women, who have previously been written off as heretical, pathological, or simply "minor." Careful historical study of the theology and the political struggles of such figures typically results in a very different perspective on the original and continuing influence of the individual. For example, Jeanne Guyon (1648–1717), who for centuries was dismissed as a foolish, unbalanced, and insubordinate woman with little to offer theologically, has been newly retrieved as an adept mystic and theologian whose clash with Jacques-Benigne Bossuet (1627–1704) instigated his vicious campaign of defamation against her. Thus her authority in her own time and her potential value as an authority for today have been significantly reevaluated.

One vein of such research is explicitly theological. Most mystics articulate their claim to authority in terms of having been radically claimed by God, thus in some way becoming mediators of the divine for others. Research on the mystics' theological self-understanding strives to clarify how each one situates her- or himself within the ongoing tradition and, at the same time, creatively reformulates it with the freshness

---

[1] Gershom Scholem, "Mysticism and Society," *Diogenes* 58 (Summer 1967): 15.

born of profound encounter with God. Often the resultant theologies are startlingly innovative, as when Hadewijch (mid-thirteenth century) claimed the right to speak for God on the basis of her precreational existence with God, or when Julian of Norwich (d. after 1416) redefined the possibilities of female authority by her profound theological reflections on Christ in female roles such as "mother" and "prostitute." This research usually aims to give the mystics renewed authority within the community of faith as they are retrieved and reappropriated as resources for contemporary theologians.

Another prominent vein of research, however, prescinds from the theological framework and simply asks the question of how the mystics' authority was created, controlled, and contested within human social networks. The thought of Michel Foucault has been very influential in this area of scholarship. For Foucault, knowledge and selfhood are always contingent, and authority emerges only in an ongoing contested negotiation among human parties. Foucault argues that "power must be understood in the first instance as the multiplicity of force relations immanent in the sphere in which they operate and which constitute their own organization.... power is not an institution, and not a structure; neither is it a certain strength we are endowed with; it is the name that one attributes to a complex strategical situation in a particular society."[2] From this perspective, reports of "experiences of God" are among the rhetorical strategies that people use to assert authority (their own or that of others) against the claims of others. Laurie Finke articulates this perspective when she says that mysticism "is not a manifestation of the individual's internal affective states but a set of cultural and ideological constructs that both share in and subvert orthodox religious institutions."[3]

The Foucauldian approach is often employed by feminists to explore the subversive and transgressive potential of female mysticism in relation to the systematic exclusion of women from the elite structures within the church. Sarah Beckwith, for example, builds on Luce Irigaray's assertion that mysticism is the "model feminine discourse" when she writes that "if the construction of the masculine as such depends on the repression of the feminine and its relegation to the role of other, the feminine is, for that very reason ... the potential source of subversion, for she is

---

[2] Michel Foucault, *The History of Sexuality*, vol. 1, *An Introduction*, trans. Robert Hurley (New York: Pantheon, 1978), pp. 92-3.

[3] Laurie A. Finke, "Mystical Bodies and the Dialogics of Vision," in *Maps of Flesh and Light: The Religious Experience of Medieval Women Mystics*, ed. Ulrike Wiethaus (Syracuse, NY: Syracuse University, 1993), p. 29.

in the position to return, to dislocate the very unity that posits her as other, to disrupt, disperse, and displace the masculine parameters that establish law and reason."[4] Beckwith finds this exemplified in, among others, Margery Kempe (ca. 1373–after 1438), who refused the typical religious roles provided for women in fourteenth-century England while writing unusually detailed accounts of her florid mystical devotions and the trouble they got her into. Beckwith sees Kempe as a mystic who played her feminine role as the Other with a vengeance, deploying it in a manner that startled and often enraged the masculine power structures of her day.

In sum, at least three distinctive paradigms of the relation between authority and mysticism can be found operative in contemporary research; often, more than one of these paradigms is operative in a single research project:

(1) A theological paradigm presumes that ultimate authority belongs to God and that authentic mysticism mediates that authority into human lives. Discernment of authenticity is a key issue for this paradigm.
(2) An emancipatory paradigm regards authority as either juridical or charismatic, and sees mystics (especially women) as bearers of charismatic authority that can challenge and change oppressive juridical structures.
(3) A postmodern paradigm understands authority as deployed in a complex and dynamic web of social relations. Mystics are cast into a place in this web from which they exercise force that shakes and bends it. The ensuing reactions may result in a reordering of relations, but there is no necessary value judgment about whether the end state is "better" or "worse" than the first.

The following historical survey refers to elements of each of these paradigms as it reviews the changing patterns of the relationship between Christian mysticism and authority.

In early Christianity there was no concept of mysticism, but rather there was a belief that the mystery of God – that is, God's hidden reality – has been revealed in Jesus and can be known by human beings. In the early third century, Origen (d. 254) articulated a theology rooted in the conviction that the most profound access to the mystery of Christ is

---

[4] Sarah Beckwith, "A Very Material Mysticism: The Medieval Mysticism of Margery Kempe," in *Gender and Text in the Later Middle Ages*, ed. Jane Chance (Gainesville: University Press of Florida, 1996), pp. 197,196.

through contemplative study of the scriptures within the church. Belief in the mystical and intellectual authority of the scriptures as revealed Word of God became the theological norm to guide any discernment of specific claims to divine knowledge. Most texts from this period that are included in standard anthologies of Christian mysticism, such as some of the writings of Origen, Gregory of Nyssa (335–94), and Augustine (354–430), present their claim to authority in terms of revealing the hidden meaning of scripture, rather than on reports of personal experience. This theological paradigm had built into it an assumption that the clergy, especially bishops, would be the primary holders of mystical authority and, moreover, would always have the prerogative of judging those who made mystical claims.

Not surprisingly, this assumption was contested from the start. For example, with the second-century rise of Montanism or "New Prophecy," whose adherents practiced severe asceticism and had ecstatic visions of the approaching second coming of Christ, the leadership role of women prophets became a major issue. The movement, and especially its female leaders Priscilla and Maximilla, was rejected and vilified by the clergy. Two centuries later, another challenge came from the Messalians or "praying ones," who believed in praying always (to the exclusion of work) so that one could drive out the inner demon and be experientially filled with the Holy Spirit. The reason for their rejection, however, probably had more to do with conflicts with the local clergy, who regarded as heretical the Messalians' claim of apostolic authority and of a right to material support from the people. It was through debates such as these that the lines of Christian institutional authority began to be set in place. Its linchpins were scripture and the hierarchical structure of the ordained clergy, with the latter holding the power to preach and administer the sacraments.

When, in the fourth century, Constantine allowed Christianity to be practiced freely in the Roman Empire, the power of wealth and state violence were allied with the church's own structures of authority. Around the same time, the desert movements in Egypt, Palestine, and Syria began to burgeon. There, a model of charismatic authority emerged: through a life intensively committed to asceticism and prayer, the holy *abba* or *amma* came to participate in the authoritative discourse of the scriptures and thus could speak a "word" tailored to each individual person or situation. These holy persons were often accorded secular as well as spiritual authority, being called upon to settle disputes and exercise local leadership. Athanasius's (d. 373) *Life of Antony*, which would become a touchstone text for later mystical movements, had as one of its chief purposes the presentation of this charismatic form of authority as entirely obedient to, and supportive of, the juridical authority of the bishops.

This model was also soon institutionalized, as the *abbas* and *ammas* gave way to the abbots and abbesses of the medieval monasteries. Meanwhile, the gap between what Rodney Stark calls the "church of piety" – those pursuing holiness, mainly in the monasteries – and the "church of power" widened. The Gregorian reform of the late eleventh century strengthened the power of the papacy, clergy, and sacraments, in particular the Eucharist. As the church placed more and more value on the authority of the male clergy, it also began excluding women even from the semiclerical roles of blessing, hearing confessions, and leading double monasteries, roles that abbesses had previously exercised. During this same period, local bishops were in the process of losing much of their secular power, with the result that many of them began to assert a more coercive form of spiritual authority. As groups such as the Cathars and Waldensians challenged church authority and gained large followings, threatened church leaders began major campaigns against them. All this forms the backdrop for the dramatic conflict between claims to extraordinary experiences of the divine and the mediating role of the church during the late eleventh to sixteenth centuries.

Bernard of Clairvaux (1090–1153) is a key figure for understanding a significant shift in the understanding of the authority of mystical experience at this time. Bernard could not have been more steeped in the classical tradition of the *auctoritates* – the scriptures and authoritative ancient authors. Yet at the same time he declared that the "book of experience" was as necessary a theological source as the traditional "book of creation" and "book of scripture." This shift opened the door to a vastly wider participation of women in developing mystical traditions. Very few women had access to the education, let alone the social roles, that would enable them to speak or write in the classically authoritative style. To the "book of experience," however, they had equal – or perhaps even greater – access. On that basis, women soon began to articulate their own theologies of the authority of mystical experience. Hildegard of Bingen (1098–1179), for example, was endowed with an extraordinary gift of visions. She accepted her culture's assertion of feminine "inferiority" but turned it around by affirming that, since "God's power is perfected in weakness," the female is uniquely apt as the chosen vessel of God's prophetic message for the world. A similar theology would appear in many guises throughout the coming years as justification for the authority of mystical women.

A model of complementarity between the "masculine" power of office and the "feminine" power of mystical charism began to take hold. In a number of the Eucharistic visions of Gertrude of Helfta (1256–1301/2), for example, she actually took the role of the priest and formed a direct channel of grace to her monastic sisters. In the words of Bynum, Christ gave Gertrude and her sisters "an authorization to do and be much of what contemporaries understood by evangelism, and his authorization was far more direct and final than any office or tradition could be."[5] Gertrude did not, however, understand her mystical authority as fundamentally subversive of dominant church traditions; rather, her visions supported the antiheretical efforts of the institutional church by emphasizing the Eucharist, priesthood, and humanity of Christ.

What we see already beginning to develop during the early thirteenth century is a pattern that will play out repeatedly over the next two centuries: women mystics envisage and claim female spiritual authority in strong and creative ways, and this is endorsed and even encouraged by members of the clergy insofar as it supports the clergy's own agenda. Public authority for most women mystics depended heavily on the active support of clerics, who in many cases were the ones who wrote down and promoted the women's teachings. This became increasingly the case after 1215, when the Fourth Lateran Council mandated yearly confession. The confessional relationship became the forum within which mystical women both received support in naming and exploring their experiences and were intensively scrutinized for their orthodoxy.

The council also instituted the office of the inquisitor, whose processes were designed to ferret out and eliminate heresy. By the fourteenth century, those claiming extraordinary experiences of God were increasingly running afoul of these procedures. The most noted example is Marguerite Porete, who was burned at the stake in 1310. On the theological level, the problem with Marguerite was her assertion that the individual self and will are annihilated in union with God, so that God acts directly through the person and the practice of the sacraments and virtues is no longer necessary. This was perceived by some clerics as a claim to mystical authority superseding that of the institutional church and its sacraments. Marguerite's fatal choice, however, was her refusal to cooperate with the inquisitorial process. Thus, even though

---

[5] Caroline Walker Bynum, "Women Mystics in the Thirteenth Century," in *Holy Feast and Holy Fast: The Religious Significance of Food to Medieval Women* (Berkeley: University of California, 1987); Caroline Walker Bynum, *Fragmentation and Redemption: Essays on Gender and the Human Body in Medieval Religion* (New York: Zone, 1991), p. 251.

her teachings had the support of some noted theologians, she was condemned as an obdurate heretic. Ironically, her *Mirror of Simple Souls* was quickly attributed to a male author and continued its circulation as an admired mystical text. Its spiritual authority, once disassociated from the voice of a supposedly insubordinate woman, was not challenged.

Marguerite, however, was in certain significant ways not a typical medieval woman mystic. Much more common was the appeal to a vision in which God gives the woman her mission of communicating what she has learned in her mystical prayer. Also, Marguerite did not somatize her mysticism in the way most others did. Many women mystics creatively reconfigured the cultural association of women with bodiliness and nurturance into a source of authority by claiming it as a special intimacy with the humanity of Christ, who himself became flesh and food. According to Bynum, this literal *imitatio Christi* lies behind such bodily enactments as extreme fasting, the stigmata, mystical illnesses, and miraculous exuding of liquids and odors. Dyan Elliott points out, however, that this somatization was "sculpted" by clerics as part of the inquisitorial search for proof of orthodox doctrines on the humanity of Christ and the Eucharist. Women's sanctity was increasingly judged by whether they could produce these somatic proofs – which, in many cases, were "profound threats to a woman's physical well-being."[6] By rejecting the "proofs" of visions and physical suffering, Marguerite was rejecting the accepted routes to female mystical authority within her culture.

Male mystics, meanwhile, usually gained authority by a less convoluted alliance with elite authority. Men much more rarely affirmed the value of visions, and even those who did so less often appealed to their visions as their primary justification for having a right to be heard. A partial exception is Rupert of Deutz (ca. 1075–1129), but even in his case the visions directly led to his choice to be ordained – that is, to claim clerical authority. More typical is Walter Hilton (d. 1396), a cleric who made fidelity to the institutional church a linchpin to the normative Christian mystical path.

By the fifteenth century, new pressures led to a damping down of the influence of mystics. Tensions at the popular level, due to overpopulation, changes in climate, and stress among elites in relation to the Great Schism, led to escalating anxiety about witchcraft and diabolical conspiracies. Before long, pocketbook-sized exorcism manuals were being widely distributed and the somatic manifestations of mysticism that had previously been rewarded with acclaim were increasingly regarded with

---

[6] Dyan Elliott, *Proving Woman: Female Spirituality and Inquisitional Culture in the Later Middle Ages* (Princeton, NJ: Princeton University, 2004), p. 298.

alarm. The model of complementarity, in which mystical women were seen as potentially gifted with an alternative charismatic form of authority, imploded as clerical structures rigidified and exerted increasing control. The widespread use of the exorcistic rites, in the words of Nancy Caciola, "represented a repeated performative enactment of ecclesiastical triumph over alternative sources of power or authority."[7]

These trends continued in the early modern era. Nonetheless, some who are called mystics are still able to find a place within orthodox traditions. The most outstanding example is Teresa of Avila (1515–82), whose astuteness in working within the confessional relationship and creatively employing rhetoric to gain authority within and outside of her religious community has been much studied. Her repeated assertions of humility, obedience, and fidelity to the institutional church, as well as her ability to obtain the support of a network of influential clerics, enabled her to pick her way through the minefield of inquisitorial surveillance. From Teresa's time onward, however, mysticism was increasingly associated with intense affectivity and marginalized as rationalism and clerical control were set ever more firmly in place. A visionary such as Anne Catherine Emmerich (1774–1824) could develop a following, but mainstream society regarded her more as a curiosity than as an authority, and she was subject to frequent brutal investigations.

A new focus of interest began to emerge in the late nineteenth and early twentieth centuries as thinkers sometimes turned to apophatic mysticism as a way around Immanuel Kant's (1724–1804) insistence that the human mind cannot know the "real" (*noumena*) but only appearances (*phenomena*). In this view, authentic mystical knowledge is an immediate contact with reality that is ineffable from the point of view of ordinary human intelligence. This approach tends to give considerable intellectual authority to mystical descriptions of the experience of God in terms of ineffability, but little to accounts of encounters involving visions, raptures, and trances. Although this selectivity sometimes distorts the complex character of the human experience of God's mystery, it also undergirds a shift of attention to the mystical as manifested in spiritual figures who do not have visions or ecstasies. Examples are Thérèse of Lisieux (1873–97) and, more recently, Mother Teresa of Calcutta (1910–97), both of whom describe an overpowering "night of faith" that is paradoxically both an absence and a presence of God.[8]

[7] Nancy Caciola, *Discerning Spirits: Divine and Demonic Possession in the Middle Ages* (Ithaca, NY: Cornell University, 2003), p. 267.
[8] See Mary Frohlich, "Desolation and Doctrine in Thérèse of Lisieux," *Theological Studies* 61 (2000): 261–79; Mary Frohlich, "Thérèse of Lisieux and Jeanne d'Arc: History, Memory, and Interiority in the Experience of Vocation," *Spiritus* 6 (2006):

Postmodern thinkers go further with these ideas. Jacques Derrida, for example, develops the idea of the "mystical foundation of authority,"[9] that which cannot be named that occurs whenever we choose justice. When we choose justice and begin to enact it within the forms of human authority, however, it once again takes on a name and becomes deconstructible. Thus human authority always bears the trace of its "mystical foundation," but it is also always moving away from that foundation. Jean-Luc Marion argues that mystical life is a dwelling in radical unknowing that is, at the same time, a convicted certainty of the life of God restructuring our lives. For Marion, this leads back to acceptance of the institutional authority of the church, which is the social body that bears this restructured life within history. Institutional authority, however, would be empty without the authority of holiness – that is, a life visibly transformed by mystical reality.

Meanwhile, in the last third of the twentieth century, burgeoning popular interest in mysticism permitted both dead and living mystics to regain a renewed measure of attention and influence. At this popular level, interest often focused on the intense and unusual character of the mystics' experience, as well as on their power to spark subversive movements in opposition to oppressive ecclesial structures.

Questions about the intrinsic authority deriving from mystical experience, as well as those concerned with its relation to human networks of authority, remain very much alive. Although the theological, emancipatory, and postmodern paradigms of authority are still very much in play, much of current interest seems to be equally driven by a psychological paradigm that envisions authority as the power to effect interior transformation, whether in oneself or others. Future research may examine more closely how these different paradigms (or perhaps yet others) affect both the mystics' and the researchers' assessments of their relation to authority.

173–94; Ann W. Astell, "Facing Each Other: Saint Thérèse of Lisieux and Emmanuel Levinas," *Spiritus* 4 (2004): 24–43; Joann Wolski Conn, "Thérèse of Lisieux: Far From Spiritual Childhood," *Spiritus* 6 (2006): 68–89; and Phyllis Zagano and C. Kevin Gillespie, "Embracing Darkness: A Theological and Psychological Case Study of Mother Teresa," *Spiritus* 10 (2010): 52–75.

[9] Jacques Derrida, "Force of Law: The 'Mystical Foundation of Authority,'" in *Deconstruction and the Possibility of Justice*, ed. Drucilla Cornell (London: Routledge, 1992), pp. 1–67.

20 Gender
ALISON WEBER

As an abstraction, Christian mysticism is a religious experience for which sexual difference and gender roles are irrelevant. Whether one focuses on mysticism as infused knowledge of divine mysteries, a transitory noetic state of consciousness, or a complex of corporeal and cognitive practices, Christian mysticism conveys the promise of Galatians 3:28: "There is no longer Jew or Greek, there is no longer slave or free, there is no longer male and female; for all of you are one in Christ Jesus."[1] But although spiritual equality is a matter of Christian doctrine, gender has had a profound impact on the perception of individual mystics and has played a fundamental role in determining how those individuals are remembered. Furthermore, gender roles have shaped the performance of mysticism – the acts, words, and gestures with which mystics have presented themselves to others.

Undoubtedly gender continues to play a role in contemporary practices of Christian spirituality. For the purposes of this essay, however, I focus on the years from 1200 to 1800, a period that encompasses what Bernard McGinn describes as the flowering and decline of Christian mysticism. Furthermore, I take a broad view of mysticism that considers not only noetic states but also coterminous practices and phenomena such as penitential asceticism, visionary and prophetic gifts, demonic possession, and imputations of sanctity. It might well be argued that this approach distorts mysticism's meaning as infused knowledge of God and exaggerates the importance of asceticism and supernatural favors in the life of the mystic. I believe, however, that this broader approach is appropriate for the periods under consideration, for mystical knowing was closely associated with what the mystic gave through suffering, received from God, and had available to give to others.

---

[1] The New Oxford Annotated Bible. New Revised Standard Version, 3rd ed. (Oxford: Oxford University Press, 2001).

I am grateful for the suggestions from Anne J. Schutte and James Amelang, who read early drafts of this essay.

MYSTICISM AND THE SEX/GENDER DISTINCTION

During the second half of the twentieth century, the female mystic emerged as a pivotal figure as several disciplines converged on the question of women's almost universal cultural subordination. A fundamental premise for much subsequent scholarship was the sex/gender distinction. The distinction, the result of a fruitful dialogue between cultural anthropologists and feminist historians, asserts that sex is biologically determined but gender is historically constructed. Gender, defined as the social roles deemed appropriate for men and women, does not proceed naturally and inevitably from biological sex. That is, in different ways throughout history, cultures have defined specific mental and emotional characteristics, aptitudes, and deficiencies as "feminine" or "masculine." Likewise, societies have identified specific economic, political, and cultural activities as appropriate for one sex to the exclusion of the other. An important corollary of the sex/gender distinction is that the "constructedness" of gender roles is almost always occluded, because gender is perceived as the natural and universal consequence of biological sex. A second corollary is that gender is a relational construct; what is "feminine" is defined as that which is not "masculine" and vice versa. Furthermore, in patriarchal societies this binary opposition assigns women to the place of a depreciated "Other," whose perceived difference is fundamental for establishing male identity and dominance. This is not to say that gender studies can be reduced to the history of women's oppression. Contemporary scholarship recognizes that gender roles can constrain men as well as women and acknowledges that, in particular circumstances, men and women have collaborated to contest gender roles and the injustices that can result from them. By the same token, it is important to note that not all work on gender is based on radical constructionism; some scholars hold that biological sex accounts, to some degree, for the historically variable manifestations of gender. Nevertheless, a common concern in this field is to make unacknowledged gender assumptions explicit and thereby come to a better understanding of the power dynamics that undergird them.

"THE NEW MYSTICISM," GENDER, AND THE BODY

Historians of Christianity agree that around 1200 there was a remarkable shift in the practice of Christian mysticism. As Bernard McGinn explains, the "new mysticism" of the thirteenth and fourteenth centuries was marked by several significant developments: secularization (the idea that it is not necessary to flee the world to have an immediate knowledge of God), democratization (the conviction that it was possible for all Christians, not just monks and nuns, to enjoy God's presence), feminization (the prominence of women as mystics), and vernacularization (the dissemination of mystical writing in vernacular language and genres). These developments made mystical ideas and practices available to women to an unprecedented extent. Enthusiastically embracing the affective piety of the mendicant orders, women devoted themselves to penitential practices and methodical mental prayer, and also aspired to nondiscursive, contemplative prayer.

Although there are considerable differences among female mystics, and although no forms of mystical practice or expression are exclusive to women, it is possible to outline certain common features. First, female mystics struggled with the issue of authority in ways that were not required of male clerics.[2] Second, female mystics frequently employed a fervent, erotic language, figuring the pursuit of God as love madness. Third, female mysticism is strongly associated with charismatic graces, such as visions, locutions, and ecstasies. Finally, late medieval women's spirituality was characterized by extreme penitential practices.[3]

Why was it that women's spirituality was so intensely focused on the body – moreover, on the suffering body? The prevailing answer to this question from the eighteenth to the early twentieth century was that women's inherent emotional fragility and physical weakness made them susceptible to psychosomatic illnesses. Specifically, as Jean-Martin Charcot (1825–93) and Sigmund Freud (1856–1939) proposed, mystics were hysterics; religious ecstasy was essentially a conversion phenomenon resulting from repressed sexuality. Around the middle of the twentieth century, some historians, theologians, and philosophers began to challenge this view of female mysticism. French feminist philosophers notably demanded that serious attention be paid to the creativity of female mystics who "spoke" through their symptoms and thus succeeded in subverting culturally imposed restrictions on their expressive and sexual freedom. Luce Irigaray, for example, famously proclaimed that female mysticism represented "the only place in Western history where woman speaks and acts in such a public way."[4]

[2] On this issue, see also the essays in this volume by Veerle Fraeters, Dyan Elliott, and Mary Frohlich.
[3] This overview of "the new mysticism" is indebted to Bernard McGinn, *The Presence of God: A History of Western Christian Mysticism*, vol. 3, *The Flowering of Mysticism: Men and Women in the New Mysticism (1200–1350)* (New York: Crossroad, 1998).
[4] Luce Irigaray, "La Mystérique," in *Speculum of the Other Woman* (Ithaca, NY: Cornell University Press, 1974), pp. 191–202, at 191.

Beginning in the 1980s, several pioneering studies by Caroline Walker Bynum approached the question of women's somatic spirituality from within a more specific historical and theological context. Drawing on a wide array of sources, Bynum chronicled how late medieval women's *devotio* was marked by an intense desire to imitate the life of Christ through self-inflicted suffering such as flagellation, extreme fasting, and sleep deprivation. She also noted that certain paramystical phenomena – such as receiving the stigmata, falling into ecstasy, or surviving on the Eucharistic host alone – were preferentially associated with women. Bynum's explanation for these phenomena was in part functionalist: while men could avail themselves of a wider range of socially sanctioned religious acts, women's practice of *imitatio Christi* was of necessity performed within the domestic sphere and on the intimate landscape of their own bodies. Penitential practices such as self-starvation, furthermore, compensated women for their exclusion from apostolic roles and endowed them with the power to perform acts of evangelical charity, to shame uncharitable parents, or to rebuke neglectful priests.[5] Bynum went beyond functionalism, however, to interrogate the symbolic power of somatic spirituality. She argued that, although women were identified with sinful flesh (as men were associated with reason and spirit), medieval conceptions of the body were not strictly dualistic and misogynist. The doctrine of the Incarnation also associated the flesh – and the female as fleshly – with Christ's humanity. In medieval devotion, therefore, "control, discipline, even torture of the flesh is ... not so much the rejection of physicality as the elevation of it – a horrible yet delicious elevation – into a means of access to the divine."[6] Although Bynum conceded that religious women had clearly internalized the negative value placed on them by their culture and urged her readers not to forget the pain and isolation that accompanied their quests, her overall emphasis was on the transcendental significance that women's somatic spirituality held for medieval men and women: "Created and redeemed by God, [the female body] was a means of encounter with him. Healed and elevated by grace, it was destined for glory at the Last Judgment."[7]

---

[5] Caroline Walker Bynum, *Jesus as Mother: Studies in the Spirituality of the High Middle Ages* (Berkeley: University of California Press, 1982); Caroline Walker Bynum, *Holy Feast and Holy Fast: The Religious Significance of Food to Medieval Women* (Berkeley: University of California Press, 1987).

[6] Caroline Walker Bynum, "The Female Body and Religious Practice in the Later Middle Ages," in *Fragmentation and Redemption: Essays on Gender and the Human Body in Medieval Religion* (New York: Zone, 1991), pp. 181–238, at p. 182.

[7] Ibid., p. 238.

Subsequent scholarship in this area, although profoundly influenced by Bynum's work, has been more cautious regarding the positive significance of embodied spirituality. While some scholars emphasize the mystics' achievement in using their words and bodies to challenge or circumvent clerical control, others warn that women's power was often limited to a restricted sphere. Sarah Beckwith assesses the situation pessimistically:

> [Female *imitatio Christi*] is a strategy that never attempts, that is unable to attempt, to break the mould of its subjection. Indeed it cannot, for it is the very equation of victimisation, passivity, subjection with femininity that allows the Christian inversion its paradoxical triumph. But like a serf becoming king, it is a deposition, a usurpation that changes the terms but never the structure; and so the nature of the change must remain severely limited.[8]

For historians like Jo Ann McNamara, the relationship between women's embodied piety and women's power depends on historically specific circumstances. Taking a long view, McNamara traces an arc of feminine power that began with successful collaborations between spiritual women and clerics during the eleventh century, peaked during the Great Schism (1378–1417) when clerics found women to be useful allies against heretics, and declined in the fifteenth century, after the French theologian Jean Gerson (1363–1429) had initiated the battle to discredit female mysticism and reaffirm the magisterial authority of the priesthood.[9] Much subsequent historical research follows this model of framing embodied spirituality – and its self-actualizing or self-destructive potential – within the context of changing alliances, institutional and legal developments, and other historical circumstances.

Scholars have also questioned the supposition that late medieval women's spirituality was primarily enacted through the body. Most notably, Amy Hollywood observes that this characterization relies heavily on hagiographical presentations by male clerics and ignores the mystical texts authored by women. Penitential asceticism and paramystical phenomena are not intrinsic to the writings of medieval female mystics such as Hadewijch (mid-thirteenth century), Mechthild of Magdeburg

---

[8] Sarah Beckwith, "A Very Material Mystic: The Medieval Mysticism of Margery Kempe," in *Medieval Literature: Criticism, Ideology and History*, ed. David Aers (Brighton, UK: Harvester, 1986), pp. 34–57, at p. 54.

[9] Jo Ann McNamara, "The Need to Give: Suffering and Female Sanctity in the Middle Ages," in *Images of Sainthood*, ed. Renate Blumenfeld-Kosinski and Timea Szell (Ithaca, NY: Cornell University Press, 1991), pp. 199–221.

(d. 1282), and Gertrude of Helfta (d. 1301/2). Rather, "there is overwhelming evidence that ... women themselves were more concerned with issues closely paralleling those important to the male mendicant orders: the meaning of the apostolic life ... and the relationship between the active imitation of Christ and the search for unity with the divine."[10]

Early modern scholars have also challenged the idea that women's spirituality was centered on the suffering or eroticized body. Teresa of Avila (1515–82), Marie of the Incarnation (1599–1672), and Barbe Acarie (1566–1618) and her circle of *dévotes* came to see mystical favors as God's means of fortifying and inspiring the individual for a life of apostolic service. Although penitential piety undoubtedly played an important role in the lives of many women, it is apparent that its practice throughout the life of individual mystics was less consistent than we have assumed. The task for historians of religion is to understand how the competing impulses to suffer and serve played out in different contexts and how social attitudes toward women channeled these impulses.

GENDER, "LIVING SAINTS," AND EARLY MODERN MYSTICISM

Advances in the historical study of gender have coincided productively with developments in the study of hagiography. In 1969, Pierre Delooz, declaring that "saints are saints for other people," advocated a new approach to sainthood, based not on an analysis of individual saints but on their significance within the network of their social relationships.[11] In 1980, the Italian historian Gabriella Zarri integrated analysis based on gender and the construction of sanctity in a foundational article on female "living saints," a term she coined to describe individuals who, during their lifetime and independently of official designation, gained a reputation for saintliness. Although not all living saints were mystics (or vice versa), Zarri observed that during the first decades of the sixteenth century in Italy, an extraordinary number of cults grew up around women whose mystical favors were conflated with thaumaturgical and prophetic powers. In some cases, women's mystical capabilities won them roles as spiritual teachers, reformers, and antagonists of demons,

---

[10] Amy Hollywood, *The Soul as Virgin Wife: Mechthild of Magdeburg, Marguerite Porete, and Meister Eckhart* (Notre Dame, IN: University of Notre Dame Press, 1995), p. 26.

[11] Pierre Delooz, "Towards a Sociological Study of Canonized Sainthood in the Catholic Church," in *Saints and Their Cults: Studies in Religious Sociology, Folklore and History*, ed. Stephen Wilson (Cambridge: Cambridge University Press, 1984), pp. 189–216, at pp. 193, 197.

roles that nevertheless sometimes left them exposed to accusations of fakery. The fortunes of these women faded after 1530, a phenomenon that Zarri attributes to a number of factors, including a return to traditional gender roles following the restoration of civic order, increased suspicion of reformist agendas in the wake of the Protestant Reformation, and a shift toward a new model of saintliness based on heroic virtue rather than thaumaturgical power.[12] Zarri's work underscores the need to study early modern mysticism in relation to related phenomena such as possession and exorcism, thaumaturgy, and prophecy – while taking into consideration local religious needs and overarching shifts in doctrine and ecclesiastical politics.

Recent studies on the discernment of spirits in the late medieval and early modern period have productively traced the evolution of gendered attitudes regarding women's spiritual capacities. During this period, guides to distinguishing true charismatic gifts proliferated. In this literature, the question of how to assess female mystics was particularly troubling. Were their ecstasies, visions, and auditions gifts from God? Were they instead deceptions of the devil, wont, as Saint Paul warned, to disguise himself as an angel of light? If the phenomena were demonic, was the woman who experienced them an innocent victim or the devil's accomplice? Or were female mystics simply frauds, hungry for power and attention? The literature of discernment drew heavily on misogynistic notions that defined women as mentally inferior to men, more sensual, devious, and more easily deceived by the devil. Furthermore, as Moshe Sluhovsky has recently argued, early modern Catholicism established an increasingly close correspondence between the effects of mysticism and diabolic possession, based on the fear that the passivity of the will during contemplative prayer could leave the soul susceptible to demonic assaults. These suspicions reached a peak during the late seventeenth century, when women's charismata were more likely to be discredited as the effects of possession, delusion, or fraudulence than esteemed as spiritual gifts.[13] Although the criteria for discernment were, in theory, gender neutral and reflected the church's long-standing mistrust of the

[12] Gabriella Zarri, "Living Saints: A Typology of Female Sanctity in the Early Sixteenth Century," in *Women and Religion in Medieval and Renaissance Italy*, ed. Daniel Bornstein and Roberto Rusconi (Chicago: University of Chicago Press, 1992), pp. 219–303. This essay was originally published in Italian in 1980.
[13] Moshe Sluhovsky, *Believe Not Every Spirit: Possession, Mysticism and Discernment in Early Modern Catholicism* (Chicago: University of Chicago Press, 2007). For the late medieval period see also Dyan Elliott, *Proving Women: Female Spirituality and Inquisitorial Culture in the Later Middle Ages* (Princeton, NJ: Princeton University Press, 2004).

spiritual aspirations of *"idiotae"* (the ignorant masses), women were doubly discredited as unlearned and as Eve's heirs.

MYSTICISM, GENDER, AND WRITING

Literary scholarship on late medieval and early modern mysticism in the last three decades has proceeded on several fronts. Philological, psychological, and textual studies have been complemented by performative and rhetorical analyses grounded in historical context. Much recent work has been directed to understanding how some women evaded the Pauline exhortation that "women keep silent in the churches" and, in certain circumstances, gained a public voice. It has been argued, for example, that mystics like Teresa of Avila and her followers developed a repertoire of rhetorical strategies that allowed them to avoid the appearance of usurping the magisterial prerogative of the clergy. Scholars have also examined the way that female mystics collaborated with priests who transcribed, preached, or otherwise disseminated their revelations. There is now a considerable body of work on spiritual autobiographies, generally produced, as was Teresa's *Life*, in response to a confessor's command that the mystic detail her spiritual methods and favors. Scholarship has revealed that despite the undeniable control that the confessor exercised over these autobiographies-on-command, the genre did afford some women opportunities to examine their inner lives, defend their religious experiences, and even engage in spiritual teaching by embedding theological statements within their confessions. Although some confessors acted as censors, others collaborated in producing a text that would advance mutual goals. Kathleen Myers has proposed the term mystic triad to describe the collaboration between the visionary woman, clerical mediator, and divine author of the mystical discourse.[14] Whether the focus is on transcribed oral expression or female-authored texts, the trend in scholarship is away from the paradigm of the solitary female writer or speaker and toward models based on interactive authorship, rhetoric, and the social dimensions of textual transmission.

In general, recent literary studies have tended to deemphasize the erotic component of mystical language, treating the mystics' erotic vocabulary as only one of several metaphorical codes. This reluctance to take mysticism's sexual language at face value probably reflects a

---

[14] Kathleen Myers, "The Mystic Triad in Colonial Mexican Nuns' Discourse: Divine Author, Visionary Scribe, and Clerical Mediator," *Colonial Latin American History Review* 6 (1997): 479–524.

rejection of earlier characterizations of the mystics as hysterics. Nancy Partner, however, has made a spirited defense of the historical validity of psychoanalytic approaches to mysticism. She argues that to see women's mystic experiences as hysterical "is not to denigrate them or dismiss them, but rather to see clearly and with sympathy the extreme distress and thwarting of women's lives, and the lengths to which they were sometimes driven for expression and relief."[15] We are faced with the absence of unmediated access to this psychic past. Any definitive consensus on whether mystics' erotic language gave voice to sexual longings or guilt – or whether the sensations they described were, properly speaking, sexual – seems highly unlikely.

MYSTICISM AND MASCULINITY

As the previous discussion indicates, most scholars of gender and mysticism have concentrated on women, motivated, perhaps, by the need to compensate for the omissions of traditional history. But gender, it bears repeating, is a relational concept. There is, furthermore, an important body of research on male mystics and what they reveal about historically variable notions of masculinity. Once again, Bynum's research was foundational. In *Jesus as Mother: Studies in the Spirituality of the High Middle Ages*, Bynum called attention to the extensive use of feminine imagery in the works of male mystical writers. Nuptial mysticism, in which the soul is cast as Christ's desiring bride, gave men a unique opportunity to explore a feminine subject position. To paraphrase Irigaray, we might say that mystical texts are one of the few spaces in Western history where men are allowed to identify with emotions that their culture would have them disown as "feminine." We must be wary, however, of assigning a transhistorical meaning to such discourse, which may be more or less transgressive in different contexts. By the same token, we cannot assume that the nuptial or nurturing language of male writers necessarily endorsed spiritual egalitarianism or translated into practical solidarity with women.

It is also apparent that holiness was an arena within which gender norms were not always rigidly demarcated. Richard Kieckhefer's study of three representative saints from the fourteenth century, two female and one male, demonstrated that their hagiographers emphasized similar saintly virtues – the patient endurance of suffering, humility, fervent

---

[15] Nancy F. Partner, "Reading the Book of Margery Kempe," *Exemplaria* 3 (1991): 29–66, at p. 63.

penitence, scrupulosity, and the experience of rapture.[16] Jodi Bilinkoff has shown that in the seventeenth-century Catholic world, aspiring holy men engaged in extreme penitential practices and were expected to demonstrate the presumed feminine virtues of docility, humility, and deference to clerical authority.[17] The implications of male versus female performance of these virtues, however, await further scrutiny. How men and women chose to display docility or humility – and how such displays were interpreted by their witnesses – were undoubtedly influenced by expectations regarding gender and rank.

As we have seen, the control clerics exercised over women's interior spiritual lives – the authority to examine, test, and judge their experiences – was indisputable. However, recent scholarship has also called attention to the deep friendships that sometimes developed between men and spiritually exceptional women. Writing on the late medieval period, John Coakley has described how clerics were sometimes drawn to holy women with "a fascination rooted in the conviction that the women possessed some essential spiritual quality or gift lacking in themselves."[18] The close relationship between Catherine of Siena (1347–80) and Raymond of Capua (1330–99) served as a model for collaboration between many confessors and aspiring female saints throughout Catholic Europe and in the New World from the early sixteenth into the eighteenth century. Although female penitents often reported suffering at the hands of unsympathetic or cruel spiritual directors, others eventually found soul mates with whom they formed deeply satisfying intimate bonds. Post-Tridentine clerics, like their medieval counterparts, also sought out spiritually gifted women whose humility, they believed, made them conduits of divine messages withheld from arrogant men.[19] We are thus reminded that there are multiple gender discourses within Christianity. The discourse of women's mental and moral inferiority, to be sure, often trumped that of spiritual equality. But the words of Thessalonians 5:19–21 – "Do not quench the spirit. Do not despise the words of prophets, but test everything" – also sanctioned a discourse

---

[16] Richard Kieckhefer, *Unquiet Souls: Fourteenth-Century Saints and Their Religious Milieu* (Chicago: University of Chicago Press, 1984).

[17] Jodi Bilinkoff, "Navigating the Waves (of Devotion): Toward a Gendered Analysis of Early Modern Catholicism," in *Crossing Boundaries: Attending to Early Modern Women*, ed. Jane Donawerth and Adele Seeff (Newark: University of Delaware Press, 2000), pp. 161–72.

[18] John W. Coakley, *Women, Men, and Spiritual Power: Female Saints and Their Male Collaborators* (New York: Columbia University Press, 2006), p. 2.

[19] Jodi Bilinkoff, *Related Lives: Confessors and Their Female Penitents, 1450–1759* (Ithaca, NY: Cornell University Press, 2005).

that conceded complementary or even superior powers to exceptional women. This does not mean that the consequences of such male/female friendships were invariably benign or that the fruits of collaboration were shared equally. Whatever the particular power dynamics, these associations can nevertheless give us a keener understanding of how men constructed their masculine identities through relationships with women.

GENDER, BAROQUE MYSTICISM, AND THE EIGHTEENTH-CENTURY REVIVAL

If in the popular imagination mysticism is a medieval phenomenon, it is now evident that charismatic styles of spirituality flourished during the seventeenth century and survived well into the eighteenth century. Despite official efforts to discourage charismatic enthusiasm, mysticism continued to thrive, especially in monastic settings. José Luis Sánchez Lora has attributed the particular character of baroque mysticism in seventeenth-century Spain to a number of factors, including the widespread cult of Teresa of Avila (canonized in 1622), the popularity of contemplative and hagiographic literature, ubiquitous images of saints in ecstasy, and the required practice of mental prayer in reformed orders. Whether encouraged by their confessors and prioresses or inspired by their own readings, many nuns aspired to mystical contemplation, Sánchez Lora suggests, as an escape from the monotonous life of strict enclosure and as a form of self-assertion.[20]

Another salient feature of baroque spirituality in Spain that extended to other parts of the Catholic world was extreme penitential asceticism. Eschewing the moderate asceticism advocated in the Tridentine era, baroque mystics wore hair shirts, flagellated themselves, and engaged in other forms of corporeal humiliation. Although prioresses and spiritual directors bore the responsibility to curb a nun's excessive zeal for self-mortification, they were not always able or willing to do so. Despite abundant warning regarding the dangers of excessive penance, many women pursued – and often found confessors willing to endorse – the path of holiness through bodily pain. As noted previously, baroque spirituality was not exclusively female; however, it has yet to be determined whether the reforms regarding canonization procedures promulgated during the pontificate of Urban VIII (1623–44) – and the subsequent

---

[20] José Luis Sánchez Lora, *Mujeres, conventos y formas de la religiosidad barroca* (Madrid: FUE, 1988).

censure of extravagant forms of religiosity during the second half of the seventeenth century – had a greater impact on men than women.

The early decades of the seventeenth century in France also witnessed a resurgence of penitential asceticism. Women played a key role in this religious revival as exemplars and leaders. As the penitential impulse waned in the 1630s, pious women worked alongside men in redirecting religious fervor toward charitable ends. In their mature years, mystics like Marie of the Incarnation and Madame Guyon (1648–1717) abandoned and even disparaged extreme asceticism and sensible favors.[21] As Barbara Diefendorf observes, if asceticism and charity are two distinct religious impulses in women's religiosity, they are nonetheless closely linked.[22] The neglected topic of eighteenth-century spirituality is also receiving attention. Marina Caffiero, for example, describes a late-eighteenth-century renewal of mysticism on the Italian peninsula, one in which lower-class women played an important role in the Church's campaign to re-Christianize men lost to secular rationalism.[23] How the mystics – and the gender ideals associated with them – were deployed to advance the agendas of early modern religious and political entities is yet another productive area of research. Together, these studies illustrate the limitations of a model based on the steady progress from medieval forms of piety to more rational and restrained modern spirituality, or on one based on a sharp distinction between penitential and apostolic spirituality.

CONCLUSION

In surveying the relation between gender and mysticism from 1200 to 1800 we find both continuity and change. Women's exclusion from the priesthood, justified on the basis of their ineradicable difference from Christ, stands as a salient example of the continuity of women's subordination and exclusion. Christianity's assimilation of medieval medical and philosophical discourses predicated on the idea of women as defective men must count as another example of how gendered notions

---

[21] Marie-Florie Bruneau, *Women Mystics Confront the Modern World: Marie de l'Incarnation (1588–1672) and Madame Guynon (1648–1717)* (Albany: State University of New York Press, 1998).

[22] Barbara Diefendorf, *From Penitence to Charity: Pious Women and the Catholic Reformation in Paris* (Oxford: Oxford University Press, 2004).

[23] Marina Caffiero, "From the Late Baroque Mystical Explosion to the Social Apostolate, 1650–1850," in *Women and Faith: Catholic Religious Life in Italy from Late Antiquity to the Present*, ed. Gabriella Zarri and Lucetta Scaraffia (Cambridge, MA: Harvard University Press, 1999), pp. 176–204.

arising at a particular historical moment can have remarkable longevity. But we now also appreciate how the fault lines among different gender discourses within Christianity resulted in a changing panorama of relations between the sexes and between women and the Church. Mysticism sometimes allowed essentialism to work in women's favor, as putatively feminine carnality and abjection endowed them with Christ-like qualities. Conversely, when men, attracted to a feminine soteriology of suffering, chose to assume a subject position culturally defined as feminine, they paradoxically made the very constructedness of gender visible.

In the last thirty-five years, scholarship has thus moved from approaching mysticism as a peculiarly female malady to considering whether mystical practices offered women paths of resistance and self-actualization. The concepts of resistance and self-actualization have, in turn, been refined by the awareness of how mysticism sometimes gave rise to unexpected collaborations between men and women and between social groups. Attention to a wider range of texts and geographies has also called into question the generalization that there was a steady decline in women's spiritual power from the late fourteenth to the eighteenth century. Finally, studies of gender and mysticism have served to complicate the paradigm of male domination and female repression within the Church. Historically, mysticism has been remarkably protean in its capacity to challenge and confirm traditional gender roles, to open and foreclose opportunities for women, and to uplift and denigrate them. For many Christians during the period under consideration, mysticism undoubtedly provided models of behavior that reified the notion of women as emotional rather than rational beings, unsuited for apostolic roles in the Church. But mysticism also served to exalt and enable women, in their own eyes and in the eyes of others, male and female. For still others, the possibility of union with a loving God promised that ultimately sex was irrelevant and that human notions of what men and women must be and do were meaningless.

21 Sexuality

CONSTANCE M. FUREY

How should we interpret Teresa of Avila's (1515–82) visceral description of being pierced by an angel's arrow? "In his hands I saw a great golden spear, and at the iron tip there appeared to be a point of fire. This he plunged into my heart several times so that it penetrated to my entrails. When he pulled it out, I felt that he took them with it, and left me utterly consumed by the great love of God. The pain was so severe that it made me utter several moans. The sweetness caused by this intense pain is so extreme that one cannot possibly wish it to cease, nor is one's soul then content with anything but God."[1] Punctured, consumed by love, moaning with a sweet pain, oblivious to all other sensations, Teresa insists that readers attend to her physical pleasure. This is the moment of ecstasy captured in Bernini's sculpture of Teresa, which portrays her swooning under an angel, her hand splayed out to the side, a bare foot flung out from beneath her robes, her face twisted upward with her mouth falling open, her eyelids half-closed, and her pupils rolled back.

The twentieth-century psychoanalyst, Jacques Lacan, bluntly proclaims that we're looking at an orgasmic woman ("she's coming. There's no doubt about it").[2] This is a conclusion many modern readers find inescapable, if also somehow unseemly. "It got embarrassing," a student of mine recently confessed after reading this passage, "as soon as she started moaning." This embarrassment implies two things: that there is something sexual about this saint and that a saint's sexuality makes us uncomfortable. It should also convey that our understanding of sexuality does not match Teresa's. Note that Teresa presented this experience as painful and pleasurable but not shameful. Although Teresa lived in a time of rampant fears about women's sexual susceptibility and several

---

[1] Teresa of Avila, *The Autobiography of Teresa of Avila*, trans. E. Allison Peers (New York: Doubleday, 1991), p. 275.
[2] Jacques Lacan, *On Feminine Sexuality: The Limits of Love and Knowledge, Book XX: Encore, 1972–73*, trans. Bruce Fink (New York: Norton, 1998), p. 76.

of her contemporaries who claimed divine inspiration were indicted for licentious behavior, the authorities who carefully vetted Teresa's visions and writings did not object to or excise this one.[3]

We are often told that religious texts are not about sexuality and that claims to the contrary betray our own obsessions. In cultures (including premodern and parts of early modern Europe) where physical privacy is relatively rare and asceticism widely esteemed, the body conspicuously signifies much besides sex. People concentrate just as much, if not more, on bodily decay, nourishment, fertility, sensory perceptions, and the physicality of spiritual discernment.[4] Moreover, sexualized interpretations of mystical texts by or about women have perpetuated the fetishization of women's bodies. Many of the most extreme somatic experiences attributed to female mystics have been relayed to us by male confessors who may have had more at stake in the physicality of the experience than did the women themselves.[5] Given this, we should not be surprised that a male sculptor chose to dramatize Teresa's corporeal ecstasy, rather than some other scene, and that it is this statue, rather than Teresa's text, that Lacan directs us to view for indubitable proof that she was orgasmic ("you need but go to Rome and see the statue by Bernini").[6]

Wary of these pitfalls, many who study mysticism disavow the topic of sexuality altogether or argue that the longing expressed in mystical texts is erotic rather than sexual. Unburdened by charges of anachronism,

---

[3] Mary Giles, "Francisca Hernández and the Sexuality of Religious Dissent," in *Women in the Inquisition: Spain and the New World*, ed. Mary Giles (Baltimore, MD: The Johns Hopkins University Press, 1999), pp. 75–97. See also Alison Weber, *Teresa of Avila and the Rhetoric of Femininity* (Princeton, NJ: Princeton University Press, 1990).

[4] A point influentially elaborated by Caroline Walker Bynum. See esp. Caroline Walker Bynum, "The Body of Christ in the Later Middle Ages: A Reply to Leo Steinberg" and "The Female Body and Religious Practice in the Later Middle Ages," in *Fragmentation and Redemption: Essays on Gender and the Human Body in Medieval Religion* (New York: Zone Books, 1991), pp. 85–6, 92, 182. For discussions of the shortcomings of Bynum's approach in light of her own subtle analysis of the body, see Richard Rambuss, *Closet Devotions* (Durham, NC: Duke University Press, 1998), pp. 43–9; Karma Lochrie, "Mystical Acts, Queer Tendencies," in *Constructing Medieval Sexuality*, ed. Karma Lochrie, Peggy McCracken, and James S. Schultz (Minneapolis: University of Minnesota Press, 1997), pp. 182–4; and Sarah Salih, "When Is a Bosom Not a Bosom? Problems with 'Erotic Mysticism'" in *Medieval Virginities*, ed. Anke Bernau, Ruth Evans, and Sarah Salih (Toronto: University of Toronto Press, 2003), pp. 18–20.

[5] Amy Hollywood, *The Soul as Virgin Wife: Mechthild of Magdeburg, Marguerite Porete, and Meister Eckhart* (Notre Dame, IN: University of Notre Dame Press, 1995), pp. 27–39.

[6] Lacan, *On Feminine Sexuality*, p. 76.

eroticism has a proud pedigree in Christian mysticism. The sixth-century theologian Pseudo-Dionysius declared *eros* the eminent power of "unifying, binding, and joining." Eroticism encompasses the interplay of divine love and human desire and the quest for union that characterize mystical texts.[7] So why talk about sexuality as well? Because if eroticism connotes yearning and fulfillment, arousal and frustration, deferral and satisfaction, the category of sexuality more specifically keeps our eyes trained on the physicality of these sensations and desires. In studying sexuality in Christian mysticism, we take our cue from the fact that many mystic writers wrote about somatic pleasure and pain, that they described bodies – their own bodies and the body of God – pierced, wounded, aroused, panting, bleeding, sucking, languishing, exulting, enlarging, and diminishing. Describing desire and unity in these terms, mystical texts deny distinctions between metaphoric and literal language and demonstrate the inseparability of body and language.[8]

This means the sexual language is not "merely" metaphorical, but also that these texts are not hard shells we can crack open to find the sexual experience inside. In an article bluntly called "Did Mystics Have Sex?" the medievalist Nancy Partner rightly observes that ignoring sexuality means turning a blind eye to some of the most provocative features of mystical texts, but she underscores how narrow this approach can be when she concludes that mystical texts reveal how mystics responded to the "heavy weight of sexual restriction" by sublimating their desire. Mystics did not have sex, but they wanted to.[9]

This binary approach stops short just at the point where mystical sexuality gets interesting. The problem with analyzing sexuality in mystical texts is not so much that we see sex everywhere, but that our notions of what sexuality entails are too limited. Sex is not something one simply has or lacks, just as sexual desire is not merely fulfilled or repressed. It is true that sexuality – as a concept that emerged during the eighteenth century – signifies a conflation of desire and identity

---

[7] Pseudo-Dionysius, *The Divine Names and Mystical Theology*, trans. John D. Jones (Milwaukee, WI: Marquette University Press, 1980), p. 145. See also Bernard McGinn, "God as Eros," in *New Perspectives on Historical Theology: Essays in Memory of John Meyendorff*, ed. Bradley Nassif (Grand Rapids, MI: Eerdmans, 1996), pp. 189–209.

[8] See Lochrie, "Mystical Acts"; and Amy Hollywood, "Sexual Desire, Divine Desire; or, Queering the Beguines," in *Toward a Theology of Eros*, ed. Virginia Burrus and Catherine Keller (New York: Fordham University Press, 2006), pp. 119–33.

[9] Nancy F. Partner, "Did Mystics Have Sex?' in *Desire and Discipline: Sex and Sexuality in the Premodern West*, ed. Jacqueline Murray (Toronto: University of Toronto Press, 1996), pp. 302, 307. See also Patricia Dailey, "The Body and Its Senses," in this volume.

unthinkable in earlier periods and remarkably formative in our own. The dichotomized concept of sexuality that prevails today shapes reality just as much for those who resist as those who embrace the iron bond between genital acts, gendered desire, and identities. But it is also true that this modern notion of sexuality as a fixed identity is inadequate to the variety and nuance of the desiring body.[10] Mystical sexuality is about the intense pleasure and pain that bodies inflict and receive and about the ecstasy, standing outside oneself, the breathless arousal and rhythmic satisfactions that come from, and in, this experience. To say, as we all now do, that this happens in the body is not in any way to displace the importance of language, for we might as well say this happens in language. The sexuality these texts express cannot, moreover, easily be plotted along a grid with the dichotomy of heterosexuality or homosexuality on one axis, and abstinence or intercourse on the other.[11]

Exploring mysticism's sexuality instead requires us to trace the serpentine descriptions of physical arousal and interactions between bodies and between selves. This is where Lacan leads if we follow him past his seeming fixation on Teresa's orgasm. Dismissive of Freud and his followers, who wrongly "reduce the mystical to questions of fucking," Lacan instead concentrates on how the physical descriptions in mystical texts convey ecstasy, ex-stasis, the experience of standing outside or

---

[10] Eve Kosofsky Sedgwick succinctly summarizes the "irreducible incoherence" of the view held by most moderately to well-educated Western people, that, on the one hand, the object of sexual desire is fixed and constitutes one's identity, and, on the other hand, that sexual desire is "an unpredictably powerful solvent of stable identities." See Eve Kosofsky Sedgwick, *Epistemology of the Closet* (Berkeley: University of California Press, 2008), p. 85. See also Michel Foucault, *History of Sexuality*, vol. 2, *The Use of Pleasure*, trans. Robert Hurley (New York: Vintage Books, 1990), p. 8, and his statement, in one of the many prefaces he wrote to this volume, that he turned to antiquity in order to study what he called the "experience of the flesh" rather than the "experience of sexuality." Michel Foucault, *The Foucault Reader*, ed. Paul Rabinow (New York: Random House, 1984). See also Arnold I. Davidson, *The Emergence of Sexuality: Historical Epistemology and the Formation of Concepts* (Cambridge, MA: Harvard University Press, 2001), pp. 30–65.

[11] Medievalists have been particularly good at making this point. See *Constructing Medieval Sexuality: Premodern Sexualities*, ed. Louise Fradenburg and Carla Freccero (New York: Routledge, 1996); Caroline Dinshaw, *Getting Medieval: Sexualities and Communities, Pre- and Postmodern* (Durham, NC: Duke University Press, 1999); Jeffrey Jerome Cohen, *Medieval Identity Machines* (Minneapolis: University of Minnesota Press, 2003); Karma Lochrie, *Heterosyncrasies: Female Sexuality When Normal Wasn't* (Minneapolis: University of Minnesota Press, 2005), pp. 47–70; and Hollywood, "Sexual Desire." See also Virginia Burrus, *The Sex Lives of Saints: An Erotics of Ancient Hagiography* (Philadelphia: University of Pennsylvania Press, 2004).

beyond oneself.¹² The sexual language in mystical texts thereby equates transcendence with embodied intersubjectivity.¹³

Let us return to Teresa and her angel. How do we understand this body? How do we read her words? If we locate this vision in the context of the chapter in Teresa's *Autobiography* in which it appears, it becomes clear that Teresa's ecstasy is an antidote to isolation or self-containment, to her fear that all she experiences is a product of her own imagination. In her intense encounter with another being, felt in and through the body, in sensations of being contorted, aroused, and altered, Teresa manifests what Luce Irigaray holds to be the main virtue of ecstatic mystical texts – they draw and erase boundaries by claiming a self distinct from and united with another. Crucially, they do this by expressing how the circumscribed body experiences sensations that seem to exceed the body. Mystical sexuality thereby configures bodily finitude not just in terms of lack but also in terms of possibility, of the possibility that the skin and bones and nerves and blood that separate us one from another might also draw us out of ourselves, join us to another, through the sensations evoked by a caress or embrace, by piercing or rubbing.¹⁴ This means that the sexual imagery and acts described in mystical texts – in texts that imagine extraordinary interactions with a deity – present a sexuality that is not about the body only, and not solely about sensual, intimate encounters between two (or more) bodies, but about the way that these encounters dislocate the embodied self, reimagining it in spaces and forms not regularly inhabited. In these texts, as we will see in the examples that follow, the bounded, discrete body becomes the site (and inspiration) for claims about how boundaries and selves might change or dissolve.

SEXUALITY AND THE SONG OF SONGS

The strangeness of mystical sexuality takes inspiration from a conventional source, the Song of Songs. Before the twelfth century, Christians usually read the Song of Songs allegorically, as a text about the relationship between Christ and his Church or Christ and Mary. But the

---

[12] Lacan, *On Feminine Sexuality*, p. 147.
[13] Amy Hollywood, *Sensible Ecstasy: Mysticism, Sexual Difference, and the Demands of History* (Chicago: University of Chicago Press, 2002), p. 5. This remarkable book, along with Hollywood's other work, deeply informs my thinking on this and other lessons to be learned from mysticism.
[14] Luce Irigaray, *Speculum of the Other Woman*, trans. Gillian C. Gill (Ithaca, NY: Cornell University Press, 1974), p. 200.

Cistercian monk Bernard of Clairvaux and other twelfth-century exegetes instead lingered over the Song of Song's marital and sexual imagery to describe the intimate connection between Christ and the believer.[15] Bernard coined a new term when he described the Song of Songs as the "book of experience," and his work marks the emergence of experiential mysticism characterized not only by language of mystical marriage but also of erotic encounters between the believer and Christ.[16] Writings by or about experiential mystics are often viscerally somatic and unconcerned to stress the metaphoric nature of this imagery.[17] So Beatrice of Nazareth (d. 1268) describes the "fever of love" that seemed to consume her body: "veins bursting, blood spilling, marrow withering, bones softening, the heart burning, the throat parching, so that the body in its every part feels this inward heat."[18] Gertrude of Helfta (d. 1301/2) uses similar images as she expands Bernard of Clairvaux's description of how the word penetrates the believer: "I felt as though an ineffable light from your divine eyes were ... softly penetrating. At first it was as though my bones were being emptied of all the marrow, then even the bones with the flesh were dissolved so that nothing was felt to exist in all my substance save that divine splendor which, in a manner more delectable than I am able to say, playing within itself, showed my soul the inestimable bliss of utter serenity."[19] Gertrude and Beatrice's contemporary, Angela of Foligno (d. 1309), reported that when God lovingly called her his daughter, "all the members of my body thrilled with delight."

---

[15] Ann Astell, *The Song of Songs in the Middle Ages* (Ithaca, NY: Cornell University Press, 1990), pp. 4–15; Denys Turner, *Eros and Allegory: Medieval Exegesis of the Song of Songs* (Kalamazoo, MI: Cistercian Publications, 1995), pp. 47–81; Stephen Moore, "The Song of Songs in the History of Sexuality," in *God's Beauty Parlor and Other Queer Spaces in and around the Bible* (Stanford, CA: Stanford University Press, 2001).

[16] See the essay in this volume by Amy Hollywood.

[17] Bernard McGinn, *The Presence of God: A History of Western Christian Mysticism*, vol. 2, *The Growth of Mysticism: Gregory the Great through the Twelfth Century* (New York: Crossroad, 1994), pp. 165, 185–93, 207–10; Bernard McGinn, *The Presence of God: A History of Western Christian Mysticism*, vol. 3, *The Flowering of Mysticism: Men and Women in the New Mysticism (1200–1350)* (New York: Crossroad, 1998), pp. 155–70. For the argument that mysticism became more erotic because of the influence of courtly love literature, see Barbara Newman, *From Virile Woman to WomanChrist* (Philadelphia: University of Pennsylvania Press, 1995), pp. 137–67, esp. 137–9.

[18] Beatrice of Nazareth, "Seven Manners of Loving," in *Mediaeval Netherlands Religious Literature*, trans. and intro. E. Colledge (Leiden, The Netherlands: Sythoff, 1965), p. 23.

[19] Gertrude of Helfta, *The Herald of Divine Love*, trans. Margaret Winkworth (New York: Paulist Press, 1993), p. 126. For Bernard's version see, e.g., Sermon 2, in *On the Song of Songs*, trans. Killian Walsh and Irene Edmonds, 4 vols. (Kalamazoo, MI: Cistercian Publications 1971–80), vol. 1, pp. 6–15.

Intimately united with Christ in the sepulchre "she had first of all kissed Christ's breast, then kissed his mouth ... then placed his hand on her other cheek, pressing herself closely to him."[20] James of Vitry's life of Marie of Oignies (d. 1213) describes her "resting with her Bridegroom" in bed for three days: "The more she felt God, the more her desire increased. She was tormented, she cried out and begged that He remain and to prevent him from leaving, she embraced Him within her arms and tearfully prayed that he show Himself more to her."[21]

Teresa of Avila's sixteenth-century commentary on the Song of Songs, which ecclesial authorities ordered her to burn, dwelt on the most erotic lines in the biblical text: "Let Him kiss me with a Kiss of His mouth" and "Thy breasts are better than wine for they give off fragrance of sweet odours."[22] This culminates in a passage that draws the maternal and erotic together; the interweaving of bride and nursing child, bridegroom and nursing mother, one who nourishes and one who pleasures, reveals how difficult it is to differentiate between the desires for food and touch, sleep and sex, between arousal and satisfaction:

> But when this most wealthy Spouse desires to enrich and comfort the Bride still more, He draws her so closely to Him that she is like one who swoons from excess of pleasure and joy and seems to be suspended in those Divine arms and drawn near to that sacred side and to those Divine breasts. Sustained by that Divine milk with which her Spouse continually nourishes her and growing in grace so that she may be enabled to receive His comforts, she can do nothing but rejoice. Awakening from that sleep and heavenly inebriations, she is like one amazed and stupefied.[23]

Responding to those who wondered whether God couldn't find more suitable images, Teresa defended the Song of Song's maternal eroticism as "the language used by the Holy Spirit."[24] This is a language not only of physicality but also of relationality. As she explains in her *Autobiography*, Teresa found that distress or despair is marked, above all, by a feeling of intense loneliness. What she receives through her

---

[20] Angela Foligno, *The Complete Works*, trans. Paul Lachance (New York: Paulist Press, 1993), pp. 148, 182.
[21] James of Vitry, *The Life of Marie d'Oignies*, trans. Margot King (Saskatoon, SK: Peregrina Publishing, 1987), p. 84.
[22] Teresa of Avila, "Conceptions of the Love of God," in *The Complete Works of Saint Teresa of Jesus*, trans. E. Allison Peers (London: Sheed and Ward, 1982), vol. 2, pp. 352–99. Also see Weber, *Teresa of Avila*, pp. 115–17.
[23] Teresa of Avila, "Conceptions," p. 359.
[24] Ibid., p. 360.

visions and raptures is the experience of finding that "the most sacred humanity becomes our Companion."[25]

So the chapter describing ecstasy in Teresa's *Autobiography* is framed by her insistence that she must escape herself and the limits of her imagination through tactile intimacy: "How could we picture Christ's humanity by merely studying the subject or form any impression of His great beauty by means of the imagination?"[26] Thus she equates the feeling of "dying with the desire to see God" with the experience of being "incapable of containing" herself and insists that this desire is not internal. It is not a "physical restlessness within the breast" or an "uncontrollable devotional feeling" nor is it an experience that she initiates, for "the soul does not try to feel the pain of the wound caused by the Lord's absence." What she seeks to describe instead is the experience of being consumed by another. Teresa first likens this to being cast into a fire, but then represents it instead as being pierced by an arrow that is "driven into the very depths of the entrails, and sometimes into the heart, so that the soul does not know either what is the matter with it or what it desires." Like an aphrodisiac, the arrow leads the heart to "hate itself for the love of this Lord."[27] In place of the undifferentiated conflagration signified by fire, Teresa's arrow conveys the force of desire that alters one's sense of bodily boundaries; disturbing, desirous encounters subsume self-love and enable love of God.[28]

The physicality of this event is vital, even though Teresa also impugns the body. In *Interior Castle*, she emphasizes that mystical marriage has nothing to do with physical sensations, "for this secret union takes place in the deepest center of the soul."[29] Yet she destabilizes this claim with her incarnational theology, especially evident in passages that ruminate on Christ's physicality – on the color of his eyes and his height, on the turmoil and confusion, and then certainty and security Teresa feels when pondering the sight of his hands and his face, and on the details of his body before and after his death.[30] Steeped in the incarnation, Teresa equates experiencing God with the exhilaration caused

---

[25] Teresa of Avila, *Autobiography*, pp. 193, 250.
[26] Ibid., p. 268.
[27] Ibid., p. 273.
[28] The close connections between physical force, divine possession, and sexual pleasure are evident in the fact that the medieval Latin term *raptus* signified all three. See Dyan Elliott, "The Physiology of Rapture and Female Spirituality," in *Medieval Theology and the Natural Body*, ed. Peter Biller and A. J. Minnis (York: York Medieval Press, 1997); and Dyan Elliott's contribution to this volume.
[29] Teresa of Avila, *Interior Castle*, in *The Complete Works*, vol. 2, p. 334.
[30] Teresa of Avila, *Autobiography*, pp. 259, 269.

by seeing, touching, or being pierced by another. If this should not be "reduced" to sex, neither does it exclude sex. As Karma Lochrie explains, mystical desire is "queer in its effects – exceeding and hyperbolizing its own conventionality and fracturing the discourses of mystical love and sex."[31] Mystical sexuality – the physical abandon caused by fantasmatic or sensory contact with other bodies – viscerally conveys that we are never wholly self-contained, never fully bounded, never fully in control of bodies or of language.

MYSTICISM AND MARRIED SEX

The medieval Catholic mystics whose sexual language has been so richly theorized had taken some sort of vow of celibacy, and so even if we eschew simplistic theories of sublimation – that they fantasized about sex because they were not having sex – we might well speculate that rejecting normative sexual activity enabled people to reimagine sexuality in intense, creative, subversive, and excessive terms. But married Christians, and even communities of married Christians, could produce equally sexualized texts, as Nicolaus Ludwig, Count Zinzendorf (1700–60) and the eighteenth-century Moravians attest.

Zinzendorf, a pietist Lutheran, deeply influenced the Moravians with his controversial, ecstatic mystical writings. Christ's side wound, variously apprehended as tomb, womb, and vagina, became the focal point of devotion for Moravian men and women alike in mystical texts and hymns, simultaneously undermining and reinforcing gender differences. Thus a Moravian hymn encourages men to bathe their "maleness" in Christ's blood, even as it represents them in ungendered terms as receptacles or vessels of what they receive from Christ: "Oh holy covenant slit, oh holy wound, govern the true maleness of the sinful creatures whom you have sanctified as a marriage vessel with the circumcision blood."[32] The "maleness" sanctified by Christ's blood becomes the metaphoric site of marriage, but Moravians literalized this connection to intercourse between men and women with instructional cards for married couples.

---

[31] Lochrie, "Mystical Acts," p. 183.
[32] *Das Litaneye-Büchlein nach der bey den Brüdern dermalen hauptsächlich gewöhnlichen Singe-Weise von neuem revidirt, und in dieser bequemen Form ausgegeben von dem Cantore Fratrum Ordinario*, 4th ed. (Barby, 1757), pp. 193–4; see also *The Litany-book, According to the Manner of Singing At present mostly in Use among the BRETHREN, Again revised, translated from the 4th German ed.* (London, 1759), p. 174, cited in Craig Atwood, "Sleeping in the Arms of Christ: Sanctifying Sexuality in the Eighteenth-Century Moravian Church," *Journal of the History of Sexuality* 8, no. 1 (1997): 33, n. 26.

These cards, adorned with representations of Christ's wound, direct couples on where and how to have sex and exhort men, for example, to read aloud an appropriate prayer as they ejaculated.[33]

In representing the wound in terms most often associated with female genitalia, however, the Moravians extend a long tradition of medieval iconography. Medieval writers demonstrate that this feminized image need not have only feminized connotations. The spear that penetrated the male Christ's body released salvific blood, and the wound was thus linked to fertility, nurturance, and healing. The medieval mystic Angela Foligno, for example, described how Christ directed her to drink the blood "freshly flowing from his side" so it might cleanse her. Writers also likened the wound to the clefts in the rock described in Song of Songs 2:14 ("My dove in the clefts of the rock, in the crannies of the wall, show me your face, let your voice sound in my ears"), and so Christ's body is both rock hard, impenetrable, and yet also full of holes or crannies where, as Bernard of Clairvaux imagines, the beloved could imbibe sweet honey.[34] The exegetical, allegorical creativity of medieval writers was in no way confined by a strict delineation between male and female, or masculine and feminine qualities such as penetration versus nurturing care.

In linking the vaginal wound to heterosexual marital sex, the Moravians seem, by contrast, to bind it to a binary notion of sexuality. Yet the play of images in their texts cannot finally be characterized as upholding marital sex over celibacy, or heterosexuality over homosexuality. Thus Zinzendorf laments that men are not able to "throw themselves bluntly with heart and body into the Savior's arms" because they are not able "to conceive, as the sisters do," but he also describes how a man, "captivated by the person of Jesus," discards his social identity to become "a playmate for the marriage bed of the blessed Creator and eternal Husband of the human soul."[35] The Moravians reinforced a male-female binary based on genital differences through their liturgical

---

[33] These images are reproduced and discussed in Aaron Fogleman, *Jesus Is Female: Moravians and the Challenge of Radical Religion in Early America* (Philadelphia: University of Pennsylvania Press, 2007), pp. 73–86.

[34] Cited in Amy Hollywood, "'That Glorious Slit': Irigaray and the Medieval Devotion to Christ's Side Wound," in *Luce Irigaray and Premodern Culture: Thresholds of History*, ed. Elizabeth D. Harvey and Theresa Krier (New York: Routledge, 2005), pp. 105–25. See Bernard of Clairvaux, *On the Song of Songs*, vol. 3, p. 142.

[35] Peter C. Erb, ed., *Pietists: Selected Writings* (New York: Paulist Press, 1983), p. 323; and Zinzendorf, "Berlin Reden," foreword to the sermons to the men, in *Hauptschriften in sechs Bänden*, ed. Erich Beyreuther and Gerhard Meyer, 6 vols. (Hildesheim: G. Olms, 1962), vol. 1, 6 (unnumbered).

devotions to Christ's penis and Mary's womb.[36] Directed to men and women alike, however, this devotional literalism could also destabilize the assumption of heterosexuality. These texts push our attention away from judgments concerning normativity or subversion by foregrounding the more subtle but equally important dynamic of how bodies and people shift and change in relation to one another.

If Moravians imagined mystical sex as a transformative model for marital sex, many other mystical texts seem to present it as a substitution. Consider Ann Lee (d. 1784), the founder of the Shakers, who refused to have sex with her husband and then, according to her followers, proclaimed Christ her husband and lover.[37] When Margery Kempe (d. ca. 1439) did the same thing four hundred years earlier, she reported that Christ told her a wife must be "homely" with her husband, "therefore must I needs be homely with you." Christ further explained that he would "lie in your bed with you ... and you may boldly, when you are in your bed, take me to you as your wedded husband ... and therefore you may boldly take me in the arms of your soul and kiss my mouth, my head, and my feet as sweetly as you will."[38]

These somatic details, typical of medieval experiential mysticism, are not common by Lee's time, and several scholars have argued that the eighteenth century marks an important historical shift: just as the rise of somatic, erotic mysticism can be dated to the thirteenth century and attributed in part to the influence of courtly literature as well as to the emergence of new kinds of religious movements, so too the decline has something to do with the conventions of eighteenth-century romance literature and evangelical revivalism.[39] Lee is reported to have spoken about her body becoming skeletal and of being born into a new flesh, "like the flesh of an infant."[40] She is also reportedly described feeling the blood of Christ washing throughout her soul and body and bearing the marks of Christ on her body. But Susan Juster argues that Lee was one of the only eighteenth-century American prophetic figures to claim

---

[36] Atwood, "Sleeping in the Arms of Christ," p. 26.

[37] *Testimonies of the Life, Character, Revelations, and Doctrines of Our Ever Blessed Mother Ann Lee* (Hancock, MA, 1816), pp. 206-7, 212-13 (hereafter cited as *1816 Testimonies*). See also Jean Humez, ed., *Mother's First-Born Daughters: Early Shaker Writings on Women and Religion* (Bloomington: Indiana University Press, 1993), p. 28, n.8.

[38] Margery Kempe, *The Book of Margery Kempe*, trans. B. A. Windeatt (New York: Viking Penguin, 1985), ch. 36, pp. 126-7.

[39] Ruth Bloch, "Changing Conceptions of Sexuality and Romance in Eighteenth-century America," *William and Mary Quarterly* 60, no. 1 (2003): 13-42.

[40] Humez, *1816 Testimonies*, pp. 47-8.

somatic incorporation into Christ, and Lee bequeathed no other visions of being physically aroused by Christ or God. Phyllis Mack similarly argues that "the boundaryless, almost liquefied eroticism" found in the texts of seventeenth-century Quaker visionaries (both male and female) and the bridal mysticism pervasive among the Moravians are largely absent from works produced by eighteenth-century Methodists, even in hymns that exhort the believer to sit in Christ's side wound. "For eighteenth-century religious seekers," Mack concludes, "spiritual enlightenment was experienced, not in the ecstasy of the purified body, but in the dominance of mind *over* body."[41] According to Mack, grotesque or excessive details or proud depictions of insanity or rapture are not readily found in modern mystical texts. (Flannery O'Connor's stories readily remind us of the limits of Mack's generalization, for O'Connor represents the mysticism of Pentecostalism and some forms of Catholicism in vivid descriptions of Christians apprehending divine power. But it remains the case that these manifestations of mysticism are no longer as prevalent as they once were.)

Yet this narrative of historical change can obscure what Kempe's and Lee's very different representations of claiming Christ as a spousal lover have in common: the divine replacement is not best understood as a substitute, if by this we imagine either that the one is very much the same as the other or that the divine represents a static ideal that can compensate for all the failures of their human husbands. In both cases, although clearly with less evidence in the case of Lee, the relationship with Christ is described as relational, as interactive and changeable, as constituted through aspirations and specific behaviors and the particularities of contact, of touch and reaction, between two beings.

The continuities and changes in mystical sex are suggested in two final examples. In 1793, Catherine Livingston Garrettson, just home from church where she heard a sermon on Christ's injunction to "love the Lord thy God with all thy heart," found herself blissfully in the presence of God, caught up in "remarkable operations" that led her to wonder, "does temptation mix itself with the work of God?" God was still with her the next day; enflamed with love "I find the body is not large enough for the Capatious Spirit which dwells within. It now seems as if it would burst thro' the Clay temenent [sic] in Acts of love and surrender to its Cheif [sic] Good."[42] Like countless mystical writers before

[41] Phyllis Mack, "Religious Dissenters in Enlightenment England," in *History Workshop Journal* 49 (2000): 1–23, on p. 7.
[42] Diane Helen Lobody, "Lost in the Ocean of Love: The Mystical Writings of Catherine Livingston Garrettson," PhD diss., Drew University, 1990, pp. 276–7.

her, Garrettson found the interpretive key to this experience in the Song of Songs: "I am my beloved's and my beloved is mine." When, weeks later, she again felt "Jesus reigning in me and filling soul and body with his blissful presence" she cried out, like Paul, "it is no more I that live but Christ living in me" – citing Galatians 2:20, a text quoted in analogous contexts by writers as diverse as Pseudo-Dionysius and Madame Guyon (d. 1717).[43] As we track the variable excitement about ecstasy and arousal, and thus about sexuality, in Christian mysticism, we learn also about the centrality and elasticity of these canonical texts.

When we come across a passage from a nineteenth-century Southern Methodist describing how when Jesus "draws nigh ... the effulgent beams of his brightness have overcome me ... I burn, I melt, I blaze, I sicken, all faint with love divine ... the fire of Jesu's love hath taken possession of all my soul and every vein beats with young life and sweet salvation," we confront an ecstasy that, like Teresa's, seeks to convey that intersubjective bodily experience can enact transcendence. The author, Sarah Jones, wrote another passage even more closely related to our opening scene from Teresa: "my adorable Jesus unveiled his rosy face; and his sparkling eyes almost made me faint: I fell on the ground and again pitched glory unto Heaven, it darted like lightening, and the thunderbolt struck somewhere about **** I thought."[44] Jones's omission suggests a lack of confidence; this marks the historical gap between a sixteenth-century Catholic nun who wrote for sisters and confessors steeped in exegesis of the Song of Songs and other visionary devotional texts, and a nineteenth-century Protestant wife and mother informed instead by emotional revivalism. But the crossed-out word also underscores that the effect of the penetration is more important than the location. Mystical sexuality is about the intense pleasure and pain that bodies inflict and receive, and about the ecstasy, standing outside oneself, the rhythmic arousal and breathless pleasure that come from and in this experience.

---

[43] Ibid., p. 288.
[44] Quoted in Cynthia Lynn, "Passion, Desire, and Ecstasy: The Experience of Religion of Southern Methodist Women, 1770–1810," in *The Devil's Lane: Sex and Race in the Early South*, ed. Catherine Clinton and Michele Gillespie (Oxford: Oxford University Press, 1997), pp. 179, 180.

22 Time and Memory
PATRICIA DAILEY

> Forgetting the created
> Memory of the creator
> Awareness of the inner
> And always loving the beloved
>
> Saint John of the Cross, The Sum of Perfection

> At the beginning, as in the ancient shaman or Hindu forms of *mystics*, there is a rhythm. Where does it come from? No one knows.... The sounds, resembling fragments of refrain, form an uncanny memory, prior to meaning. One would be hard put to say what it is the memory of: it recalls something that is not a past; it awakens what the body does not know about itself.
>
> Michel de Certeau, The Mystic Fable

Mystical texts are riddled by different forms of temporal expression: by dates that mark the contiguity of liturgical hours and visions, by memories of divine visitations, by a desire to inhabit a memory of the imitation of Christ, by promises of divine love and hope for a future moment of perfection in God. Generally speaking, two different times are expressed, one chronological or historical and the second atemporal or eternal, a time outside of time, the time of God, which is not subject to change or to mediation and remains identical with itself. This Augustinian model, inherited by many Christian mystics, posits a human existence necessarily mediated by time, one that aspires to the promise of eternal salvation or union by means of memory.[1]

---

[1] Although mystical texts often focus on the historical time of Christ's crucifixion, the meaning is allegorical while not necessarily futural: its true meaning does not refer to a distant future, but to the immanent present of suffering with Christ and becoming "what we already are," to use a phrase of Hadewijch's. The mystic refashions the traditional reading of history's relation to literal and allegorical truth, exemplified by Hugh of Saint Victor (1096–1141): "The literal is the narrative of history, expressed in the basic meaning of the letter. Allegory is when, by means of this event in the story ...

The expression of time in mystic texts is complex, for the texts invoke a memory that does not find its source in everyday experience. The term experience is misleading, for the mystic text invokes the memory of what I will call an unlived experience: it invokes a memory, like the imitation of Christ, that is lived only as a promise. It invokes a memory, like the memory of union with the divine, that lies outside of time, anchored in the realm of the eternal.[2] As Michel de Certeau notes, the rhythm of the mystic text "recalls an uncanny memory, prior to meaning ... it recalls something that is not a past."[3] Like a postmemory (of scripture and traditions of exegesis, perhaps) that traverses generations and "characterizes the experience of those who grow up dominated by narratives that preceded their birth" and thus have no direct historical access to its referent, the memory of the mystic does not belong, properly speaking, to the individual person who recalls it.[4] Yet rather than postmemory, I would call this memory prememory, for it is oriented to something that claims to be before history and before space. Here I will show how the mystic text is structured and constituted by this prememory of an unlived experience, and how it attempts to bridge disparate temporalities through a performative dimension of the text and of the body. I explore how different kinds of memory are used or invoked by the mystical text and the ensuing temporal effects: how, for example, objects and images, or artificial memory, prompt associations and feelings that allow for mnemonic recall and affective incarnations of Christ's Passion; how dates and hours work as temporal markers in accessing the atemporal; how texts function as forms of collective memory that may be countersigned by a confessor or monastic community; and how the memory of this unlived experience is structured like that

---

another action is signified, belonging to past or present or future time." Hugh of Saint Victor, "The Three Best Memory Aids for Learning History," in *The Medieval Craft of Memory*, ed. Mary Carruthers and Jan M. Ziolkowski (Philadelphia: University of Pennsylvania Press, 2002), p. 39. By contrast, the mystic text refashions this distinction, in allowing the desired eternal to be hosted by the present while not identical with it.

[2] I agree with Michael Scanlon when he argues that "for Augustine, salvation is redemption *from* the perpetual perishing that is history – it is not the redemption *of* history. The fulfillment of Christian hope is transhistorical in God's eternity beyond history." Michael Scanlon, "Arendt's Augustine," in *Augustine and Postmodernism*, ed. John Caputo and Michael Scanlon (Bloomington: Indiana University Press, 2005), p. 169.

[3] Michel de Certeau, *The Mystic Fable* (Chicago: University of Chicago Press, 1992), p. 297.

[4] I am referring to Marianne Hirsch's use of the term postmemory to characterize the memory of the children of Holocaust survivors. See Marianne Hirsch, "Past Lives: Postmemories in Exile," *Poetics Today* 17, no. 4 (Winter 1996): 559–686, p. 559.

of a traumatic event, reconfiguring the interrelation between meaning, experience, language, event, and time.

The memory of the mystic belongs to the atemporal and eternal soul, universal in nature: John Tauler (ca. 1300–61) reminds us that "Saint Augustine says that the soul has a hidden abyss, untouched by time and space.... Here the soul has its eternal abode."[5] In his short poem *The Sum of Perfection*, Saint John of the Cross (1542–91) phrases this paradoxical recall in terms of a double movement: remembering the creator (what Augustine calls recalling God within by means of the memory of the image of God in which humanity was created), and forgetting the created, that is, forgetting all that is bound to historical time, creation, the self, and the distraction of thought – in short, to all that exists under the sign of separation from God. As the *Cloud of Unknowing* emphasizes, "just as this cloud of unknowing is above you, between you and your God, so you must put beneath you a cloud of forgetting, between you and all the creatures that have ever been made."[6] For John of the Cross, as for many mystics, this movement assumes the figure of love, and its ultimate end is the remnant of love that effaces all but itself, the living memory of the divine.

Many mystical texts explicitly set one foot in the material of historical time, tethering awareness of the divine to a specific date or hour. The mystic anchors her memory, nonexperience, or text in a shared time and space, in a similar (although not identical) fashion as she may rely upon the mnemonic function of external objects; both exist in counterpoint to the atemporal and inner nature of mystical experience or consciousness. "One day when I had been walking solitarily abroad and was coming home, I was taken up in the love of God," writes George Fox, the seventeenth-century Quaker.[7] The date is often paired with the cyclical time of liturgical ritual: Hadewijch, the thirteenth-century Brabant beguine writes, "It was at Matins on the feast *In nativitate beatae Mariae* [on the Nativity of the Blessed Mary] and after the Third Lesson something wonderful was shown me in the spirit."[8] Ignatius of Loyola's (1491–1556) *Spiritual Diaries* are prompted by the cycles of the mass: "The First Day of Lent. [Ash Wednesday]. Wednesday [February 27]. Upon entering the

---

[5] John Tauler, *Sermons*, trans. Maria Shrady and Joseph Schmidt (New York: Paulist Press, 1985), p. 89.
[6] James Walsh, ed., *The Cloud of Unknowing*, (New York: Paulist Press, 1981), ch. 5, p. 128.
[7] George Fox, *An Autobiography*, ed. Rufus M. Jones (Philadelphia: Philadelphia Friends' Book Store, 1903), p. 84.
[8] Hadewijch, *Complete Works*, trans. Columba Hart (New York: Paulist Press, 1980), Vision 9, p. 285. Slightly modified citation.

chapel, during prayer, I perceived deeply in my heart ... the Most Holy Trinity and Jesus."[9] Henry Suso's (d.1366) *Little Book of Eternal Wisdom* begins, "A Dominican friar was once standing before a crucifix after matins."[10] This coupling of the mystical text and a form of dating or embeddedness in communal time performs several functions: first, it allows for a textual and temporal pivot between historical (or cyclical) and eternal time; second, it complements the text's function as testimony and record of a spiritual experience; and third, it provides a model for future meditation on and desired union with God.

As a pivot between at least two times, the mystical text is a narrative that bears witness to the manifestation of the divine and to a way of approaching God. Liturgical calendars and hours also function as manifestations of the divine, reorganizing the material of history into a manifestation and lived experience of the Bible and thereby enabling what Susan Boynton calls performative exegesis. The mystical text functions as a testimonial of biblical or spiritual truth, the experience of which counters the communal nature of ritual in that it cannot be shared, it can only promise to be on an individual basis.[11] Because the mystic text claims to bear witness to the mystery of God, to a secret of how God dwells and is manifest in the paradoxical hiddenness of the soul, the text functions as a form of testimony. It asks for the faith of the reader or listener and attests to a spiritual truth that is both absolutely singular and universal. It implicitly or explicitly claims to have access to a time outside of time, the memory of which is marked by time and is temporalized by the language of the text itself.

The difference between liturgical and mystical time may be further understood in terms of mysticism's interiorization of its Pauline influence. While Christian mysticism inherits the incommensurability of the eternal from Augustine, it claims a Pauline legacy that asserts the realization of the mystery of God. For Paul, the *mysterion*, the divine mystery, is the accomplishment or realization of God's design or image in Christ (*syn Christo*), first hidden from human beings and then made manifest. Important here is that Paul insists on the now (*nyn*), of the realization of the mystery between humanity and God.[12] In this now-time,

---

[9] Ignatius of Loyola, *The Spiritual Exercises and Selected Works*, ed. George E. Ganss (New York: Paulist Press, 1991), p. 251.

[10] Henry Suso, "The Little Book of Eternal Wisdom," in *Henry Suso: The Exemplar, with Two German Sermons*, trans. Frank Tobin (New York: Paulist Press, 1989), p. 207.

[11] See Susan Boynton, "Performative Exegesis in the Fleury *Interfectio Puerorum*," *Viator* 29 (1998): 39–64.

[12] See Romans 8:18; 11:5; 12:2.

the *mysterion* may be known and lived by the members of the church, the *corpus mysticum*, in the form of the sacrament. Mysticism takes this one step further in claiming an experience or consciousness of the mystery, often through the figure of Christ, the temporal manifestation of divinity par excellence. While mystics may place an importance on the historical Christ, many mystics shift the emphasis from the historical event to the figure of Christ as promise that may be accessed in a moment hosted by the present.

Meister Eckhart (d. 1328) radicalizes the temporal possibility of this moment, proposing that the present implicitly always hosts an immanent "now" (what Tauler calls an "instant") that may bridge historical and eternal time. In his sermons, he configures the now-time as an eternal rebirth in God, available to the individual soul:

> God creates the world and all things in a present now [*in einem gegenwärtigen Nun*], and the time which passed a thousand years ago is as present and near to God as the time which is now [*die Zeit, die jetzt ist*]. As for the soul that remains in a present now [*in einem gegenwärtigen Nun*], the Father gives birth to his only-begotten Son into it, and in this same birth the soul is born back into God. All this is one birth.[13]

In another of his German sermons, he writes that

> three things hinder us from hearing the Eternal word. The first is corporality, the second multiplicity, the third temporality [*Zeitlichkeit*]. If a person had passed beyond these three things, he would live in eternity, in the spirit, in oneness, and in the vast solitude; and there he would hear the Eternal word.[14]

Although the articulation of the "now" and its relation to eternal rebirth is complex, Eckhart provides a way of understanding the role of the text in relation to this "now" time, which promises to free the soul from its temporal constraints. On the theological level, the text makes an assertion about temporal relationships between the soul and God, and, as I have shown, it must paradoxically temporalize its assertions about the eternal, given that it uses language to do so. On a textual level, Eckhart's sermons often speak of this rebirth in the present or past (with reference to "the time which passed" or to what "God creates"), yet he often uses

---

[13] Meister Eckhart, *Teacher and Preacher*, trans. Bernard McGinn and Frank J. Tobin (New York: Paulist Press, 1986), Sermon 10, p. 265.
[14] Ibid., Sermon 12, p. 267.

a modal verb in appealing to an individual's approach to the mystery ("This is how that person should be who wants to do x or y").

This textual and verbal shuttling, what I called earlier a temporal pivot between a divine "is" or "was" and an explicit (or implicit) human "should," "would," and thus "will" or "may be," brings together disparate temporalities within the mystic text. While at the theological level, Eckhart's ecstatic "now" promises to bridge historical and eternal time for the individual's soul, so too does his text promise to bridge historical and eternal time, in providing a virtual index – the reflection of an invisible matrix – of how times conjoin, thus providing an example for the individual to follow. Whether the text is a sermon, vision, or poem – whatever the form of the mystic text – the atemporal shadows the language of the text as its double. The eternal echoes through the text in the modal tense, in the promise of an instant to come that is always already there. Whether the text explicitly articulates this promise in the urgency of a "should" or a "will be," the promise will always underlie the text in the possibility of repetition for the individual who follows.

The Protestant mystic Johann Arndt (1555–1621) makes the prescriptive aspect of the text even clearer, and urges that the text's addressee seek God through the figure of the kingdom within: "In order to understand me rightly in this Third Book [*True Christianity*], know that it is intended to point out how you are to seek and find the kingdom of God in yourself (Lk 17:21)."[15] As with many mystics, in Arndt, the figure for the atemporal is conjoined with the topographical. For Saint Gregory of Nyssa (335–94), it is articulated as an apprehension of a graphic trace. Using an image that recalls the Aristotelian image of the writing tablet, he notes that "the measure of what is accessible to you is in you.... God has imprinted upon your constitution replicas of the good things in his own nature, as though stamping wax with the shape of a design."[16] The sense of following an imprint is expressed by Saint Francis of Assisi (1181/2–1226) in a prayer asking that we follow in Christ's footprints, "May we be able to follow / in the footprints of Your beloved Son."[17] Although the imprint may be read as a figure of the image of God within us or of the Christic trace engendered by the imitation of Christ, the figural aspect of the memory of the eternal may also be transposed into the register of affect. Not only does

---

[15] Johann Arndt, *True Christianity*, trans. Peter Erb (New York: Paulist Press, 1979), p. 221.

[16] Gregory of Nyssa, *Homilies on the Beatitudes*, ed. Hubertus R. Drobner and Albert Viciano (Leiden, The Netherlands: Brill, 2000), p. 70.

[17] Francis of Assisi, "A Prayer of St. Francis," in *Francis and Claire: The Complete Works*, trans. Regis J. Armstrong and Ignatius Brady (New York: Paulist Press, 1982), p. 61.

the mystic text speak about the atemporal as imprint or as now-time and propose a way of apprehending it, it can also be affected by it, in terms of its way of speaking about it, that is, in the poetic impact of apophatic language, and in the way it affects the soul.

William of Saint Thierry (ca. 1085–1148) explains that "memory brings the thoughts that arise from these good things to the intellect so that they can be given form as an *affectus* [in the soul] ... [thus becoming] the joy of a person who has found delight."[18] As the soul may bear a trace of this imprint, so may the body of the mystic. John of the Cross speaks of how God affects the soul's memory in terms of a divine touch:

> God effects in the soul what it is incapable of acquiring. God usually grants these divine touches, which cause certain remembrances of Him, at times when the soul is least expecting or thinking of them. Sometimes they are produced suddenly through some remembrance, which may only concern some slight detail. They are so sensible that they sometimes cause not only the soul, but also the body to tremble.[19]

Whereas Eckhart's text provides temporal figures for internal pivots toward the eternal, and Gregory and John of the Cross use spatial and affective figures for internal recollection, the body and the experience of touch and pain are important figures for women's mystical texts of the Middle Ages and early modern period, as if the body provided a mnemonic record for a memory that cannot yet be perceived or comprehended, only felt. As Michel de Certeau explains, "one would be hard put to say what it is the memory of: it recalls something that is not a past; it awakens what the body does not know about itself."[20]

In a significant number of women's mystical texts, the play of time, memory, affect, body, language, and the eternal is attenuated to the point of staging a form of temporal drama that unfolds in dislocated temporalities. Medieval mystics or visionaries such as Julian, Hadewijch, and Hildegard of Bingen (1098–1179) claim, after the fact, to experience a visitation or vision, which occurs in time, often on a specific date or a specific hour. However, the vision is outside of time, in that the mystic's inner body or soul experiences an awareness or proximity to the

---

[18] William of Saint Thierry, "Golden Letter," in *The Essential Writings of Christian Mysticism*, ed. and trans. Bernard McGinn (New York: Random House, 2006), pp. 254–5.

[19] John of the Cross, *Selected Writings*, ed. Kieran Kavanaugh (New York: Paulist Press, 1987), p. 139.

[20] Certeau, *The Mystic Fable*, p. 297.

divine, which may be beyond the grasp of language. Like the unassimilated memory of a traumatic event, this unlived experience continues to haunt the mystic, often in the somatic form of bodily pain. Hildegard writes, almost in the spirit of public confession, that after years of keeping her vision silent, "I was forced by a great pressure of pains to manifest what I had seen and heard."[21] The body's pain carries within it the force of those memories that the soul can no longer contain. For Julian, the writing of the *Showings* is delayed: she receives her revelations on May 13, 1373, yet it is only "fifteen years after and more" that her question as to their meaning is "answered in spiritual understanding" and she is able to compose her text.[22]

This temporal syncopation of event, meaning, and time has a similar structure to what Freud calls belatedness and Jean Laplanche calls afterwardsness, both describing the latency of trauma.[23] Initially grasped "only in the very inaccessibility of its occurrence," like the wounding nature of traumatic experience, the divine visitation is silenced for lengths of time and is not fully understood when it happens.[24] For the mystic, the vision accrues meaning over time, as the mystic attains spiritual growth and understanding. Yet the divine visitation is never completely understood, for the mystic never attains complete identification with the source of her experience. Although the mystic may often assert in the vision that she "saw and understood," the content of this understanding remains elusive even when put into writing, for it is God, not the mystic, who is its source. Whatever understanding is permitted is delayed; consequently, the event is only fully experienced and comprehended with its articulation in language. It is as though historical time has to catch up with the envelope of an atemporal experience, which is

[21] Peter Dronke, *Women Writers of the Middle Ages: A Critical Study of Texts from Perpetua (d. 203) to Marguerite Porete (d. 1310)* (Cambridge: Cambridge University Press, 1984), p. 145.
[22] Julian of Norwich, *Showings*, trans. and ed. Edmund College and James Walsh (New York: Paulist Press, 1978), p. 342.
[23] See Sigmund Freud, *Beyond the Pleasure Principle*, trans. James Strachey (New York: W. W. Norton, 1990); Jean Laplanche, *Life and Death in Psychoanalysis*, trans. Jeffrey Mehlman (Baltimore, MD: The Johns Hopkins University Press, 1976); and Jean Laplanche, "Notes on Afterwardsness," in *Jean Laplanche: Seduction, Translation, Drives*, ed. John Fletcher and Martin Stanton (London: ICA editions, 1993), pp. 217–27.
[24] Cathy Caruth, *Unclaimed Experience* (Baltimore, MD: The Johns Hopkins University Press, 1996), p. 18. Dominick LaCapra warns of the dangers of sacralizing and aestheticizing trauma in forging parallels with the experience of divine transcendence. See Dominick LaCapra, *History in Transit: Experience, Identity, Critical Theory* (Ithaca, NY: Cornell University Press, 2004), pp. 117–32.

not delivered at the moment it occurs, but is postdated to the time it is hosted in language and only then to the time of the affective register. As Cathy Caruth argues, "the experience of trauma, the fact of latency, would thus seem to consist, not in the forgetting of a reality that can hence never fully be known, but in an inherent latency within the event itself."[25] For the mystic, the incision of the eternal into the fabric of the everyday occurs as a disruptive occurrence that can only be absorbed and given a belated meaning, one experienced retroactively, as if for the first time.

In Julian's description of her *Showings*, a form of artificial memory seems to lead to the content of her vision. As she lies in bed with her desired life-threatening illness, she stares at a crucifix, prompting the fulfillment of her request for a bodily sight of the passion of Christ. The crucifix is an external sign, a condensation of Christ's Passion that provides for internal mnemonic recall and imitation, allowing her to first see Christ's bleeding head. Then, through the association of painful images of Christ's bleeding face, she is enabled in the time of the vision to participate in the historic event of Christ's crucifixion through compassion and imitation. The vision thus allows for a virtual restaging of historical time, but in the register of eternal time, the time of her soul's salvation.

In her eighth vision, a vision of the soul's victory over time, Hadewijch inverts the sense of the subject of recall, describing her return and departure from herself as though she were the object of recall and not the subject of memory. She writes as though the vision of victory over time *recalled her*, recalling her from her body to an originary eternity to which she belongs. At the end of the vision a figure speaks out to her:

> And [the Lord Champion] said: "Return again into your material being [*materie*] and let your works blossom forth. The blows of enmity are drawing near you. But you return as victor over all, for you have conquered all." Then I came back in myself as someone in new severe pain, and so I shall remain being until the day when I am again recalled to the experience from which I then turned away.[26]

Hadewijch's vision is signed by her return into her body, yet she waits to be recalled again to the experience shown to her in her vision, in the hoped-for event of another vision, if not in the hope of a triumph over

---

[25] Caruth, *Unclaimed Experience*, p. 17.
[26] Hadewijch, *Complete Works*, p. 284.

time in death. The vision promises Hadewijch a form of afterlife – in its prefiguration of the ultimate triumph, to be recalled away from the body, once and for all, and be delivered from historical time in the eternity of salvation. This inversion of recall also shows that the memory does not find its origin in the mystic, but in God. It is not her memory, but the memory of God, in the strange sense of the subjective and objective genitive. Although the mystic makes uses of her memory of the divine, often through contemplation of the living memory of God, who is Christ himself, ultimately the mystic attests that it is the divine that recalls her back to her origin, leaving behind her earthly body.

For Julian, the afterlife of the text also displays both senses of the genitive, attesting to her own spiritual practices as well as to the work of the divine in her, but its afterlife is of a different kind. At the very end of her *Showings*, she notes that the

> book is begun by God's gift and his grace, but it is not yet performed, as I see it. For charity, let us all join with God's working in prayer, thanking, trusting, rejoicing, for so will our good Lord be entreated, by the understanding which I took in all his own intention, and in the sweet words where he says most happily: I am the foundation of your beseeching.[27]

"Not yet performed," the book, a record of divine revelations, pleads for a continuation of its work – for a continuation according to what has already begun in the book itself, by God's gift and grace, that is, to what already performs as the work of the book, not as Julian's work, but God's. The book thus functions as a record or memory of the work of God in her, a work that must also be continued, in her actions and in her performance of Christ's Passion. Memory is not merely a turning to the past or to time immemorial, but also a guide to the timelessness of the future. The memory of God's work, God's memory of divinity working through her and by extension through all of his creatures, asks yet again to be hosted by the body in the promise of an ultimate and timeless performance.

---

[27] Julian, *Showings*, p. 342.

Select Bibliography of Christian Mystical Texts up to around 1750

Aelred of Rievaulx. *Treatises and the Pastoral Prayer*. Trans. Theodore Berkeley, Mary Paul Macpherson, and R. Penelope Lawson. Kalamazoo, MI: Cistercian Publications, 1971.
———. *The Mirror of Charity*. Trans. Elizabeth Connor. Kalamazoo, MI: Cistercian Publications, 1990.
———. *Spiritual Friendship*. Trans. Mark F. Williams. Scranton, PA: University of Scranton Press, 1994.
Angela of Foligno. *The Complete Works*. Trans. Paul Lachance. New York: Paulist Press, 1993.
Anselm of Canterbury. *The Prayers and Meditations of St. Anselm*. Trans. Benedicta Ward. Harmondsworth, UK: Penguin Books, 1973.
Arndt, Johann. *True Christianity*. Trans. Peter Erb. New York: Paulist Press, 1978.
Athanasius. *The Life of Antony and the Letter to Marcellinus*. Trans. Robert C. Gregg. New York: Paulist Press, 1980.
Augustine. *On Christian Doctrine*. Trans. D. W. Robertson Jr. Indianapolis: Bobbs-Merrill, 1958.
———. *On the Psalms*. Trans. Scholastica Hebgin and Felicitas Corrigan. 2 vols. Westminster, MD: Newman Press, 1960–1.
———. *The Literal Meaning of Genesis*. Trans. John Hammond Taylor. 2 vols. New York: Newman Press, 1982.
———. *Confessions*. Trans. Henry Chadwick. Oxford: Oxford University Press, 1991.
Barratt, Alexandra, ed. *Women's Writing in Middle English*. London: Longman, 1992.
Basil of Caesarea. *The Letters*. Trans. Roy J. Deferrari. 4 vols. Cambridge, MA: Harvard University Press, 1926–34.
Beatrice of Nazareth. "Seven Manners of Loving." In *Mediaeval Netherlands Religious Literature*. Trans. E. Colledge. Leiden, The Netherlands: Sythoff, 1965.
Benedict of Nursia. "The Rule of Saint Benedict." In *RB 1980: The Rule of Saint Benedict*. Ed. Timothy Fry. Collegeville, MN: The Liturgical Press, 1981.
———. *The Rule of Benedict*. Ed. and trans. Bruce L. Vernarde. Cambridge, MA: Harvard University Press, 2011.
Bernard of Clairvaux. *On the Song of Songs*. Trans. Killian Walsh and Irene Edmonds. 4 vols. Kalamazoo, MI: Cistercian Publications, 1971–80.

———. *On Loving God.* Trans. Emero Stiegman. Kalamazoo, MI: Cistercian Publications, 1995.

Bérulle, Pierre de. "Discourse on the State and Grandeurs of Jesus." In *Bérulle and the French School: Selected Writings.* Ed. William M. Thompson. Trans. Lowell M. Glendon. New York: Paulist Press, 1989.

Blamires, David, trans. *The Book of the Perfect Life: Theologia deutsch – theologia Germanica.* Walnut Creek, CA: AltaMira Press, 2003.

Bonaventure. *The Soul's Journey into God; The Tree of Life; The Life of Saint Francis.* Trans. Ewert Cousins. New York: Paulist Press, 1978.

Cassian, John. *The Conferences.* Trans. Boniface Ramsey. New York: Newman Press, 1997.

———. *The Institutes.* Trans. Boniface Ramsey. New York: Newman Press, 2000.

Cassiodorus. *Explanation of the Psalms.* Trans. P. G. Walsh. 2 vols. New York: Paulist Press, 1990–1.

Catherine of Siena. *The Dialogue.* Trans. Suzanne Noffke. New York: Paulist Press, 1980.

———. *The Letters of Catherine of Siena.* Trans. Suzanne Noffke. Tempe, AZ: Medieval and Renaissance Texts and Studies, 2000.

Cawley, Martinus, trans. *Send Me God: The Lives of Ida the Compassionate of Nivelles, Nun of La Ramée, Arnulf, Lay Brother of Villers, and Abundus, Monk of Villers.* Turnhout, Belgium: Brepols, 2003.

Denck, Hans. *Selected Writings of Hans Denck 1500–1527.* Ed. E. J. Furcha. Lewiston, NY: Edwin Mellen Press, 1989.

Eckhart, Meister. *The Essential Sermons, Commentaries, Treatises and Defense.* Trans. Edmund Colledge and Bernard McGinn. New York: Paulist Press, 1981.

———. *German Sermons and Treatises.* Trans. M. O'C. Walshe. 3 vols. London: Watkins, 1979–87.

———. *Teacher and Preacher.* Trans. Bernard McGinn with Frank Tobin and Elvira Borgstadt. New York: Paulist Press, 1986.

Elisabeth of Schönau. *The Complete Works.* Trans. Anne L. Clark. New York: Paulist Press, 2000.

Erb, Peter C., ed. *Pietists: Selected Writings.* New York: Paulist Press, 1983.

Evagrius of Pontus. *The Greek Ascetic Corpus.* Trans. Robert E. Sinkewicz. Oxford: Oxford University Press, 2003.

Feiss, Hugh, ed. *On Love: A Selection of Works by Hugh, Adam, Achard, Richard, and Godfrey of St. Victor.* Turnhout, Belgium: Brepols, 2011.

Fénelon, François de Salignac de la Mothe-. *Selected Writings.* Ed. and trans. Chad Helms. New York: Paulist Press, 2006.

Francis of Assisi. *Francis and Claire: The Complete Works.* Trans. Regis J. Armstrong and Ignatius Brady. New York: Paulist Press, 1982.

Francis of Sales. *Treatise on the Love of God.* Trans. Henry Benedict Mackey. Westminster, MD: Newman Press, 1953.

Fox, George. *An Autobiography.* Ed. Rufus M. Jones. Philadelphia: Ferris and Leach, 1903.

Gerson, Jean. *Early Works.* Trans. Brian Patrick McGuire. New York: Paulist Press, 1998.

Gertrude of Helfta. *Spiritual Exercises.* Trans. Gertrud Jaron Lewis and Jack Lewis. Kalamazoo, MI: Cistercian Publishers, 1989.
———. *The Herald of Divine Love.* Trans. Margaret Winkworth. New York: Paulist Press, 1993.
Gregory the Great. *Morals on the Book of Job.* Trans. John Henry Parker. 3 vols. Oxford and London: J. G. F. and J. Rivington, 1844.
———. *Dialogues.* Trans. Odo John Zimmerman. Washington, DC: The Catholic University of America Press, 1959.
———. *The Homilies of St. Gregory the Great on the Book of the Prophet Ezekiel.* Trans. Theodosia Gray. Etna, CA: Center for Traditionalist Orthodox Studies, 1990.
Gregory of Nyssa. *The Life of Moses.* Trans. Abraham J. Malherbe and Everett Ferguson. New York: Paulist Press, 1978a.
———. *The Lord's Prayer; The Beatitudes.* Trans. Hilda C. Graef. New York: Paulist Press, 1978b.
Guigo I. *The Meditations of Guigo I, Prior of the Charterhouse.* Trans. A. Gordon Mursell. Kalamazoo, MI: Cistercian Publications, 1995.
Guigo II. *The Ladder of Monks and Twelve Meditations: A Letter on the Contemplative Life.* Trans. Edmund Colledge and James Walsh. Kalamazoo, MI: Cistercian Publications, 1981.
Guyon, Jeanne Marie Bouvier de la Motte. *The Autobiography of Madame Guyon.* Trans. Thomas Taylor Allen. New Canaan, CT: Keats Publishing, 1980.
Habig, Marion, ed. *St. Francis of Assisi: Writings and Early Biographies; English Omnibus of the Sources for the Life of Saint Francis.* Chicago: Franciscan Herald, 1973.
Hadewijch. *Complete Works.* Trans. Columba Hart. New York: Paulist Press, 1980.
———. *Poetry of Hadewijch.* Trans. Marieke Van Baest. Leuven, Belgium: Peeters, 1998.
Hildegard of Bingen. *Scivias.* Trans. Columba Hart and J. Bishop. New York: Paulist Press, 1990.
Hilton, Walter. *The Scale of Perfection.* Trans. John Clark and Rosemary Dorward. New York: Paulist Press, 1991.
Hugh of Saint Victor. *Didascalicon.* Trans. Jerome Taylor. New York: Columbia University Press, 1961.
———. *On the Sacraments of the Christian Faith.* Trans. Roy J. Deferrari. Cambridge: Medieval Academy of America, 1976.
Ignatius of Loyola. *Letters of St. Ignatius of Loyola.* Trans. William J. Young. Chicago: Loyola University Press, 1959.
———. *The Spiritual Exercises and Selected Works.* Ed. George E. Ganss. New York: Paulist Press, 1991a.
———. *The Constitutions of the Society of Jesus.* Trans. George E. Ganss. New York: Paulist Press, 1991b.
James of Vitry. *The Life of Marie d'Oignies.* Trans. Margot H. King and Hugh Feiss. In *Mary of Oignies: Mother of Salvation.* Ed. Anneke B. Mulder-Bakker. Turnhout, Belgium: Brepols, 2006.
John Chrysostom. *On the Incomprehensible Nature of God.* Trans. Paul W. Harkins. Washington, DC: The Catholic University of America, 1984.

John of the Cross. *The Collected Works of Saint John of the Cross*. Trans. Kieran Kavanaugh and Otilio Rodriguez. Washington, DC: Institute of Carmelite Studies, 1979.

Julian of Norwich. *The Writing of Julian of Norwich: A Vision Showed to a Devout Woman and a Revelation of Love*. Ed. Nicholas Watson and Jacqueline Jenkins. University Park: Pennsylvania State University Press, 2006.

Kempe, Margery. *The Book of Margery Kempe*. Ed. Lynn Staley. New York: Norton, 2000.

Marguerite of Oingt. *Writing of Marguerite of Oingt Medieval Prioress and Mystic*. Trans. Renate Blumenfeld-Kosinski. Cambridge: D. S. Brewer, 1997.

Marguerite Porete. *The Mirror of Simple Souls*. Trans. Ellen Babinsky. New York: Paulist Press, 1993.

McGinn, Bernard, ed. *The Essential Writings of Christian Mysticism*. New York: Modern Library, 2006.

Mechthild of Magdeburg. *The Flowing Light of the Godhead*. Trans. Frank Tobin. New York: Paulist Press, 1998.

Molinos, Miguel de. *The Spiritual Guide*. Trans. Robert P. Baird. New York: Paulist Press, 2010.

Nicholas of Cusa. *Selected Spiritual Writings*. Trans. H. Lawrence Bond. New York: Paulist Press, 1997.

Origen. *The Song of Songs: Commentary and Homilies*. Trans. R. P. Lawson. New York: Newman Press, 1957.

———. *Commentary on the Epistle to the Romans, Books 1–5*. Trans. Thomas P. Scheck. Washington, DC: Catholic University of America Press, 2001.

Osuna, Francisco de. *The Third Spiritual Alphabet*. Trans. Mary E. Giles. New York: Paulist Press, 1981.

Petroff, Elisabeth Alvilda, ed. *Medieval Women's Visionary Literature*. Oxford: Oxford University Press, 1986.

Pseudo-Dionysius. *The Complete Works*. Trans. Paul Rorem and Colm Luibhéid. New York: Paulist Press, 1987.

Pseudo-Macarius. *The Fifty Spiritual Homilies; and, the Great Letter*. Trans. George A. Maloney. New York: Paulist Press, 1992.

Richard of Saint Victor. *The Twelve Patriarchs; The Mystical Ark; Book Three of the Trinity*. Trans. Grover A. Zinn. New York: Paulist Press, 1979.

Rolle, Richard. *The Fire of Love*. Trans. Clifton Wolters. Harmondsworth, UK: Penguin, 1972.

———. *The English Writings*. Trans. Rosalind S. Allen. New York: Paulist Press, 1988.

Ruusbroec, John. *The Spiritual Espousals and Other Works*. Trans. James A. Wiseman. New York: Paulist Press, 1985.

Savage, Anne and Nicholas, Watson, ed. and trans. *Anchoritic Spirituality: Ancrene Wisse and Associated Works*. New York: Paulist Press, 1991.

Stallings-Taney, C. Mary, Francis X. Taney, and Anne Miller, eds. *Meditations on the Life of Christ*. Asheville, NC: Pegasus Press, 2000.

Suso, Henry. *The Exemplar, with Two German Sermons*. Trans. Frank Tobin. New York: Paulist Press, 1989.

Tauler, John. *Sermons*. Trans. Maria Shrady. New York: Paulist Press, 1985.

Teresa of Avila. *The Collected Works of St. Teresa of Avila.* Trans. Kieran Kavanaugh and Otilio Rodriguez. 3 vols. Washington, DC: Institute of Carmelite Studies, 1987.

Thomas of Cantimpré. *The Collected Saint's Lives: Christina the Astonishing, Margaret of Ypres, Lutgard of Aywières, and Abbot John of Cantimpré.* Ed. Barbara Newman and Margot King. Turnhout, Belgium: Brepols, 2008.

Van Engen, John, ed. and trans. *Devotio Moderna: Basic Writings.* New York: Paulist Press, 1988.

Walsh, James, ed. and trans. *The Cloud of Unknowing.* New York: Paulist Press, 1981.

Ward, Benedicta, trans. *The Sayings of the Desert Fathers: The Alphabetical Collection.* Kalamazoo: MI: Cistercian Publications, 1984.

———. trans. *Wisdom of the Desert Fathers: Systematic Sayings from the Anonymous Series of the Apopthegmata Patrum.* Oxford: SLG Press, 1986.

Wesley, John and Charles Wesley. *Selected Writings and Hymns.* Ed. Frank Whaling. New York: Paulist Press, 1981.

William of Saint Thierry. *On the Nature and Dignity of Love.* Trans. Geoffrey Webb and Adrian Walker. London: Mowbray, 1956.

———. *The Enigma of Faith.* Trans. John D. Anderson. Kalmazoo, MI: Cistercian Publications, 1974.

———. *On Contemplating God; Prayer; Meditations.* Trans. Sister Penelope. Kalamazoo, MI: Cistercian Publications, 1977.

———. *The Golden Epistle: A Letter to the Brethren at Mont Dieu.* Trans. Theodore Berkeley. Kalamazoo, MI: Cistercian Publications, 1980.

———. *Exposition on the Song of Songs.* Trans. Columba Hart. Kalamazoo, MI: Cistercian Publications, 1989.

Select Bibliography of Modern Works Related to the Study of Western Christian Mysticism

Aers, David and Lynn Staley. *Powers of the Holy: Religion, Politics, and Gender in Late Medieval English Culture.* University Park: Pennsylvania State University Press, 1996.

Ahlgren, Gillian T. W. *Teresa of Avila and the Politics of Sanctity.* Ithaca, NY: Cornell University Press, 1996.

Astell, Ann. *The Song of Songs in the Middle Ages.* Ithaca, NY: Cornell University Press, 1990.

———. "Facing Each Other: Saint Thérèse of Lisieux and Emmanuel Levinas." *Spiritus* 4 (2004): 24–43.

Atwood, Craig. "Sleeping in the Arms of Christ: Sanctifying Sexuality in the Eighteenth-Century Moravian Church." *Journal of the History of Sexuality* 8, no. 1 (1997): 25–51.

Bagger, Matthew. *Religious Experience, Justification, and History.* Cambridge: Cambridge University Press, 1999.

———. *The Uses of Paradox: Religion, Self-Transformation, and the Absurd.* New York: Columbia University Press, 2007.

Beckman, Patricia Z. "The Power of Books and the Practice of Mysticism in the Fourteenth Century: Heinrich of Nördlingen and Margaret Ebner on Mechthild's *Flowing Light of the Godhead*." *Church History* 76 (2007): 61–83.

Beckwith, Sarah. "A Very Material Mysticism: The Medieval Mysticism of Margery Kempe." In *Medieval Literature: Criticism, Ideology, History.* Ed. David Aers. New York: St. Martins, 1986.

———. *Christ's Body: Identity, Culture, and Society in Late Medieval Writings.* New York: Routledge, 1993.

———. "Passionate Regulation: Enclosure, Ascesis, and the Feminist Imaginary." *South Atlantic Quarterly* 93 (1994): 803–24.

———. *Signifying God: Social Relation and Symbolic Act in the York Corpus Christi Plays.* Chicago: University of Chicago Press, 2001.

Bell, David. *What Nuns Read: Books and Libraries in Medieval English Nunneries.* Kalamazoo, MI: Cistercian Publications, 1995.

Bell, Rudolph. *Holy Anorexia.* Chicago: University of Chicago Press, 1985.

Bell, Rudolph and Cristina Mazzoni. *The Voices of Gemma Galgani: The Life and Afterlife of a Modern Saint.* Chicago: University of Chicago Press, 2003.

Bell, Susan. "Medieval Women Book Owners: Arbiters of Lay Piety and Ambassadors of Culture." *Signs* 7 (1982): 742–68.

Bilinkoff, Jodi. *The Avila of Saint Teresa: Religious Reform in a Sixteenth-Century City.* Ithaca, NY: Cornell University Press, 1992.

———. "Navigating the Waves (of Devotion): Toward a Gendered Analysis of Early Modern Catholicism." In *Crossing Boundaries: Attending to Early Modern Women.* Ed. Jane Donawerth and Adele Seeff. Newark: University of Delaware Press, 2000.

———. *Related Lives: Confessors and Their Female Penitents, 1450–1759.* Ithaca, NY: Cornell University Press, 2005.

Bestul, Thomas. *Texts of the Passion: Latin Devotional Literature and Medieval Society.* Philadelphia: University of Pennsylvania Press, 1996.

———. "Antecedents: The Anselmian and Cistercian Contributions." In *Mysticism and Spirituality in Medieval England.* Ed. William F. Pollard and Robert Boenig. Woodbridge, UK: Boydell and Brewer, 1997.

Boff, Leonardo. "The Need for Political Saints: From a Spirituality of Liberation to the Practice of Liberation." *Cross Currents* 30, no. 4 (1980–1): 369–76.

Boon, Jessica. "Trinitarian Love Mysticism: Ruusbroec, Hadewijch, and the Gendered Experience of the Divine." *Church History* 72 (2003): 484–503.

Bouyer, Lous, Jean LeClercq, and François Vandenbroucke. *The Spirituality of the Middle Ages.* Trans. Benedictines of Holme Eden Abbey. London: Burnes and Oates, 1968.

Boynton, Susan. "Performative Exegesis in the Fleury *Interfectio Puerorum.*" *Viator* 29 (1998): 39–64.

———. "Religious Soundscapes: Liturgy and Music." In *The Cambridge History of Christianity: Christianity in Western Europe c. 1100-c.1500.* Ed. Miri Rubin and Walter Simons. Cambridge: Cambridge University Press, 2009.

Brantley, Jessica. *Reading in the Wilderness: Private Devotion and Public Performance in Late Medieval England.* Chicago: University of Chicago Press, 2007.

Bruneau, Marie-Florine. *Women Mystics Confront the Modern World: Marie de l'Incarnation (1599–1672) and Madame Guyon (1648–1717).* Albany: State University of New York Press, 1998.

Burton-Christie, Douglas. *The Word in the Desert: Scripture and the Quest for Holiness in Early Christian Monasticism.* New York: Oxford University Press, 1993.

———. "The Place of the Heart: Geography and Spirituality in *The Life of Antony.*" In *Purity of Heart in Early Christian Ascetic and Monastic Literature.* Ed. Harriet A. Luckman and Linda Kulzer. Collegeville, MN: The Liturgical Press, 1999.

———. "Listening, Reading, Praying: Orality, Literacy and Early Monastic Spirituality." *Anglican Theological Review* 83, no. 2 (2001): 5–25.

Bynum, Caroline Walker. *Docere Verbo et Exemplo: An Aspect of Twelfth-Century Spirituality.* Missoula, MT: Scholars Press, 1979.

———. *Jesus as Mother: Studies in the Spirituality of the High Middle Ages.* Berkeley: University of California Press, 1982.

———. "Women Mystics and Eucharistic Devotion in the Thirteenth Century." *Women's Studies* 11 (1984): 179–214.

———. *Holy Feast, Holy Fast: The Religious Significance of Food to Medieval Women.* Berkeley: University of California Press, 1987.

———. *Fragmentation and Redemption: Essays on Gender and the Human Body in Medieval Religions*. New York: Zone Books, 1991.

———. "Why All the Fuss about the Body? A Medievalist's Perspective." *Critical Inquiry* 22 (1995): 1–33.

———. "Violent Imagery in Late Medieval Piety." *German Historical Institute Bulletin* 30 (2002): 3–36.

———. *Wonderful Blood: Theology and Practice in Late Medieval Northern Germany and Beyond*. Philadelphia: University of Pennsylvania Press, 2007.

———. *Christian Materiality: An Essay on Religion in Late Medieval Europe*. New York: Zone Books, 2011.

Caciola, Nancy. *Discerning Spirits: Divine and Demonic Possession in the Middle Ages*. Ithaca, NY: Cornell University Press, 2003.

———. "Breath, Heart, Guts: The Body and Spirits in the Middle Ages." In *Demons, Spirits, Witches: Communicating with the Spirits*. Ed. Gábor Klaniczay and Éva Pócs. Budapest: Central European University Press, 2005.

Caffiero, Marina. "From the Late Baroque Mystical Explosion to the Social Apostolate, 1650–1850." In *Women and Faith: Catholic Religious Life in Italy from Late Antiquity to the Present*. Ed. Gabriella Zarri and Lucetta Scaraffia. Cambridge, MA: Harvard University Press, 1999.

Carlson, Thomas. *Indiscretion: Finitude and the Naming of God*. Chicago: University of Chicago Press, 1999.

———. *The Indiscrete Image: Infinitude and the Creation of the Human*. Chicago: University of Chicago Press, 2008.

Carrera, Elena. *Teresa of Ávila's Autobiography: Authority, Power and the Self in Mid-Sixteenth Century Spain*. London: MHRA and Maney Publishing, 2005.

Carruthers, Mary. *The Book of Memory: A Study of Memory in Medieval Culture*. Cambridge: Cambridge University Press, 1990.

———. *The Craft of Thought: Meditation, Rhetoric, and the Making of Images, 400–1200*. Cambridge: Cambridge University Press, 1998.

Casey, Michael. *A Thirst for God: Spiritual Desire in Bernard of Clairvaux's Sermons on the Song of Songs*. Kalamazoo, MI: Cistercian Publications, 1988.

Certeau, Michel de. *Heterologies: Discourse on the Other*. Trans. Brian Massumi. Minneapolis: University of Minnesota Press, 1986.

———. "Mysticism." *Diacritics* 22 (1992a): 11–25.

———. *The Mystic Fable. Vol.1. The Sixteenth and Seventeenth Centuries*. Trans. Michael B. Smith. Chicago: Chicago University Press, 1992b.

Coakley, John. *Women, Men, and Spiritual Power: Female Saints and Their Male Collaborators*. New York: Columbia University Press, 2006.

Cognet, Louis. *Post-Reformation Spirituality*. Trans. P. J. Hepburne-Scott. London: Burns and Oates, 1959.

Colledge, Edmund and J. C. Marler. "'Poverty of the Will': Ruusbroec, Eckhart and *The Mirror of Simple Souls*." In *Jan van Ruusbroec: The Sources, Content and Sequels of His Mysticism*. Ed. Paul Mommaers and Norbert De Paepe. Leuven, Belgium: Leuven University Press, 1984.

Constable, Giles. *Three Studies in Medieval Religious and Social Thought*. Cambridge: Cambridge University Press, 1995.

Coward, Harold and Toby Foshay, eds. *Derrida and Negative Theology*. Albany: State University of New York Press, 1992.

Cré, Marleen. *Vernacular Mysticism in the Charterhouse: A Study of London, British Library, MS Additional 37790*. Turnhout, Belgium: Brepols, 2006.

Daley, Brian. "Finding the Right Key: The Aims and Strategies of Early Christian Interpretation of the Psalms." In *Psalms in Community: Jewish and Christian Textual, Liturgical, and Artistic Traditions*. Ed. Harold W. Attridge and Margot E. Fassler. Atlanta, GA: Society of Biblical Literature, 2003.

Derrida, Jacques. *Acts of Religion*. Ed. Gil Anidjar. New York: Routledge, 2002.

Despres, Denise. *Ghostly Sights: Visual Meditation in Late Medieval Literature*. Norman, OK: Pilgrim Books, 1989.

Dinshaw, Carolyn. *Getting Medieval: Sexualities and Communities, Pre- and Postmodern*. Durham, NC: Duke University Press, 1999.

Driver, Stephen D. *John Cassian and the Reading of Egyptian Monastic Culture*. New York: Routledge, 2002.

Dronke, Peter. *Women Writers of the Middle Ages: A Critical Study of Texts from Perpetua (d. 203) to Marguerite Porete (d. 1310)*. Cambridge: Cambridge University Press, 1984.

Duffy, Eamon. *The Stripping of the Altars: Traditional Religion in England, c. 1400–c. 1580*. New Haven, CT: Yale University Press, 1992.

Dupré, Louis. *Passage to Modernity: An Essay in the Hermeneutics of Nature and Culture*. New Haven, CT: Yale University Press, 1993.

Dupré, Louis and Don E. Saliers, eds. *Christian Spirituality: Post-Reformation and Modern*. New York: Crossroad, 1991.

Dutton, Elisabeth M. *Julian of Norwich: The Influence of Late-Medieval Devotional Compilations*. Woodbridge, UK: D. S. Brewer, 2008.

Dyas, Dee, Valerie Edden, and Roger Ellis, eds. *Approaching Medieval English Anchoritic and Mystical Texts*. Cambridge: D. S. Brewer, 2005.

Dysinger, Luke. *Psalmody and Prayer in the Writings of Evagrius Ponticus*. Oxford: Oxford University Press, 2005.

Elliott, Dyan. "The Physiology of Rapture and Female Spirituality." In *Medieval Theology and the Natural Body*. Ed. Peter Biller and Alistair Minnis. Woodbridge, UK: York Medieval Press/Boydell and Brewer, 1997.

———. "*Dominae* or *Dominatae?* Female Mystics and the Trauma of Textuality." In *Women, Marriage, and Family in Medieval Christendom: Essays in Memory of Michael M. Sheehan, C. S. B.* Ed. Constance Rousseau and Joel Rosenthal. Kalamazoo, MI: Medieval Institute Publications, 1998.

———. *Fallen Bodies: Pollution, Sexuality, and Demonology in the Middle Ages*. Philadelphia: University of Pennsylvania Press, 1999.

———. "True Presence/False Christ: The Antinomies of Embodiment in Late Mediaeval Spirituality." *Mediaeval Studies* 64 (2002): 241–65.

———. *Proving Woman: Female Spirituality and Inquisitional Culture in the Later Middle Ages*. Princeton, NJ: Princeton University Press, 2004.

———. *The Bride of Christ Goes to Hell: Metaphor and Embodiment in the Lives of Pious Women, 200–1500*. Philadelphia: University of Pennsylvania Press, 2012.

Emery, Kent, Jr. and Joseph Wawrykow, ed. *Christ among the Medieval Dominicans: Representations of Christ in the Texts and Images of the Order of Preachers*. Notre Dame, IN: University of Notre Dame Press, 1998.

Endean, Philip. *Karl Rahner and Ignatian Spirituality*. Oxford: Oxford University Press, 2001.
Erler, Mary C. *Women, Reading, and Piety in Late Medieval England*. Cambridge: Cambridge University Press, 2002.
Evans, G. R. "*Mens Devota*: The Literary Community of the Devotional Works of John of Fécamp and St. Anselm." *Medium Aevum* 43 (1974): 105–15.
Fassler, Margot E. "Composer and Dramatist: 'Melodious Singing and Freshness of Remorse.'" In *Voice of the Living Light: Hildegard of Bingen and Her World*. Ed. Barbara Newman. Berkeley: University of California Press, 1998.
———. "Music for the Love Fest: Hildegard of Bingen and the Song of Songs." In *Women's Voices across Musical Worlds*. Ed. J. Bernstein. Boston: Northeastern University Press, 2003a.
———. "Hildegard and the Dawn Song of Lauds: An Introduction to Benedictine Psalmody." In *Psalms in Community: Jewish and Christian Textual, Liturgical, and Artistic Traditions*. Ed. Harold W. Attridge and Margot E. Fassler. Atlanta, GA: Society of Biblical Literature, 2003b.
Finke, Laurie A. "Mystical Bodies and the Dialogics of Vision." In *Maps of Flesh and Light: The Religious Experience of Medieval Women Mystics*. Ed. Ulrike Wiethaus. Syracuse, NY: Syracuse University, 1993.
Fleming, John. *An Introduction to the Franciscan Literature of the Middle Ages*. Chicago: Franciscan Herald Press, 1977.
Fogleman, Aaron. *Jesus Is Female: Moravians and the Challenge to Radical Religion in Early America*. Philadelphia: University of Pennsylvania Press, 2007.
Forman, Robert, ed. *The Problem of Pure Consciousness: Mysticism and Philosophy*. Oxford: Oxford University Press, 1990.
Fraeters, Veerle. "Handing on Wisdom and Knowledge in Hadewijch of Brabant's Book of Visions." In *Women and Experience in Later Medieval Writing: Reading the Book of Life*. Ed. Anneke B. Mulder-Bakker and Liz Herbert McAvoy. New York: Palgrave Macmillan, 2009.
Frohlich, Mary. "Spiritual Discipline, Discipline of Spirituality: Revisiting Questions of Definition and Method." *Spiritus* 1 (2001): 65–78.
———. "Critical Interiority." *Spiritus* 7 (2007): 77–81.
Fulton, Rachel. *From Judgment to Passion: Devotion to Christ and the Virgin Mary, 800–1200*. New York: Columbia University Press, 2002.
———. "Taste and See That the Lord Is Sweet (Ps. 33:9): The Flavor of God in the Monastic West." *Journal of Religion* 86 (2006): 169–204.
Giles, Mary. "Francisca Hernández and the Sexuality of Religious Dissent." In *Women in the Inquisition: Spain and the New World*. Ed. Mary Giles. Baltimore, MD: The Johns Hopkins University Press, 1999.
Green, D. H. *Women Readers in the Middle Ages*. Cambridge: Cambridge University Press, 2007.
Grundmann, Herbert. *Religious Movements in the Middle Ages*. Trans. Steven Rowan. Notre Dame, IN: University of Notre Dame Press, 1995[1935].
Hadot, Pierre. *Philosophy as a Way of Life: Spiritual Exercises from Socrates to Foucault*. Trans. Michael Chase. Oxford: Blackwell, 1995.
Hamburger, Jeffrey F. *The Rothschild Canticles: Art and Mysticism in Flanders and the Rhineland Circa 1300*. New Haven, CT: Yale University Press, 1990.

———. *The Visual and the Visionary: Art and Female Spirituality in Late Medieval Germany*. New York: Zone Books, 1998.

———. "Speculations on Speculation: Vision and Perception in the Theory and Practice of Mystical Devotions." In *Deutsche Mystik im abendländischen Zusammenhang: Neu erschlossene Texte, neue methodische Ansätze, neuetheoretische Konzepte*. Ed. Walter Haug and Wolfram Schneider-Lastin. Tübingen, Germany: Niemeyer, 2000.

———. "The 'Various Writings of Humanity': Johannes Tauler on Hildegard of Bingen's *Liber Scivias*." In *Visual Culture and the German Middle Ages*. Ed. Kathryn Starkey and Horst Wenzel. London: Palgrave Macmillan, 2005.

Hamburger, Jeffrey F. and Anne-Marie Bouché, eds. *The Mind's Eye: Art and Theological Argument in the Middle Ages*. Princeton, NJ: Princeton University Press, 2006.

Harmless, William. *Desert Christians: An Introduction to the Literature of Early Monasticism*. New York: Oxford University Press, 2004.

Harrison, Anna. "'Oh! What Treasure Is in this Book?' Writing, Reading, and Community at the Monastery of Helfta." *Viator* 39, no. 1 (2008): 75–106.

Heinonen, Meri. "Brides and Knights of Christ: Gender and Body in Later Medieval German Mysticism. PhD diss., University of Turku, Finland, 2007.

Herbert-McAvoy, Liz. *Authority and the Female Body in the Writings of Julian of Norwich and Margery Kempe*. Cambridge: D. S. Brewer, 2004.

Hindmarsh, D. Bruce. "'End of Faith as Its Beginning': Models of Spiritual Progress in Early Evangelical Devotional Hymns." *Spiritus* 10 (2010): 1–21.

Hobbins, Daniel. "The Schoolman as Public Intellectual: Jean Gerson and the Late Medieval Tract." *American Historical Review* 108 (2003): 1308–35.

———. *Authorship and Publicity before Print: Jean Gerson and the Transformation of Late Medieval Learning*. Philadelphia: University of Pennsylvania Press, 2009.

Holder, Arthur, ed. *The Blackwell Companion to Christian Spirituality*. Oxford: Blackwell, 2006.

Hollywood, Amy. *The Soul as Virgin Wife: Mechthild of Magdeburg, Marguerite Porete, and Meister Eckhart*. Notre Dame, IN: University of Notre Dame Press, 1995.

———. "Suffering Transformed: Marguerite Porete, Meister Eckhart, and the Problem of Women's Spirituality." In *Meister Eckhart and the Beguine Mystics*. Ed. Bernard McGinn. New York: Continuum, 1997.

———. "Inside Out: Beatrice of Nazareth and Her Hagiographers." In *Gendered Voices: Medieval Saints and Their Interpreters*. Ed. Catherine Mooney. Philadelphia: University of Pennsylvania Press, 1999.

———. *Sensible Ecstasy: Mysticism, Sexual Difference, and the Demands of History*. Chicago: University of Chicago Press, 2002.

———. "Mysticism, Death and Desire in the Work of Hélène Cixous and Catherine Clément." In *Religion in French Feminist Thought: Critical Perspectives*. Ed. Morny Joy, Kathleen O'Grady, and Judith L. Poxon. New York: Routledge, 2003.

———. "'That Glorious Slit': Irigaray and the Medieval Devotion to Christ's Side Wound." In *Luce Irigaray and Premodern Culture: Thresholds of History*. Ed. Theresa Krier and Elizabeth D. Harvey. New York: Routledge, 2004.

———. "Sexual Desire, Divine Desire: or, Queering the Beguines." In *Toward a Theology of Eros*. Ed. Virginia Burrus and Catherine Keller. New York: Fordham University Press, 2006.

———. "Mysticism and Transcendence." In *The Cambridge History of Christianity: Christianity in Western Europe, c. 1100–c. 1500*. Ed. Miri Rubin and Walter Simons. Cambridge: Cambridge University Press, 2009.

Howells, Edward. *John of the Cross and Teresa of Avila: Mystical Knowing and Selfhood*. New York: Crossroad Publishing Company, 2002.

Idel, Moshe and Bernard McGinn, eds. *Mystical Union and Monotheistic Faith: An Ecumenical Dialogue*. New York: Macmillan, 1989.

Irigaray, Luce. *Speculum of the Other Woman*. Trans. Gillian C. Gill. Ithaca, NY: Cornell University Press, 1985.

———. *Sexes and Genealogies*. Trans. Gillian C. Gill. New York: Columbia University Press, 1993.

James, William. *The Varieties of Religious Experience: A Study in Human Nature*. Harmondsworth, UK: Penguin, 1982 [1902].

Jantzen, Grace. *Power, Gender, and Christian Mysticism*. Cambridge: Cambridge University Press, 1995.

Katz, Steven T., ed. *Mysticism and Philosophical Analysis*. Oxford: Oxford University Press, 1978.

———. ed. *Mysticism and Religious Traditions*. Oxford: Oxford University Press, 1983.

———. ed. *Mysticism and Language*. Oxford: Oxford University Press, 1992.

Kerby-Fulton, Kathryn. *Books under Suspicion: Censorship and Tolerance of Revelatory Writing in Late Medieval England*. Notre Dame, IN: University of Notre Dame Press, 2006.

Kessler, Herbert. *Spiritual Seeing: Picturing God's Invisibility in Medieval Art*. Philadelphia: University of Pennsylvania Press, 2000.

Kessler, Michael and Christian Sheppard, eds. *Mystics: Presence and Aporia*. Chicago: University of Chicago Press, 2003.

Kieckhefer, Richard. *Unquiet Souls: Fourteenth-Century Saints and Their Religious Milieu*. Chicago: University of Chicago Press, 1984.

Kocher, Suzanne. *Allegories of Love in Marguerite Porete's* Mirror of Simple Souls. Turnhout, Belgium: Brepols, 2008.

Lacan, Jacques. *On Feminine Sexuality: The Limits of Love and Knowledge, Book XX: Encore, 1972–73*. Trans. Bruce Fink. New York: Norton, 1998.

Laird, Martin. "The 'Open Country Whose Name Is Prayer': Apophasis, Deconstruction, and Contemplative Practice." *Modern Theology* 21, no. 1 (2005): 141–55.

Largier, Niklaus. "Inner Senses, Outer Senses: The Practice of Emotions in Medieval Mysticism." In *Codierungen von Emotionen im Mittelalter/ Emotions and Sensibilities in the Middle Ages*. Ed. C. Stephen Jaeger and Ingrid Kasten. Berlin: De Gruyter, 2003.

———. *In Praise of the Whip: A Cultural History of Arousal*. Trans. Graham Harman. New York: Zone Books, 2007.

———. "Medieval Mysticism." In *The Oxford Handbook of Religion and Emotion*. Ed. John Corrigan. Oxford: Oxford University Press, 2008.

———. "Mysticism, Modernity, and the Invention of Aesthetic Experience." *Representations* 105 (2009): 37–60.

LeClercq, Jean. *The Love of Learning and the Desire for God: A Study of Monastic Culture*. Trans. Catherine Misrahi. New York: Fordham University Press, 1974.

Lerner, Robert. *The Heresy of the Free Spirit in the Later Middle Ages*. Berkeley: University of California Press, 1972.

———. "Ecstatic Dissent." *Speculum* 67 (1992): 33–57.

———. "New Light on *The Mirror of Simple Souls*." *Speculum* 85 (2010): 91–116.

Lipton, Sara. "'The Sweet Lean of the Head': Writing about Looking at the Crucifix in the High Middle Ages." *Speculum* 80 (2005): 1172–1208.

———. "Images and their Use." In *The Cambridge History of Christianity: Christianity in Western Europe, c.1100–c.1500*. Ed. Miri Rubin and Walter Simons. Cambridge: Cambridge University Press, 2009.

Lobody, Diane Helen. "Lost in the Ocean of Love: The Mystical Writings of Catherine Livingston Garrettson." PhD diss., Drew University, 1990.

Lochrie, Karma. *Margery Kempe and Translations of the Flesh*. Philadelphia: University of Pennsylvania Press, 1991a.

———. "The Language of Transgression: Body, Flesh, and Word in Mystical Discourse." In *Speaking Two Languages: Traditional Disciplines and Contemporary Theory in Medieval Studies*. Ed. Allen J. Frantzen Jr. Albany: State University of New York Press, 1991b.

———. "Mystical Acts, Queer Tendencies." In *Constructing Medieval Sexuality*. Ed. Karma Lochrie, Peggy McCracken, and James S. Schultz. Minneapolis: University of Minnesota Press, 1997.

Lossky, Vladimir. *The Mystical Theology of the Eastern Church*. Trans. Fellowship of Saint Alban and Saint Sergius. London: James Clark, 1957.

Louth, Andrew. *The Origins of the Christian Mystical Tradition: From Plato to Denys*. New York: Oxford University Press, 2007.

Lubac, Henri de. *Medieval Exegesis*. Vol. 2. *The Four Senses of Scripture*. Trans. E. M. Macierowski. Grand Rapids, MI, and Edinburgh: William Eerdmans and T. & T. Clark, 2000.

Lynn, Cynthia. "Passion, Desire, and Ecstasy: The Experiential Religion of Southern Methodist Women, 1770–1810." In *The Devil's Lane: Sex and Race in the Early South*. Ed. Catherine Clinton and Michele Gillespie. Oxford: Oxford University Press, 1997.

Mack, Phyllis. *Visionary Women: Ecstatic Prophecy in Seventeenth-Century England*. Berkeley: University of California Press, 1992.

———. "Religious Dissenters in Enlightenment England." *History Workshop Journal* 49 (2000): 1–23.

Marion, Jean-Luc. "In the Name: How to Avoid Speaking of 'Negative Theology.'" In *God, the Gift, and Postmodernism*. Ed. John D. Caputo and Michael J. Scanlon. Bloomington: Indiana University Press, 1999.

Matter, Ann E. *The Voice of My Beloved: The Song of Songs in Western Medieval Christianity*. Philadelphia: University of Pennsylvania Press, 1990.

Mazzoni, Cristina. *Saint Hysteria: Neurosis, Mysticism, and Gender in European Culture*. Ithaca, NY: Cornell University Press, 1996.

McGinn, Bernard. *The Presence of God: A History of Western Christian Mysticism*. Vol. 1. *The Foundations of Mysticism: Origins to the Fifth Century*. New York: Crossroad, 1991.
———. *The Presence of God: A History of Western Christian Mysticism*. Vol. 2. *The Growth of Mysticism: Gregory the Great through the Twelfth Century*. New York: Crossroad, 1994a.
———. ed. *Meister Eckhart and the Beguine Mystics*. New York: Continuum, 1994b.
———. "God as Eros." In *New Perspectives on Historical Theology: Essays in Honor of John Meyendorff*. Ed. Bradley Nassif. Grand Rapids, MI: Eerdmans, 1996a.
———. "Mysticism." In *The Oxford Encyclopedia of the Reformation*. Ed. Hans J. Hillerbrand. Oxford: Oxford University Press, 1996b.
———. *The Presence of God: A History of Western Christian Mysticism*. Vol. 3. *The Flowering of Mysticism: Men and Women in the New Mysticism (1200–1350)*. New York: Crossroad, 1998.
———. "The Four Female Evangelists of the Thirteenth Century: The Invention of Authority." In *Deutsche Mystik im Abendländischen Zusammenhang: Neue Erschlossene Texte, Neue Methodische Ansatze, Neue Theoretische Konzeptee*. Ed. Walter Haug and Wolfram Schneider-Lastin. Tübingen, Germany: Max Niemeyer Verlag, 2000.
———. *The Mystical Thought of Meister Eckhart: The Man from Whom God Hid Nothing*. New York: Crossroad, 2001a.
———. "The Language of Inner Experience in Christian Mysticism." *Spiritus* 1 (2001b): 157–71.
———. "*Vere tu es Deus absconditus*: The Hidden God in Luther and Some Mystics." In *Silence and the Word: Negative Theology and Incarnation*. Ed. Oliver Davies and Denys Turner. Cambridge: Cambridge University Press, 2002.
———. "'Evil-Sounding, Rash, and Suspect of Heresy': Tensions between Mysticism and Magisterium in the History of the Church." *Catholic Historical Review* 90, no. 2 (2004): 193–212.
———. *The Presence of God: A History of Western Christian Mysticism*. Vol. 4. *The Harvest of Mysticism in Medieval Germany*. New York: Crossroad, 2005.
———. "Regina quondam...." *Speculum* 83 (2008a): 817–39.
———. "Mystical Consciousness: A Modest Proposal." *Spiritus* 8 (2008b): 44–63.
McGuire, Brian Patrick. *Jean Gerson and the Last Medieval Reformation*. University Park: Pennsylvania State University Press, 2005.
McIntosh, Mark. *Mystical Theology: The Integrity of Spirituality and Theology*. Oxford: Blackwell, 1998.
McNamer, Sarah. "The Origins of the *Meditationes vitae Christi*." *Speculum* 84 (2009a): 905–55.
———. *Affective Meditation and the Invention of Medieval Compassion*. Philadelphia: University of Pennsylvania Press, 2009b.
Meale, Carole, ed. *Women and Literature in Britain, 1100–1500*. Cambridge: Cambridge University Press, 1993.
Merton, Thomas. *Contemplation in a World of Action*. Garden City: Doubleday, 1971 [1965].

———. *Conjectures of a Guilty Bystander.* Garden City, NJ: Doubleday, 1989 [1966].

Minnis, Alastair and Rosylynn Voaden, eds. *Medieval Holy Women in the Christian Tradition c. 1100–c. 1500.* Turnhout, Belgium: Brepols, 2010.

Mooney, Catherine M. "The Authorial Role of Brother A. in the Composition of Angela of Foligno's Revelations." In *Creative Women in Medieval and Early Modern Italy: A Religious and Artistic Renaissance.* Ed. E. Ann Matter and John Coakley. Philadelphia: University of Pennsylvania Press, 1994.

———. ed. *Gendered Voices: Medieval Saints and Their Interpreters.* Philadelphia: University of Pennsylvania Press, 1999.

Moore, Rosemary. *The Light in Their Consciences: The Early Quakers in Britain 1646–1666.* University Park: Pennsylvania State University Press, 2000.

Moore, Stephen. *God's Beauty Parlor and Other Queer Spaces in and around the Bible.* Stanford, CA: Stanford University Press, 2001.

Myers, Kathleen. "The Mystic Triad in Colonial Mexican Nuns' Discourse: Divine Author, Visionary Scribe, and Clerical Mediator." *Colonial Latin American Historical Review* 6 (1997): 479–524.

Newman, Barbara. *Sister of Wisdom: Saint Hildegard's Theology of the Feminine.* Berkeley: University of California Press, 1987.

———. *From Virile Woman to WomanChrist.* Philadelphia: University of Pennsylvania Press, 1995.

———. "Possessed by the Spirit: Devout Women, Demoniacs, and the Apostolic Life in the Thirteenth Century." *Speculum* 73 (1998): 733–70.

———. "The Mirror and the Rose: Marguerite Porete's Encounter with the *Dieu D'Amours.* In *The Vernacular Spirit: Essays on Medieval Religious Literature.* Ed. Renate Blumenfeld-Kosinski et al. New York: Palgrave, 2002.

———. *God and the Goddesses: Vision, Poetry, and Belief in the Middle Ages.* Philadelphia: University of Pennsylvania Press, 2003.

———. "What Did It Mean to Say 'I Saw'? The Clash between Theory and Practice in Medieval Visionary Culture." *Speculum* 80 (2005): 6–41.

———. "The Visionary Texts and Visual Worlds of Religious Women." In *Crown and Veil: Female Monasticism from the Fifth to the Fifteenth Centuries.* Ed. Jeffrey F. Hamburger and Susan Marti. New York: Columbia University Press, 2008.

Oberman, Heiko A. "Some Notes on the Theology of Nominalism: With Attention to Its Relation to the Renaissance." *Harvard Theological Review* 53 (1960): 47–76.

———. "*Simul Gemitus et Raptus:* Luther and Mysticism." In *The Dawn of the Reformation.* Grand Rapids, MI: Eerdmans, 1992.

Ohly, Friedrich. *Sensus Spiritualis: Studies in Medieval Significs and the Philology of Culture.* Trans. Kenneth J. Northcott. Chicago: University of Chicago Press, 2005.

Olson, Linda and Kathryn Kerby-Fulton, eds. *Voices in Dialogue: Reading Women in the Middle Ages.* Notre Dame, IN: University of Notre Dame Press, 2005.

Ozment, Steven E. "*Homo viator*: Luther and Late Medieval Theology." In *Reformation in Medieval Perspective.* Ed. Steven E. Ozment. Chicago: Quadrangle Books, 1971.

———. *Mysticism and Dissent: Religious Ideology and Social Protest in the Sixteenth Century.* New Haven, CT: Yale University Press, 1973.

———. *The Age of Reform 1250–1550: An Intellectual and Religious History of Late Medieval and Reformation Europe*. New Haven, CT: Yale University Press, 1980.

Partner, Nancy F. "Reading the Book of Margery Kempe." *Exemplaria* 3 (1991): 29–66.

———. "Did Mystics Have Sex?" In *Desire and Discipline: Sex and Sexuality in the Premodern West*. Ed. Jacqueline Murray and Konrad Eisenbichler. Toronto: University of Toronto Press, 1996.

Paulsell, Stephanie. "Writing and Mystical Experience in Marguerite d'Oingt and Virginia Woolf." *Comparative Literature* 44, no. 3 (1992): 249–67.

———. "*Scriptio divina*: Writing and the Experience of God in the Works of Marguerite d'Oingt." PhD diss., University of Chicago, 1993.

———. "*Scriptio divina*: Women, Writing and God." *The Spire* 26, no. 1 (2005): 10–17.

Perez-Romero, Antonio. *Subversion and Liberation in the Writings of St. Teresa of Avila*. Atlanta, GA: Rodophi, 1996.

Pickering, F. P. "Notes on Late Medieval German Tales in Praise of *Docto Ignorantia*." *Bulletin of the John Rylands Library Manchester* 24, no. 1 (1940): 121–37.

Poor, Sara S. *Mechthild of Magdeburg and Her Book: Gender and the Making of Textual Authority*. Philadelphia: University of Pennsylvania Press, 2004.

———. "Women Teaching Men in the Medieval Devotional Imagination." In *Partners in Spirit: Men, Women, and Religious Life in Germany, 1100–1500*. Ed. Fiona J. Griffiths and Julie Hotchin. New York: Brepols, forthcoming.

Pranger, M. B. *Bernard of Clairvaux and the Shape of Monastic Thought: Broken Dreams*. Leiden, The Netherlands: Brill, 1994.

———. *The Artificiality of Christianity: Essays on the Poetics of Monasticism*. Stanford, CA: Stanford University Press, 2002.

Proudfoot, Wayne. *Religious Experience*. Berkeley: University of California Press, 1985.

Raitt, Jill, Bernard McGinn, and John Meyendorff, eds. *Christian Spirituality II: High Middle Ages and Reformation*. New York: Crossroad, 1987.

Rambuss, Richard. *Closet Devotions*. Durham, NC: Duke University Press, 1998.

Rudy, Gordon. *Mystical Language of Sensation in the Later Middle Ages*. New York: Routledge, 2002.

Ruffing, Janet, ed. *Mysticism and Social Transformation*. Syracuse, NY: Syracuse University Press, 2001.

Saenger, Paul. *Space between Words: The Origins of Silent Reading*. Stanford, CA: Stanford University Press, 1997.

Salih, Sarah. "When Is a Bosom Not a Bosom? Problems with 'Erotic Mysticism.'" In *Medieval Virginities*. Ed. Anke Bernau, Ruth Evans, and Sarah Salih. Toronto: University of Toronto Press, 2003.

Sargent, Michael. "Walter Hilton's *Scale of Perfection*: The London Manuscript Group Reconsidered." *Medium Aevum* 52 (1983): 189–216.

Scheepsma, Wybren. *The Limburg Sermons: Preaching in the Medieval Low Countries at the Turn of the Fourteenth Century*. Trans. David F. Johnson. Leiden, The Netherlands: Brill, 2008.

Schiewer, Regina D. "Sermons for Nuns of the Dominican Observance Movement." In *Medieval Monastic Preaching*. Ed. Carolyn Muessig. Boston: Brill, 1998.

Schmidt, Leigh Eric. *Hearing Things: Religion, Illusion, and the American Enlightenment*. Cambridge, MA: Harvard University Press, 2000.

———. "The Making of Modern 'Mysticism.'" *Journal of the American Academy of Religion* 71 (2003): 273–302.

———. *Restless Souls: The Making of American Spirituality – From Emerson to Oprah*. San Francisco: Harper, 2005.

———. *Heaven's Bride: The Unprintable Life of Ida C. Craddock, American Mystic, Scholar, Sexologist, Martyr, and Madwoman*. New York: Basic Books, 2010.

Schürmann, Reiner. *Meister Eckhart: Mystic and Philosopher*. Bloomington: Indiana University Press, 1978.

Sells, Michael. *Mystical Languages of Unsaying*. Chicago: University of Chicago Press, 1994.

Sheldrake, Philip. "Christian Spirituality as a Way of Living Publicly: A Dialectic of the Mystical and the Prophetic." *Spiritus* 3, no. 1 (2003): 19–37.

Simons, Walter. "Reading a Saint's Body: Rapture and Bodily Movement in the Vitae of Thirteenth-Century Beguines." In *Framing Medieval Bodies*. Ed. Sara Kay and Miri Rubin. Manchester, UK: University of Manchester, 1994.

———. *Cities of Ladies: Beguine Communities in the Medieval Low Countries, 1200–1565*. Philadelphia: University of Pennsylvania Press, 2001.

———. "'Staining the Speech of Things Divine': The Uses of Literacy in Medieval Beguine Communities." In *The Voice of Silence: Women's Literacy in a Men's Church*. Ed. Thérèse de Hemptinne and María Eugenia Góngora. Turnhout, Belgium: Brepols, 2004.

Sluhovsky, Moshe. *Believe Not Every Spirit: Possession, Mysticism and Discernment in Early Modern Catholicism*. Chicago: University of Chicago Press, 2007.

Smalley, Beryl. *The Study of the Bible in the Middle Ages*. 3rd. ed. Notre Dame, IN: University of Notre Dame Press, 1982.

Soelle, Dorothee. *The Silent Cry: Mysticism and Resistance*. Minneapolis, MN: Fortress Press, 2001.

Somerset, Fiona. "Excitative Speech: Theories of Emotive Response from Richard Fitzralph to Margery Kempe." In *The Vernacular Spirit*, ed. Renate Blumenfeld-Kosinski, Duncan Robertson, and Nancy Bradley Warren. New York: Palgrave, 2002.

Southern, R. W. *Western Society and the Church in the Middle Ages*. Middlesex, UK: Penguin, 1970.

———. *Saint Anselm: A Portrait in a Landscape*. Cambridge: Cambridge University Press, 1990.

Stang, Charles M. "Dionysius, Paul and the Significance of the Pseudonym." In *Rethinking Dionysius the Areopagite*. Ed. Sarah Coakley and Charles M. Stang. Oxford: Wiley-Blackwell, 2008.

———. "'Being Neither Oneself Nor Someone Else': The Apophatic Anthropology of Dionysius the Areopagite." In *Apophatic Bodies: Negative Theology, Incarnation and Relationality*. Ed. Chris Boesel and Catherine Keller. New York: Fordham University Press, 2009.

———. *Apophasis and Pseudonymity in Dionysius the Areopagite*. Oxford: Oxford University Press, 2012.
Stewart, Columba. *Cassian the Monk*. New York: Oxford University Press, 1998.
———. "Imageless Prayer and the Theological Vision of Evagrius Ponticus." *Journal of Early Christian Studies* 9, no. 2 (2001): 173–204.
Stock, Brian. *The Implications of Literacy: Written Language and Models of Interpretation in the Eleventh and Twelfth Centuries*. Princeton, NJ: Princeton University Press, 1983.
Suydam, Mary A. and Joanna E. Ziegler, eds. *Performance and Transformation: New Approaches to Late Medieval Spirituality*. New York: Saint Martin's Press, 1999.
Swanson, R. N. *Religion and Devotion in Europe, c. 1215–c.1515*. Cambridge: Cambridge University Press, 1995.
Szarmach, Paul, ed. *An Introduction to the Medieval Mystics of Europe*. Albany: State University of New York Press, 1984.
Tamburello, Dennis. *Union with Christ: John Calvin and the Mysticism of St. Bernard*. Louisville, KY: Westminster John Knox Press, 1994.
Taves, Ann. *Fits, Trances, and Visions: Experiencing Religion and Explaining Experience from Wesley to James*. Princeton, NJ: Princeton University Press, 1999.
———. *Religious Experience Reconsidered: A Building-Block Approach to the Study of Religion and Other Special Things*. Princeton, NJ: Princeton University Press, 2009.
Taylor, Andrew. *Textual Situations: Three Medieval Manuscripts and Their Readers*. Philadelphia: University of Pennsylvania Press, 2002.
Taylor, Robert. "The Old French 'Cistercian' Translations." In *Medieval Translators and Their Craft*. Ed. Jeanette Beer. Kalamazoo, MI: Medieval Institute Publications, 1989.
Turner, Denys. *Eros and Allegory: Medieval Exegesis of the Song of Songs*. Kalamazoo, MI: Cistercian Publications, 1995a.
———. *The Darkness of God: Negativity in Christian Mysticism*. Cambridge: Cambridge University Press, 1995b.
Underhill, Evelyn. *Mysticism: A Study in the Nature and Development of Man's Spiritual Consciousness*. London: Methuen, 1911.
Van Engen, John. *Sisters and Brothers of the Common Life: The Devotio Moderna and the World of the Later Middle Ages*. Philadelphia: University of Pennsylvania Press, 2008.
Vauchez, André. *The Spirituality of the Medieval West: From the Eighth to the Twelfth Century*. Trans. Colette Friedlander. Kalamazoo, MI: Cistercian Publications, 1993.
Voaden, Rosalynn. "God's Almighty Hand: Women Co-Writing the Book." In *Women, The Book, and the Godly*. Ed. Leslie Smith and Jane H. M. Taylor. Cambridge: D. S. Brewer, 1995.
———. ed. *Prophets Abroad: The Reception of Continental Holy Women in Late-Medieval England*. Woodbridge, UK: D. S. Brewer, 1996.
———. *God's Words, Women's Voices: The Discernment of Spirits in the Writing of Late-Medieval Women Visionaries*. Woodbridge, UK: Boydell Press, 1999.

Watson, Nicholas. *Richard Rolle and the Invention of Authority.* Cambridge: Cambridge University Press, 1991.

———. "Censorship and Cultural Change in Late-Medieval England: Vernacular Theology, the Oxford Translation Debate, and Arundel's Constitutions of 1409." *Speculum* 70 (1995): 822–64.

———. "Desire for the Past." *Studies in the Age of Chaucer* 21 (1999): 59–97.

Weber, Alison. *Teresa of Avila and the Rhetoric of Femininity.* Princeton, NJ: Princeton University Press, 1990.

———. *Approaches to Teaching Teresa of Ávila and the Spanish Mystics.* New York: The Modern Language Association of America, 2009.

Weil, Simone. *The Notebooks of Simone Weil.* 2 vols. Trans. Arthur Wills. London: Routledge, 1956.

———. *Waiting For God.* Trans. Emma Craufurd. New York: Harper and Row, 1973.

Williams, Rowan. *The Wound of Knowledge: Christian Spirituality from the New Testament to St. John of the Cross.* London: Darton, Longman, and Todd, 1979.

———. *Teresa of Avila.* London: Geoffrey Chapman, 1991.

———. "Religious Experience in the Era of Reform." In *Companion to Theology.* Ed. Peter Bryne and Leslie Houlden. London: Routledge, 1995.

Windeatt, Barry. "Constructing Audiences for Contemplative Texts: The Example of a Mystical Anthology." In *Imagining the Book.* Ed. Stephen Kelly and John J. Thompson. Turnhout, Belgium: Brepols, 2005.

Winston-Allen, Anne. *Convent Chronicles: Women Writing about Women and Reform in the Late Middle Ages.* University Park: Pennsylvania State University Press, 2004.

Wogan-Browne, Jocelyn, Ian R. Johnson, and Ruth Evans, eds. *The Idea of the Vernacular: An Anthology of Middle English Literary Theory, 1280–1520.* University Park: Pennsylvania State University Press, 1999.

Yannaras, Christos. *Elements of Faith: An Introduction to Orthodox Theology.* Edinburgh: T. and T. Clark, 1991.

Zarri, Gabriella. "Living Saints: A Typology of Female Sanctity in the Early Sixteenth Century." In *Women and Religion in Medieval and Renaissance Italy.* Ed. Daniel Bornstein and Roberto Rusconi. Chicago: University of Chicago Press, 1992.

Zieman, Katherine. *Singing the New Song: Literacy and Liturgy in Late Medieval England.* Philadelphia: University of Pennsylvania Press, 2008.

Author and Artist Index

Abelard (1079–1142), 61n7, 94–5
Achard of Saint Victor (d. 1170/1), 94, 99
Adam of Saint Victor (d. 1143), 94
Aelred of Rievaulx (1110–67), 90, 161, 229, 236
Alan of Lille (ca. 1128–1202/3), 75n46, 289
Albert the Great (d. 1280), 192, 206
Alcher of Clairvaux (ca. 1160), 179
Alexander of Hales (d. 1245), 190
Alexander Nequam (d. 1217), 161
Alfonso of Jaén (1327–89), 231
Altensteig, John (fl. early sixteenth century), 283, 287
Althusser, Louis, 69n25
Ambrose of Milan (d. 397), 202
Andrew of Saint Victor (d. 1175), 94
Angela of Foligno (d. 1309), 188, 199, 231–2, 333, 337
Anselm of Bec (ca. 1033–1109) (also known as Anselm of Canterbury), 81, 158–60, 165, 168
Anselm of Haverberg (ca. 1095–1158), 93
Antony (d. 356), 38, 44–51, 57–8, 309

Aristotle (384–22 BCE), 146
Arndt, Johann (1555–1621), 209, 346
Asad, Talal, 69n25
Athanasius of Alexandria (d. 373), 44, 309–10
Augustine of Canterbury (d. 604), 245
Augustine of Hippo (354–430), 1–2, 2n3, 12, 17, 24–5, 59, 143, 148–50, 158, 160, 175–9, 188, 190, 202, 211–15, 261–5, 287, 309, 343–4: *Confessions*, 1–3, 12, 100, 150, 261–2, 264, 310, 322
Aune, David E., 264–5n2
Averill, James R., 298–300

Basil of Caesarea (d. 379), 59, 138, 142–3
Baudonivia (sixth/seventh centuries), 191
Beach, Alison I., 60n3, 70n26, 71n80
Beatrice of Nazareth (d. 1268), 108, 184, 198, 231–2, 333
Beaufort, Margaret (1444–1509), 236
Beckwith, Sarah, 307–8, 319
Benedetta Carlini (d. 1661), 195
Benedict of Aniane (d. 821), 60

Benedict of Nursia (ca. 480–547), 57, 60, 60n5, 65–6, 178–80
Benet of Canfield (1562–1611), 118
Bening, Simon (1483–1561), 284
Bernard of Clairvaux (1090–1153), 27–8, 63n9, 74–8, 86–91, 160, 164, 184, 191–3, 204, 208, 229–30, 241–6, 267–8, 296, 310, 337
Bernini, Giovanni (1598–1680), 272, 328–9
Bérulle, Pierre de (1575–1629), 131–4, 209–10
Bilinkoff, Jodi, 118n12
Boff, Leonardo (b. 1938), 211–12, 221
Bonaventure (1221–74), 15, 102, 163–5, 171–2, 192, 197–8, 206, 230, 236
Bossuet, Jacques-Benigne (1627–1704), 306
Brakke, Dave, 39n7, 49n26
Bridget of Sweden (d. 1373), 188, 195, 231–3, 238, 245–6
Brown, Peter, 41n9, 49n26
Bruno the Carthusian (ca. 1030–1101), 86
Bynum, Caroline Walker, 272, 274, 306, 311–12, 318, 323

Calvin, John (1509–64), 126
Cassian, John (d. ca. 435), 10, 13–16, 24, 37, 49, 53–4, 57, 65–70, 76, 149, 156, 159, 170, 175–7
Cassiodorus (d. ca. 585), 149, 167, 262
Catherine of Genoa (1447–1510), 116, 232n25
Catherine of Siena (1347–80), 194, 198–9, 231n24, 233, 238, 324
Certeau, Michel de (1925–86), 6n10, 7n12

Charcot, Jean-Martin (1825–93), 317
Christina the Astonishing (d. 1224), 195
Clement of Alexandria (ca. 150–ca. 215), 138
Constable, Giles, 70n29
Crean, John E., Jr., 62n8

Daley, Brian, 66n17
Denck, Hans (ca. 1500–27), 128–9
Denis the Carthusian (1403–71), 237–8
Diemut of Wessobrunn, 71n30
Dionysius the Areopagite (also cited as Pseudo-Dionysius the Areopagite) (early sixth century), 13, 17, 24, 137, 140, 143–6, 155–6, 161, 164, 192, 237, 258–61, 287, 330
Dominic Guzman (ca. 1171–1221), 99
Dorothea of Hof (late fifteenth century), 248–51
Dorothea of Montau (d. 1394), 195, 199
Douceline of Digne (d. 1274), 195–6

Ebner, Margaret (d. 1351), 188, 234–5, 239n48
Eckhart, Meister (d. 1328), 3, 19, 79n59, 103–4, 110, 120, 192, 196–7, 204–20, 232–4, 249, 286–7, 345, 347
Egbert/Ekbert of Schönau (twelfth century), 183, 240
Elisabeth of Schönau (d. 1164), 183–4, 229

Elisabeth of Toss ("Elizabeth of Hungary"), 233
Elizabeth of Spalbeek (1246–1304), 275
Elliott, Dyan, 194n23, 335n28
Elsbeth Stagel (d. ca. 1360), 240
Elsbeth of Stoffeln (fl. fourteenth century), 291
Emmerich, Anne Catherine (1774–1824), 313
Erasmus, Desiderius (ca. 1469–1536), 117, 119
Evagrius of Pontus (d. 390), 37, 49–51, 55–7, 202–3
Evans, Gillian R., 75n46

Fassler, Margot E., 60n3, 64–5n12
Fénelon, François de Salignac de la Mothe (1651–1715), 210
Fishlake, Thomas (fourteenth century), 236
Fitzralph, Richard (fl. mid-fourteenth century), 296–7, 303
Foucault, Michel, 307, 333n10
Fox, George (1624–91), 130, 343
Francis of Assisi (1181/2–1226), 15, 100–1, 193, 195, 346
Francis of Osuna (ca. 1492–1540), 117
Francis of Sales (d. 1622), 210
Freud, Sigmund (1856–1939), 317, 331, 348

Garrettson, Catherine Livingston (eighteenth century), 339
Geert Grote (d. 1384), 235–6
Geoffrey of Saint Victor (d. 1194), 94
Gerson, Jean (d. 1429), 197–8, 208, 235n37, 237–8, 319

Gertrude the Great of Helfta (1256–1301/2), 77, 152–5, 172, 176–7, 231, 289–90, 311, 319–20, 333
Goehring, James, 47n22
Golitzin, Alexander, 255n11
Gould, Graham, 40n8
Granada, Luis de (mid-sixteenth century), 118n12
Green, D. H., 275n31
Gregory the Great (ca. 540–604), 60, 152, 178, 180, 269
Gregory of Nazianzos (330–90), 138
Gregory of Nyssa (ca. 335–ca. 394), 60n5, 138, 202, 309, 346–7
Gregory Palamas (ca. 1296–1359), 142–5
Griffiths, Fiona J., 73n39
Griffiths, Paul E., 301–2
Guerric of Igny (d. 1157), 90
Guibert of Tournai (d. 1284), 229, 231
Guigo I (d. 1136), 160, 262
Guigo II (d. 1193), 13, 152, 160, 171–2, 262–3
Gûte Tuschelin (fourteenth century), 291
Guyon, Jeanne Marie Bouvier de la Motte (1648–1717), 79n59, 210, 306, 326

Hadewijch (active ca. 1250), 19, 25, 77–9, 107–10, 112n94, 183–7, 205, 231, 235, 269–71, 307, 319–20, 343, 347, 349
Hadot, Pierre, 48n23
Harmless, William, 38–9n6
Heidegger, Martin (1889–1976), 145
Heloise (d. 1164), 61, 61n7
Henry of Nördlingen (fourteenth century), 234–5, 245

Hildegard of Bingen (1098–1179), 23–4, 28, 60n3, 72–9, 229, 240–1, 244–5, 262, 282, 310, 347–8; *Scivias*, 23, 78, 240, 244–5, 282
Hilduin of Saint Denys (ninth century), 143
Hilton, Walter (d. 1396), 169–70, 176–7, 236–7, 312
Hindmarsh, D. Bruce, 15n22, 33n41, 64n10
Hollywood, Amy, 78n56, 79n59, 272n22, 274–5, 319, 332n13
Hugh of Fouilloy (d. 1172–74), 93–4
Hugh of Saint Victor (1096–1141), 13, 95–9, 155, 161, 167, 176–7, 192, 229, 267n10, 268, 287–9
Hugh of Saumur (1024–1109), 82
Hutchinson, Ann (1591–1643), 77

Ida of Louvain (ca. 1065–1139), 272–3
Ignatius of Loyola (1491–1556), 131–2, 211–12, 217–18, 343–4
Irigaray, Luce, 307, 317, 332
Irlam, Shaun, 27n35, 31n38
Isaac of Stella (d. 1169), 90
Isadore of Seville (d. 636), 158, 178, 262

Jacopone da Todi (d. 1306), 109–10
James of Maerlant (thirteenth century), 231n22
James of Milan (thirteenth/fourteenth century), 163
James of Vitry (d. 1240), 192–3, 198, 334
James of Voragine (d. 1298), 57
James, William (1842–1910), 2n4
Jay, Martin, 66n19
Jerome (d. 420), 142

Joachim of Fiore (1132–1202), 91
John Chrysostom (ca. 347–407), 138, 255–8
John of Climacus (d. ca. 606), 44
John of the Cross (1542–91), 27n35, 79n59, 118–19, 122–4, 155–6, 209, 235, 343, 347
John of Dalyatha (ca. eighth century), 260–1
John of Damascus (d. 749), 168
John of Fécamp (d. 1078), 80–6, 111, 159, 165, 168
John Nider (1380–1438), 248
John the Scot Eriugena (ca. 815–77), 192
Johnson, Penelope D., 60n3
Julian of Norwich (d. aft. 1416), 188, 231, 237, 245, 307, 347–50

Kant, Immanuel (1724–1804), 313
Kempe, Margery (d. aft. 1438), 30, 188, 237, 308, 338

Lacan, Jacques, 328–32
Lambert li Bègues (mid-twelfth century), 229
Largier, Niklaus, 31–2, 271, 272n22
Lawrence, C. H., 61n6
LeClercq, Jean, 65n16, 69n25, 147, 157, 243
Lee, Ann, Mother (d. 1784), 30, 338
Lichtman, Maria, 196–7n34
Lossky, Vladimir (d. 1948), 145–6
Louth, Andrew, 38n5
Ludolph of Saxony (d. 1377), 163
Luis of León (1528–91), 118
Lutgard of Aywières (d. 1246), 195

Luther, Martin (1483–1546), 31–2, 114–19, 124–7, 132

Mack, Phyllis, 33n41, 339
Mande, Henry (d. 1431), 112
Mangegold of Lautenbach (ca. 1030–ca. 1103), 86
Margaret of Oingt (d. 1310), 187–8, 262, 274
Marguerite Porete (d. 1310), 3, 19–21, 79n59, 108, 112, 192, 196–7, 206, 208–9, 227–9, 231–3, 238, 245, 262–3, 303, 311–12
Marie of the Incarnation (neé Barbe Acarie) (1566–1618), 131, 210, 320
Marie of the Incarnation (neé Marie Guyart) (1599–1672), 320, 326
Marquard of Lindau (d. 1392), 248
Martin, Annick, 39n7
Mary of Oignies (d. 1213), 192–3, 198, 334
Maximus the Confessor (d. 662), 57, 142, 144–5, 204
McGinn, Bernard, 2n3, 38n5, 41–2, 60n5, 66–7n19, 70n28, 75n46, 103n67, 115, 119, 240, 252–3, 258, 265n3, 298, 300, 306, 315–17
Mechthild of Hackeborn (1241–99), 77, 231, 233
Mechthild of Magdeburg (ca. 1207–82), 19, 108, 184, 186, 205, 231, 234–5, 240, 246–8, 272–3, 319–20
Meersseman, G., 230n18
Merton, Thomas (1915–68), 211–12, 218–20
Methley, Richard (d. 1527/28), 237

Mitchell, Margaret M., 256–8
Molinos, Miguel de (1628–97), 354
Monica (Augustine of Hippo's mother), 1–3
Moore, Rosemary, 33n41

Nemes, Balázs J., 246n29
Newman, Barbara, 333n17
Newton, John (1725–1807), 64n10
Nicholas of Cusa (ca. 1400–64), 118, 238
Nietzche, Friedrich (1844–1900), 145
Norbert of Xanten (ca. 1080–1134), 86

O'Connor, Flannery (1925–65), 339
Origen of Alexandria (185–254), 5, 57, 74, 148–51, 169–70, 201–2, 212, 265, 308–9
Osuna, Francisco de (ca. 1492–ca. 1540), 117
Otto of Passau (fl. 1380), 248

Pachomius (d. ca. 346), 59
Peter the Chanter (d. 1197), 170
Peter Damian (ca. 1007–72), 82, 86
Peter Lombard (d. 1160), 95, 190n8
Peters, Gerlach (d. 1411), 112
Peuntner, Thomas (d. 1429), 248
Philip of Clairvaux (thirteenth century), 275
Philip of Harvengt (d. 1183), 93
Philo (ca. 15–10 BCE–ca. 45–50 CE), 253–5
Pico della Mirandola (1463–93), 118

Plato (d. ca. 348/7 BCE), 137, 139
Plotinus (d. 270), 2, 200, 202, 253
Pranger, M. Burcht, 63n9
Proclus (410/412–85), 139–40, 258, 260
Pseudo-Dionysius the Areopagite (early sixth century). *See* Dionysius the Areopagite

Rahner, Karl (1904–84), 133, 267n10
Raymond of Capua (1330–99), 198–9, 324
Regnault, Lucien, 40n8
Richard of Saint Victor (d. 1173), 91, 97–9, 161, 181, 229, 267n10, 268, 283, 289
Rolle, Richard (d. 1349), 168, 175–7, 233, 236, 245, 297–8, 300, 303
Rosenwein, Barbara, 73n39
Rousselot, Pierre, 98
Rubenson, Samuel, 39n7
Rudolf of Biberach (ca. 1270–1326), 269
Rudolph, Conrad, 63n9
Ruh, Kurt, 249n28, 250n30
Rupert of Deutz (ca. 1075–1129), 76–7, 229, 312
Ruusbroec, John (d. 1381), 208, 228n7, 233, 235, 245, 299–300, 303

Sartre, Jean Paul (1905–80), 145
Schmidt, Leigh Eric, 6n10, 32n40
Sedgwick, Eve Kosofsky, 331n10
Sheldrake, Philip, 41n9
Shepard, Thomas (1605–49), 77
Simons, Walter, 112n94

Smith, Ted A., 33n41
Soelle, Dorothee (1929–2003), 211–12, 220
Soubirous, Bernadette (d. 1879), 188
Stăniloae, Dumitru, 144
Stephen of Muret (d. 1124), 85
Stephen of Sawley (d. 1252), 173
Stock, Brian, 25n32, 75n46
Suso, Henry (1295–1366), 22, 103n67, 192, 208, 232–5, 240, 245, 248, 287, 344
Symeon the New Theologian (949–1022), 142

Tauler, John (d. 1361), 103n67, 116, 208, 245, 282, 286, 343, 345
Taves, Ann, 33n41
Teresa of Avila (1515–82), 117–24, 209, 313, 320, 322, 328–9, 333–5, 340
Teresa of Calcutta, Mother (1910–97), 313
Theodore of Mopsuestia (ca. 350–428), 266
Thérèse of Lisieux (1873–97), 27n35, 313
Thomas Aquinas (ca. 1225–74), 102, 155, 176, 189–90
Thomas of Cantimpré (d. ca. 1270), 195, 354
Thomas Gallus (d. 1246), 206
Thomas à Kempis (d. 1471), 236
Thornton, Robert (fifteenth century), 172
Tipson, Baird, 33n41, 77n51
Turner, Denys, 79n59

Urban VIII (1623–44), 325–6
Ubertino da Casale (d. ca. 1329–41), 163

Underhill, Evelyn (1875–1941), 155, 363
Underhill, James, 6n10

Van Engen, John, 74n41
Vanna of Orvieto (d. 1306), 195
Vernarde, Bruce L., 60n3
Vincent of Beauvais (d. ca. 1264), 244

Wesley, Charles (1707–78), 355
Wesley, John (1703–91), 355
William of Auvergne (d. 1249), 197

William of Champeaux (active early twelfth century), 94
William of Saint Martin (fl. 1250), 244
William of Saint Thierry (ca. 1085–1148), 28, 90, 180, 204, 229–30, 268–9, 271n18, 347

Yannaras, Christos, 144

Zarri, Gabriella, 320–1
Zinzendorf, von, Count, Nicolas Ludwig (1700–60), 129, 336–7

General Index

Abram/Abraham, 253–5
action (*actio*), 130, 133, 211–22: contemplation ranked against, 213–15; as transient activity, 213. *See also* contemplation (*contemplatio*)
Adam and Eve, 190, 321–2
affect (*affectus*), 67–8, 162, 171, 182, 206, 267, 294, 297, 303. *See also* emotion
affirmation, 12, 140–1, 143
agency, 46, 272, 275
allegory/allegorical interpretation, 5, 13–14, 27n24, 148–9, 202, 304
alumbrados, 121
Anabaptists, 32, 127, 129
anachoresis, 43–7
anagogical interpretation, 149, 181, 187
analogy, 139–41, 144
anéantissement (self-abnegation), 132
angels, 179, 183, 188, 197, 240
annihilation, 3, 19–21, 108, 228, 295
anthropology/anthropologists, 300–1, 316
apophasis: apophatic theology, 12, 19, 78n56, 137–46, 155–6, 215–16, 283, 287, 311; negative theology (*via negativa*), 20, 137, 249
Apophthegmata Patrum, 51 and passim
apostles, 85, 168, 227, 258
aridity. *See* dark night of the soul
Ark of the Covenant, 284
asceticism/ascetic practice, 9–10, 61, 84, 92, 191, 326, 329
Augustinian rule. *See* "The Rule of Augustine"
authority, 9, 26–8, 110–12, 128, 183–4, 245, 248, 305–14: challenges to, 309–13; charismatic, 305, 309–10, 317, 321; in Christian theology, 305; coercive, 310; cultural differences in, 305, 316; early Christianity and, 308–9; elite, 305–6; experiences of God and, 307; feminist scholars studying, 306; institutional, 314; intellectual, 313; juridical, 310; male clergy and, 310, 319; mystical foundation of, 314; as power of authorship, 305; recluses, 60n3; theological, 306–7; three paradigms relating to

mysticism, 308; women's, 310–13
authorship, 241–7, 305, 322

baptism, 127, 201
beatitudes, 227
beguines. *See* women, religious
Benedictine monasticism, 57, 59–79: ascetic details in, 61; cenobitism and, 74n41; children and, 70–1; daily life in, 60–1; Divine Office in, 148; John of Fécamp and, 80–6; knowledge transmission and, 71; manual labor in, 61, 64, 70–1; nursing the sick and, 70; obedience, chastity, and poverty in, 70; physical discipline in, 70–1n19; prayer in, 64–9; reading and, 64, 69–70; reform of, 11, 87–92; song and chant in, 71–9
Benedictine rule. *See Rule of Benedict*
Bible, 5, 14, 32, 70, 74, 102, 117, 147–9, 179, 305, 344. *See also* Hebrew Bible; New Testament; Vulgate
blind/blinding, 89, 142, 277, 283–5
body/embodiment, 25, 29–30, 189–90, 264–76, 312, 319, 329
books: attitudes toward, 248; customaries, 74; manuscripts bound into, 242; production of, 71, 147–8, 250; as record of God's work, 350; senses in form of, 272n22
Books of Hours, 148, 172
"bridal mysticism," 76, 90, 125–6, 154–5, 182, 186, 191–5, 202–4, 209, 271, 333–4, 339. *See also* gender; sexuality

Canons: canons of Prémontre, 85; canons of Saint Augustine, 115; canons of Saint Victor, 86; Dominican, 230n18; regular canons, 84–6, 92–9, 105; rule of Aachen, 84; secular canons, 84
Cappadocian Fathers, 144–5
cardinal virtues, 227
Carmelites, 100–1, 117, 122–4, 131
cataphasis, 12, 78n56, 137–46. *See also via positiva*
Cathar heresy, 310
Catholic Reformation, 114–17, 124, 131, 235, 239
celibacy, 69, 336–7
cenobitism, 74n41
chant, 65, 71, 152, 168, 185
charismatic graces, 305, 309–10, 317
charity, 170, 198–9, 212–18, 269n15, 318, 326
Christ: divinity of, 161; doctrine of the whole, 213; erotic encounters of, 333–4; feminization of, 272, 307, 336–8; as food, 273, 312; God born in us, 128; as God's loving concern, 201; hidden sense of, 271n18; historical, 127, 345; humanity of, 81–2, 161–3, 311–12, 318; as husband substitute, 338; the incarnate, 2, 201, 280, 318; loving his Church, 332–6; Martha, Mary, and, 212–13; meditation on the life and death of, 15n22; physicality of, 335; presence of, 45–6; as promise, 345; relationship with,

Christ (cont.)
133–4, 186–7; salvific mysteries of, 209–10; Satan appearing as, 197; side wound of, 284, 336–40; in Suso's texts, 232–3. *See also* Passion, Christ's; God; Trinity
the church, 14, 20, 28, 149, 202, 208, 305, 307, 309–14
clairvoyance, 184
clergy/clerics, 22, 28–9, 198, 225, 241: authority and, 28, 305, 309–19, 322, 325; meditation and, 165; as mentors of women, 186–8, 197–9; pastoral care, 93; private prayers and, 168
The Cloud of Unknowing, 236–7, 343
commandments, 63, 161, 186, 214, 227, 282
community, 7, 45–59, 123–4, 129–31
compilations, 24, 243–5
Complutensian Polyglot Bible, 117
composition (*operatio*), 13, 24
confession, 225, 247, 310, 313, 322
confraternities, 116
consciousness, 66–7n19
"Constitutions of Arundel" (1407), 237
contemplation (*contemplatio*), 4–6, 9–10, 21, 60n5, 116, 152: action and, 211–22; Augustine's ranking of works and, 213–15; as entrapment's opposite, 267; as eternal repose, 213; as highest goal, 212; liberation work and, 211; manuscripts and, 242; meditation and, 160, 180; stages of, 164, 192; works and, 213. *See also* action (*actio*); *theôria*
contemplativus in liberation, 211
conversation, 15n22, 240–1, 243
conversion, 32–3n41, 88–9, 100, 151, 197, 250, 317
convents, 76, 91, 106–7, 234, 247, 291
copying. *See* duplication of texts
Council of Constance (1414–18), 198
Council of Trent (1545–63), 125, 131, 133–4
Council of Vienne (1311–12), 120
Courtly love, tradition or literature, 107–8, 194, 233–4, 333n17, 338
creation of the world, 2, 12, 72, 95, 102–3, 133, 150, 162, 202, 283, 287, 343
the creed (*credo*), 227, 230
crucifix, 126, 128, 185, 197
crucifixion, 271n18, 284, 335

daily living, 9, 40, 60–1, 213
dangerous texts, 241, 250
darkness, 142–4, 146, 155–6, 299–300
dark night of the soul (aridity), 27n24, 122–3, 126–7, 155
democratization, 11, 22, 114–16, 124–7, 133–4, 188, 219–20, 228, 316–17
demons/demonic forces, 44, 46–9, 52, 175–6, 179, 188
the desert, 45–6, 48, 83, 207
desert fathers and mothers, 9, 40n8, 101, 148, 159, 179, 309
desire, sexual or equally intense, 10, 19, 30, 54, 66–8, 107–8, 161,

180–2, 187, 204, 228, 262, 270, 284, 290, 318, 330–1, 334–6
detachment, 78n56, 215, 250
Devotio Moderna (New Devotion), 235–6
devotional practice/writing, 147, 149–51, 159, 165, 184, 238, 241–2, 267
dialectics, 81–2, 86
dignity, 117–18, 161
discernment of spirits (*diakrisis*), 48, 188, 197–8, 238, 321–2
Divine Office, 60n3, 64n12, 71–3, 148, 168, 174
Dominicans, 85, 99–100, 115, 225
drink, 41, 61, 182, 214, 263, 337
duplication of texts, 23, 25, 92, 230, 234, 235n36, 241
Dutch language, 6n10, 226, 231n22
dying, 51, 149, 264

ears/hearing, 89, 121, 162, 185, 264, 267n10, 269, 272, 337
eating, 41, 91, 152, 272–3
ecstasy: desire and jubilation in, 181: Dionysius and, 192; Eucharist and, 185, 193–4; experience of God's presence in, 78n56; feminine in twelfth and thirteenth centuries, 182–7, 193–6; images of saints in, 325; mystic's path and, 154–5; rapture distinguished from, 190; senses and, 182; sexuality and, 331; in Teresa of Avila's *Autobiography*, 335–6; visions of light and, 98
ecstatic union, 21, 107–8: language of, 122; of seeing God, 180

emanation (and return), 3, 12, 19, 140–1
embodiment. *See* body
emotion, 26, 27n24, 54, 148, 159–62, 294–304: basic, 300–1; cognitive states and, 301; in prayer and meditation, 271–2; as recent invention, 294; shaped by its culture, 298–302; undervalued, 295. *See also* affect; feeling; love
English language, 6n10, 226, 242–3
enthusiasm, 31n38, 32, 171, 325
epectesis, 44
eros, 19, 30, 89–90, 144–5, 202, 205, 329–30. *See also* eroticism; love; *Minne*; sexuality
eroticism, 19, 24, 30, 89, 188, 202–5, 209–10, 234, 292, 322–4, 329–30, 333–4, 338–9
eschatology, 16–17n2
eternity, 7, 30, 265, 341–2, 346
Eucharist, 5–6, 185, 193–4, 201, 225, 273, 290–1, 311–12, 344–5. *See also* host; sacraments
evangelicals, 32–3n41, 190n8
excessus mentis, 16–17, 37, 181, 187, 189
Exodus, 55, 280, 284–5
exorcism, 312–13, 321
experience, sexual and/or religious, 1, 5, 7, 9–11, 16–33, 66n19, 78n56, 79n59, 314–15, 322–4, 328–35, 339–50
exterior human being (outer person). *See* exteriority
exteriority, 119–34, 211, 218, 220, 264–76
extromission, 285–6

faith, 32, 63, 74, 81, 96, 99, 124–7, 131, 153, 175, 193, 221, 270, 282, 285, 296
feeling, 16, 26, 54, 65, 67–8, 108, 217, 275, 294–8, 302–4, 334–5, 342
femininity, 29, 109, 182–7, 232–3, 307–8, 310–11, 316, 319, 323–4, 327, 337
fire, image of, 37, 56, 182, 335. See also prayer, fiery
Fourth Lateran Council (1215), 225–6, 311
Franciscans, 100, 115, 117, 162, 225
French language, 6n10, 226, 230, 242–3
French mysticism (seventeenth century), 209–10, 280
French Oratory, 131, 133–4
"Friends of God," 234

Gelassenheit. See letting go
gender, 29, 315–27: affecting who's remembered and how, 315; baroque mysticism and, 325–6; biological sex versus, 316; Christ and, 336–8; discourses about in Christianity, 324–5; eighteenth-century mystic revival and, 325; emotion construed by, 300–1; gender differences and Moravians, 336–40; male-female friendships, 324; mysticism, writing, and, 322; "new mysticism" and, 240, 316–20; shifting concepts of, 338. See also feminine; masculine
Genesis, 16–17, 148, 150, 152, 178, 188, 253–4, 287

German History Bible (1467), 278–9
German language, 6n10, 226, 232, 242–3, 247
God: eye of, 286; face of, 278–9; invisibility of, 278; love of, 164; marriage of the soul to, 154–5; memory of, 350; one and three, 140; self-revelation of, 137; transmitting his words, 240–51. See also Christ; Trinity
Gospels, 148, 167, 282
grace, 64, 67, 166–7, 169–70, 179, 208, 228, 311
Great Schism (1378–1429), 312, 319
Greek Christian tradition, 5, 144–5
Greek philosophy, 5, 137–8, 144–5, 200–2, 212, 264

hagiography/hagiographical literature, 17–18, 45, 195, 230, 319, 325
"Hail Mary" (*Ave Maria*), 16, 167, 172, 227, 235
hearing. See ears
heaven, 56, 81, 147, 152, 173–4, 178, 205, 257, 265, 273, 340, 350
Hebrew Bible, 64n12, 137, 147, 178, 201–2, 282
hell, 64, 128, 227
heresy (and heretics), 3, 20–1, 84, 103, 112, 196–7, 206, 210, 227–8, 230, 232, 243, 311
Heresy of the Free Spirit, 120, 207–8, 232, 249–50
hermits, 62, 84
hesychasts, 142–3
hierarchy, abolishment of, 124–8, 241, 249

General Index 383

history/historians, 300–1, 316, 318, 322
Holy Spirit, 127, 205, 309. *See also* Trinity
honey, 268–9, 272–3
host, Eucharistic, 185, 194, 273, 291–2, 318. *See also* Eucharist; sacraments
humanism, 11, 114, 116–19, 133–4
Humiliati/e, 104
hunger, 43–4, 238, 270–1, 290

idiotae (the illiterate), 226, 282, 289–90, 322
illumination. *See* light
images/imagination, 25, 63n9, 162–3, 178, 182, 185, 192, 267, 277
imago dei, 103, 179, 183, 265
imitation of Christ, 15, 101n63, 236, 273–5, 318, 346–7
imitatio Pauli (the imitation of Paul), 257
immanence, 3–4, 7, 25, 30, 128
incarnation, 26, 133, 140–1, 213, 342
incomprehensibility of God, 138, 143
inebriation, 18, 99, 182, 191, 334
ineffability, 2n4, 6–7, 89, 145, 163–4, 187, 259, 277–8, 305, 333
informal religious movements, 11, 104–13
the inner mountain, 47, 57–8
inner transformation, 6–7, 54, 68
inquisition, 11n94, 118, 120–1, 206, 311–12
intellect/intellectuals, 2–3, 178–9, 190–1, 202–3, 205–97
intercession, 73, 170

interiority, 7n11, 11, 66n17, 71n31, 114, 119–34, 191, 211, 216, 220, 229, 264–76
intromission, 285–7
introspection, 14–15, 32–3n41, 85, 158–9, 162–3, 301
Italian language, 6n10, 226, 231n24, 242

Jesus. *See* Christ
Jewish influences, 94, 147, 150–1, 278, 280, 282
Job, 74, 162, 179, 270
John of the New Testament, 190, 212–13, 273, 280, 284–5
justice, 125, 175, 187, 220–2, 290, 314, 316

kataphasis. *See* cataphasis
kisses, 151, 154–5, 271n18
knowing/knowledge, 67, 71, 75, 79, 82, 93, 96–7, 111–12, 138–47, 165, 170

ladders, 13, 152, 160
laicization, 11, 114, 116, 124–34
laity, 8–11, 16, 163–5, 172, 225–7, 242
Latin, 5, 22, 64n12, 225–39: clergy and, 22–3, 110, 225–7, 231–41, 263; international public for, 229; mnemonic terms linked to God, 265
lectio divina, 13–16, 71n31, 147–56, 158, 160–1, 184. *See also* reading
letting go (*Gelassenheit*), 45, 103–4, 126–9
liberation theology, 21, 211–12, 220–1

light, 13, 55–6, 122, 142, 155, 175, 179, 232, 244
literacy, 10–11, 83, 147, 163, 198, 226, 242
literature, secular, 229, 233
litteratus/illitteratus, 226
liturgy, 7, 64–6, 69, 71–4, 77–9, 140–7, 167, 184–5, 343–4
"living saints," 320
locutions, 317
logismoi, 50–3
Lollards, 237
Lord's Prayer. *See* "Our Father" (*Pater Noster*)
love, 1–3, 10, 20–1, 64, 67, 98, 142–6, 148, 153: burning of, 297; divine love and human desire, 330; double face of, 214; knowledge and, 27n26; love of God, 159–60, 162, 175, 180, 192; love of neighbor, 212; perfection through, 227–8; union different from, 299. *See also* eros; *Minne*
Low Countries, 91, 93–4, 104, 106–8, 165, 182, 187, 192
Luke, 21, 148, 212–13

magisterial reformation, 32, 134
manual labor, 40–1, 64, 70–1, 86
manuscripts, 23, 70n26, 231, 240–4: fragmented, 243, 246–7. *See also* duplication of texts; writing; transmission
married sex, 194n23, 336–40
martyrs, 180–4
"Martyr's Synod," 129
Mary and Martha, 107, 212–18, 220
Mary, the mother of God (the Virgin Mary), 72–3, 88, 183, 188, 284, 332
masculinity, 29, 232–3, 284n15, 307–8, 311, 316, 323–5, 337
Mass, 127, 168, 194, 247. *See also* Eucharist
materiality, 267, 272–6
material possessions, 1, 50, 73, 101, 129
mediation, 2, 15, 67, 119, 131, 306, 341
meditation (*meditatio*), 9–10, 13–14, 16, 21, 32–3n41, 51, 147–8, 151–3, 157–65: on God's Word, 180; as ladder rung, 160–1; as mental activity, 158; monastic, 157, 165; narratives, 157–8; on past, present, and future, 161; as physical activity, 158; prayer training and, 157, 175; as spiritual practice, 157; in written form, 157
meditationes vitae Christi (meditations on the life of Christ), 15, 162
memory of the divine, 343: prememory, 342; texts as collective, 342; time and, 341–50; of a time outside of time, 344; of traumatic events, 342–3, 347–9; union by means of, 341; of unlived experience, 342
memory/memorization, 31, 157, 161–2, 185, 294: functioning like a stomach, 264; living mendicant orders, 11, 99–104, 205, 287
mercy, 89, 164, 170, 213, 229
metaphor, 3, 160–1, 201, 204
Methodism, 15n41, 32–3n41, 33n12
mind: *excessus mentis*, 16–17, 37, 181, 187, 189: of God, 19, 169,

205; expanded, 2, 13, 56, 76, 90, 97, 141, 159, 167, 190, 206, 255, 262, 264, 283, 289, 339

Minne, 107, 112n94, 269–70. *See also* Eros; Love

monasticism: adult recruits for, 87; cenobitical, 59, 62, 91; distracted monks and, 82–3; early, 37–58, 157n1; Eastern monasticism, 4n5, 57; in eleventh and twelfth centuries, 82; eremitical, 91; experimental, 42; guidelines for daily life in, 243; Jacob's ladder and, 152; lay monks, 87; meditation in, 165; sarabites, 62; spiritual life, steps to, 152–3, 155; traditions of origin, 8; vision controlled in, 290; wandering monks and, 43–4; Western monasticism, 86. *See also* Benedictine monasticism

Monastic reform: Carthusians, 91–2, 160; Cistercians, 28, 152, 160; Cluny, 86; Gorze, 82; texts aimed at, 243; monasteries: as physical and imaginary place, 43; as school for the Lord's service, 62–3; ties with local leaders, 61n6; the world and, 212, 218–19

Montanism (also known as "The New Prophecy"), 309

Moravians, 129–31, 134, 336–40

Moses, 55–6, 137, 180, 190, 203, 279, 284–5

mystery, 142, 344–5

mysticism: Augustinian model of time and, 341; baroque, 325–6; in beguine life, 107; condemnations of (1300–1700), 120–1; definitions of, 8n15, 39, 41–2; desire different in, 328–36; early Christianity and, 308–9; emotion, religion, and experience of, 299–300; exterior reform and, 119–34; "false," 2n4, 4–5, 207–8, 210; folk psychology challenged by, 302; gender and who's remembered, 315; inner sources of, 119–34; liberation and, 211–12; male mystics researched, 323–5; married sex and, 336–40; in modernity, 31; mystical body, 273; "new mysticism," 240, 316–20; opposite bodily entrapment, 267; paradigms relating to authority in, 308; performance, gender, and, 315; politics and, 220; sex disavowed in study of, 329–30; somatization and, 312–13, 318; temporalities within mystic text, 346; term's sources and meanings, 5–8; texts' patterns over time, 229–39; transmission of mystical tests, 240–51; "true," 4–5, 207–8; vernacular flowering of, 228–39; visuality and, 277–93; women's self-actualization and, 327; writing, gender, and, 322

negative language, 138–9, 203
negative theology. *See* apophasis
neighbor, 21, 88–9, 212, 214–15, 218
Neoplatonism, 2–3, 19, 118–19, 128, 146, 178, 286
"New Devout," 112

New Testament, 129, 147–8, 201–2
nuns. *See* women, religious

obedience, 62, 69, 83–4
oblates, 87
"observance movement," 251
the One, 2, 10, 53–5, 139–40, 154, 200, 202
opus dei, 65
oratio. *See* prayer (*oratio*)
Oratory of Divine Love, 116
order of Friars Minor. *See* Franciscans
order of Preachers. *See* Dominicans
order of the Virgin Mary of Mount Carmel. *See* Carmelites
Orthodox theology, 144–6
"Our Father" (*Pater Noster*), 16, 167–8, 171–4, 227, 230, 235

pain, 30, 48, 122, 170, 318, 325, 328, 330–1, 335, 340, 347–9. *See also* suffering
paper, 242
paradox, 5, 13, 155–6, 228, 277, 344
paramystical phenomena, 111, 198–9
parchment, 242, 244–5
Passion, Christ's, 15n22, 81, 131–2, 161–2, 183, 342
pastoral theology, 85, 93, 249
Paul, 24, 148, 170, 178, 180, 183, 278, 284–5, 287–8, 321
peace, 138, 198–9
penitence/penitential practices, 84, 317–18, 324
Pentecostalism, 32–3n41

performance, 23, 226, 242, 267, 273–4, 315, 344, 350
philosophy/philosophers, 4, 137–8, 144–5, 199–202, 212, 300–1, 317
physical force, 335n28
Pietism, 32–3n41, 74n41
"The Pious Miller's Wife," 250–1
Platonism, 137, 139
pleasure, 1, 30, 51, 189, 328, 330–1, 334, 335n28, 340
poetry, 96, 118, 142, 153
possession, 199–200, 220, 254–7, 315, 321, 335n28, 340
poverty, 19, 55, 69, 83, 99, 106
practice, 7–10, 69n21, 165, 171, 212, 298
praise, 3–4, 64, 88, 141, 148, 175–6
prayer (*oratio*), 13–16, 21, 32–3n41, 158, 167–77: Anglo-Irish (eighth century), 159; apophatic theology and, 144; in Benedictine life, 64, 69; before modern mysticism, 7–10; clergy and, 73, 168; as comfort, 175; common, 10, 40; as confession, 176; fiery, 16, 37–8, 68, 169–70, 174; impossible, 50–1; incense like, 174; intercessions, 170; as ladder rung, 13, 152, 171–2; length of, 169, 176; meditation and, 158, 160; modern mysticism disengaged from, 7; private, 168; psalms and hymns integral to, 168; rhetorical modes of, 170–1; of Saint Ambrose, 81; scripture and, 147–56, 168–9; supplications, 170, 176; as surrender, 176; thanksgivings, 170; women and

contemplative, 317; in a word, 168; work and, 211, 221
preaching, 7–8, 11, 84, 98–104, 110, 115, 129–30, 186, 207, 247–9, 256, 309
Premonstratensian, 93, 105
pride, 50–1, 71, 88, 100, 297–8
print, 23, 115, 236, 239, 242, 244, 251
prophets, 178, 183–4, 237, 246, 254–5, 282, 309
proseuche, 51–6
prosoche, 47–51
Protestant Reformation/ Protestantism, 31–2, 33n41, 114–34, 321
Psalms/Psalter, 10, 15n22, 16, 64n12, 66–9, 71–9, 148: ecstatic vision and, 184; integral to the practice of prayer, 168, 173–4; meditation on, 157–8
pseudonymous writing, 12, 24, 137, 230n20, 259–60
psychology/psychologists, 26, 199, 209, 300–1, 314, 322–3
Puritanism, 32–3n41, 77n51

Quakers, 114, 130–1, 134, 339, 343. *See also* Society of Friends
Quietist Controversy (Quietism), 120–1, 210, 217

Rachel and Leah, 214
racism, 123, 219
Radical Reformation, 12, 121–3, 127–31, 134, 208–9
rapture (*raptus*), 3, 16–18, 189–9: definition of, 189–91; into evil, 197; female mystics and, 193–6; in Hebrew Bible/New Testament, 190; heretic trials and, 196–7; physical abstraction and, 189–90
ratio triplex, 283–4
reading, 7–8, 10, 13, 21, 23, 32–3n41, 40, 64, 70n28, 147, 152, 156: embodiment transformed through, 272n22; in five stages of spiritual ascent, 171; as meditation, 157, 160
recitation, 147, 157
recluses, 105–6, 226, 229
reformation: early modern, 12, 114–34; of heretical error, 241; magisterial, 12; vernaculars flowering because of, 239. *See also* Catholic Reformation; Protestant Reformation
regula (rules of life), 59
repentance, 146, 151
revelation, 12, 21–2, 29, 78, 96, 111, 132, 137, 142–6, 179, 183, 186–8, 191–8, 237, 241–2, 280, 290, 348
Roman Catholicism, 12, 32, 70–7, 114–19, 124–8, 131–4, 144, 209, 228n11, 235, 238–9, 321, 324, 335, 339
Roman Empire, 309
"The Rule of Augustine," 11, 60n3, 84, 92–3
Rule of Benedict, 10, 14, 59–65, 83–4, 88–9, 92, 148, 152, 158

sacraments, 20, 42, 95, 102, 105, 108, 112–19, 121, 227, 247, 268, 309–11
sacra pagina, 147–56
saints, 1, 3–4, 183, 245, 305, 325
Satan, 197, 321

scripture (*scriptio divina*): knowledge illuminated by, 265–6: Luther's theology and, 32, 125; meditating on, 15, 54, 82, 165; Radical Reformation and, 128–30; reciting, 9–10, 40; senses and, 27. See also *lectio divina*

Second Vatican Council, 133

seeing: contemplation in terms of, 283: with eye of the heart, 292; inner sight, 267n10, 272; as synonym for divine knowledge, 269; seeing God, 180–1, 184–6, 189, 207

Seelengrund, 128

self-abnegation. See *anéantissement*

self-examination. See introspection

senses, 3, 9, 25–7, 182, 185, 192, 264–76: in book form, 272n22; doubling of, 269–70; emotion, 294; hierarchy of, 284, 287; spiritual, 268

sermons, 244, 247

sexuality, 29–30, 328–40: Bernini's sculpture and, 328–9; consummation by God, 328; ecstatic, 328–9; images relating to, 328, 332–3, 335; limited notions about, 330–1; married sex and mysticism, 336–40; maternal and erotic interwoven, 334; Moravian mystics and, 336–9; painful, 328–31; physical arousal in texts, 331–2; pleasurable, 328–31; Quaker visionaries and, 339; repressed, 317, 328–9; Shakers and, 338

Shakers, 30, 338

side wound, Christ's, 284, 336, 339

sight. See seeing

silence, 13, 40, 61, 277, 322

sin, 159–60, 164, 249

"Sister Catherine Treatise," 111–12, 248–50

sleep, 41, 61, 91, 102, 215, 252, 263, 318, 334

Society of Friends (Quakers), 130–1, 134

Society of Jesus, 217–18

solitude, 4, 40, 60, 91

Solomon, 148, 181, 280

song, 65–6, 71–9, 107, 109–10, 148–9, 153

Song of Songs, 27–8, 74–8, 88–9, 148–55, 182, 184, 191, 202–4, 209, 230, 268, 332–7

soul, 2–5, 18, 20, 30, 67n20, 78n56, 178, 181, 207, 228, 238, 249–50: feeling and, 295; inner human being and, 264–5; physiognomy for, 264; secret union in center of, 335

Spanish language, 6n10

Spanish mysticism (sixteenth century), 209

speaking, 111, 171, 240

speculation (*speculatio*), 289

spiritual senses. See senses

stigmata, 101, 173, 193, 198–9, 318

suffering, 48–9, 275, 312, 317–19, 325–6

syneisactism, 105

Synod of Aachen (817), 61

taste, 267n10, 268–9, 272, 283

teachers/teaching, 68, 71, 82, 94, 101–3, 107, 110, 215, 225, 241, 249–50, 320, 322

tears, 17, 161, 176, 296, 303
tertiaries, 105, 109, 226
texts, mystical, 17, 22–4, 30, 118, 151, 205, 229–37, 240–56, 264, 268, 272–4, 286, 298, 319, 323, 329–32, 336–9, 341–3, 347; See duplication of texts; manuscripts; writing; transmission
Theologia Deutsch, 116, 126–8
theôria, 6, 82, 202, 212
time, 7, 30–1, 341–50: atemporal or eternal, 341, 343, 346; chronological or historical, 341; out of time, 344; timelessness, 350; victory over, 349
tomb, 46, 48, 336
touch, 25, 30, 75, 141, 182, 187, 267, 270–2, 334–6, 339, 347
trances, 192, 198–9
transcendence, 2–4, 6–7, 30, 318
transformation, 122–4, 209–10, 266
translation, 7n12, 22, 87, 92, 163, 234–6
transmission, 7n12, 22–3, 240–51, 274
trauma, 342–3, 347–9
Trinity, 89, 150, 182, 202–3, 205, 207, 268, 287. See also Christ; God; Holy Spirit
tropological understanding, 149, 156

Union (*unio mystica*), 32–3n41, 119–20, 123, 125–6, 200–10: as advance into darkness, 138; ecstatic, 107–8, 154–6; erotic, 205–6, 209–10; kiss of mouth as, 151; language of, 200; love different from, 299; memory of union with the divine, 342; mystical, 18, 202–3; optimism about, 11; steps to, 152, 191–2, 204; union of distinction, 18; union without distinction, 19, 21, 78n56, 200, 202–3, 205, 207–8, 210; *unitas spiritus*, 18–19, 202, 208, 210; unitive experience, 3–6, 10
universities, 117, 225, 237

Vernacular languages, 5, 7n13, 22, 109–10, 152, 163, 205, 225–39, 244, 246, 317
via negativa, 162, 220. See also apophasis
via positiva, 162, 220. See also cataphasis
via transformativa, 220
Victorines, 96, 143, 163–5
vision (*visio*), 4–6, 16–18, 21, 26, 28, 60n5, 178–88: beatific, 180–1; corporeal, 181; ecstatic, 180–7; eyes of the heart and mind, 179; faith aspiration through, 285; false, 4–5, 188, 207–8; feminine in twelfth and thirteenth centuries, 182–7; intellect and, 178–9; as knowing, 178; meaning accrued over time, 348–9; men devaluing, 312; mystery beyond the power of, 280–1; prescribed visualizations, 188; rapture as a higher form of, 178; specific time of, 347–8; spiritual, 181, 238; strictly controlled in monastic settings, 290; theories of, 285–6; three kinds of, 178, 190; transmission of, 240; true,

vision (*visio*) (*cont.*)
  4–5, 188, 207–8. *See also* seeing
visions, 77, 78n56, 182–8, 347–8:
  of Bernadette Soubirous, 188;
  of Ezekiel and Revelation, 179;
  of Gertrude, 173; of Hadewijch,
  77–9, 185–7, 343, 349–50; of
  Hildegard, 244–5; of Julian, 267,
  349–50; of Margery Kempe,
  188; of Marguerite of Oingt,
  274; at Ostia, 2; Peter and
  Paul's, 190
visuality, 277–93
Vulgate, 64n12, 190n7

Waldensians, 85, 310
wilderness, 46
will, 294
Wisdom, 1–3, 232–3, 268
witchcraft, 312–13
women, religious, 22, 71:
  Augustinian rule and, 60n3;
  authority struggles and, 317;
  beguines, 84, 106–12, 115,
  192–3, 205, 232; collaboration
  with clerics among, 319;
  contemplative aspirations
  of noble, 165; cultural
  suppression of, 316; deference
  to authority among, 110–12;
  as devotional works' audience,
  163; ecstatic in twelfth and
  thirteenth centuries, 182–7;
  erotic elements and, 317, 320,
  322–3; flesh connections in
  mysticism, 274–5; image of
  God less bright in, 183; in
  informal movements, 105; late
  medieval spirituality and, 101;
  lectio divina and, 184–5; made
  flesh, 273, 280; meditation
  among, 182; mysticism not
  uniform among, 109; nuns,
  105–6, 152–3, 183, 231–2, 291;
  psychosomatic illness and,
  317; Quaker, 130; rapture and,
  192–3; as readers of vernacular
  writings, 226, 229; and the
  Rule of Benedict, 61; sexuality
  and, 29–30; spiritual authority
  of, 311; suppressing female
  visionaries, 198; temporal,
  textual drama, 347; texts by and
  about, 76; transmitting God's
  Word, 240–51; union with
  God, 28; vernacular mystical
  texts by, 232n15; visionaries
  consulted, 184; visions among,
  17; the Word, 1–3, 10, 180, 207,
  248; writing by, 17, 227–37
writing, 24–5, 32–3n41, 186, 225–
  51: as emotional sharing tool,
  297–8; transmission of vision
  through, 274; women's suffering
  written up by men, 275

"The Young Woman of Two and
  Twenty," 250–1

CPSIA information can be obtained
at www.ICGtesting.com
Printed in the USA
LVHW090111100120
643090LV00001B/34/P